Seeking the Truth

Edited by Richard M. Reinsch II

Seeking THE *Truth*

AN ORESTES BROWNSON ANTHOLOGY

The Catholic University of America Press
Washington, D.C.

The paper used in this publication meets the minimum requirements of American National Standards for Information Science—Permanence of Paper for Printed Library Materials, ANSI Z39.48-1984.
∞

Image on title page: O.A. Brownson. Print Collection, Miriam and Ira D. Wallach Division of Art, Prints and Photographs, The New York Public Library, Astor, Lenox and Tilden Foundations

Library of Congress Cataloging-in-Publication Data
Names: Brownson, Orestes Augustus, 1803–1876, author.
Title: Seeking the truth : an Orestes Brownson anthology / edited by Richard M. Reinsch II.
Description: Washington, D.C. : The Catholic University of America Press, 2016. | Includes bibliographical references and index.
Identifiers: LCCN 2016023638 | ISBN 9780813228617 (pbk. : alk. paper)
Subjects: LCSH: Philosophy, American—19th century.
Classification: LCC B908.B61 R45 2016 | DDC 191—dc23
LC record available at https://lccn.loc.gov/2016023638

READER AIDED BY A GRANT
FIGURE FOUNDATION
IN SEARCH OF THE LUMEN

For Evelyn, the love of my life, mother of our mighty platoon

CONTENTS

ACKNOWLEDGMENTS

I owe a tremendous debt to several scholars who aided me in my understanding of Orestes A. Brownson and gave me guidance in structuring the introduction and essays selected for this anthology. Brownson can be credited with writing over twenty volumes of first-rate essays on an array of subjects and controversies. The plan to combine his work into a single volume was a difficult one, and bringing it to completion required me to walk with him through the social, religious, and political tumults that he encountered in the nineteenth century. To that end, I am thankful to several people who gave me direction.

First, many thanks to Peter Lawler for his scholarship on Brownson, which provided my own introduction to Brownson's life and work. His comments and advice as I was preparing this volume improved the final product greatly. Gregory Butler's work on Brownson has also been enormously beneficial to me. His comments on the introduction and shape of the work refined it. Robert Moffit's expertise on Brownson and his willingness to offer his expertise, indeed, encouragement on this project spurred me forward. My Liberty Fund colleague Hans Eicholz provided important criticism and gave a rich historical context on the path I was endeavoring to walk with Brownson. For that, I am grateful. G. M. Curtis, my friend and critic, provided feedback that improved this book significantly. Of more importance was his counsel that I can be confident in the intrinsic worth of this project if, at its end, I can speak to Brownson as my witness and know that I have kept faith with his life and work. I hope that I have at every turn.

I am indebted to my employer Liberty Fund for providing me significant research support, which enabled to me to compile this volume. My period of study leave in 2013 was invaluable in completing this anthology. Moreover, the spirit of our work at Liberty Fund is that the calling of understanding the freedom and responsibility of the human person is a task that doesn't end. I hope that with this volume, I contribute a small piece to that noble work.

To my wife, Evelyn, thank you for the time and understanding you have graciously extended to me in preparing this book—a task made even more difficult with your carrying our fifth child, John Paul, during its last phase. Thank you for showing me the gift of love, of forgiveness, and for showing our children the grace of your motherhood. I am always yours.

INTRODUCTION

Orestes Brownson's American Search for the Truth

Orestes A. Brownson was a seeker who lived in the service of truth. His search and the commitments he forged stand as our gain, even if they both impressed and confused his contemporaries and later biographers. He was alternately seen as an irascible prophet, an unsteady weathervane, or brilliant. Lord Acton thought Brownson possessed the ablest mind of America and implored him to accept John Henry Newman's invitation to be Lecturer Extraordinary at his Catholic University of Ireland.[1] James Russell Lowell made the charge of weathervane with *A Fable for Critics* that observed that

He shifts quite about, then proceeds to expound
That 't is merely the earth, not himself, that turns round,
And wishes it clearly impressed on your mind
That the weathercock rules and not follows the wind;
Proving first, then as deftly confuting each side,
With no doctrine pleased that's now somewhere denied,
He lays the denier away on the shelf,
And then—down beside him lies gravely himself.

Brownson's twentieth-century biographer Arthur Schlesinger Jr. observed that he "took almost every side of every hot question and was a sledgehammer controversialist at every step along his tempestuous path."[2] As descriptions of Brownson, these terms are not wholly wrong, but they obscure his central focus of finding the truth wherever it led him. Evidence for the authenticity of his questing is found in his philosophical, religious, and political conversions.

He migrated through Presbyterianism, universalism, skepticism, unitarianism, and transcendentalist thought, and finally at age forty-one to Catholicism. Politically, he found himself anticipating socialism in the 1830s, then, turning into a disciple of John Calhoun's states' rights constitutionalism, before incorporating his criticisms of mass democracy into a unique philosophical defense of the Constitution that would emerge in full bloom during the Civil War. In doing so, Brownson was willing to admit error, and he was willing to tell others how wrong, he thought, they had been. Russell Kirk argued that Brownson

> stands in the first rank of American men of ideas.... Perhaps the very versatility of the man has made it difficult for professors to fit him into any convenient category. For Brownson was a political philosopher of a high order, a religious essayist of brilliance, a literary critic of force and discernment, a serious journalist ... and one of the shrewdest observers of American character and institutions we ever have been blessed with.[3]

These observations underscore the depth and breadth of Brownson's intellectual life.

Life could only be freely lived if done so in the service of truth. The strength of this conviction inspired his study, his writing, and his willingness to stand alone and to be despised publicly at times. As such, Brownson believed in fervent disagreement and debate when necessary.[4] Although his differences with other voices were intense, they were not malicious, nor is there evidence that they were for power or personal aggrandizement.

If much of late modern thought can be characterized as dualistic, fractured, and subjective, Brownson's questing was that of a modern intellectual using modern philosophical resources in dialogue with premodern and classical sources to recover the ground the dialectical whole to knowledge. Therefore, the intellectual quest must contemplate the natural and the supernatural, reason and faith, religion and science, the various levels and forms of political authority, the beginning and the end of man, and the relationships that exist among these sets of inquiries. Resulting from Brownson's study of these universal questions is also a particular application of his learning. Brownson, unlike almost any other American figure, illuminates the promises and the limitations of American institutions while also seeking to edify its experiment with republican self-government.

Brownson's life, in its several phases, turns, and allegiances, has remained noteworthy for his rejection of modern pragmatism's aim to obtain material comfort in service of man's desires while de-emphasizing deeper concerns for philosophical and spiritual truth.[5] Therefore, Brownson's writings, born from his existential wranglings, were addressed to our authentic human longings to know the truth about ourselves. To study Brownson is to learn from a man whose first concern was to be open to the truth about what it means to be a human person.[6] Unlike pragmatism, which simply shrugs off such concerns, Brownson returned again and again to the searching questions of human existence. In this quest, he was open to insights and knowledge from sources apart from reason itself.

Reason, Brownson asserted, might ask questions that it is unable to answer. The true philosopher would insist on pursuing such inquiries even if they led beyond the limited horizon of pure reason. Brownson thought that faith and reason, far from being incompatible, reinforced each other. In fact, reason, Brownson noted, found evidence in revelation for truths reason could never have discovered on its own. Human equality was one prime example Brownson, like Tocqueville, pointed to. Reason might confidently ground its defense of equality of persons, but its binding normative truth was never one it could have reached without revelation. Reason itself, Brownson thought, was insufficient: "Let philosophy go as far as it can, but let the philosopher never for a moment imagine that human reason will ever be able to understand itself."[7]

Brownson's metaphysical speculation dismissed the rational sufficiency of the God of the deists. Such rejection was made because Brownson came to affirm that life was lived by communion, and this was predicated on the person's experiencing reality as a free and relational being. The personal, incarnate God of Christian revelation supplies the foundation of our relational nature by best accounting for human freedom that is the singular exception within a clockwork universe. In Brownson's understanding of communion, freedom, and the questions freedom poses find a profoundly new foundation and method for its realization in time; that is, a personal being has a personal creator whom he can love and is loved by it.

Christian theology, for Brownson, aids what we can know through reason about ourselves and nature. We have divine and natural support for the experiences we have of ourselves as free persons. In this manner, Brownson's argument connects with the encyclical *Deus Caritas Est*, where Pope Benedict XVI compared the God who loves man to the God Aristotle looked to as the supreme object of man's contemplation. "The divine power that Aristotle at the height of Greek philosophy sought to grasp through reflection, is indeed for every being an object of desire and of love—and as the object of love this divinity moves the world—but in itself it lacks nothing and does not love: it is solely the object of love. The one God in whom Israel believes, on the other hand, loves with a personal love."[8] This should lead, Brownson held, to a profoundly different ground for a liberal politics precisely because the person found his authentic freedom in love of man and God. Politics is transcended by and must support these truths of human freedom and existence.

Early Life

Born in 1803 in Vermont, Brownson spent his early life in the Green Mountain State. The death of Brownson's father when Brownson was six left his mother alone to raise five children. Unable to provide for the family, she left Brownson and his twin sister to be raised by neighbors. Because he was an autodidact, his capabilities emerged almost immediately. As a child he read the King James Bible, Watt's *Psalms and Divine Songs* and *The Franklin Primer*, and Jonathan Edward's *History of the Redemption*, among others. Brownson reported that in his adolescent years, he moved on to John Locke's *Essay on Human Understanding*, Pope's *Homer*, *Robinson Crusoe*, *Arabian Knights*, and various books on American history and economy.[9] Brownson memorized most of the Bible by the time he was fourteen.[10]

Brownson's adopted family gave him the elements of their informally practiced Congregationalism. His youth was short-lived. This does not appear to be the result of material hardship, but that Brownson assumed the cares of adulthood from an early age. At fifteen, he returned to his mother and other siblings in New York. Here, Brownson lived in a region of religious excitement and the incredible movement of people. The energy of western New York was fueled by people on the move geographically, religiously, and economically. In short, these unsettled circumstances of Brownson's early life certainly shaped his own intellectual and religious curiosity in a vital way.

Ever the seeker, Brownson's first religious commitment was made at eighteen to the Presbyterian Church based on his personal experience of grace, but he left soon after joining. Later, Brownson claimed that the rejection of reason by Presbyterian theology and its consequent rigidity led him to discount its teachings.[11] Man must be taken in full, and if reason could not be affirmed by a theology, Brownson held, then so much for such a theology. Changes in thought were mirrored by changes in occupation.

Brownson learned the printing trade at a newspaper, tutored, taught school, became a Universalist minister, and fell in love with Sally Healy, the daughter of a family he had tutored. They married in 1827 and had eight children. Two sons died in the Civil War that Brownson vigorously defended. In time, Brownson became a scholar, an orator, a journalist, and a man of profound philosophical, religious, and political commitments.

Brownson plunged into deep intellectual waters on a dizzying array of issues and ideas that rose to prominence in public discussion in America and Europe. He ranged widely on American constitutionalism, and various social and political issues such as education, immigration, slavery, feminism, among others. Furthermore, Brownson penned significant criticisms of Immanuel Kant's a priori forms of synthetic knowledge, John Henry Newman's evolutionary account of Christian doctrine, and Georg Hegel's philosophy of history, among other ideas of great thinkers.[12]

Brownson, then, developed over the years into a preeminent public intellectual of the nineteenth century. All of this was fueled in part and supported by his learning in such languages as Greek, Latin, Italian, German, Spanish, and French, which enabled him to encounter classic and contemporary works of Western thought in their original voice. His writing in political philosophy conveyed a thorough understanding of Greek, Roman, and medieval sources. Much of his disdain for many of the moderns resulted from what he believed was the unreality of their political thought. His knowledge of American political thought is evident in his acute grasp of ongoing debates over federal power in the nineteenth century.[13]

Brownson's studies included the English medieval political experience as a leading teacher of law and liberty.[14] The English lawyers John Fortescue, Edward Coke, and William Blackstone and the English clergymen John of Salisbury and Richard Hooker instilled in Brownson a belief that the rule of law stood under constant threat from encroaching power. In nineteenth-century terms, this threat came from majoritarian democracy, Brownson observed. As such, Brownson emphasized preserving the fundamental precepts and rules of the common law as decisive for individual liberty.[15] He astutely identified the tendencies of legislatures to codify and proliferate statute laws at the expense of common law liberties, which, he believed, had grounded private relations in history, reason, and practice. Other significant points of departure in Brownson's journey include Aristotle's *Politics* and Aquinas's legal and political writings, along with Francisco Suárez and Robert Bellarmine on the foundations of lawful government.[16]

Union and Progress

Brownson was a political radical in his early adulthood. Biographer R. A. Herrera succinctly observed that during this period, he frequently associated Christianity with democracy in a potent form of liberation theology that employed Christianity to perfect social and political democracy.[17] Indeed, in the late 1820s he was close to protosocialists Robert Owen and Francis Wright, contributing to their journal the *Free Inquirer*. A member of the New York Workingmen's Party, he urged labor and wage reform and the abolition of inheritance, proposals that were far to the left of the mainstream opinion. But Brownson's purposes, in reality, were more agrarian than socialist. He believed in uniting labor and capital in the person, an idea he thought was subverted by industrial capitalism.

In his illuminating study, Gregory Butler argued that Brownson as a Universalist minister—ordained in 1826—had inverted the symbols of Christianity.[18] For Brownson, in his younger days, reason and free inquiry had led him to the conclusion that basic Christian doctrines are without any reasonable grounding. Brownson referred to himself as a Christian, not because he believed in the supernatural doctrines of the faith but because of his conviction that Christ was an example of radical social reform. As such, Brownson sought to use Christ as an instrument for summoning the people's best energies for social and political transformation.[19] Brownson was, in effect, pragmatically offering Christ as a symbol in support of an egalitarian order.

Brownson commentator Patrick Carey observed of Brownson's early diary entries that even his belief in salvation was caught up with his intense focus on ameliorating social evils. Salvation doctrine had too narrowly focused on securing eternal life for the believer. An expanded focus, Brownson thought, should be on salvation as means for relieving social inequities.[20] This belief in the necessity of organized religion for achieving a new man and a new church explains why Brownson broke with the conventional socialism seen in Owen and Wright. Owen and Wright's calls for reform were predicated on an imminent transformation motivated by a quest for justice. Brownson insisted that religion was the only means that could really supply such motivation.

After being expelled from the Universalist Church in 1829 because of his declining biblical faith, among other reasons, Brownson stated, "The only God I recognized was the divine in man, which I supposed to be the real meaning of the Christian doctrine of the Incarnation, the mystery of Emmanuel, or God with us, God manifest in the flesh."[21] Brownson proclaimed himself "a friend of man" and lived a period of skepticism, and he remained in Ithaca until the summer of 1832 when he moved to Walpole, New Hampshire, to begin his Unitarian ministry. He would emerge from his biblical doubting by reading Unitarian pastor William Ellery Channing's sermon "Likeness to God," a work that he found enormously influential, prompting his return to active ministry.[22] This sermon convinced him that man possessed an internal, intuitive revelation of God. Religion was a natural part of man. As such, man's desire for God could never be erased from his being. Brownson, under Channing's influence, embraced the divine within and experienced Christianity anew.[23]

Brownson soon arrived in Massachusetts and was installed in 1834 as pastor of the First Congregational Church in Canton, Massachusetts, sixty miles south of Boston. Here, Brownson began a ministry deeply devoted to the "mental and moral elevation of the laboring class." He put into practice the Christian ministry he believed was called for in the modern industrializing age, a faith that would edify workers by giving them moral, social uplift and that would not seem irrelevant or indifferent to their hardscrabble circumstances. Inspiring Brownson in this regard was the French humanitarian and philosopher Saint-Simon. In the essay "Memoir of Saint-Simon," Brownson noted that "[h]e [Saint-Simon] speaks no longer, as before, to the learned. He turns to the industrious classes and devotes then years to the work of making them comprehend the new social rank they are destined to hold."[24] Present in Saint-Simon, Brownson discerned, is the notion of a hierarchical organization of society, religious in its conception, that compels humanity forward. This, too, found favor with Brownson and informed much of his sermon and writing output.[25] The essay "The Church of the Future" and his first book, *New Views of Christianity, Society, and the Church*, most clearly evidence Brownson's notion that a new church for a new man and society must be built to inspire progress. These ideas remained evident in Brownson's writings until his conversion to the Catholic Church roughly a decade later in 1844.

Brownson moved to Boston in 1836, settling in the suburb of Chelsea, to meld together a progressive religious organization with an ambitious scope. He founded The Society for Christian Union and Progress to foster unity among Christians in Boston with the expansive hope that it would become the model for the church of the future. Of note was the growing concern expressed to Brownson by Unitarian leaders of the increasingly unchurched working class in Boston and the dissatisfaction, if not apathy, toward religion these leaders thought present in other classes.[26] Brownson attempted to address this problem by finding the ground of Christian truth. Now the Christian syncretist, Brownson united the affirmations of different Christian sects and downplayed their differences. This work of unification, however, was meant to serve the larger goal of human progress toward equality.

Brownson believed that a great man must reunite the scattered sheep of Christianity as Moses, John the Baptist, and Jesus had done with their witness.[27] To this end, Brownson required a "representative man" who would provide a new birth of the spirit. Needless to say, no such prophet was forthcoming, and this left Brownson to proclaim the twofold objectives of the Society: Christian unification and the progress of man. His opening sermon for the society, "The Wants of the Time," delivered in Boston's Lyceum Hall in 1836, advanced this dual mission by emphasizing the profound social dimension of the New Covenant:

> I say again that Jesus was emphatically the teacher of the masses, the prophet of the workingmen if you will, of all those who "labor and are heavy laden" Were I to repeat his words in this city or elsewhere, with the intimation that I believed they meant something, were I to say, as he said, "It is easier for a camel to go through the eye of a needle, than for a rich man to enter the kingdom of heaven," and to say it in a tone that indicated I believed he attached any meaning to what he said, you would call me a "radical," an "agrarian," a "trades unionist," a "leveler," a "disorganizer," or some other name equally barbarous and horrific."[28]

In Boston, Brownson worked out the key elements of his progressive religious and philosophical project. He sermonized that Christianity and democracy are deeply interwoven and contain the authentic gospel of Jesus. In understanding this social truth of the gospel, a new catholicity of Christianity could emerge.

During his Boston sojourn, Brownson published his first book in 1836 entitled *New Views of Christianity, the Society, and the Church*, which expressed in grand form the idea of humanitarian progress made possible through Christian unification with such unification profoundly shaping the American polity.[29] In this essay, Brownson's radical thought coalesced around the interrelatedness of religion, philosophy, and political reform. The stated object was to a build a new church that will harmonize spirit and matter (atonement) and, from this organization, would emerge the energy for greater social reforms. As Brownson stated in correspondence to George Bancroft the same year that *New Views* was published, "I am trying to democratize religion and philosophy."[30]

Catholicism, Brownson observed, had condemned matter and exalted the spirit, much to man's great confusion. This error in thinking and practice was inverted by Protestantism, which exalted matter over the spirit. With Catholicism being dead in the modern era, Brownson urged, and Protestantism having ceased its progress with the chaos of the French Revolution, a new birth of religious truth was now called for.[31] The proper harmony of spirit and matter required atonement, Brownson stated, but such atonement can only come if we know that "human nature is well made ... its elements are true and divine. And this is the hidden sense of that symbol of the God-Man. That symbol teaches all who comprehend it, to find divinity in humanity, and humanity in divinity. By presenting us God and man united in one person, it shows us that both are holy."[32]

Brownson acknowledged later that he exaggerated Catholic and Protestant teachings on matter and spirit to undergird his own philosophy of history and its completion in the doctrine of the atonement as redefined by Brownson. Catholicism does not regard matter as inherently evil nor does Protestantism emphasize a this-worldliness to the exclusion of a life in the spirit or a preparation for eternal life.[33] Brownson's astounding argument was an attempt to construct a historical narrative in the service of an ideology by emphasizing partial truths and generalities about institutions, religions, and social movements. Brownson's rendering of the past and present is of a piece with his project of a future human happiness.

Brownson's pantheist argument built upon the work of French philosopher Victor Cousin who has "demonstrated that humanity, nature, and God have precisely the same laws, that what we find in nature and humanity we may also find in God.... This at once destroys all antithesis between spirit and matter, between God and man."[34] With great similarity, Channing's sermon "Likeness to God," which Brownson held to the same rank as the Sermon on the Mount, proclaimed that "in ourselves are the elements of the Divinity." Channing's theology uncovered for Brownson that "the God-Man indicates not the antithesis of God and man; nor does it stand for a being alone of its kind; but it indicates the homogeneousness of the human and divine natures."[35] The atonement, as properly understood by Channing, became the basis for progress to "correct our estimate of man, of the world, of religion and of God, and remodel all our institutions." Progress, Brownson held, is the proof of our liberty and the highest activity man can pursue. "God," Brownson observed, "gave his richest gift when he gave the capacity for progress. This capacity is the chief glory of our nature, the brightest signature of its divine origin and the pledge of its immortality."[36]

Historian Perry Miller remarked that in this intellectual period Brownson was trying fundamentally to reground the American polity because he believed its Enlightenment basis was proving insufficient for a democratic age.[37] Individual freedom, apart from cohesive spiritual and moral union of the people, was only a release that would drive the republic apart as every citizen went their own way without a common history that could unite them in progress. Miller's insight was not only correct on this particular part of Brownson's intellectual journey, but comprehended Brownson's overall project. Brownson believed that much of the Enlightenment was doomed to failure, the signs of which were already evident to him. America's founding would also fail if other resources were not brought in to complete its experiment in self-government, republican institutions, and liberty. Although Brownson's progressive politics and pantheist-sounding theology would change, his commitment to finding a better ground for American constitutionalism and its corresponding virtues led him to his greatest work, *The American Republic*, which I discuss later in this chapter.

Much of Brownson's radical thought was inseparable from Channing's influence. For Brownson, this meant that individuals possessed the divine spark within, and thus had privileged access to truth. Individuals could intuitively believe in the Christian faith apart from belief in revelation and in New Testament miracles. More powerfully, man could establish the kingdom of God on earth.

Brownson evinced the characteristic modern experience of intense frustration over the presence of inequalities and other evils, Gregory Butler concluded.[38] In rejecting the Jewish-Christian teaching of man as the in between, being capable of receiving eternal love despite being caught in time, Brownson understood "human beings solely in terms of an inner-worldly pursuit of comfort and happiness." Slighting a transcendental reference point for human longing and pain, Brownson emphasized the need for action over thought, pragmatic realization of material equality over the contemplation and study of "nursery tales ... obsolete creeds, silly tracts, foolish catechisms, or stupid folios of polemical theology." Instead, the crucial part, for Brownson, was to find "the best means of procuring food, clothing, and shelter."[39]

Brownson aimed at an "original equality" for all members of the human family.[40] His rhetoric soared in this regard, evincing an ambitious future not unlike that final state of communist utopia detailed by Karl Marx, where there are abundant goods and limitless freedom. "Men," Brownson said, "will be free in their persons, free to pursue happiness, and free to enjoy the good of their labors. Amid this freedom, industry will awake and all will be enabled to find a competent support. Temptations to vice will be removed; crimes will become less and less frequent till they finally disappear, and our jails and penitentiaries be thrown open, or converted to abodes of virtue and happiness."[41] The ambition for the future that Brownson displayed was utopian and demonstrated his confidence in salvation by technique.

Brownson taught that the American achievement of independence from Great Britain should be understood as a world transformative event, beneficial for humanity in its progression to equality. In his 1834 "Independence Day Address at Dedham, Massachusetts," Brownson urged on his hearers a universal, exemplary truth for July 4:

> We have come together to celebrate Freedom's Birthday. Not the Birthday of Freedom merely for this country, but for the world, for man universally. There was a deeper meaning in that Declaration of the Congress of '76 to which we have just listened than that of the political independence of this country. That independence was indeed declared, that independence has indeed been won and defended by deeds of heroism and self-sacrifice, unsurpassed in the world's history, but it enters for only a small affair into what should occupy our thoughts on this day.... A higher and holier triumph than that of arms, or even that of the political independence of any country, excites the warm emotions of our hearts and calls forth our sympathy. We celebrate the triumph of humanity. No limited horizon confines us today. A boundless heaven spreads out over us and the whole human race comes within the scope of our vision.[42]

This dramatic public intervention by Brownson called for social equality as the full realization of the political equality of citizens. As such, the Declaration of Independence, which Brownson invoked as the animating spirit of the American republic, is currently an unfulfilled document. Achieving its principles requires more than equality before law. Brownson contended for "laws which shall not only speak the same language to all, but which shall have the same meaning for all, the same practical effect upon all."

One manifestation of this principle will be to end the separation of capital and labor, which is "a worm gnawing into the very heart of that tree of liberty which our fathers have planted."[43] Brownson thought that the split that industrial capitalism has worked between capital and labor was unjust because it produced idlers who obtain the fruits of all the labor while those who were actually productive were poor. Thus, a permanent inequality was etched into American institutions, betraying the country's noble inheritance. Brownson's address concluded with a paean to education as the most fitting means for effecting and reintroducing equality into America: "We want a republican education, an education which shall accustom the child from the first to see things valued according to their worth—not in the market—but in themselves.... In a word we want an education that shall breathe into the child that very spirit which dictated the assertion, 'God has created all men equal.'"[44]

Brownson argued that American political institutions supported man's need for liberation. "The idea," Brownson said, "which lies at the bottom of our institutions, is the supremacy of Man.... Here is to be established and developed the sovereignty of Man." So we have, according to Brownson, "the American idea. This idea in the political world is translated by universal suffrage."[45] Progress, liberty, and education of humanity are among the nation's goals to accomplish. Brownson's conception of America soared even higher in *New Views*, where he declared that "[o]ur republic sprang into being, and the world leaped with joy that a man child was born.... A new paradise was imagined forth for man, inaccessible to the serpent, more delightful than that which Adam lost, and more attractive than that which the pious Christian hopes to gain."[46]

In his 1840 essay "The Laboring Classes," he called for a thoroughgoing social equality for workers and the poor by ending the division between capital and labor. The essay was Brownson's most radical political statement. He predicted that "the great work for this age and the coming, is to raise up the laborer, and to realize in our own social arrangements and in the actual condition of all men, that equality between man and man, which God has established between the rights of one and those of another."[47] One striking fact of this essay is its anticipation of Karl Marx's denunciation of system and structural inequality that cannot be remedied by moral reform, only by revolution and comprehensive change.[48] On this point, Brownson announced,

> [T]he evil we speak of is inherent in all our social arrangements, and cannot be cured without a radical change of those arrangements.... Continue our present system of trade, and all its present evil consequences will follow, whether it be carried on by your best men or your worst.... The only way to get rid of its evils is to change the system, not its managers. The evils of slavery do not result from the personal characters of slave masters. They are inseparable from the system, let who will be masters. Make all your rich men good Christians, and you have lessened not the evils of existing inequality in wealth.... You must abolish the system or accept its consequences.[49]

Education must be oriented to the goal of unrelenting social progress, and Christians would understand the significance their faith places upon them for the emancipation of the working classes. Part of effecting this change was the abolition of the priesthood. Brownson spoke not only to the Catholic Church but to any ecclesial body that authorizes and maintains a structure of religious leadership who mediate God's ways to man as well. The quasi-revolutionary quality of the essay is evident in its thoroughly democratic Christianity calling the believer to resuscitate the "Christianity of Christ" by zealously working for social reform.[50] The church, Brownson intoned, currently stood as a stumbling block to these efforts that the contemporary believer was called to.

His political program called for an end to the power of "Banks over the government, and [to] place the government in the hands of the laboring classes themselves."[51] Brownson never specified which banks but seems to have in mind a broad selection of banks that enable the national system of commerce, which enables the oppression of the laboring class. Second, he called for an end to the hereditary descent of property. Such property must "become the property of the state" to be used equitably for the rising generation. This particular reform, Brownson stated, would not "be effected peaceably ... only by the strong arm of physical force. It will come, if it ever come at all, only at the conclusion of war, the like for which the world as yet has never witnessed."[52] Brownson concluded that this last measure is too much for the present condition of humanity but that the time has come for open discussion of the possibility and justice of achieving it. To be sure, Brownson did not call for the abolition of private property, but key elements of his analysis eerily anticipate the socialist theorizing that will dominate Western political thought until that ideology's existential failure.

The reaction and fallout that Brownson experienced from the essay were intense and wide ranging. Brownson later reported that in publishing "The Laboring Classes" he knew he was inviting scorn and isolation for himself, even so, Brownson defended the essay vigorously noting that he had not called for the abolition of Christianity, private property, and the market. However, the soaring proclamations of the essay easily committed it to denunciation. Complicating matters was that Brownson believed that the Democratic Party was the political vehicle for the enactment of his liberation program, and he had allied himself with it. No deep philosophical affinity attracted Brownson to the Democrats. In part he did not believe that forming a third party would prove efficacious to his goals. Therefore, he sought to shape and influence the party he believed was closest to the laborers whom Brownson wanted to elevate. As a court philosopher for the Democratic Party, their Whig opponents pinned Brownson's essay on the Democrats during the 1840 elections, tarring the party by association. Brownson was humiliated. The Democrats were defeated, and the Whigs, whom Brownson thought deceitful of the electorate, won.

How easily, Brownson wondered, had majoritarian political principles cut both ways? That people had accepted and celebrated the craven Whig campaign of William Henry Harrison as the candidate of "a log cabin and hard cider" was too much for Brownson. He took the entire political episode as evidence disproving his egalitarian belief in democracy's perfective potential. Citizens stood revealed as persons without discernment and independent judgment. The merely clever had prevailed.

A Reforming Mind

The negative repercussions Brownson experienced during the 1840 election season surely fueled his more conservative approach to government. However, in an 1838 essay titled "Democracy," Brownson had argued his deep-seated disagreement with the notion that the sovereign people were the masters of government. Brownson's analysis of the ease with which democracy can become authoritarian is worth repeating, as is his argument that freedom can exist within a democracy only if it is acknowledged that a body of truth transcends both ruler and ruled, state and man. He inquired of democracy,

> Are the people the highest? Are they ultimate? And are we bound in conscience to obey whatever it may be their good pleasure to ordain? If so, where is individual liberty? If so, the people taken collectively, are the absolute master of every man taken individually. Every man, as a man, then, is an absolute slave. Whatever the people, in their collective capacity; may demand of him, he must feel himself bound in conscience to give. No matter how intolerable the burdens imposed, painful and needless the sacrifices required, he cannot refuse obedience without incurring the guilt of disloyalty; and he must submit in quiet, in silence, without even the moral right to feel that he is wronged.[53]

Sovereignty of the people, Brownson argued, cleaved law and liberty into broken pieces that cannot be melded together despite the insistence of democratic reformers. For democracy to be a regime of liberty it required a standard of truth that could be appealed to as justly supporting the regime and its laws. "Why," Brownson asked, "ought I to do this or that particular thing?" When men are true to their "higher convictions," they demand a standard beyond the proclamation of the king, the aristocracy, or the majority will. "Every man feels that he has a right to do whatever is just and that it is his duty to do it. Whatever he feels to be just, he feels to be legitimate, to be law, to be morally obligatory. Whatever is unjust, he feels to be illegitimate, to be without obligation, and to be that which it is not disloyalty to resist." In this vein, Brownson's final verdict was that "witness is borne to an authority above the individual, above kings, nobilities, and people, and to the fact, too, that the absolute sovereign is justice. Justice is then the sovereign, the sovereign of sovereigns, the king of kings, lord of lords, the supreme law of the people, and of the individual."[54]

Brownson's essay demonstrated that his mind was deeply unsatisfied with the modern philosophical foundations of democracy. The majoritarian will of the people could not be the basis of authority. Paradoxically, in the "Democracy" essay, Brownson's lofty conception of the state, his belief that it was called to realize social equality, led him to reject the common understanding of popular sovereignty. Brownson located in mass democracy an almost perennial lack of wisdom. If America was to tutor and elevate man, care for the downtrodden, and be a force for progress, then an authority above the people was needed, he thought, to guide and restrain democracy. This belief in a transcendent moral authority as crucial to American republicanism became a central part of Brownson's maturing political thought.

Brownson's desire for release from Enlightenment political and philosophical categories owed to his observations that the sovereignty of reason was unable to explain man's deepest purposes. Reason as understood by the continental Enlightenment enfeebled human thought because it could not make sense of objective reality, Brownson argued. As such, man under the tutelage of modern philosophy became locked in his own mind, unable to describe reality. Brownson's search for a comprehensive approach rejecting modern rationalism found full expression in transcendentalism, a movement that he helped define as its most philosophical member, even if his role has been little noted.[55]

As an intellectual grouping, transcendentalism can be broadly articulated as a reaction to Enlightenment rationalism. American transcendentalists were post-Kantians who believed that the theology of their former Unitarian religion was rationalistic, starving man's spirit. The reason of the Enlightenment, they argued, eviscerated belief in God, immortality, freedom, or an inspired life. The materialism of Enlightenment thought could not speak to the human spirit in its full dimensions.[56] Instead, transcendentalists pointed to German idealism (Fichte, Schelling, Goethe) or, following Brownson, to the French eclecticism of Victor Cousin or to the English idealism of Coleridge and Carlyle as the basis of a new spiritual philosophy.

Transcendentalism emphasized change, development, and spiritual revitalization of the self by subordinating nature to the spirit and emphasizing the "authentic self" against a materialistic and commercial civilization. As Patrick Carey summarized the transcendentalists believed American life with its focus on gain had become a society antithetical to the authentic self. Accordingly, the movement placed reason below the inspirations of nature, as such, and it tended toward the identification of God and man and God and nature. This ultimately, Brownson concluded, amounted to pantheism that believed man emanated from God.

The transcendentalist Brownson somehow cohered with the Unitarian Brownson during his ministry in Boston during the 1830s. Brownson taught that man was able, through rational effort, to reach the model man of Jesus Christ and perfect himself. Contrary to orthodox Christian teaching, man was not alienated from God.[57] However, Brownson was also disturbed by the subjectivism of leading transcendentalists that gave short shrift to reason. Ultimately, the refusal of the transcendentalist school to contemplate God, man, reason, and nature in their distinctive capacities turned Brownson from the movement. Although transcendentalism was a potent form of romantic reaction, its pantheist conclusions proved deeply problematic for Brownson.

If Brownson had once looked to transcendentalism for its idealist tendencies, his critical engagement with transcendentalism was the moment when Brownson finally began to reject much of the political, philosophical, and religious categories of thought that had dominated his mind. Prompting this further discovery was transcendentalism's subjectivism that issued, Brownson concluded, from its belief that nature was divinity. From this point, transcendentalists argued that man could find the truth not by reason or lived experience but by sinking into his nature, which, Brownson noted, must be an irrational one. The consequence was that man was left with himself and all the forces that lurked inside him as his guide. Elements such as reason, historical religion, and tradition were dismissed as relevant guides for the individual. Such a position was possible for the transcendentalists because they believed man to be an emanation of God. The transcendentalists sought union or identity between nature and the spirit of man because nature was truth, part of divinity itself. Ralph Waldo Emerson had proclaimed as much in his Harvard Divinity School Address that urged students to realize the divine within themselves.

While Brownson qualified his criticisms in certain cases, his study of Victor Cousin led him to sharply question the movement. Philosophically, Brownson upheld with most transcendentalists the belief in the divine light within the person and that man could know divinity intuitively, but this was not, he stressed, a personal and subjective knowing, as many transcendentalists believed. Rather, this was an impersonal, spontaneous light that every person possessed. Man's experience of God was concrete. This light is better stated as a primitive revelation that is a gift to man, existing prior to man's senses and reflection but that he is capable of grasping and understanding through reflection even as it conditions that process. Cousin's eclecticism, which I have sketched here, melded with Kantian a priori conditioning of knowledge with Scottish Common Sense philosophy. It guided Brownson's increasingly critical approach to transcendentalism, giving him resources to repudiate its inward turn because the person's knowledge of God is not a subjectively shaped understanding.

Brownson had also long held that Christ was just an idea in the mind of God, whose virtues were being externally realized by people in time. This Christian idealism was now rejected by Brownson as he grappled with the subjective forms of spirituality put forward by transcendentalism, most notably, Emerson. What unfolded in Brownson's mind is that Christian revelation, to be true, required history, tradition, and external forms of practice by believers. In short, something factual had to be revealed for the religion to be worth following. Brownson now understood that without a historical Christ, transcendentalist pantheism was inevitable. The historical Christ, backed by a theology of the Incarnation, was the most compelling evidence that God was distinct from his works and not identical to them.

Brownson came to repudiate transcendentalism in no uncertain terms:

> [Transcendentalism is] the last stage on this side of nowhere, the logical and historical evolution of Protestantism. It is the Gospel turned upside-down and exalts the inferior soul, the seat of concupiscence, placing it above man's spiritual nature. The Transcendentalists are not reasoners, but 'seers' who believe that passion and imagination are superior to reason.... [W]e will not believe them till they tell us what they see.[58]

In a powerfully worded condemnation of his friend Ralph Waldo Emerson's widely noted Harvard Divinity School Address, Brownson said, that its rule was to "obey thyself" and "follow thy instincts, follow thy inclinations, live as thou listest." But this was lacking, Brownson thought, in the wisdom that people needed to live well. "Strike out the idea of something above man to which he is accountable, make him accountable only to himself, and why shall he not live as he listest?" We must, Brownson counseled, obey a power higher than our will. Brownson added that Emerson's address amounted "to another name for self-worship."[59]

Some have argued that Emerson's Divinity School Address earned him the title of America's first "death of God" theologian.[60] This is certainly Brownson's critique, charging Emerson, in effect, with an inability to locate any truth other than that found in man's intuition and private sense of the good. As such, Emerson placed man over God. Brownson's dialogue with Emerson compelled him to look deeply into a doctrine of personal emancipation. The pursuit of Emerson's ideal, Brownson noted, would license the rapacious to inherit the earth.

Life by Communion

In the 1840s Brownson began to gravitate to orthodox Christianity and then to Catholicism in 1844. Two doctrines are foremost here in his journey. One is the freedom of God, or Brownson's belief that God is free to create and is not detached from his creation as in the rationalist deist conception. Second, Brownson accepted from French philosopher Pierre Leroux his doctrine that man progresses by a threefold communion with nature, with society, and with God.[61] The great crisis Brownson navigated was the epistemological crisis introduced by Descartes and deepened by Kant. The effectual truth of modern philosophy was that it insulated the person within his own mind, preempting knowledge of the objective world. Brownson acutely understood this and believed that it needed to be remedied with a systematic philosophy that again connected the human subject with the external world on an objective basis.

Leroux's thought achieves this epistemological feat by noting that man as a subject required for his progress an objective element to commune with. Man was an incomplete being without nature and the reality of an intelligible world that existed apart from his subjective thought. Leroux argues that man's subjective capacity is raised by interaction with the objective world. This was, most crucially, a statement of humility about man's capacities:

> Having settled it that man does not suffice for himself in the intellectual order, that he cannot think without thinking what is not himself, or without the concurrence of that object with the subject.... Man lives and can live only by communion with what is not himself. In himself alone, cut off from all not himself, he is neither progressive nor a living being.... He cannot lift himself, but must be lifted, by placing him in communion with a higher and elevating object.[62]

Such communion also meant that man's progress in history was distinct but not separable from the providence of God whose presence in human affairs was constant. This further entailed providential men by which the human race advanced.[63]

Equally significant in Brownson's discovery of a divine support for philosophic realism is the notion of the freedom of God as an affirmation of human personhood. He stated, "This threw a heavy burden from my shoulders, and in freeing God from his assumed bondage to nature, unschackled my own limbs, and made me feel that in God's freedom I had found a sure pledge of my own." Moreover, Brownson equated the God he formerly believed in as one subject to "inexorable general laws," but he now understood that "God binds nature, nature cannot bind him." As Brownson argued, "[e]ither we must give up all ground for piety, or suffer Providence to intervene in the affairs of the world, and of the human race."[64]

Brownson's understanding of the freedom of God emerged from a profound causal link of divine personhood with human personhood. We experience ourselves as free and relational beings not chained to impersonal nature. Is there real support, however, for this authentic subjectivism? Or is this experience of freedom and love an illusion? Brownson believes that the best evidence we have for grounding our experiences of ourselves as free and relational beings is in the personal God who is the logical causal foundation for our personhood.

Brownson held that a being like man, who is actuated by love, and everywhere exists in communities, has his personhood given to him by a free and personal God. The freedom of God combines with Leroux's life by communion doctrine to emphasize that the human person advances through relationships with God, other human beings, and with nature in the form of property. Thus, the subjectivism of modern philosophy, Brownson argued, is a heresy and definitive proof for this charge is found in the relationships of communion that bind the human person and shape his existence. Accounting for freedom is paramount in Brownson's argument for communion.

The person subjectively experiences himself as a free, relational being who must wonder if there is an ultimate foundation for his personhood. Ancient thinkers were unable to ground man's subjectivity and his freedom in anything that was explanatory of this perceived freedom. The god of Aristotle is a principle, a what, ontologically incapable of concern or love for man. He is the deist god of clock making who separates himself from his creation after he puts it in motion. But how do you derive a who, or a person, from a what, or a god, that is a principle?

Implicit in Brownson's formulation is that nature is not "self-sufficient, to understand nature as possessing a purpose within itself, is the basic error of pagan philosophy, and is therefore 'pantheistic.'"[65] The personal, incarnated God of Christian revelation supplies this ground of personhood and does so not by obliterating the distinction between time and eternity, God and man but through mediation by way of the second member of the Trinity, Jesus Christ. Thus, man is shown God's infinite love for him through God becoming man and lifting man's estrangement from God by his death and resurrection. Our relational freedom and the questions it poses finds a profoundly new foundation and method for its realization in time, that is, a personal being has a personal creator whom he can love and is loved by it. Man must work from what he believes best explains his capacities for reason, judgment, happiness, love, and loyalty. Christian revelation had opened to reason the belief that man's end was in a God of love.

Brownson ultimately converted to Roman Catholicism by way of both of these notions and the support they give to philosophic realism and the free and relational personhood of God. On his conversion, the last of his ecclesial commitments, Brownson gave ultimate attribution to the doctrine of grace and the sacraments. He also noted that traditional Catholic teachings alone would not have brought him into the church. The intellectual tendencies of the modern world that enfold the unbeliever make reception of Catholic theology almost impossible. Brownson observed that his own preparation could serve as a model for the church as it confronts the contrasting spirits of the age and presents itself to the modern world, "especially in this age, when objections are drawn from philosophy rather than history, from feeling rather than logic."

From 1842 onward, consistent with his adaptation of Leroux's philosophy of communion and belief in the freedom of God, Brownson's political thought will relinquish its perfectionist quest and come to terms with the natural drama of political life. Politics, Brownson articulated, finds natural support in man's rational and reflective capacities. Moreover, communion with other persons under the just authority of law enables true human flourishing.

Brownson's understanding of republicanism was guided by the need for both liberty and authority to inform each other in their respective capacities. That is, man's duties and corresponding rights to fulfill them fundamentally constrain the state's powers over him, a revolution in human thought and practice made possible by Christianity, Brownson noted.[66] But this means that individual rights are only possible in the light of authority, or man's need to exercise responsibility in the use of his rights to a truth that transcends human invention but is yet comprehensible and discoverable by human agency. In short, rights are bound with a trust the individual must have to a personal God who has created an intelligible world. Only in this metaphysical light that finds a basis for natural law existing above both ruler and ruled can republican government find an enduring center.

Compelling evidence of Brownson's affirmation of republican government, qualified by an insistence on its limitations, is his brief discussion of the Declaration of Independence in his classic 1865 work *The American Republic: Its Constitution, Tendencies and Destiny*. Peter Lawler noted that Brownson confirmed the natural rights conclusions of the Declaration but not its methodology in reaching those conclusions.[67] That is, Brownson affirmed the equality of human persons as a fact but one that has become self-evident through Christian revelation, which philosophy cannot help but now affirm. Human beings are equal because they are equally created. This subtle shift undermined, Brownson contended, a key aspect of social contract thinking, evident in the Declaration of Independence: self-sovereignty as the origin of government. Thus, government is not founded on man by his consent but is entrusted to him from God:

> But as, under the law of nature, all men are equal, or have equal rights as men, one man has and can have in himself no right to govern another; and as man is never absolutely his own, but always and everywhere belongs to his Creator, it is clear that no government originating in humanity alone can be a legitimate government. Every such government is founded on the assumption that man is God, which is a great mistake—is, in fact, the fundamental sophism which underlies every error and sin.[68]

Brownson's maturation as a thinker further evidences itself in his coming to terms with much of modern political thought. The trajectory of Brownson's mind, in many respects, had always been a rejection of modern political notions of self-interest, individualism, the social contract and the belief that theory or reason operating apart from history, tradition, settlement, religion, and language, among other particulars, would found an enduring polity. Brownson's criticism focused on the unbound nature of modern political tendencies.

Law with Liberty

A series of critical essays published between 1845 and 1855 evidence Brownson's reformed social and political thought. In his 1845 essay "Catholicity Necessary to Sustain Political Liberty," Brownson argued in a tone similar to but stronger than Alexis de Tocqueville that democracy without religion becomes humanitarian ideology that will consume the regime of liberty it is meant to foster and protect. A religion that has been democratized to irrelevance no longer inspires and challenges its adherents. Therefore, it poses no barrier to the immense attractions of worldly powers and interests dominating democratic government and society. Brownson argued that democratic society must retain the sense of limits and an attachment to finding justice in their civic relations. An isolating individualism, Brownson related, is democracy's termination point if it loses touch with a religion that exists above the people.[69]

Rejecting his earlier favorable anticipation of Marxist ideology in "The Laboring Classes," Brownson's three essays "Socialism and the Church,"

"Channing on the Church and Social Reform," and "Channing on Christendom and Socialism" repudiated socialism as a heresy that apes Christian charity and solidarity while promising an even greater fulfillment of these virtues through vast structural change.[70] Socialism's theft of Christian virtues is its great strength:

> Socialism conceals from the undiscriminating multitude its true character, and appealing to the dominant sentiment of the age and to some of the strongest natural inclinations and passions, it asserts itself with a terrific power, and rolls on in its career of devastation and death with a force that human beings, in themselves, are impotent to resist. Men are assimilated to it with all the power of their nature, and by all their reverence for religion.[71]

In "Liberalism and Socialism," Brownson listed the deficiencies in both ideologies insofar as they reduce man's social and political existence to abstract doctrines of popular sovereignty or egalitarianism without asking what is true and false in both of these conceptions and fully reckoning with the complex requirements necessary for free societies to endure.[72] Insofar as socialism had any truth, it consisted in human solidarity. Human beings, are, after all, equal by the divinely created law of nature, Brownson noted, but the socialist demands an end to inequality, tout court. In this socialism pursues an end so grand that the means to effectuate it wreak greater havoc than the problems posed by social and economic inequality. Brownson observed that the socialism of necessity calls for the state to invent new forms of morality and to enforce them against the people. Instead, Brownson emphasized reforms for the working class that are consistent not only with men's legitimate needs for solidarity but also with the person's need for family, property, political society, and religion for his integral development. Undoing these associations in pursuit of an egalitarian society is madness, Brownson judged.

Brownson's essay also addressed a continental European liberalism that insisted on the natural rights of the sovereign individual possessed as their birthright apart from any authoritative preliberal traditions. The problem with this liberalism, Brownson thought, is its constricted belief that the individual and the state were the only two densities of modern society that were needed for a free and decent regime. The individual armed with a bevy of rights before the state was likely to be swallowed by a collectivism made possible by the elimination of various types and scales of communities that stood between the individual and the state. There would, it follows, be no context for individualism. This would make individual freedom an incomprehensible status that would end in citizens being left to their own devices, delinked from their neighbors, seeking refuge within the tutelary modern state. As Peter Lawler noted, this analysis aligns Brownson with Alexis de Tocqueville's reflections on the arts of associations that stave off an omnicompetent state by linking men with one another in shared pursuits.[73] Returning to Brownson's evolved position that we are free and relational beings as opposed to autonomous individuals, the tragedy of democracy was its tendency to reduce the person to an individualism that could not contemplate the institutions of freedom. Absent the proper contexts for its exercise, freedom loses to equality's siren calls to relink man through the ministrations of the modern state.

Another essential practice necessary to elevate the human spirit within modern democracy is religious freedom, Brownson prominently argued in several essays. These essays place Brownson firmly within nineteenth-century Catholic liberalism and proclaim his commitment to the religion clauses of the First Amendment as the best legal security for religious freedom in the world:

> What we assert is, not what is called theological tolerance, but what is called civil tolerance. Error has no rights, but the man who errs has equal rights with him who errs not. The civil authority is incompetent to discriminate between truth and error, and the church is a spiritual kingdom without force, or the mission to employ it for the one or against the other. The weapons of her warfare are spiritual not carnal; consequently, before the secular or human authority, whether of churchmen or statesmen, truth and error must stand on the same footing and be equally protected in the equal rights of the citizen. All sects should be equal before the civil law, and each citizen protected in the right to choose and profess his own religion, which we call his conscience.[74]

Brownson deftly argued that America's constitutional commitment to religious freedom is no mere concession to religious exercise or a point of tolerance, but instead is an affirmation of the liberty of the citizen to situate himself before God.[75] America recognizes the reality of human conscience and its search for transcendent meaning and seeks at the level of fundamental legal principle to protect this individual pursuit, even recognizing that religious practice will be stronger as a result, with this redounding to the country's larger advantage. While we have no direct evidence that John Courtney Murray read Orestes Brownson's writings on this or any other matter, the close similarity between Brownson's defense of religious liberty and the grounds for this freedom in *Dignitatis Humanae* of the Second

Vatican Council, the American document, largely authored by Murray, is manifest.

Brownson, unlike James Madison in his much-noted "Memorial and Remonstrance against Religious Assessments," moved beyond a defense of religious liberty that solely focused on the individual in isolation from the church or corporate religious body. He defended the ancient concept of freedom of the church and its insistence that the church possesses internal freedom to propose its truth, to teach and govern its members, and to speak freely to the social and political order that it inhabits. This is the great truth of the American constitutional order, Brownson observed. Here, the church is free to speak and practice freely with no undue interference from government:

> My church is my right, is included in my right as an American citizen; and she has the right to be here, because I have the right myself to be here, and to have my own religion.... The liberty of the Catholic Church is her liberty to be here as the Catholic Church, as herself, and to hold and to do all that she teaches belongs to her as the church of God. She must be free to be here with all that she teaches is everywhere binding on the consciences of the faithful.[76]

Liberty of conscience, Brownson stated, can only be recognized and upheld when the liberty of the church is included within the broader protections of religious liberty. If not, should the freedom of the church be disavowed, then "my liberty of conscience as a citizen, is not recognized and protected. But, if recognized and protected, she has all that she can receive from the government."[77]

The American Republic

Brownson's deep-seated rejection of social contract thought owed to his belief that it inevitably led to the interlocking vices of modern political life: anarchism and consolidation. Social contract thought lacked an external referent higher than man's will, that could limit, shape, and condition it. As such, the highest being was man who would self-create government by consent as a protection against death and to secure property rights.[78] But, Brownson asked, is this limited philosophical conception of limited government true?

Orestes Brownson articulated that the modern project of social contract theory as explicated by Thomas Hobbes, John Locke, and Jean Jacques Rousseau failed to understand the complex relationship between the nature of the human person and political order. Within the strictures of social contract theory, there is a scientific deconstruction of man to provide for a new foundation of political sovereignty. The division of man's being into manageable parts for political order is first hypothetical and then made actual through its ability to reshape man's understanding of himself from a relational, created being to an individual whose purposes are defined by a self-interested willing and choosing.

This was, for Brownson, not an item of idle philosophical speculation. Social contract theory, he observed, was the most consistent teaching among the American founders for explaining their act of independence and forging of the Constitution. America accepted the theory

> as modified by asserting that the individual delegates instead of surrendering his rights to civil society, was generally adopted by the American people in the last century, and is still the more prevalent theory with those among them who happen to have any theory or opinion on the subject. It is the political tradition of the country. The state, as defined by the elder Adams, is held to be a voluntary association of individuals. Individuals create civil society, and may uncreate it when they judge advisable.[79]

Brownson quoted the Declaration of Independence to emphasize his point regarding the pervasiveness of the social contract theory within the American political tradition. Government "derives its just powers from the consent of the governed."[80] Brownson's opposition emerged from his deep reading of the Western political tradition that had articulated the naturalness of political authority, the person's inbuilt need for society, and with Christian revelation, man's relational capacity, and his end in God, which gives his life a purpose beyond government, forever circumscribing its powers.

The purpose of the state of nature, Brownson argued in extended fashion, is to remove man from authority, civilization, and religion. The person must stand as a sovereign agent of the political order. Russell Hittinger observed that this appeal is "to no authority other than what is first in the mind ... under the authority of no pope, prince, or scripture."[81] Thus does authority emerge from individuals making agreements on "what is (or seems) self-evident" apart from any higher order of law or obligation save for what the contracting individual wills.[82]

For Brownson, the social contract theorists affirm what they first deny. Persons who roam the state of nature and finally calculate that it is in favor of their self-interest to consent to a contract that will found a political society must first have had a notion of the social setting to begin with. That is, achieving political society requires a profound awareness of man's social condition and dependency on others.[83] But, how, Brownson wondered, on its own terms, by its very operation, could the state of nature ever provide such knowledge?

> The advocates of the theory deceive themselves by transporting into their imaginary state of nature their views, habits, and capacities of the civilized man.... But these are no representatives of the primitive man in the alleged state of nature. These primitive men have no experience, no knowledge, no conception even of civilized life, or of any state superior to that in which they have thus far lived. How then can they, since, on the theory, civil society has no root in human nature, but is a purely artificial creation, even conceive of civilization, much less realize it?[84]

Brownson's lengthy interrogation of an actual basis for the state of nature teaching uncovers its sheer imaginativeness, placing before us its determined attempt to teach individuals how to be sovereigns who construct a politics that will permit the mastery of nature. Brownson's definitive answer to the social contract teaching is in the concept of territorial democracy he learned from Benjamin Disraeli and which forms part of his constitutional argument in *The American Republic* that I discuss in the next section.

Brownson's political arguments challenge the democratic symbols many Americans now accept regarding our constitutional order. Much of this democratic takeover of American republicanism emerged in Brownson's time. He sought to repel it as a hostile infection threatening the continued existence of American constitutionalism. Perhaps George Bancroft, the German educated historian and sometime friend of Brownson, best articulated the American mind of the mid nineteenth century. Bancroft argued that America could only be understood as a democratic nation par excellence whose mission is to deepen internally this revolution. American institutions were founded by and must be led by democracy. It followed, according to Bancroft, that America's principle and its confidence must be in *vox populi est vox Deo*. Brownson's critical reflections on Bancroft's scholarship as storytelling in the service of democratic ideology home in on its slighting of America's republican Constitution.

Brownson inquired, "Was unyielding democratic revolution in the minds of the founding generation, Brownson inquired?" Finding this notion false on several levels, he argued that legitimate government served the human person but utilized republican forms that hemmed in the people's worst propensities, creating space for reflection and choice for the good.

Accordingly, separation of powers, federalism, religious liberty, the presidential veto, and the common law were all proof, for Brownson, that the majority will is to be constantly seasoned and tutored by deliberation and delay. Of significance, Brownson argued, is that the unwritten foundation of the American Constitution points to truths higher than the majority will. Man had ends beyond government, and republican limitations on government served the person's true north in this regard.

This was the significance of the elusive notion of the common good, Brownson stated. The form of government was not sufficient to protect liberty or the higher goods that citizens sought. For that, the statesman and the citizen must focus on the end of government rather than the form. Man's highest purposes were not coextensive with government or society itself but did require social and political institutions to support man's way to their fulfillment. The truth about republicanism is that it profoundly engages man's natural capacity for politics. Accordingly, American constitutionalism serves the common good by facilitating and not hindering what Brownson called communion of man with man (society), man with property (economics), and man with God (religious life).[85]

This teaching brought Brownson into substantial conflict with much of modern political thought, including certain aspects of the American founding. If man's life was best realized by living in communion with others and with God, then man lived amid a thicket of goods. Brownson argued that communion with others in society necessarily requires love and loyalty for its goods to be realized. The strongest elements of modern political thought: egoistic individualism, self-interest as a political organizing concept, the sufficiency of reason, and flattening of religion, Brownson believed, were deliberate detours from the truth about man and his freedom.

This appropriately brings us to *The American Republic*, a work that Brownson stated was his most mature political thought and his "last on politics or government, and must be taken as the authentic, and the only authentic statement of my political views and convictions."[86] In this book, he sets forth his thoughts on the foundations of government and the particular excellence of the American political order. America, Brownson discerned, is best understood through its unwritten constitution and the notion of territorial democracy. Brownson's book is a philosophically complex argument on the origin of government and law and the application of these principles by Brownson to the American Constitution. Moreover, Brownson wrote this book in search of the American constitutional soul at the end of the horrific Civil War, which demonstrated, he thought, the failure of American statesmen to understand the genius of the American order in its origins, principles, and the political calling placed on it. I can only here provide a general description of its many arguments and alert the reader to pertinent passages for further study.

The great principles of politics "have their origin and ground in the great, universal, and unchanging principles of the universe. Hence, I have labored to show the scientific relations of political to theological principles, the real principles of all science, as of all reality. An atheist, I have said, maybe a politician; but if there were no God, there could be no politics."[87] Brownson is explicit, politics is a natural pursuit of relational beings created by a personal god. "Man," he said, "is a dependent being.... He lives not in himself, but lives and moves and has his being in God. He exists, develops, and fulfills his existence only by communion with God, through which he participates of the divine being and life. He communes with God through the divine creative act and the Incarnation of the Word, through his kind, and through the material world."[88] Life by communion in Brownson's conception of politics confirms our relational nature that finds its natural expression in political activity.

From the creative act of God we know, Brownson observed, that man is everywhere "born and lives in society, and can be born and live nowhere else.... Hence, wherever man is found he is found in society, living in more or less strict intercourse with his kind." From this Brownson concluded that "[a]s society is a necessity of man's nature, so is government a necessity of society."[89] And this government when properly understood is a positive force for justice, solidarity, and liberty, a law-giving body that protects rights as it promotes the common good. Brownson believed that the Augustinian conception of government as a force that prohibits evil was only partially correct, for government's office is "positive as well as negative."[90]

His expansive aim was to articulate the providential mission of America:

> Its idea is liberty, indeed, but liberty with law, and law with liberty. Yet its mission is not so much the realization of liberty as the realization of the true idea of the state, which secures at once the authority of the public and the freedom of the individual—the sovereignty of the people without social despotism, and individual freedom without anarchy. In other words, its mission is to bring out in its life the dialectic union of authority and liberty, of the natural rights of man and those of society. The Greek and Roman republics asserted the state to the detriment of individual freedom; modern republics either do the same, or

> assert individual freedom to the detriment of the state. The American republic has been instituted by Providence to realize the freedom of each with advantage to the other.[91]

This providential mission issues from America's unique origins, from the fact that its "constitution has no prototype in any prior constitution." Such originality, Brownson asserted, "has been overlooked by the great majority even of our own statesmen."[92] The key is to understand America's given origins. For this, the statesman must look to the initial deposit of religious, cultural, and political orderings that America had received. This was the unwritten or providential constitution of a country. The written law memorialized, as it were, this foundation with law. The more significant role, however, was in the unwritten norms and mores, and to this, Brownson stressed, deference and humility were owed.

In stating this argument, Brownson rejected the social contract teaching that an unattached mass of people ex nihilo create government and a body of law based on self-interest. Something must first determine the people. Before the state there is a common history, language, religion, and forms of law that cohere a people into a body making them capable of pursuing a common political project, that is, the providential constitution. This enables the written political articulation, the actual organization of the state, to occur. So political life requires limits, boundaries, and definition for citizens to assert their will; something must first be there to receive it. Attempting to replace or discard the unwritten constitution was "state suicide."

In the United States, the citizen was a member of a state and a national government. In this, it reflected the preexisting political settlement of the colonies. Brownson believed two facts are salient: the colonies had instinctually united in their push for independence from the British Empire, and as subjects of the Crown, they had voiced their political grievances through their colonial political bodies. The colonies themselves, Brownson noted, had united both as a protest against abuses of their English liberties and then to declare independence. Once achieved, an independent America, in time, jettisoned the Articles of Confederation, its wartime constitution. This rejection was an affirmation of experience in favor of a political articulation more suited to the actual unity of the colonies during their war for independence. Accordingly, the Articles had been an immature declaration of state sovereignty, one made of necessity without sufficient reflection on events.

The failure and lethargy in actually governing that had been incentivized by the Articles was proof that it was a misplaced layer on America's unwritten constitutional foundation. The constitutional framework of 1787 properly expressed the dialectical form of national and state political organization in America. In its best light, Brownson urged, the national (general) and state (particular) governments are not inevitable competitors and are called to realize in their work man's natural requirements that move from the local community outward to larger spheres of interaction.

Territorial democracy articulated that political power belonged to a bounded territory as a matter of public right. The true emphasis of territorial democracy is on the territorial as opposed to the personal basis of power. Brownson pointed to Greece and Rome to illustrate the concept. Athens "introduced the principal of territorial democracy," and subdivided power "into demes or wards." The foremost principle demonstrated was "loyalty of all citizens" to Athens, not to a particular ruler or ruling group.

The Senate body in Rome politically organized the undifferentiated mass into a body politic governed by public rule. Only those heads of households that were "tenants of the sacred territory of the city, which has been surveyed and marked by the god Terminus," were entitled to govern in the Senate. Political rule was legitimated by the Roman legal principle of land ownership. Brownson formulated that here was "the introduction of an element which is not patriarchal, and which transforms the patriarch or chief of a tribe into the city or state, and founds the civil order, or what is now called civilization. The city or state takes the place of the private proprietor, and territorial rights take the place of purely personal rights."[93]

Territorial democracy related the Constitution of 1787 to the attachment of the people to the actual bounded political territories, federal and state. The sovereign is the organic, territorial people bounded by law. This political and legal relationship was not created by the people, however. This is of crucial significance. Brownson asserted that the idea of the people as a sovereign mass creating by will and consent their government is false as a matter of fact and right. Accordingly, power was bounded by a given political settlement and had to be exercised as a trust that was responsible both to God and to citizens for its actions.

Territorial democracy Brownson thought is integral to American government because it distinguishes the republican form of government from modern political tendencies that claim to exemplify republicanism but, ultimately, are a slow return to barbaric political forms. As Brownson explained,

> [t]he most marked political tendency of the American people has been, since 1825, to interpret their government as a pure and simple democracy, and to

> shift it from a territorial to a purely popular basis, or from the people as the state, inseparably united to the national territory or domain, to the people as simply population, either as individuals or as the race. Their tendency has unconsciously, therefore, been to change their constitution from a republican to a despotic, or from a civilized to a barbaric constitution.[94]

Modern democrats locate sovereignty in the individual or in the collective. Brownson's concern is that either location does admit at the level of principle a limit to state power, and, as such, fails to understand the genius of American constitutional order. To thwart the limitless claims of sovereignty in modern political thought, Brownson articulated the notion of law, obligation, and right being fixed to the territory where it is exercised as a public trust. In this regard, Brownson observed that "[t]he people of the United States are sovereign only within the territory or domain of the United States, and their sovereignty is a state, because fixed, attached, or limited to that specific territory. It is fixed to the soil, not nomadic."[95]

Since sovereignty consists only of the territorially constituted people, then the particular requirements of the polity shape public deliberation and responsibility. For America, territorial democracy is exemplified by the division of powers that go beyond mere institutions or separation of classes and interests. Thus, Brownson called for America "to realize that philosophical division of powers of government which distinguish it from both imperial and democratic centralism."[96] America's constitutional structure distinguishes general relations and interests from particular relations and interests. Thus, state and federal powers have their own particular spheres but must also form the "interdependent" work of constitutional government. As such, territorial democracy provides the architecture of devotion to federalism and the separation of powers in the American system.

The Civil War, however, provided unfortunate evidence of an America that failed to realize its distinctive constitution. The duties of the general and of the particular as they were to be exercised by the federal and state governments, respectively, had been conflated with demands for centralized power by both Northern and Southern politicians. The result had been the defeat of the South and its slave economy. This was a proper result, Brownson thought, but it was fraught with dangers if the war's victory would be enlisted on the side of "humanitarian democracy" and efface the limits, boundaries, and rights of the American constitutional system.[97] "The tendency now is, as to the Union, consolidation, and as to the particular state, humanitarianism, socialism, or centralized democracy."[98] Brownson feared that the "higher law of humanity" appealed to by the humanitarians would become the dominant element of American politics. Against its drumbeating for equality and progress, the Constitution's limitations would prove impotent.

To stave off this threat of humanitarian democracy, Brownson pointed to the South. The particular qualities of the South included its defense of a robust conception of liberties. In this the Southerners challenged the state's comprehensive claims on behalf of collective ideals. This vindicated a significant principle of liberty denied by the humanitarians who were willing "to lose the individual in the race." The Southerners, however, were likely to still err in not properly understanding the social nature of government, seeing only the protection of property rights and individual interests as its purpose. This meant that territorial government and its notion of public trust must still be vindicated to preserve the division of powers within government.[99]

Conclusion

Brownson suspended his *Brownson Quarterly Review* in 1864. He claimed that failing health was the cause, but surely the declining subscription rate by Southerners owing to his support for the federal government, which was never compensated for by a sufficient level of increased Northern subscriptions, was the biggest reason. Brownson had also supported the radical Republican candidate John C. Frémont against Lincoln in the 1864 election and was humiliated when Frémont pulled out of the race. He did, however, gain time to write *The American Republic* during this period. Brownson reintroduced the *Brownson Quarterly Review* in 1873, ending it shortly before his death in 1876, with essays on, among other subjects, federalism and various constitutional questions, the Civil War Amendments, and the rights of women and blacks that displayed common attitudes of the period. These essays are evidence of a man worried about social and political changes and what they will mean for American constitutionalism and its structural principle federalism. Brownson supported the equality of blacks under law, but did not think that the Fourteenth Amendment should be enlisted in a broad effort to effectuate equality for newly freed slaves.[100] In fact, Brownson believed the Fourteenth Amendment had been unconstitutionally ratified and was a threat to federalism and the constitutional balance it upheld.[101]

Brownson viewed black suffrage as a political right that was earned and given by the community rather than a the natural right as urged by the radical Republicans. There was, accordingly, no immediate necessity for an Amendment to effectuate it. This makes his defense of emancipation somewhat ambivalent, even though he affirmed the citizenship of freed blacks after the Civil War. They had supported the Union and had fought and died for its preservation. Accordingly, citizenship had become a matter of justice. The terms of that citizenship, however, were not as simple for Brownson. When the contemporary reader recalls Brownson's fear of an impending humanitarian democracy in post–Civil War America, said reader might understand though not agree with his concerns that enlightened politicians might enlist blacks in a movement for a leveling equality that would dismiss the restrictions on power contained in the American Constitution.

On women, Brownson feared that the women's rights movement would obliterate all distinctions of sex before law. This he judged to be part of the humanitarian thrust that would build an order of autonomy and bury the relations proper to men and women in family. The result would be a confused social and political order.[102] Here, however, Brownson judged too broadly. His insistence that women should only be mothers, even as he acknowledged examples of their great leadership, failed to acknowledge the complex roles and patterns that women might pursue. However, readers can disagree with Brownson on his judgments regarding the condition of freed slaves and women but still understand his concerns that a humanitarian zeitgeist was motivating many of the claimants. Behind what many regard as the legitimate claims of women's equality, Brownson, perhaps rightly, discerned an indiscriminate claim of autonomism that would set men and women against or apart from one another rather than as complementary and distinct. Evidence from the contemporary feminist movement suggests that he was correct in certain respects with regard to the long arc of women's rights in America.

Unable to write regularly and his health now failing, Brownson left Elizabeth, New Jersey, in 1875 and moved to the home of his favorite son, Henry Jr., in Detroit, Michigan. His health never recovered. Brownson died in 1876, the day after Easter, having received the sacraments of confession and the Eucharist. Notre Dame, whose founder, Edward Sorin, had once offered Brownson a teaching position at the college, had his body later exhumed and buried in a crypt in the Sacred Heart Chapel on campus. His unpublished papers reside at the university.

Brownson's legacy is found in his intellectual journey, one that continually challenged the fractured nature of modern discourse. In his contributions we are treated to the distinctness and unity of the natural and the supernatural, science and philosophy, politics and religion, democracy and limited government, education and the individual, among other notions, as the grand themes that should guide the minds of scholars and the cultured public. This prolific output, even its more premature and excessive judgments, stressed the dialectical whole of knowledge.

At the center for Brownson is the relational God that he reintroduced to denizens of modernity. The ultimate ground of his conversion from pseudosocialism and his American liberation theology is the freedom of God to create and sustain his creation. Brownson witnessed firsthand modernity's detachment from God and the tendency of democratic society to move from orthodox religious belief to an identification with a humanitarian, therapeutic spirit recognizing no principled limits to its reformative power. Brownson's writings place before us the opposite tendency. His course is a man who moves from pantheism to the relational God who provides real support for human freedom and individuality.

The sheer volume and variety, to say nothing of the turns his judgments take, make his writings challenging for the contemporary reader to discern. Confidence, however, can finally be had in Brownson's desire to understand and comprehend being and the human person through language using the ideas and practices of religion, philosophy, history, and even politics. To walk in the intellectual paths he trod is to engage in a quest for truth as a relational person whose end is in his beginning. This is the unity of Brownson's amazing life.

PART I | Union and Progress

ONE

An Essay on the Progress of Truth

No. I

MR. EDITOR:

I this week commence a series of numbers on the progress of moral reform throughout the world. I shall continue them if I have leisure and health, until I either exhaust my subject or my knowledge. The importance and interesting nature of this subject, as well as my own method of treating it, will be unfolded as I proceed, hence need not be labored in an exordium.—As a motto to my inquiry I select Isaiah, chap. xxxv. 1.

> The wilderness and the solitary place shall be glad for them; and the desert shall rejoice and blossom like the rose.

The final emancipation of the human race from sin, misery and death is a source of pleasing contemplation, and may justly employ the attention of those, who despair of ever finding consolation from the prospective improvement of man while an inhabitant of this sublunary state. At a convenient time, we should not hesitate to wing imagination through regions of ether, and survey a beatified universe bending around the throne of Light,

From the *Gospel Advocate and Impartial Investigator,* vol. 5 (November 17, 1827): 361–62, (November 24, 1827): 369–71, (December 8, 1827): 385–87, (December 15, 1827): 393–94; vol. 6 (January 19, 1828): 24–26, (February 2, 1828): 46–47, (February 17, 1828): 55–56, (March 1, 1828): 68–69, (March 15, 1828): 87–90.

bursting amid the rays of Jehovah's love; but the present requires us to consider what amelioration the progress of Truth will make in the condition of human society below.

Whatever bliss there may be in store for us in that unseen world to which we are all hastening, the present is all we can call our own. We are now inhabitants of the earth, and our chief inquiry should be—how can we render it a pleasing and desirable habitation? I am a believer in life and immortality beyond the grave; but I am not ambitious of being one of that number who forget earth for heaven—who, to ensure the joys of that invisible kingdom, forego the rational pleasures of this.

The present generation owes a duty to all succeeding ones. The course we take will have a greater or less effect upon the morals or happiness of our latest prosperity. We live not for ourselves alone; we are connected with all nations, all generations of men. Let us not, then, because we expect soon to remove to some distant clime, demolish or suffer to decay, the institutions necessary to give peace and felicity to our successors. There are those, who think, if our future welfare or happiness after death be secured, there is no necessity of troubling ourselves about our condition here; and if this generation was the last of the human race, there would be some force in the consideration. But "one generation passeth and another cometh, but the earth abideth forever." The parent finds sufficient inducement to labor, that he may secure his child a competent support; the philanthropist looks through futurity to ages yet unborn, and, while his bosom swells with the prospect, he invokes the genius of improvement to transmit them such institutions as shall preserve external peace and internal tranquility—to transmit them such a fund of knowledge, that the evils with which we and our forefathers have been afflicted, may never reach them.

Is this no inducement to labor? Look back then upon past ages; what deplorable ignorance has debased the human mind! Man has been the slave of both civil and ecclesiastical tyrants. The dignity of his nature has been forgotten amid the bigotry and superstition with which he has been governed. At one time, he is seen rushing with ruthless fury against his brother; at another bowing and cringing before a God of his own manufacture—the property of a fellow lordling, who supports the luxury of his table with the produce of his blood—the dupe of designing hypocrites, who make him sick, that they may be paid for curing him—filled with a zeal for God, fired with enthusiasm for his law, he is seen dealing forth death upon all whose zeal and enthusiasm are different from his own. Robbed by the political despot of the right of pursuing happiness and enjoying the fruit of his labor—divested by the priest of the liberty of conscience and all the felicity of mental independence, he rises in gaudy ignorance or splendid poverty, in the most abject servitude and the most degrading superstition. A prey to all the evils of this physical constitution and the calamities incident to life, rendered thrice doubly severe by his own folly and the exorbitant exactions of his brethren; war sweeps off its millions, carries mourning to as many cottages, and childlessness to as many mothers. Theological wrangling, intestine divisions and domestic discord, destroys what little repose might otherwise have been received! Say, ye friends of the human race! do you wish those evils to go down to posterity? have you no anxiety to remove these evils, that the wrongs and outrages which you have suffered may not be entailed upon your offspring?

But if these considerations have no weight with the philanthropist of the day, it only shows the degradation of their minds, the narrowness of their conceptions, and the feeble claim they have to the name they assume; and no stronger argument is required to show the importance of a reformation throughout the world. Those, however, who can join in the prospective improvement of our race while here reason sufficient to call forth their exertions will contemplate with delight the improvement itself and linger with inexpressible gratitude to God, on the certainty it will in due time be effected.

The improvement of which we speak, or the reformation which we desire, is one that will recognize the original equality of the human family—secure to them all the rights which nature has given them, whether as individuals or members of society. The government of the country recognizes many of our original rights and in a good degree secures them. The reformation we seek, will base all institutions whether civil or ecclesiastical, upon this original equality, and will call forth all the energies of statesmen, moralists or divines to preserve it. Government will then aim at the good of the governed; political, and other rulers will be the servants, not the masters of the people–will be chosen for the good of the whole, not of a few, and be supported from a conviction of their utility, not because they have been born to hereditary advantages, or been forced upon us by circumstances over which our partiality for ancient usages would give us no control.

Men will then be free in their person, free to pursue happiness, and free to enjoy the good of their labors. Amid this freedom, industry will awake and all will be enabled to find a competent support. Temptations to vice will be removed; crimes will become less and less frequent till they finally disappear, and our jails and penitentiaries be thrown open, or converted to abodes of virtue and happiness.

The mind will then have recovered its independence; conscience will not then be bound by the fetters of priestcraft; but it will become the monitor to virtue, the friend of mankind—will entwine around each heart the cords of fraternal affection, and no more break a brother on the wheel or burn him at the stake. Reason will have regained her long lost dominions; her mild and gentle laws will extend peace through all her empire, and preserve the quietness and felicity of every bosom. The happy children of men will form the cheerful circle around the evening fire, give free exercise to all the kind and benevolent feelings of the heart, with no gloomy personage to destroy their heaven born harmony, with his furious declamations and horrid denunciations! Implicit faith in unintelligible dogmas will find no adherents. Each will claim the right of examination; whatever is not congenial with facts, corroborated by universal experience, will be laid aside as a remnant of ancient superstition.

Religion will then rest for its support on a knowledge of human nature, not on the assertions of ignorant or interested men. It will not be a fruitful source of unhappy contention, will not tend to alienate the affections of brethren, nor drive them to the commission of the foulest crimes that ever blackened the page of history; but it will encourage all those good actions, cherish all those kind feelings, render all that mutual assistance which our dependant situation requires.

Such is the improvement we seek, such is the reformation that will be accomplished when men shall have recovered mental independence, and shall dare reason on the nature and propriety of existing institutions; when they shall acknowledge no law but *reason*, no religion but *justice*, no morality but *humanity* in all its forms.

No. II

The opposition to the emancipation of the human race from the bondage of their numerous masters, will be long and obstinate. There are so many notions abroad; so many vague and inconsistent theories are proclaimed by the learned, and enforced by those who claim the direction of the public mind, upheld by those in authority, and eagerly embraced by the multitude; the simple dictates of reason—the plain injunctions of morality, are so readily consigned to forgetfulness, that he who comes forward with a plain and rational scheme, is in danger of being doomed to suffer the contempt of the ignorant, and the persecution of the designing.

The experiment has been fairly tried: to the advocates of a blind and unnatural religion, and to the adherents of a cruel and despotic policy, every indulgence has been granted; we have listened with the most profound attention; we have believed with the most yielding credulity, and obeyed with the most persevering enthusiasm. The popular instructions, from their first existence, have contended earnestly for "the faith"—extolled the purity of their principles, and the wonderful efficacy of their instructions in making society virtuous and man universally happy. Alas! discord has marked their proceedings, confusion their preaching; and notwithstanding man was totally depraved at first, he has been growing worse ever since!

The circumstances of the age call aloud for reform. There has been so much tinsel; so many pretences have been made; so much noise about religion and divine communications has been heard; that men, whose minds have been enlightened by science—whose hearts are warmed by philanthropy, and whose bosoms bleed with compassion for the human race, have turned with disgust from everything bearing such a recommendation, and sought in nature alone, a remedy for infatuated man. They may have gone so far; but every truly enlightened mind will reject with disdain every notion that contradicts the great principles of universal existence, or supersedes the necessity of studying them. I am no enemy to religion; but I would listen with attention, and examine with the most vigilant caution; whatever is not conducive to our happiness while here, I reject as unworthy our attention. Happy would it be for all men, if they would come to this conclusion. But the obstacles to be surmounted in coming to this are many. They rise like mountains, and we tremble as we survey the broadness of their base and the sublimity of their tops. The errors of antiquity are so numerous and so tenaciously embraced, that no wonder timorous souls are despondent. No improvement can be effected while men retain their veneration for institutions merely because they are ancient; nor until many, who now labor with the most persevering assiduity to perpetuate such veneration, shall cease from their pernicious task, and turn their attention to ascertain what is beneficial to man in his social and individual capacity. But the struggle to accomplish this will be long and arduous. Princes who hold their power on the precarious tenure of artificial distinctions in the human family, will be unwilling to enlighten their subjects. Truth is dreaded by them, for they well know the right, by which they govern, has no existence in the nature of things. Should people learn, the God of the Universe made all men originally equal, privileged classes would lose their prerogatives, and be reduced to a level with the rest of mankind. Kings would then depend on the suffrages of their subjects for their election. This, the crowned heads of the earth well know. Hence it was, they saw with consternation the independence of this country, and armed their united forces against republican France. It is the apprehension that truth may enter the dark recesses of their deluded, degraded subjects, that binds together the "Holy Alliance" of Europe, and it is this that drives them to extinguish every ray of liberty that might for a moment illume the darkness of despotism!

Kings and potentates will, from a regard to their own interests, oppose any innovation upon the old order of things. Their power is founded in ignorance, supported by arbitrary and unnecessary distinctions, and has no recommendation but its hoary age. Consequently they have nothing so much to fear as a spirit of inquiry, and close investigation. Such a spirit would undermine the thrones on which they are seated, and trample in the dust every vestige of their tyranny! They will, it must be expected, use every exertion in their power to prevent any alteration in the condition of their people.

Our religious education, and the nature of our ecclesiastical institutions, are much more powerful obstacles in the march of improvements. These form an impediment much more difficult to remove, because supported by more stubborn, more numerous, and more complicated prejudices. It is here too, where reformation is most needed. Whoever has turned over the historic page and traced man through his *religious* career, has wandered in the midst of crime, through scenes the most foul and horrible that fancy can paint. Man, thought, doomed to suffer from the physical circumstances of his condition—though he is a child of sickness and distress—affected by every change in this ever changing state, may forget the whole, in the magnitude and numberless variety of the evils he has heaped upon him by his pretended *spiritual assistants*!

From time immemorial men have formed themselves into religious associations; and under the pretence of superior activity, of more successfully promoting their own and their brethren's welfare, have presumed to dictate to the world what it must believe, and what ceremonies it must observe. To over awe the mind and make it submissive to what all the better feelings of the heart oppose, inspiration has been pretended, and the voice of the Almighty has been made to sanction errors too absurd to be believed on less authority. The venders of this inspiration have usurped an undue ascendency over the lives and consciences of men, as degrading to those who obey as it is profitable to those who rule.

Particular churches have been established, and the priest has promised heaven to all who unite, and denounced the most horrid doom upon all who refuse. A creed was drawn up for the church; the more unintelligible the better, because the aid of the priest in its explication becomes thus the more necessary; a system of external duties is enjoined, the more absurd, or the farther removed from common utility the better, for its observance thus more clearly draws the line of distinction between those who belong to the church, and those denominated the world. All that is required to maintain the purity of one's character, is to believe this unintelligible creed, and damn all who doubt it; to perform the external duties enjoined, which usually consist in assembling together, making a few grimaces and genuflections, repeating over parrot like, a few unmeaning words, in doing penance, supporting the church, and treating with infinite contempt or extreme cruelty all who pay less reverence to such pious *indispensables*. This maintains one's claim to holiness, opens to him the doors of the church here, and of heaven hereafter—gives him a passport to regions of glory, and entitles him to endless beatitude in the mansions of felicity.

A class of men have been produced—fanatics, who have labored with a zeal and perseverance worthy a better cause, which, had they been properly directed, would have done honor to themselves, and been of the highest utility to man. But alas! their zeal was not according to knowledge. They have been deceived by an unreal form—they have contended for a phantom—overlooked the great duties of justice and humanity—encouraged a blind worship, for they knew not what—tolerated a bigoted, superstitious religion equally derogatory from God, and unprofitable to man.

Antiquity is replete with instruction. So many valuable lessons are taught by her examples that we should frequently recur to her sacred archives. The farther our retrospection runs, the more have we to deplore—more prevalent and more absurd is the superstition. Implicit reliance on the priest, augur, soothsayer, Sybil, or whatever name designated their character, comprised nearly the whole of man's moral and religious duties. The priests were mere tools of state; whatever they taught was designed to promote the interest of their masters, or to advance their own ambitious prospects. Thus it was with the priests of Greece, of Rome, and many of the oriental nations. Their religion was upheld for the express purpose of exacting that submission, and that support, which they despaired of otherwise obtaining. And the whole machinery was as much regulated by the state government, as any other department of state police. The philosophers, indeed, discarded the silly and absurd tales of which their religion was composed; they would have labored to enlighten the minds and lead men to the practice of moral virtue, but the infatuated multitude, ever true to the hand that oppresses them, were the first to condemn any effort made for amelioration.

The Jewish theocracy, however useful it might have been in its first establishment, soon became no better than that of other nations. The priests usurped nearly all the power, and seemed to regard little else than the receiving of their tithes and other offerings. They uttered, to be sure, the most horrid denunciations if the people thought for themselves, or became weary of their hierarchy. If the people worshipped Baal, not withstanding they themselves had made the worship of the true God too grievous to be borne, they usually succeeded in overwhelming the nation with calamity, and when led away captive by their enemies, told them it was the just resentment of the Almighty for their apostasy. But all this was apparently not because they cared more for one religion than another, only to support that one which best supported them.

No. III

Jesus Christ, about 18 centuries ago, appeared. He digested the crude notions of religion, then prevalent—selected from the systems already known, what was universally obligatory, to which he made some new accessions, and finally gave us a religion of reason and common sense, as pure, doubtless, as the circumstances of our condition require. His tragical death and the subsequent preaching of his disciples gave his doctrine a rapid and wide extension; but it had not sooner gained ascendency over the ancient religion, than those in authority sought to make it subservient to state policy, dependant on courts and levees.

Christianity was diverted from its natural course, and instead of ameliorating the condition of man, making him more happy by making him virtuous, it uncapt the bottomless pit and permitted monsters of cruelty and blood to fill the earth with rapine and war.—The sickly wretch substituted for the fair daughter of heaven, never softened the heart, never called into action the virtuous principles of our nature, but allowed the appetites all their force, and the passions to rage uncontrolled.

Be sound in the faith, tell a religious experience, and support the church, was a passport through the society of the holy here, and to the regions of the glorified hereafter! This maintained the sanctity of one's character, regardless of moral goodness, and this being all that was required, little more was sought. Justice and mercy fell into disrepute, humanity was unknown, and common sympathy consigned to the land of forgetfulness. Zeal for the Church usurped the place of every other virtue. Then were seen swarms of mendicants pillaging the scanty pittance of the villagers, for which they gave indeed a few *holy relicks*, such as "sanctified rice."

Tears which saints had wept,
A thousand years in vials kept.

Then were seen hordes of monks who cloaked every species of iniquity under the sacred garb of piety, constantly laboring to increase the wealth and independence of the church. Then, too, holy enthusiasm raged. Mothers, without a complaint, could see their sons and wives their husbands, turn from their warm embrace, confined in the dungeon of the Inquisition, brought before the *Ghostly Father*, or burned on the *Auto da Fe*!

Different in forms, but the same in spirit, are the religionists of the present day. Men, professedly holy, do not hesitate to declare from the desk, the supposed guardian of virtue, that the abandoned profligate is less dangerous in society, and more likely to be saved than the honest upright citizen, renowned for his benevolence and general humanity. Faith is raised over morality, and those who style themselves sound in *that*, arrogate to themselves all that is correct in theory, or virtuous in practice, and denounce the most horrid doom upon all who do not bear the same character.

They have an ardent love for God, manifest great anxiety to maintain the glory of his power and the honor of his character. They are ever ready to let him save, from endless woe, souls which his veracity stands pledged to make eternally miserable. But alas! they have so much to do to assist Omnipotence, they are unable to regard the wants of a neighbor. Or, if they have time to bestow a casual glance upon the necessities of a brother, their benevolence evaporates in prayer for his never dying soul, while the body is left to starve!

Men frequently change the name of their sect while they retain the spirit of their former opinions. The primitive Christians, with few exceptions, retained all the distinctive features of the several systems of faith from which they had been converted. A Jewish Christian was in general still a Jew, except in name and the observance of some few ceremonies. Papal Rome was Pagan Rome, under a new appellation. Images of gods were replaced by pictures of Christ and his Apostles, deified heroes by canonized saints, and the Pantheon became as much crowded with the one as it had been with the other.

The beads, crucifixes and holy trinkets, had in so much reverence by thousands of *nominal* Christians, are good evidence, that the gospel of Christ, in the manner it was preached, has not much elevated their conceptions of things, or given them any very exalted ideas of God or his service. The superstitious members of the Roman and Greek churches who regard these trifles, are no more worshippers of the true God, than were the blind votaries of Bacchus, Hercules or Apollo; nor indeed Protestants who place their highest sanctity in the observance of certain days or ceremonies—they are as much idolators as were the deluded adorers of Wodin or Thor.

Most European nations, together with the civilized part of America, embrace unanimously the Christian religion; but it is not unfrequently, we find the spirit of that blessed doctrine exhibited in much greater perfection by the untutored natives of our forests. The *meek and humble* disciple of Christ, may blush for his own want of goodness when he marks the native generosity of the savage. Little research is necessary to show the rational man, that the boasted religions of the day, bear strong marks of consanguinity to the long since obsolete superstitions of ages we hope may never return.

The religions of Greece and Rome are condemned, and justly. No man of common sense, but discards the Deistical notions of the Orientals, and the arrogant pretensions of the Pharisees of Palestine; but the most popular sentiments of our time are only a gross compound of them all, in which each ingredient retains all its peculiarities. The man that should draw a parallel of ancient faith, particularly of the Pharisees, with the most approved modern notions would be pronounced a severe satirist on the faith, and if he was in the synagogue would soon be cast out.

The directors of our opinions have discovered this identity, and to prevent any evil which might fall upon themselves, have very discreetly forbid the comparison, and prohibited investigation and the exercise of our own understanding. The reformer wishes to convince the people, the notions they imbibe are supported neither by reason or revelation; he is commanded to lay reason aside, and is told the priest, *who cannot lie*, has declared these notions to be inspired. He refers them back to their origin, explains the causes which gave them their birth, the reasons which first gained them notoriety, and the circumstances which have perpetuated their existence to the present time: the vengeance of the clerical despot here, and the threatened wrath of Omnipotence hereafter, is the reward he receives for his benevolent intentions.

The Reformer expostulates:—"God has made man a rational being; can he be displeased with the exercise of the noblest faculty he has given us? The notions you imbibe, O people! are unreasonable and contradictory; they are dishonorable to God and injurious to man. The consequences of such sentiments are seen in that spirit of contention which pervades every department of society—in the readiness with which parents, for the love of God, can discountenance their children, and children their parents for the same cause—in the alienated affections of brethren—the hostility, the animosity with which brother attacks brother, and sister rails against sister. O peace! heaven-born word! there is musick in thy name, but alas! theological wrangling has driven thee from our bosoms, and banished thee from our dwellings! The domestic circle is invaded, and tranquility forsakes the fire-side! Malice and rage arm the priest—Fanaticism the multitude! Ignorance and cupidity urge them on and tho' *Religion* may flourish, *Happiness* is gone. Where is the calm and dignified Christian? Where is the man that dare assert the independence of the mind? Where the society not torn by contending factions? Where the community not distracted by intestine broils and the heart-withering conduct of professed religionists? O whither has wandered the genius of Christianity! Whither has fled the native benevolence and forbearance of the human heart? God of Love! restore to man the exercise of his reason, that in contending for religion, he may not destroy everything worthy the name!"

O the lover may
Distrust that look which steals his soul away:
The babe may cease to think that it can play
With heaven's rainbow; alchemists may doubt
The shining gold their crucible gives out:
But Faith —fanatic Faith—once wedded fast
To some dear falsehood, hugs it to the last.

The appeal to facts—to the benevolent feelings of the heart, but enrages the deluded votaries of a blind and unnatural religion, and calls down upon him who makes it the curses and indignation of the ignorant, the superstitious, the bigoted and the designing. "Licentious innovator!" "Infidel!" "Blasphemer of God and Reviler of the Saints!" are the honorable epithets he received and the names by which posterity shall learn the extent of his philanthropy.

Men have so long been taught to distrust their own reason—so long heard enforced, as the only means of their eternal salvation, receive implicitly what the priest shall dictate,—that the great body of the people have forgotten that all were originally equal, and endowed with the same right to judge for themselves. They consider the various notions transmitted them by circumstances of which they never think, are absolutely necessary to maintain proper reverence for the God of heaven; they consider them sacred as the light of Jehovah's throne, and they would sooner part with life itself than renounce them. They believe their eternal all is at stake, if they do not swallow all the ancient whims however absurd or pernicious—all, all is gone! A place of eternal, inconceivable torture remains as their inevitable doom!

No. IV

The least reflection, one would suppose, might convince the most skeptical that this excessive veneration—this implicit reliance, is the result of the craft of a class of man, who wish to revel in luxury without sharing the common burden. That man must be grossly infatuated who imagines the All-wise Parent of nature has suspended the eternal weal of his children upon the contingency of their believing certain religious dogmas. The religious opinions of the age may, indeed, have been transmitted to us from remote antiquity; they may be consecrated by the blood of martyrs, and endeared by the memory of our fathers who believed them; but the man who disclaims all authority but reason, and all creeds but truth, will consider all these external ornaments of little importance, and every argument founded upon them he will ever treat with contempt.

The grand secret is disclosed. No man is against reason, until reason is against him. People that reason cannot be duped. In order to maintain their authority over our minds, priests have told us it is offensive to god, that we exercise this noble faculty. Should men reason, the injustice of their practices would be discovered, and the solidity of their claims be called in question.

Many of those sentiments which have been outstripped by the improvements in natural and moral science, were, no doubt, in their first establishment useful. The first preachers of them considered them true, and very likely proclaimed them with the benevolent intention of ameliorating the condition of man. It was probably by the same desire, that they were induced to represent them as coming from God; and with the wish of insuring them a cordial reception, they were also led to make it criminal to doubt their truth. But ambitious men converted the precautious, those philanthropists had to preserve their sentiments, to a source of individual aggrandizement, assuming to themselves the prerogatives of the Most High—pretending to be under the immediate influence of his spirit, they declared to the people, "whatever we do, however absurd or pernicious in its tendency is suggested by the Holy Ghost, and you will be torn by demons if you do not believe it."

A traffic in human souls the most deleterious in its consequences was carried on by these spiritual merchandizers; but the people, however much oppressed and borne down by the heavy burdens they had to bear, must not complain, because their complaining would be against Heaven, whose vengeance would flash instant death upon them if they dared murmur against his will.

They brought forward their sacred books, written in a style and language wholly unintelligible to the great body of the people. These books they said were from God, and no one must expect salvation that has the audacity to doubt them. To the complaint from the people that they could not understand these books, they answered, "true, many things in them are hard to be understood, which many wrest to their own destruction, but god has conferred on his servants, *the priests*, the privilege of understanding them; believe what we say, give us of your substance to support us, and our children and we will guide you to heaven."

If the people complained the doctrines preached were unreasonable or contradictory; they were answered, what is contradictory to *us*, may be perfectly consistent to God—with him doubtless black and white are the same. What to short-sighted man appears unreasonable may be perfectly reasonable to say, infinite goodness may produce infinite evil, and still retain the character of infinite goodness.

Thus wearied with undue usurpations, the mind lost its elasticity, and finally yielded itself an abject slave to it spiritual master, placed unbounded confidence in what he taught, and obeyed with the most persevering enthusiasm what he commanded. The evil effects of such a state of things have come down to us. The cloven-footed monster which preyed upon our ancestors has come hither to embitter our felicity, and to render us gloomy vassals to clerical dominion.

Adventurous spirits from the old world have felled our forests,—converted the wilderness into a fruitful field—erected on the fastnesses of wild beasts, cities which bid fair to rival the numbers, wealth, commerce and refinement of any which Europe can boast. Liberty has given additional splendor to our noon day sun; freedom has brightened the fires of our evening skies, and mental independence has given verdure to our fields and beauty to our landscapes. Here the care worn son of despotic climes has found a home; oppressed virtue an asylum; and bleeding humanity, driven from the courts of tyrants, a retreat.

The enemies of the human race have cut their way to our peaceful shores,—have entered our paradise, coiled themselves around the tree of knowledge, and are now presenting us the "death-distilling fruit." The claims, which the inhabitants of the old world are already beginning to spurn, are brought hither to bind the sons of those fathers, who taught the world by their example to discard every species of tyranny.

My country! more is thy peril, greater is they danger, than when the gigantic power of a trans-Atlantic prince sent its minions to ravage thy courts and destroy thy women and children. A direful doom awaits thee; the chains of a more dreadful slavery are even now clanking in thy ears;—repose not too much confidence in the virtue of thy sons—the mode of attack is secret and the movements of the enemy are silent.

A clerical hierarchy is threatened us, and the utmost vigilance is requisite to avert the impending danger. The leaders of the grand enterprise are as crafty as they are ambitious. The missionary cause, like the Crusades against the Infidels, was thrown out to engage the great body of the people, that the engine might move unobserved. The sympathies of the people were enlisted by many a pathetic description of poor heathens dropping into hell; the purse was opened—money was at the disposal of the reverend dignitaries who had shown so much compassion upon the wretched pagans.

They sought, as the next step, the superintendence of literature—they have obtained the management of nearly all the seminaries of learning; and, to make their triumph complete, they established their Sabbath schools, introduced their tracts and other books fraught with their own peculiarities, and thus they could begin with the infant and attend him through all the stages of this education. Immense power has thus been thrown into their hands; and they hold in their hands, to use their own exaggerated expression, "the lever that moves the moral world." In this department their plan has succeeded.

One thing remains to be accomplished—this done, and their plan has succeeded in every part. This thing, is to get the supreme control of our political institutions. This, indeed, *remains* to be done; but there is some fear it may be nearer effected than any philanthropist is willing to believe. The proposal that none but Christians should be elected to any office—the attempt to persuade the freemen of these states to vote for no man unless he belong to some church, if it succeeds, will pave the way to designate the particular church; and when such a measure has succeeded, a majority of the favored church will compose the grand council of the nation. Woe be to thee, O Columbia, when that shall be the case.

No. V

The preceding numbers may seem rather an essay on the progress of error, but the exposition they contained was deemed necessary to point out the nature of the evils to be removed, and to exhibit some of the obstacles which ever have had and probably ever will have a tendency to impeded the march of truth. The task was by no means pleasing. To trace the mind in its downward course is an ungrateful employment calculated to arouse the angry feelings and call forth the resentment of those whose lives and errors may be discovered and exposed, without receiving the commiseration of even those who wish to see mankind more virtuous, consequently more happy.

The benevolent heart weeps in sorrow over the follies, the aberrations and inconsistencies of the children of men; it deeply deplores their misery and wretchedness, the severity with which they oppress each other; anxious for their amelioration it raises its inquiries—"Indulgent God! Is man eternally ordained to be the dupe and slave of man! Shall he never regain his independence, and be free to exert his mental powers in the acquisition of knowledge; be free to study the works of his Creator, and while his bosom glows with gratitude to his Heavenly Father, be free to repose with confidence on the paternal affection of the Sovereign of nature? The opposition to this has been already stated. It is aided by all the powers of darkness, but it is hoped the remainder of this essay will evince the "omnipotence of truth," and bring to weary and disconsolate man, the joyful intelligence that it shall prevail to the annihilation of error, and to the eternal banishment of evils which have so long afflicted the human race.

Nature gave to man the law of liberty, and entwined a desire for independence around every fibre of his heart. Amid all the usurpations o tyrants under all the oppressions so liberally heaped upon him, some secret thought recurs to his native dignity; he rises enraged at the shackles of his slavery, indignant spurns the thought and demands his rank in the scale of being. He may be misled, he may mistake the road to the land of Freedom, he may deceive himself in the choice of means, to promote his felicity, but he will never relinquish the attempt. His errors shall serve to correct him, and his follies shall teach him wisdom.

A cursory view of the past may be profitable, towards enabling us duly to appreciate the present and to form rational conjectures respecting what may hereafter prevail.

The origin of the world is involved in impenetrable darkness; and notwithstanding some may assert, it had its birth only the other day, the man who "knows how little can be known" will be convinced that the period is so remote that it is useless to expect any minute details of its infantile history. Whether man lived alone or in society in that early stage of its existence, what language they spoke, or what opinions they formed are alike hidden from the sharpest ken of those who live at this lapse of time. What passed before the flood, together with a number of years since, may be delivered over to lawless poets and the lovers of fiction to be peopled with such inhabitants as their prolific imaginations may choose to create. These also who are dissatisfied with the present, and despair of finding anything better in the unexplored regions of futurity, may paint to themselves a golden scene in those days long since forgotten. Then perhaps the earth yielded her fruit without culture and man found a rich supply without labor; then perhaps the heavens wore perpetual sunshine and the fields were clothed with continual verdure, uniting at all times the hopes of spring with the enjoyments of autumn; then the air may have been pure and man a stranger to disease may have reclined in the ambrosial abode or basked amid beds of flowers, free from want or satiety, pain of body or remorse of mind; then too the morning may have been vocal with his hymns of praise, and the evening may have repeated his devotions to his God; but alas! very different is the picture since history has usurped the province of fable, and too faithfully recorded the follies, the crimes and sufferings of mankind.

The earliest records in our possession represent the inhabitants of the earth as divided into petty hordes, continually making war upon each other subsisting by the chase, pastorage, some rude agriculture and plunder. They united under a chief, in whose abilities they could place confidence, who led them forth to battle, but returned them to an equality with the rest when the object was attained or when the war was over. In time of peace the father governed his family without submitting to the authority of a higher tribunal; in cases, however, where the interests of the tribe or nation were involved, the whole were summoned and the deliberations of the most experienced were listened to with profound reverence and their advice followed little deviation.

Religion was then but little more than that respect due to a superior, or that reverence due from a child to its father, together with gratitude to those who were considered benefactors of the community. Under the patriarchal form of government every father was the priest in his own family, as may easily be seen is the history of Abraham. Religion being then free from the doubt and mysticism in which it has since been involved, was easily learned and easily practiced, hence the necessity of a person to devote himself wholly to explaining and enforcing it, was unfelt.

The relations given of Osis, Bacchus, and Jupiter show plainly enough what was the early situation of men and also what was the character of the Gods they worshipped. Men must indeed be ignorant when it becomes necessary to have a God to teach them agriculture; but it was said of Osiris a principal deity among the Egyptians, that while king of that country, he had taken unwearied pains, to civilize his subjects and to teach them to cultivate their lands. Hence he was represented by the *Apis* or Ox, because that animal being the most useful one in tilling the ground, was the most proper emblem to perpetuate the memory of him who had taught the art.

The *Oak* was sacred to Jupiter because he first taught men to live upon acorns. Men could not have advanced far in the knowledge of things, when they deified a man for showing them acorns were good to eat, nor could this simple act become a proof of his divinity.

Many became Gods because they had *killed* some monster, such as the Minotaur the Hydra, &c. It is not however to be supposed that the most ignorant considered these as creatures of the world; they only served them as benefactors of the country to which they belonged, or for which they had done them signal services. It *is* true they were worshipped, but probably at first, the worship was nothing more than a decent respect paid to their memories by those who felt themselves under obligations to them for the utility of their lives. But the poets and orators who celebrated their achievements and enumerated their virtues, in their exaggerated strain, represented them as a superior order of beings, inhabitants of the stars or the celestial regions, who had submitted to privation and distress on earth for the benefit of its inhabitants, but had now departed, returned to their former place of residence and were looking for sacrifice and offering, as due for the benefits they had conferred. Hence perhaps, the first ideas entertained of a superior being: hence originated the fables and absurdities of the heathen Mythology.

It is admitted the poets and philosophers, speaking of Osiris, Bacchus, or Jupiter address him as "the *greatest* and *best* of beings, the *father of Gods and men*" but this must be understood rather as complimentary than as conveying their real sentiments, for the accounts which the same persons give of their god in other places are utterly inconsistent with such declarations. The words of De la Motte in reply to Madame Davier may be properly introduced in this place: "What! could Homer seriously believe Jupiter to be the Creator of gods and men? Could he think him the father of his own father Saturn, whom he drove out of heaven, or of Juno his sister and his wife, of Neptune and Pluto his brothers or of the nymphs who had charge of him in his childhood, or of the giants who made war upon him and would have dethroned him if they had then arrived at the age of manhood? How well his actions justify the Latin epithets, *Optimus Maximus*, so often given him, all the world knows."

The idea of one supreme Being, Creator of all things seems not to have made any part of the religious creeds on antiquity. The ancients deified men and paid them religious worship. They erected temples to the sun, moon, and the hosts of heaven, they dedicated altars to the hidden virtue of mere astrological conceits, and sacrificed to the elements of nature; but the worship of the true God was unknown.

Abraham during the early part of his life was an idolator, and his views of God for a long time were extremely defective. The supposition that God required him to offer up on sacrifice his beloved son Isaac, argues great ignorance of the perfections of the Deity, for which he was justly reproved by the voice that called to him just as he was about to stretch forth the sacrificial knife. Abraham no doubt showed in this act his willingness to obey

God, and notwithstanding he tried in respect to the nature of his duty the readiness he had to discharge it, was accounted to him for righteousness.

However exalted were the conceptions which Moses had of the attributes of Jehovah, if he be the author of the book of Genesis he certainly was far from having found him out to perfection. He frequently represents him as moving from place to place, also as being disappointed, grieving and repenting for what he had done; all which when applied to the Deity must be grossly improper; for if he move from one place to another he cannot be Omniscient, and if he be disappointed his wisdom must be finite, and if he repent, he cannot be immutable. This is not urged as an argument against the Divine authenticity of the book, for the state of the human mind at that time necessarily required an imperfect system, for one that was perfect would have exceed its powers of comprehension.

No. VI

The most extraordinary increase of divine light which the records of antiquity have preserved, is to be found in the system of religion and politicks established by Moses, the great Prophet and Lawgiver of the Jews. To us it is a matter of perfect indifference, by what means he received the knowledge of that system, whether by inspiration or philosophical research—whether his ideas of God were wholly original with himself, or collected from the opinions of different theologians—whether the ritual he instituted, the sacrifices and offerings he enjoined upon his followers, were invented by him, modified from the existing practices of other nations or sects with which he had become acquainted; since it is only at the institution itself we look, and for its correctness and real utility in producing the happiness of mankind we inquire.

Many of the ideas Moses entertained of Jehovah, are such as the most enlightened theologians of all subsequent ages even to the present, have held in the highest estimation, and are such as the most skeptical respecting the divine authority of the bible, must pronounce to be in accordance with an eternal truth. He called Him an Almighty Being, the Creator of all worlds and all beings, the Father of the spirits of all flesh. He considered Him one and indivisible, without any particular form or likeness by which he could be represented. Thus far Moses and the Christian philosopher agree. The physical character and essence (if the terms mean anything) of God, were as clearly understood, and as fully made known by him as by any of his successors; for indeed, no one that knows his own weakness will ever expect to have any clear conceptions upon a subject so far exceeding the sublimest flight of human thought. With regard to the moral character of God, the same cannot be said. There runs through the whole of the Mosaick economy, traces of partiality in the Being it professes to adore, and it cannot be denied, his character is drawn rather from the suggestions of man's dark understanding than according to the light which the beauty, order, and utility of nature everywhere sheds with divine effulgence upon our eyes. The right for one nation to extirpate another, not sparing even the women and children, and to possess their land, is not now admitted by those who can pretend to have any correct views of justice; and the prince who should profess to have received from God a commission to such effect, would be looked upon by all judicious persons either as a gross impostor, designing to turn the religious prejudices of the people to the channel of his own ambition, or as a mad man more fit to be inmate of an insane hospital, than to hold the reins of government. The case of the Canaanites rests on the same ground for a justification, and it is presumed no Christian believes the moral perfection of his God, would allow him to issue such a commission at this time, however proper it might have been in the days of Moses and Joshua.

The declaration contained by the second precept of the Decalogue, that Jehovah is "a jealous God visiting the iniquities of the fathers upon the children to the third and fourth generations," if it be understood as teaching that God punishes the children for the crimes of their parents, is certainly opposed to every principle of moral equity, if we, at this period can be supposed to have any correct idea of the term.

Moses seems to have been too contracted in his views of the providence of God. His regard for all His children. He seems to convey the idea, (and it is certain his followers obtained it,) that Jehovah held all the world in abhorrence but themselves, and that the children of Israel were the only nation on earth on which he had the least compassion. Perhaps this may be justified. All the world were idolators, and it accordingly became necessary for Moses, who abhorred idolatry, to place the strongest guards possible around his people to prevent them from adopting the odious practice. Hence it might have been necessary to impress his followers with the idea that God hated idolators. The guard, strong as it was, however, did not prevent them from embracing the idolatry of the nations which surrounded them.

Moses made no distinction between moral and ceremonial duties. The want of this distinction though probably unfelt at the time his system was established, soon became the occasion of great neglect of the substantial virtues, and very useful in enabling those who had the desire, to make the observance of the *form* pass for the *power* of godliness. The externals of religion as they are usually called are nothing of themselves, and are to be valued only according to their power of leading men "to do justly, to love mercy, and to walk humbly with their God."

Moses erred in establishing so many rites and ceremonies. His numerous sacrifices and offerings, whether considered as gifts, designed to express the devotion of those who made them, or as expiatory, intended to atone for the commission of moral evil, and to placate the Deity, evince clearly enough, his want of proper notions of the Divinity, and due attention to that kind of worship which a God of absolute perfection must demand of his intelligent creatures. But in this he excused, as in the case of divorcement, they were permitted on account of their hardness of heart or gross conceptions of the people. Still it may be urged, the effect of so many rites and ceremonies was to draw off the attention of the worshipper from the substance, and lead him to depend only on the shadow. The writers of the 50th psalm, the 1st chapter of Isaiah and the 6th of Micah, have adopted a more rational, and it is presumed a more correct sentiment on this subject, and may be adduced as a strong argument to prove that the ideas of religion among the Jewish prophets, had improved, or approximated the truth during the lapse of days from Moses to Micah.

The ideas of punishment found in the laws contained in the system under examination seem to have too much of the nature of revenge. The penal code seems calculated to nourish a vindictive spirit, rather than that mild lenient, and which experience, as well as the gospel, has proved to be most conducive to the felicity of society, and consequently most pleasing to God.

An "eye for an eye," was their proverb among themselves; and their most approved method for redressing a wrong, was to inflict the same degree of injury upon the offender which had this singular advantage, it doubled the amount of suffering by making two evils where was but one before. The same as would be the case, a man burns down my house, burn down his so that both our families may be left destitute. The most unreasonable exactions was their demand from those in their power: hence, one reason why they were so much detested by the nations by which they were surrounded. Supposing God hated all the world but themselves, and believing he had designed to heap upon all nations except their own, the most severe judgments they arrogated to themselves the province of interpreters of his will, and presumed to measure out his justice according to their own ideas of the desert of *their*, and by consequence, his enemies.

The admission of slavery was another imperfection in the Mosaick system. This, however, seems to have been the besetting evil of all the political systems of antiquity; and it must be said, in palliation of the Jewish Lawgiver, that he made many wise and benevolent regulations to alleviate the condition of the slaves he permitted his followers to hold.

Another defect was in blending his civil and ecclesiastical affairs. This had a tendency to encourage encroachment upon the rights of the people by the priests, and to produce servile or superstitious disposition on the part of the governed. This was actually the case. No priests ever encroached more upon the prerogatives of the people than the Jewish and no people were ever more blindly devoted to their priests than the Jews.

No. VII

It is not intended by pointing out some of the defects of the Mosaic system, to lessen the real value of that institution; but merely to evince the fact that the most perfect of the numerous systems of religion transmitted us from remote ages does not contain that clear and consistent view of the moral perfections of the Almighty, nor that comprehensive, correct and satisfactory detail of the various duties belonging to our individual and social relations which the general diffusion of knowledge at this time would lead us to expect from a system formed under the immediate direction of the Most High.

If Christians are in the habit of admitting the divine authenticity of the Jewish scriptures, they should also recollect that the institution itself was abolished by the introduction of Christianity. If the institution had been perfect, it should have remained; but inasmuch as a system of religion given by God has superseded this, we are at perfect liberty to consider it defective and to examine the correctness of the several parts or the beauty and utility of the whole in the same manner we would had it been of human origin.

Christ did not hesitate to pronounce some of its maxims incorrect and to give new ones in their place: "Ye have heard that it has been said, 'an eye for an eye, a tooth for a tooth;' but I say unto you, resist not the injurious."

See Matthew 5:38, 39. His decision in the case of divorcement was very different from Moses, and may serve to explain the reason of many other of the laws found in his code. See Matthew 19:7, 8. The disposition of the Jews was so intractable and the state of improvement was such that different laws would have been either useless or pernicious.

But he who loves truth and desires to follow the sacred injunctions will not ask for scriptural authority to convince him that that is wrong which comes in contact with enlightened understanding, or to give him liberty to express his honest convictions when from the best information he can obtain the cause of religion and humanity require it. To conceal fraud is to be an accomplice of imposition and to be silent when we have discovered it is to declare our friendship for the original perpetrators. If we have ascertained that the creeds of our brethren contain error united with truth, we ought to invite and assist them to make a separation that they reject that which is bad but hold fast that which is good.

There is no intention in the writer of this article, by telling the world there are imperfections in the Mosaic system, to weaken their faith in the Christian religion; but he would, by exciting them to an examination of the subject, induce those who wish to know the truth to study the Christian instead of the Jewish Scriptures. For the Jewish being given to a man in a state less improved and less refined admits many things which would be improper under the Christian dispensation.

People have generally imagined the Jewish Scriptures did not contain all the truth; yet all they did contain was truth. A greater error need not be imbibed. This was the very case with the Jews; and, to convince them of this mistake, the apostles labored long and hard. No fact is or can be clearer, than that the new dispensation contains things in opposition to the old. Hence, as Christians, we should form our sentiments from the new. If we wish to be Jews we may study the old.

Divines know these things but they continue to practice on the maxim, "It is no harm to deceive a man to his benefit." The experiment has been tried, but all deception is found to be against the best interests both of the deceiver and the deceived; and though a partial good may sometimes be practiced, yet seldom, if ever, is it sufficient to overbalance the evil. Priests suppose that because we have hitherto been taught that the Bible was every word of it dictated by the Spirit of God, if they should now disclose the truth that some of it does not contain sentiments proper for us to believe, we would reject the whole. Hence, to make people believe the truth, we must preach a certain mixture of falsehood and we must become dishonest for the benefit of mankind. This language is too degrading; it is more than the independent spirit of man can bear. It says to a fellow being, "You are incapable of managing your own concerns; your ears are such you must not hear the truth, but you must have some one to oversee your affairs and preach to you falsehood." Can anything be more insulting? Can there by anything more destructive to everything valuable in the human bosom, or virtuous in human society? And who is the being that presumes to read this language in our ears; is it a God? No, it is a frail mortal, like ourselves, as ignorant and equally liable to err. Let then the lesson return to himself and let him say how he should be pleased to have such language pronounced in his own ears. Honesty is the best policy; and he who has not sufficient independence to speak what he believes to be truth is not fit to be a teacher or to have the least concern with instructing mankind.

From an examination of the Mosaic system it is learned that the best system of antiquity could boast would not be called perfect now. Other systems there were, but they were inferior to this and may therefore be permitted to rest in the tombs where for ages they have been inured. The Mosaic was a great advance from the idolatry which preceded it. The prophets made many improvements in the religion left by Moses; but it was still imperfect.

No. VIII

On commencing the inquiry into ancient opinions, I intended to run over the various systems of religion which had, at different times, occupied the attention of mankind, and to have marked the gradual improvement of each, that encouragement might be afforded to the almost despairing philanthropist that truth was progressive; and it may confidently be expected that the revolutions of the future will accelerate its march, as well as those of the past; but I found myself laboring to prove what few will deny: and also exhibiting that kind of proof which but few would appreciate. The question—"*Cui bono*?"—also occurred: What benefit will it be to mankind, to call from the tombs, where for ages they have been inurned, the ashes of those errors which employed the cogitation of the speculative and contemplative—which fired the zeal of the enthusiastic, or promoted the designs of the ambitions for enslaving mankind and trampling on the ruins of all that is noble or endearing in the human bosom? All that we can say with certainty is that man acquires his knowledge by observation and experience. Time enlarges experience and continual researches extend our observations; hence, every generation may leave it successor an increasing fund of knowledge, which may be transmitted, still enlarged, to later prosperity.

In conformity to this maxim, we find antiquity, or the remotest period of which we can obtain any record, was extremely ignorant. The true character of God was unknown; man's moral and religious obligations but vaguely perceived and improperly enforced; physical and intellectual science had no name; the true principles of philosophizing or the rules to be observed in our search after truth were undiscovered; hence little can be found to satisfy the mind of the inquirer—he returns in disgust, and seek relief in contemplating the present, or expatiating in the boundless expanse of futurity. But as you come down you find an improvement. As men acquire leisure for study, they detect old errors, but generally substitute new ones in their place, which again, in their turn, give way to others more lately invented.

Formerly men pretended to a great deal more knowledge than they do now; but since we have abated some in our pretensions, I am inclined to believe we are, in reality, more knowing; for there is more truth than poetry in Pope's definition of wisdom—"to know how little can be known." Most of the moral, religious, and philosophical systems which we have received from our ancestors, are merely hypothetical. They elicit genius, but it is often of an unchastened kind. Their authors had mental greatness, perhaps superior to ours, but they were deficient in science or a true knowledge of nature.

Time was when the priests were in possession of all the knowledge, as well as the religion of the community: and experience has shown us very clearly how willing this class of people are to enlighten the great mass of mankind. Now they do indeed labor to diffuse knowledge, but they did not do it until the laity came in possession of it by other means. Had priests pursued the course which the policy of that body suggested as the most proper, we might perhaps, at this time, been bowing down to Egypt's "dok ox," as the fit object of our religious veneration; or, perhaps, fashioning with Aaron the golden calf, as the emblem of the God of nature. But they have been driven from their policy and have been compelled to resign the keys of science, and to relinquish their exclusive claims to the chair of literature. The keys of heaven and hell they are indeed permitted to retain, but the great body of the people believe they have neither power to open the one or shut the other.

The ancients may be excused in some degree for the absurdity of their religious system, for they depended wholly upon their priests; and as priests always delight to arouse the credulous by marvelous stories and astonishing miracles, we may suppose they revealed them in all the wild luxuriance of mysticism, and dealt out to the gaping multitude without measure, the pious absurdities of their midnight dreams, and the holy raptures of their unlicensed, yet unreproved imaginations. Their dreams and raptures may now supply matter for an evening tale, and may excite our risibility or raise our indignation at their impositions upon their brethren; but they will not gain a moment's credence, or create the least regret that they are never to return. With these remarks we bid adieu to those airy castles and fantastic fabrics which once employed the imaginations, and excited the hopes and fears of mankind; for though God may have spoken to them face to face, they were subject to the same law that governs us. The tree of knowledge must wait the nourishment of slow experience before it can expand its branches, afford shade or beauty, yield fragrance or fruit.

Christianity had done much for mankind. But alas! the best system is of no avail to minds still slumbering in the cells of ignorance. Though its rays beam with power, they cannot pierce at once the mighty deep of superstition; nor can their warmth penetrate in a moment the icy heart of the ingot and melt it to philanthropy. It has done much and much is now doing; but it would have done more if men had known at its first exhibition, what bitter experience has since taught, that, though science is not religion, she is the handmaid of religion. There may be science without religion, but religion cannot claim much purity nor usefulness without science. But science has flourished under the fostering sun of Christianity, and its reciprocal influence has heightened that sun, expanded his rays, and given him a more agreeable and a more permanent warmth.

One circumstance which now exists, promises to be of vast utility in enlarging the boundaries of our knowledge. Philosophers now build on experiment. The fondness for hypotheses and love of theorizing, which so long checked the growth of knowledge, are now in some measure laid aside for matters of fact, and it is now ascertained to be folly to build on conjecture, or to pretend to know that which we have never seen or investigated with any of our senses. True philosophy now attempts to analyze nature, exhibit her various phenomena, but not to explain them. The composition of bodies is ascertained, and the changes to which they are liable, are, in many instances predicted. The mind also is subjected to the same analysis; its susceptibilities developed, and the various classes of its changes, as they are affected by its relation to matter or to itself are defined. The same rule, the same method, is finding its way into religion, and the most beneficial results may be anticipated.

No. IX

Science has shed her "lucid rays" over many nations and the most abject slaves of ignorance have caught a glimpse—faint indeed, but sufficiently powerful to make them dissatisfied with their condition, and to enable them to meditate some amelioration. The invention of the art of printing has furnished the philanthropist with successful weapons, to combat the foes of the human race and vindicate the cause of wisdom and virtue. Armed by this invention, he has already shaken thrones, filled the hearts of tyrants with dismay and the courts of despotism with consternation! The mighty fabric of bigotry and superstition, which cost the labor of ages to erect and which were cemented by the blood of millions, already trembled to their foundations before his successful attacks. Several nations have been compelled to throw off the burden of political servitude and others have been obliged to abate the rigor of their institutions and the severity of their laws.

The enlightened benefactors of mankind, a few years since in this country, lighted the beacon of universal emancipation. Europe saw the illumination, France assembled in its rays increased its effulgence. Did she fall? She reflected splendor as she "kissed the dust." From her temporary defeat we are enabled to learn the rules of our future exertions to avoid the rock on which she split and the whirl-pool in which she was tossed. The march of liberty may be more slow hereafter than was anticipated but what is lost in severity will be gained in permanency. But France shall rise. The republican principles of her revolution, though now apparently dormant shall yet spring up and yield a plenteous harvest. Her martyred patriots still live in her bleeding memory, and sooner shall the enemies of the human race arrest the sun in his progress or roll back the wheels of nature, than prevent the resuscitation of the cause for which they bled and its complete triumph over the tyrannical principles which have for a time obscured its glory!

The overgrown power of the Pope of Rome, has become little more than nominal. The splendid dome of Popery, erected from the spoils of almost every heathen temple and ornamented with the paintings of almost every heathen artist, is nearly demolished. The "bulls" of the Vatican are now regarded as harmless things, and their thunderings cease to terrify mankind. The church which was not improperly styled the "mother of harlots" has begun her reformation and bids fair to outstrip her daughters in this laudable work. Calvinism has had its day. There have been converts that could gravely declare that man a heretic who did not believe "God has not created all men to like estate but to some has fore-appointed life and to others death and as they were created to the one or the other so they were elected to eternal life or reprobated to misery inconceivable, and themselves thus elected or reprobated were eternally and unchangeably designed and so definite that one cannot be added or diminished, and all this for the manifestation of his sovereign mercy and his vindictive justice. But where is the man that will now boldly advocate in all its native deformity this consummation of absurdity and cruelty, this focus in which all the objectionable parts of the most objectionable theories ever dreamed of by man have concentrated their power?

We have Calvinists in name, but they are most of them ashamed of the peculiar tenets of the successful champions of malevolence, whose name they bear. Every sober minded man among them is much more solicitous to conceal these doctrines or to give them a more inviting dress than he is to exhibit them as believed by our ancestors. Edwards and Hopkins in our country, men possessing by no means shall abilities have endeavored to reconcile the *decretum horribile* of Calvinism with the universal benevolence of God, and notwithstanding they have concluded it is best upon the whole, to compel a part to weep eternally in hell that the righteous in heaven may have their bliss consummated, they have borne testimony strong as was in their power to the fact that God is a being of universal benevolence—a truth when once admitted by the mind puts in the back ground all those imaginary fears and burning bells which Calvin placed in the front.

The Church of England though originally Calvinist or nearly so, now pays very little attention to the doctrine of election and reprobation—except it be to discountenance it. She indeed retains her thirty-nine articles but they have not much control over the sentiments of the clergy in general.

The Methodists sprang up in the last century and although in point of doctrine they have done little more than to declaim against the horrid tenets of the Reformer of Geneva[1] they have by their unwearied exertions done much to benefit in many places the lower classes of mankind—these unfortunate persons whom the clergy of more popular churches have generally treated with neglect.

These are indeed trifling considerations when our minds take in the vast family of man, but as they show that the most enlightened religious institutions are purifying themselves, we catch the hope that they will soon be prepared to instruct the more ignorant and to shed the rays of truth upon the benighted parts of our earth. They show, the spirit of investigation is abroad, and however powerful or obstinate the enemies it has to encounter, it will never return till wreathed with laurels of victory. These apparently minute consequences show us there is a redeeming principle in human society and however slow may be its operations it will finally produce a glorious renovation.

The last century has done much, and should the same exertions be made and be attended by the same success for one hundred years to come the world will appear almost entirely different from what it was one hundred years back. The work is begun, and the first obstacles are surmounted. The path now before us is plain, and as the wheel of improvement acquires celerity from its own motion the remaining part of the road will be run with more quickness, ease, and safety than that already traversed.

The labors of our predecessors though apparently feeble produce astonishing results and instead of wondering why we are no further advanced we should rather wonder why we have progressed so far. A few centuries back the world was in darkness and "gross darkness covered the people," a senseless jargon disturbed the schools, a philosophy was taught which had little effect but to render more imperious the gloom if ignorance which brooded over the nations. War in its grossest forms and in its most malignant aspect was multiplied to an extent which threatened the world with depopulation. This "horrid monster" is now made to wear a milder garb, and much is done to render his march tolerable. That philosophy is discarded and a new one commenced which rests on experiment not conjecture for its authority. That jargon is no longer heard and our seminaries have learned it is their province to teach their subjects *things* rather than words.

Improvements in navigation have brought all nations within the vicinity of each other. Commerce has made us acquainted with all. The art of printing will convey to all, almost instantaneously the discoveries of each. Hence what we gain cannot be lost. Our discoveries and improvements are embodied in so many books and read in so many different languages that nothing less than a universal conflagration can destroy the whole.

True, many nations are yet ignorant, barbarous and savage, and exhibit a faithful picture of what all once were, but missionaries are flying with the wind to each; and though what they carry is of no great consequence they will open with them a communication, make us acquainted with their language, manners and customs and enable us to transfuse through their ignorance mass those truths which at once correct the head and amend the heart. It is thus the arts of the enemy shall operate to his own ruin, and the efforts made to extend the dominions of priest-craft be the means of its final overthrow. One, however, would naturally suppose there was a shorter and more direct road to the desired object. But all men are not philosophers, but few reflect seriously on the propriety or impropriety of the measures they adopt. The majority of mankind are borne along the tide of things as passion or belief gives the impulse, without attempting to correct their progress or even to inquire where they are likely to land. Men are governed more by their prejudices than by their reason and these are generally so obstinate that nothing short of miscarriage can subdue their power. Experience is surely a dear school but we have a great many who will learn in no other way and some not even in this. Hence the march of truth has sometimes been by a circuitous route. The obstacles which impeded her footsteps were not always to be surmounted at once. She has many times, apparently, slackened her progress and permitted the fables of men to pave for her a way to certain victory. Such is the Missionary scheme contemplated either as to the motives of its founders or the measures adopted to carry it into execution. Contemptible indeed is the motive. It is no other than to spread there unintelligible doctrines, sometimes strangely called the "doctrines of grace" among the Heathen—those doctrines which must excite the ridicule or disquiet of every man's mind that is freed from the leading strings of his mother. Contemptible and worse are the measures adopted to prosecute this scheme. But I will not mention them for may posterity never learn how grossly depraved were the most popular religionists of the 19th century. The selling of Joseph into Egypt was not commendable in itself considered but the consequences were good, and the same perhaps may hereafter be said of the Missionary scheme. The same perhaps too of the petty institutions of sabbath schools. When the first lessons taught are veneration for the church which adopt them. These and all similar measures will finally produce a reaction. Woe then to the pride of their abettors, for it shall receive a deadly wound!

Truth is the pebble in the lake and however small at first are the circles, or however, slow they may succeed each other, they will continue till they have spread over the whole surface. Truth has already disclosed to the once despised inhabitants of the southern half of our Continent the balm of personal liberty and national independence, she armed them against tyrants that oppressed, she led them to victory and though her triumph be not yet complete she will finally spread a richer wealth over the sand than the silver of Potosi or the gold of Mexico could purchase. The wrongs of Montezuma shall be avenged and science flourish over all the territory beheld by the disgraceful conqueror of the Inca of Peru.

Greece shall emerge from the gloom of Turkish vassalage; science and literature revisit the land of Plato; liberty triumph again on the plains of Marathon and be maintained by the justice of Aristides. Nor here shall end the march of Truth. India shall behold her effulgence—cast aside her idol gods—recognize the original equality of the human family—treat them all as brethren, and worship with gratitude the common Father of all. The Minstrel of Zion shall retake his harp from the willow and heavenly music shall re-echo from the mountains of Jerusalem. Nor ye sable sons of Africa shall truth forget to light the darker features of your doom. Distant, yes, ye degraded men, distant is the day, but come it shall to restore to you the rights to which nature and nature's God entitle you, and give your long abused country its place among the nations of the earth. Ye wanderer's of Arabia's desert, and ye tribes that roam the forest, a glorious sun shall shed his enlightening beams upon your desolations. Showers shall distill their genial influence upon your land, and the desert shall be glad with the rest, and the wilderness and the solitary place rejoice and blossom as the rose. The Genius of emancipation is hurrying over the world—he bears on his wings the long wished for relief, and fast as the wheel of improvement can move, it shall be borne to you.

Such are the suggestions of hope—such are the conclusions warranted by a review of the past and the contemplation of the present. Philanthropists, awake! your exertions shall be crowned with success. Regard not the proscriptions of the ignorant and the designing. Disapprobation from those who are incapable of perceiving the value of your labors, and from those who have no desire to witness the renovation you wish to produce, you must expect, but be not discouraged. Posterity will reap the fruit of your toil, and the unbounded felicity which you may transmit to future generations will fully compensate you for any sacrifices you may be compelled to make. Let your voices be heard! Ye friends of Truth, of Science, of Liberty, and Religion in its purity, break your long silence, let the echo of your voices ring back from every quarter—man shall be free! Tyranny, whether civil or ecclesiastical, shall be annihilated—wars shall cease—contentions end. Peace and unbroken harmony shall reign wherever the voice of man is heard or wherever the sun emits his golden beams.

TWO

Free Enquirers

Those who call themselves Orthodox may be sure of our respectful attention, long as we are able to write, but they will pardon us if we leave our examinations of the validity of their claims to pay our compliments to another class who are making some noise in our little world.

This class is composed of Deists, Sceptics, Free Enquirers, and Materialists. By the by, a friend, more timorous than discerning, whispered in our ear the other day that somebody thought the editor of the *Gospel Advocate* had a strong claim to admission into this honorable corps. Be this as it may, our sentiments are neither the better nor the worse for any supposed coincidence between them and those advocated by the classes we have mentioned. We, however, wish our friends to look at our statements, and if what we allege for facts be true, they must not censure us, for we cannot make truth bend to their wishes nor to our own. Each one must bend himself to the truth, or else he will always find cause for dissatisfaction. But our readers need not be alarmed. For, before we conclude to dispense with the Gospel—to abjure our Savior, and relinquish our hope in a future state of existence, we shall change the name of our paper—our friends shall have timely warning.

But it was the Free Enquirers we proposed to notice. How numerous this class may be we cannot say, nor is it of much consequence. The organs

From *The Gospel Advocate and Impartial Investigator* 7 (March 21, 1829): 89–90.

of the party, in this country, are the *Free Enquirer*, lately published at New Harmony, but now transferred to New York; *The Correspondent* published also at New York, and one or two more publications, we believe, though we have no knowledge of any except these two.

The *Free Enquirer* is edited by Miss Frances Wright, Robert Dale Owen, and R. L. Jennings. Miss Wright is a lady of talents and of no small philosophical acquisition. Did we believe in transmigration of souls, we might think old Epicurus had re-appeared in the person of Miss Wright, different from what he appeared in the Garden, only in the acquisition of a few feminine graces, and perhaps a few visionary notions, common to both sexes. We mean this as no reproach, for we consider Epicurus best deserving the name of philosopher, of any one antiquity can boast. We were agreeably surprised to find Dr. Good, in his Book of Nature, has not been ashamed to rescue the name of this philosopher from the reproach which has so long deceived the world.

Miss Wright's avowed object is to improve the condition of the human race. This is a good object. We can wish her success in this; for anyone who can feel, knows there is need enough. We have seen two of her lectures on knowledge. We approve them, and indeed we have advanced the same principles both in our sermons and our essays. There is nothing in the lectures which should alarm the honest enquirer after truth.

It will, however, be remarked these lectures are only abstract principles. Perhaps we should differ in our deductions from these principles, and in our application of them to the improvement of the human race. We believe, however, Miss Wright would in carrying her first principles out in detail, leave man destitute of all religious notions, and deprive him of the benefit of all written laws. Man must have religion. He has always had some kind, and to us there appears nothing better calculated to elevate his conceptions and ennoble his nature, than the religion of Jesus. Written laws, and indeed all government, would be unnecessary, if mankind were just; but whether all can be made so is very doubtful to us. Man is a bundle of appetites and passions, irregular and violent in their operations. Some government will be necessary until his nature is changed, which we think will require more power than the *Free Enquirer* can exert. And whether the change would make man the better is a matter of doubt. Some things are beautiful in theory, but are the reverse in practice. Miss Wright has a *beau ideal*, perhaps good, but most probably like all ideal beings, better suited to some other world than to this.

Her co-editors, Mr. Owen and Mr. Jennings, we presume, are of the same sentiments with herself. They are men of no mean abilities. Mr. Owen has been the principal acting editor of the *Enquirer* for some time past. We have read his productions with pleasure. He is a good natured man. Cares little about any man's God or creed; and, what we like him for, he always keeps his temper and manifests a truly catholic spirit. But we should think him blest or curst with too much philosophical indifference, to work any extensive revolution. Men are successful in proportion to their zeal, not to their knowledge. Of Mr. Jennings we know little; some few of his articles we have seen, which elicit some talent.

The *Correspondent* is edited by George Houston, and is very different in character from the *Free Enquirer*. The *Enquirer* may certainly claim the praise of liberality, but the *Correspondent*, in the rancor of sectarianism, may contest the palm with the most staunch, thorough-going orthodox publications of the day. Mr. Houston will pardon our freedom, but we think if he cannot exhibit as powerful arguments as religionists, he can match them in variance. And if he does not believe the orthodox creed, he seems not much deficient in its spirit.

Fools and knaves, dupes and impostors, are the charitable epithets he heaps upon us poor creatures, who are so old fashioned as to believe the Bible. Alas for the believer in the Bible! He can expect no mercy at the hands of the relentless editor. We have sometimes thought if the spirit which breathes in his paper should become predominant, that we foolish creatures who cling to the religion of Jesus, would be put to death, merely that the land might be purged of the enemies to his beautiful theory. Though upon second thought we conclude it would be like the spirit of all sects when in power, treat kindly all who submit. Mr. Houston has suffered imprisonment for his sentiments. He, no doubt, feels acutely. We would make all allowances necessary. But we do think one precept from that book he despises would be comfortable to his feelings. It is the precept which requires us to forgive our enemies.

The sentiments of this paper are such as are held by modern Deists, or, perhaps Materialists; we have not read the paper attentively. The value of such sentiments have been pretty well tested. We are not very sure they will be useful to the world. We do not, however, deny the editors of these papers the right to circulate their sentiments. They have the same right we have to circulate ours. But still we do not perceive their peculiar worth.

Both these papers attack religion. If they hurled their blows at superstition only, it would be well. It may be the result of education, it may be folly; but we have found religion very comfortable to our feelings. When we were overwhelmed with adversity (and we have been), it was not a little consoling to reflect the world is under the control of a wise, powerful and good Being. Who will cause all things to work together for good, and that our light affliction here, will work for us a far more exceeding weight of glory.

We are opposed to superstition, to bigotry, and to false systems of religion. But we have not yet become so *enlightened* as to be pleased with universal skepticism, or with the cold unfeeling dreams of the Deist, or colder speculations of the Materialist. Creation loses its beauty, the world its charms, when we consider it the fortuitous production of chance or to blind necessity. And then, to think we live, toil a few days, sink into the grave and are no more, is not well calculated to prompt exertion, or to keep up our spirits amid the numerous incidents of life.

But if these editors will convince us (and we are willing to be convinced) that their course is calculated to regenerate the world, and make man universally happy, they may then have our good wishes and our co-operation. They go too fast for us. We condemn them not, but would say, the progress of truth is always slow, and they, in our opinion, far outstrip her in the race.

THREE

Memoir of Saint-Simon

[This is a review of various works written by the followers of Claude Henri de Rouvroy, Comte de Saint-Simon.

1. *Doctrine of Saint-Simon. Exposition. First Year.* 1828–9. Third edition, revised and enlarged.
2. *Saint-Simonian Doctrine. General summary of the Exposition made in 1828–9. From the Revue Encyclopédique.* Second edition.
3. *Saint-Simonian Religion. Central Instruction.* From *l'Organisateur.*
4. *Letter to the President of the Chamber of Deputies.*]

Everybody has heard of the Saint-Simonians, a new sect of philosophers, politicians, and religionists which a few years ago appeared in France. They made much noise and attracted no little attention for a time, by the novelty of some of their notions, and by the enthusiasm with which they supported them. It is said, how truly we know not, that they have latterly run into many wild and mischievous extravagancies, and that the day of their glory is past. However this may be, they have left indelible traces of their new system on the philosophical and religious opinions of France; and since they are now making their appearance in England, and since we have seen it stated that they intend visiting this country, we have thought it not too late to be both interesting and profitable to give a more detailed account of their

From *The Unitarian* (June 1834), 279–89.

doctrines than is within the reach of our readers generally. In this article, however, we can do little more than furnish some notices of Saint-Simon himself, the prophet of the sect, which we collect almost entirely from the works before us.

Claude Henri Saint-Simon, son of the Duc de Saint-Simon, the author of the "Memoirs," was born April 17, 1760, of one of the noble families of France, which traces its descent, through the Counts of Vermandois, from Charlemagne. He had early a presentiment of his destined greatness, and from the age of seventeen he caused himself to be awakened in the morning with the words, "GET UP, COUNT, YOU HAVE GREAT THINGS TO DO." His heated imagination presented before him the royal founder of his family, who foretold to him that to the glory of having produced a great monarch should be added through him that of producing a great philosopher.

He entered the military service at seventeen, and the year after came into this country, where he made five campaigns with distinction, under the orders of Bouillié and Washington. He became acquainted with Franklin, and studied the political organization of our United States; for while here he busied himself much more with political science than with military tactics, for which he had no great fondness. It is from this period that he dates his philosophic tendency. "The war" [of the American revolution], he says, "in itself did not interest me; but its object interested me very much, and this enabled me to support its labours without repugnance. 'I will the end,' I often said, 'I should then will the means.' But my disgust for the trade of arms was complete, so soon as I saw peace approach. From that moment I saw clearly what was to be my future career. My vocation was not to be a soldier. I was carried to a very different and, I may say, an opposite kind of activity. To study the development of the human mind, and afterwards to labour to perfect civilization,—such was the object I proposed to myself, and to which I devoted myself without repose, consecrating to it my whole life. This new kind of activity began then to engross all my powers. The remainder of my stay in America was employed in meditating on the great events I had witnessed, in seeking to discover their causes and to foresee their results. I saw then that the American revolution must signalize a new political era, necessarily determine an important progress in general civilization, and cause great changes in the social order then existing in Europe."

Scarcely had he returned to Europe when he was called upon to witness the breaking out of the French revolution. This spectacle, at once magnificent and terrible, could not fail to affect him deeply; but looking beyond the vulgar horizon, into the future as well as into the past, he was able to distinguish its causes and to appreciate its results. He saw in this grand event the practical application of the theories founded by the reformers in the fifteenth and sixteenth centuries, and popularised by the philosophers in the eighteenth century,—the legitimate destruction of a moral and social order which no longer responded to the interests and the sentiments of society; and at the same time he saw that this crisis, called to prepare the soil for the seed, contained in itself no germ of reorganization, and that it could be definitively terminated only by the production of a new principle of social classification. To discover this principle, bring it out, and establish it, was what he considered his mission. He viewed the French revolution as having only a destructive mission,—necessary, important, but incomplete for humanity; and therefore, instead of being carried away by its current, as were nearly all whose sympathies were like his, he applied himself to the accumulation of the materials required for the erection, on the ruins of the old, of a new social edifice, to remain, to improve in beauty, grandeur, strength, and symmetry forever.

His first care was to procure the pecuniary resources necessary for his work. To this end he engaged in some immense financial speculations, which were crowned with great success. "I desired fortune," he said, "only as the means of organizing a grand industrial establishment, to found a school to perfect science, in a word, to contribute to the progress of light, and to the melioration of the fate of humanity." The grand establishment was organized, but it failed; and his partner, who did not share his philanthropic, or, as some may say, visionary views, separated from him, much to Saint-Simon's disadvantage, whose ability to manage pecuniary matters, alone, does not seem 'to have been of the highest order.

However, faithful to the plan he had traced, he employed the feeble remains of his fortune saved from the ruin of the establishment, the attempted industrial and scientific school, to perfect his own scientific education. His object was to introduce into the French school a grand scientific theory which should embrace all the sciences and all the facts of science. But this required preliminary labours. It was necessary to know the actual condition of science and the history of its discoveries. Seven years were devoted to these preliminary labours. He did not confine himself to libraries. He sat down opposite the Polytechnic School; he contracted a friendship with several of its professors, and employed three years with their aid in making himself master of the current knowledge respecting inorganic bodies. Good cheer, good wine, much attention to the professors, to whom his purse was open, seem to have made them communicative, and to have procured him all the facilities he could desire. "I had, however," he says, "great difficulties to surmount. My brain had lost its malleability; I was no longer young. But I enjoyed some advantages, extended travels, the intercourse of able men which I sought and obtained, an early education by d'Alembert, an education which had woven me a metaphysical net so compact that no important fact could pass through it."

After three years, in 1801, he left the Polytechnic School and seated himself near that of Medicine. Here he formed a connection with the physiologists, and did not leave them till he had obtained a full knowledge of their general ideas on organic bodies. He then visited England, Switzerland, and a part of Germany. "My object," he says, "in going to England was to inform myself whether the English had discovered any new general ideas. I returned, assured that they had upon their stocks no new capital idea." His opinion of Germany was a little more favourable. "I brought from Germany the conviction that general science was yet in its infancy in that country, since it was there founded on mysticism; but I conceived a hope of its ultimate progress, on seeing the whole of that great nation passionately engaged in a scientific direction."

Saint-Simon did not content himself with studying the sciences and the learned; he wished to know artists and their inspirations, and to compare their genius with that of scientific speculators. His house, thus, for a year, became the resort of the most distinguished men in Paris of both classes. Seven years had now been employed in forming an acquaintance with the various branches of human knowledge, and he felt himself able to draw up an inventory of the scientific wealth of Europe.

But now commenced his severest trials, his greatest labours. His fortune, shaken by the failure of the "grand establishment," was wholly dissipated by his pursuit after knowledge. His friends deserted him. From this time he must live in want, in suffering, in humiliation. He must remain *alone with the consciousness of what he is*, and for a long time this consciousness proved itself able to sustain his courage. His first occupation was to recast philosophy. Napoleon had said to the Institute, "Give me an account of the progress of science since 1789. Tell me what is the actual state of science, and what are the means necessary to make it advance." The Institute replied to this magnificent question merely by a series of partial, historical reports, which being tied together by no general view could give to science no real impulse. Saint Simon undertook to remedy this defect. He conceived and executed his *Introduction aux Travaux Scientifiques du XIXe Siècle*, in two volumes quarto, a great work, in which he deposited the germ of most of the ideas he afterwards developed. In this work he demonstrates for the human race what Bacon had for the individual, that intellectual activity has two general, alternate modes of operation, *analysis* and *synthesis*, the mode *à priori*, and the mode *à posteriori*; he makes it appear that science, considered in the assemblage of all the men who cultivate it passes successively, but at distant intervals of time, from *analysis* to *synthesis*, from the search after facts to the construction of theories; that the greatest step which the human mind can be made to take in the direction of the sciences is to determine the proper time to pass from one mode to the other; he takes it upon him to prove that the learned of Europe, for a century engaged in the paths of analysis, have sufficiently explored them, and that they ought to abandon them for a general or synthetic point of view. In a word, he required the learned to return to the point of view of Descartes, which they had entirely forgotten for that of Newton. "Descartes," he says to them, "had monarchized science. Newton republicanized it, he *anarchized* it. You are only learned anarchists, you deny the existence, the supremacy of a general theory." He afterwards enumerated the principal conceptions of the learned during the 17th and 18th centuries, particularly that of Condorcet on the progressive development of the human race. He furnished the means for the study of this development, a study elevated by him to the rank of a positive science. The learned did not regard him, but the future will comprehend him.

But it was chiefly in reference to a social and political end that he sought to stimulate the zeal of the learned. The destructive wars which followed the French revolution made him feel every day more vividly the necessity of reorganizing a general doctrine and a central European power. Preoccupied, as he was at this epoch, with the importance of the sciences, it was to the scientific that he addressed himself to realize his project. He wished to elevate them to the height of such a mission. "From the 15th century up to this day," he says to them, "the institution which united the European nations, and curbed the ambition of people and of kings, has been successively enfeebled. It is now completely destroyed. A general war, a fearful war, a war which threatens to devour the whole European population, has already existed for twenty years and harvested many millions of men. You alone can reorganize European society. Time presses—blood flows—hasten to declare yourselves." But he spoke in vain. The learned were as little moved by the anarchy of Europe as by the anarchy of science. Saint-Simon did not know, at this moment, that it was from HIMSELF ALONE must proceed the doctrine and the men capable of reestablishing unity, order, harmony.

The year eighteen hundred and fourteen arrives. Always ardent to pursue under the most suitable form the object from which he never in any circumstances allowed himself to be diverted, he abandons the direction essentially speculative, which till now he has followed, to engage in political labours. He soon perceives the new character which the development of industry must impart to society and to the forms of government. He speaks no longer, as before, to the learned. He turns to the industrious classes, and devotes ten years to the work of making them comprehend the new social rank they are destined to hold. He writes and publishes successively several works, but they produced no great sensation. He who labours for the industrious classes does nobly, but he must not expect to be very readily comprehended not very cordially thanked. But let no one on this account desert them. They curse the hand that would unloose their fetters, only because they fear its design is to rivet them firmer. At this period of his life Saint-Simon presents himself in a touching attitude. He lived in poverty, in want, in neglect. He laboured incessantly, in his own opinion for the good of his fellow-beings; yet no one thanked him; no one aided him; no one cheered him onward; but all united in loading him with obloquy and abuse. "These fifteen days," he writes, "I have lived on bread and water. I have laboured without fire. I have sold everything, even to my wearing apparel, to defray the expense of some copies of my work. It is the passion for science and public happiness, it is the desire to find the means for terminating, in a gentle manner, the fearful crisis in which all European society is engaged, that has plunged me into this distress. It is therefore without a blush that I avow my wants, and solicit the assistance needed to put me in a condition to continue my work."

One day, one single day, in this terrible situation, scorned and abandoned by the very men for whom his life was a perpetual sacrifice, his courage fails him. He doubts his mission; he is in despair; he asks, he wills, he seeks to die. His hand is armed against himself; the ball grazes his forehead. "But his hour is not yet come." His work must not be left incomplete. He has created a philosophy of the sciences, a philosophy of industry; he must live long enough to find the religion destined to unite the two creations. He must now be the prophet of the law of love. "God," say his disciples, in apostrophizing him, "God has left thee to fall only to prepare thee for a still grander initiation; and see, from the bottom of the abyss he raises thee, exalts thee even to himself. He sheds over thee the religious inspiration which vivifies, sanctifies, renews thy whole being. Henceforth it is no longer the learned man, no longer the workingman, that speaks. A hymn of love escapes from his mutilated body. THE DIVINE MAN IS MANIFEST. 'New Christianity' is given to the world!—Moses *promised* to mankind universal brotherhood; Jesus Christ *prepared* it; Saint-Simon *realizes* it. The Church *really* Universal is about to be born. The reign of Caesar ends; a pacific takes the place of a military society; and the Universal Church governs the temporal as well as the spiritual, in the outer as well as in the inner court. Science is holy, industry is holy, for they seem to improve the condition of the poorest classes and to bring them near to God. Priests, the learned, the industrious, these are the whole society; chiefs of the priests, chiefs of the learned, chiefs of the industrious, these are the whole government. And all *good* is the *good* of the church, and every profession is a religious function, a grade in the social hierarchy. To each one according to his capacity, to each capacity according to its works. The reign of God is at hand. All prophecies are fulfilled. Saint-Simon, now thou mayest die, for THOU HAST DONE GREAT THINGS."

Saint-Simon closed his career with his religious work called *New Christianity*. He died the 19th of May, 1825, in obscurity, in want, attended by his only disciple, who received his last revelations and who became the chief of the sect. If we may believe his disciples, Saint-Simon was a man of exalted worth. His only passion, according to them, was the public good. Liberty, industry, philosophy in all that it has of the sublime were the constant themes of his meditations. He had an almost unequalled nobleness of soul and of sentiment. His conversation was clear, lively, brilliant, able in a few hours to make perceptible and palpable, ideas which it would require volumes fully to develop. He never talked of himself. He discarded all the factitious distinctions of society, and shone by himself alone, by the man that was in him. His genius was great, but his heart was greater. All his ideas passed through his heart. He was never known to complain of a single human being, although he had made many ingrates. He had an inconceivable simplicity of manner, always seized the tone and placed himself within the reach of the one who enjoyed his conversation; and such was his flexibility of mind that while the wisest carried away the hope of returning to profit by his conversation, the ignorant left him with the idea that they had instructed him. He was lavish of his thoughts, cared not who profited by them, provided they were diffused. It was his delight to collect around him young men, the men of the future, and to procure them the means of opening to themselves an honourable career by their labours or their writings. No selfishness was discovered to sully the beauty of his character. He knew how to acquire wealth, had acquired it more than once, but his regard for the interests of others and little care for his own made him diffuse it faster than he could obtain it. "If there were not generosity in the heart," said he, "it would always be a good calculation."

His enemies, indeed, allege many things against him. The most important is that he was a very troublesome beggar. His disciples do not deny the charge; they allege that it was his desire to do mankind good that reduced him to beggary. They, however, do not pretend that he was perfect. They consider him not as the type of perfection, but of an eternal progress towards perfection. They see in him an advance prophetic of the advance of humanity. They think he ascended high the ladder whose steps, through the infinite, lead up to God. He leaped an immense chasm, and now lends a helping hand to his disciples to leap the same, and to place themselves by his side. He ended a thousand times greater than he began; and death does not interrupt his eternal progress. "Great God!" say his disciples, "he is and always will be before thy face; he is and always will be *with us*, *in us*. It will always be by him that we shall develop ourselves and make our way to thee. The being of Saint-Simon, growing more and more perfect, is at each moment made up of all that we can conceive of love, of wisdom, and beauty under a human form. It is to the being composed of these that our worship, our admiration, and our souls are devoted. Old religions, wholly *stationary*, have the type of what they reverence in the past; our religion, wholly *progressive*, places it in the future; and one of the finest results of our progress is that we every day become able to represent our type to ourselves under a more attracting and a more perfect form."

This may be a little mystical to those of our readers who have long had thinking made easy to them. It is not the man they worship. It is not the man Saint-Simon they reverence. They pay their homage to the progress he manifested, to the truths he disclosed, and to the passionate love of humanity which controlled him. They revere him as a model for them to imitate only in his progress, and in the object towards which he directed his labours. They do not look at him as he was in the past, to see what they should be; they look at him where his continued progress has elevated him, and thus gather strength to press onward and upward after him.

With the Saint-Simonians everything is progress, everything changes to man's conception as he advances. God enlarges, becomes pure, wise, and beautiful, in proportion as the mind that contemplates him enlarges, becomes pure, clothed with wisdom, and adorned with beauty. This idea is undoubtedly just. The God of the ignorant is not the God of the enlightened. Every man has a God of his own, exactly proportioned to his degree of mental and moral progress. That which a man worships is always the highest worth of which he can form any conception. The negro ascribes to his ill shapen *fétiche* the highest excellence he can conceive, and you must enlarge his mental and moral capacity before he can worship a God of higher and more moral attributes. You change not the object of man's worship by changing the name of his God. The Jew, who ascribed to his Jehovah no higher qualities than the Greeks did to Jupiter, was no more a worshipper of the true God than they. The same is true of the Christian. If mankind worship the true God now any more than formerly, it is because there has been an advance, because the human mind has grown and become able to take in the idea of a purer, sublimer, and more beautiful Divinity.

We delight to apply this thought to Christianity somewhat as the Saint-Simonians apply it to their prophet. Christianity is to every Christian the type of moral and religious perfection; but that type varies in different ages, in different individuals, and even in the same individual at different epochs of his life. Christianity, in the minds of those who embraced it in the early centuries, was a low thing to what it is now. No matter what it was in the mind of its Author; where it was embraced it was measured not by his mind, but by the minds of those who embraced it. It can never in any mind mean a greater degree of moral and religious perfection than that mind is capable of receiving, understanding, appreciating. There must be almost an infinite difference between Milton's Christianity and that of the Abbé Paris. Still, one was a Christian, as well as the other. One age, one sect is Christian, as well as another, when compared with itself. Each is modeled after the same type, each takes in the highest worth of which it can form any conception. But the type stands for an amount exactly proportioned to the progress which has been made. Christianity, then, can never be outgrown. We may pursue an eternal career of progress, and at each step will the term Christianity enlarge its meaning, and the word Christ designate purer, lovelier, sublimer worth!

But to return. Saint-Simon, viewed as he may be, was undoubtedly no ordinary man. His views are those of no ordinary mind. They bear the stamp of originality, of a mind in pursuit of variety, in love with the beautiful, and, in its own estimation, wedded to humanity, and longing to redeem, exalt, and make it happy and forever more happy. We have dwelt long upon his career, perhaps too long for the patience of our readers; but we delight to trace such a character, we find instruction in its very extravagancies. We shall take up his system as developed by his disciples, as we find time and room.

FOUR

An Address, Delivered at Dedham, on the Fifty-Eighth Anniversary of American Independence, July 4, 1834

FRIENDS AND FELLOW CITIZENS,

We must have cold hearts, if they do not beat with warm emotions on the return of this day; we must have dull spirits, if they be not stirred by the proud recollections of the anniversary we have met to celebrate.

No party victory, no triumph of ephemeral interests, calls us together on this day. We have met to commemorate an event dear to humanity—an event in which man throughout the world has a deep and lasting interest, in which he may find matter for sympathy, gratulation and hope. We have come together to celebrate Freedom's Birthday. Not the Birthday of freedom, merely, for this country, but for the world, for man universally.

There was a deeper meaning in that Declaration of the Congress of '76, to which we have just listened, than that of the political independence of this country. That independence was indeed, declared, that independence has indeed been won and defended by deeds of heroism and self-sacrifice, unsurpassed in the world's history, but it enters for only a small affair into what should occupy our thoughts on this day. The struggle between the

Originally published by H. Mann, printer (Dedham, Mass., 1834).

then feeble colonies and the mother country, deserves all the eulogiums it has received, but we are not here merely to recall it. A higher and a holier triumph than that of arms, or even that of the political independence of any country, excites the warm emotions of our hearts and calls forth our sympathy. We celebrate the triumph of humanity. No limited horizon confines us today. A boundless heaven spreads out over us and the whole human race comes within the scope of our vision.

I pray you, Fellow Citizens, not to take a narrow view of the American Revolution. There was more in that Revolution than the American and British armies. The past and the future were there. The spirit of immobility and the spirit of progress met there in terrible conflict; humanity all entire, was there, and ours was but the battle ground where it conquered the power to take another step forward in its eternal career of improvement. In that Revolution there were debated not merely the interests of a few colonists and their descendants, but man's whole future was debated and decided. We should then look beyond the battle ground, beyond the contending armies, to the cause then in question, to the principle which came out from the battle triumphant. To that cause, to that principle, sacred be this day. Sacred be this day, not merely to military triumph, not merely to deeds of heroism, nor of patriotism, but to the progress of the human race, to the political redemption and social installation of humanity.

The cause in question fifty-eight years ago this day, was that of the human race, the principle then declared was the equality of mankind. "All men are created equal," is the noble sentence that embodies the doctrine contended for by the Congress of '76, maintained and triumphantly established by the revolutionary army. I will not say that at that epoch, the assertion "all men are created equal," was suspected of the deep and full meaning we now assign it. I am not certain that the signers of the Declaration of Independence intended to assert by it anything more than the political equality of different communities, and the right of each community to choose its own form of government. But Providence makes men the unwitting instruments of advancing his designs, and often puts into their mouths words big with a meaning they little suspect, and sometimes with a meaning they are little able to appreciate. The time had come for the great principle of equality for which Christianity during so many ages had been paving the way, to be ushered in and set to work in the affairs of the world; and Providence so overruled it, that our fathers in asserting the rights of communities, asserted those of individuals, and in declaring one community's rights equal to those of another, uttered that soul-kindling truth, man equals man, man measures man, the world over.

I know of no topic more appropriate to this day than this great truth of man's equality to man. I therefore ask your indulgence to some desultory, perhaps common place, comments upon it, which I am desirous to bring before you, and which I should be glad to bring before the whole American people.

In speaking of equality, I pray you not to misinterpret me. There is a sense in which it is not true that "all men are created equal." It is not true that all men are born with the same capacities. There are original differences, intellectual, moral and physical, which no education that ever has been and which I venture to predict, none that ever will be devised can overcome. One child is born weak and sickly, another strong and healthy; one is quick and another is slow to learn; one can take in only isolated facts, dwell only on the minuteness of detail, another rises to causes and delights to trace first principles; one has no perception of the beautiful, sees nothing in nature to admire, and never rises to contemplate anything higher than food, clothing and shelter; another seizes upon the ideal of the beautiful, detaches it, re-embodies it, in forms before which all real beauty grows pale; one from the earliest moments is sweet tempered, another is sour tempered; one from a very early period is deeply affected by religious considerations, draws all his delight from meditating on God, the human soul, heaven and eternity, another cannot be made to think seriously of anything which goes above or beyond this present life. In these and a thousand other instances men are not, and we do not believe they ever will be, equal. We infer this from all experience, and from all acquaintance with human organization and with the reciprocal action of mind and matter. And I by no means mean to assert that in these respects and in others of a like kind, "all men are created equal."

When I contend for equality, that all men are created equal, I mean that all have a common nature, are brothers of the same family, heirs of the same inheritance, having the same general faculties, the same general wants, and the same general elements of knowledge and virtue. I mean that all have equal rights, that in all our social intercourse and relations, in all our governmental and educational provisions, man should be considered as measuring man. In a word, I mean that one man has no rights over another which that other has not over him, and that no one should have the power to derive any benefit from another without giving to that other a full, an exact equivalent.

I here mean something more than that specious kind of equality which English and French statesmen and some even in our country would give us, that is, simply equality before the laws. There are too many at home and abroad who have no higher notions of equality, or at least who contend that no other equality is practicable or consistent with social order. I am not able to express the abhorrence I feel for this doctrine. It is plausible, but it has no soundness. Its terms are popular, but its spirit is consistent with a very gross system of privilege. It is by doctrines like this that the enemies of the people contrive to mislead and enslave them.

There may be a great and most mischievous inequality, even in those countries where no man is above the laws. Laws may be framed so as to be very unequal in their influence upon different classes of society, and that too, without bearing on their face the marks of the least inequality. One class of community may have no temptations to steal, but very great temptations to defraud, to overreach, to oppress the poor; another class may be strongly and almost exclusively, tempted to steal; a law then punishing fraud, overreaching, or oppression, with a simple fine, while it punished stealing with death or imprisonment, would be anything but equal in its practical effect. And in fact, even in those countries where equality before the laws is recognized, the laws are generally framed so as to fall with the most tremendous weight upon offences to which the poor are almost exclusively exposed.

Imprisonment for debt is a case in point. The rich, the poor, the honest, and the dishonest are before this law, so far as its face is concerned, equal. But the rich man cannot be imprisoned for debt unless it be his choice; the dishonest have generally address enough to escape, and consequently to all practical purposes, it is a law exclusively against the honest poor man. Is there not here, and in cases like these, a distinction, and a most odious distinction tolerated by government? Yet in these and a thousand other cases that might be mentioned, all are equal before the laws. He who transgresses the law incurs its penalty. And what boots it that it is so, if the laws are made so as to strike only one part of community, and that too, the part it ought especially to protect?

I mean then by equality, if not that all men have equal capacities, at least something more than equality before the laws. I not only ask for equality before the laws, but for equal laws—for laws which shall not only speak the same language to all, but which shall have the same meaning for all, the same practical effect upon all. All have the same rights, and I ask that these rights be in no instance invaded, that all be in a situation to demand them, to defend them if attacked, and to enjoy them freely and fully.

Those of our orators who have no higher ambition than to flatter the people, inflate national vanity, and show themselves off in rounded periods, tell us that equality, even in this broad sense, is already gained in this country. But no such thing. We have equality in scarcely any sense worth naming. Will you pretend that we are equal as long as a large portion of our community lies at the mercy of any political demagogue who knows how to veil his liberticide designs under a pretended love of the *dear* people? Will you say that we are equal while all our higher seminaries of learning are virtually closed to all except the rich? Equal while we have those who are born with the right to live in luxury and idleness, while there are others who are born with only the rights to starve if they do not work? Equal, while one part of community can and do lay under contribution the labor of the other, make it the means of their wealth and power, and the means too of riveting the firmer the chains of those who perform it? I allude not here to negro slavery. I allude to that marked distinction which exists all over the world and which is everyday becoming more glaring in our own country, between the working men and the idlers, between those who produce and are poor and those who produce not and are rich; between those who perform all the productive labor and those who are crafty enough, *enterprising* enough, to obtain all its fruits. I allude here to what may seem to you no evil, but to me it is an evil, an evil of immense magnitude, one which lies at the bottom of nearly all the social evils which exist among us. And as long as this evil exists we are not free. There is a worm gnawing into the very heart of that tree of liberty which our fathers have planted.

Is my language severe? Be it so. I am not here to flatter. I stand not here to boast what a free, enlightened, and virtuous people we are. I would not utter a note of discord to mar the harmony which the recollections of this day should always produce; but I cannot avoid saying that we are not that free, enlightened and virtuous people our fourth of July orators and our political demagogues have made us believe we are. We have boasted too much. We must become more modest. Our freedom is written on paper, our equality is registered in our Constitutions, but of what avail is that, if it be not written in our hearts and registered in our souls?

We have a constantly besetting sin. We compare ourselves not with our own future, but with the people and institutions of the old world. Because in some respects we really are less wicked than they, we infer that we are as good as we can or ought to be; because our institutions really are better than theirs we conclude they are the best we ought to desire. We flatter ourselves that because we have taken one step, that we have run the whole career of improvement; that because we have begun well, that we have nothing further to do but to applaud ourselves for what we have done. Here is our besetting sin. Here is the rock on which we are liable to split. We look backward, not forward; to what we have done rather than to what we should do, and compare ourselves with what others are instead of comparing ourselves with what we may and ought to be.

God, in his providence, has assigned to the American people an important mission. He has given it us in charge to prove what man is, to develop his whole nature, and show of what he is capable. As the first step towards the completion of this mission, we are to bring out and carry into practice that grand, comprehensive principle, "All men are created equal." This we have not yet done. Our mission is only begun. We have only started in the race, and let us not sit down and fold our hands as if we had reached the goal and won the race. But let us be aware that we have done nothing, if we stop where we are. Our motto must be,—"Onward, onward, till the work be done."

And do not, I entreat you hastily conclude, that all is done that can be done. Beware how you infer, because there never has been a greater degree of equality in any country than already exists in ours, that none greater is desirable or attainable. Beware, how you set bounds to human improvement. Providence, nature, nor grace has ever yet said to man in his progressive career, "Hitherto shalt thou come, but no further." We are in but the infancy of the world, in but the first, faint dawnings of civilization. Time and the progress of events have it in charge to unfold and nourish in that creature man, now so weak, so contemned, a moral and social growth not yet dreamed of by the firmest of the believers in his indefinite perfectibility. There are wrapped up in the bottom of his soul, the germs of lofty and deathless energies, which go beyond, immeasurably beyond and above the strongest, the sublimest, he has as yet been able to exhibit. Far, far is he from having attained his full height. Let thought stretch its pinions and soar to the highest point it can reach and man in his upward flight shall yet rise above it.

Let not this be doubted. There is in the belief of this a kindling power, a something which gives us a lofty enthusiasm and creates within us the energy to realize it. Let no one forget that one law of our nature, one which distinguishes us from the brute, is Improvement. The beaver of today builds not his house with more skill, makes it not more convenient than did the beaver of four thousand years ago. He has not surpassed the first of his race. He knows no progress. But man has outstripped his ancestors. Generation improves upon generation, and the school boy of today is above the wisest of the Greeks. Let us not overlook nor underrate man's power of progress. Let us not, when a noble object is proposed, one for which all the better part of our nature cries out, let us not be deterred from pursuing it by the objection, "It never has been, therefore it cannot be." This is the cowardly sluggard's objection. What! Has there been no progress? Has there never been gained at one epoch nothing which did exist before that epoch? What! Have I only dreamed of the creations of science, of industry, and genius? Is it a dream, that mariner's compass which opens a pathway in the deep and brings together the most distant corners of the earth? Is it a dream, that Art of Printing, an art that electrifies the mass of mind, creates a universe of thought and opens a medium of intercourse between all nations and all ages? Is it a dream, that bold navigator who discovered this new world, and led the way to this mighty republic and to all the civilized life on this western hemisphere? Is it a dream, those proud triumphs of science which have subdued nature, discloses to us new worlds embedded in what were once counted simple elements, which have snatched the lightning from the clouds and guided the harmless fire? Is it a dream, the discovery and application of the wonders of Steam which makes the ships walk the sea regardless of wind or tide? Is it a dream, this free government, this splendid creation of human wisdom, which we so loudly and so justly boast, whose origin we this day commemorate? And yet all these are modern things. None of the ancients knew them. They have come out from Christianity, and some of them have come up into life within our own memories. Either these are dreams, the flitting visions of a distempered fancy, or things may take place at one epoch, which had no existence before it. In other words, there has been, there is, there may be, a progress. Man even in his infancy has done wonders, what will he not do in his manhood?

Let us then bid adieu to the arguments of those who have eyes only for the past, and who exert themselves only to keep the human race from marching to its end. Let us bid adieu to the spirit of immobility and imbibe the spirit of movement, the spirit whose look is upward and whose motion is onward. The equality I have designated is not impracticable. It is a truth which we must bring out of the abstract and clothe with life and activity.

God never made one portion of mankind to live in idleness, in uselessness, and in luxury, and another part to live in toil and want; he never made some to be masters and some to be slaves, some to live and grow rich by skillfully, not to say dishonestly, availing themselves of the labors of others—the many to be "hewers of wood and drawers of water" to the few. God has never done this. He created all men with equal rights, and made one capable of measuring another. He created all of "one blood," made them to be brothers, fellow beings, to aid, not to worry and devour each other. This is a truth taught us from Heaven. It is a distinguishing doctrine, as it is one of the brightest signatures of the divine origin of Christianity. Christianity teaches it by declaring him alone the greatest who best serves the human race. "He who would be greatest among you, let him become your servant." And dare we say that here is a truth taught us, a duty enjoined upon us by religion itself, that is impracticable? And what is it that makes it impracticable, if it be so? It is nothing but our conviction that it is impracticable, nothing but the continual cry that it is impossible. It is this that unmans us and keeps us back in a condition we should have long since outgrown. To him that believeth all things are possible. If ye had faith as a grain of mustard seed, ye might remove mountains. It is the want of faith, the want of full conviction in its practicability that renders it impracticable. Take hold of the work with both hands, let your minds, your hearts, your very souls be in it, and no matter how difficult it is, you will accomplish it; mountains will give way before you, and your path will become smooth and easy. Men can, men must, men will realize the equality for which I am contending. I see them pursuing it, I hear them crying out for it, and heaven and earth shall pass away sooner than they shall not obtain it.

But they will gain it not by a miracle. It must, as must all improvements in man's moral and social condition, be obtained by natural means, by the exertion of those powers which God has given us. Our present work is to realize this equality. How shall it be done? Important question have I asked—one on the right answer to which much depends for our country's future and for the future of humanity. How shall we realize, not in our professions and in our paper constitutions, but in our social condition, intercourse and relations, that equality is recognized—I will say taught, enjoined, in Christianity, and adopted as the basis of our political institutions? We have not yet done it. There is a striking discrepancy between our practice and the theory we avow. We have borne witness to a degree of equality which we have not yet created. How shall we do it?

Not by government alone. We cannot legislate our citizens into the equality we desire. Government, in fact, is much more limited in the sphere of its operations, than is commonly imagined. In its best state, its mission is mostly negative. It is charged merely to prevent one man from invading the rights of another; to maintain an "open field and fair play" to individual genius and enterprise. In countries overrun with despotism, a free government may seem to be the greatest good to be desired, the greatest God can bestow; but our own experience may teach us that it does not embosom and necessarily bring along with it, every good. We have a free government. Here all offices are open to merit alone, and the whole body of the people are free to elect whom they will to be their servants or the agents of their power. But look at the men who sometimes fill high stations. Can you believe they are, one half of them, the choice of the people? I know the people may be deceived, but never so as to prefer some men who have filled some of the highest offices in their gift. We all know that party management, the intrigues of party leaders render the right of suffrage in, perhaps, a majority of cases where it is worth having, a nullity. A few individuals of one party get together and make a nomination, a few individuals of another party make another nomination, and my boasted right of suffrage is dwindled down to a choice between these two nominations. I may dislike them both, but unless I choose not to vote at all or throw my vote away, I must vote for one or the other.

But pass over this, let all party management and party sins sleep in forgetfulness, suppose the people select the men they really prefer, always elect the very best men in the state or nation, and very little is gained. No matter how good laws are, they will remain on your statute books a dead letter unless demanded by the public; and the public if ignorant or immoral, or but feebly moral, will not be very likely to demand any very good laws. A community in which privilege obtains, in which inequality prevails, will not often be very unanimous, in demanding or in obeying laws which have an equalizing tendency, which seek the good of the poorest and most numerous class instead of that of the richest, smallest and most highly favored class.

I value a free government, a popular government, ay, if you will, a democratic government, for I have not a feeling about me that is not democratic. But a free government is powerless without a free people. No matter how much freedom you incorporate into your paper constitutions, you can never have any more practiced than is written in the hearts and on the characters of the people. I therefore expect little from government, I ask little but to be let alone. Its nature is never to lead, but to follow. The people must precede it, opinion must go before it. If the people go right government cannot go wrong. If the people love right character, liberty and equality will be maintained, let what will be the character of the government, and whoever may be the men entrusted with its management. We sometimes express fears for our government, we sometimes fear that our free institutions may become a prey to some aspiring demagogue who will succeed in erecting a throne of despotism on the ruins of our temple of liberty. It may be so. But it will not be so because that demagogue is wicked, is talented and powerful; but because the people will have become corrupt, because liberty will no longer be written in their hearts, and because they will have ceased to have any freedom in their souls. It is, then, of comparatively little consequence, that fierce contention we witness among politicians. I view with almost perfect indifference the contests between the great leading parties which now distract our country. They are only struggles between those who *have* and those who *want* office. The country, humanity, moral and social progress are not in those struggles. We must leave them, and, to a certain degree, legislative enactments, take our stand upon higher and holier ground, and speak directly to the people as moral, intelligent, religious and social beings. We must dare look on truth and dare hold it up, that by its light there may be formed just such characters as we need to support our free institutions.

I know of but one means of introducing the equality and of effecting that moral and social reform in our country and throughout the world, which every good man sighs and yearns for, and that means is education. I do not mean ability to read and write, and cipher, with a smattering of geography and grammar, and the catechism in addition. I mean Education, the *formation* of *character*, the moral, religious, intellectual, and physical training, disciplining, of our whole community. Our common schools do not do this. They are better than nothing, but they do not educate us. Our higher seminaries may do something toward educating us, but little towards fitting us for our mission. They educate us to be fond of distinctions, to be fond of popularity, and to look with contempt on the people. And glad am I that no more of our community are able to give their children *such* an education.

We want a republican education, an education which shall accustom the child from the first to see things valued according to their worth—but in themselves; an education which shall raise our children above the factitious distinctions of society, which now pervert our judgments, and which shall teach them to value every man according to his intrinsic worth, without any regard to his position in society, and even without any reference to the length of his purse or to the firmness of his coat. In a word we want an education that shall breathe into the child that very spirit which dictated the assertion, "God has created all men equal;" that very spirit which filled the hearts, nerved the souls of our fathers and made them stake life, property and honor, in defiance of a transatlantic tyrant, and in defence of the rights of man—which shall breathe into the child the very spirit of that gospel which is glad tidings to the poor, which declares, "blessed are the poor for theirs is the kingdom of heaven," that we all have one Father, and that we all are members of the same vast brotherhood of humanity—an education which shall make us feel that man wherever seen is our brother, woman wherever found is our sister, and he who injures a human being commits an offence against us, he who wrongs a man wrongs us, the arrow that wounds another's heart has sped deep into our own—an education that shall make us good Christians, give us firm and manly characters, consistent with truth and full of love to mankind.

We have now no such education. We have indeed little support for liberty or morality. We have established a free government, but we have done comparatively nothing to preserve it. We have declared ourselves in favor of Freedom and left that Freedom to take care of itself. There is no such thing amongst us as education of our children in reference to their moral and social destination, in reference to those duties which devolve upon them as citizens of this republic—of this republic which God in his providence has appointed to be the school whence are to go out the doctrines and the men destined to regenerate the world.

The education we now patronize, teaches us no doctrines of equality, none of philanthropy. Our first lesson is to make a good bargain, our second to get rich, our third to look out for ourselves, and our fourth and last is that if some are unhappy, if our wealth has been the occasion of others' poverty, if unholy distinctions prevail, we must thank God we are not among the wretched, and the wretched must believe for their consolation, that the distinctions in society of which they complain, are, as a writer in a popular periodical has it, "the express appointment of God."

Long as such an education is the best we have, we cannot accomplish our mission, we cannot perform that grand and beneficent work which Deity has assigned us. The fact is, we forget the millions, we fix our eyes and the eyes of our children on the few. We covet and teach them to covet their wealth and their distinctions. We legislate for the few, not for the many. Our legislators seem not aware that there are such creatures as workingmen in existence, except in the penal part of their legislation. They legislate for capitalists, landholders, stockholders, corporations, master mechanics, and those generally who make use of the labors of others, but very seldom for the journeyman mechanic, the laborers in your factories, and those generally who perform physical labor of community, unless indeed they have some law with a severe penalty to enact; then, indeed, the workingman is by no means neglected. But in this I blame not our legislators. They seldom know any better. They do not know that such a thing as the people exists, or if they do, they know that they were raised to their dignity of legislators by deserting the people and that they must continue to desert or neglect them or lose it. This is an evil, and one that cannot be removed unless our children are taught that the people are the human race, and that he alone has any moral worth who devotes himself without reserve to their greatest good, unless we give to our children that republican education I have pointed out, and form them, not to despise the people, not to be masters of the people, but servants of the people, to raise themselves and to carry the people up with them.

And not only a few children must be educated in this way, but all the children of our whole community. All need it, all have a right to it, all may demand it. Society is bound to give it, and if it does not it forfeits its right to punish the offender. And not one sex alone must be educated, but the children of both sexes. Woman's is the more important sex, and if but one half of our race can be educated, let it be woman, instead of man. Woman forms our character. She is with us through life. She nurses us in infancy, she watches by us in sickness, soothes in distress, supports us in adversity and cheers us in the melancholy of old age. The rank determines that of the race. If she be high minded and virtuous with a soul thirsting for that which is lofty, true and disinterested, so is it with the race. If she be light and vain, with her heart set only on trifles, fond alone of pleasure—alas! For the community where she is so, it is ruined! Let all then, all the children of both sexes, have this republican education for which I contend. And all the coming generations may have it. We have only to will it. There is nothing we cannot do if we but will to do it. We talk much about education. We speak of its vast importance, of its absolute necessity, but seem to imagine that talking is enough. But we must will it. We must act. We must take hold of the work, take hold of it in earnest, put forth all our energies, and rest not till it be done.

Let there be once established a system of equal, republican education, of an education for all the children of our land, whether rich or poor, male or female, an education which shall be such as our position in the moral, political, religious, and philosophical world demands, and the equality on which I have dwelt will be obtained, our government will be firmly established, our free institutions will begin to unfold their beauty, man will prove that he is capable of self government, humanity will disclose its mighty power of progress, and we shall have accomplished our mission. The light of our example will then reach the darkest corners of the earth, all nations will then turn towards us with admiration and for guidance. Freedom will be vindicated, liberty will become universal, all the world will be free, all will be peace, love, and progress towards perfection. Noble result! By the eye of faith I see the auspicious day when it shall be so, dawn on the world. I see the moment draw near, when man shall no longer see an enemy in man, when wars shall end, tyrannies be abolished, and oppression cease, and "every man sit under his own vine and fig tree with none to molest or make afraid."

Young men! ye who are full of the future, whose souls are full of energy, and whose hearts burn to do grand and glorious deeds, 'tis yours to hasten that day. Your fathers have done nobly. They have begun a magnificent work, but it is yours to finish it. The mission of your fathers is ended. They have departed. Gone are they who so nobly dared, so bravely struggled, to gain you a country and liberty for the world! Gone are they who signed that immortal paper which has this day been read in our hearing. Gone are they who stood firm, in those days which "tried men's souls." I see but there and there one, lingering behind as if unwilling to quit the scene till they can bear some good tidings from you, their children, to those who have preceded them. And gone too is He whose soul was full of chivalry, whose heart was full of the love of humanity, Liberty's Representative and champion in two worlds! He is gone! and you are left alone. Alone, young men, to your own energies and philanthropy. A grand and comprehensive work is bequeathed you. The men of the revolution have given it to you in charge to regenerate the world. Prove yourselves equal to your mission. And ere long free principles and just practice will become universal; man will prove himself equal to his destiny, act worthy of his lofty nature and heavenly origin. Imbibe the spirit which animated the hearts and nerved the souls of your fathers fifty-eight years ago, and you will extend your influence from circle to circle till it spread over the whole of human society—and the song of freedom, of peace and love resound from every corner of the earth and rise in swellings trains to mingle with the full chorus of angels and the blest above.

Young men! look forward with full faith to such a glorious consummation; fix your eyes upon it; march towards it, as steadily and as firmly as your fathers did to win the political liberty we now boast. Contemplate the inspiring vision; let it fill your souls with a noble enthusiasm, and believe nothing gained till you have realized it. Feel that you live only for man, and that your mission is to set him forward with more rapid strides towards that perfection after which his soul hungers and thirsts. Make this the end of all your exertions, and never tire in this work of philanthropy. Do this, and you will preserve your country free; do this and you will regenerate the world. Do this, and all posterity shall bless your memories, and God himself approve your conduct and welcome you to heaven.

FIVE

New Views of Christianity, Society, and the Church

To the members and friends of the society for Christian Union and Progress, this little volume is inscribed as a token of affection and esteem, by the author

Preface

It must not be inferred from my calling this little work New Views, that I profess to bring forward a new religion, or to have discovered a new Christianity. The religion of the Bible I believe to be given by the inspiration of God, and the Christianity of Christ satisfies my understanding and my heart. However widely I may dissent from the Christianity of the Church, with that of Christ I am content to stand or fall, and I ask no higher glory than to live and die in it and for it.

I believe my views are somewhat original, but I am far from considering them the only or even the most important views which may be taken of the subjects on which I treat. Those subjects have a variety of aspects, and all their aspects are true and valuable. He who presents any one of them does a service to Humanity; and he who presents one of them has no occasion to fall out with him who presents another, nor to claim superiority over him.

Originally published by James Munro and Company (Boston, 1836).

Although I consider the views contained in the following pages original, I believe the conclusions, to which I come at last, will be found very much in accordance with those generally adopted by the denomination of Christians, with whom it has been for some years my happiness to be associated. That denomination, however, must not be held responsible for any of the opinions I have advanced. I am not the organ of a sect. I do not speak by authority, nor under tutelage. I speak for myself and from my own convictions. And in this way, better than I could in any other, do I prove my sympathy with the body of which I am a member, and establish my right to be called a Unitarian.

In what I have written here, as well as in all I have written elsewhere and on other occasions, I have aimed to set an example of free thought and free speech. I ask no thanks for this, for it was my duty and I dared not do otherwise. Besides, theology can never rise to the rank and certainty of a science, till it be submitted to the free and independent action of the human mind.

It will at once be seen that I have given only a few rough sketches of the subjects I have introduced. Many statements appear without the qualifications with which they exist in my own mind, many parts are doubtless obscure for the want of fuller developments, and the whole probably needs to be historically verified. But I have done all I could without making a larger book, and a larger book I could hope that nobody would buy or read. I may hereafter fill up my sketches and complete my pictures; but it would have been useless in the present state of the public mind to attempt more than I have done.

For my literary sins I have a right to some indulgence. My early life was spent in far other pursuits than those of literature. I make no pretensions to scholarship. For all my other sins—except those of omission for which I have given a valid excuse—I ask no indulgence. I hope I shall be rigidly criticized. He who helps me correct my errors is my friend.

Those who feel any interest in "The Society for Christian Union and Progress"—a society collected during the past summer, and of which I am the minister—may find in this volume the principles on which that society is founded, and the objects it contemplates. To the members of that society and to those who have listened to my preaching these views will not be new.

If any of my readers wish to pursue the subject touched upon in my Introduction, I would refer them to Benjamin Constant's great work *De la Religion considerée dans sạ Source, ses Formes et ses Developpements*, or *On Religion Considered in Its Source, Its Forms, and Its Developments*, to *Religion and the Church*, a book by Dr. Follen, which he is now publishing in a series of numbers; and especially to Friedrich Schleiermacher's work *Ueber die Religion: Reden an die Gebildeten unter ihren Verächten*, or *Discourses on Religion, addressed to the Cultivated among its Despisers*, a work which produced a powerful sensation in Germany when it first appeared, and one which cannot fail to exert a salutary influence on religious inquiry among ourselves. A friend, to whom I am proud to acknowledge myself under many obligations, has translated this work in the course of his own private studies, and I cannot but hope that he may be induced before long to publish it.

With these remarks I commit my little work to its fate. It contains results to which I have come only by years of painful experience; but I dismiss it from my mind with the full conviction, that He, who has watched over my life and preserved me amidst scenes through which I hope I may not be called to pass again, will take care that if what it contains be false it shall do no harm, and if it be true that it shall not die.

O. A. B.
BOSTON, NOV. 8, 1836

Contents

Introduction

Religion is natural to man and he ceases to be man the moment he ceases to be religious.

This position is sustained by what we are conscious of in ourselves and by the universal history of mankind.

Man has a capacity for religion, faculties which are useless without it, and wants which God alone can satisfy. Accordingly wherever he is, in whatever age or country, he has—with a few individual exceptions easily accounted for—some sort of religious notions and some form of religious worship.

But it is only religion, as distinguished from religious institutions, that is natural to man. The religious sentiment is universal, permanent, and indestructible; religious institutions depend on transient causes, and vary in different countries and epochs.

As distinguished from religious institutions, religion is the Conception, or Sentiment, of the Holy, that which makes us think of something as Reverend, and prompts us to revere it. It is that indefinable something within us which gives a meaning to the words Venerable and Awful, which makes us linger around the Sacred and the Time-hallowed, the graves of heroes or of nations,—which leads us to launch away upon the boundless expanse, or plunge into the mysterious depths of Being, and which, from the very ground of our nature, like the Seraphim of the prophet, is forever crying out, "Holy, holy, holy, is the Lord of hosts; the whole earth is full of his glory."

Religious institutions are the forms with which man clothes his religious sentiment, the answer he gives to the question, What is the Holy? Were he a stationary being, or could he take in the whole of truth at a single glance, the answer once given would be always satisfactory, the institution once adopted would be universal, unchangeable, and eternal. But neither is the fact. Man's starting point is the low valley, but he is continually—with slow and toilsome effort it may be—ascending the sides of the mountain to more favorable positions, from which his eye may sweep a broader horizon of truth. He begins in ignorance, but he is ever growing in knowledge.

In our ignorance, when we have seen but little of truth, and seen that little but dimly, we identify the Holy with the merely Terrible, the Powerful, the Inscrutable, the Useful, or the Beautiful; and we adopt as its symbols, the Thunder and Lightning, Winds and Rain, Ocean and Storm, majestic River or placid Lake, shady Grove or winding Brook, the Animal, the Bow or Spear by means of which we are fed, clothed, and protected; but as Experience rolls back the darkness, which made all around us appear huge and spectral, purges and extends our vision, these become inadequate representatives of our religious ideas; they fail to shadow forth the Holy to our understandings; and we leave them and rise to that which appears to be free from their limited and evanescent nature, to that which is Unlimited, All-sufficient, and Unfailing.

We are creatures of growth; it is, therefore, impossible that all our institutions should not be mutable and transitory. We are forever discovering new fields of truth, and every new discovery requires a new institution, or the modification of an old one. We might as well demand that the sciences of physiology, chemistry, and astronomy should wear eternally the same form, as that religious institutions should be unchangeable, and that those which satisfied our fathers should always satisfy us.

All things change their forms. Literature, Art, Science, Governments, change under the very eye of the spectator. Religious institutions are subject to the same universal law. Like the individuals of our race, they pass away and leave us to deck their tombs, or in our despair, to exclaim that we will lie down in the grave with them. But as the race itself does not die, as new generations crowd upon the departing to supply their places, so does the reproductive energy of religion survive all mutations of forms, and so do new institutions arise to gladden us with their youth and freshness, to carry us farther onward in our progress, and upward nearer to That which "'is the same yesterday, today, and forever."

Chapter I: Christianity

About two thousand years ago, mankind, having exhausted all their old religious institutions, received from their heavenly Father through the ministry of Jesus of Nazareth a new institution which was equal to their advanced position, and capable of aiding and directing their future progress.

But this institution must be spoken of as one which was, not as one which is. Notwithstanding the vast territories it acquired, the mighty influence it once exerted over the destinies of humanity, and its promises of immortality, it is now but the mere shadow of a sovereign, and its empire is falling in ruins. What remains of it is only the body after the spirit has left it. It is no longer animated by a living soul. The sentiment of the Holy has deserted it, and it is a by-word and a mockery.

Either then Jesus did not embrace in his mind the whole of truth, or else the Church has at best only partially realized his conception.

No institution, so long as it is in harmony with the progress of the understanding, can fail to command obedience or kindle enthusiasm. The Church now does neither. There is a wide disparity between it and the present state of intellectual development. We have discovered truths which it cannot claim as its own; we are conscious of instincts which it disavows, and which we cannot, or will not, suppress. Whose is the fault? Is it the fault of Humanity, of Jesus, or of the Church?

Humanity cannot be blamed, for Humanity's law is to grow; it has an inherent right to seek for truth, and it is under no obligation to shut its eyes to the facts which unfold themselves to its observation. It is not the fault of Jesus, unless it can be proved that all he contemplated has been realized, that mankind have risen to as pure, and as happy a state as he proposed; have indeed fully comprehended him, taken in his entire thought, and reduced it to practice. Nobody will pretend this. The fault then must be borne by the Church.

The Church even in its best days was far below the conception of Jesus. It never comprehended him, and was always a very inadequate symbol of the Holy as he understood it.

Christianity, as it existed in the mind of Jesus, was the type of the most perfect religious institution to which the human race will, probably, ever attain. It was the point where the sentiment and the institution, the idea and the symbol, the conception and its realization appear to meet and become one. But the contemporaries of Jesus were not equal to this profound thought. They could not comprehend the God-Man, the deep meaning of his assertion, "I and my Father are one." He spake as never man spake—uttered truths for all nations, and for all times; but what he uttered was necessarily measured by the capacity of those who heard him—not by his own. The less never comprehends the greater. Their minds must have been equal to his in order to have been able to take in the full import of his words. They might—as they did—apprehend a great and glorious meaning in what he said; they might kindle at the truths he revealed to their understandings, and even glory in dying at the stake to defend them; but they would invariably and inevitably narrow them down to their own inferior intellects, and interpret them by their own previous modes of thinking and believing.

The Disciples themselves, the familiar friends, the chosen Apostles of Jesus, notwithstanding all the advantages of personal intercourse and personal explanations, never fully apprehended him. They mistook him for the Jewish Messiah, and even after his resurrection and ascension, they supposed it to have been his mission to "restore the kingdom to Israel." Though commanded to preach the Gospel to "every creature," they never once imagined that they were to preach it to any people but the Jewish, till the circumstances, which preceded and followed Peter's visit to Cornelius the Roman Centurion, took place to correct their error. It was not till then that any one of them could say, "Of a truth, I perceive that God is no respecter of persons; but in every nation he that feareth him and worketh righteousness is accepted with him." If this was true of the Disciples, how much more true must it have been of those who received the words of Jesus at second or third hand, and without any of the personal explanations or commentaries necessary to unfold their meaning?

Could the age, in which Jesus appeared, have comprehended him, it would have been superior to him, and consequently have had no need of him. We do not seek an instructor for our children in one who is not able to teach them. Moreover, if that age could have even rightly apprehended Jesus, we should be obliged to say his mission was intended to be confined to that age, or else to admit that the human race was never to go beyond the point then attained. Either Jesus did not regard the Future of Humanity, or he designed to interrupt its progress, and strike it with the curse of immobility; or else he was above his age and of course not to be understood by it. The world has not stood still since his coming; the Church has always considered his kingdom as one of which there is to be no end; and we know that he was not comprehended, and that even we, with the advantage of nearly two thousand years of mental and moral progress, are far—very far—below him.

If the age in which Jesus appeared could not comprehend him, it is obvious that it could not fully embody him in its institutions. It could embody no more of him than it could receive, and as it could receive only a part of him, we must admit that the Church has never been more than partially Christian. Never has it been the real body of Christ. Never has it reflected the God-Man perfectly. Never has it been a true mirror of the Holy. Always has the Holy in the sense of the Church been a very inferior thing to what it was in the mind and heart and life of Jesus.

But we must use measured terms in our condemnation of the Church. We must not ask the man in the child. The Church did what it could. It did its best to "form Christ" within itself, "the hope of glory," and was up to the period of its downfall as truly Christian, as the progress made by the human race admitted. It aided the growth of the human mind; enabled us to take in more truth than it had itself received; furnished us the light by which we discovered its defects; and by no means should its memory be cursed. Nobly and perseveringly did it discharge its duty; useful was it in its day and generation; and now that it has given up the ghost, we should pay it the rites of honorable burial, plant flowers over its resting place, and sometimes repair thither to bedew them with our tears.

To comprehend Jesus, to seize the Holy as it was in him, and consequently the true idea of Christianity, we must, from the heights to which we have risen by aid of the Church, look back and down upon the age in which he came, ascertain what was the work which there was for him to perform, and from that obtain a key to what he proposed to accomplish.

Two systems then disputed the Empire of the World; Spiritualism represented by the Eastern world, the old world of Asia, and Materialism represented by Greece and Rome.[1] Spiritualism regards purity or holiness as predicable of Spirit alone, and Matter as essentially impure, possessing and capable of receiving nothing of the Holy,—the prison house of the soul, its only hindrance to a union with God, or absorption into his essence, the cause of all uncleanness, sin, and evil, consequently to be contemned, degraded, and as far as possible annihilated. Materialism takes the other extreme, does not recognize the claims of Spirit, disregards the soul, counts the body everything, earth all, heaven nothing, and condenses itself into the advice, "Eat and drink, for tomorrow we die."

This opposition between Spiritualism and Materialism presupposes a necessary and original antithesis between Spirit and Matter. When Spirit and Matter are given as antagonist principles, we are obliged to admit antagonism between all the terms into which they are respectively convertible. From Spirit is deduced by natural generation, God, the Priesthood, Faith, Heaven, Eternity; from Matter, Man, the State, Reason, the Earth, and Time; consequently to place Spirit and Matter in opposition, is to make an antithesis between God and Man, the Priesthood and the State, Faith and Reason, Heaven and Earth, and Time and Eternity.

This antithesis generates perpetual and universal war. It is necessary then to remove it and harmonize, or unite the two terms. Now, if we conceive Jesus as standing between Spirit and Matter, the representative of both—God-Man—the point where both meet and lose their antithesis, laying a hand on each and saying, "Be one, as I and my Father are one," thus sanctifying both and marrying them in a mystic and holy union, we shall have his secret thought and the true Idea of Christianity.

The Scriptures uniformly present Jesus to us as a mediator, the middle term between two extremes, and they call his work a mediation, a reconciliation—an atonement. The Church has ever considered Jesus as making an atonement. It has held on to the term at all times as with the grasp of death. The first charge it has labored to fix upon heretics has been that of rejecting the Atonement, and the one all dissenters from the predominant doctrines of the day, have been most solicitous to repel is that of "denying the Lord who bought us." The whole Christian world, from the days of the Apostles up to the moment in which I write, have identified Christianity with the Atonement, and felt that in admitting the Atonement they admitted Christ, and that in denying it they were rejecting him.

Jesus himself always spoke of his doctrine, the grand Idea which lay at the bottom of all his teaching, under the term "Love." "A new commandment give I unto you, that ye love one another." "By this shall all men know that ye are my disciples, if ye have love one to another." John, who seems to have caught more of the peculiar spirit of Jesus than any of the Disciples, sees nothing but love in the Gospel. Love penetrated his soul; it runs through all his writings, and tradition relates that it at length so completely absorbed him that all he could say in his public addresses was, "Little children, love one another." He uniformly dwells with unutterable delight on the love which the Father has for us and that which we may have for him, the intimate union of man with God, expressed by the strong language of dwelling in God and God dwelling in us. In his view there is no antagonism. All antithesis is destroyed. Love sheds its hallowed and hallowing light over both God and Man, over Spirit and Matter, binding all beings and all Being in one strict and ever-lasting union.

The nature of love is to destroy all antagonism. It brings together; it begetteth union, and from union cometh peace. And what word so accurately expresses to the consciousness of Christendom, the intended result of the mission of Jesus, as that word peace? Every man who has read the New Testament feels that it was peace that Jesus came to effect,—peace after which the soul has so often sighed and yearned in vain, and a peace not merely between two or three individuals for a day, but a universal and eternal peace between all conflicting elements, between God and man, between the soul and body, between this world and another, between the duties of time and the duties of eternity. How clearly is this expressed in that sublime chorus of the angels, sung over the manger-cradle—"Glory to God in the highest, on earth peace and good-will to men!"

Where there is but one term there is no union. There is no harmony with but one note. It is mockery to talk to us of peace where one of the two belligerent parties is annihilated. That were the peace of the grave. Jesus must then save both parties. The Church has, therefore, with a truth it has never comprehended, called him God-Man. But if the two terms and their products be originally and essentially antagonist; if there be between them an innate hostility, their union, their reconciliation cannot be effected. Therefore in proposing the union, in attempting the Atonement, Christianity declares as its great doctrine that there is no essential, no original antithesis between God and man; that neither Spirit nor Matter is unholy in its nature; that all things, Spirit, Matter, God, Man, Soul, Body, Heaven, Earth, Time, Eternity, with all their duties and interests, are in themselves holy. All things proceed from the same Holy Fountain, and no fountain sendeth forth both sweet waters and bitter. It therefore writes "Holiness to the Lord" upon everything, and sums up its sublime teaching in that grand synthesis, "Thou shalt love the Lord thy God with all thy heart and mind and soul and strength, and thy neighbor as thyself."

Chapter II: The Church

The aim of the Church was to embody the Holy as it existed in the mind of Jesus, and had it succeeded, it would have realized the Atonement; that is, the reconciliation of Spirit and Matter and all their products.

But the time was not yet. The Paraclete was in expectation. The Church could only give currency to the fact that it was the mission of Jesus to make an atonement. It from the first misapprehended the conditions on which it was to be effected. Instead of understanding Jesus to assert the holiness of both Spirit and Matter, it understood him to admit that Matter was rightfully cursed, and to predicate holiness of Spirit alone. In the sense of the Church then he did not come to atone Spirit and Matter, but to redeem Spirit from the consequences of its connection with Matter. His name therefore was not the Atoner, the Reconciler, but the Redeemer, and his work not properly an atonement, but a redemption. This was the original sin of the Church.

By this misapprehension the Church rejected the mediator. The Christ ceases to be the middle term uniting Spirit and Matter, the *hilasterion*, the mercy-seat, or point where God and man meet and lose their antithesis, the Advocate with the Father for Humanity, and becomes the Avenger of Spirit, the Manifestation of God's righteous indignation against Man. He dies to save mankind, it is true, but he dies to pay a penalty. God demands man's everlasting destruction; Jesus admits that God's demand is just, and dies to discharge it. Hence the symbol of the cross, signifying to the Church an original and necessary antithesis between God and man which can be removed only by the sacrifice of justice to mercy. In this the Church took its stand with Spiritualism, and from a mediator became a partisan.

By taking its stand with Spiritualism the Church condemned itself to all the evils of being exclusive. It obliged itself to reject an important element of truth, and it became subject to all the miseries and vexations of being intolerant. It became responsible for all the consequences which necessarily result from Spiritualism. The first of these consequences was the denial that Jesus came in the flesh. If Matter be essentially unholy, then Jesus, if he had a material body, must have been unholy; if unholy, sinful. Hence all the difficulties of the Gnostics—difficulties hardly adjusted by means of a Virgin Mother and the Immaculate Conception; for this mode of accommodation really denied the God-Man, the symbol of the great truth the Church was to embody. It left the God indeed, but it destroyed the Man, inasmuch as it separated the humanity of Jesus by its very origin from common humanity.

Man's inherent depravity, his corruption by nature followed as a matter of course. Man by his very nature partakes of Matter, is material, then unholy, then sinful, corrupt, depraved. He is originally material, therefore originally a sinner. Hence original sin. Sometimes original sin is indeed traced to a primitive disobedience, to the Fall; but then the doctrine of the Fall itself is only one of the innumerable forms which is assumed by the doctrine of the essential impurity of Matter.

From this original, inherent depravity of human nature necessarily results that antithesis between God and man which renders their union impossible and which imperiously demands the sacrifice of one or the other. "Die he or justice must." Man is sacrificed on the cross in the person of Jesus. Hence the Vicarious Atonement, the conversion of the Atonement into an Expiation. But, if man was sacrificed, if he died as he deserved in Jesus, his death was eternal. Symbolically then he cannot rise. The body of Jesus after his resurrection is not material in the opinion of the Church. He does not rise God-Man, but God. Hence the absolute Deity of Christ, which under various disguises has always been the sense of the Church.

From man's original and inherent depravity it results that he has no power to work out his own salvation. Hence the doctrine of Human Inability. By nature man is enslaved to Matter; he is born in sin and shaped in iniquity. He is sold to sin, to the world, to the devil. He must be ransomed. Matter cannot ransom him; then Spirit must,—and "God the mighty Maker" dies to redeem his creature—to deliver the soul from the influence of Matter.

But this can be only partially effected in this world. As long as we live, we must drag about with us this clog of earth—matter—and not till after death, when our vile bodies shall be changed into the likeness of Christ's glorious body, shall we be really saved. We are not then saved here; we only hope to be saved hereafter. Hence the doctrine which denies holiness to man in this world, which places the kingdom of God exclusively in the world to come, and which establishes a real antithesis between heaven and earth, and the means necessary to secure present well-being and those necessary to secure future blessedness.

God has indeed died to ransom sinners from the grave of the body, to redeem them from the flesh, to break the chains of the bound and to set the captive free; but the effects of the ransom must be secured; agents must be appointed to proclaim the glad tidings of salvation, to bid the prisoner hope, and the captive rejoice that the hour of release will come. Hence the Church. Hence too the authority of the Church to preach salvation—to save sinners. And as the Church is composed of all who have this authority and of none others, therefore the dogma, "Out of the Church there is no salvation."

The Church is commissioned; it is God's agent in saving sinners. It is then his representative. If the representative of God, then of spirit. In its representative character, that is, as a Church, it is then spiritual, and if spiritual, holy; and if holy, infallible. Hence the Infallibility of the Church.

The Holy should undoubtedly govern the Unholy; Spirit then should govern Matter. Spirit then is supreme; and the Church as the representative of Spirit must also be supreme. Hence the Supremacy of the Church.

The Church is a vast body composed of many members. It needs a head. It should also be modeled after the Church above. The Church above has a supreme head, Jesus Christ: the Church below should then have a head, who may be its center, its unity, the personification of its wisdom and its authority. Hence the Pope, the Supreme Head of the Church, Vicar of Jesus, and Representative of God.

The Church is a spiritual body. Its supremacy then is a spiritual supremacy. A spiritual supremacy extends to thought and conscience. Hence on the one hand the Confessional designed to solve cases of conscience, and on the other Creeds, Expurgatory Indexes, Inquisitions, Pains and Penalties against Heretics.

The spiritual order in heaven is absolute; the Church then as the representative of that order must also be absolute. As a representative it speaks not in its own name, but in the name of the power it represents. Since that power may command, the Church may command; and as it may command in the name of an absolute sovereign, its commands must be implicitly obeyed. An absolute sovereign may command to any extent he pleases—what shall be believed as well as what shall be done. Hence Implicit Faith, the Authority which the Church has alleged for the basis of Belief. Hence too prohibitions against reason and reasoning which have marked the Church under all its forms, in all its phases and divisions and subdivisions.

Reason too is human; then it is material; to set it up against Faith were to set up the Material against the Spiritual; the Human against the Divine; Man against God: for the Church being God by proxy, by representation, it has of course the right to consider whatever is set up against the faith it enjoins as set up against God.

The Civil Order, if it be anything more than a function of the Church, belongs to the category of Matter. It is then inferior to the Church. It is then bound to obey the Church. Hence the claims of the Church over civil institutions, its right to bestow the crowns of kings, to place kingdoms under ban, to absolve subjects from their allegiance, and all the wars and antagonism between Church and State.

The spiritual order alone is holy. Its interests are then the only interests it is not sinful to labor to promote. In laboring to promote them, the Church was under the necessity of laboring for itself. Hence its justification to itself of its selfishness, its rapacity, its untiring efforts to aggrandize itself at the expense of individuals and of states.

As the interests of the Church alone were holy, it was of course sinful to be devoted to any others. All the interests of the material order, that is, all temporal interests, were sinful, and the Church never ceased to call them so. Hence its perpetual denunciation of wealth, place and renown, and the obstacles it always placed in the way of all direct efforts for the promotion of well-being on earth. This is the reason why it has discouraged, indeed unchurched, anathematized, all efforts to gain civil and political liberty, and always regarded with an evil eye all industry not directly or indirectly in its own interests.

This same exclusive Spiritualism borrowed from Asia, striking Matter with the curse of being unclean in its nature, was the reason for enjoining Celibacy upon the Clergy. An idea of sanctity was attached to the ministerial office, which it was supposed any contact with the flesh would sully. It also led devotees, those who desired to lead lives strictly holy, to renounce the flesh, as well as the world and the devil, to take vows of perpetual celibacy and to shut themselves up in Monasteries and Nunneries. It is the origin of all those self-inflicted tortures, mortifications of the body, penances, fastings, and that neglect of this world for another, which fill so large a space in the history of the Church during what are commonly called the "dark ages." The Church in its theory looked always with horror upon all sensual indulgences. Marriage was sinful, till purified by Holy Church. The song and the dance, innocent amusements, and wholesome recreations, though sometimes conceded to the incessant importunities of Matter, were of the devil. Even the gay dress and blithesome song of nature were offensive. A dark, silent, friar's frock was the only befitting garb for nature or for man. The *beau ideal* of a good Christian was one who renounced all his connections with the world, became deaf to the voice of kindred and of friends, insensible to the sweetest and holiest emotions of humanity, immured himself in a cave or cell, and did nothing the livelong day but count his beads and kiss the crucifix.

Exceptions there were; but this was the Idea, the dominant tendency of the Church. Thanks, however, to the stubbornness of Matter, and to the superintending care of Providence, its dominant tendency always found powerful resistance, and its Idea was never able fully to realize itself.

Chapter III: Protestantism

Everything must have its time. The Church abused, degraded, vilified Matter, but could not annihilate it. It existed in spite of the Church. It increased in power, and at length rose against Spiritualism and demanded the restoration of its rights. This rebellion of Materialism, of the material order against the Spiritual, is Protestantism.

Matter always exerted a great influence over the practice of the Church. In the first three centuries it was very powerful. It condemned the Gnostics and Manicheans as heretics, and was on the point of rising to empire under the form of Arianism. But the Oriental influence predominated, and the Arians became acknowledged heretics.

After the defeat of Arianism, that noble protest in its day of Rationalism against Mysticism, of Matter against Spirit, of European against Asiatic ideas, the Church departed more and more from the Atonement, and became more and more arrogant, arbitrary, spiritualistic, papistical. Still Matter occasionally made itself heard. It could not prevent the celibacy of the clergy, but it did maintain the unity of the race and prevented the re-establishment of a sacerdotal caste, claiming by birth a superior sanctity. It broke out too in the form of Pelagianism, that doctrine which denies that man is clean gone in iniquity, and which makes the material order count for something. Pelagius was the able defender of Humanity when it seemed to be deserted by all its friends, and his efforts were by no means unavailing.

Matter asserted its rights and avenged itself in a less unexceptionable form in the Convents, the Monasteries and Nunneries, among the clergy of all ranks, in that gross licentiousness which led to the reformation attempted by Hildebrand; and finally it ascended—not avowedly, but in reality—the papal throne, in the person of Leo X.

The accession of Leo X to the papal throne is a remarkable event in the history of the Church. It marks the predominance of material interests in the very bosom of the Church itself. It is a proof that whatever might be the theory of the Church, however different it claimed to be from all other powers, it was at this epoch in practice the same as the kingdoms of men. Poverty ceased in its eyes to be a virtue. The poor mendicant, the barefooted friar, could no longer hope to become one day the spiritual head of Christendom. Spiritual gifts and graces were not now enough. High birth and royal pretensions were required; and it was not as a priest, but as a member of the princely House of Medici that Leo became Pope.

The object of the Church had changed. It had ceased to regard the spiritual wants and welfare of mankind. It had become wealthy. It had acquired vast portions of this world's goods, and its great care was to preserve them. Its interests had become temporal interests, and therefore it needed, not a spiritual Father, but a temporal prince. It is as a prince that Leo conducts himself. His legates to the Imperial, English and French Courts, entered into negotiations altogether as ambassadors of a temporal prince, not as the simple representatives of the Church.

Leo himself is a sensualist, sunk in his sensual pleasures, and perhaps a great sufferer in consequence of his excesses. It is said he was an Atheist, a thing more than probable. All his tastes were worldly. Instead of the sacred books of the Church, the pious legends of Saints and Martyrs, he amused himself with the elegant but *profane* literature of Greece and Rome. His principal secretaries were not holy monks but eminent classical scholars. He revived and enlarged the University at Rome, encouraged human learning and the arts of civilization, completed St. Peter's, and his reign was graced by Michael Angelo and Raphael. He engaged in wars and diplomacy and in them both had respect only to the goods of the Church, or to the interests of himself and family as temporal princes.

Now all this was in direct opposition to the theory of the Church. Materialism was in the papal chair, but it was there as a usurper, as an illegitimate. It reigned in fact, but not in right. The Church was divided against itself. In theory it was Spiritualist, but in practice it was Materialist. It could not long survive this inconsistency, and it needed not the attacks of Luther to hasten the day of its complete destruction.

But Materialism must have become quite powerful to have been able to usurp the papal throne itself. It was indeed too powerful to bear patiently the name of usurper; at least to be contented to reign only indirectly. It would be acknowledged as sovereign, and proclaimed legitimate. This the Church could not do. The Church could do nothing but cling to its old pretensions. To expel Materialism and return to Hildebrand was out of the question. To give up its claims, and own itself Materialist, would have been to abandon all title to even its material possessions, since it was by virtue of its spiritual character that it held them. Materialism—as it could reign in the Church only as it were by stealth—resolved to leave the Church and to reign in spite of it, against it, and even on its ruins. It protested, since it had all the power, against being called hard names, and armed itself in the person of Luther to vindicate its rights and to make its claims acknowledged.

The dominant character of Protestantism is then the insurrection of Materialism, and what we call the Reformation is really a Revolution in favor of the material order. Spiritualism had exhausted its energies; it had done all it could for Humanity; the time had come for the material element of our nature, which Spiritualism had neglected and grossly abused, to rise from its depressed condition and contribute its share to the general progress of mankind. It rose, and in rising it brought up the whole series of terms the Church had disregarded. It brought up the state, civil liberty, human reason, philosophy, industry, all temporal interests.

In Protestantism, Greece and Rome revived and again carried their victorious arms into the East. The Reformation connects us with classical antiquity, with the beautiful and graceful forms of Grecian art and literature, and with Roman eloquence and jurisprudence, as the Church had connected us with Judea, Egypt and India.

Chapter IV: Protestantism

That Protestantism is the insurrection of Matter against Spirit, of the material against the spiritual order, is susceptible of very satisfactory historical verification.

One of the most immediate and efficient causes of Protestantism was the Revival of Greek and Roman Literature. Constantinople was taken by the Turks, and its scholars and the remains of Classical Learning which it had preserved were dispersed over Western Europe. The Classics took possession of the Universities and the Learned, were studied, commented on, appealed to as an authority paramount to that of the Church and—Protestantism was born.

By means of the Classics, the scholars of the Fifteenth Century were introduced to a world altogether unlike and much superior to that in which they lived—to an order of ideas wholly diverse from those avowed or tolerated by the Church. They were enchanted. They had found the Ideal of their dreams. They became disgusted with the present; they repelled the civilization effected by the Church, looked with contempt on its Fathers, Saints, Martyrs, Schoolmen, Troubadours, Knights and Minstrels, and sighed and yearned and labored to reproduce Athens or Rome.

And what was that Athens and that Rome which seemed to them to realize the very Ideal of the Perfect? We know very well today what they were. They were material; through the whole period of their historical existence, it is well known that the material or temporal order predominated over the spiritual. They are not that old spiritual world of the East which reigned in the Church. In that old world—in India for instance—where Spiritualism has its throne, Man sinks before God, Matter fades away before the presence of Spirit, and Time is swallowed up in Eternity. Industry is in its incipient stages, and the state scarcely appears. There is no history, no chronology. All is dateless and unregistered. An inflexible and changeless tyranny weighs down the human race and paralyzes its energies. Ages on ages roll away and bring no melioration. Everything remains as it was, monotonous and immovable as the Spirit it contemplates and adores.

In Athens and Rome all this is reversed. Human interests, the interests of mankind in time and space, predominate. Man is the most conspicuous figure in the group. He is everywhere, and his imprint is upon everything. Industry flourishes; commerce is encouraged; the state is constituted, and tends to democracy; citizens assemble to discuss their common interests; the orator harangues them; the aspirant courts them; the warrior and the statesman render them an account of their doings and await their award. The People—not the Gods—will, decree, make, unmake or modify the laws. Divinity does not become incarnate, as in the Asiatic world, but men are deified. History is not Theogony, but a record of human events and transactions. Poetry sings heroes, the great and renowned of earth, or chants at the festal board and the couch of voluptuousness. Art models its creations after human forms, for human pleasure or human convenience. They are human faces we see; human voices we hear; human dwellings in which we lodge and dream of human growth and human melioration.

There are Gods and temples, and priests and oracles, and augurs and auguries, it is true; but they are not like those we meet where Spiritualism reigns. The Gods are all anthropomorphous. Their forms are the perfection of the human. The allegorical beasts, the strange beasts, compounded of parts of many known and unknown beasts which meet us in Indian, Egyptian and Persian Mythology, as symbols of the Gods, are extinct. Priests are not a caste as they are under Spiritualism, springing from the head of Brahma and claiming superior sanctity and power as their birth-right, but simple police officers. Religion is merely a function of the state. Socrates dies because he breaks the laws of Athens—not, as Jesus did—for blaspheming the Gods. Numa introduces or organizes Polytheism at Rome for the purpose of governing the people by means of appeals to their sentiment of the Holy; and the Roman "Pontifex Maximus" was never anything more than a master of police.

This in its generality is equally a description of Protestantism, as might indeed have been asserted beforehand. The epoch of the Revival of Classical Literature must have been predisposed to Materialism or else it could not have been pleased with the Classics, and the influence of the Classics must have been to increase that predisposition, and as Protestantism was a result of both, it could be nothing but Materialism.

In classical antiquity religion is a function of the state. It is the same under Protestantism. Henry the Eighth of England declares himself supreme Head of the Church, not by virtue of his spiritual character, but by virtue of his character as a temporal prince. The Protestant princes of Germany are protectors of the Church; and all over Europe, there is an implied contract between the State and the Ecclesiastical Authorities. The State pledges itself to support the Church on condition that the Church support the State. Ask the kings, nobility, or even church dignitaries, why they support religion, and they will answer with one voice, "Because the people cannot be preserved in order, cannot be made to submit to their rulers, and because civil society cannot exist, without it." The same or a similar answer will be returned by almost every political man in this country; and truly may it be said that religion is valued by the protestant world as a subsidiary to the state, as a mere matter of police.

Under the reign of Spiritualism all questions are decided by authority. The Church prohibited reasoning. It commanded, and men were to obey or be counted rebels against God. Materialism, by raising up man and the state, makes the reason of man, or the reason of the state, paramount to the commands of the Church. Under Protestantism, the state in most cases, the individual reason in a few, imposes the creed upon the Church. The King and Parliament in England determine the faith which the clergy must profess and maintain; the Protestant princes in Germany have the supreme control of the symbols of the Church, the right to enact what creed they please.

Indeed the authority of the Church in matters of belief was regarded by the Reformers as one of the greatest evils, against which they had to contend. It was particularly against this authority that Luther protested. What he and his coadjutors demanded, was the right to read and interpret the Bible for themselves. This was the right they wrested from the Church. To have been consequent they should have retained it in their hands as individuals; it would then have been the right of private judgment and, if it meant anything, the right of the reason to sit in judgment on all propositions to be believed. To this extent, however, they were not prepared to go. Between the absolute authority of the Church, and the absolute authority of the individual reason, intervened the authority of the state. But as the state was material, the substitution of its authority for the authority of the Church was still to substitute the Material for the Spiritual.

But the tendency, however arrested by the state, has been steadily towards the most unlimited freedom of thought and conscience. Our fathers rebelled against the authority of the state in religious matters as well as against the authority of the Pope. In political and industrial speculations, the English and Americans give the fullest freedom to the individual reason, Germany has done it to the greatest extent in historical, literary and philosophical, and to a very great extent, in theological matters, and France does it in everything. All modern philosophy is built on the absolute freedom and independence of the individual reason; that is, the reason of humanity, in opposition to the reason of the church or the state. Descartes refused to believe in his own existence but upon the authority of his reason; Bacon allows no authority but observation and induction; Berkeley finds no ground for admitting an external world, and therefore denies it; and Hume finding no certain evidence of anything outward or inward, doubted philosophically of all things.

Philosophy is a human creation; it is the product of man, as the universe is of God. Under Spiritualism, then, which—in theory—demolishes man, there can be no philosophy; yet as man, though denied, exists, there is a philosophical tendency. But this philosophical tendency is always either to Skepticism, Mysticism, or Idealism. Skepticism, that philosophy which denies all certainty, made its first appearance in modern times in the Church. The Church declared the reason unworthy of confidence, and in doing that gave birth to the whole skeptical philosophy. When the authority of the Church was questioned and she was compelled to defend it, she did it on the ground that the reason could not be trusted as a criterion of truth, and that there could be no certainty for man, if he did not admit an authority independent of his reason,—not perceiving that if the reason were stuck with impotence there would be no means of substantiating the legitimacy of the authority.

On the other hand, the Church having its point of view in Spirit, consulted the soul before the body, became introspective, fixed on the Inward to the exclusion of the Outward. It overlooked the Outward; and when that is overlooked it is hardly possible that it should not be denied. Hence Idealism or Mysticism.

Under the reign of Materialism all this is changed. There is full confidence in the reason. The method of philosophizing is the experimental. But as the point of view is the Outward—Matter—Spirit is overlooked; Matter alone admitted. Hence philosophical Materialism. And philosophical Materialism, in germ or developed, has been commensurate with Protestantism. When the mind becomes fixed on the external world, inasmuch as we become acquainted with that world only by means of our senses, we naturally conclude that our senses are our only source of knowledge. Hence SENSUALISM, the philosophy supported by Locke, Condillac, and even by Bacon, so far as it concerns his own application of his method. And from the hypothesis that our senses are our only inlets of knowledge, we are compelled to admit that nothing can be known which is not cognizable by some one or all of them. Our senses take cognizance only of Matter; then we can know nothing but Matter. We can know nothing of the spirit or soul. The body is all that we know of man. That dies, and there ends man—at least all we know of him. Hence no immortality, no future state. If nothing can be known but by means of our senses, God, then, inasmuch as we do not see him, hear him, taste him, smell him, touch him, cannot be known; then he does not exist for us. Hence Atheism. Hence Modern Infidelity, in all its forms, so prevalent in the last century, and so far from being extinct even in this.

The same tendency to exalt the terms depressed by the Church is to be observed in the religious aspect of Protestantism. Properly speaking, Protestantism has no religious character. As Protestants, people are not religious, but co-existing with their Protestantism, they may indeed retain something of religion. Men often act from mixed motives. They bear in their bosoms sometimes two antagonist principles, now obeying the one, and now the other, without being aware that both are not one and the same principle. With Protestants, religion has existed; but as a reminiscence, a tradition. Sometimes, indeed, the remembrance has been very lively, and seemed very much like reality. The old soldier warms up with the recollections of his early feats, and lives over his life as he relates its events to his grandchild,—

Shoulders his crutch and shows how fields are won.

If the religion of the Protestant world be a reminiscence, it must be the religion of the Church. It is, in fact, only Catholicism continued. The same principle lies at the bottom of all Protestant churches, in so far as they are churches, which was at the bottom of the Church of the middle ages. But Materialism modifies their rites and dogmas. In the practice of all, there is an effort to make them appear reasonable. Hence Commentaries, Expositions, and Defences without number. Even where the authority of the reason is denied, there is an instinctive sense of its authority and a desire to enlist it. In mere forms, pomp and splendor have gradually disappeared, and dry utility and even baldness have been consulted. In doctrines, those which exalt man and give him some share in the work of salvation have gained in credit and influence. Pelagianism, under some thin disguises or undisguised, has become almost universal. The doctrine of man's inherent Total Depravity, in the few cases in which it is asserted, is asserted, more as a matter of duty than of conviction. Nobody, who can help it, preaches the old-fashioned doctrine of God's Sovereignty, expressed in the dogma of unconditional Election and Reprobation. The Vicarious Atonement has hardly a friend left. The Deity of Jesus is questioned, his simple Humanity is asserted and is gaining credence. Orthodox is a term which implies as much reproach as commendation; people are beginning to laugh at the claims of councils and synods, and to be quite merry at the idea of excommunication.

In Literature and Art there is the same tendency. Poetry in the last century hardly existed, and was, so far as it did exist, mainly ethical or descriptive. It had no revelations of the Infinite. Prose writers under Protestantism have been historians, critics, essayists, or controversalists; they have aimed almost exclusively at the elevation or adornment of the material order, and in scarcely an instance has a widely popular writer exalted God at the expense of Man, the Church at the expense of the State, Faith at the expense of Reason, or Eternity at the expense of Time. Art is finite, and gives us busts and portraits, or copies of Greek and Roman models. The Physical sciences take precedence of the Metaphysical, and faith in Railroads and Steamboats is much stronger than in Ideas.

In governments, the tendency is the same. Nothing is more characteristic of Protestantism, than its influence in promoting civil and political liberty. Under its reign all forms of governments tend towards the Democratic. "The King and the Church" are exchanged for the "Constitution and the People." Liberty, not Order, is the word that wakes the dead, and electrifies the masses. A social science is created, and the physical well-being of the humblest laborer is cared for, and made a subject of deliberation in the councils of nations.

Industry has received in Protestant countries its grandest developments. Since the time of Luther, it has been performing one continued series of miracles. Every corner of the globe is explored; the most distant and perilous seas are navigated; the most miserly soil is laid under contribution; manufactures, villages and cities spring up and increase as by enchantment; canals and rail-roads are crossing the country in every direction; the means of production, the comforts, conveniences and luxuries of life are multiplied to an extent hardly safe to relate.

Such, in its most general aspect, in its dominant tendency, is Protestantism. It is a new and much improved edition of the Classics. Its civilization belongs to the same order as that of Greece and Rome. It is in advance, greatly in advance, of Greece and Rome, but it is the same in its groundwork. The Material predominates over the Spiritual. Men labor six days for this world and at most but one for the world to come. The great strife is for temporal goods, fame or pleasure. God, the Soul, Heaven, and Eternity, are thrown into the back ground, and almost entirely disappear in the distance. Right yields to Expediency, and Duty is measured by Utility. The real character of Protestantism, the result to which it must come, wherever it can have its full development, may be best seen in France, at the close of the last century. The Church was converted into the Pantheon, and made a resting place for the bodies of the great and renowned of earth; God was converted into a symbol of the human reason, and man into the Man-Machine; Spiritualism fell, and the Revolution marked the complete triumph of Materialism.

Chapter V: Reaction of Spiritualism

What I have said of the Protestant world cannot be applied to the present century without some important qualifications. Properly speaking, Protestantism finished its work and expired in the French Revolution at the close of the last century. Since then there has been a reaction in favor of Spiritualism.

Men incline to exclusive Spiritualism in proportion to their want of faith in the practicability of improving their earthly condition. This accounts for the predominance of Spiritualism in the Church. The Church grew up and constituted itself amidst the crash of a falling world, when all it knew or could conceive of material well-being was crumbling in ruins around it. Greece and Rome were the prey of merciless barbarians. Society was apparently annihilated. Order there was none.—Security for person, property, or life, seemed almost the extravagant vagary of some mad enthusiast. Lawless violence, brutal passion, besotting ignorance, tyrants and their victims, were the only spectacles presented to win men's regard for the earth, or to inspire them with faith and hope to labor for its improvement. To the generation of that day, when the North disgorged itself upon the South, the earth must have appeared forsaken by its Maker, and abandoned to the Devil and his ministers. It was a wretched land; it could yield no supply; and the only solace for the soul was to turn away from it to another and a better world, to the world of spirit; to that world where tyrants do not enter, where wrongs and oppression, sufferings and grief, find no admission; where mutations and insecurity are unknown, and where the poor earth-wanderer, the time-worn pilgrim, may at length find that repose, that fullness of joy which he craved, which he sought but found not below. This view was natural, it was inevitable; and it could lead only to exclusive spiritualism—mysticism.

But when the external world has been somewhat meliorated, and men find that they have some security for their persons and property, that they may count with some degree of certainty on tomorrow, faith in the material order is produced and confirmed. One improvement prepares another. Success inspires confidence in future efforts. And this was the case at the epoch of the Reformation. Men had already made great progress in the material order in their temporal weal. Their faith in it kept pace with their progress, or more properly, outran it. It continued to extend till it became almost entire and universal. The Eighteenth Century will be marked in the annals of the world for its strong faith in the material order. Meliorations on the broadest scale were contemplated and viewed as already realized. Our Republic sprang into being, and the world leaped with joy that "a man child was born." Social progress and the perfection of governments became the religious creed of the day; the weal of man on earth, the spring and aim of all hopes and labors. A new paradise was imaged forth for man, inaccessible to the serpent, more delightful than that which Adam lost, and more attractive than that which the pious Christian hopes to gain. We of this generation can form only a faint conception of the strong faith our fathers had in the progress of society, the high hopes of human improvement they indulged, and the joy too big for utterance, with which they heard France in loud and kindling tones proclaim LIBERTY and EQUALITY. France for a moment became the center of the world. All eyes were fixed on her movements. The pulse stood still when she and her enemies met, and loud cheers burst from the universal heart of Humanity when her tricolored flag was seen to wave in triumph over the battle field. There was then no stray thought for God and eternity. Man and the world filled the soul. They were too big for it. But while the voice of Hope was yet ringing, and *Te Deum* shaking the arches of the old Cathedrals,—the Convention, the reign of Terror, the exile of patriots, the massacre of the gifted, the beautiful and the good. Napoleon and the Military Despotism came, and Humanity uttered a piercing shriek, and fell prostrate on the grave of her hopes!

The reaction produced by the catastrophe of this memorable drama was tremendous. There are still lingering among us those who have not forgotten the recoil they experienced when they saw the Republic swallowed up, or preparing to be swallowed up, in the Empire. Men never feel what they felt but once. The pang which darts through their souls changes them into stone. From that moment enthusiasm died, hope in social melioration ceased to be indulged, and those who had been the most sanguine in their anticipations, hung down their heads and said nothing; the warmest friends of Humanity apologized for their dreams of Liberty and Equality; Democracy became an accusation, and faith in the perfectibility of mankind a proof of disordered intellect.

In consequence of this reaction, men again despaired of the earth; and when they despair of the earth, they always take refuge in heaven; when man fails them, they always fly to God. They had trusted materialism too far—they would now not trust it at all. They had hoped too much—they would now hope nothing. The future, which had been to them so bright and promising, was now overspread with black clouds; the ocean on which they were anxious to embark was lashed into rage by the storm, and presented only images of dismasted or sinking ships and drowning crews. They turned back and sighed for the serene past, the quiet and order of old times, for the mystic land of India, where the soul may dissolve in ecstasy and dream of no change.

At the very moment when the sigh had just escaped, that mystic land reappeared. The English, through the East India Company, had brought to light its old Literature and Philosophy, so diverse from the Literature and Philosophy of modem Europe or of classical antiquity, and men were captivated by their novelty and bewildered by their strangeness. Sir William Jones gave currency to them by his poetical paraphrases and imitations; and the Asiatic Society by its researches placed them within reach of the learned of Europe. The Church rejoiced, for it was like bringing back her long lost mother, whose features she had remembered and was able at once to recognize. Germany, England, and even France became Oriental. Cicero, and Horace, and Virgil, Aeschylus, Euripides, and even Homer, with Jupiter, Apollo and Minerva were forced to bow before Hindu Bards and Gods of uncouth forms and unutterable names.

The influence of the old Braminical or spiritual world, thus dug up from the grave of centuries, may be traced in all our Philosophy, Art and Literature. It is remarkable in our poets. It moulds the form in Byron, penetrates to the ground in Wordsworth, and entirely predominates in the Schlegels. It causes us to feel a new interest in those writers and those epochs which partake the most of Spiritualism. Those old English writers who were somewhat inclined to mysticism are revived; Plato, who travelled in the East and brought back its lore which he modified by Western genius and molded into Grecian forms, is reedited, commented on, translated and raised to the highest rank among philosophers. The middle ages are reexamined and found to contain a treasure of romance, acuteness, depth and wisdom, and are deemed by some to be "dark ages" only because we have not light enough to read them.

Materialism in Philosophy is extinct in Germany. It is only a reminiscence in France, and it produces no remarkable work in England or America. Phrenology, which some deem Materialism, has itself struck Materialism with death in Franz Gall's Work, by showing that we are conscious of phenomena within us which no metaphysical alchemy can transmute into sensations.

Protestantism, since the commencement of the present century, in what it has peculiar to itself, has ceased to gain ground. Rationalism in Germany retreats before the Evangelical party; the Genevan Church makes few proselytes; English and American Unitarianism, on the plan of Priestley and Belsham, avowedly material, and being, as it were, the jumping-off place from the Church to absolute infidelity, is evidently on the decline. There is probably not a man in this country, however much and justly he may esteem Priestley and Belsham, as bold and untiring advocates of reason and of Humanity, who would be willing to assume the defence of all their opinions. On the other hand Catholicism has revived, offered some able apologies for itself, made some eminent proselytes and alarmed many Protestants, even among ourselves. Indeed everywhere is seen a decided tendency to Spiritualism. The age has become weary of uncertainty. It sighs for repose. Controversy is nearly ended, and a sentiment is extensively prevailing, that it is a matter of very little consequence what a man believes, or what formulas of worship he adopts, if he only have a right spirit. Men, who a few years ago were staunch Rationalists, now talk of Spiritual Communion; and many, who could with difficulty be made to admit the inspiration of the Bible, arc now ready to admit the inspiration of the sacred books of all nations; and instead of stumbling at the idea of God's speaking to a few individuals, they see no reason why he should not speak to everybody. Some are becoming so spiritual that they see no necessity of matter; others so refine matter that it can offer no resistance to the will, making it indeed move as the spirit listeth; others still believe that all wisdom was in the keeping of the priests of ancient India, Egypt, and Persia, and fancy the world has been deteriorating for four thousand years, instead of advancing. Men go out from our midst to Europe, and come back half Catholics, sighing to introduce the architecture, the superstition, the rites and the sacred symbols of the middle ages.

A universal cry is raised against the frigid utilitarianism of the last century. Money-getting, desire for worldly wealth and renown, are spoken of with contempt, and men are evidently leaving the Outward for the Inward, and craving something more fervent, living and soul-kindling. All this proves that we have changed from what we were; that, though Materialism yet predominates and appears to have lost none of its influence, it is becoming a tradition; and that there is a new force collecting to expel it. Protestantism passes into the condition of a reminiscence. Protestant America cannot be aroused against the Catholics. A mob may burn a convent from momentary excitement, but the most protestant of the Protestants among us will petition the Legislature to indemnify the owners. Indeed Protestantism died in the French Revolution, and we are beginning to become disgusted with its dead body. The East has reappeared, and Spiritualism revives; will it again become supreme? Impossible.

Chapter VI: Mission of the Present

We of the present century must either dispense with all religious instructions, reproduce Spiritualism or Materialism, or we must build a new Church, organize a new institution free from the imperfections of those which have been.

The first is out of the question. Men cannot live in a perpetual anarchy. They must and will embody their ideas of the True, the Beautiful, and the Good—the Holy, in some institution. They must answer in some way the questions: What is the Holy? What is the true destination of Man?

To reproduce Spiritualism or Materialism, were an anomaly in the development of Humanity. Humanity does not traverse an eternal circle; it advances; it does not come round to its starting-point, but goes onward in one endless career of progress towards the Infinite, the Perfect.

Besides, it is impossible. Were it desirable, neither Spiritualism nor Materialism can to any considerable extent, or for any great length of time, become predominant. We cannot bring about that state of society which is the indispensable condition of the exclusive dominion of either.

Spiritualism just now revives; its friends may anticipate a victory; but they will be disappointed. Spiritualism, as an exclusive system, reigns only when men have no faith in Material interests; and in order to have no faith in material interests, we must virtually destroy them; we must have absolute despotism, a sacerdotal caste, or we must have another Decline and Fall like that of the Roman Empire, and a new irruption like that of the Goths, Vandals and Huns.

None of these things are possible. There are no more Goths, Vandals, or Huns. The North of Europe is civilized. Northern and central Asia is in the process of civilization through the influence of Russia; England is mingling the arts and sciences of the West with the Spiritualism of India; France and the colony of Liberia secure Africa; the Aborigines of this continent will in a few years have vanished before the continued advance of the European races; merchants and missionaries will do the rest. No external forces can then ever be collected to destroy civilization and compel the human race to commence its work anew.

Internally, modern civilization has nothing to fear. It contains no seeds of destruction. A real advance has been made. A vast fund of experience has been accumulated and is deposited in so many different languages, that we can hardly conceive it possible that it should be wholly lost or greatly diminished. The Art of Printing, unknown to Greek and Roman civilization, multiplies books to such an extent, that it is perfectly idle to dream of any catastrophe, unless it be the destruction of the world itself, which will reduce them to a few precious fragments like those left us of classical antiquity.

There is, too, a remarkable difference in the diffusion of knowledge. In the best days of classical antiquity, the number of the enlightened was but small. The masses were enveloped in thick darkness. Now the masses have been to school, and are going to school. The millions, who then were in darkness, now behold light springing up. The loss of one individual, however prominent he may be, is not felt. Another is immediately found to fill his place.

Liberty exists also to a much greater extent. The rights of man are better comprehended and secured. The individual man is a greater being than he was in Greece or Rome. He has a higher consciousness of his worth, and he is more respected, and his interests are felt to be more sacred.

Labor has become more honorable. In Greece and Rome labor was menial; it was performed by slaves, at least by the ignorant and brutish. Slavery is disappearing. It has only a small corner of the civilized world left to it. As slavery disappears, as labor comes to be performed by freemen, it will rise to the rank of a liberal profession, and men of character and influence will be laborers.

The improvements in the arts of production have become so extensive and the means of creating and accumulating wealth are so distributed, and the amount of wealth has already become so great and is shared by so many, that it is impossible that there should ever come again a scene of general poverty and wretchedness to make men despair of the earth, and abandon themselves wholly to the dreams of a spirit-land. There must always remain something to hope from the material order, and consequently, whatever may be the influence of a sudden panic, or a momentary affright, always a check to the absolute dominion of Spiritualism.

Nor can Materialism become sovereign again. It contains the elements of its own defeat. The very discipline, which Materialism demands to support itself, in the end neutralizes its dominion. As soon as men find themselves well off in a worldly point of view, they discover that they have wants which the world does not and cannot satisfy. The training demanded to ensure success in commercial industrial enterprises, or politics, strengthens faculties which crave something superior to commerce, to mere industry, or to politics. The merchant would not be always estimating the hazards of speculation; he dreams of his retirement from business, his splendid mansion, his refined hospitality, a library, and studious ease; the mechanic looks forward to a time when he shall have leisure to care for something besides merely animal wants; and the politician to his release from the cares and perplexities of a public life, to a quiet retreat, to a dignified old age, spent in plans of benevolence, in aiding the cause of education, religion, or philosophy. This low business world, upon which the moralist and the divine look down with much sorrow, is not quite so low after all, as they think it. It is doing a vast deal to develop the intellect. It is full of high and expanded brows.

It is true that money getting, mere physical utility has at this moment a wide influence, and may absorb the mind and heart quite too much. Still the evil is not unmixed. That man, who tortures his brain, spends his days and nights to accumulate a fortune, is much superior to him who is content to rot in poverty, who has no courage, no energy to attempt to improve his condition. He is a better member of society, is worth more to humanity. It is a great day, even for spiritualism, when all the people of a country are carried away in an industrial direction. Speculation may be rife, frauds may be common; many may become rich by means they care not to make known; many may become discontented; there may be much striving this way and that, much effort to get up, keep up, to pull or to push down; but the many will sharpen their faculties, and gain the leisure and the means and the disposition to attend to the spiritual part of their being. It does my heart good to witness the industrial activity of my countrymen. I see very clearly the evils which attend it; but I also see every year the general level rising, and the moral and intellectual power increasing. So is it too with our political struggles. They quicken thought, give the people the use of language, a consciousness of their power, especially of the power of mind, and upon the whole they do much to elevate the general character. Those quiet times we look back upon and regret, either were not as quiet as we think them, or they were quiet because they had not enough of thought to move them. They were as still, but too often as putrid, as the stagnant pool.

The science which is now introduced into commerce, into the mechanic arts and agricultural pursuits, and which is every day receiving a greater extension and new applications, while it preserves the material order, also keeps alive the spiritual, and gives us a check against the absolute ascendancy of Materialism.

We cannot then go back either to exclusive Spiritualism, or to exclusive Materialism. Both these systems have received so full a development, have acquired so much strength, that neither can be subdued. Both have their foundation in our nature, and both will exist and exert their influence. Shall they exist as antagonist principles? Shall the spirit forever lust against the flesh, and the flesh against the spirit? Is the bosom of Humanity to be eternally torn by these two contending factions? No. It cannot be. The war must end. Peace must be made.

This discloses our Mission. We are to reconcile spirit and matter; that is, we must realize the atonement. Nothing else remains for us to do. Stand still we cannot. To go back is equally impossible. We must go forward, but we can take not a step forward, but on the condition of uniting these two hitherto hostile principles. PROGRESS is our law and our first step is UNION.

The union of Spirit and Matter was the result contemplated by the mission of Jesus. The Church attempted it, but only partially succeeded, and has therefore died. The time had not come for the complete union. Jesus saw this. He knew that the age in which he lived would not be able to realize his conception. He therefore spoke of his "second coming." The Church has always had a vague presentiment of its own death, and the birth of a new era when Christ should really reign on earth. For a long time the hierophants have fixed upon ours as the epoch of the commencement of the new order of things. Some have gone even so far as to name this very year, 1836, as the beginning of what they call the Millennium.

The particular shape which has been assigned to this new order, this "latter day glory," the name by which it has been designated, amounts to nothing. That some have anticipated a personal appearance of Jesus, and a resurrection of the saints, should not induce us to treat with disrespect the almost unanimous belief of Christendom in a fuller manifestation of Christian truth, and in a more special reign of Christ in a future epoch of the world. All the presentiments of Humanity are to be respected. Humanity has a prophetic power. "Coming events cast their shadows before."

The "second coming" of Christ will be when the Idea which he represents, that is, the Idea of atonement, shall be fully realized. That Idea will be realized by a combination, a union, of the two terms which have received thus far from the Church only a separate development. This union the

Church has always had a presentiment of; it has looked forward to it, prayed for it; and we are still praying for it, for we still say, "Let thy kingdom come." Nobody believes that the Gospel has completed its work. The Church universal and eternal is not yet erected. The cornerstone is laid; the materials are prepared. Let then the workmen come forth with joy, and bid the Temple rise. Let them embody the true Idea of the God-Man, and Christ will then have come a second time; he will have come in power and great glory, and he will reign, and the whole earth will be glad.

Chapter VII: Christian Sects

This age must realize the Atonement, the union of Spirit and Matter, the destruction of all Antagonism and the production of universal peace.

God has appointed us to build the new Church, the one which shall bring the whole family of Man within its sacred enclosure, which shall be able to abide the ravages of time, and against which "the gates of hell shall not prevail."

But we can do this only by a general doctrine which enables us to recognize and accept all the elements of Humanity. If we leave out any one element of our nature, we shall have antagonism. Our system will be incomplete and the element excluded will be forever rising up in rebellion against it and collecting forces to destroy its authority.

All sects overlook this important truth. None of them seem to imagine that human nature has or should have any hand in the contraction of their theories. Instead of studying human nature, ascertaining its elements and its wants, and seeking to conform to them, every sect labors to conform human nature to its own creed. No one dreams of molding its dogmas to human nature, but everyone would mold human nature to its dogmas. Everyone is a bed of Procrustes. What is too short must be stretched, what is too long must be docked. No sect ever looks to human nature as the measure of truth; but all look to what they are pleased to call the truth, as the measure of human nature.

This were well enough if human nature had only been made of wax, or some other ductile material. But unfortunately it is very stubborn. It will not bend. It will not be mutilated. Its laws are permanent and universal; each one of them is eternal and indestructible. They war in vain who war against them. Be they good or be they bad, we must accept them, we must submit to them and do the best we can with them.

But human nature is well made, its laws are just and holy, its elements are true and divine. And this is the hidden sense of that symbol of the God-Man. That symbol teaches all who comprehend it, to find Divinity in Humanity, and Humanity in Divinity. By presenting us God and Man united in one person, it shows us that both are holy. The Father and the Son are one. Therefore we are commanded to honor the Son as we honor the Father, Humanity as Divinity, Man as well as God. But the Church has never understood this. No sect now understands it. Hence the contempt with which all sects treat human nature, and their entire want of confidence in it as a criterion of truth. They must correct themselves. "The Word was made flesh and dwelt among us."

To reject human nature and declare it unworthy of confidence as the Church did,—and as all sects now do, is—whether we know it or not—to reject all grounds of certainty, and to declare that we have no means of distinguishing truth from falsehood. Truth itself is nothing else to us than that which our nature by some one or all of its faculties compels us to believe. The fact that God has made us a revelation does not in the least impair this assertion. God has revealed to us truths which we could not of ourselves have discovered. But how do we know this? What is it but the human mind that can determine whether God has or has not spoken to us? What but the human mind can ascertain and fix the meaning of what he may have communicated? If we may not trust the human mind, human nature, how can we ever be sure that a revelation has been made? Or how distinguish a real revelation from a pretended one? By miracles? But how determine that what are alleged to be miracles, really are miracles? Or the more difficult question still, that the miracles, admitting them to be genuine, do necessarily involve the truth of the doctrines they are wrought to prove? Shall we be told that we must believe the revelation is a true one, because made by an authorized teacher? Where is the warrant of his authority? What shall assure us that the warrant is not a forgery? Have we anything but our own nature with which to answer these and a hundred more questions like them and equally important?

If human nature has the ability and the right to answer these questions, where are the limits of its ability and its right? If we trust it when it assures us God has spoken to us, and when it interprets what he has spoken, where shall we not trust it? If it be no criterion of truth, why do we trust it here? And if it be, why do we disclaim it elsewhere? Why declare it worthy of confidence in one case and not in another? It is the same in all cases, in all its degrees; and whether it testifies to that which is little, or to that which is great, it is the same, and its testimony is of precisely the same validity.

If we admit that human nature is the measure of truth,—of truth for us, human beings—then we admit that it is the criterion by which all sects must be tested. It is then the touchstone of truth. Every sect must be approved or condemned according to its decision. No sect must blame Humanity for not believing its doctrines. If after they have been fairly presented and fully comprehended they are rejected, they are proved to be false, or at least to be only partially true. It is no recommendation to advocate doctrines repugnant to human nature; nor is it any reproach to defend those which are pleasing to the natural heart. Humanity loves the truth and can be satisfied with nothing else. The sect, then, which ceases to make converts should abandon or enlarge its creed.

Sects in general are and will be slow to learn this truth. Each sect, because it has all the truth to be seen from its stand-point, takes it for granted that it has the whole truth. It does not even dream that there may be other stand-points, from which other truths may be seen or the same truths under other aspects; and therefore it concludes when its doctrines are rejected, that they are rejected because human nature is perverse or impotent, because men cannot or will not see the truth, or because they naturally hate it. Let it change its position and it will soon learn that the horizon, which it took to be the boundary of truth, was in fact only the boundary of its own vision.

All sects, however, have their truth and are serviceable to Humanity. Each one has a special doctrine which gives prominence to some one element of our nature, and is therefore satisfactory to all in whom that element predominates. But as that element, however important a one it may be, is not the whole of human nature, and as it can hardly be predominant alike in all men, no sect can satisfy entire Humanity. Each sect does something to develop and satisfy the separate elements of Humanity, but no one can develop and satisfy all the elements of Humanity and satisfy them as a whole.

Spiritualism and Materialism are the two most comprehensive sectarian doctrines which have ever been proclaimed. But neither of these is comprehensive enough. Either may satisfy a large class of wants but each must leave a class equally large unsatisfied. One has always been opposed by the other, and mutual opposition has finally destroyed them both. Humanity is still sighing for what it has not. It is seeking rest but finds none. And rest it will not find, till its untiring friends gain a standpoint, from which, as with one grand panoramic view, they may take in all its elements in their relative proportions, and exact distances, in their diversity and in their unity, till they have gone up and down the earth and collected and brought together its disjointed members, which contending sects have torn asunder, and molded them into one complete and lovely form of truth and holiness.

Where is the Christian sect that is engaged in this work? Where is the one that deems it desirable or possible? All the sects of Christendom, so far as it concerns their dominant tendency, fall into the category of Spiritualism, or into that of Materialism. Catholicism is virtually the Church of the middle ages. It is but a reminiscence. It has no life, at least no healthy existence. It belongs to Spiritualism. Calvinism, bating some few modifications produced by Protestant influence, is only a continuation of Catholicism. It is decidedly Spiritualistic. Its prayers, its hymns and homilies are deeply imprinted with Spiritualism. It repels the material order, and exhorts us to crucify the flesh, to disregard the world and to think only of God, the soul and eternity.

In the opinion of the Calvinist, the world lies under the curse of the Almighty. It is a wretched land, a vale of tears, of disease and death. There is no happiness below. It is vain, almost impious, to wish it till death comes to release us from the infirmities of the flesh. As long as we live we sin; we must carry about a weary load, an overwhelming burthen, a body of death. Man is a poor, depraved creature. He is smitten with a curse, and the curse spreads over his whole nature. There is nothing good within him. Of himself he can obtain, he can do, nothing good. He is unclean in the sight of God. His sacrifices are an abomination, and his holiest prayers are sinful. His will is perverted; his affections are all on the side of evil; his reason is deprived of its light, it is blind and impotent, and will lead those who trust to its guidance down to hell.

By its doctrine of "Foreordination," Calvinism annihilates man. It allows him no independent causality. It permits him to move only as a preordaining and irresistible will moves him. It makes him a thing, not a person, with properties but without faculties or rights. Whatever his destiny, however cruel, he has no right to complain. Spirit is absolute and has the right to receive him into blessedness or send him away into everlasting punishment, without any regard to his own wishes, merit or demerit. Hence Calvinists always give supremacy to the Spiritual order. They fled from England to this then wilderness world, because they would not conform to a Church established by the state; and when here they constituted the Church superior to the state. In theory the Pilgrims made the state a mere function of the Church. In order to be a citizen it was necessary that one should first be a church member. And for the last twenty years the great body of Calvinists throughout our whole country have been exerting all their skill and influence to raise the Church to that eminence from which it may overlook the state, control its deliberations and decide its measures.

His doctrine of "hereditary total depravity" has always compelled the Calvinist to reject Reason and to rely on Authority—to seek faith, not conviction. Protestant influences prevent him in these days from submitting to an infallible Pope, but he indemnifies himself by infallible creeds, councils, synods and assemblies. Or if these fail him, he can ascribe infallibility to the "written Word." Always does he prohibit himself the free exercise of his own understanding, and prescribe bounds beyond which reason and reasoning must not venture.

By the dogma of Christ's vicarious death, he takes his stand decidedly with Spiritualism, denies the Atonement, loses sight of the Mediator, and rejects the God-Man. He cannot then build the new Church, the Church truly universal and eternal. It is in vain that we ask him to destroy all antagonism. He does not even wish to do it; before the foundations, its origin and eternity were decreed. God and the devil, the saint and sinner, in his estimation, are alike immortal.

Universalism would seem to a superficial observer to be what we need. Its friends call it the doctrine of universal reconciliation, and they group around the love of God that which constitutes the real harmony and unity of creation. But Universalists do not understand themselves. They have a vague sense of the truth, but not a clear perception of it. As soon as they begin to explain themselves, they file off either to the ranks of Spiritualism, or of Materialism.

The larger number of Universalists, among whom is, or was, the chief of the sect, contend that all sin originates in the flesh and must end with it. The flesh ends at death, when it is deposited in the tomb; therefore, "he that is dead is freed from sin." Sin is the cause of all suffering; when sin ends, suffering ends. Sin ends at death, and therefore after death no suffering, but universal happiness.

This doctrine is as decidedly Spiritualism as oriental Spiritualism itself. If the body be the cause of all sin, it certainly deserves no respect. It is a vile thing, and should be despised, mortified, punished, annihilated. Universalists do not draw this inference, but they avoid it only by really denying that there is any sin, or at least by considering the consequences of sin of too little importance to be dreaded.

The body, however, according to this doctrine is a curse. Man would be better off without it than he is with it. It deserves nothing on its own account. Wherefore then shall I labor to make it comfortable? I shall be released from it tomorrow, and enter into a world of unutterable joy. Let my lodging tonight be on the bare ground, in the open air, destitute of a few conveniences, what imports it? Can I not afford to forego a pleasant lodging for one night, since I am ever after to be filled and overflowing with blessedness? Universalism, then, according to this exposition of it, must inevitably lead to neglect of the material order. Its legitimate result would be, not licentiousness, but a dreaming, contemplative life, wasting itself away in idleness, watching the motion of the sun, and wishing it to move faster, so that we may be the sooner translated from this miserable world, where nothing is worth laboring for, to our Father's kingdom where is music and dancing, songs and feasting forever and ever.

Universalists have, however, existing side by side with this exclusive Spiritualism, some strong tendencies to Materialism. Spiritualism and Materialism are nearly balanced in their minds, and constitute, not a union of spirit and matter, but a parallelism which has no tendency to union. But when the true doctrine of the Atonement is proclaimed, Universalists will be among the first believers. None will rejoice more than they, to see the new Church rise from the ruins of the old, and none will attend more readily or with more zeal at its consecration.

Unitarianism belongs to the material order. It is the last word of Protestantism, before Protestantism breaks entirely with the Past. It is the point towards which all Protestant sects converge in proportion as they gain upon their reminiscences. Every consistent Protestant Christian must be a Unitarian. Unitarianism elevates man; it preaches morality; it vindicates the rights of the mind, accepts and uses the reason, contends for civil freedom, and is social, charitable and humane. It saves the Son of man, but sometimes loses the Son of God.

But it is from the Unitarians that must come out the doctrine of universal reconciliation; for they are the only denomination in Christendom that labors to rest religious faith on rational conviction; that seeks to substitute reason for authority, to harmonize religion and science, or that has the requisite union of piety and mental freedom, to elaborate the doctrine which is to realize the Atonement. The orthodox, as they are called, are disturbed by their memory. Their faces are on the back side of their heads. They have zeal, energy, perseverance, but their ideas belong to the past. The Universalist can do nothing till someone arises to give them a philosophy. They must comprehend their instincts, before they can give to their doctrine of reconciliation that character which will adapt it to the wants of entire Humanity.

But Unitarians are every day breaking away more and more from tradition and every day making new progress in the creation of a philosophy which explains Humanity, determines its wants and the means of supplying them. Mind at this moment is extremely active among them, and as it can act freely it will most certainly elaborate the great doctrine required. They began in Rationalism. Their earlier doctrines were dry and cold. And this was necessary. They were called at first to a work of destruction. They were under the necessity of clearing away the rubbish of the old Church, before they could obtain a site whereon to erect the new one. The Unitarian preacher was under the necessity of raising a stern and commanding voice in the wilderness, "Prepare ye the way of the Lord, make his paths straight." He raised that voice, and the chief Priests and Pharisees in modern Judea heard and trembled, and some have gone forth to be baptized. The Unitarian has baptized them with water unto repentance, but he has borne witness that a mightier than he shall come after him, who shall baptize them with the Holy Ghost and with fire.

When the Unitarian appeared, there was on this whole earth no spot for the Temple of the living God, the temple of Reason, Love and Peace. For such a spot he contended. He has obtained it. He has begun the Temple; its foundations already appear, and although the workmen must yet work with their arms in one hand, he will see it completed, consecrated, and filled with the glory of the Lord.

Chapter VIII: Indications of the Atonement

The Church was the result of three causes, the Asiatic conquests of the Romans, the Alexandrian school of Philosophy, and the Christian movement of the people.

By the Asiatic conquests of the Romans, Spiritualism and Materialism were brought together upon the same theatre, and placed in the condition necessary to their union. Eastern and Western ideas were mingled in strange confusion throughout the whole of the Roman Empire during the first three centuries of our era, and the attempt to unite them, to combine them into a regular and harmonious system could hardly fail to be made.

This attempt was made by the Alexandrian Philosophers. These Philosophers called themselves eclectics. Their avowed object was to unite, the East and the West, European and Asiatic ideas, to reduce to a regular system the ideas of all the various schools of philosophy. They did it as perfectly as they could with the lights they had and the experiments they had made.

The Christian movement of the people was apparently very unlike that of the Alexandrian. The early Christians were the farthest in the world from being philosophers. They were inspired. They were moved by an impulse of which they asked, and could have given no account. God moved in them, and spoke through them; gave them a holy enthusiasm, a resistless energy of character, and prepared them to do, to dare and to suffer anything and everything. At his command they went forth to conquer the world, and they did conquer it; not, as it has been well remarked, by killing, but by dying.[2]

We understand today what it was that moved the early Christians. What was inspiration in them is philosophy in us. They had an instinctive sense of the synthesis of Spirit and Matter. Yet they thought nothing of Spirit and Matter. They disturbed themselves not in the least with Spiritualism and Materialism, with the East and the West, with Europe and Asia. They saw mankind sunk in sin and misery, weary and heavy laden, and they went forth strong in the Lord to raise them to virtue, to convert them to Christ and to give them rest. They did not speculate, they did not reason—they saw and felt and acted.

These and the Alexandrians met, and the Church was the result. The share of the Alexandrians in the construction of the Church has always been acknowledged to be very great. Perhaps it was greater than any have suspected. Certain it is that they furnished the Fathers their philosophy, and they may be pronounced without much hesitation, the real elaborators—not of Christianity, but—of the dogmas of the Church.

All men feel more or less the desire to account to themselves for what they are. For a time they may be carried away by a force not their own, and they may be so engrossed with varied and exciting action and events, that they have no time to think; but at the first moments of calmness and self-consciousness they will ask what has moved them, what was the power which carried them away and whither have they been borne. This was the case with the early Christians. The first excitement over, and the visits of inspiration having become less frequent, they desired to explain themselves to themselves, to give a name to the instincts they had obeyed, to the Divinity which had moved them, and to the destiny they had been fulfilling. The Alexandrians answered all their questions. They explained the Christians to themselves, and henceforth their explanations were counted Christianity.

These three causes of the old Church, or analogous ones, reappear today for the first time since that Epoch; and is not their reappearance an indication that a new Church is about to be built?

The East and the West are again on the same theatre. The British by means of their East India Company have reconquered the fatherland of Spiritualism, and brought up from the graves of ages its old Literature and Philosophy, and mingled them with those of the West, the father-land of Materialism. The Church itself has introduced not a little Spiritualism into Christian civilization, while Protestantism by encouraging the study of the classics has reproduced Greece and Rome. The two worlds, the two civilizations, the two systems to be atoned or united are now in very nearly the same relative condition as they were at the birth of the Church. They are thrown together into the crucible.

Alexandria, too, is reproduced with the modifications and improvements which two thousand years could not fail to effect. Eclecticism is declared to be the philosophy of the nineteenth century. Not one of the exclusive systems, which obtained during the last century, has now any life. Materialism is a tradition even in France; Idealism has exhausted itself in Germany, and England has no philosophy.

Schelling had at least a presentiment of Eclecticism in his doctrine of Identity; Hegel has greatly abridged the labors of its friends; Fries and his disciples observe its method, and Jacobi virtually embraced it. In our own country it has produced no great work, and perhaps will not; but it is avowed by many of the best minds among us, and is the only philosophy we have, that has not ceased to make proselytes.

In France, however, Eclecticism has received its fullest developments. M. Cousin has all but perfected it. He has presented us the last results of the philosophical labors of his predecessors and contemporaries, and furnished us with a method by which we may construct a philosophy which may truly be called the Science of the Absolute, a philosophy which need not fear the mutations of time and space, and may be sure that its sovereignty will be complete and undisputed as fast and as far as it comes to be understood.

M. Cousin has not only given us, as it were, a geometrical demonstration of the existence of Nature and of God, but he has also demonstrated that Humanity, Nature and God have precisely the same laws, that what we find in Nature and Humanity we may also find in God, and that when we have once risen to God, we may come back and find again in Nature and Humanity all that we had found in him.[3] This at once destroys all antithesis between Spirit and Matter, between God and man, gives man a kindred nature with God, makes him an image or manifestation of God, and paves the way for universal reconciliation and peace. If God be holy, man, inasmuch as he has the very elements of the Divinity, is also holy. God and man may then unite in an everlasting and holy union, Justice and Mercy kiss each other, and—all antagonism is destroyed.

The third cause, the inspiration of the people, is no less remarkable now than it was in the first centuries of our era. When God would produce a great result, one which requires the cooperation of vast multitudes, he does not merely inspire one man; he does not speak plainly in distinct propositions to a few, and leave them to speak to the many; but he gives an impulse to the masses, and carries away all the world in the direction of the object to be gained. People seem to themselves to be acting from their own impulses, and to be obeying their own convictions; but they are borne along by an invisible and resistless power towards an end of which they have a vague presentiment, but no distinct vision.

This is the case now. The time has come for a new Church, for a new synthesis of the elements of the life of Humanity. The end to be attained is Union. How would an inspiration designed to give the energy, the power to attain this end be most likely to manifest itself; in what way could it manifest itself but by giving the people an irresistible longing for union, and a tendency to unite, to associate on all occasions and for all purposes not inconsistent with union itself? And what is the most striking characteristic of this age? Is it not the tendency to association, a tendency so strong that it appears to the cool spectator like a monomania?

This tendency shows itself everywhere. All over Christendom, men seem mad for associations. They associate for almost everything, to promote science, literature, art and industry, to circulate the Bible, to distribute religious tracts, to diffuse useful knowledge, to improve and extend education, to meliorate governments and laws, to soften the rigors of the prison house, to aid the sick, to relieve the poor, to prevent pauperism, to free the slave, to send out missionaries, and to evangelize the world. And—what deserves to be remarked—all these associations, various as they are, really propose in every instance a great and glorious end. They all are formed for useful, moral, religious, philosophical, philanthropical or humane purposes. They may be badly managed, they may fail in accomplishing what they propose, but that which they propose deserves to be accomplished. Sectarians may control them; but in all cases their ends are broader than any sect, than all sects, and they alike commend themselves to the consciences and the prayers of mankind. In some of these associations, sects long and widely separated come together, and find to their mutual satisfaction that they have a common ground, and a ground which each one instinctively admits to be higher and holier than any merely sectarian ground.

This tendency too is triumphing over all obstacles. Sects, which opposed this or that association because principally under the control of this or that sect, have slowly and reluctantly ceased their opposition, and have finally acquiesced. Individuals, who for a time resorted to ridicule and abuse to check associations, are now silent, and they stand amazed as did those who listened to the Apostles on the day of Pentecost. Those who apprehended great evils from them now seek to withstand them only by counter associations. To resist them is in fact out of the question. One might as well resist the whirlwind. There is a more than human power at the bottom of them. They come from God, from a divine inspiration given to the people to build the new Church and realize the Atonement, a universal and everlasting association.

This tendency or inspiration will, in a few days, meet the Eclectic moment, if it has not already met it; and what shall prevent a result similar to that which followed the meeting of the early Christian inspiration and the Alexandrian Eclecticism? This inspiration is, indeed, at this moment, apparently blind, but it and Modern Philosophy tend to the same end. They have then the same truth at bottom. They must then have a natural affinity with one another. They will then come together. The philosophy will explain and enlighten the inspiration. They who are now mad for associations will comprehend the power which has moved them, they will see the end towards which they have been tending without their knowing it, and they will give to the philosopher in return zeal, energy, enthusiasm, and there will then be both the Light and the Force needed to construct the new Church.

And I think I see some indications that this meeting of inspiration and philosophy is already taking place. Something like it has occurred in Germany, in that movement commenced by Herder, but best represented by

Schleiermacher, a man remarkable for warmth of feeling, and coolness of thought, a preacher and a philosopher, a theologian and a man of science, a student and a man of business. It was attempted in France, where it gave birth to "Nouveau Christianisme," but without much success, because it is not a new Christianity but a new Church that is required.

But the plainest indications of it are at home. In this country more than in any other is the man of thought united in the same person with the man of action. The people here have a strong tendency to profound and philosophic thought, as well as to skillful, energetic and persevering action. The time is not far distant when our whole population will be philosophers, and all our philosophers will be practical men. This is written on almost everyman's brow in characters so plain that he who runs may read. This characteristic of our population fits us above all other nations to bring out and realize great and important ideas. Here too is the freedom which other nations want, and the faith in ideas which can be found nowhere else. Philosophers in other countries may think and construct important theories, but they can realize them only to a very limited extent. But here every idea may be at once put to a practical test, and if true it will be realized. We have the field, the liberty, the disposition and the faith to work with ideas. It is here then that must first be brought out and realized the true idea of the Atonement. We already seem to have a consciousness of this, and it is therefore that we are not and cannot be surprised to find the union of popular inspiration with profound philosophical thought manifesting itself more clearly here than anywhere else.

The representative of this union here is a body of individuals rather than a single individual. The many with us are everything, the individual almost nothing. One man, however, stands out from this body, a more perfect type of the synthesis of Eclecticism and inspiration than anyone else. I need not name him. Philosophers consult him, and the people hear his voice and follow him. His connection with a particular denomination may have exposed him to some unfriendly criticism, but he is in truth one of the most popular men of the age. His voice finds a response in the mind and in the heart of Humanity.

His active career commenced with the new century, in the place where it should, and in the only place where it could,—in the place where a Republic had been born and Liberty had received her grandest developments and her surest safeguards. There he has continued, and there he has been foremost in laying the foundation of that new Church which will soon rise to greet the morning ray, and in which a glad voice will chant the hymn of peace to the evening sun. Few men are so remarkable for their union of deep religious feeling with sound reflection, of sobriety with popular enthusiasm. He reveres God and he reverences man. When he speaks he convinces and kindles.

When Rationalism was attacked he appeared in its defence and proclaimed, in a language which still rings in our ears, the imprescriptible rights of the mind. After the first shock of the war upon Rationalism had been met, and a momentary truce tacitly declared, he brought out in an Ordination Sermon the great truth which destroys all antagonism and realizes the Atonement. In that Sermon—the most remarkable since the Sermon on the Mount—he distinctly recognizes and triumphantly vindicates the God-Man. "In ourselves are the elements of the Divinity. God then does not sustain a figurative resemblance to man. It is the resemblance of a parent to a child, THE LIKENESS OF A KINDRED NATURE." In this sublime declaration, the Son of God is owned. Humanity, after so many years of vain search for a Father, finds itself here openly proclaimed the true child of God.

This declaration gives us the hidden sense of the symbol of the God-Man. By asserting the Divinity of Humanity, it teaches us that we should not view that symbol as the symbol of two natures in one person, but of kindred natures in two persons. The God-Man indicates not the antithesis of God and man; nor does it stand for a being alone of its kind; but it indicates the homogeneousness of the human and divine natures, and shows that they can dwell together in love and peace. The Son of Man and the Son of God are not two persons but one—a mystery which becomes clear the very moment that the human nature is discovered to have a sameness with the Divine.

Chapter IX: The Atonement

The great doctrine, which is to realize the Atonement and which the Symbol of the God-Man now teaches us, is that all things are essentially holy, that everything is cleansed, and that we must call nothing common or unclean.

"And God saw everything that he had made, and behold it was very good." And what else could it have been? God is wise, powerful and good; and how can a wise, powerful and good being create evil? God is the great Fountain from which flows everything that is; how then can there be anything but good in existence?

Neither Spiritualism nor Materialism was aware of this truth. Spiritualism saw good only in pure Spirit. God was pure Spirit and therefore good; but all which could be distinguished from him was evil, and only evil and that continually. Our good consisted in resemblance to God, that is, in being as like pure Spirit as possible. Our duty was to get rid of Matter. All the interests of the material order were sinful. St. Augustine declared the flesh, that is the body, to be sin; perfection then could be obtained only by neglecting, and as far as possible, annihilating it. Materialism, on the other hand, had no recognition of Spirit. It considered all time and thought and labor bestowed on that which transcends this world as worse than thrown away. It had no conception of inward communion with God. It counted fears of punishment or hopes of reward in a world to come mere idle fancies, fit only to amuse or control the vulgar. It laughed at spiritual joys and griefs, and treated as serious affairs only the pleasures and pains of sense.

But the new doctrine of the Atonement reconciles these two warring systems. This doctrine teaches us that spirit is real and holy, that matter is real and holy, that God is holy and that man is holy, that spiritual joys and griefs, and the pleasures and pains of sense, are alike real joys and griefs, real pleasures and pains, and in their places are alike sacred. Spirit and Matter, then, are saved. One is not required to be sacrificed to the other; both may and should coexist as separate elements of the same grand and harmonious whole.

The influence of this doctrine cannot fail to be very great. It will correct our estimate of man, of the world, of religion and of God, and remodel all our institutions. It must in fact create a new civilization as much in advance of ours, as ours is in advance of that which obtained in the Roman Empire in the time of Jesus.

Hitherto we have considered man as the antithesis of all good. We have loaded him with reproachful epithets and made it a sin in him even to be born. We have uniformly deemed it necessary to degrade him in order to exalt his Creator. But this will end. The slave will become a son. Man is hereafter to stand erect before God as a child before its father. Human nature, at which we have pointed our wit and vented our spleen, will be clothed with a high and commanding worth. It will be seen to be a lofty and deathless nature. It will be felt to be Divine, and Infinite will be found traced in living characters on all its faculties.

We shall not treat one another then as we do now. Man will be sacred in the eyes of man. To wrong him will be more than crime, it will be sin. To labor to degrade him will seem like laboring to degrade the Divinity. Man will reverence man.

Slavery will cease. Man will shudder at the bare idea of enslaving so noble a being as man. It will seem to him hardly less daring than to presume to task the motions of the Deity and to compel him to come and go at our bidding. When man learns the true value of man, the chains of the captive must be unloosed and the fetters of the slave fall off.

Wars will fail. The sword will be beaten into the ploughshare and the spear into the pruning hook. Man will not dare to mar and mangle the shrine of the Divinity. The God looking out from human eyes will disarm the soldier and make him kneel to him he had risen up to slay. The warhorse will cease to bathe his fetlocks in human gore. He will snuff the breeze in the wild freedom of his native plains, or quietly submit to be harnessed to the plough. The hero's occupation will be gone, and heroism will be found only in saving and blessing human life.

Education will destroy the empire of ignorance. The human mind, allied as it is to the Divine, is too valuable to lie waste or to be left to breed only briars and thorns. Those children, ragged and incrusted with filth, which throng our streets, and for whom we must one day build prisons, forge bolts and bars, or erect gibbets, are not only oar children, our brother's children, but they are children of God, they have in themselves the elements of the Divinity and powers which when put forth will raise them above what the tallest archangel now is. And when this is seen and felt, will those children be left to fester in ignorance or to grow up in vice and crime? The whole energy of man's being cries out against such folly, such gross injustice.

Civil freedom will become universal. It will be everywhere felt that one man has no right over another which that other has not over him. All will be seen to be brothers and equals in the sight of their common Father. All will love one another too much to desire to play the tyrant. Human nature will be reverenced too much not to be allowed to have free scope for the full and harmonious development of all its faculties. Governments will become sacred; and while on the one hand they are respected and obeyed, on the other it will be felt to be a religious right and a religious duty, to labor to make them as perfect as they can be.

Religion will not stop with the command to obey the laws, but it will bid us make just laws, such laws as befit a being divinely endowed like man. The Church will be on the side of progress, and Spiritualism and Materialism will combine to make man's earthly condition as near like the lost Eden of the Eastern poets, as is compatible with the growth and perfection of his nature.

Industry will be holy. The cultivation of the earth will be the worship of God. Working- men will be priests, and as priests they will be reverenced, and as priests they will reverence themselves and feel that they must maintain themselves undefiled. He that ministers at the altar must be pure, will be said of the mechanic, the agriculturist, the common laborer, as well as of him who is technically called a priest.

The earth itself and the animals which inhabit it will be counted sacred. We shall study in them the manifestation of God's goodness, wisdom, and power, and be careful that we make of them none but a holy use.

Man's body will be deemed holy. It will be called the temple of the Living God. As a temple it must not be desecrated. Men will beware of defiling it by sin, by any excessive or improper indulgence, as they would of defiling the temple or the altar consecrated to the service of God. Man will reverence himself too much, he will see too much of the Holy in his nature ever to pervert it from the right line of Truth and Duty.

"In that day shall there be on the bells of the horses, HOLINESS UNTO THE LORD; and the pots in the Lord's house shall be as the bowls before the altar. Yea, every pot in Jerusalem and in Judah shall be Holiness unto the Lord of hosts." The words of the prophet will be fulfilled. All things proceed from God and are therefore holy. Every duty, every act necessary to be done, every implement of industry, or thing contributing to human use or convenience, will be treated as holy. We shall recall even the reverence of the Indian for his bow and arrow, and by enlightening it with a Divine philosophy preserve it.

"Pure religion, and undefiled before God and the Father is this, to visit the fatherless and the widows in their affliction, and to keep oneself unspotted from the world." Religious worship will not be the mere service of the sanctuary. The universe will be God's temple, and its service will be the doing of good to mankind, relieving suffering and promoting joy, virtue and well-being. By this, religion and morality will be united, and the service of God and the service of man become the same. Our faith in God will show itself by our good works to man. Our love to the Father, whom we have not seen, will be evinced by our love for our brother whom we have seen.

Church and State will become one. The State will be holy, and the Church will be holy. Both will aim at the same thing, and the existence of one as separate from the other will not be needed. The Church will not be then an outward visible power, coexisting with the State, sometimes controlling it and at other times controlled by it; but it will be within, a true spiritual—not spiritualistic—Church, regulating the heart, the conscience and the life.

And when this all takes place the glory of the Lord will be manifested unto the ends of the earth, and all flesh will see it and rejoice together. The time is yet distant before this will be fully realized. We are now realizing it in our theory. We assert the holiness of all things. This assertion becomes an idea, and ideas, if they are true, are omnipotent. As soon as Humanity fully possesses this idea, it will lose no time in reducing it to practice. Men will conform their practice to it. They will become personally holy. Holiness will be written on all their thoughts, emotions and actions on their whole lives. And then will Christ really be formed within, the hope of glory. He will be truly incarnated in universal Humanity, and God and man will be one.

Chapter X: Progress

The actual existence of evil, the effects of which are everywhere so visible, and apparently so deplorable, may seem to be a serious objection to the great doctrine of the Atonement, that all things are essentially good and holy; but it will present little difficulty, if we consider that God designed us to be progressive beings, and that we can be progressive beings only on the condition that we be made less perfect than we may become, that we have our point of departure at a distance from our point of destination. We must begin in weakness and ignorance; and if we begin in weakness and ignorance we cannot fail to miss our way, or frequently to want strength to pursue it. To err in judgment or to come short in action will be our unavoidable lot, until we are instructed by experience and strengthened by exertion.

But this is no ground of complaint. We gain more than we lose by it. Had we without any agency of our own been made all that by a proper cultivation of our faculties we may become, we should have been much inferior to what we now are. We could have had no want, no desire, no good to seek, no end to gain, no destiny to achieve—no employment, and no motive to action. Our existence would have been aimless, silent and unvaried, given apparently for no purpose but to be dreamed away in an eternal and unbroken repose. Who could desire such an existence? Who would prefer it to the existence we now have, liable to error, sin and misery as it may be?

Constituted as we are, the way is more than the end, the acquisition more than the possession; but had we been made at once all that is promised us by our nature, these would have been nothing; we should indeed have had the end, the possession, but that would have been all. We should have been men without having first been children. Our earlier life, its trials and temptations, its failures and its successes, would never have existed. Would we willingly forego that earlier life? Dear to all men is the memory of childhood and youth; dear too is the recollection of their difficulties and dangers, their struggles with the world or with our own passions. We may regret, do regret, suffer remorse, that we did not put ourselves forth with more energy, that the enemy with which we had to contend was not more manfully met; but who of us is the craven to wish those difficulties and dangers had been less, or that the enemy's forces had been fewer and weaker?

God gave his richest gift when he gave the capacity for progress. This capacity is the chief glory of our nature, the brightest signature of its Divine origin and the pledge of its immortality. The being which can make no farther progress, which has finished its work, achieved its destiny, attained its end, must die. Why should it live? How could it live? What would be its life? But man never attains his end; he never achieves his destiny; he never finishes his work; he has always something to do, some new acquisition to make, some new height of excellence to ascend, and therefore is he immortal. He cannot die, for his hour never comes. He is never ready. Who would then be deprived of his capacity for progress?

This capacity, though it be the occasion of error and sin, is that which makes us moral beings. Without it we could not be virtuous. A being that does not make himself, his own character, but is made, and made all he is or can be, has no free will, no liberty. He is a thing, not a person, and as incapable of merit or demerit as the sun or moon, earthquakes or volcanoes. As much superior as is a moral to a fatal action, a perfection wrought out in and by oneself to a perfection merely received, as much superior as is a person to a thing, albeit a glorious thing, so much do we gain by being made for progress, by having a capacity for virtue, notwithstanding it be also a capacity for sin, so much superior are we to what we should have been, had we been created full grown men, with all our faculties perfected.

But moral evil, by the superintending care of Providence and the free will of man, is often if not always a means of aiding progress itself. The sinner is not so far from God as the merely innocent. He who has failed is farther onward than he who has not been tried. The consequences of error open our eyes to the truth; the consequences of transgression make us regret our departure from duty and try to return; the effort to return gives us the power to return. Thus does moral evil ever work its own destruction. Rightly viewed, it were seen to be no entity, no positive existence, but merely the absence of good, the void around and within us, and which by the enlargement of our being, we are continually filling up. It is not then a person, a thing, a being, and consequently can make nothing against the doctrine, which asserts the essential holiness of all things.

But men formerly supposed evil to be a substantial existence, as much of an entity as goodness. But then came the difficulty, whence could evil originate? It could not come from a good source, for good will not and cannot produce evil. But evil exists. Then all things do not come from the same source. One good and holy God has not made whatever is. There must be more Gods than one. There must be an evil God to create evil, as well as a good God to create good. Hence the notion of two Gods, or two classes of Gods, one good and the other bad, which runs through all antiquity, and under the terms God and the Devil, is reproduced even in the Christian church.

But this notion is easily shown to be unfounded. If one of the two Gods depend on the other, then the other must be its cause, its creator. In this case, nothing would be gained. How could a good God create a bad one, or a bad God create a good one? If one does not depend on the other, then both are independent, each is sufficient for itself. A being that is sufficient for itself, that has the grounds of its existence within itself must be absolute, almighty. There are then two absolutes, two almighties; but this is an absurdity, a contradiction in terms. This notion then must be abandoned. It was abandoned, and the evil was transferred to Matter. But Matter is either created or it is not. If it be created, then it is dependent, and that on which it is dependent is answerable for its properties. How could a good God have given it evil properties? If it be not created, then it is sufficient for itself; it has the grounds of its own existence within itself; it is then absolute, almighty, and the absurdity of two absolutes, of two almighties, is reproduced.

Still we need not wonder that men, who saw good and evil thickly thrown together up and down the earth, the tares everywhere choking the wheat, should have inferred the existence of two opposite and antagonist principles, as the cause of what they saw. Nor is it at all strange that men, who felt themselves restrained, hemmed in, by the material world, who carried about with them a material body for ever importuning them with its wants and subjecting them to a thousand ills, should have looked upon Matter as the cause of all the evil they saw, felt and endured. As things presented themselves to their observation they judged rightly. We may, by the aid of a revelation, which shines farther into the darkness and spreads a clearer light around us and over the Universe than any they had received, be able to correct their errors, and to perceive that the antagonism, in which they believed, has no existence in the world of reality; but we must beware how we censure them for the views they took. They saw what they could see with their light and from their position, and we can do no more. Future generations will have more favorable positions and a stronger and clearer light than we have, and they will be to us what we are to the generations which went before us. As we would escape the condemnation of our children, so should we refrain from condemning our fathers. They did their duty, let us do ours,—serve our own generation without defaming that to which we owe our existence and all that we are. All things are holy, and all doctrines are sacred. All the productions of the ever-teeming brain of man, however fantastic or unsubstantial their forms, are but so many manifestations of Humanity, and Humanity is a manifestation of the Divinity. The Son of Man is the Incarnate God. He who blasphemes the spirit with which he works and fulfils his mission in the flesh, blasphemes the Holy Ghost. Silent then be the tongue that would lisp, palsied the hand that would write the smallest censure upon Humanity for any of the opinions it has expressed, however defective, however far from embracing the whole truth, future or more favored inquirers may And them. Humanity is holy, let the proudest kneel in reverence.

This doctrine of progress, not only accounts for the origin of evil and explains its difficulties, but it points out to us our duty. The duty of every being is to follow its destiny, to seek its end. Man's destiny is illimitable progress; his end is everlasting growth, enlargement of his being. Progress is the end for which he was made. To this end, then, it is his duty to direct all his inquiries, all his systems of religion and philosophy, all his institutions of politics and society, all the productions of genius and taste, in one word all the modes of his activity.

This is his duty. Hitherto he has performed it, but blindly, without knowing and without admitting it. Humanity has but today, as it were, risen to self-consciousness, to a perception of its own capacity, to a glimpse of its inconceivably grand and holy destiny. Heretofore it has failed to recognize dearly its duty. It has advanced, but not designedly, not with foresight; it has done it instinctively, by the aid of the invisible but safe-guiding hand of its Father. Without knowing what it did, it has condemned progress, while it was progressing. It has stoned the prophets and reformers, even while it was itself reforming and uttering glorious prophecies of its future condition. But the time has now come for Humanity to understand itself, to accept the law imposed upon it for its own good, to foresee its end and march with intention steadily towards it. Its future religion is the religion of progress. The true priests are those who can quicken in mankind a desire for progress, and urge them forward in the direction of the True, the Good, the Perfect.

Here I must close. I have uttered the words UNION and PROGRESS as the authentic creed of the New Church, as designating the whole duty of man. Would they had been spoken in a clearer, a louder and a sweeter voice, that a response might be heard from the universal heart of Humanity. But I have spoken as I could, and from a motive which I shall not blush to own either to myself or to Him to whom all must render an account of all their thoughts, words and deeds. I once had no faith in Him, and I was to myself "a child without a sire." I was alone in the world, my heart found no companionship, and my affections withered and died. But I have found Him, and he is my Father, and mankind are my brothers, and I can love and reverence.

Mankind are my brothers,—they are brothers to one another. I would see them no longer mutually estranged. I labor to bring them together, and to make them feel and own that they are all made of one blood. Let them feel and own this, and they will love one another; they will be kindly affectioned one to another, and "the groans of this nether world will cease;" the spectacle of wrongs and outrages oppress our sight no more; tears be wiped from all eyes, and Humanity pass from death to life, to life immortal, to the life of God, for God is love.

And this result, for which the wise and the good everywhere yearn and labor, will be obtained. I do not misread the age. I have not looked upon the world only out from the window of my closet; I have mingled in its busy scenes; I have rejoiced and wept with it; I have hoped and feared, and believed and doubted with it, and I am but what it has made me. I cannot misread it. It craves union. The heart of man is crying out for the heart of man. One and the same spirit is abroad, uttering the same voice in all languages. From all parts of the world voice answers to voice, and man responds to man. There is a universal language already in use. Men are beginning to understand one another, and their mutual understanding will beget mutual sympathy, and mutual sympathy will bind them together and to God.

And for progress too the whole world is struggling. Old institutions are examined, old opinions criticized, "even the old Church is laid bare to its very foundations, and its holy vestments and sacred symbols are exposed to the gaze of the multitude; new systems are proclaimed, new institutions elaborated, new ideas are sent abroad, new experiments are made, and the whole world seems intent on the means by which it may accomplish its destiny. The individual is struggling to become a greater and a better being. Everywhere there are men laboring to perfect governments and laws. The poor man is admitted to be human, and millions of voices are demanding that he be treated as a brother. All eyes and hearts are turned to education. The cultivation of the child's moral and spiritual nature becomes the worship of God. The priest rises to the educator, and the schoolroom is the temple in which he is to minister. There is progress; there will be progress. Humanity must go forward. Encouraging is the future. He, who takes his position on the "high table land" of Humanity, and beholds with a prophet's gaze his brothers, so long separated, coming together, and arm in arm marching onward and upward towards the Perfect, towards God, may hear celestial voices chanting a sweeter strain than that which announced to Judea's shepherds the birth of the Redeemer, and his heart full and overflowing, he may exclaim with old Simeon, "Lord, now lettest thou thy servant depart in peace, for mine eyes have seen thy salvation."

SIX

Emerson's Divinity School Address

Mr. Emerson's Address

This is in some respects a remarkable address,—remarkable for its own character and for the place where and the occasion on which it was delivered. It is not often, we fancy, that such an address is delivered by a clergyman in a Divinity College to a class of young men just ready to go forth into the churches as preachers of the Gospel of Jesus Christ. Indeed it is not often that a discourse teaching doctrines like the leading doctrines of this, is delivered by a professedly religious man, anywhere or on any occasion.

We are not surprised that this address should have produced some excitement and called forth some severe censures upon its author; for we have long known that there are comparatively few who can hear with calmness the utterance of opinions to which they do not subscribe. Yet we regret to see the abuse which has been heaped upon Mr. Emerson. We ought to learn to tolerate all opinions, to respect every man's right to form and to utter his own opinions whatever they may be. If we regard the opinions as unsound, false, or dangerous, we should meet them calmly, refute them if we can; but be careful to respect, and to treat with all Christian meekness and love, him who entertains them.

"*An Address Delivered before the Senior Class in Divinity College, Cambridge, Sunday Evening, 15 July, 1838.* By Ralph Waldo Emerson. Boston: James Munroe and Co., 1838. 8vo. pp. 32." From *Boston Quarterly Review* 1 (October 1838): 500–514.

There are many things in this address we heartily approve; there is much that we admire and thank the author for having uttered. We like its life and freshness, its freedom and independence, its richness and beauty. But we cannot help regarding its tone as somewhat arrogant, its spirit is quite too censorious and desponding, its philosophy as indigested, and its reasoning as inconclusive. We do not like its mistiness, its vagueness, and its perpetual use of old words in new senses. Its meaning too often escapes us; and we find it next to impossible to seize its dominant doctrine and determine what it is or what it is not. Moreover, it does not appear to us to be all of the same piece. It is made up of parts borrowed from different and hostile systems, which "baulk and baffle" the author's power to form into a consistent and harmonious whole.

In a moral point of view the leading doctrine of this address, if we have seized it, is not a little objectionable. It is not easy to say what that moral doctrine is; but so far as we can collect it, it is, that the soul possesses certain laws or instincts, obedience to which constitutes its perfection. "The sentiment of virtue is a reverence and delight in the presence of certain divine laws." "The intuition of the moral sentiment is an insight of the perfection of the laws of the soul." The moral sentiment results from the perception of these laws, and moral character results from conformity to them. Now this is not, we apprehend, psychologically true. If any man will analyze the moral sentiment as a fact of consciousness, he will find it something more than "an insight of the perfection of the laws of the soul." He will find that it is a sense of obligation. Man feels himself under obligation to obey a law; not the law of his own soul, a law emanating from his soul as a lawgiver; but a law above his soul, imposed upon him by a supreme lawgiver, who has a right to command his obedience. He does never feel that he is moral in obeying merely the laws of his own nature, but in obeying the command of a power out of him, above him, and independent of him.

By the laws of the soul, we presume, Mr. Emerson means our instincts. In his Phi Beta Kappa Address, reviewed in this journal for January, he speaks much of the instincts, and bids us "plant ourselves on our instincts, and the huge world will come round to us." The ethical rule he lays down is then, "follow thy instincts," or as he expresses it in the address before us, "obey thyself." Now if we render this rule into the language it will assume in practice, we must say, obey thyself,—follow thy instincts,—follow thy inclinations,—live as thou listest. Strike out the idea of something above man to which he is accountable, make him accountable only to himself, and why shall he not live as he listeth? We see not what restraint can legitimately be imposed upon any of his instincts or propensities. There may then be some doubts whether the command, "obey thyself," be an improvement on the Christian command, "deny thyself."

We presume that when Mr. Emerson tells us to obey ourselves, to obey the laws of our soul, to follow our instincts, he means that we shall be true to our higher nature, that we are to obey our higher instincts, and not our baser propensities. He is himself a pure minded man, and would by no means encourage sensuality. But how shall we determine which are our higher instincts and which are our lower instincts? We do not perceive that he gives us any instructions on this point. Men like him may take the higher instincts to be those which lead us to seek truth and beauty; but men in whom the sensual nature overlays the spiritual, may think differently; and what rule has he for determining which is in the right? He commands us to be ourselves, and sneers at the idea of having "models." We must take none of the wise or good, not even Jesus Christ as a model of what we should be. We are to act out ourselves. Now why is not the sensualist as moral as the spiritualist, providing he acts out himself? Mr. Emerson is a great admirer of Carlyle; and according to Carlyle, the moral man, the true man, is he who acts out himself. A Mirabeau, or a Danton is, under a moral point of view, the equal of a Howard or a Washington, because equally true to himself. Does not this rule confound all moral distinctions, and render moral judgments a "formula," all wise men must "swallow and make away with"?

But suppose we get over this difficulty and determine which are the higher instincts of our nature, those which we must follow in order to perfect our souls, and become,—as Mr. Emerson has it,—God; still we ask, why are we under obligation to obey these instincts? Because obedience to them will perfect our souls? But why are we bound to perfect our souls? Where there is no sense of obligation, there is no moral sense. We are moral only on the condition that we feel there is something which we *ought* to do. Why ought we to labor for our own perfection? Because it will promote our happiness? But why are we morally bound to seek our own happiness? It may be very desirable to promote our happiness, but it does not follow from that we are morally bound to do it, and we know there are occasions when we should not do it.

Put the rule, Mr. Emerson lays down, in the best light possible, it proposes nothing higher than our own individual good as the end to be sought. He would tell us to reduce all the jarring elements of our nature to harmony, and produce and maintain perfect order in the soul. Now is this the highest good the reason can conceive? Are all things in the universe to be held subordinate to the individual soul? Shall a man take himself as the center of the universe, and say all things are for his use, and count them of value only as they contribute something to his growth or well-being? This were a deification of the soul with a vengeance. It were nothing but a system of transcendental selfishness. It were pure egotism. According to this, I am everything; all else is nothing, at least nothing except what it derives from the fact that it is something to me.

Now this system of pure egotism, seems to us to run through all Mr. Emerson's writings. We meet it everywhere in his masters, Carlyle and Goethe. He and they may not be quite so grossly selfish as were some of the old sensualist philosophers; they may admit a higher good than the mere gratification of the senses, than mere wealth or fame; but the highest good they recognize is an individual good, the realization of order in their own individual souls. Everything by them is estimated according to its power to contribute to this end. If they mingle with men it is to use them; if they are generous and humane, if they labor to do good to others, it is always as a means, never as an end. Always is the *doing*, whatever it be, to terminate in self. Self, the higher self, it is true, is always the center of gravitation. Now is the man who adopts this moral rule, really a moral man? Does not morality always propose to us an end separate from our own, above our own, and to which our own good is subordinate?

No doubt it is desirable to perfect the individual soul, to realize order in the individual; but the reason, the moment it is developed, discloses a good altogether superior to this. Above the good of the individual, and paramount to it, is the good of the universe, the realization of the good of creation, absolute good. No man can deny that the realization of the good of all beings is something superior to the realization of the good of the individual. Morality always requires us to labor for the highest good we can conceive. The moral law then requires us to seek another good than that of our own souls. The individual lives not for himself alone. His good is but an element, a fragment of the universal good, and is to be sought never as an end, but always as a means of realizing absolute good, or universal order. This rule requires the man to forget himself, to go out of himself, and under certain circumstances to deny himself, to sacrifice himself, for a good which does not center in himself. He who forgets himself, who is disinterested and heroic, who sacrifices himself for others, is in the eyes of reason, infinitely superior to the man who merely uses others as the means of promoting his own intellectual and spiritual growth. Mr. Emerson's rule then is defective, inasmuch as it proposes the subordinate as the paramount, and places obligation where we feel it is not. For the present, then, instead of adopting his formula, "obey thyself," or Carlyle's formula, "act out thyself," we must continue to approve the Christian formula, "deny thyself, and love thy neighbor as thyself."

But passing over this, we cannot understand how it is possible for a man to become virtuous by yielding to his instincts. Virtue is voluntary obedience to a moral law, felt to be obligatory. We are aware of the existence of the law, and we act in reference to it, and intend to obey it. We of course are not passive but active in the case of virtue. Virtue is always personal. It is our own act. We are in the strictest sense of the word the cause or creator of it. Therefore it is, we judge ourselves worthy of praise when we are not virtuous. But in following instinct, we are not active but passive. The causative force at work in our instincts, is not our personality, our wills, but an impersonal force, a force *we* are not. Now in yielding to our instincts, as Mr. Emerson advises us, we abdicate our own personality, and from persons become things, as incapable of virtue as the trees of the forest or the stones of the field.

Mr. Emerson, moreover, seems to us to mutilate man, and in his zeal for the instincts to entirely overlook reflection. The instincts are all very well. They give us the force of character we need, but they do not make up the whole man. We have understanding as well as instinct, reflection as well as spontaneity. Now to be true to our nature, to the whole man, the understanding should have its appropriate exercise. Does Mr. Emerson give it this exercise? Does he not rather hold the understanding in light esteem, and labor almost entirely to fix our minds on the fact of the primitive intuition as all-sufficient of itself. We do not ask him to reject the instincts, but we ask him to compel them to give account of themselves. We are willing to follow them; but we must do it designedly, intentionally, after we have proved our moral right to do it, not before. Here is an error in Mr. Emerson's system of no small magnitude. He does not account for the instincts nor legitimate them. He does not prove them to be divine forces or safe guides. In practice, therefore, he is merely reviving the old sentimental systems of morality, systems which may do for the young, the dreamy, or the passionate, but never for a sturdy race of men and women who demand a reason for all they do, for what they approve or disapprove.

Nor are we better satisfied with the theology of this discourse. We cannot agree with Mr. Emerson in his account of the religious sentiment. He confounds the religious sentiment with the moral; but the two sentiments are psychologically distinct. The religious sentiment is a craving to adore, resulting from the soul's intuition of the Holy; the moral sense is a sense of obligation resulting from the soul's intuition of a moral law. The moral sentiment leads us up merely to universal order; the religious sentiment leads us up to God, the Father of universal order. Religious ideas always carry us into a region far above that of moral ideas. Religion gives the law to ethics, not ethics to religion. Religion is the communion of the soul with God, morality is merely the *cultus exterior*, the outward worship of God, the expression of the life of God in the soul: as James has it, "pure religion,—external worship, for so should we understand the original,—and undefiled before God and the Father is this, To visit the fatherless and widows in their affliction, and to keep himself unspotted from the world."

But even admitting the two sentiments are not two but one, identical, we are still dissatisfied with Mr. Emerson's account of the matter. The religious sentiment, according to him, grows out of the soul's insight of the perfection of its own laws. These laws are in fact the soul itself. They are not something distinct from the soul, but its essence. In neglecting them the soul is not itself, in finding them it finds itself, and in living them it is God. This is his doctrine. The soul then in case of the religious sentiment has merely an intuition of itself. Its craving to adore is not a craving to adore something superior to itself. In worshipping then, the soul does not worship God, a being above man and independent on him, but it worships itself. We must not then speak of worshipping God, but merely of worshipping the soul. Now is this a correct account of the religious sentiment? The religious sentiment is in the bottom of the soul, and it is always a craving of the soul to go out of itself, and fasten itself on an object above itself, free from its own weakness, mutability, and impurity, on a being all-sufficient, all-sufficing, omnipotent, immutable, and all-holy. It results from the fact that we are conscious of not being sufficient for ourselves, that the ground of our being is not in ourselves, and from the need we feel of an Almighty arm on which to lean, a strength foreign to our own, from which we may derive support. Let us be God, let us feel that we need go out of ourselves for nothing, and we are no longer in the condition to be religious; the religious sentiment can no longer find a place in our souls, and we can no more feel a craving to adore than God himself. Nothing is more evident to us, than that the religious sentiment springs, on the one hand, solely from a sense of dependence, and on the other hand, from an intuition of an invisible Power, Father, God, on whom we may depend, to whom we may appeal when oppressed, and who is able and willing to succor us. Take away the idea of such a God, declare the soul sufficient for itself, forbid it ever to go out of itself, to look up to a power above it, and religion is out of the question.

If we rightly comprehend Mr. Emerson's views of God, he admits no God but the laws of the soul's perfection. God is in man, not out of him. He is in the soul as the oak is in the acorn. When man fully develops the laws of his nature, realizes the ideal of his nature, he is not, as the Christians would say, god-like, but he is God. The ideal of man's nature is not merely similar in all men, but identical. When all men realize the ideal of their nature, that is, attain to the highest perfection admitted by the laws of their being, then do they all become swallowed up in the One Man. There will then no longer be men; all diversity will be lost in unity, and there will be only One Man, and that one man will be God. But what and where is God now? Before all men have realized the ideal of their nature, and become swallowed up in the One Man, is there really and actually a God? Is there any God but the God Osiris, torn into pieces and scattered up and down through all the earth, which pieces, scattered parts, the weeping Isis must go forth seeking everywhere, and find not without labor and difficulty? Can we be said to have at present anything more than the disjected members of a God, the mere embryo fragments of a God, one day to come forth into the light, to be gathered up that nothing be lost, and finally moulded into one complete and rounded God? So it seems to us, and we confess, therefore, that we can affix no definite meaning to the religious language which Mr. Emerson uses so freely.

Furthermore, we cannot join Mr. Emerson in his worship to the soul. We are disposed to go far in our estimate of the soul's divine capacities; we believe it was created in the image of God, and may bear his moral likeness; but we cannot so exalt it as to call it God. Nor can we take its ideal of its own perfection as God. The soul's conception of God is not God, and if there be no God out of the soul, out of the *me*, to answer the soul's conception, then is there no God. God as we conceive him is independent on us, and is in no sense affected by our conceptions of him. He is in us, but not us. He dwells in the hearts of the humble and contrite ones, and yet the heaven of heavens cannot contain him. He is the same yesterday, today, and forever. He is above all, the cause and sustainer of all that is, in whom we live and move and have our being. Him we worship, and only him. We dare not worship merely our own soul. Alas, we know our weakness; we feel our sinfulness; we are oppressed with a sense of our unworthiness, and we cannot so sport with the solemnities of religious worship, as to direct them to ourselves, or to anything which does not transcend our own being.

Yet this worship of the soul is part and parcel of the transcendental egotism of which we spoke in commenting on Mr. Emerson's moral doctrines. He and his masters, Carlyle and Goethe, make the individual soul everything, the center of the universe, for whom all exists that does exist; and why then should it not be the supreme object of their affections? Soul-worship, which is only another name for self-worship, or the worship of self, is the necessary consequence of their system, a system well described by Pope in his Essay on Man:

> Ask for what end the heavenly bodies shine,
> Earth for whose use? Pride answers, "'T is for mine:
> For me, kind nature wakes her genial power,
> Suckles each herb, and spreads out every flower;
> Annual for me, the grape, the rose, renew
> The juice nectareous, and the balmy dew;
> For me, the mine a thousand treasures brings;
> For me, health gushes from a thousand springs:
> Seas roll to waft me, suns to light me rise;
> My footstool earth, my canopy the skies."

To which we may add,

> While man exclaims, "See all things for my use!"
> "See man for mine!" replies a pampered goose:
> And just as short of reason he must fall
> Who thinks all made for one, not one for all.

Mr. Emerson has much to say against preaching a traditional Christ, against preaching what he calls historical Christianity. So far as his object in this is to draw men's minds off from an exclusive attention to the "letter," and to fix them on "the spirit," to prevent them from relying for the matter and evidence of their faith on merely historical documents, and to induce them to reproduce the gospel histories in their own souls, he is not only not censurable but praiseworthy. He is doing a service to the Christian cause. Christianity may be found in the human soul, and reproduced in human experience now, as well as in the days of Jesus. It is in the soul too that we must find the key to the meaning of the Gospels, and in the soul's experience that we must seek the principal evidences of their truth.

But if Mr. Emerson means to sever us from the past, and to intimate that the Christianity of the past has ceased to have any interest for the present generation, and that the knowledge and belief of it are no longer needed for the soul's growth, for its redemption and union with God, we must own we cannot go with him. Christianity results from the development of the laws of the human soul, but from a supernatural, not a natural, development; that is, by the aid of a power above the soul. God has been to the human race both a father and an educator. By a supernatural,—not an *unnatural*—influence, he has, as it has seemed proper to him, called forth our powers, and enabled us to see and comprehend the truths essential to our moral progress. The records of the aid he has at different ages furnished us, and of the truths seen and comprehended at the period when the faculties of the soul were supernaturally exalted, cannot in our judgment be unessential, far less improper, to be dwelt upon by the Christian preacher.

Then again, we cannot dispense with Jesus Christ. As much as some may wish to get rid of him, or to change or improve his character, the world needs him, and needs him in precisely the character in which the Gospels present him. His is the only name whereby men can be saved. He is the father of the modern world, and his is the life we now live, so far as we live any life at all. Shall we then crowd him away with the old bards and seers, and regard him and them merely as we do the authors of some old ballads which charmed our forefathers, but which may not be sung in a modern drawing-room? Has his example lost its power, his life its quickening influence, his doctrine its truth? Have we outgrown him as a teacher?

In the Gospels, we find the solution of the great problem of man's destiny; and, what is more to our purpose, we find there the middle term by which the creature is connected with the Creator. Man is at an infinite distance from God; and he cannot by his own strength approach God, and become one with him. We cannot see God; we cannot know him; no man hath seen the Father at any time, and no man knoweth the Father, save the Son, and he to whom the Son reveals him. We approach God only through a mediator; we see and know only the Word, which is the mediator between God and men. Does Mr. Emerson mean that the record we have of this Word in the Bible, of this Word, which was made flesh, incarnated in the man Jesus, and dwelt among men and disclosed the grace and truth with which it overflowed, is of no use now in the church, nay, that it is a let and a hindrance? We want that record, which is to us as the testimony of the race, to corroborate the witness within us. One witness is not enough. We have one witness within us, an important witness, too seldom examined; but as important as he is, he is not alone sufficient. We must back up his individual testimony with that of the race. In the Gospel records we have the testimony borne by the race to the great truths it most concerns us to know. That testimony, the testimony of history, in conjunction with our own individual experience, gives us all the certainty we ask, and furnishes us a solid ground for an unwavering and active faith. As in philosophy, we demand history as well as psychology, so in theology we ask the historical Christ as well as the psychological Christ. The church in general has erred by giving us only the historical Christ; but let us not now err, by preaching only a psychological Christ.

In dismissing this address, we can only say that we have spoken of it freely, but with no improper feeling to its author. We love bold speculation; we are pleased to find a man who dares tell us what and precisely what he thinks, however unpopular his views may be. We have no disposition to check his utterance, by giving his views a bad name, although we deem them unsound. We love progress, and progress cannot be effected without freedom. Still we wish to see certain sobriety, a certain reserve in all speculations, something like timidity about rushing off into an unknown universe, and some little regret in departing from the faith of our fathers.

Nevertheless, let not the tenor of our remarks be mistaken. Mr. Emerson is the last man in the world we should suspect of conscious hostility to religion and morality. No one can know him or read his productions without feeling a profound respect for the singular purity and uprightness of his character and motives. The great object he is laboring to accomplish is one in which he should receive the hearty cooperation of every American scholar, of every friend of truth, freedom, piety, and virtue. Whatever may be the character of his speculations, whatever may be the moral, philosophical, or theological system which forms the basis of his speculations, his real object is not the inculcation of any new theory on man, nature, or God; but to induce men to think for themselves on all subjects, and to speak from their own full hearts and earnest convictions. His object is to make men scorn to be slaves to routine, to custom, to established creeds, to public opinion, to the great names of this age, of this country, or of any other. He cannot bear the idea that a man comes into the world today with the field of truth monopolized and foreclosed. To every man lies open the whole field of truth, in morals, in politics, in science, in theology, in philosophy. The labors of past ages, the revelations of prophets and bards, the discoveries of the scientific and the philosophic, are not to be regarded as superseding our own exertions and inquiries, as impediments to the free action of our own minds, but merely as helps, as provocations to the freest and fullest spiritual action of which God has made us capable.

This is the real end he has in view, and it is a good end. To call forth the free spirit, to produce the conviction here implied, to provoke men to be men, self-moving, self-subsisting men, not mere puppets, moving but as moved by the reigning mode, the reigning dogma, the reigning school, is a grand and praiseworthy work, and we should reverence and aid, not abuse and hinder him who gives himself up soul and body to its accomplishment. So far as the author of the address before us is true to this object, earnest in executing this work, he has our hearty sympathy, and all the aid we, in our humble sphere, can give him. In laboring for this object, he proves himself worthy of his age and his country, true to religion and to morals. In calling, as he does, upon the literary men of our community, in the silver tones of his rich and eloquent voice, and above all by the quickening influence of his example, to assert and maintain their independence throughout the whole domain of thought, against every species of tyranny that would encroach upon it, he is doing his duty; he is doing a work the effects of which will be felt for good far and wide, long after men shall have forgotten the puerility of his conceits, the affectations of his style, and the unphilosophical character of his speculations. The doctrines he puts forth, the positive instructions, for which he is now censured, will soon be classed where they belong: but the influence of his free spirit, and free utterance, the literature of this country will long feel and hold in grateful remembrance.

SEVEN

The Laboring Classes

Thomas Carlyle unquestionably ranks among the ablest writers of the day. His acquaintance with literature seems to be almost universal, and there is apparently no art or science with which he is not familiar. He possesses an unrivalled mastery over the resources of the English tongue, a remarkably keen insight into the mysteries of human nature, and a large share of genuine poetic feeling. His works are characterized by freshness and power, as well as by strangeness and singularity, and must be read with interest, even when they cannot be with approbation.

The little work, named at the head of this article, is a fair sample of his peculiar excellencies, and also of his peculiar defects. As a work intended to excite attention and lead the mind to an investigation of a great subject, it possesses no ordinary value; but as a work intended to throw light on a difficult question, and to afford some positive directions to the statesman and the philanthropist, it is not worth much. Carlyle, like his imitators in this country, though he declaims against the destructives, possesses in no sense a constructive genius. He is good as a demolisher, but pitiable enough as a builder. No man sees more clearly that the present is defective and unworthy to be retained; he is a brave and successful warrior against it, whether reference be had to its literature, its politics, its philosophy, or its religion; but when the question comes up concerning what ought to be, what should

Boston Quarterly Review , volume 3, published by Benjamin H. Greene (Boston, 1840).

take the place of what is, we regret to say, he affords us no essential aid, scarcely a useful hint. He has fine spiritual instincts, has outgrown materialism, loathes skepticism, sees clearly the absolute necessity of faith in both God and man, and insists upon it with due sincerity and earnestness; but with feelings very nearly akin to despair. He does not appear to have found as yet a faith for himself, and his writings have almost invariably a skeptical tendency. He has doubtless a sort of faith in God, or an overwhelming Necessity, but we cannot perceive that he has any faith in man or in man's efforts. Society is wrong, but he mocks at our sincerest and best directed efforts to right it. It cannot subsist as it is; that is clear: but what shall be done to make it what it ought to be, that he saith not. Of all writers we are acquainted with, he is the least satisfactory. He is dissatisfied with everything himself, and he leaves his readers dissatisfied with everything. Hopeless himself, he makes them also hopeless, especially if they have strong social tendencies, and are hungering and thirsting to work out the regeneration of their race.

Mr. Carlyle's admirers, we presume, will demur to this criticism. We have heard some of them speak of him as a sort of soul-quickener, and profess to derive from his writings fresh life and courage. We know not how this may be. It may be that they derive advantage from him on the homeopathic principle, and that he cures their diseases by exaggerating them; but for ourselves we must say, that we have found him anything but a skillful physician. He disheartens and enfeebles us; and while he emancipates us from the errors of tradition, he leaves us without strength or courage to engage in the inquiry after truth. We rise from his writings with the weariness and exhaustion one does from the embraces of the Witch Mara. It is but slowly that our blood begins to circulate again, and it is long before we recover the use of our powers. Whether his writings produce this effect on others or not, we are unable to say; but this effect they do produce on us. We almost dread to encounter them.

Mr. Carlyle would seem to have great sympathy with man. He certainly is not wanting in the sentiment of Humanity; nor is he deceived by external position, or dazzled by factitious glare. He can see worth in the socially low as well as in the socially high; in the artisan as well as the noble. This is something, but no great merit in one who can read the New Testament. Still it is something, and we are glad to meet it. But after all, he has no true reverence for Humanity. He may offer incense to a Goethe, a Jean Paul, a Mirabeau, a Danton, a Napoleon, but he nevertheless looks down upon his fellows, and sneers at the mass. He looks down upon man as one of his admirers has said, "as if man were a mouse." But we do not wish to look upon man in that light. We would look upon him as a brother, an equal, entitled to our love and sympathy. We would feel ourselves neither above him nor below him, but standing up by his side, with our feet on the same level with his. We would also love and respect the common-place mass, not merely heroes and sages, prophets and priests.

We are moreover no warm admirers of Carlyle's style of writing. We acknowledge his command over the resources of our language, and we enjoy the freshness, and occasional strength, beauty, and felicity of his style and expression, but he does not satisfy us. He wants clearness and precision, and that too when writing on topics where clearness and precision are all but indispensable. We have no patience with his mistiness, vagueness, and singularity. If a man must needs write and publish his thoughts to the world, let him do it in as clear and as intelligible language as possible. We are not aware of any subject worth writing on at all, that is already so plain that it needs to be rendered obscure. Carlyle can write well if he chooses; no man better. He is not necessarily misty, vague, nor fantastic. The antic tricks he has been latterly playing do not spring from the constitution of his mind, and we must say do by no means become him. We are disposed ourselves to assume considerable latitude in both thought and expression; but we believe every scholar should aim to keep within the general current of his language. Every language receives certain laws from the genius of the people who use it, and it is no mark of wisdom to transgress them; nor is genuine literary excellence to be attained but by obeying them. An Englishman, if he would profit Englishmen, must write English, not French nor German. If he wishes his writings to become an integral part of the literature of his language, he must keep within the steady current of what has ever been regarded as classical English style, and deny himself the momentary éclat he might gain by affectation and singularity.

We can, however, pardon Carlyle altogether more easily than we can his American imitators. Notwithstanding his manner of writing, when continued for any considerable length, becomes monotonous and wearisome, as in his *History of the French Revolution*,—a work which, with all its brilliant wit, inimitable humor, deep pathos, and graphic skill, can scarcely be read without yawning,—yet in his case it is redeemed by rare beauties, and marks a mind of the highest order, and of vast attainments. But in the hands of his American imitators, it becomes puerile and disgusting; and what is worthy of note is, that it is adopted and most servilely followed by the men among us who are loudest in their boasts of originality, and the most intolerant to its absence. But enough of this. For our consolation, the race of imitators is feeble and short-lived.

The subject of the little work before us, is one of the weightiest which can engage the attention of the statesman or the philanthropist. It is indeed, here, discussed only in relation to the working classes of England, but it in reality involves the condition of the working classes throughout the world,—a great subject, and one never yet worthily treated. Chartism, properly speaking is no local or temporary phenomenon. Its germ may be found in every nation in Christendom; indeed wherever man has approximated a state of civilization, wherever there is inequality in social condition, and in the distribution of the products of industry. And where does not this inequality obtain? Where is the spot on earth, in which the actual producer of wealth is not one of the lower class, shutout from what are looked upon as the main advantages of the social state?

Mr. Carlyle, though he gives us few facts, yet shows us that the condition of the workingmen in England is deplorable, and every day growing worse. It has already become intolerable, and hence the outbreak of the Chartists. Chartism is the protest of the working classes against the injustice of the present social organization of the British community, and a loud demand for a new organization which shall respect the rights and well-being of the laborer.

The movements of the Chartists have excited considerable alarm in the higher classes of English society, and some hope in the friends of Humanity among ourselves. We do not feel competent to speak with any decision on the extent or importance of these movements. If our voice could reach the Chartists we would bid them be bold and determined; we would bid them persevere even unto death; for their cause is that of justice, and in fighting for it they will be fighting the battles of God and man. But we look for no important results from their movements. We have little faith in a John Bull mob. It will bluster, and swagger, and threaten much; but give it plenty of porter and roast-beef, and it will sink back to its kennel, as quiet and as harmless as a lamb. The lower classes in England have made many a move since the days of Wat Tyler for the betterment of their condition, but we cannot perceive that they have ever effected much. They are doubtless nearer the day of their emancipation, than they were, but their actual condition is scarcely superior to what it was in the days of Richard the Second.

There is no country in Europe, in which the condition of the laboring classes seems to us so hopeless as in that of England. This is not owing to the fact, that the aristocracy is less enlightened, more powerful, or more oppressive in England than elsewhere. The English laborer does not find his worst enemy in the nobility, but in the middling class. The middle class is much more numerous and powerful in England than in any other European country, and is of a higher character. It has always been powerful; for by means of the Norman Conquest it received large accessions from the old Saxon nobility. The Conquest established a new aristocracy, and degraded the old to the condition of Commoners. The superiority of the English Commons is, we suppose, chiefly owing to this fact.

The middle class is always a firm champion of equality, when it concerns humbling a class above it; but it is its inveterate foe, when it concerns elevating a class below it. Manfully have the British Commoners struggled against the old feudal aristocracy, and so successfully that they now constitute the dominant power in the state. To their struggles against the throne and the nobility is the English nation indebted for the liberty it so loudly boasts, and which, during the last half of the last century, so enraptured the friends of Humanity throughout Europe.

But this class has done nothing for the laboring population, the real *proletarii.* It has humbled the aristocracy; it has raised itself to dominion, and it is now conservative,—conservative in fact, whether it call itself Whig or Radical. From its near relation to the workingmen, its kindred pursuits with them, it is altogether more hostile to them than the nobility ever were or ever can be. This was seen in the conduct of England towards the French Revolution. So long as that Revolution was in the hands of the middle class, and threatened merely to humble monarchy and nobility, the English nation applauded it; but as soon as it descended to the mass of the people, and promised to elevate the laboring classes, so soon as the starving workman began to flatter himself, that there was to be a revolution for him too as well as for his employer, the English nation armed itself and poured out its blood and treasure to suppress it. Everybody knows that Great Britain, boasting of her freedom and of her love of freedom, was the life and soul of the opposition to the French Revolution; and on her head almost alone should fall the curses of Humanity for the sad failure of that glorious uprising of the people in behalf of their imprescriptible, and inalienable rights. Yet it was not the English monarchy, nor the English nobility, that was alone in fault. Monarchy and nobility would have been powerless, had they not had with them the great body of the English Commoners. England fought in the ranks, nay, at the head of the allies, not for monarchy, not for nobility, nor yet for religion; but for trade and manufactures, for her middle class against the rights and well-being of the workingman; and her strength and efficiency consisted in the strength and efficiency of this class. Now this middle class, which was strong enough to defeat nearly all the practical benefit of the French Revolution, is the natural enemy of the Chartists. It will unite with the monarchy and nobility against them; and spare neither blood nor treasure to defeat them. Our despair for the poor Chartists arises from the number and power of the middle class. We dread for them neither monarchy nor nobility. Nor should they. Their only real enemy is in the employer. In all countries is it the same. The only enemy of the laborer is your employer, whether appearing in the shape of the master mechanic, or in the owner of a factory. A Duke of Wellington is much more likely to vindicate the rights of labor than an Abbot Lawrence, although the latter may be a very kind-hearted man, and liberal citizen, as we always find Blackwood's Magazine more true to the interests of the poor, than we do the Edinburgh Review, or even the London and Westminster.

Mr. Carlyle, contrary to his wont, in the pamphlet we have named, commends two projects for the relief of the workingmen, which he finds others have suggested,—universal education, and general emigration. Universal education we shall not be thought likely to depreciate; but we confess that we are unable to see in it that sovereign remedy for the evils of the social state as it is, which some of our friends do, or say they do. We have little faith in the power of education to elevate a people compelled to labor from twelve to sixteen hours a day, and to experience for no mean portion of the time a paucity of even the necessaries of life, let alone its comforts. Give your starving boy a breakfast before you send him to school, and your tattered beggar a cloak before you attempt his moral and intellectual elevation. A swarm of naked and starving urchins crowded into a school-room will make little proficiency in the "Humanities." Indeed, it seems to us most bitter mockery for the well-dressed, and well-fed to send the schoolmaster and priest to the wretched hovels of squalid poverty,—a mockery at which devils may laugh, but over which angels must weep. Educate the working classes of England; and what then? Will they require less food and less clothing when educated than they do now? Will they be more contented or more happy in their condition? For God's sake beware how you kindle within them the intellectual spark, and make them aware that they too are men, with powers of thought and feeling which ally them by the bonds of brotherhood to their betters. If you will doom them to the external condition of brutes, do in common charity keep their minds and hearts brutish. Render them as insensible as possible, that they may feel the less acutely their degradation, and see the less clearly the monstrous injustice which is done them.

General emigration can at best afford only a temporary relief, for the colony will soon become an empire, and reproduce all the injustice and wretchedness of the mother country. Nor is general emigration necessary. England, if she would be just, could support a larger population than she now numbers. The evil is not from over population, but from the unequal repartition of the fruits of industry. She suffers from over production, and from over production, because her workmen produce not for themselves but for their employers. What then is the remedy? As it concerns England, we shall leave the English statesman to answer. Be it what it may, it will not be obtained without war and bloodshed. It will be found only at the end of one of the longest and severest struggles the human race has ever been engaged in, only by that most dreaded of all wars, the war of the poor against the rich, a war which, however long it may be delayed, will come, and come with all its horrors. The day of vengeance is sure; for the world after all is under the dominion of a Just Providence.

No one can observe the signs of the times with much care, without perceiving that a crisis as to the relation of wealth and labor is approaching. It is useless to shut our eyes to the fact, and like the ostrich fancy ourselves secure because we have so concealed our heads that we see not the danger. We or our children will have to meet this crisis. The old war between the King and the Barons is well-nigh ended, and so is that between the Barons and the Merchants and Manufacturers, —landed capital and commercial capital. The business man has become the peer of my Lord. And now commences the new struggle between the operative and his employer, between wealth and labor. Every day does this struggle extend further and wax stronger and fiercer; what or when the end will be God only knows.

In this coming contest there is a deeper question at issue than is commonly imagined; a question which is but remotely touched in your controversies about United States Banks and Sub Treasuries, chartered Banking and free Banking, free trade and corporations, although these controversies may be paving the way for it to come up. We have discovered no presentiment of it in any king's or queen's speech, nor in any president's message. It is embraced in no popular political creed of the day, whether christened

Whig or Tory, *Juste-milieu* or Democratic. No popular senator, or deputy, or peer seems to have any glimpse of it; but it is working in the hearts of the millions, is struggling to shape itself, and one day it will be uttered, and in thunder tones. Well will it be for him, who, on that day, shall be found ready to answer it.

What we would ask is, throughout the Christian world, the actual condition of the laboring classes, viewed simply and exclusively in their capacity of laborers? They constitute at least a moiety of the human race. We exclude the nobility, we exclude also the middle class, and include only actual laborers, who are laborers and not proprietors, owners of none of the funds of production, neither houses, shops, nor lands, nor implements of labor, being therefore solely dependent on their hands. We have no means of ascertaining their precise proportion to the whole number of the race; but we think we may estimate them at one half. In any contest they will be as two to one, because the large class of proprietors who are not employers, but laborers on their own lands or in their own shops will make common cause with them.

Now we will not so belie our acquaintance with political economy, as to allege that these alone perform all that is necessary to the production of wealth. We are not ignorant of the fact, that the merchant, who is literally the common carrier and exchange dealer, performs a useful service, and is therefore entitled to a portion of the proceeds of labor. But make all necessary deductions on his account, and then ask what portion of the remainder is retained, either in kind or in its equivalent, in the hands of the original producer, the workingman? All over the world this fact stares us in the face, the workingman is poor and depressed, while a large portion of the non-workingmen, in the sense we now use the term, are wealthy. It may be laid down as a general rule, with but few exceptions, that men are rewarded in an inverse ratio to the amount of actual service they perform. Under every government on earth the largest salaries are annexed to those offices, which demand of their incumbents the least amount of actual labor either mental or manual. And this is in perfect harmony with the whole system of repartition of the fruits of industry, which obtains in every department of society. Now here is the system which prevails, and here is its result. The whole class of simple laborers are poor, and in general unable to procure anything beyond the bare necessaries of life.

In regard to labor two systems obtain; one that of slave labor, the other that of free labor. Of the two, the first is, in our judgement, except so far as the feelings are concerned, decidedly the least oppressive. If the slave has never been a free man, we think, as a general rule, his sufferings are less than those of the free laborer at wages. As to actual freedom one has just about as much as the other. The laborer at wages has all the disadvantages of freedom and none of its blessings, while the slave, if denied the blessings, is freed from the disadvantages. We are no advocates of slavery, we are as heartily opposed to it as any modern abolitionist can be; but we say frankly that, if there must always be a laboring population distinct from proprietors and employers, we regard the slave system as decidedly preferable to the system at wages. It is no pleasant thing to go days without food, to lie idle for weeks, seeking work and finding none, to rise in the morning with a wife and children you love, and know not where to procure them a breakfast, and to see constantly before you no brighter prospect than the almshouse. Yet these are no unfrequent incidents in the lives of our laboring population. Even in seasons of general prosperity, when there was only the ordinary cry of "hard times," we have seen hundreds of people in a not very populous village, in a wealthy portion of our common country, suffering for the want of the necessaries of life, willing to work, and yet finding no work to do. Many and many is the application of a poor man for work, merely for his food, we have seen rejected. These things are little thought of, for the applicants are poor; they fill no conspicuous place in society, and they have no biographers. But their wrongs are chronicled in heaven. It is said there is no want in this country. There may be less than in some other countries, but death by actual starvation in this country is we apprehend no uncommon occurrence. The sufferings of quiet, unassuming but useful class of females in our cities, in general seamstresses, too proud to beg or to apply to the alms-house, are not easily told. They are industrious; they do all that they can find to do; but yet the little there is for them to do, and the miserable pittance they receive for it, is hardly sufficient to keep soul and body together. And yet there is a man who employs them to make shirts, trousers, etc., and grows rich on their labors. He is one of our respectable citizens, perhaps is praised in the newspapers for his liberal donations to some charitable institution. He passes among us as a pattern of morality, and is honored as a worthy Christian. And why should he not be, since our *Christian* community is made up of such as he, and since our clergy would not dare question his piety, lest they should incur the reproach of infidelity, and lose their standing, and their salaries? Nay, since our clergy are raised up, educated, fashioned, and sustained by such as he? Not a few of our churches rest on Mammon for their foundation. The basement is a trader's shop.

We pass through our manufacturing villages; most of them appear neat and flourishing. The operatives are well dressed, and we are told, well paid. They are said to be healthy, contented, and happy. This is the fair side of the picture; the side exhibited to distinguished visitors. There is a dark side, moral as well as physical. Of the common operatives, few, if any, by their wages, acquire a competence. A few of what Carlyle terms not inaptly the *body-servants* are well paid, and now and then an agent or an overseer rides in his coach. But the great mass wear out their health, spirits, and morals, without becoming one whit better off than when they commenced labor. The bills of mortality in these factory villages are not striking, we admit, for the poor girls when they can toil no longer go home to die. The average life, working life we mean, of the girls that come to Lowell, for instance, from Maine, New Hampshire, and Vermont, we have been assured, is only about three years. What becomes of them then? Few of them ever marry; fewer still ever return to their native places with reputations unimpaired. "She has worked in a Factory," is almost enough to damn to infamy the most worthy and virtuous girl. We know no sadder sight on earth than one of our factory villages presents, when the bell at break of day, or at the hour of breakfast, or dinner, calls out its hundreds or thousands of operatives. We stand and look at these hard working men and women hurrying in all directions, and ask ourselves, where go the proceeds of their labors? To the man who employs them, and for whom they are toiling as so many slaves, is one of our city nabobs, reveling in luxury; or he is a member of our legislature, enacting laws to put money in his own pocket; or he is a member of Congress, contending for a high tariff to tax the poor for the benefit of the rich; or in these times he is shedding crocodile tears over the deplorable condition of the poor laborer, while he docks his wages twenty-five per cent; building miniature log cabins, shouting Harrison and "hard cider." And this man too would fain pass for a Christian and a republican. He shouts for liberty, stickles for equality, and is horrified at a Southern planter who keeps slaves.

One thing is certain; that of the amount actually produced by the operative, he retains a less proportion than it costs the master to feed, clothe, and lodge his slave. Wages is a cunning device of the devil, for the benefit of tender consciences, who would retain all the advantages of the slave system, without the expense, trouble, and odium of being slave-holders.

Messrs. Thome and Kimball, in their account of the emancipation of slavery in the West Indies, establish the fact that the employer may have the same amount of labor done 25 percent cheaper than the master. What does this fact prove, if not that wages is a more successful method of taxing labor than slavery? We really believe our Northern system of labor is more oppressive, and even more mischievous to morals, than the Southern. We, however, war against both. We have no toleration for either system. We would see a slave a man, but a free man, not a mere operative at wages. This he would not be were he now emancipated. Could the abolitionists effect all they propose, they would do the slave no service. Should emancipation work as well as they say, still it would do the slave no good. He would be a slave still, although with the title and cares of a freeman. If then we had no constitutional objections to abolitionism, we could not, for the reason here implied, be abolitionists.

The slave system, however, in name and form, is gradually disappearing from Christendom. It will not subsist much longer. But its place is taken by the system of labor at wages, and this system, we hold, is no improvement upon the one it supplants. Nevertheless the system of wages will triumph. It is the system which in name sounds more honest than slavery, and in substance is more profitable to the master. It yields the wages of iniquity, without its opprobrium. It will therefore supplant slavery, and be sustained—for a time.

Now, what is the prospect of those who fall under the operation of this system? We ask, is there a reasonable chance that any considerable portion of the present generation of laborers, shall ever become owners of a sufficient portion of the funds of production, to be able to sustain themselves by laboring on their own capital, that is, as independent laborers? We need not ask this question, for everybody knows there is not. Well, is the condition of a laborer at wages the best that the great mass of the working people ought to be able to aspire to? Is it a condition,—nay can it be made a condition,—with which a man should be satisfied; in which he should be contented to live and die?

In our own country this condition has existed under its most favorable aspects, and has been made as good as it can be. It has reached all the excellence of which it is susceptible. It is now not improving but growing worse. The actual condition of the working-man today, viewed in all its bearings, is not so good as it was fifty years ago. If we have not been altogether misinformed, fifty years ago, health and industrious habits, constituted no mean stock in trade, and with them almost any man might aspire to competence and independence. But it is so no longer. The wilderness has receded, and already the new lands are beyond the reach of the mere laborer, and the employer has him at his mercy. If the present relation subsist, we see nothing better for him in reserve than what he now possesses, but something altogether worse.

We are not ignorant of the fact that men born poor become wealthy, and that men born to wealth become poor; but this fact does not necessarily diminish the numbers of the poor, nor augment the numbers of the rich. The relative numbers of the two classes remain, or may remain, the same. But be this as it may; one fact is certain, no man born poor has ever by his wages, as a simple operative, risen to the class of the wealthy. Rich he may have become, but it has not been by his own manual labor. He has in some way contrived to tax for his benefit the labor of others. He may have accumulated a few dollars which he has placed at usury, or invested in trade; or he may, as a master workman, obtain a premium on his journeymen; or he may have from a clerk passed to a partner, or from a workman to an overseer. The simple market wages for ordinary labor, has never been adequate to raise him from poverty to wealth. This fact is decisive of the whole controversy, and proves that the system of wages must be supplanted by some other system, or else one half of the human race must forever be the virtual slaves of the other.

Now the great work for this age and the coming, is to raise up the laborer, and to realize in our own social arrangements and in the actual condition of all men, that equality between man and man, which God has established between the rights of one and those of another. In other words, our business is to emancipate the proletaries, as the past has emancipated the slaves. This is our work. There must be no class of our fellow men doomed to toil through life as mere workmen at wages. If wages are tolerated it must be, in the case of the individual operative, only under such conditions that by the time he is of a proper age to settle in life, he shall have accumulated; enough to be an independent laborer on his own capital,—on his own farm, or in his own shop. Here is our work. How is it to be done?

Reformers in general answer this question, or what they deem its equivalent, in a manner which we cannot but regard as very unsatisfactory. They would have all men wise, good, and happy; but in order to make them so, they tell us that we want not external changes, but internal; and therefore instead of declaiming against society and seeking to disturb existing social arrangements, we should confine ourselves to the individual reason and conscience; seek merely to lead the individual to repentance, and to reformation of life; make the individual a practical, a truly religious man, and all evils will either disappear, or be sanctified to the spiritual growth of the soul.

This is doubtless a capital theory, and has the advantage that kings, hierarchies, nobilities,—in a word, all who fatten on the toil and blood of their fellows, will feel no difficulty in supporting it. Nicholas of Russia, the Grand Turk, his Holiness the Pope, will hold us their especial friends for advocating a theory, which secures to them the odor of sanctity even while they are sustaining by their anathemas or their armed legions, a system of things of which the great mass are and must be the victims. If you will only allow me to keep thousands toiling for my pleasure or my profit, I will even aid you in your pious efforts to convert their souls. I am not cruel; I do not wish either to cause, or to see suffering; I am therefore disposed to encourage your labors for the souls of the workingman, providing you will secure to me the products of his bodily toil. So far as the salvation of his soul will not interfere with my income, I hold it worthy of being sought; and if a few thousand dollars will aid you, Mr. Priest, in reconciling him to God, and making fair weather for him hereafter, they are at your service. I shall not want him to work for me in the world to come, and I can indemnify myself for what your salary costs me, by paying him less wages. A capital theory this, which one may advocate without incurring the reproach of a disorganizer, a jacobin, a leveller, and without losing the friendship of the rankest aristocrat in the land.

This theory, however, is exposed to one slight objection, that of being condemned by something like six thousand years' experience. For six thousand years its beauty has been extolled, its praises sung and its blessings sought, under every advantage which learning, fashion, wealth, and power can secure; and yet under its practical operations, we are assured, that mankind, though totally depraved at first, have been growing worse and worse ever since.

For our part, we yield to none in our reverence for science and religion; but we confess that we look not for the regeneration of the race from priests and pedagogues. They have had a fair trial. They cannot construct the temple of God. They cannot conceive its plan, and they know not how to build. They daub with untempered mortar, and the walls they erect tumble down if so much as a fox attempt to go up thereon. In a word they always league with the people's masters, and seek to reform without disturbing the social arrangements which render reform necessary. They would change the consequents without changing the antecedents, secure to men the rewards of holiness, while they continue their allegiance to the devil. We have no faith in priests and pedagogues. They merely cry peace, peace, and that too when there is no peace, and can be none.

We admit the importance of what Dr. Channing in his lectures on the subject we are treating recommends as "self-culture." Self-culture is a good thing, but it cannot abolish inequality, nor restore men to their rights. As a means of quickening moral and intellectual energy, exalting the sentiments, and preparing the laborer to contend manfully for his rights, we admit its importance, and insist as strenuously as anyone on making it as universal as possible; but as constituting in itself a remedy for the vices of the social state, we have no faith in it. As a means it is well, as the end it is nothing.

The truth is the evil we have pointed out is not merely individual in its character. It is not, in the case of any single individual, of any one man's procuring, nor can the efforts of any one man, directed solely to his own moral and religious perfection, do aught to remove it. What is purely individual in its nature, efforts of individuals to perfect themselves, may remove. But the evil we speak of is inherent in all our social arrangements, and cannot be cured without a radical change of those arrangements. Could we convert all men to Christianity in both theory and practice, as held by the most enlightened sect of Christians among us, the evils of the social state would remain untouched. Continue our present system of trade, and all its present evil consequences will follow, whether it be carried on by your best men or your worst. Put your best men, your wisest, most moral, and most religious men, at the head of your paper money banks, and the evils of the present banking system will remain scarcely diminished. The only way to get rid of its evils is to change the system, not its managers. The evils of slavery do not result from the personal characters of slave masters. They are inseparable from the system, let who will be masters. Make all your rich men good Christians, and you have lessened not the evils of existing inequality in wealth. The mischievous effects of this inequality do not result from the personal characters of either rich or poor, but from itself, and they will continue, just so long as there are rich men and poor men in the same community. You must abolish the system or accept its consequences. No man can serve both God and Mammon. If you will serve the devil, you must look to the devil for your wages, we know no other way.

Let us not be misinterpreted. We deny not the power of Christianity. Should all men become good Christians, we deny not that all social evils would be cured. But we deny in the outset that a man, who seeks merely to save his own soul, merely to perfect his own individual nature, can be a good Christian. The Christian forgets himself, buckles on his armor, and goes forth to war against principalities and powers, and against spiritual wickedness in high places. No man can be a Christian who does not begin his career by making war on the mischievous social arrangements from which his brethren suffer. He who thinks he can be a Christian and save his soul, without seeking their radical change, has no reason to applaud himself for his proficiency in Christian science, nor for his progress towards the kingdom of God. Understand Christianity, and we will admit, that should all men become good Christians, there would be nothing to complain of. But one might as well undertake to dip the ocean dry with a clam-shell, as to undertake to cure the evils of the social state by converting men to the Christianity of the Church.

The evil we have pointed out, we have said, is not of individual creation, and it is not to be removed by individual effort, saving so far as individual effort induces the combined effort of the mass. But whence has this evil originated? How comes it that all over the world the working classes are depressed, are the low and vulgar, and virtually the slaves of the non-working classes? This is an inquiry which has not yet received the attention it deserves. It is not enough to answer, that it has originated entirely in the inferiority by nature of the working classes; that they have less skill and foresight, and are less able than the upper classes, to provide for themselves, or less susceptible of the highest moral and intellectual cultivation. Nor is it sufficient for our purpose to be told, that Providence has decreed that some shall be poor and wretched, ignorant and vulgar; and that others shall be rich and vicious, learned and polite, oppressive and miserable. We do not choose to charge this matter to the will of God. "The foolishness of man perverteth his way, and his heart fretteth against the Lord." God has made of one blood all the nations of men to dwell on all the face of the earth, and to dwell there as brothers, as members of one and the same family; and although he has made them with a diversity of powers, it would perhaps, after all, be a bold assertion to say that he has made them with an inequality of powers. There is nothing in the actual difference of the powers of individuals, which accounts for the striking inequalities we everywhere discover in their condition. The child of the plebeian, if placed early in the proper circumstances, grows up not less beautiful, active, intelligent, and refined, than the child of the patrician; and the child of the patrician may become as coarse, as brutish as the child of any slave. So far as observation on the original capacities of individuals goes, nothing is discovered to throw much light on social inequalities.

The cause of the inequality, we speak of, must be sought in history, and be regarded as having its root in Providence, or in human nature, only in that sense in which all historical facts have their origin in these. We may perhaps trace it in the first instance to conquest, but not to conquest as the ultimate cause. The Romans in conquering Italy no doubt reduced many to the condition of slaves, but they also found the great mass of the laboring population already slaves. There is everywhere a class distinct from the reigning class, bearing the same relation to it, that the Gibbeonites did to the Jews. They are principally *colons*, the cultivators for foreign masters, of a soil of which they seemed to have been dispossessed. Who has dispossessed them? Who has reduced them to their present condition,—a condition which under the Roman dominion is perhaps even ameliorated? Who were this race? Whence came they? They appear to be distinct from the reigning race, as were the Helotae from the Doric-Spartan. Were they the aborigines of the territory? Had they once been free? By what concurrence of events have they been reduced to their present condition? By a prior conquest? But mere conquest does not so reduce a population. It may make slaves of the prisoners taken in actual combat, and reduce the whole to tributaries, but it leaves the mass of the population free, except in its political relations. Were they originally savages, subjugated by a civilized tribe? Savages may be exterminated, but they never, so far as we can ascertain, become to any considerable extent "the hewers of wood and drawers of water" to their conquerors. For our part we are disposed to seek the cause of the inequality of conditions of which we speak, in religion, and to charge it to the priesthood. And we are confirmed in this, by what appears to be the instinctive tendency of every, or almost every, social reformer. Men's instincts, in a matter of this kind, are worthier of reliance than their reasonings. Rarely do we find in any age or country, a man feeling himself commissioned to labor for a social reform, who does not feel that he must begin it by making war upon the priesthood. This was the case with the old Hebrew reformers, who are to us the prophets of God? with Jesus, the Apostles, and the early Fathers of the Church? with the French democrats of the last century; and is the case with the Young Germans, and the Socialistis, as they call themselves in England, at the present moment. Indeed it is felt at once that no reform can be effected without resisting the priests and emancipating the people from their power.

Historical research, we apprehend, will be found to justify this instinct, and to authorize the eternal hostility of the reformer, the advocate of social progress, to the priesthood. How is it we ask, that man comes out of the savage state? In the savage state, properly so called, there is no inequality of the kind of which we speak. The individual system obtains there. Each man is his own center, and is a whole in himself. There is no community, there are no members of society; for society is not. This individuality, which, if combined with the highest possible moral and intellectual cultivation, would be the perfection of man's earthly condition, must be broken down before the human race can enter into the path of civilization, or commence its career of progress. But it cannot be broken down by material force. It resists by its own nature the combination of individuals necessary to subdue it. It can be successfully attacked only by a spiritual power, and subjugated only by the representatives of that power, that is say, the priests.

Man is naturally a religious being, and disposed to stand in awe of invisible powers. This makes, undoubtedly, under certain relations, his glory; but when coupled with his ignorance, it becomes the chief source of his degradation and misery. He feels within the workings of a mysterious nature, and is conscious that hidden and superior powers are at work all around him, and perpetually influencing his destiny; now wafting him onward with a prosperous gale, or now resisting his course, driving him back, defeating his plans, blasting his hopes, and wounding his heart. What are his relations to these hidden, mysterious, and yet all-influencing forces? Can their anger be appeased? Can their favor be secured? Thus he asks himself. Unable to answer, he goes to the more aged and experienced of his tribe, and asks them the same questions. They answer as best they can. What is done by one is done by another, and what is done once is done again. The necessity of instruction, which each one feels in consequence of his own feebleness and inexperience, renders the recurrence to those best capable of giving it, or supposed to be the best capable of giving it, frequent and uniform. Hence the priest. He who is consulted prepares himself to answer, and therefore devotes himself to the study of man's relations to these invisible powers, and the nature of these invisible powers themselves. Hence religion becomes a special object of study, and the study of it a profession. Individuals whom a thunder-storm, an earthquake, an eruption of a volcano, an eclipse of the sun or moon, any unusual appearance in the heavens or earth, has frightened, or whom some unforeseen disaster has afflicted, go to the wiseman for explanation, to know what it means, or what they shall do in order to appease the offended powers. When reassured they naturally feel grateful to this wise-man; they load him with honors, and in the access of their gratitude raise him far above the common level, and spare him the common burdens of life. Once thus distinguished, he becomes an object of envy. His condition is looked upon as superior to that of the mass. Hence a multitude aspire to possess themselves of it. When once the class has become somewhat numerous, it labors to secure to itself the distinction it has received, its honors and its emoluments, and to increase them. Hence the establishment of priesthoods or sacerdotal corporations, such as the Egyptian, the Braminical, the Ethiopian, the Jewish, the Scandinavian, the Druidical, the Mexican, and Peruvian.

The germ of these sacerdotal corporations is found in the savage state, and exists there in that formidable personage called a *jongleur*, juggler, or conjurer. But as the tribe or people advances, the juggler becomes a priest and the member of a corporation. These sacerdotal corporations are variously organized, but everywhere organized for the purpose, as that arch rebel, Thomas Paine, says, "of monopolizing power and profit." The effort is unceasing to elevate them as far above the people as possible, to enable them to exert the greatest possible control over the people, and to derive the greatest possible profit from the people.

Now if we glance over the history of the world, we shall find, that at the epoch of coming out of the savage state, these corporations are universally instituted. We find them among every people; and among every people at this epoch, they are the dominant power, ruling with an iron despotism. The real idea at the bottom of these institutions, is the control of individual freedom by moral laws, the assertion of the supremacy of moral power over physical force,—a great truth, and one which can never be too strenuously insisted on; but a truth which at this epoch can only enslave the mass of the people to its professed representatives, the priests. Through awe of the gods, through fear of divine displeasure, and dread of the unforeseen chastisements that displeasure may inflict, and by pretending, honestly or not, to possess the secret of averting it, and of rendering the gods propitious, the priests are able to reduce the people to the most wretched subjection, and to keep them there; at least for a time.

But these institutions must naturally be jealous of power and ambitious of confining it to as few hands as possible. If the sacerdotal corporations were thrown open to all the world, all the world would rush into them, and then there would be no advantage in being a priest. Hence the number who may be priests must be limited. Hence again a distinction of clean and unclean is introduced. Men can be admitted into these corporations only as they descend from the priestly race. As in India, no man can aspire to the priesthood unless of Braminical descent, and among the Jews unless he be of the tribe of Levi. The priestly race was the ruling race; it dealt with science, it held communion with the Gods, and therefore was the purer race. The races excluded from the priesthood were not only regarded as inferior, but as unclean. The Gibeonite to a Jew was both an inferior and an impure. The operation of the principles involved in these considerations, has, in our judgment, begun and effected the slavery of the great mass of the people. It has introduced distinctions of blood or race, founded privileged orders, and secured the rewards of industry to the few, while it has reduced the mass to the most degrading and hopeless bondage.

Now the great mass enslaved by the sacerdotal corporations are not emancipated by the victories which follow by the warrior caste, even when those victories are said to be in behalf of freedom. The military order succeeds the priestly; but in establishing, as it does in Greece and Rome, the supremacy of the state over the church, it leaves the great mass in the bondage in which it finds them. The Normans conquer England, but they scarcely touch the condition of the old Saxon bondmen. The Polish serf lost his freedom, before began the Russian dominion, and he would have recovered none of it, had Poland regained, in her late struggle, her former political independence. The subjection of a nation is in general merely depriving one class of its population of its exclusive right to enslave the people; and the recovery of political independence, is little else than the recovery of this right. The Germans call their rising against Napoleon a rising for liberty, and so it was, liberty for German princes and German nobles; but the German people were more free under Napoleon's supremacy than they are now, or will be very soon. Conquest may undoubtedly increase the number of slaves; but in general it merely adds to the number and power of the middle class. It institutes a new nobility, and degrades the old to the rank of commoners. This is its general effect. We cannot therefore ascribe to conquest, as we did in a former number of this journal, the condition in which the working classes are universally found. They have been reduced to their condition by the priest, not by the military chieftain.

Mankind came out of the savage state by means of the priests. Priests are the first civilizers of the race. For the wild freedom of the savage, they substitute the iron despotism of the theocrat. This is the first step in civilization, in man's career of progress. It is not strange then that some should prefer the savage state to the civilized. Who would not rather roam the forest with a free step and unshackled limb, though exposed to hunger, cold, and nakedness, than crouch an abject slave beneath the whip of the master? As yet civilization has done little but break and subdue man's natural love of freedom; but tame his wild and eagle spirit. In what a world does man even now find himself, when he first awakes and feels some of the workings of his manly nature? He is in a cold, damp, dark dungeon, and loaded all over with chains, with the iron entering into his very soul. He cannot make one single free movement. The priest holds his conscience, fashion controls his tastes, and society with her forces invades the very sanctuary of his hearty and takes command of his love, that which is purest and best in his nature, which alone gives reality to his existence, and from which proceeds the only ray which pierces the gloom of his prison-house. Even that he cannot enjoy in peace and quietness, nor scarcely at all. He is wounded on every side, in every part of his being, in every relation in life, in every idea of his mind, in every sentiment of his heart. O, it is a sad world, a sad world to the young soul just awakening to its diviner instincts! A sad world to him who is not gifted with the only blessing which seems compatible with life as it is—absolute insensibility. But no matter. A wise man never murmurs. He never kicks against the pricks. What is is, and there is an end of it; what can be may be, and we will do what we can to make life what it ought to be. Though man's first step in civilization is slavery, his last step shall be freedom. The free soul can never be wholly subdued; the etherial fire in man's nature may be smothered, but it cannot be extinguished. Down, down deep in the center of his heart it burns inextinguishable and forever, glowing intenser with the accumulating heat of centuries; and one day the whole mass of Humanity shall become ignited, and be full of fire within and all over, as a live coal; and then—slavery, and whatever is foreign to the soul itself, shall be consumed.

But, having traced the inequality we complain of to its origin, we proceed to ask again what is the remedy? The remedy is first to be sought in the destruction of the priest. We are not mere destructives. We delight not in pulling down; but the bad must be removed before the good can be introduced. Conviction and repentance precede regeneration. Moreover we are Christians, and it is only by following out the Christian law, and the example of the early Christians, that we can hope to effect anything. Christianity is the sublimest protest against the priesthood ever uttered, and a protest uttered by both God and man; for he who uttered it was God-Man. In the person of Jesus both God and Man protest against the priesthood. What was the mission of Jesus but a solemn summons of every priesthood on earth to judgment, and of the human race to freedom? He discomfited the learned doctors, and with whips of small cords drove the priests, degenerated into mere money changers, from the temple of God. He instituted himself no priesthood, no form of religious worship. He recognized no priest but a holy life, and commanded the construction of no temple but that of the pure heart. He preached no formal religion, enjoined no creed, set apart no day for religious worship. He preached fraternal love, peace on earth, and good will to men. He came to the soul enslaved, "cabined, cribbed, confined," to the poor child of mortality, bound hand and foot, unable to move, and said in the tones of a God, "Be free; be enlarged; be there room for thee to grow, expand, and overflow with the love thou wast made to overflow with."

In the name of Jesus we admit there has been a priesthood instituted, and considering how the world went, a priesthood could not but be instituted; but the religion of Jesus repudiates it. It recognizes no mediator between God and man but him who dies on the cross to redeem man; no propitiation for sin but a pure love, which rises in a living flame to all that is beautiful and good, and spreads out in light and warmth for all the chilled and benighted sons of mortality. In calling every man to be a priest, it virtually condemns every possible priesthood, and in recognizing the religion of the new covenant, the religion written on the heart, of a law put within the soul, it abolishes all formal worship.

The priest is universally a tyrant, universally the enslaver of his brethren, and therefore it is Christianity condemns him. It could not prevent the reestablishment of a hierarchy, but it prepared for its ultimate destruction, by denying the inequality of blood, by representing all men as equal before God, and by insisting on the celibacy of the clergy. The best feature of the Church was in its denial to the clergy of the right to marry. By this it prevented the new hierarchy from becoming hereditary, as were the old sacerdotal corporations of India and Judea.

We object to no religious instruction; we object not to the gathering together of the people on one day in seven, to sing and pray, and listen to a discourse from a religious teacher; but we object to everything like an outward, visible church; to everything that in the remotest degree partakes of the priest. A priest is one who stands as a sort of mediator between God and man; but we have one mediator, Jesus Christ, who gave himself a ransom for all, and that is enough. It may be supposed that we, protestants, have no priests; but for ourselves we know no fundamental difference between a catholic priest and a protestant clergyman, as we know no difference of any magnitude, in relation to the principles on which they are based, between a protestant church and the catholic church. Both are based on the principle of authority; both deny in fact, however it may be in manner, the authority of reason, and war against freedom of mind; both substitute dead works for true righteousness, a vain show for the reality of piety, and are sustained as the means of reconciling us to God without requiring us to become god-like. Both therefore ought to go by the board.

We may offend in what we say, but we cannot help that. We insist upon it, that the complete and final destruction of the priestly order, in every practical sense of the word priest, is the first step to be taken towards elevating the laboring classes. Priests are, in their capacity of priests, necessarily enemies to freedom and equality. All reasoning demonstrates this, and all history proves it. There must be no class of men set apart and authorized, either by law or fashion, to speak to us in the name of God, or to be the interpreters of the word of God. The word of God never drops from the priest's lips. He who redeemed man did not spring from the priestly class, for it is evident that our Lord sprang out of Judea, of which tribe Moses spake nothing concerning the priesthood. Who in fact were the authors of the Bible, the book which Christendom professes to receive as the word of God? The priests? Nay, they were the inveterate foes of the priests. No man ever berated the priests more soundly than did Jeremiah and Ezekiel. And who were they who heard Jesus the most gladly? The priests? The chief priests were at the head of those who demanded his crucifixion. In every age the priests, the authorized teachers of religion, are the first to oppose the true prophet of God, and to condemn his prophecies as blasphemies. They are always a let and a hindrance to the spread of truth. Why then retain them? Why not abolish the priestly office? Why continue to sustain what the whole history of man condemns as the greatest of all obstacles to intellectual and social progress.

We say again, we have no objection to teachers of religion, as such; but let us have no class of men whose profession it is to minister at the altar. Let us leave this matter to Providence. When God raises up a prophet, let that prophet prophesy as God gives him utterance. Let every man speak out of his own full heart, as he is moved by the Holy Ghost, but let us have none to prophesy for hire, to make preaching a profession, a means of gaining a livelihood. Whoever has a word pressing upon his heart for utterance, let him utter it, in the stable, the market-place, the street, in the grove, under the open canopy of heaven, in the lowly cottage, or the lordly hall. No matter who or what he is, whether a graduate of a college, a shepherd from the hill sides, or a rustic from the plough. If he feels himself called to go forth in the name of God, he will speak words of truth and power, for which Humanity shall fare the better. But none of your hireling priests, your "dumb dogs" that will not bark. What are the priests of Christendom as they now are? Miserable panders to the prejudices of the age, loud in condemning sins nobody is guilty of, but silent as the grave when it concerns the crying sin of the times; bold as bold can be when there is no danger, but miserable cowards when it is necessary to speak out for God and outraged Humanity. As a body they never preach a truth till there is none whom it will indict. Never do they as a body venture to condemn sin in the concrete, and make each sinner feel "thou art the man." When the prophets of God have risen up and proclaimed the word of God, and, after persecution and death, led the people to acknowledge it to be the word of God, then your driveling priest comes forward, and owns it to be a truth, and cries "cursed of God and man is he who believes it not." But enough. The imbecility of an organized priesthood, of a hireling clergy, for all good, and its power only to demoralize the people and misdirect their energies, is beginning to be seen, and will one day be acknowledged. Men are beginning to speak out on this subject, and the day of reckoning is approaching. The people are rising up and asking of these priests whom they have fed, clothed, honored, and followed. What have ye done for the poor and friendless, to destroy oppression, and establish the kingdom of God on earth? A fearful question for you, O ye priests, which we leave you to answer as best ye may.

The next step in this work of elevating the working classes will be to resuscitate the Christianity of Christ. The Christianity of the Church has done its work. We have had enough of that Christianity. It is powerless for good, but by no means powerless for evil. It now unmans us and hinders the growth of God's kingdom. The moral energy which is awakened it misdirects, and makes its deluded disciples believe that they have done their duty to God when they have joined the church, offered a prayer, sung a psalm, and contributed of their means to send out a missionary to preach unintelligible dogmas to the poor heathen, who, God knows, have unintelligible dogmas enough already, and more than enough. All this must be abandoned, and Christianity, as it came from Christ, be taken up, and preached and preached in simplicity and in power.

According to the Christianity of Christ no man can enter the kingdom of God, who does not labor with all zeal and diligence to establish the kingdom of God on the earth; who does not labor to bring down the high, and bring up the low; to break the fetters of the bound and set the captive free; to destroy all oppression, establish the reign of justice, which is the reign of equality, between man and man; to introduce new heavens and a new earthy wherein dwelleth righteousness, wherein all shall be as brothers, loving one another, and no one possessing what another lacketh. No man can be a Christian who does not labor to reform society, to mould it according to the will of God and the nature of man; so that free scope shall be given to every man to unfold himself in all beauty and power, and to grow up into the stature of a perfect man in Christ Jesus. No man can be a Christian who does not refrain from all practices by which the rich grow richer and the poor poorer, and who does not do all in his power to elevate the laboring classes, so that one man shall not be doomed to toil while another enjoys the fruits; so that each man shall be free and independent, sitting under "his own vine and fig tree with none to molest or to make afraid." We grant the power of Christianity in working out the reform we demand; we agree that one of the most efficient means of elevating the workingmen is to Christianize the community. But you must Christianize it. It is the Gospel of Jesus you must preach, and not the gospel of the priests. Preach the Gospel of Jesus, and that will turn every man's attention to the crying evil we have designated, and will arm every Christian with power to effect those changes in social arrangements, which shall secure to all men the equality of position and condition, which it is already acknowledged they possess in relation to their rights. But let it be the genuine Gospel that you preach, and not that pseudo-gospel, which lulls the conscience asleep, and permits men to feel that they may be servants of God while they are slaves to the world, the flesh, and the devil; and while they ride roughshod over the hearts of their prostrate brethren. We must preach no Gospel that permits men to feel that they are honorable men and good Christians, although rich and with eyes standing out with fatness, while the great mass of their brethren are suffering from iniquitous laws, from mischievous social arrangements, and pining away for the want of the refinements and even the necessaries of life.

We speak strongly and pointedly on this subject, because we are desirous of arresting attention. We would draw the public attention to the striking contrast which actually exists between the Christianity of Christ, and the Christianity of the Church. That moral and intellectual energy which exists in our country, indeed throughout Christendom, and which would, if rightly directed transform this wilderness world into a blooming paradise of God, is now by the pseudo-gospel, which is preached, rendered wholly inefficient, by being wasted on that which, even if effected, would leave all the crying evils of the times untouched. Under the influence of the Church, our efforts are not directed to the reorganization of society, to the introduction of equality between man and man, to the removal of the corruptions of the rich, and the wretchedness of the poor. We think only of saving our own souls, as if a man must not put himself so out of the case, as to be willing to be damned before he can be saved. Paul was willing to be accursed from Christ, to save his brethren from the vengeance which hung over them. But nevertheless we think only of saving our own souls; or if perchance our benevolence is awakened, and we think it desirable to labor for the salvation of others, it is merely to save them from imaginary sins and the tortures of an imaginary hell. The redemption of the world is understood to mean simply the restoration of mankind to the favor of God in the world to come. Their redemption from the evils of inequality, of factitious distinctions, and iniquitous social institutions, counts for nothing in the eyes of the Church. And this is its condemnation.

We cannot proceed a single step, with the least safety, in the great work of elevating the laboring classes, without the exaltation of sentiment, the generous sympathy and the moral courage which Christianity alone is fitted to produce or quicken. But it is lamentable to see how, by means of the mistakes of the Church, the moral courage, the generous sympathy, the exaltation of sentiment, Christianity does actually produce or quicken, is perverted, and made efficient only in producing evil, or hindering the growth of good. Here is wherefore it is necessary on the one hand to condemn in the most pointed terms the Christianity of the Church, and to bring out on the other hand in all its clearness, brilliancy, and glory the Christianity of Christ.

Having, by breaking down the power of the priesthood and the Christianity of the priests, obtained an open field and freedom for our operations, and by preaching the true Gospel of Jesus, directed all minds to the great social reform needed, and quickened in all souls the moral power to live for it or to die for it; our next resort must be to government, to legislative enactments. Government is instituted to be the agent of society, or more properly the organ through which society may perform its legitimate functions. It is not the master of society; its business is not to control society, but to be the organ through which society effects its will. Society has never to petition government; government is its servant, and subject to its commands.

Now the evils of which we have complained are of a social nature. That is, they have their root in the constitution of society as it is, and they have attained to their present growth by means of social influences, the action of government, of laws, and of systems and institutions upheld by society, and of which individuals are the slaves. This being the case, it is evident that they are to be removed only by the action of society, that is, by government, for the action of society is government.

But what shall government do? Its first doing must be an undoing. There has been thus far quite too much government, as well as government of the wrong kind. The first act of government we want, is a still further limitation of itself. It must begin by circumscribing within narrower limits its powers. And then it must proceed to repeal all laws which bear against the laboring classes, and then to enact such laws as are necessary to enable them to maintain their equality. We have no faith in those systems of elevating the working classes, which propose to elevate them without calling in the aid of government. We must have government, and legislation expressly directed to this end.

But again what legislation do we want so far as this country is concerned? We want first the legislation which shall free the government, whether State or Federal, from the control of the Banks. The Banks represent the interest of the employer, and therefore of necessity interests adverse to those of the employed; that is, they represent the interests of the business community in opposition to the laboring community. So long as the government remains under the control of the Banks, so long it must be in the hands of the natural enemies of the laboring classes, and may be made, nay, will be made, an instrument of depressing them yet lower. It is obvious then that, if our object be the elevation of the laboring classes, we must destroy the power of the Banks over the government, and place the government in the hands of the laboring classes themselves, or in the hands of those, if such there be, who have an identity of interest with them. But this cannot be done so long as the Banks exist. Such is the subtle influence of credit, and such the power of capital, that a banking system like ours, if sustained, necessarily and inevitably becomes the real and efficient government of the country. We have been struggling for ten years in this country against the power of the banks, struggling to free merely the Federal government from their grasp, but with humiliating success. At this moment, the contest is almost doubtful,—not indeed in our mind, but in the minds of no small portion of our countrymen. The partisans of the Banks count on certain victory. The Banks discount freely to build "log cabins," to purchase "hard cider," and to defray the expense of manufacturing enthusiasm for a cause which is at war with the interests of the people. That they will succeed, we do not for one moment believe; but that they could maintain the struggle so long, and be as strong as they now are, at the end of ten years constant hostility, proves but all too well the power of the Banks, and their fatal influence on the political action of the community. The present character, standing, and resources of the Bank party, prove to a demonstration that the Banks must be destroyed, or the laborer not elevated. Uncompromising hostility to the whole banking system should therefore be the motto of every working man and of every friend of humanity. The system must be destroyed. On this point there must be no misgiving, no subterfuge, no paliation. The system is at war with the rights and interest of labor, and it must go. Every friend of the system must be marked as an enemy to his race, to his country, and especially to the laborer. No matter who he is, in what party he is found, or what name he bears, he is, in our judgment, no true democrat, as he can be no true Christian.

Following the distinction of the Banks, must come that of all monopolies, of all PRIVILEGE. There are many of these. We cannot specify them all; we therefore select only one, the greatest of them all, the privilege which some have of being born rich while others are born poor. It will be seen at once that we allude to the hereditary descent of property, an anomaly in our American system, which must be removed, or the system itself will be destroyed. We cannot now go into a discussion of this subject, but we promise to resume it at our earliest opportunity. We only say now, that as we have abolished hereditary monarchy and hereditary nobility, we must complete the work by abolishing hereditary property.[1] A man shall have all he honestly acquires, so long as he himself belongs to the world in which he acquires it. But his power over his property must cease with his life, and his property must then become the property of the state, to be disposed of by some equitable law for the use of the generation which takes his place. Here is the principle without any of its details, and this is the grand legislative measure to which we look forward. We see no means of elevating the laboring classes which can be effectual without this. And is this a measure to be easily carried? Not at all. It will cost infinitely more than it cost to abolish either hereditary monarchy or hereditary nobility. It is a great measure, and a startling. The rich, the business community, will never voluntarily consent to it, and we think we know too much of human nature to believe that it will ever be effected peaceably. It will be effected only by the strong arm of physical force. It will come, if it ever comes at all, only at the conclusion of war, the like of which the world as yet has never witnessed, and from which, however inevitable it may seem to the eye of philosophy, the heart of Humanity recoils with horror.

We are not ready for this measure yet. There is much previous work to be done, and we should be the last to bring it before the legislature. The time, however, has come for its free and full discussion. It must be canvassed in the public mind, and society prepared for acting on it. No doubt they who broach it, and especially they who support it, will experience a due share of contumely and abuse. They will be regarded by the part of the community they oppose, or maybe thought to oppose, as "graceless varlets," against whom every man of substance should set his face. But this is not, after all, a thing to disturb a wise man, nor to deter a true man from telling his whole thought. He who is worthy of the name of man, speaks what he honestly believes the interests of his race demand, and seldom disquiets himself about what may be the consequences to himself. Men have, for what they believed the cause of God or man, endured the dungeon, the scaffold, the stake, the cross, and they can do it again, if need be. This subject must be freely, boldly, and fully discussed, whatever may be the fate of those who discuss it.

PART II | The Recovery of Ordered Liberty

EIGHT

The Mediatorial Life of Jesus

REVEREND AND DEAR SIR,

My apology, if an apology be needed, for addressing you on the Mediatorial Life of Jesus, is in the position which you occupy among the friends of liberal inquiry, the influence your writings have had in forming my own religious opinions and character, and the generous friendship which you have long shown me personally, in good report and in evil.

You, sir, have been my spiritual father. Your writings were the first to suggest to me those trains of thought, which have finally ended in raising me from the darkness of doubt to the warm sun-light of a living faith in God, in the Bible as God's Word, and in Jesus Christ as the mediator between God and man, and as the real Savior of the world through his life, death and resurrection. I can never cease to be grateful for the important services you have rendered me, nor can I forget the respect and indulgence you have shown me notwithstanding all my short comings, and the steadiness with which you have cheered and sustained me, when the world grew dark around me, and hope was dying out of my soul.

You know, sir, somewhat of the long and painful struggles I have had in working my way up from unbelief to the high table-land of the Christian's faith and hopes; you have borne with me in my weakness, and have not

A Letter to Rev. William Ellery Channing, D.D. Originally published by Charles C. Little and James Brown (Boston, 1842).

been disposed to condemn me because I was not able, with a single bound, to place myself on that elevation. You have not been one to despise my lispings and stammerings; but while others have treated me rudely, denying me all love of truth, and all sense of goodness, you have continued to believe me at bottom honest and sincere. From my heart, sir, I thank you. I feel that you have been a true friend, and that I may open my mind and heart to you without reserve. You will receive with respect whatever comes forth from an ingenuous heart, whether it find a response in your own severer judgment or not.

You know that many years ago I was a confirmed unbeliever. I had lost; not my unbelief, but my hostility to religion, and had even to a certain extent recovered my early religious feelings, when a friend, now no more, read me one day your sermon on *Likeness to God*, preached at the ordination of Frederic A. Farley, Providence, R.I., 1828. My friend was an excellent reader, and he entered fully into the spirit of the sermon. I listened as one enchanted. A thrill of indescribable delight ran through my whole soul. I could have leaped for joy. I seemed suddenly to have found a father. To me this was much. I had never known an earthly father, and had often had I wept when I had heard, in my boyhood, my playmates, one after another, say "my father." But now, lone and deserted as I had felt myself, I too had become a son, and could look up and say, "my father" around and say, "my brothers."

The train of thought then suggested, pursued with fidelity, led me to believe myself a Christian, and to resume my profession as a Christian preacher. But when I first came into this community as a preacher, my Christianity was pretty much all comprised in two articles, the Divinity of Humanity, and the brotherhood of the race,—which I had learned from your sermon. These two articles suffered me as a preacher to dwell only on the dignity and worth of human nature, and the importance of making this dignity and worth acknowledged in all men, however high, or however low. But this I thought enough. I was honest, I was sincere in avowing myself a Christian, all deficient as I now believe my faith was; and consequently, I could not admit the justice of the charge of infidelity which was brought on all sides against me. So far as sincerity of purpose and honesty of conviction were concerned, I knew myself a believer, and thought I had a right to be treated as a believer. You were one of the few to acknowledge that right.

In looking back, sir, on the ten years which have passed, or nearly passed away, since I had the honor and the pleasure of first meeting you personally, I am now satisfied that I came among my Unitarian brethren with a faith quite too contracted for the wants of a real Christian, and with my bosom torn by two contrary tendencies. I had a strong tendency to religion, and to religious faith; but at the same time, unconsciously, another tendency, of quite an opposite character. This last tendency, really the weakest of the two, was almost the only one noted by the public, and hence, the almost universal accusation of infidelity of which I became the subject.

This last tendency has shown itself in my efforts to find the grounds of religion in human nature, to discover in the pure reason the evidences of religious faith, and to resolve the providences of God, as manifested in extraordinary men, prophets and messiahs, into the ordinary operations of Nature. But, in my preaching and writings, I have given altogether more prominence to this tendency than it really had in my own mind, in the persuasion that by so doing, I could recommend the Gospel to unbelievers. I am now satisfied that in this I not only exposed myself to undeserved reproach, but committed a great mistake as a matter of mere policy. The best way to convert unbelievers to the Gospel, is to preach the Gospel, the whole Gospel, and nothing but the Gospel. Preach God's truth as he has revealed it, in simplicity, and with fidelity; it will not fail to do its work. Nevertheless, though injustice was done to me, by a misconstruction of my motives, yet this tendency which had originally made me an unbeliever still subsisted to a considerable extent, and under its influence I sometimes uttered things irreconcilable with my present views of the Gospel.

The truth is, sir, that I have come but slowly and perhaps reluctantly into the Christian faith. I embraced at once the two articles I have named, but I have been slow to go far beyond. I have disputed the ground inch by inch, and have yielded only when I had no longer any ground on which to stand. The debate in my mind has been going on for the last ten years, which have been to me, taken as a whole, years of much severer internal conflict than they have been of external conflict, severe as this last, as you well know, has actually been.

You must permit me to say, that from the first, I have had some misgivings. In my happiest moments my thought has never been clear to myself, and I have felt that there was more in it than I had mastered. With more than tolerable powers of utterance, both as a speaker and as a writer, I have never been able to utter a thought that I was willing to accept when reflected back from another mind. Neither friend nor enemy has ever seemed to understand me; and I have never seen a criticism from a friendly or an unfriendly hand, with but one single exception, in which there was the remotest allusion to the thought I seemed to myself to have had in writing the piece criticized. Discovering that I was not understood, or rather misunderstood, I have from time to time changed my point of view and my phraseology, with the hope of being able to communicate my real thought. All in vain. I have only gained a sneer for my versatility and frequent changes of opinions. I have at times wondered at this; but I am satisfied that it was owing to the contrary tendencies at work in my mind, and to the fact, that I had not fully mastered what I wished to say, and therefore had only lisped and stammered, instead of articulating clearly and distinctly.

You must pardon me, for saying so much of myself. I have wished to confess, explain, and then forget. The difficulties under which I labored, I think, through the blessing of God, I have finally been able to overcome. I think I see wherein my past faith was defective, and why I have heretofore been unable to speak so as to be understood. I think, moreover, that I am now able to solve several problems which have troubled other and greater minds than mine, to throw light on several questions connected with Jesus as Mediator, and to point out the ground on which both Unitarians and Trinitarians may unite as brothers, with "one Lord, one faith, one baptism."

I have sir, finally attained to a view of the plan of a world's salvation through a Mediator, which I think reconciles all conflicting theories, discloses new wisdom in that plan, and enables us to take, in its most obvious and literal sense, without any subtlety or refinement, what the scriptures say of Jesus, and of salvation through his life. The Gospel becomes to me now a reality, and the teachings of the New Testament throughout realities, having their corresponding facts in the positive world. The views to which I have attained appear to me to be new, grand, and of the greatest importance. If I am not deceived they enable us to demonstrate with as much certainty as we have for our own existence several great and leading doctrines of the church universal, which have heretofore been asserted as great and holy mysteries, but unproved and unexplained. I think I can show that no small portion of the Bible, which is generally taken figuratively, is susceptible of a literal interpretation, and that certain views of the Mediator, and his Life, from which, our Unitarian friends have shrunk, are nevertheless true, and susceptible of a philosophical demonstration. I think, sir, I am able to show that the doctrine that human nature became depraved through the sin of Adam, and that it is redeemed only through the obedience of Christ; that the doctrine which teaches us that the Mediator is truly and indissolubly God-man, and saves the world by giving literally his life to the world, are the great "central truths" of Christianity, and philosophically demonstrable.

This, if it can be done, you will admit is important, and must involve a theological revolution. My purpose in writing you this letter, is to call your attention to the method by which it can be done, and to ask your judgment on that method. If I am right, I know you will rejoice with me, for the result will prove to be that higher manifestation of religious truth which you and so many others have been looking for, and asserting, must come.

Before I proceed to lay before you the important views themselves, I must be allowed to say a word as to the means by which I have attained to them; I do this that I may not arrogate to myself what does not belong to me. I have little other merit in attaining to these views than that of following out to their legitimate conclusions, certain philosophical principles, which I have been assisted by others to obtain. The great principle which underlies the whole, I became master of about one year ago. I saw, at once its immense reach in the region of metaphysics: but did not see at the time very clearly its importance in the social world, or the religious world. Leroux, in his work on *Humanité*, discovered to me its social applications. In endeavoring to point out, in a sermon a few Sundays since, this social application, which seemed to me to give new significance to the Communion, I perceived suddenly the theological application, of the principle in question, and the flood of light it throws on long-controverted dogmas. This theological application, which I am about to point out, is all that I claim as original with myself, and all that I claim as novel in the views of which I speak. I really then have done nothing, and pretend to do nothing, but to make an original application of principles which have been discovered for me by others. I say this, because I am sometimes accused of plagiarism, and sometimes lauded for being original. I have never yet claimed to be an original thinker; I have no ambition to be thought an original thinker. I might perhaps have deserved the credit of originality some twelve or fourteen years ago. I lived then far away from books and from the society of intelligent men; but men have gained great credit in this city since I have been here, by doing little more than echo the doctrines which I then put forth, or which may be found at least in germ in what I, an untutored backwoodsman, then wrote and published. But since I came into this community, I have read what I could, and have sought to obtain a knowledge of just views, and to present just views to the public, without caring whether they originated with me, or with others. But in fact many views which I have put forth, and which it is presumed that I must have borrowed from others, have really been original with me. This is the case with certain doctrines on property which I hold in common with the Saint-Simonians, also certain views as to the influence of property on politics and legislation, which are similar in some respects to those of Harrington, etc. But after all, the great inquiry of every man should be for the truth, and the truth he should be willing to accept, let it come from what source it may. Our own reputations for originality should never weigh one feather. The only truly original mind after all, is the mind that can readily assimilate and reproduce from itself the truth that comes to it.

In the doctrines I am about to present, I claim no originality. I merely claim originality for the process by which I demonstrate their philosophical truth. The doctrines have been taught ever since the time of Jesus; they have never, before this attempt of mine, so far as my knowledge extends, been demonstrated. What I have to offer on the main subject of this Letter, I shall take the liberty to arrange under three general heads.

I. Whence comes the Mediator?
II. What is his work?
III. What is the method by which he performs it?

These three inquiries will cover the whole ground that I wish at present to occupy, or that is necessary to enable me to bring out all the peculiar views I am anxious to set forth concerning Jesus as the Mediator and Savior of the world.

Whence comes the Mediator? I should not detain you a moment with this inquiry, were it not that there is a tendency in some minds among us, to rank Jesus in the category of ordinary men. I do not say that any among us question his vast superiority over all other men of whom history retains any record, but in this superiority they see nothing supernatural, no special interposition of Providence. Jesus was a man of greater natural endowments, and of more devout piety, truer and deeper philanthropy than other men. He has exerted a great and beneficial influence on the world, will perhaps continue to exert a beneficial influence for some time to come; but he is divine, it is said, in no sense in which all men are not divine, in no sense in which nature is not divine. He had a larger nature, and was truer to it, than other men, and this is all wherein he was distinguished from other men, or had any special divinity.

Persons who entertain this view, speak of him in very respectful, I may almost say, in very flattering terms. Their praise is high, warm, and no doubt sincere. But they do not seem to regard him as having been, in the strict sense of the term, a "providential man." He is providential only in that vague and unsatisfactory sense in which all nature, all men, and all events are providential. They do not look upon him as having been, in the plain, ordinary sense of the terms, sent from God to be the redeemer and savior of the world. They give a very loose explanation of the text, "God so loved the world that he gave his only begotten Son to die, that whosoever should believe on him might not perish, but have everlasting life." Jesus was the "Son of God" as all men are sons of God, and in no other sense, and "was given" as all men are given, and not otherwise. This is a conclusion, you are aware, to which some among us have come.

The same tendency which leads thus far, leads even farther. It not only reduces Jesus to the category of ordinary men, but, as might be expected, it does the same by Moses and the prophets, by the apostles, and, indeed, by all who have generally been regarded as having been specially sent from God for the instruction and improvement of mankind. These men have not spoken to us from God, words given them by a higher power, and in a name above all names, but out of their own hearts, from their own deep but natural experience. Their utterances are, no doubt, worthy of our respect. We may be refreshed by reading them, as by all genuine utterances, in which men are true to their great natures. The Bible, of course, ceases to be a book divinely inspired, a book authoritative, fit to be appealed to as decisive on matters lying beyond human experience; though it remains a very good book, containing many striking passages, much genuine poetry, some fine myths, some touching narratives, even some philosophy, and worthy to stand on the scholar's shelf with Homer, Shakespeare, Sir Thomas Brown, and Emanuel Swedenborg.

This tendency might go farther still. The state of mind and heart which leads us to wish to exclude all special providence or interposition of the Deity from the person of Jesus, and the Bible and its authors, would, if followed to its legitimate result, lead us to exclude God from the moral world altogether. When excluded from the moral world, he of course will not be retained in the natural world, and then is God wholly excluded from the universe. We are then without God, and God, if he be at all, is only an Epicurean God, who reposes at an infinite distance from the universe, disturbing himself with its concerns not at all.

It seems to me, sir, that this tendency, which neither you nor I have wholly escaped, is a tendency to resolve God into the laws of nature,—the laws of the moral world, and those of the natural world. Now what is this but a tendency to sink God in nature, to lose him entirely, that is, to become atheists. I do not mean to say that you or I have been affected by this tendency to any very great extent, but you know that it has manifested itself in our midst. We have found it in our friends; we have met with it in our parochial visits; we have seen it in the doctrines put forth by men who profess to have outgrown the past; and indeed it has been the decided tendency of the literature and science of Christendom for the last century and a half. Men have deified nature, boasted the perfection and harmony of her laws, forgetful that there are such things as volcanos, earthquakes, noxious damps and poisonous effluvia, blight and mildew. They shrink from admitting the doctrine of Providence. In reading ancient history they seek to resolve all that is marvelous or prodigious into natural laws and some entire religious sects are so afraid of the interposition of God, that they say men are rewarded and punished according to the "natural laws." They see no longer the hand of God, but great Nature.

Out from the heart of nature rolled,
The burdens of the Bible old;
The litanies of nations came,
Like the volcano's tongue of flame,
Up from the burning core below,—
The canticles of love and woe.

But I need hardly say to you that this whole tendency is anti-religious, and productive, in every heart that indulges it, of decided irreligion. The scriptures everywhere represent the agents and ministries of our instruction and improvement as sent by a heavenly Father. Noah, Abraham, Moses, David, Isaiah, Peter, James, John, and Paul, are always called of God, and sent. They come to us not of their own accord; they speak to us not in their own name, but as ambassadors for God. God gives to each a special mission, and sends him on an errand of love and mercy to his tribe, nation, or race. This is the only view compatible with religion.

When we resolve God into the laws of nature, whether as called the laws of the moral world or of the natural world, we have nothing remaining but nature. Nature, when there is no God seen behind it, to control it, to do with it as he will, in fact, that wills to overrule its seeming evil for real good, is a mere Fate, an inexorable Destiny, a dark, inscrutable, resistless Necessity. It has no freedom, no justice. It sweeps on regardless of what it crushes or carries away before it; now with its lightnings striking down the old man in his sins, and now the infant in its innocence. Where is the ground for religious emotion—religious exercise? All is fixed, irrevocable. What shall we do? Or wherefore attempt to do anything? We may fear and tremble at the darkness before and behind us, but wherefore love, or be grateful? We may be anxious about the future, but wherefore pray? We may wish to be forgiven our sins, but who can forgive them? What is the ground of penitence and pardon?

Prayer, many amongst us have felt, is quite useless, if not improper, saving as a sort of aesthetic exercise, saving its spiritual effect on the one who prays. Forgiveness of sins men have seemed, to a very great extent, to consider as altogether out of the question. They either seek on the one hand a scapegoat, a substitute, someone to suffer for their sins, in their place, or they say God leaves us to the *natural* consequences of our deeds. There is no God, who of his own free grace, pardons the sinner, and receives and embraces the returning prodigal.

In fact, sir, not a few among us, though they admit, in words, that there is a God, do virtually deny his existence, by failing to believe in his freedom. You have contended for human freedom, and declared that man is annihilated just in proportion as his freedom is abridged. You may say as much of God. Freedom and sovereignty are one and the same. It has been felt that God has hedged himself in by natural laws, laws of his own establishing, so that he is no longer free to hear and answer prayer, or to comfort and forgive the penitent. God acts undoubtedly in accordance with invariable and eternal laws, but these laws are not the *natural* laws, not laws which he has enacted, but the laws of his own being; that is to say, he acts ever in conformity with himself, according to his own immutable will. The laws which he is not free to violate are not laws out of himself, but which he himself is. "That is to say again, God is not free to be other than himself, and in this fact he is proved to be absolutely free."

This tendency to resolve God into nature, is unscriptural and fatal to religion. Either we must give up all pretensions to religion or follow an opposite tendency. Either we must give up all ground for piety, or suffer Providence to intervene in the affairs of the world, and of the human race. We must also guard with great care against all disposition to revolt at this intervention. The true religious theory requires us to regard the authors of the Bible as supernaturally endowed, as sent specially by our Father on special missions, and the Bible therefore as a supernatural book, belonging to a different category from that of all other books.

According to this view, we must regard Jesus, not as *coming* but as *sent*, not as raising himself up to be the Mediator, but as having been raised up by the Father in heaven. He is from God, who commends his love to us by him. It is God's grace, not human effort or human genius, that provides the Mediator. It is impossible then to press Jesus into the category of ordinary men. He stands out alone, distinct, peculiar. This much, I must be permitted to assume in regard to Jesus, if I am to concern myself with Christianity at all. In answer then to the question, Whence comes the Mediator? I reply, from God, "whoso loved the world that he gave his only begotten Son to die, that whosoever should believe on him might not perish but have everlasting life."

II

But, assuming that God sent the Mediator, what did he send him to do? What was the work to be done for human redemption and sanctification? In other words, what is the condition in which the Gospel assumes the human race to be *without Christ*, and from which God, through the mediation of Christ, is represented as saving it? A great question this, and one on which I feel that I cannot so fully sympathize with your views as I once did. You say, in the sermon to which I have already alluded, that "In ourselves are the elements of the Divinity. God, then, does not sustain a figurative resemblance to man. It is the resemblance of a parent to a child, the likeness of a kindred nature." I am not sure that I catch your precise meaning in these sentences, but from these and from your writings generally, I infer that you hold man to be created with a *nature* akin to that of the Divinity. In other words, man is created with a divine nature, and therefore the human and divine must be at bottom identical. This is the doctrine I have been accustomed to draw from your writings, and which is termed, amongst your admirers, the doctrine of the Divinity of Humanity.

This doctrine, which you have set forth on so many occasions, with all the power of your rich and fervid eloquence, I must needs believe is the real parent of that deification and worship of the human soul, which has within a few years past manifested itself among our transcendentalists. Men more ardent but less discriminating than yourself, have seized upon this expression, "in ourselves are the elements of the Divinity," and have inferred that God is nothing but the possibility of man. In your stead, I presume the expression only means that it is in ourselves that we find the germs, not of

God, but of the idea of God. Others, however, have interpreted you differently, and have gone so far as to say that God is merely the complement of humanity; and some whom we have been loath to call insane, have not illogically though absurdly proceeded to say of themselves, "*I* am God;" "I and my Father are one,"—thus interpreting of the human soul, all that is said in the Bible of Jesus, of the Logos, and therefore by implication all that is said of the Infinite God.

You will not understand me to intimate that you have had any sympathy with this extravagant, not to say blasphemous conclusion, which not a few of our friends have drawn from what they have supposed to be your premises. I know well that while you have wished to defend the freedom of those who have drawn it, and to do justice to the moral purity of their characters, you have shrunk from the conclusion itself. Yet, you must allow me to say, that I feel that you have in some measure warranted this deification and worship of the human soul. Assuming the divinity of human nature as the starting point, as you do, I see not well how a logical mind, not restrained by an abundant stock of good sense, can avoid coming to this conclusion. I must confess that I cannot see how one can avoid it, save at the expense of his consistency.

I certainly shall not deny that there is something divine in man; but I do deny that what is divine in man is original in his nature, save as all nature is divine, inasmuch as it is the work of God, and made at bottom,—if one may so speak, and mean anything,—out of divine substance. But you nor I have ever intended to favor pantheism. We do not therefore confound nature with God, any more than we do God with nature. I see not, then, how it is possible for man in any intelligible or legitimate sense of the word, to be *naturally* divine. The two terms seem to me to involve a direct contradiction. There is something divine in the life of man, I am willing to own; but this divinity which you find there, I think has been communicated to man, super-induced upon his nature, if I may so speak, by the grace of God through our Lord Jesus Christ. The error which I seem to myself to find in your view of man is, that you assume his *natural* likeness to God, that he contains, as essential elements of his nature, the elements of the Divinity. I am unable to reconcile with this fact of possessing a divine nature, my own experience, or the recorded experience of the race. Man, if so lofty, so divine, having in himself the elements of God, and therefore of infinity, should not be so foolish, so weak, and so wicked as we know him to have been in all past ages, and as we find him to be even in ourselves. It does well enough now and then for declamation to talk of man's likeness to God, but alas! few there are who have not been obliged, by painful experience, to exclaim with the Hebrew prophet, "it is not in man that walketh to direct his steps."

Allow me to say, that I think it is an error to assume that Christianity takes the divinity of humanity as its point of departure. Christianity seems to me to assume throughout as its point of departure, man's sinfulness, depravity, alienation from God and heaven. It treats man everywhere as a sinner, as morally diseased, morally dead, and its work is always to restore him to moral life and health; not to a consciousness of the greatness and divinity of his soul, but to righteousness, to a spiritual communion and union with God. And after all, is not this view the true one? Is not man a sinner? Who is there of us, however exalted or however low our estate, cultivated or uncultivated our minds, however pure and blameless may be our lives, that does not bear on his heart the damning stain of sin? Who has not exclaimed, nay, who does not perpetually exclaim, "I am a sinner; the good I should I do not, and the evil that I should not that I do. O wretched man that I am, who shall deliver me from the body of this death?" The universal conscience of the race bears witness to the fact that all men sin, and come short of the glory of God. All religions are so many additional witnesses to this fact, for they are all so many methods dictated to man, or devised by him, for getting rid of sin, and placing himself at one with God.

This much you, I know, will admit, however it may or may not be reconcilable with what you say of man's divinity. But I think Christianity goes farther than this. It assumes not only that all men are actual sinners, but also that human nature itself has been corrupted, is depraved, so that men by nature are prone to do evil. This is the doctrine which I know you have opposed; but I think I can present it in a light in which you will not refuse to accept it; because I see how I can accept it, and find also a place for the doctrine which you yourself have so much at heart.

This doctrine of the depravity of human nature is, you will admit, a doctrine of universal tradition. With me tradition is always good evidence when its subject-matter is not intrinsically improbable. This is, I am aware, a broad principle, but I am able to demonstrate its soundness. The pure reason is always incompetent to decide on questions which go out of the department of mathematics. In what concerns the race, tradition is the criterion of certainty, only we must not forget that the individual man must be free to sit in judgment on the question, what is or is not tradition. The doctrine of human depravity is admitted on all hands to be a doctrine of universal tradition. If men were not universally conscious of its truth, of its conformity to what they know of themselves, how could they universally believe it? If it were false, it would be right in the face and eyes of what each one knows of himself, and we should naturally expect to find it universally rejected. Men cannot even by your rich and kindling eloquence, which is seldom surpassed, be made to believe, to any great extent, in your doctrine of the divinity of humanity. Even those of us the most anxious to embrace it, find ourselves unable to do so. We are too conscious of our own weakness and unworthiness. If the opposite doctrine were not more true to our experience, we should find equal difficulty in believing that.

Moreover, the Scriptures seem to me to teach very clearly, that the actual sins of mankind, are not all the difficulties in the way of our salvation, that are to be overcome. I will say nothing now of Genesis; I confine myself to the New Testament. Paul teaches, beyond all question, that all men died in Adam, that through Adam sin entered into the world, and by sin a corruption of human nature. It was through the disobedience of one man that many, the many, that is, all men, were made sinners. Thus John, when he points to Jesus, says, "Behold the Lamb of God which takes away the *sin* of the world." He does not say *sins*, but *sin*, that is, the original depravity of human nature.

Experience also, I think, indicates at least that there is in all men, even now, an undercurrent of depravity, by virtue of which men, if left to themselves, delight in sin rather than in holiness. Children are not always the sweet innocents we sometimes pretend. The little rogues not unfrequently show animation, spirit, intelligence only when doing some mischief. Moreover, if human nature were not depraved, if it were what you represent it, and if there were no sin but actual sin, how could there be even actual sin? How comes it to pass that men, pure by nature, and possessing in themselves the very elements of God, do no sooner begin to develop their pure and godlike nature than they sin? What is it that works in us, and manifests itself in our acts? Is it not human nature? Since then the workings of this nature are unquestionably sinful, must not the nature itself be depraved?

I am willing to admit that the doctrine of human depravity, has assumed a form which is somewhat objectionable. Not indeed because it has been said to be total, that is, extending to and over all the faculties of the human soul. For the human soul is not many, but one, and acts ever as unity. It would be grossly absurd then to assume that one phasis of it could remain undepraved while another was depraved. Sin also blunts the intellect as well as corrupts the heart. They who have pleasure in unrighteousness are easily deluded. They are the pure in heart who see God. But the error has been in assuming perfection as the point of departure for man and nature, and therefore in considering the imperfection we now see in man and nature to be the result of a fall from a perfect state. A fall from such a state is inconceivable. But man being originally created imperfect, as he must have been, naturally, if not inevitably, sinned, and this sin necessarily corrupted human nature.

I say *necessarily*. Grant me what you will not deny, that the first man, whether called Adam or not, sinned, and the doctrine of the inherent, hereditary depravity of human nature follows inevitably, necessarily. This may seem to be a strong statement, but I can justify it.

The old doctrine on this subject is that God made a covenant with Adam, by virtue of which Adam became the Federal Head of humanity, so that all his posterity should be implicated in his transgression. I do not like the term *covenant*. Say that God so created man, and subjected him to such a law of life, that the first man could not sin without involving all his posterity in his sin, and you will say what I believe to be the strict truth. But how can this be? Shall the innocent be involved in the fate of the guilty? They are so in nature, and in this life, to some extent, in providence. This world does not realize our conceptions of justice. Hence the promise and the hope of another. But this is not the point.

Philosophy has succeeded in demonstrating what everybody has always believed without perceiving its full significance,—that we are dependent beings, and are in no case and in no sense able to live by and in ourselves alone. Man can no more *live* by himself alone, than he can *exist* alone. Cut him off from all communion with nature, and could he live? Cut him off from all communication with other men, with his race, would he not die? Does not man die in solitude? In perfect solitude could he ever be said to live, that is to live a human life? Could any of his affections, moral, religious, social, or domestic, be ever developed? Certainly not. Here then is a fact of immense importance.

Let us begin by distinguishing *life* from *being*. To be is not necessarily to live. Inorganic matter is, but we can hardly say that it *lives*. To live is to manifest. But no being except God the self-existent, and the self-living being, is able to manifest itself by itself alone. There is no act, no function that man can perform in a state of perfect isolation. He cannot think without thinking himself as the subject of the thought, and thinking something not himself as its object. He has the capacity to love, but he cannot manifest it, that is live it, without loving; and he cannot love without loving something, some object. This which I say of love I may say of all of man's capacities, whether physical, intellectual, sentient, or sentimental. To deny this, and to assume that man can in any case be his own object, were to assume that man is capable of living in himself alone; which would imply that he, like the infinite God is self-existent and self-living.

If to live is to manifest ourselves, and if we cannot manifest ourselves without communion with an object which we are not, it follows that our life is at once subjective and objective. A man's life is not all in himself. It is in himself and in his object—the object by means of which he lives. This, if we say man is a dependent being, insufficient for himself, is what we necessarily affirm.

Now man's object, by communion with which he lives, is other men, God, and nature. With God and nature he communes only indirectly. His direct, immediate object is other men. His life, then, is in himself and in other men. All men are brought by this into the indissoluble unity of one and the same life. All become members of one and the same body, and members one of another. The object of each man is all other men. Thus do the race live *in solido*, if I may use a legal term, the objective portion of each man's life being indissolubly in all other men, and, therefore, that of all men in each man.

It follows necessarily from this oneness of the life of all men, that no one member can be affected for good or evil, but the whole body, all humanity in space, time and eternity must actually or virtually be affected with it.

Assume now, that the first man sinned, and it is a fair presumption that he did sin, to say the least. This man must have been the object by virtue of communion with which his children were enabled to live. They could not live without an object, and he must be that object. Life is indissolubly subjective and objective. He must furnish the objective portion of their life. This portion of their life must partake of his moral character. He had polluted himself by sin. This pollution is necessarily transmitted by virtue of the fact that he is their object, to them, who corrupted in the objective portion of their life, must needs be corrupted in the subjective portion.

Adam's sin must necessarily have been transmitted to his children, not solely by natural generation, as some have contended, but by moral generation. Nor could it stop there. His children must have been the object of their children, and thus have transmitted it to them. These again must have transmitted it to a later generation; and thus, since the preceding generation furnishes always the objective portion of the life of the succeeding generation, it must necessarily be transmitted from generation to generation forever, or till the race should cease to exist; unless the current were arrested and rolled back by a foreign power.

Bearing in mind this law of life, which philosophy has succeeded in demonstrating without once suspecting its application, and I think you will agree with me in accepting the doctrine in question, in believing that Paul meant what he said, when he said that all die in Adam, and that through the disobedience of one man all were made sinners, and that, therefore, death hath passed upon all men. I think, also, that you will agree that the Church generally, with which we have both warred on this point, has been right in asserting original sin, and the innate, hereditary depravity of human nature. The Church seems to me to have erred only in considering this depravity, hereditary by virtue of a covenant or imputation, on the one hand, or by natural generation on the other. It is hereditary by virtue of the fact stated, that the preceding generation always furnishes the objective portion of the life of the succeeding generation, and without the objective portion the subjective portion would be as if it were not.

This principle of life which I have set forth is one of an immense reach. It shows at a glance the terrible nature of sin. In sin this principle is reversed, but is not destroyed. It operates for evil as, when in its normal condition, it does for good. By virtue of this principle, sin, whatever its degree, however great or however slight, by whomsoever committed, necessarily propagates itself, and must continue to propagate itself eternally, if not arrested by the sovereign grace of God. Humanity has originally in itself no more inherent power to overcome it than a body once set in motion has to arrest itself. How little then do they know of the true philosophy of life, who treat sin as if it were a light affair!

I am now prepared to answer the question, what is the work to be done? It is to redeem human nature from its inherent depravity, communicate to it a new and divine life, through which individuals' may be saved from actual transgression, and raised to fellowship with the Father, by which they shall become really sons of God, and joint-heirs of a heavenly inheritance.

III

Having now determined the work there was for a Mediator to perform, I pass in the third and last place to consider the method by which he performs it; and I think I shall succeed in demonstrating the truth of the four following positions which are held by the Church generally.

1. Man naturally does not and cannot commune directly with God, and therefore can come into fellowship with him only through a Mediator.
2. This Mediator must be at once and indissolubly, in the plain literal sense of the terms, very God of very God, and very man of very man; and so being very God of very God, and very man of very man, he can literally and truly mediate between God and men.
3. Jesus saves man, redeems him from sin, and enables him to have fellowship, as John says, with the Father, by giving his life literally not only for him but to him.
4. Men have eternal life, that is, live a true normal life, only so far forth as they live the identical life of Jesus. "He that hath the Son hath life"; "he that hath not the Son hath not life"; "except ye eat the flesh and drink the blood of the Son of Man ye have no life in you."

These are strong positions, and such as we Unitarians have not generally embraced in a very literal sense; but I think I can show them to be not only tenable, but positions that we may accept without giving up anything we now have, that we really value. They may require us to enlarge our faith, but not to alter or abandon it. Nay, they are virtually implied in what we are every day preaching.

Jesus says, in answer to a question put to him by Thomas, "I am the way, the truth, and the life." These words have a profound significance, and a literal truth, which I confess I for one have been but slow to comprehend. I confess, sir, that I have honestly believed, that we might have a very sufficient Christianity without including the historical person we call Jesus; not indeed that I have ever failed, in my own view of Christianity, to include him. But I have taught from the pulpit, and from the press, that Christianity did not necessarily and could not be made to stand or fall with the fact whether there ever was or was not such a person as Jesus. This I now see was a grave error. Christ, the literal person we call Christ, is Christianity. All begins and ends with him. To reject him historically is to reject Christianity. This is the truth which they have had who have accused some of us of advocating the "latest form of infidelity," though under other aspects we who have been so accused, have been much farther from infidelity than our accusers.

The fact is, sir, that the language, in which the Catholic or Universal Church clothes the doctrines I have set forth in the propositions enumerated, has prevented a large number of us from seeing the realities concerned. Many of us have even believed that there were no realities there, that the doctrines of the Church do not concern realities at all, but mere covenants, bargains, imputations, legal fictions, etc. Finding no reality under the symbols of the Church, we have concluded them to be empty forms, with which it were useless for us to attempt to satisfy the wants of either our minds or our hearts. We consequently rejected them, and sought to find what we needed in the everlasting truth and nature of things. All well enough up to a certain point; but we sought it unfortunately in the *abstract* truth and nature of things, not in *real life*. Consequently Jesus became to us a law, an abstract principle- according to which man was made. This has been the case with myself in nearly all that I have written. In my *New Views*, Jesus has for me a high *representative* value. But having once attained to the principle represented, to the everlasting truth signified, I felt that the representative became as unnecessary, as the scaffolding after the temple is erected. This is the vice of Mr. Parker's South Boston Sermon, and of my Review of it.

On the other hand were our Unitarian friends of what has been called the old school. These with great truth hung on to the person and life of Jesus, and accused us who sought to resolve Jesus into an abstract law of the moral world, of rejecting Christianity altogether. But they did not help our difficulties. True they retained a personal Jesus, but they did not seem to us to retain any great matter for him to do; and when they talked of the importance of his life they failed to show us that importance. With the best intentions in the world, we could not see how, except in words, they made out that Jesus was anything more than a very exemplary sort of a man, a very zealous and able reformer, whom we should do well to respect and to remember along with Plato, Alfred, Luther and Swedenborg. We felt that there must be a deeper, a more permanent Christ than this, and we sought him, as I have intimated, in abstract philosophy.

You, sir, I know have said much of the life of Christ, and have spoken of its intimate relation to Christianity; but I confess that I do not find its importance according to your views, save as an example, and as well fitted to give force and efficacy to his instructions. You seem to me to make Jesus the way, and the truth, an example for man to imitate, and a teacher, through his life as well as through his words, of the truth; although I find, in what you say of him, I admit, almost a presentiment of the fact that he is the Life. Now, I apprehend that Christendom feels very deeply that Jesus was something more to humanity than a picture hung up on the cross for the world to gaze at, and something more, too, than a teacher of truth; for as a mere teacher, I apprehend he has slight claims to originality. I have been unable to find a single doctrine, a single precept, absolutely peculiar to the New Testament. It will hardly do to stop with Jesus as an eminent teacher and true model man. We have all felt, nay, we all feel, that something more was necessary. As a model man, he serves us very little purpose, because we see him in but a very few of the relations of life, and because his perfections are above, altogether above the reach of us human beings. If none could be Christians but those who can be in all respects what he is, we should have no Christians. Taken as a mere teacher, the Gospel histories become to us almost a farce. The little that is brought forth in this way hardly justifies the prodigies recorded.

Allow me to say again, that I think there is a significance in what Jesus says, when he says, "I am the way, the truth and the life," which those of us who have asserted the abstract Christ, and those of us who have reduced Jesus to the capacity of an exemplar and teacher of truth and righteousness, have not attained unto,—a significance which once attained unto, will save the one class of us from our alleged coldness, and the other from our abstractions, and give to us all what we and the world need—Life.

I begin by assuming that the finite cannot commune directly with the infinite. Like does not and cannot commune with unlike. Moreover, the finite when regarded as depraved, all will agree, cannot commune, hold fellowship with infinite holiness. Man then could not commune directly with God; both because finite and because sinful. Then he must remain ever alienated from God, or a medium of communion, that is, a Mediator, must be provided. And this Mediator must of course be provided by the Infinite, and not by the finite. It would be absurd to say that man, unable to commune with God, can nevertheless provide a medium of communion with him. God must provide it. That is, he must condescend, come down to the finite, down to man, and by so doing, take man up to himself.

The Mediator, or medium of communion must needs be both human and divine. For if it do not touch man on the one hand, and God on the other, it cannot bring the two together, and make them one. Moreover, it must be really, literally, and indissolubly human and divine, God-man; not figuratively, symbolically, or mythically, for the Gospel deals only with realities. Types and shadows disappeared with the Mosaic dispensation.

Now, if you will recall what I have said of life, and the law of life, you will see at once how truly, and how literally Jesus was this Mediator between God and man. To live is to manifest oneself, and no being, except the self-living Being, God, can manifest itself save by communion with some object. Life, then, in all beings, but the Unbegotten, is at once subjective and objective. This is the principle of life, which philosophy has demonstrated beyond the possibility of cavil.

Jesus, you admit, to say the least, was an extraordinary personage. I have already shown in this Letter that he does not belong to the category of ordinary men. He is special, distinct, peculiar. Say now that God takes humanity, in the being we term Jesus, into immediate communion with himself, so that he is the direct object by means of which Jesus manifests himself. The result would be life; that life, like all derivative life, at once subjective and objective, must necessarily be, in the strictest sense of the terms, human and divine, the life of God and the life of man, made indissolubly one. For God being the object, would be the objective portion, and man being the subject would be the subjective portion, which united is God-man. Here is the Mediator at once God-man, and that in no figurative sense, in no overstrained, refined sense, but all simply and literally, as the most simple-minded must understand the terms.

According to this view, it is the Life that mediates; that is, the Mediator is the Living Jesus, not Jesus the latent, the unmanifested, and, therefore, to all practical purposes the same as no Jesus at all. The Living Jesus, the Life, is the Christ, and the Christ is then, what Paul and the Church have always asserted, "GOD MANIFEST IN THE FLESH." How true, now, is what Jesus said, "I am the way, the truth, and the Life!" All those passages which speak of Jesus Christ as the Son of God, the only begotten of the Father, become now literally true. Christ is literally the Son of God, begotten of the Father by spiritual generation, and being born from the immediate communion of the human and divine, is in the strictest sense in which you can use the terms, very God of very God, and very man of very man; and as God, distinguishable, as the Church has always contended, from God the Father only as the begotten must needs be distinguishable from the unbegotten.

If I am right in this, Jesus lived not as we do, merely by virtue of communion with other men and nature, but by virtue of immediate and unrestrained communion with God. The Scriptures nowhere represent Jesus as living an independent, an underived life. He is begotten of the Father; he is the Son; and he says expressly that he lives *by* the Father. I need on this point make no quotations. He never professes to live without the Father, but professes to live always by the Father and in the Father.

Now Jesus being at once God and man in his life, answers precisely the condition of a Mediator between God and man. God and man are nothing to us save so far as they are living. They do not exist for us only so far forth as they live. Jesus is all to us in his life. The Jesus men saw and communed with was the life of Jesus, the Living Jesus, that is to say, the Christ. Being human he was within the reach of human beings, and being at the same time indissolubly God, by communing with him they necessarily communed with God. Whoso touched him, laid his hand on God. "Have I been so long with thee, and yet hast thou not known me, Philip? He that hath seen me, hath seen the Father."

It is the Life that mediates. Jesus, I have said, so has said the Church, saves the world by communicating to it his life, not as a life for them to look at, to contemplate as an example, and to seek to copy, to imitate, but for them literally to live, to be *their* life. This is now quite explicable. Jesus was placed in the world in the midst of men. Men communed with him while he was in the flesh. Then by the very principle of life already stated, he must have become the objective portion of their life. Then his life literally enters into and becomes an inseparable portion of the life of those human beings, say his disciples, who lived in and by communion with him. He was the object to his disciples; then, the objective portion of their life, by virtue of which their subjective life was developed.

But the human race lives, as we have seen, *in solido*; all are members of one and the same body, and members one of another. There is a oneness of life which runs through them all, making them so strictly one, that the whole must feel whatever affects any one. The slightest vibrations in the heart of the least significant member are felt through the mighty heart of the whole. Consequently, the very moment that this new life of Jesus was communicated to the disciples, it was communicated virtually to the race. The disciples became objects with which others communed, and by means of their communion with others, necessarily imparted this life to others, by virtue of that very principle of life by which they had received it, and by virtue of which, when reversed, we have seen the sin of Adam necessarily extended to all his posterity. By the fact that one generation overlaps another, and thus becomes its objective life, the generation in which Christ appeared must necessarily transmit it to its successor, and that successor to its successor, and thus generation carry it on to generation, so long as the succession of generations should last.

This doctrine of the transmission of the Life from generation to generation, is denied by no sect, to my knowledge, except the Baptists, who seem to me to mistake more fundamentally the real character of Christianity, than any other sect to which the Protestant reformation has given birth. In all other churches it is borne witness to by the doctrine of infant baptism. Children are baptized because it is felt that there is a sense in which the children of elect or believing parents are born into the kingdom. Infant baptism, then, has an important meaning. It is the symbol of a vital doctrine of Christianity, which is, to my understanding, rejected by all those who admit only baptism of adults, on voluntary profession of faith. The same doctrine of the transmission of the life from man to man in time and space, by what I have termed spiritual generation, is borne witness to by what is termed apostolic succession. Without meaning to accept this last doctrine, in its episcopal sense, I must say that I see a great truth which it covers. This divine life was communicated to the world through the apostles, and mainly through those who succeeded them in the ministry. A virtue evidently, according to the principle of life, must have been communicated by the apostles to their successors. They who have not received this virtue cannot be true ministers of Jesus. For how can I communicate to others the divine life of Jesus, if I have not myself received that life? The doctrine of apostolic succession teaches us simply that the church has held that this divine life is communicable from man to man by spiritual generation. Hence with singular propriety has she called her clergy, *spiritual fathers.* Every true clergyman is the father of his flock, and verily begets in them a true life. The error of the church has been in supposing that this life could be communicated by laying on of the hands of the presbytery. Probably, however, at bottom, nothing more has ever been meant by this, than that the communion between us who are to minister at the altar and the apostles, and through them with Jesus, must be real and unbroken. And if the view I have taken be true, this communion depends on no arbitrary ceremony; it is real, and the very principle of life itself prevents it from being interrupted in any case whatever. Perhaps also, if we were really filled with this divine life, as we should be, we might impart somewhat of it, merely by the laying on of hands.

We see, now, how Jesus can be literally the Mediator between God and men, and how by the fact that he lived in communion with men, he must communicate his life to the world, to human nature, so that it must become henceforth the life of humanity, a new life, by virtue of which the human race comes under a new dispensation, and is able, so to speak, to commence a new series. Assume what we have assumed, that this life is at once human and divine, we can readily perceive that its introduction into the life of humanity would redeem humanity from the corruption which was by Adam, so that what Paul says must be literally true, "As in Adam all die, even so in Christ shall all be made alive." And this discloses the necessity of regarding the life of Jesus as supernatural, superhuman. The life of any man would pass into the life of all men as I have shown must have passed the life of Jesus; but unless that life was a life above that of humanity, it could not redeem humanity, and raise it to a higher life. The merit of the life of Jesus, and the reality of the redemption by him, must be then in exact proportion to his divinity. To deny his divinity would be the denial of all in Christianity worth affirming.

Happily this divinity is easily demonstrated; at least, we can easily demonstrate the supernatural, the superhuman character of the life of Jesus. It is historically demonstrable that the life of Jesus was altogether superior to the age in which he lived. He must then have lived in communion with an object which that age, and therefore nature, could not furnish; that is to say, in communion with an object above the world, above nature, superhuman. Here then is his supernatural character established at once. Then the introduction of his life into humanity was a redemption of humanity. He becomes then our Redeemer, the Father of a new age.

Nor is this all. By virtue of the fact that the life of Jesus has passed into the life of humanity, humanity is able to commune with God. Through Jesus who is our life, we have access to the Father, may come into communion, as John says, into *fellowship*, with him. Then we may live in communion with God, and consequently be every moment deriving new life and strength from him. Thus the life of Jesus does not grow fainter and fainter as echoed by generation after generation, but stronger and stronger, as the path of the just grows brighter and brighter into the perfect day. Hence his life becomes more powerful unto life than the sin of Adam was unto death, and so through Jesus we shall be more than conquerors. This is what Paul means when he says, "not as the offense so is the free gift; for if by one man's offense death reigned by one, *much more* they which receive abundance of grace shall reign through one Jesus Christ." "But where sin abounded grace did *much more* abound." Life is stronger than death and must be ultimately victorious, especially since by virtue of the indwelling Christ, which is our life, we have access to the Father and can renew our life at the Fountain of Life itself day by day.

I intended to adduce a large number of passages of Scripture in support of these views, but I have not room, nor is it necessary. These passages will readily occur to all who are familiar with the writings of John and Paul. They always speak of Christ and Christianity as the Life. "That," says John, in his first Epistle, "that which was from the beginning which we have heard, which we have seen with our eyes, which we have looked upon, and our hands have handled, of the Word of Life; (for the Life was manifested, and we have seen it, and bear witness, and show unto you, that eternal Life, which was with the Father, and was manifested unto us;) that which we have seen and heard, declare we unto you, *that ye may have fellowship with us*; AND TRULY OUR FELLOWSHIP IS WITH THE FATHER AND WITH HIS SON JESUS CHRIST." This is quite to my purpose. But here is a passage more so still. Jesus says, "As the living Father hath sent me, and as I live by the Father, even so he that eateth me shall live by me." *As the living Father has sent me*. The Father hath life in himself, and needeth not others in order to be able to live. This self-living Life hath sent me. *As I live by the Father*. Here is the assertion of the fact that Jesus lives by communion with the Father, and therefore of the fact that his life is indissolubly God-man. *Even so he that eateth me shall live by me*. Eating is merely a figurative expression for partaking, receiving. It is not the literal flesh, for the flesh profiteth nothing, that we are to receive and assimilate, but the spirit, the very life of Jesus. To those who thus receive him, he is the object with whom they commune, and they live by him precisely as he lives by the Father; and as he by living by the Father lives the life of God immediately, so they by living by him do live the life of God mediately.

This view gives new meaning to the doctrine of brotherhood. You have done much to make us all feel that whatever our condition in life, or position in society, we are all brothers, members of one and the same great family. But the doctrine I am bringing out goes even further, and shows us that the relation subsisting between men is actually more intimate than that which we ordinarily express by the term brotherhood. All men are not only members of one family, but they are all members one of another. The life of each man is indissolubly in himself and in all other men. The injury done to the life of one man is an injury done to the life of all men: the least significant member, however incrusted with filth or polluted with sin, cannot suffer but the whole body must suffer with him. Regard for our own welfare and disinterested regard for others may combine then to ameliorate the moral, intellectual, and physical condition of mankind. Here is the doctrine that shall give power to the preacher, the philanthropist, the genuine reformer, whether moral or social.

This intimate relation of all men in the unity of one and the same life, explains the Eucharist or Communion. That rite of the church is not merely commemorative of the last supper of Jesus with his disciples. All Christianity clusters around it, centers in it; for all Christianity is in this one word COMMUNION. Jesus was the living bread which came down from heaven to give life to the world. This Life, the new Life, Eternal Life, the Life by living which we are redeemed from sin and united to God, could be communicated to the world, only by virtue of a communion between Jesus and his disciples, and to the rest of mankind in time and space only by communion with them. The great fact here affirmed is that the life of Jesus is communicated to the world, and spread from man to man according to the very principle of human life itself. It becomes human life, and men become one with Jesus, and one with God, just in proportion as it is lived. Then in order to enable all men to live this life, we must seek to facilitate the means of communion for all men in both time and space. This translated into practical life will be the organization of all our domestic and social institutions in obedience to the strictest order and most unrestrained freedom compatible with order. Nay, our domestic and social order, instead of being a check on freedom, should be so organized as to be the support of freedom, or of man's uninterrupted communion with man, according to the normal wants of his nature and his life.

We may now understand and accept what is said of the dignity of human nature. Taken as we find it today, in the bosom of Christian civilization, it unquestionably has a recuperative energy, even, if you will, a divine worth. My objection to what you have alleged of human nature, is that you affirm it of human nature originally and universally. You and the church in some respects agree. Both speak of human nature today, without intimating that the mission of Christ has in the least affected it. If human nature were always what you say, I cannot conceive what need there was of a Redeemer; if it be now what the church generally affirms, that is, inherently and totally depraved, I am equally unable to conceive what the Redeemer has done.

If there be any truth in the doctrine of life as I have set it forth; if there be any truth in the alleged fact that the Life of Jesus was a new life, a life *above the human life of the age in which he came*; then assuredly has the coming of Jesus redeemed human nature, and communicated to it higher and diviner elements. Human nature is not to-day what it was before the coming of Jesus. In speaking of human nature, meaning thereby the powers and capacities of man, we must have regard to chronology. It is false, what we say, that human nature is the same in all ages. The law of human life is the same in all ages; but that life is never the same for two successive generations, or else where were the idea of progress, without which the whole plan of Providence would be inexplicable? To assert that human nature is the same to-day that it was before the coming of Christ, is to "deny the Lord that bought us;" because it either denies that Jesus has come at all, or that he has come to any effect.

The coming of Jesus has communicated a new life to the race, which by means of *communion* of man with man shall extend to all individuals. This new life has not as yet, we all know, wholly overcome and effaced the death which was by Adam; but it is in the heart of humanity, an incorruptible seed, I had almost said, a seminal principle of divinity. The humanity of today has in its life, which is the indwelling Christ, the Christ that was to be with us unto the end of the world, a redeeming power, a recuperative energy, by virtue of which it is able to come into fellowship with the Father, and thus work out its own salvation. The possession of this principle, this energy, this life, literally, as I have endeavored to prove, the Christ, is that wherein human nature differs now from what it was before Jesus came. Then it had in its life no redeeming principle, now it has. This divinity is not it, but Christ formed within it, the hope of glory. Human nature in some sense then I own possesses to-day the divine worth you claim for it; not by virtue of its own inherent right, but by virtue of its union through the law of life to Christ, who is our head, and who is one with God. This union virtually complete, is actually incomplete. To complete it, and therefore to make all men one in Christ, and through him one with the Father, thus fulfilling his prayer, as recorded in the seventeenth chapter of John's Gospel, is the work to be done, towards which Christian civilization is tending, and to which all true Christians direct all their efforts, individual and social. We may be even far from this glorious result as yet, and we may even be in ourselves weak and inefficient; but the Life is in the world; Christ has entered into the life of humanity; the Word has become Flesh, and dwells among us; and as individuals and as a race we may do all things through Christ strengthening us. We can effect this, because God works in us both to will and to do. By communion with Jesus, we derive life, as I have said, from God himself; we are led by the Spirit of God, are sons of God; clothed upon with a life, majesty, and power, before which the empire of darkness and sin must be as chaff before the wind. We are placed at one with God. All things then are for us. The winds are our messengers, and flames of fire our ministers. Even the spirits shall obey us. Who can set bounds to our power, since our strength is not ours, but God's; since our life is hid in God, in whom we dwell, and who through his Son dwells in us. O, sir, I believe it will prove to be literally true, what Jesus said, "he that believeth on me, greater works than these shall he do." We know little of the power, of the moral force with which to overcome the world, true fellowship of man with man in the life and spirit of Jesus will give us. God is for us, who can be against us? Here, sir, is my hope. The world lieth in wickedness; man preys upon man; discordant sounds of wrongs, outrages and grief and death strike my ear on every hand; but I despair not; Christ is our life, because he lives we shall live also; Christ is our life, a true life, and I fear not but life will finally swallow up death in victory, and the new heavens and the new earth, wherein dwelleth righteousness, become a glorious reality, an everlasting inheritance for the generations of men.

Longer I would detain you; I would endeavor to show that by virtue of the law of life which binds in one indissoluble whole all the individuals of the race in space, time, and eternity, the mission of Jesus must therefore necessarily be retroactive, extending back to the first born man as well as forward to the latest born; thus giving a meaning to what is said of his preaching to the spirits in prison, to the inhabitants of the world before the flood, and also a meaning to the practice of baptizing for the dead, of which Paul speaks. But this would carry me too far for my present purpose. I can only say, that this law of life appears to me to be a key to most of the mysteries connected with our faith. It throws a flood of light on many, very many points, which have hitherto been dark and perplexing. It gives to the whole Gospel an air of reality; nay, makes it a living reality. We get rid of all types and shadows, symbols and myths, representative, symbolical, or mythical interpretations. We are able now to take the Gospel as it is, with docile minds, and in simplicity of heart, in its plain obvious sense, without any mystical refinement or philological subtlety.

For myself, sir, I value the view I have presented, because it removes all doubts with regard to the origin of the Bible. Here is a doctrine of Life contained in the New Testament, which has been asserted, preached, believed, denied, controverted, for eighteen hundred years, unproved, unexplained, and pronounced by all the world to be inexplicable, and held to be a mystery by its most devout and enlightened believers. The latest discoveries of philosophy furnish us a key to this mystery, and instantly it is plain, simple, demonstrable. Now, am I to believe that man could have found out and written, what it has taken the race eighteen hundred years of close study to be able to begin to see the reasonableness of? Believe so who can; I cannot. In this simple fact alone, I see that in writing the New Testament there was employed a superhuman mind, and a mind which after eighteen hundred years of growth none of us can equal. For I see there depths which philosophy is yet in no condition to sound. But when every discovery in philosophy but tends to make more apparent and certain the truth of the Book, can I for a moment hesitate to believe that these depths, when sounded, will be found to contain the richest treasures of divine love and wisdom? The Bible is therefore removed at once out of the category of ordinary books, and I can clasp it to my heart as the Word of God, in which is recorded the truths I am to believe, and contained ample authority for asserting them. Though I have come slowly to this conclusion, do not believe that I have come so slowly as my writings would seem to indicate, as they who know me best can readily testify. I have seemed to the world to have altogether less faith in the Bible than I have really had, because, as you well know, I have for these last ten years been laboring to bring under religious influences, a class of minds to whom the Bible is an offense rather than an authority. All I say now is that the view I have presented, shows so much wisdom and beauty in the New Testament, so much and so profound truth, altogether beyond the age in which the book was written, that I feel more deeply than ever its supernatural character; and am more and more willing to yield to it as an authority. I can take it now all simply, and do not feel called upon to refine away any portion of it.

I have now, I feel, a doctrine to preach. I can preach now, not merely make discursions on ethics and metaphysics. The Gospel contains now to me not a cold abstract system of doctrine, a collection of moral apothegms, and striking examples of piety and virtue. It points me to Life itself. Metaphysical studies have indeed brought me, through the blessing of God, to the understanding of the doctrine, but having come to it, it suffices for itself. I now need to know nothing but Jesus and him crucified. I can shut up all books but the Bible and the human heart, and go forth and preach Christ crucified, to the Jew a stumbling-block, and to the Greek foolishness no doubt, but to them that are called, Christ the power of God, and the wisdom of God. I have something besides abstract speculations and dry moral precepts, or mysterious jargon to offer. I have the doctrine of Life, the Word of Life to proclaim. I have an end to gain; it is to bring men into communion with each other, so that the Word of Life may have free course among them, and be glorified in binding them together in that love wherewith God hath loved us.

I feel too, that I can now go and utter the very word this age demands. That word is COMMUNION. The age is waiting for it. It is sick of divisions, sick of mere forms, wearied and disgusted with mere cant; no better pleased with mere metaphysical speculations; impatient of dry disquisitions, and of cold, naked abstractions. It demands Life and Reality. Away with your formulas; away with your seeming and make-believe! Life and Reality; give us Life and Reality! Life and Reality we can give, for such the Gospel now proves itself to be. The doctrine that man lives by communion with man, and through the life derived from Jesus with God, will bring us together on one platform, in the unity of life itself, and the church will become one in Christ, "from whom the whole body fitly joined together, and compacted by that which every joint supplieth, according to the effectual working in the measure of every part, maketh increase of the body unto the edifying of itself in love;"—the church shall in very deed become one and universal, and be the living body of our Lord, and the race will speak with one tongue, have one faith, one Lord, one baptism. The great doctrine of Life may now be preached, and whoso preaches that will bring the world to the Life, and through the Life save it from death and raise it to God.

Nor is this all. With this doctrine of life, I feel that I may go forth in a higher name than my own. I was wrong some time since, as I was understood, in saying that man should not presume to speak to man authoritatively in the name of God, although I was right in my own thought. What I wished to protest against was, an artificial priesthood, the members of which by virtue of their membership, should deem themselves authorized to speak to us, nay, to command us in the name of God. My protest was against man-made priests, priests after the order of Aaron, whose authority is in their gown and band. These were the priests I said we must destroy, and for saying which my wise countrymen abused me from one end of the Union to the other. But priests in this sense, I say now, away with. They are dumb dogs that will not bark. They are foolish builders that daub with untempered mortar; blind leaders of the blind; spoilers not feeders of the flock. Yes, away with them, if such there be. Let us have priests after the order of Melchizedek; priests anointed with an unction from the Holy One, whose tongues are touched with a live coal from off God's altar; whose authority is engraved by the great head of the church on their very hearts. These are the priests that we want, and the only ones we want,—priests of God's calling, not man's.

Nevertheless no man should attempt to preach unless he may speak in a higher name than his own. Man is a poor, frail worm of dust, and what is his authority worth? Let me speak in my own name, who will hear, nay, who ought to hear? I feel, and so does every man feel, when he rises to preach, that is, if he have any humility, that he is insufficient and altogether unworthy. How can I speak? These are older, wiser, more learned, nay, it may be, better than I. Have I the presumption to stand up to instruct, to warn, admonish, rebuke, exhort? Nay, I cannot. I cannot preach; I can only reason, discuss, or dispute; I must not speak from the height of the Christian pulpit, as one having authority, but from the level of the multitude I address. Every minister, worthy of the name, has felt this. For years I felt it, and never pretended to preach. I addressed the people who came to hear me. I discoursed to them as well as I could, but did not preach. I could not preach. I had no authority to preach; except the laying on of the hands of the presbytery, and that I felt was not sufficient. But now I feel that I have authority, because now I can say "the doctrine is not mine." I have God's truth to preach, and I go to preach it not in my own name, nor in the name of any man, nor any set of men, but on the authority of God's Word. So far as I am true to the doctrine, so far as I am faithful to the Life, I know God will speak through me, and give efficacy to the word.

More I would say, but enough. I have addressed you with freedom, but I trust not with disrespect. I have spoken freely of myself, for I have wished to make certain explanations to the public concerning my faith. I have spoken earnestly, for the view which I have presented of the mediatorial Life of Jesus has deeply affected me. I have been verging toward it for years; some of my friends tell me they had obtained it some time ago from my public communications; but I myself have not seen it clearly until within a few weeks. Had I seen it earlier, the obscurities and seeming inconsistencies with which I have been charged, I think would never have occurred. I have found it a view which clears up for me my own past, and enables me to preserve the continuity between the past of humanity, its present, and its future. More than all this; it has touched my heart, and made me feel an interest in the Gospel, in my fellow men, and in the upbuilding of God's kingdom on the earth, deep as my interest has long been in these subjects, which I have never known before. What before was mere thought has now become love; what was abstraction has become life; what was merely speculation has become downright, living earnestness. God is to me my Father; Jesus my life; mankind my brethren. I see mankind practically divided, worrying and devouring each other, and my heart bleeds at the wrong they do each other; and I have no thought, no wish but to bring them back to unity and fraternity in Christ Jesus; so that we may all be one. My early profession I therefore resume, with a love for it I never felt before. I resume it because my heart is full and would burst could it not overflow. I must preach the Gospel. Necessity is laid upon me, and woe is me if I do not.

Forgive the liberty I have taken, and believe me, as ever,

YOURS, WITH SINCERE RESPECT,
O. A. BROWNSON

NINE

Demagoguism

It is universally conceded, that republics, especially democracies, can subsist only by means of the virtue and intelligence of the people; but it does not appear to have been very generally considered, that democracies, or popular forms of government, which, through suffrage and eligibility, admit the great mass of the population to a share in the administration, have a strong tendency to counteract the very virtues on which their permanence and utility depend.

Our political history, we think, demonstrates this latter position, beyond the reach of cavil or doubt, to all who have accustomed themselves to look a little below the surface of things. Here, in this matter, the boasted maxim of political economy, that demand creates a supply, does not hold good. Looking at what we were in the beginning, and at what we now are, it may well be doubted, whether another country in Christendom has so rapidly declined as we have, in the stern and rigid virtues, in the high-toned and manly principles of conduct, essential to the stability and wise administration of popular government.

We commenced our national existence with many peculiar advantages, and advantages wholly independent of our peculiar political institutions. We began our labors on a virgin soil, in a new country, of vast extent, great

"Party Machinery. Mr. Van Buren and the Presidency. Civic Virtue." From *Brownson's Quarterly Review* 1 (January 1844): 84–104.

internal resources, and remote from the vicious and corrupting examples of the Old World. We were, for the most part, an agricultural people, sparse, not crowded into towns and cities, with plenty of new and fertile lands, easy to be obtained, and yielding a rich and immediate reward to the cultivator. Our wants were few, our manners and tastes were simple, and life with us was uniform and little exposed to vicious temptations. Government had little to do, for all moved on harmoniously, as it were, of itself. It must have been a bad government, indeed, that could, at once, have corrupted us, and hindered our growth and prosperity. So were we in the outset; but so are we no longer. Our population has become comparatively dense; our new lands are exhausted, or have receded so far in the distance as to be no longer of easy access, or attainable at all by the inhabitants of the older States, who have not some little capital in advance. We have become a populous and a wealthy country, a great manufacturing and trading people, as well as a great agricultural people; we are separating, more and more, capital and labor, and have the beginnings of a constantly increasing *operative* class, unknown to our fathers, doomed always to be dependent on employment by the class who represent the capital of the country, for the means of subsistence, and therefore to die of hunger and nakedness, when employment fails them; we are brought, by improvements in steam navigation, alongside of the Old World, into immediate contact with its vicious and corrupt civilization; we are no longer isolated, no longer a simple, primitive people; our old manners have passed, or are rapidly passing, away; our increasing wealth brings in with it luxury, poverty, and distress, as well as refinement, and a more general culture.

Here is what we have become. It is now, under these altered circumstances both of the country and the people, that the virtues of our institutions are put to the test. These institutions have as yet had no severe trial. The peculiar advantages of our position are sufficient to account for all the superiority, under a moral and social point of view, we have hitherto exhibited. But, if, with these advantages, our institutions have suffered us so to deteriorate, will they suffice to restore us to our former elevation? Nay, if, with these advantages, we have, under these institutions, fallen nearly to a level with the Old World, and shown a rapid decline in the stern and rigid virtues, the high-toned and manly qualities we are accustomed to boast in our ancestors, unparalleled in other Christian nations, not excepting even England, to what can we attribute so lamentable a fact, but to our peculiar institutions themselves? The result, to which we have come, is attributable to no slight or accidental cause, but to a deep-seated and constantly operating cause, and this cause can be found nowhere, but in our peculiar form of government.

In speaking of the decline we have experienced in the stern, rigid, high-toned virtues of our population, we are far from implying, or wishing to imply, that we have fallen below even the more advanced nations of the Old World; and, in assuming, that our political institutions, taken independently of the accidental advantages of our position, have not produced such unmixed good as our noisy politicians pretend, we are equally far from implying, or wishing to imply, that we are not even yet in a moral and social condition much superior to that of any other people. What we mean to assert is, that, under a moral and social point of view, we have not maintained our former relative superiority. We are still in advance of the Old World; but by no means so far in advance as we were in the outset; and, considering the many obstacles the several nations of the Old World have had to encounter, and the much we have had in our peculiar position in our favor, we have, relatively speaking, fallen behind them, and show a deterioration, of which they set us no example. France, Germany, England, even Spain, have, during the period of our national existence, made no inconsiderable efforts at national regeneration, and each and all of them have, we believe, commenced the upward movement, while we alone have actually deteriorated.

Assuming this to be a fact, there must be, in the nature of our peculiar institutions, some inherent and permanent cause of this deterioration. And this we solemnly believe to be the case. In this world, good and evil grow together, and often spring from the same root. The matter of vice and virtue, as Milton has remarked, is not unfrequently the same. As you recede from one evil, you strike upon another; and as you secure a new advantage, you expose yourself to a new danger. This has been our experience as a people. We have escaped many, perhaps the heaviest, of the political evils of the Old World; but, in return, have exposed ourselves to evils, from which the Old World is comparatively free. These evils, to which we have exposed ourselves, are by no means so great, or so difficult to guard against, or to counteract, as to induce us, for a moment, to balance our institutions with those of any other people; or to ask ourselves, if we have done wisely in adopting, or shall do wisely in sustaining them. With all the evils to which they expose us, they are the best, at least, for us, that the world has ever seen, or that we can even conceive of. All we insist on is, that they do expose us to evils, which demand our sleepless vigilance, and all our wisdom and energy, to counteract. They will not, as it were, go of themselves, of themselves create all the virtue essential to their wise and just administration.

A delusion had seized the world about the time of our national birth, that all the evils, the human race suffers, are owing to bad government; and that a wisely constituted government will, as it were, of itself cure them. Hence, we fell into the mistake of feeling, that our institutions would take care of themselves, and work out for us, without any special agency of our own, that higher social good towards which our minds and hearts were turned. But bad government itself must have a cause, and can have no cause but the ignorance, the vice, the selfishness, and the indolence, of the people; and the best of institutions will produce only mischievous results, if not wisely and virtuously administered; and wisdom and virtue, in our case, to secure the right sort of administration, must not only be generally diffused among the people, but be brought to bear directly on the administration itself.

Another delusion, at the same epoch, seized the more advanced nations of Christendom; namely, that the people could *make* the constitution, and that nothing was wanting to secure its successful practical working, but to intrust it to the care of the people. The desideratum of the time was to get rid of bad governments, of tyrannical and oppressive rulers. It was felt, that the people, if admitted into the government, would have so deep an interest in good government, that they would never submit to bad government, or suffer the government to become bad; and that their own interest would lead them to resist all tyrannical and oppressive magistrates, and to invest none with power who would not exercise it for the common good. All this was plausible, and taking; but it obviously placed the dependence for good government, not on the virtue of the people, on their sense of duty, and power of sacrifice; but on their *sense of interest.* Their own sense of their own interest would lead them to institute good government, and to insist on wise and equitable administration. But, in throwing a people back upon their sense of their own interest, leaving them, nay, teaching them, to be governed by their own views of their own interest, do we not, necessarily, destroy the very virtues essential to the maintenance of wise and good government? Do we not set up interest as the ruling motive? And, when interest becomes the ruling motive of a people, will not each individual struggle, not to administer the government for the good of all, but to make it a machine for promoting his own private ends?

The principle of the political order sought to be introduced, and on which the statesmen and politicians relied for securing the practical benefits to be expected from government, was to pit the selfishness of one against the equal selfishness of another; or, as we may express it, UNIVERSAL COMPETITION. The principle of competition is selfishness. Leave, then, free scope to the selfishness of all, and the selfishness of each will neutralize the selfishness of each, and we shall have for result,—Eternal Justice, wise and equitable government, shedding its blessings, like the dews of heaven, upon all, without distinction of rank or condition! Truly, this were putting vice to a noble use, and proposing a transmutation of the base metals into the precious, far surpassing that dreamed of by the old alchemists, in their insane pursuit of the philosopher's stone. But the success of the theory would not have given the result anticipated. From absolute negation how obtain an affirmative? Assuming the absolute equality of all, and that, in all cases, the selfishness of one will exactly balance the selfishness of another, the result will be zero, that is to say, absolutely nothing. But assuming the *inequality* of the social elements, and that the selfishness of one is not, in all cases, the exact measure of the selfishness of another, then they in whom selfishness is the strongest will gain the preponderance, and, having the power, must, being governed only by selfishness, wield the government for their own private ends. And this is precisely what has happened, and which a little reflection might have enabled any one to have foretold. The attempt to obtain wise and equitable government by means of universal competition, then, must always fail. But this is not the worst. It, being a direct appeal to selfishness, promotes the growth of selfishness, and, therefore, increases the very evil from which government is primarily needed to protect us.

Nor is this all. Alongside of this principle of universal competition, lay that of RESPONSIBILITY TO THE PEOPLE. Responsibility of the civil magistrate to the people was, no doubt, asserted with a good motive, for the purpose of establishing the right of the people to divest the agents of authority of all power, in case they abused it; and also as a restraint on these agents themselves, who, knowing that if they abused their trusts the people could dismiss them, would be induced, by all their love of power and place, to use their power for the common good. Here, again, the same attempt to convert the base metals into the precious, to make selfishness produce the effects of the loftiest virtue. But the old alchemists did not discover the philosopher's stone. We have not yet discovered any method by which lead can be converted into silver or gold. Selfishness is selfishness, and will be selfish, say and do what we will. And, therefore, instead of taking care not to abuse its trusts, so as not to lose place or power, it only set its wits at work to secure the confidence of the people, by professing the greatest respect for their virtue and intelligence, and a willingness at all times to bow to their will, and to do all their bidding. Selfishness became a courtier, and sought to gain its ends by flattering the sovereign people, and by *seeming* to have no interest but theirs. It would not tyrannize and oppress with the strong hand, by bidding defiance to popular power; but it would do it by sly cunning, by subtle arts, and plunder the people, and enrich itself, by their own consent, at least with their own hands. If it pleased the people, and gained their confidence, it was enough; no matter by what means.

The result, therefore, of making all officers of government, and all aspirants to office, feel their responsibility to the people, has been simply to encourage demagoguism, and to cover the land with swarms of greedy and unprincipled demagogues. To gain place, or power, I must please the people; and the readiest way of pleasing the people, the only way practicable to selfishness, is to flatter them, to defer to them, to adopt their opinions, to take the law from them, and never to resist them, or seek to change their course, let it lead where it may. Selfishness, then, becomes a TIME-SERVER; seeks not for truth and justice, but for what is popular; asks not, What is right? but simply, What will the people say? It has no opinions of its own. It runs athwart no popular prejudice; treads on none of the people's corns; is non-committal on all points on which the public mind has not declared itself; and is tolerant to all incipient errors, for they may become popular tomorrow. It is prudent, sleek, decorous. It has no rough edges, no angular points, and thrusts its elbow into no man's ribs. Its face has a settled smile; and its voice is soft, gentle, insinuating. It is calm, dispassionate, mild, deliberate. It is free from rage, from hurry, and "bides its time." If it fails to-day, it will succeed to-morrow. "The sober second thought of the people" will set all right, and place it at the top of the ladder. Hence, all manly devotion to the truth, all earnestness in the defence of the right, all firm resistance to popular error and delusion, all bold and vigorous efforts to advance the people, and carry on individual and social progress, are out of place, and must be quietly left by the way; for they might endanger our popularity, offend, perhaps, the majority, and prevent us from securing the objects of our ambition.

We draw here no fancy sketch; we are, unhappily, painting from the life. One sees the original everywhere. The evil has become great and menacing. We have lost our manliness; we have sacrificed our independence; we have become tame and servile, afraid to say that our souls are our own, till we have obtained permission of the public to say so, or at least till we have pretty well ascertained that it will not be *unpopular* to say so. The tameness and servility of American literature are almost universally admitted. It has no manliness, no reach, no depth, no aspiration. It seeks to win popular favor, not to correct public sentiment; to echo public opinion, not to form it.

Now this, we contend, is a natural result of the principle of *responsibility to the people*, contended for by our politicians. If you repeat always to your statesmen, "Remember your accountability to the *people*," you must expect them to ask always, not, What is right? but, What is popular? And when you have led your statesmen to do so, made popular opinion their guide, you have made it so for all who aspire to place or power; and then you have made it so for the great body of your whole community, and not in relation to politics only, but in relation to every department of life. Popularity will become the leading object of ambition, and popular opinion the standard of morality. The public will intervene everywhere. The minister of religion will court the public, and the pulpit will soften or suppress the unpopular truth. All will be done with a view to immediate popular effect; and what will not tend to secure immediate popularity will be looked upon as a blunder, or, at best, as a crime. In such a state as this, how can there be the virtue necessary to sustain wise, equitable, and efficient government? In such a state as this we indisputably are; and to such a state as this, if not our institutions themselves, at least the doctrines in regard to them, with which we commenced our political career, have a direct, if not an inevitable, tendency to reduce us. Here is the weak side of our political order, and here is what must always be the result of a political order, which rests for its support on Selfishness, on Interest, on universal Competition, and Responsibility to the popular will. Here is *the* danger to which we are peculiarly exposed, and against which, if we love our country, and desire the prevalence of justice, we must be always on our guard.

It is useless to undertake to deny what we have here stated, and useless to undertake to prove, that popular governments have not a direct tendency to create a multitude of demagogues, and to make what is popular the standard of what is right, or proper to be undertaken. Popular governments are favorable, by the freedom of competition they maintain, to commerce, to industry, to great material prosperity, *for a time*, so long as there remains a large body of the people as yet uncorrupted,—so long as the selfish principle they foster has not yet become universal. But, as soon as this principle, on which they are founded, reaches the heart of the community, and the scramble for wealth, for place, and for power, affects all classes, and becomes universal, all sorts of prosperity come to a standstill, and the state falls to pieces by its own internal vice and rottenness. What are called free states are always marked by a sudden and surprising activity, by a sudden and surprising prosperity, and by almost as sudden and surprising a decline and fall. And this lies in the nature of things, unless, independent of the government proper, there be in the community a counteracting and conservative principle. On this point, if we will neglect the lessons of antiquity, (for our experiment is not so new as we sometimes boast), we do not well to neglect the lessons of our own experience. No man can attentively study our political history, and analyze with some care our popular institutions, but must perceive, and admit, that our state contains the seeds of its own dissolution, and seeds, which have already begun to germinate. Unless the tendency, we have thus far obeyed, can be arrested, and a stronger and more effectual conservative principle be brought in to our relief, all hopes of a successful issue must be abandoned.

We feel how very unpalatable all this must be to our countrymen, and how ill it must be received. It will be easy to ascribe it to our own diseased imagination, or disappointed ambition; it will be easy to ascribe it to a growing distrust of our institutions, to a hankering after other forms of government, or to a love of singularity, or of notoriety. All this it is easy to say, and all this unquestionably will be said, and be believed by not a few. There are a thousand voices interested in silencing the still small voice of truth; and may do so. But, alas! the truth remains the same, and the evil exists not the less, conceal we it never so effectually from the eyes of the spectator. The evil is there. The cancer eats into the very vitals, and death must, sooner or later, ensue. We may say what we will of the physician who warns us of our danger, who bids us seize time by the forelock, and apply the remedy before it has become irremediable; we may dismiss him, and call in another, who will tell us smooth things, that there is no danger, that we may eat, drink, dance, sing, and be merry, as usual; but this will avail us nothing. The cancer is there, and eats, eats, never the less.

But we have not closed the catalogue of our dangers. The root of all is in the attempt, with a mere negative quantity, to obtain a positive, out of selfishness to bring forth virtue. This attempt, as we have seen, makes selfishness the ruling principle of the whole community. The great object of action, then, so far as government is concerned, is to make it the means of promoting, not the public good, but private interest. But to suppose, that it can promote equally the private interest of all, is absurd; or even of a majority. It can, in the nature of things, promote the private interest of only the few. Then there must be some contrivance by which the few can control its operations, and secure to themselves its advantages, in the language of the day, "the spoils." This contrivance, we may express by the word PARTY. There may still be in the country some remains of virtue, some reminiscences of the doctrine, that we ought to seek the public good. They who share these reminiscences might, if free to act according to their own convictions and sense of duty, trouble us, and thwart our schemes. We must control them by means of party organization and party usages, and substitute devotion to party, for devotion to the public, and thus make even the virtues of the people subservient to our selfish purposes. Hence springs up a system of party tactics, from which this country has more to fear, than from any other one cause whatever.

This system, if we have rightly learned it,—and we have learned it from the intimate personal associates of the distinguished man who is at present its most brilliant representative,—is in substance this: In a republican government, everything must be done by means of party. Our first effort, therefore, must be to get, and to keep, our party in the majority. We must never propose any measure likely to throw it, or to keep it, in the minority. If we keep our party in the majority, we can, from time to time, through it, propose and carry such measures as we may judge to be proper, or expedient. Mark this. The *first* object is, not, to find out and support what is for the public good, but, by organization and discipline, to get, and to keep, our party in the ascendency. *After this*, if we can serve the public without falling into the minority, well and good; if not, why just as well and good, provided we only hold on—*to the offices*. Nothing can be worse than this. Regular organized parties, in a republican government, organized with a view to permanence, so as to make it the primary duty of the citizen to support them, are fraught with the greatest danger to liberty. They are contrivances to override the constitution, and to enable a minority to rule the majority. They are machines constructed for the express purpose of centralizing power, for the express benefit of the intriguing politicians, who, by getting hold of the crank, may work then as they please. The only parties really defensible in a free government, are such as naturally and spontaneously spring up, and group themselves around different views of governmental policy. These come when they should, last as long as the difference of policy lasts, and then dissolve of themselves. They come, accomplish their object, and disappear.

But having determined that all is to be done by and through party, and that our primary duty is to labor for the organization and ascendency of our party, the next thing to be insisted on is, *Fidelity to the party, and strict adherence to its usages,*—the surrender of all individual opinions, convictions, and preferences, to the decision of the party, which decision, be it understood, is always to be effected by the aforesaid politicians who have hold of the crank. This throws the whole business into the hands of central committees, and deprives the great mass of the citizens of all free voice in the determination of measures, or in the selection of candidates. These committees, often self-constituted, or, if not, chosen by a feeble minority, arrange everything, and leave to the citizens at large, or to the great mass of the party, nothing to do, but to accept their arrangements, and support their nominations, or to assume the responsibility of throwing the government into the hands of the opposing party.

To keep the ranks of the party full, to prevent members from breaking away and asserting their independence, appeals are now made to the lowest and most corrupting passions of the human heart. The individual, who shows himself a little uneasy, or disposed to kick at the party traces, must be denounced, thrown over, and declared to be an enemy, and no longer entitled to the confidence of the party. Thus men must be kept in the party, and faithful to its usages, decisions, and nominations, not by attachment to its principles and measures, but through fear, that, if they assert their independence, they will lose their share of "the spoils."

Now, fasten this doctrine on the country, and let it become our settled mode of disposing of all political matters, and our liberties, and the whole action of the government, will be at the mercy of the sly, cunning, adroit, intriguing, selfish demagogues, whom our country, as we have seen, has a direct and strong tendency to multiply.

And here, we must be permitted to say, is a strong reason why the American people should pause and deliberate long, before restoring Mr. Van Buren to the high office from which, in 1840, they so indignantly ejected him. It cannot be denied, that Mr. Van Buren is the most conspicuous representative of this system of party management, in the country. The system itself has been perfected, and to no inconsiderable extent was founded, by him and his more immediate political associates. He is intimately connected with it; owes to it all the political elevation he has ever received, and relies on it alone for his restoration to the presidency. He has no hope but in its influence; his restoration would, therefore, be a direct sanction of the system by the American people, and go far towards fastening it upon the country beyond the reach of future redress. In this view of the case, the reelection of Mr. Van Buren, whatever his personal worth, would be a dangerous precedent, and a most serious public calamity.

In 1840, such was the state of certain great public questions, and such Mr. Van Buren's position, that all those of us, who felt deeply the importance of completing the financial policy commenced under his administration, were obliged either to vote for him, or to vote against our principles. But there is no necessity of driving us again to this severe alternative. Moreover, his defeat was not an unmixed evil, for it was not wholly owing to the opposition of the American people to the leading measures, or rather *measure*,—for it had but one,—of his administration; but, to no inconsiderable extent, to the obnoxious system of party management he represented. We are not sure but the determination to get rid of that system—the caucus system—had as much to do in effecting his defeat, as opposition to the Independent Treasury. Men had grown weary of party tyranny, and disgusted with its machinery. That this gave to the Opposition no little of their strength is pretty clearly evinced by the fact, that no sooner were Mr. Van Buren and his caucus system believed to be out of the way, than the Republican party was stronger than ever. State after State returned, and gave their votes for the principles and measures of government, they had persisted, under him and his tactics, in voting down. The whole party, throughout the Union, gave a sudden spring, as if freed from some superincumbent weight, which had hitherto pressed it to the earth, and prevented all free movement. It was a general jubilee; and men seemed to say, "Now republican principles can have a free development, and a certain triumph."

Considerate men, who had stood by Mr. Van Buren, and made no inconsiderable sacrifices to sustain him, felt, after all, that his defeat had its good side, in that it might tend to break up the old party organization, demolish its machinery, and leave men a measure of freedom to labor for the public good. They felt that all was not lost; nay, that the gain might possibly, in the long run, overbalance the loss. Mr. Van Buren, they felt, was out of the way; and this, in itself, was no trifling gain. Hope sprang up afresh, and, in the buoyancy of their hearts, they were disposed to treat him with all tenderness, to tread lightly on his faults, to forget the injuries he had inflicted on the Republican cause, and to magnify, as much as possible, his virtues and public services. His defeat softened prejudice and disarmed hostility, and all were disposed to follow him to private life with marked respect, if not with gratitude. They felt, that, since he was no longer in the field, the disasters of the campaign could he easily repaired; and that the Republican forces, marshalled again, under new leaders, with fresh hopes, and the natural stimulus of recently recovered freedom, would be in no danger of a future defeat. There was reason and justice in all this. But the reappearance of Mr. Van Buren upon the stage changes the whole aspect of affairs. He comes not alone, but as the chief of a band, which the country had devoutly hoped was dispersed, never to be collected again. He comes as the representative of the same old corrupt and corrupting system of party tactics, followed by the same swarm of greedy spoilsmen, with their appetite for plunder sharpened by the few years' abstinence they have been forced, through the remains of the original virtue and patriotism of the country, to practice. Gratify his wishes, restore him to the place he is personally soliciting, and we lose all that was good in the defeat of the Republican party in 1840, and retain only the evil. We restore, what, with an almost unheard of effort, the country had thrown off, and place the Republican party in the condition in which it must be defeated again, or the country be inevitably ruined.

These are, no doubt, hard things to be said of a man who has once filled the high office of president of these United States; but, if Mr. Van Buren had been at all worthy of that high office, they never would have been said; for he would, on his defeat, have retired, and remained thenceforth in private life. The fact, that he is now before the public, soliciting to be restored to that office from which the country ejected him with indignation and disgust, is a proof of his moral unfitness for the place to which he aspires, and of the justice and wisdom of the people in ejecting him. He loses all the sympathy his defeat excited, forfeits all the respect with which generous hearts always follow the fallen, and all the sacredness that ordinarily belongs to those who have filled high office. He stands before us, simply as an aspirant for the highest honor in the gift of the American people, and not an aspirant relying on his own personal merits and eminent public services, but on a system of party tactics and caucus machinery, which cannot be countenanced for a moment, without the most serious detriment to liberty, and the grossest indignity to civic virtue. Under these circumstances, he must expect to have hard things said of him, at least hard things to be *thought* of him, by every man capable of distinguishing between the virtues of the citizen and the virtues of the partisan. He voluntarily provokes the severest censure from every enlightened friend of his country, and of her republican institutions. It is too much to ask us to restore the old caucus system, the old party machinery, and reinstate all the old drill sergeants, by whose means our liberties have been jeopardized, and our Republic brought to the very edge of the precipice. It is too much to expect us quietly, now after so much has been done, to clear the onward path of republicanism; now after Providence has so signally intervened in our favor against those who had for so long a time provoked its indignation, to replace the old impediments swept away by the whirlwind of 1840, by rallying again around the very man, who, of all others in the Union, relies most on these very impediments for success, and who cannot be ignorant, that, if it were not for the party contrivances which stifle the free voice of the people, he would never be solicited to leave, even for a moment, the classic shades of Lindenwold.

We have spoken of the peculiar dangers to which institutions like ours are exposed. These dangers are great and threatening; they have already acquired an alarming force, and seem almost ready to break upon us with overwhelming fury; but we do not look upon them as inevitable, or irremediable. We may guard against them, and shelter ourselves almost, if not wholly, against all ill consequences. But our protection against them is in the virtue of the people, in their firmness to resist the tendency to selfishness, which our institutions themselves naturally generate; and we must add, in their virtue, not merely as *subjects* of the government, but as *citizens*.

Here, where suffrage is so nearly universal, the great body of the adult male population sustain to the government a two-fold relation,—the relation of *subject*, and the relation of *citizen*. As subjects, they are held to allegiance; their virtue is loyalty, and their duty obedience; as citizens, they are constituent elements of the government itself, and share in the administration.

A faithful discharge of all their duties as subjects will not secure the ends of good government. Good government demands, not only strict obedience to the laws, but just laws, and wise administration. The justice of the laws, and the wisdom of the administration, depend on the virtue and intelligence of the people, not in their capacity of subjects, but in their capacity of citizens. The republican form of government will prove a total failure, unless the citizens, acting as constituent elements of the government, carry into its administration loyalty to Eternal Justice; that stern integrity, and disinterested devotion to the public, which will force the government, in all its practical workings, to seek, always and everywhere, the greatest good of each individual subject, whether high or low, rich or poor.

The chief danger, to which our republican institutions are exposed, does not lie in the disloyalty of the people when acting as subjects, but in their venality and corruption when acting as citizens,—in their increasing want of devotion to the public good, and increasing efforts to convert the government into a machine for promoting their own purely private and selfish ends,—each regardless of the evils he may cause it to inflict on others.

This distinction has not, we apprehend, been always made, nor sufficiently insisted upon. The teachers of morality, whether from the pulpit or the press, when insisting on the necessity of popular virtue to sustain popular government, have confined themselves mainly, to the virtue of the subject, that is, obedience to the laws, and the faithful discharge of the several duties involved in the various private relations of man with man; and it is still this obedience, and these private virtues, that our clergy have chiefly in view, when they speak of the necessity of religion as the support of popular government. Here is one great reason why we have so many tolerable subjects, who are grossly corrupt citizens; and why, with no mean share of private morality, we have scarcely the semblance of civic virtue. There has been, with us, in a deeper sense than is commonly implied, a total separation of Church and State. Religion and morality, in a political point of view, afford us little or no protection, because they are seldom brought to bear upon the people in their capacity of citizens. They will be sufficient for our wants, only when we are made to feel by our moral and religious teachers, that we must carry with us, in our capacity of citizens, all the singleness of purpose, all the firmness to resist temptation, and all the self-denial, and disinterested devotion to the Supreme Law, that we are required to have in our capacity of subjects, or private individuals.

Doubtless, the cultivation and growth of our virtues as subjects will tend to strengthen and confirm our virtues as citizens; but, on the other hand, the neglect of our virtues as citizens will tend to corrupt and destroy our virtues as subjects. I carry my selfishness with me into the discharge of my duties as a citizen, and I seek to make laws, or to administer the government, for my own private benefit. But I make the laws. If they are against my interest, why should I obey them? If I obey selfishness in making the laws, I shall be very apt to obey it in keeping them; and if I am corrupt in what concerns the public, I shall not long remain pure in what concerns individuals. We would not underrate the virtues of the subject, but, in their effects, the virtues of the citizen, in a country like ours, are of far more vital importance. The former affect few, and those only for a short period; the latter affect millions, and it may be through a thousand generations. Our religious and moral teachers should, then, bring the whole force of religion and morality to bear upon our conduct as citizens. The citizen, as distinguished from the subject, is a public officer; in voting, he acts in a public capacity; exercises, not a private right, but a public trust; and, therefore, is bound to vote, not according to his private interests or feelings, but according to his most solemn convictions of the public good. No citizen has a right to say, "My vote is my own, and I may give it for whom I please." The consequences of his vote do not concern himself alone. In voting, he acts for others, no less than for himself. It is not, then, what he is willing to submit to for himself, that should govern him, but what he has the right to fasten upon those with whom he is associated. The citizen, who deposits his vote, should, then, do it under a deep and solemn feeling of his accountability, both to his fellow-citizens, or subjects, and to the Great Moral Governor of the Universe. He, who trifles with his vote, trifles with a sacred trust; he who trifles with his vote, or suffers it to be tampered with by others, is as guilty as would be the Christian who should trifle with the most solemn act of his religion. He who gives his vote for the party, or the man, he cannot in conscience approve, and thus aids in fastening, what he cannot but believe an injury, on his country, is worse than a thief and a robber. He is a traitor to his God, his country, and his race. Here, no more than elsewhere, can there be the least compromise with duty, without guilt. To the citizen, as to the man, God says, "My son, give me thy heart." We must be made, as citizens, to feel this, and to act accordingly, or all is lost. Wise and just government cannot long coexist with the utter profligacy of the great mass of our citizens, as citizens. The citizens will impress upon the government their own want of public spirit and integrity. Our great danger lies here,—in our want of high-toned, stern, uncompromising civic virtue.

It is not our design, in this Journal, which is devoted mainly to the discussion of first principles, to mingle in the party strife about special measures or particular men; but there are times, when men and principles are so interlinked, that it is impossible to disjoin them, and treat them separately. Such is, in our view, the present. We have reached such a crisis in our political affairs, that almost everything depends, not on the party which now succeeds, but on the *man* we elect president. The great labor should now be to elect a president of the country, not the mere chief of a party,—a man who will go into office, and reform the administration, and wield the whole force of the government against the spoilsmen, and do all that he can, constitutionally, to arrest the tendency to suffer the politics of the country to lie under the control of the demagogues, as they have been for the last fifteen years. We want a man of high moral integrity, of a high order of intellect, of great firmness, decision, and energy of character, who shall look more than four years ahead; a man who is above all party trickery, and who disdains all appeal to party machinery as the means of his elevation; a man, in one word, the very opposite, in all his moral qualities and party relations, of Mr. Van Buren. We want a man at the head of the government who *is* a man, feeling his accountability to his Maker, and his duty to sacrifice himself, if need be, for the good of his country, and the moral and social elevation of his countrymen.

Now, it strikes us, that it is time for the sound portion of the people, disregarding all old party lines, and laying aside, for the moment, even favorite party measures, to rally around some such man, whether he has heretofore been called a Democrat or a Whig. Greater questions are at stake, than Bank or No-bank, Tariff or Free Trade. The very existence of our Republic, the very existence of our government, as it existed in the minds and the hearts of our fathers, and as capable of being a guaranty of individual liberty and public prosperity, is at stake. If the right man, if a statesman, instead of a partisan, be placed now in the presidential chair, the circumstances of the country are such, that he can give to the political action of the country a healthy direction, and aid in our restoration to civic virtue. He can dash the hopes of the spoilsmen, and rescue the government from those who would make it an instrument of plundering the many for the benefit of the few. We have carried our ultraism, on both sides, far enough, and, go we with the *extreme right*, or the *extreme left*, ruin alike awaits us.

We trust this appeal does not come too late. Sensible men, in all parts of the country, are beginning to feel, that the success of the partisans of Mr. Van Buren, or those of Mr. Clay, representing as they do the opposite extremes, would be fraught with the most serious injury. Corruption has spread far and wide; the two armies of demagogues are marshaled, their drill sergeants are at work day and night; but it is to be hoped, that there is yet a sufficient number not enrolled in either of these divisions, to save the Republic. Let these men, who want justice and free government, make themselves heard before it is too late; let them select their man; let them rally to his support; and they will succeed. If not, if they fail, they will have the imperishable glory of having failed in a noble effort for a righteous cause. But they will not fail. There is a moral majesty in the movements of honest men and firm patriots, before which the unprincipled and corrupt cannot stand a moment. They will succeed. The moral forces of the universe are all with those who contend for the right, and let it not be said, that already the chains of party are so firmly riveted on our limbs, and our lips so closely fastened with its padlocks, that we cannot move nor speak.

TEN

Catholicity Necessary to Sustain Popular Liberty

By popular liberty, we mean democracy; by democracy, we mean the democratic form of government; by the democratic form of government, we mean that form of government which vests the sovereignty in the people as population, and which is administered by the people, either in person or by their delegates. By sustaining popular liberty, we mean, not the introduction or institution of democracy, but preserving it when and where it is already introduced, and securing its free, orderly, and wholesome action. By Catholicity, we mean the Roman Catholic Church, faith, morals, and worship. The thesis we propose to maintain is, therefore, that without the Roman Catholic religion it is impossible to preserve a democratic government, and secure its free, orderly, and wholesome action. Infidelity, Protestantism, heathenism may institute a democracy, but only Catholicity can sustain it.

Our own government, in its origin and constitutional form, is not a democracy, but, if we may use the expression, a limited *elective* aristocracy. In its theory, the representative, within the limits prescribed by the Constitution, when once elected, and during the time for which he is elected, is, in his official action, independent of his constituents, and not responsible to

From *Brownson's Quarterly Review* 2 (October 1845): 514–30.

them for his acts. For this reason, we call the government an elective aristocracy. But, practically, the government framed by our fathers no longer exists, save in name. Its original character has disappeared, or is rapidly disappearing. The Constitution is a dead letter, except so far as it serves to proscribe the modes of election, the rule of the majority, the distribution and tenure of offices, and the union and separation of the functions of government. Since 1828, it has been becoming in practice, and is now, substantially, a pure democracy, with no effective constitution but the will of the majority for the time being. Whether the change has been for the better or the worse, we need not stop to inquire. The change was inevitable, because men are more willing to advance themselves by flattering the people and perverting the Constitution, than they are by self-denial to serve their country. The change has been effected, and there is no return to the original theory of the government. Any man who should plant himself on the Constitution, and attempt to arrest the democratic tendency,—no matter what his character, ability, virtues, services,—would be crushed and ground to powder. Your Calhouns must give way for your Polks and Van Burens, your Websters for your Harrisons and Tylers. No man, who is not prepared to play the demagogue, to stoop to flatter the people, and, in one direction or another, to exaggerate the democratic tendency, can receive the nomination for an important office, or have influence in public affairs. The reign of great men, of distinguished statesmen and firm patriots is over, and that of the demagogues has begun. Your most important offices are hereafter to be filled by third and fourth rate men, men too insignificant to excite strong opposition, and too flexible in their principles not to be willing to take any direction the caprices of the mob—or the interests of the wire-pullers of the mob—may demand. Evil or no evil, such is the fact, and we must conform to it.

Such being the fact, the question comes up, How are we to sustain popular liberty, to secure the free, orderly, and wholesome action of our practical democracy? The question is an important one, and cannot be blinked with impunity.

The theory of democracy is, Construct your Government and commit it to the people to be taken care of. Democracy is not properly a government; but what is called the government is a huge machine contrived to be wielded by the people as they shall think proper. In relation to it the people are assumed to be what Almighty God is to the universe, the first causes the medial cause, the final cause. It emanates from them; it is administered by them, and for them; and, moreover, they are to keep watch and provide for its right administration.

It is a beautiful theory, and would work admirably, if it were not for one little difficulty, namely,—*the people are fallible, both individually and collectively, and governed by their passions and interests, which not unfrequently lead them far astray, and produce much mischief.* The government must necessarily follow their will; and whenever that will happens to be blinded by passion, or misled by ignorance or interest, the government must inevitably go wrong; and government can never go wrong without doing injustice. The government may be provided for; the people may take care of that; but who or what is to take care of the people, and assure us that they will always wield the government so as to promote justice and equality, or maintain order, and the equal rights of all, of all classes and interests?

Do not answer by referring us to the virtue and intelligence of the people. We are writing seriously, and have no leisure to enjoy a joke, even if it be a good one. We have too much principle, we hope, to seek to humbug, and have had too much experience to be humbugged. We are Americans, American born, American bred, and we love our country, and will, when called upon, defend it, against any and every enemy, to the best of our feeble ability; but, though we by no means rate American virtue and intelligence so low as do those who will abuse us for not rating it higher, we cannot consent to hoodwink ourselves, or to claim for our countrymen a degree of virtue and intelligence they do not possess. We are acquainted with no salutary errors, and are forbidden to seek even a good end by any but honest means. The virtue and intelligence of the American people are not sufficient to secure the free, orderly, and wholesome action of the government; for they do not secure it. The government commits, every now and then, a sad blunder, and the general policy it adopts must prove, in the long run, suicidal. It has adopted a most iniquitous policy, and its most unjust measures are its most popular measures, such as it would be fatal to any man's political success directly and openly to oppose; and we think we hazard nothing in saying, our free institutions cannot be sustained without an augmentation of popular virtue and intelligence. We do not say the people are not capable of a sufficient degree of virtue and intelligence to sustain a democracy; all we say is, they cannot do it without virtue and intelligence, nor without a higher degree of virtue and intelligence than they have as yet attained to. We do not apprehend that many of our countrymen, and we are sure no one whose own virtue and intelligence entitle his opinion to any weight, will dispute this. Then the question of the means of sustaining our democracy resolves itself into the question of augmenting the virtue and intelligence of the people.

The press makes readers, but does little to make virtuous and intelligent readers. The newspaper press is, for the most part, under the control of men of very ordinary abilities, lax principles, and limited acquirements. It echoes and exaggerates popular errors, and does little or nothing to create a sound public opinion. Your popular literature caters to popular taste, passions, prejudices, ignorance, and errors; it is by no means above the average degree of virtue and intelligence which already obtains, and can do nothing to create a higher standard of virtue or tone of thought. On what, then, are we to rely?

"On Education," answer Frances Wright, Abner Kneeland, the Hon. Secretary of the Massachusetts Board of Education, and the Educationists generally. But we must remember that we must have virtue and intelligence. Virtue without intelligence will only fit the mass to be duped by the artful and designing; and intelligence without virtue only makes one the abler and more successful villain. Education must be of the right sort, if it is to answer our purpose; for a bad education is worse than none. The Mahometans are great sticklers for education, and, if we recollect aright, it is laid down in the Koran, that every believer must at least be taught to read; but we do not find their education does much to advance them in virtue and intelligence. Education, moreover, demands educators, and educators of the right sort. Where are these to be obtained? Who is to select them, judge of their qualifications, sustain or dismiss them? The people? Then you place education in the same category with democracy. You make the people through their representatives the educators. The people will select and sustain only such educators as represent their own virtues, vices, intelligence, prejudices, and errors. Whether they educate mediately or immediately, they can impart only what they have and are. Consequently, with them for educators, we can, by means even of universal education, get no increase of virtue and intelligence to bear on the government. The people may educate, but where is that which takes care that they educate in a proper manner. Here is the very difficulty we began by pointing out. The people take care of the government and education; but who or what is to take care of the people, who need taking care of quite as much as either education or government?—for, rightly considered, neither government nor education has any other legitimate end than to take care of the people.

We know of but one solution of the difficulty, and that is in RELIGION. There is no foundation for virtue but in religion, and it is only religion that can command the degree of popular virtue and intelligence requisite to insure to popular government the right direction and a wise and just administration. A people without religion, however successful they may be in throwing off old institutions, or in introducing new ones, have no power to secure the free, orderly, and wholesome working of any institutions. For the people can bring to the support of institutions only the degree of virtue and intelligence they have; and we need not stop to prove that an infidel people can have very little either of virtue or intelligence, since, in this professedly Christian country, this will and must be conceded us. We shall, therefore, assume, without stopping to defend our assumption, that religion is the power or influence we need to take care of the people, and secure the degree of virtue and intelligence necessary to sustain popular liberty. We say, then, if democracy commits the government to the people to be taken care of, religion is to take care that they take proper care of the government, rightly direct and wisely administer it.

But what religion? It must be a religion which is above the people and controls them, or it will not answer the purpose. If it depends on the people, if the people are to take care of it, to say what it shall be, what it shall teach, what it shall command, what worship or discipline it shall insist on being observed, we are back in our old difficulty. The people take care of religion; but who or what is to take care of the people? We repeat, then, what religion? It cannot be Protestantism, in all or any of its forms; for Protestantism assumes as its point of departure that Almighty God has indeed given us a religion, but *has given it to us not to take care of us, but to be taken care of by us*. It makes religion the ward of the people; assumes it to be sent on earth a lone and helpless orphan, to be taken in by the people, who are to serve as its dry nurse.

We do not pretend that Protestants say this in just so many words; but this, under the present point of view, is their distinguishing characteristic. What was the assumption of the Reformers? Was it not that Almighty God had failed to take care of his Church, that he had suffered it to become exceedingly corrupt and corrupting, so much so as to have become a very Babylon, and to have ceased to be his Church? Was it not for this reason that they turned reformers, separated themselves from what had been the Church, and attempted, with such materials as they could command, to reconstruct the Church on its primitive foundation, and after the primitive model? Is not this what they tell us? But if they had believed the Son of Man came to minister and not to be ministered unto, that Almighty God had instituted his religion for the spiritual government of men, and charged himself with the care and maintenance of it, would they ever have dared to take upon themselves the work of reforming it? Would they ever have fancied that either religion or the Church could ever need reforming, or, if so, that it could ever be done by human agency? Of course not. They would have taken religion as presented by the Church as the standard, submitted to it as the law, and confined themselves to the duty of obedience. It is evident, therefore, from the fact of their assuming to be reformers, that they, consciously or unconsciously, regarded religion as committed to their care, or abandoned to their protection. They were, at least, its guardians, and were to govern it, instead of being governed by it.

The first stage of Protestantism was to place religion under the charge of the civil government. The Church was condemned, among other reasons, for the control it exercised over princes and nobles, that is, over the temporal power; and the first effect of Protestantism was to emancipate the government from this control, or, in other words, to free the government from the restraints of religion, and to bring religion in subjection to the temporal authority. The prince, by rejecting the authority of the Church, won for himself the power to determine the faith of his subjects, to appoint its teachers, and to remove them whenever they should teach what be disapproved, or whenever they should cross his ambition, defeat his oppressive policy, or interfere with his pleasures. Thus was it and still is it with the Protestant princes in Germany, with the temporal authority in Denmark, Sweden, England, Russia,—in this respect also Protestant,—and originally was it the same in this country. The supreme civil magistrate makes himself sovereign pontiff, and religion and the Church, if disobedient to his will, are to be turned out of house and home, or dragooned into submission. Now, if we adopt this view, and subject religion to the civil government, it will not answer our purpose. We want religion, as we have seen, to control the people, and through its spiritual governance to cause them to give the temporal government always a wise and just direction. But, if the government control the religion, it can exercise no control over the sovereign people, for they control the government. Through the government the people take care of religion, but who or what takes care of the people? This would leave the people ultimate, and we have no security unless we have something more ultimate than they, something which they cannot control, but which they must obey.

The second stage in Protestantism is to reject, in matters of religion, the authority of the temporal government, and to subject religion to the control of the faithful. This is the full recognition in matters of religion of the democratic principle. The people determine their faith and worship, select, sustain, or dismiss their own religious teachers. They who are to be taught judge him who is to teach, and say whether he teaches them truth or falsehood, wholesome doctrine or unwholesome. The patient directs the physician what to prescribe. This is the theory adopted by Protestants generally in this country. The congregation select their own teacher, unless it be among the Methodists, and to them the pastor is responsible. If he teaches to suit them, well and good; if he crosses none of their wishes, enlarges their numbers, and thus lightens their taxes and gratifies their pride of sect, also well and good; if not, he must seek a flock to feed somewhere else.

But this view will no more answer our purpose than the former; for it places religion under the control of the people, and therefore in the same category with the government itself. The people take care of religion, but who takes care of the people?

The third and last stage of Protestantism is Individualism. This leaves religion entirely to the control of the individual, who selects his own creed, or makes a creed to suit himself, devises his own worship and discipline, and submits to no restraints but such as are self-imposed. This makes a man's religion the effect of his virtue and intelligence, and denies it all power to augment or to direct them. So this will not answer. The individual takes care of his religion, but who or what takes care of the individual? The state? But who takes care of the state? The people? But who takes care of the people? Our old difficulty again.

It is evident, from these considerations, that Protestantism is not and cannot be the religion to sustain democracy; because, take it in which stage you will, it, like democracy itself, is subject to the control of the people, and must command and teach what they say, and of course must follow, instead of controlling their passions, interests, and caprices.

Nor do we obtain this conclusion merely by reasoning. It is sustained by facts. The Protestant religion is everywhere either an expression of the government or of the people, and must obey either the government or public opinion. The grand reform, if reform it was, effected by the Protestant chiefs, consisted in bringing religious questions before the public, and subjecting faith and worship to the decision of public opinion,—public on a larger or smaller scale, that is, of the nation, the province, or the sect. Protestant faith and worship tremble as readily before the slightest breath of public sentiment, as the aspen leaf before the gentle zephyr. The faith and discipline of a sect take any and every direction the public opinion of that sect demands. All is loose, floating,—is here to-day, is there tomorrow, and, next day, may be nowhere. The holding of slaves is compatible with Christian character south of a geographical line, and incompatible north; and Christian morals change according to the prejudices, interests, or habits of the people,—as evinced by the recent divisions in our own country among the Baptists and Methodists. The Unitarians of Savannah refuse to hear a preacher accredited by Unitarians of Boston.

The great danger in our country is from the predominance of material interests. Democracy has a direct tendency to favor inequality and injustice. The government must obey the people; that is, it must follow the passions and interests of the people, and of course the stronger passions and interests. These with us are material, such as pertain solely to this life and this world. What our people demand of government is, that it adopt and sustain such measures as tend most directly to facilitate the acquisition of wealth. It must, then, follow the passion for wealth, and labor especially to promote worldly interests.

But among these worldly interests, some are stronger than others, and can command the government. These will take possession of the government, and wield it for their own especial advantage. They will make it the instrument of taxing all the other interests of the country for the special advancement of themselves. This leads to inequality and injustice, which are incompatible with the free, orderly, and wholesome working of the government.

Now, what is wanted is some power to prevent this, to moderate, the passion for wealth, and to inspire the people with such a true and firm sense of justice, as will prevent any one interest from struggling to advance itself at the expense of another. Without this, the stronger material interests predominate, make the government the means of securing their predominance, and of extending it by the burdens which, through the government, they are able to impose on the weaker interests of the country.

The framers of our government foresaw this evil, and thought to guard against it by a written Constitution. But they entrusted the preservation of the Constitution to the care of the people, which was as wise as to lock up your culprit in prison and entrust him with the key. The Constitution, as a restraint on the will of the people, or the governing majority, is already a dead letter. It answers to talk about, to declaim about, in electioneering speeches, and even as a theme of newspaper leaders, and political essays in reviews; but its effective power is a morning vapor after the sun is well up.

Even Mr. Calhoun's theory of the Constitution, which regards it not simply is the written instrument, but as the disposition or the constitution of the people into sovereign states united in a federal league or compact, for certain purposes which concern all the states alike, and from which it follows that any measure unequal in its bearing, or oppressive upon any portion of the confederacy, is *ipso facto* null and void, and may be vetoed by the aggrieved state, —this theory, if true, is yet insufficient; because, 1. It has no application within the State governments themselves; and because, 2. It does not, as a matter of fact, arrest what are regarded as the unequal, unjust, and oppressive measures of the Federal government. South Carolina, in 1833, forced a compromise, but in 1842, the obnoxious policy was reversed, is pursued now successfully, and there is no State to attempt again the virtue of State interposition. Not even South Carolina can be brought to do so again. The meshes of trade and commerce are so spread over the whole land, the controlling influences of all sections have become so united and interwoven, by means of banks, other moneyed corporations, and the credit system, that henceforth State interposition becomes practically impossible. The Constitution is practically abolished, and our Government is virtually, to all intents and purposes, as we have said, a pure democracy, with nothing to prevent it from obeying the interest or interests which for the time being can succeed in commanding it. This, as the Hon. Caleb Cushing would say, is a "fixed fact." There is no restraint or predominating passions and interests but in religion. This is another "fixed fact."

Protestantism is insufficient to restrain these, for it does not do it, and is itself carried away by them. The Protestant sect governs its religion, instead of being governed by it. If one sect pursues, by the influence of its chiefs, a policy in opposition to the passions and interests of its members, or any portion of them, the disaffected, if a majority, change its policy, if too few or too weak to do that, they leave it and join some other sect, or form a new sect. If the minister attempts to do his duty, reproves a practice by which his parishioners "get gain," or insists on their practicing some real self-denial not compensated by some self-indulgence, a few leading members will tell him very gravely, that they hired him to preach and pray for them, not to interfere with their business concerns and relations; and if he does not mind his own business, they will no longer need his services. The minister feels, perhaps, the insult; he would be faithful; but he looks at his lovely wife, at his little ones. These to be reduced to poverty, perhaps to beggary,—no, it must not be; one struggle, one pang, and it is over. He will do the bidding of his masters. A zealous minister in Boston ventured, one Sunday, to denounce the modern spirit of trade. The next day, he was waited on by a committee of wealthy merchants belonging to his parish, who told him he was wrong. The Sunday following, the meek and humble minister publicly retracted, and made the *amende honorable*.

Here, then, is the reason why Protestantism, though it may institute, cannot sustain popular liberty. It is itself subject to popular control, and must follow in all things the popular will, passion, interest, ignorance, prejudice, or caprice. This, in reality, is its boasted virtue, and we find it commended because under it the people have a voice in its management. Nay, we ourselves shall be denounced, not for saying Protestantism subjects religion to popular control, but for intimating that religion ought not to be so subjected. A terrible cry will be raised against us. "See, here is Mr. Brownson," it will be said, "he would bring the people under the control of the Pope of Rome. Just as we told you. These Papists have no respect for the people. They sneer at the people, mock at their wisdom and virtue. Here is this unfledged Papistling, not yet a year old, boldly contending that the control of their religious faith and worship should be taken from the people, and that they must believe and do just what the emissaries of Rome are pleased to command; and all in the name of liberty too." If we only had room, we would write out and publish what the anti-Catholic press will say against us, and save the candid, the learned, intellectual, and patriotic editors the trouble of doing it themselves; and we would do it with the proper quantity of Italics, small capitals, capitals, and exclamation points. Verily, we think we could do the thing up nearly as well as the best of them. But we have no room. Yet it is easy to foresee what they will say. The burden of their accusation will be, that we labor to withdraw religion from the control of the people, and to free it from the necessity of following their will; that we seek to make it the master, and not the slave, of the people. And this is good proof of our position, that Protestantism cannot govern the people,—for they govern it,—and therefore that Protestantism is not the religion wanted; for it is precisely a religion that can and will govern the people, be their master, that we need.

If Protestantism will not answer the purpose, what religion will? The Roman Catholic, or none. The Roman Catholic religion assumes, as its point of departure, that it is instituted not to be taken care of by the people, but to take care of the people; not to be governed by them, but to govern them. The word is harsh in democratic ears, we admit; but it is not the office of religion to say soft or pleasing words. It must speak the truth even in unwilling ears, and it has few truths that are not harsh and grating to the worldly mind or the depraved heart. The people need governing, and must be governed, or nothing but anarchy and destruction await them. They must have a master. The word must be spoken. But it is not our word. We have demonstrated its necessity in showing that we have no security for popular government, unless we have some security that the people will administer it wisely and justly; and we have no security that they will do this, unless we have some security that their passions will be restrained, and their attachments to worldly interests, so moderated that they will never seek, through the government, to support them at the expense of justice; and this security we can have only in a religion that is above the people, exempt from their control, which they cannot command, but must, on peril of condemnation OBEY. Declaim as you will; quote our expression,—THE PEOPLE MUST HAVE A MASTER,—as you, doubtless will; hold it up in glaring capitals, to excite the unthinking and unreasoning multitude, and to doubly fortify their prejudices against Catholicity; be mortally scandalized at the assertion that religion ought to govern the people, and then go to work and seek to bring the people into subjection to your banks or moneyed corporations through their passions, ignorance, and worldly interests, and in doing so, prove what candid men, what lovers of truth, what noble defenders of liberty, and what ardent patriots you are. We care not. You see we understand you, and, understanding you, we repeat, the religion which is to answer our purpose must be *above* the people, and able to COMMAND them. We know the force of the word, and we mean it. The first lesson to the child is, *obey*; the first and last lesson to the people, individually or collectively, is, OBEY:—and there is no obedience where there is no authority to enjoin it.

The Roman Catholic religion, then, is necessary to sustain popular liberty because popular liberty can be sustained only by a religion free from popular control, above the people, speaking from above and able to command them, and such a religion is the Roman Catholic. It acknowledges no master but God, and depends only on the divine will in respect to what it shall teach, what it shall ordain, what it shall insist upon as truth, piety, moral and social virtue. It was made not by the people, but for them; is administered not by the people, but for them; is accountable not to the people, but to God. Not dependent on the people, it will not follow their passions; not subject to their control, it will not be their accomplice in iniquity and speaking from God, it will teach them the truth, and command them to practice justice. To this end the very constitution of the Church contributes. It is Catholic, universal; it teaches all nations, and has its center in no one. If it was a mere national church, like the Anglican, the Russian, the Greek, or as Louis the Fourteenth in his pride sought to make the Gallican, it would follow the caprice or interest of that nation, and become but a tool of its government or of its predominating passion. The government, if anti-popular, would use it to oppress the people, to favor its ambitious projects, or its unjust and ruinous policy. Under a popular government, it would become the slave of the people, and could place no restraint on the ruling interest or on the majority; but would be made to sanction and consolidate its power. But having its center in no one nation, extending over all, it becomes independent of all, and in all can speak with the same voice and in the same tone of authority. This the Church has always understood, and hence the noble struggles of the many calumniated popes to sustain the unity, Catholicity, and independence of the ecclesiastical power. This, too, the temporal powers have always seen and felt, and hence their readiness, even while professing the Catholic faith, to break the unity of Catholic authority, for, in so doing they could subject the Church in their own dominions, as did Henry the Eighth, and as does the emperor of Russia, to themselves.

But we pray our readers to understand us well. We unquestionably assert the *adequacy* of Catholicity to sustain popular liberty, on the ground of its being exempted from popular control and able to govern the people; and its *necessity*, on the ground that it is the only religion, which, in a popular government, is or can be exempted from popular control, and able to govern the people. We say distinctly, that this is the ground on which, reasoning as the statesman, not as the theologian, we assert the adequacy and necessity of Catholicity and we object to Protestantism, *in our present argument*, solely on the ground that it has no authority over the people, is subject to them, must follow the direction they give it, and therefore cannot restrain their passions, or so control them as to prevent them from abusing their government. This we assert, distinctly and intentionally, and so plainly, that what we say cannot be mistaken.

But in what sense do we assert Catholicity to be the master of the people? Here we demand justice; for on this point some of our former assertions have, by a profligate press, been willfully perverted. The authority of

Catholicity is spiritual, not temporal; and the only sense in which we have here urged or do urge its necessity is as the means of augmenting the virtue and intelligence of the people. We demand it as a religious, not as a political power. We began by defining democracy to be that form of government which vests the sovereignty in the people. We weighed our words and knew what we said when we gave that definition. If, then, we recognize the sovereignty of the people in matters of government, we must recognize their political right to do what they will. The only restriction on their will we contend for is a *moral* restriction; and the master we contend for is not a master that prevents them from doing politically what they will, but who, by his moral and spiritual influence, prevents them from willing what they ought not to will. The only influence on the political or governmental actions of the people which we ask from Catholicity, is that which it exerts on the mind, the heart, and the conscience;—an influence it exerts by enlightening the mind to see the true end of man, the relative value of all worldly pursuits, by moderating the passions, by weaning the affections from the world, inflaming the heart with true charity, and by making each act in all things seriously, honestly, conscientiously. The people will thus come to see and to will what is equitable and right, and will give, to the government a wise and just direction, and never use it to effect any unwise or unjust measures. This is the kind of master we demand for the people, and this is the bugbear of "Romanism" with which miserable panders to prejudice seek to frighten old women and children. Is there anything alarming in this? In this sense, we wish this country to come under the Pope of Rome. As the visible head of the Church, the spiritual authority which Almighty God his instituted to teach and govern the nations, we assert his supremacy, and tell our countrymen that we would have them submit to him. They may flare up at this as much as they please, and write as many alarming and abusive editorials as they choose or can find time or space to do,—they will not move us, or relieve themselves of the obligation Almighty God his placed them under of obeying the authority of the Catholic Church, Pope and all.

If we were discussing the question before us as a theologian, we should assign many other reasons why Catholicity is necessary to sustain popular liberty. Where the passions are unrestrained, there is license, but not liberty; the passions are not restrained without divine grace; and divine grace comes ordinarily only through the sacraments of the Church. But from the point of view we are discussing the question, we are not at liberty to press this argument, which, in itself, would be conclusive. The Protestants have foolishly raised the question of the influence of Catholicity on democracy, and have sought to frighten our countrymen from embracing it by appealing to their democratic prejudices, or, if you will, convictions. We have chosen to meet them on this question, and to prove that democracy without Catholicity cannot be sustained. Yet in our own minds the question is really unimportant. We have proved the insufficiency of Protestantism to sustain democracy. What then? Have we in so doing proved that Protestantism is not the true religion? Not at all; for we have no infallible evidence that democracy is the true or even the best form of government. It may be so, and the great majority of the American people believe it is so; but they may be mistaken, and Protestantism be true, notwithstanding its incompatibility with republican institutions. So we have proved that Catholicity is necessary to sustain such institutions. But what then? Have we proved it to be the true religion? Not at all. For such institutions may themselves be false and mischievous. Nothing in this way is settled in favor of one religion or another, because no system of politics can ever constitute a standard by which to try a religious system. Religion is more ultimate than politics, and you must conform your politics to your religion, and not your religion to your politics. You must be the veriest infidels to deny this.

This conceded, the question the Protestants raise is exceedingly insignificant. The real question is, Which religion is from God? If it be Protestantism, they should refuse to subject it to any human test, and should blush to think of compelling it to conform to anything human; for when God speaks, man has nothing to do but to listen and obey. So, having decided that Catholicity is from God, save in condescension to the weakness of our Protestant brethren, we must refuse to consider it in its political bearings. It speaks from God, and its speech overrides every other speech, its authority every other authority. It is the sovereign of sovereigns. He who could question this, admitting it to be from God, has yet to obtain his first religious conception, and to take his first lesson in religious liberty; for we are to hear God, rather than hearken unto men. But we have met the Protestants on their own ground, because, though in doing so we surrendered the vantage-ground we might occupy, we know the strength of Catholicity and the weakness of Protestantism. We know what Protestantism has done for liberty, and what it can do. It can take off restraints, and introduce license, but it can do nothing to sustain true liberty. Catholicity depends on no form of government; it leaves the people to adopt such forms of government as they please, because under any or all forms of government it can fulfill its mission of training up souls for heaven; and the eternal salvation of one single soul is worth more than, is a good far outweighing, the most perfect civil liberty, nay, all the worldly prosperity and enjoyment ever obtained or to be obtained by the whole human race.

It is, after all, in this fact, which Catholicity constantly brings to our minds, and impresses upon our hearts, that consists its chief power, aside from the grace of the sacraments, to sustain popular liberty. The danger to that liberty comes from love of the world,—the ambition for power or place, the greediness of gain or distinction. It comes from lawless passions, from inordinate love of the goods of time and sense. Catholicity, by showing us the vanity of all these, by pointing us to the eternal reward that awaits the just, moderates this inordinate love, these lawless passions, and checks the rivalries and struggles in which popular liberty receives her death blow. Once learn that all these things are vanity, that even civil liberty itself is no great good, that even bodily slavery is no great evil, that the one thing needful is a mind and heart conformed to the will of God, and you have a disposition which will sustain a democracy wherever introduced, though doubtless a disposition that would not lead you to introduce it where it is not.

But this last is no objection, for the revolutionary spirit is as fatal to democracy as to any other form of government. It is the spirit of insubordination and of disorder. It is opposed to all fixed rule, to all permanent order. It loosens everything and sets all afloat. Where all is floating, where nothing is fixed, where nothing can be counted on to be tomorrow what it is today, there is no liberty, no solid good. The universal restlessness of Protestant nations, the universal disposition to change, the constant movements of the populations, so much admired by shortsighted philosophers, are a sad spectacle to the sober-minded Christian, who would, as far as possible, find in all things a type of that eternal fixedness and repose he looks forward to as the blessed reward of his trials and labors here. Catholicity comes here to our relief. All else may change, but it changes not. All else may pass away, but it remains where and what it was, a type of the immobility and immutability of the eternal God.

ELEVEN

Authority and Liberty

A critic in this city expresses surprise that this book could have been written by a young man born and brought up in Kentucky; but we see no reason why it could not have been written by a young man as well as by an old man, and in Kentucky as well as in any other part of the Union. We suppose they read in Kentucky as well as in Massachusetts; and it is not more strange that a young Kentuckian than that a young Bostonian should expend a good deal of thought in elaborating a system compounded of sense and nonsense, truth and falsehood, common-place and crude speculation. The book certainly indicates some natural and acquired ability, but no ability peculiar to either side of the Alleghanies. The substance of it may be read any day in Schlegel, Carlyle, Macaulay, Guizot, Bancroft, and *The Boston Quarterly Review*. We have discovered nothing new or striking in the views it sets forth, or if now and then something we never met with before, it is usually something we have no desire to meet with again.

The author tells us, in his brief *advertisement*, "that it may seem presumptuous for a young, backwoodsman ... to enter the lists with Schlegel, Guizot, and Macaulay." We think it not only may *seem* so, but that it actually *is* so; for Schlegel and Guizot—to say nothing of Macaulay—are at

"*Remarks on the Past, and Its Legacies to American Society* by J. D. Nourse (Louisville, Ky.: Morton and Griswold, 1847), 16mo., pp. 223." From *Brownson's Quarterly Review*, New Series, 3 (April 1849): 138–62.

least men of varied and profound erudition. They are scholars, and have not derived their learning at second or third hand. Mr. Nourse may rival, nay, surpass them, in his ambition and self-confidence; but he must live long, and enjoy advantages of study which neither Kentucky nor Massachusetts affords, before he rivals them in anything else, or can do much else than travesty them. Not that we regard either of them as a safe guide. Guizot is eclectic and humanitarian; and Schlegel is too mystical, and too ambitious, to reduce within a theory matters which by their very nature transcend any theory the human mind can form or comprehend. Mr. Nourse has, if you will, extraordinary natural abilities, an honest and ingenuous disposition; but he has not yet begun to master the present, far less the whole past. He has a vague recognition of religion, concedes some influence to Christianity in civilizing the world; but he is without faith, and has yet to learn the very rudiments of the Christian creed. We doubt, also, whether he is able to give even the outlines of a single historical period, or of a single people or institution, with sufficient accuracy to enable them to serve as the basis of a single sound induction. One should know the *facts* of history before proceeding to construct its *philosophy*. He will forgive us, therefore, if we tell him that we do regard him as not a little presumptuous in attempting a work for which he has in reality not a single qualification. He writes, indeed, with earnestness; his style, though somewhat cramped, and deficient in freedom and ease, is dignified, simple, clear, and terse, occasionally rich and beautiful; but this cannot atone for the general incorrectness of his statements, or the crudeness and unsoundness of his speculations.

With sound premises and freed from the prejudices of his education, we doubt not, Mr. Nourse might arrive at passable conclusions; but he is ruined by his love of theorizing, his false philosophy, and his unsound theology. He may have philanthropic impulses and generous sentiments; he may mean to be a Christian, and actually believe that he is a Christian believer; but, whether he knows it or not, the order of thought which he seeks to develop and propagate is neither more nor less than the old Alexandrian Syncretism, as obtained through German Mysticism, French Eclecticism, and Boston Transcendentalism. Radically considered, his system, if system it can be called, is the old Alexandrian system, which sprang up in the third century of our era, as the rival of the Christian Church, ascended the throne of the Caesars with Julian the Apostate, and fled to Persia in the sixth century, when Justinian closed the last schools of philosophy at Athens. This system was an attempted fusion of all the particular forms of Gentilism, moulded into a shape as nearly like Christianity as it might be, and intended to dispute with it the empire of the world. It borrowed largely from Christianity,—copied the forms of its hierarchy, and many of its dogmas; which has led some in more recent times, who never consult chronology, to charge the Church with having herself copied her hierarchy, her ritual, and her principle doctrines from it. It made no direct war on the Christian Symbol; it simply denied or derided the sources whence it was obtained, and the authority which Christian faith always presupposes. It called itself *Philosophy*, and its pretension was to raise philosophy to the dignity of religion, and to do by it what Christianity professes to do by faith and an external and supernaturally accredited revelation. It was, therefore, Gentile Rationalism, and, in fact, Gentile Rationalism carried to its last degree of perfection. It is this Rationalism, met and refuted by the great Fathers of the third, fourth, and fifth centuries, that lies at the bottom of our author's thought, and which he labors to reproduce with a zeal—we cannot say ability—not unworthy of a disciple of Plotinus, Proclus, and Porphyrius.

This should not surprise us. There is nothing new under the sun. The old Gentile world exhausted human reason; and it is not possible, even with a full knowledge of all the Church teaches, taking human reason alone as the basis of our system, to surpass the old Alexandrian Syncretism, or Neoplatonism, as it is sometimes called. In constructing it, the human mind had present to it, as materials, all the labors and traditions of Gentilism in all ages and nations, and also all the teachings and traditions of Jews and Christians, as well as of the Jewish and early Christian sects and it was, from the point of view of Rationalism, the *resumé* of the whole. It was the last word of heathendom. In it Gentilism, collecting and combining all that was not the Christian Church, exerted all her forces and all her energies for a last desperate battle against the Nazarene, against the triumph of the Cross. Catholicity or Rationalism is, as everyone knows or may know, the only alternative that remains to us since the preaching of the Gospel. Impossible, then, is it to depart from Catholicity without falling back on Rationalism, and, if a little profound and consistent, upon Neoplatonism, as Rationalism in its fullness and integrity. All heresies are simply attempts to return to this Rationalism, and in it they find their complement, as may be historically as well as logically established. All your modern philosophies are regarded as profound and complete only as they approach it. Kant, Schelling, Hegel, Cousin, Leroux, De Lamennais, Hermes, Schleiermacher, Carlyle, Emerson,

Parker, all belong to the Alexandrian school, and only reproduce, more or less successfully, its teachings, and to the best of their ability renew the war it waged against the Christian Church.

It is no objection to what we assert, that the sects and many of the modern philosophies retain some or even the greater part of the Christian dogmas. Neoplatonism did as much. We must not forget that Neoplatonism is subsequent to the Christian Church; that it took its rise in the school of Ammonius Saccas, in the beginning of the third century of our era; that it received its form and development from Plotinus, who flourished about the year of our Lord 260; and that it proposed itself as the rival rather than the antagonist of Christianity. Its aim was to satisfy the ever-recurring and indestructible religious wants of the human soul, without recognizing the Christian Church, or bowing to the authority of the Nazarene. It was not the Christian doctrines, abstracted from the Christian Church, and received as philosophy on the authority of reason or even private inspirations, instead of the authority of our Lord and his supernatural commissioned teachers, that it opposed. It was willing, to accept Christianity as a philosophy, or a part of philosophy; but not as a religion, far less as a religion complete in itself and excluding all others. Hence, it, as well as the Church, taught one Supreme God existing as a Trinity in Unity, the immortality of the soul, the fall of man and the corruption of human nature, the necessity of redemption, self-denial and the practice of austere virtue; that we are bound to worship God, must live for him, and can attain to supreme felicity only in attaining to an ineffable union with him. In the simple province of philosophy it was often profound and just. In many things it and Christianity ran parallel one with the other. Not unfrequently do the Alexandrian philosophers talk like Christian Fathers, and Christian Fathers talk like Alexandrian philosophers. There is Neoplatonism in St. Gregory Nazianzen, in St. Basil, and St. Augustine. The most renowned of the Fathers studied in its schools, as distinguished Doctors now study in the schools of the philosophers of France and Germany. But Neoplatonism was at bottom a philosophy, and whatever it held from Christianity, it held as philosophy, as resting on a human, not a Divine basis. The philosophers transformed Christianity, so far as they accepted it, into a philosophy; while the Fathers made Neoplatonism, so far as they did not reject it, subservient to Christianity, to the statement and explication of Christian theology to the human understanding, keeping it always within the province of reason, and never allowing it to become the arbiter of the dogmas of faith, or to supersede or interfere with the Divine authority on which alone they were to be meekly and submissively received. The Fathers, therefore, were not less Christian for the philosophy they did not reject, nor the Alexandrians the less Gentile Rationalists for the Christian doctrines they borrowed. One may embrace, avowedly, all Christian doctrine, without approaching the Christian order, if, as Hermes proposed he embraces it as philosophy, or on the authority of reason; for the Christian, to be a Christian believer, must believe God, and therefore Christianity, because it is his supernatural word, not because it is the word of human reason or human sentiment, as contend our modern Liberal Christians.

It would be interesting to show historically the resemblance of the whole modern un-Catholic world to the old Alexandrian world represented by Plotinus, Jamblicus, Porphyrius, Proclus, and Julian the Apostate;—how each heresiarch and each modern philosopher only reproduces what the old Christian Fathers fought against and defeated,—how every progress in this boasted age of progress only tends to bring us back to the system which the Gregories, the Basils, and their associates combated from the Christian pulpit and the Episcopal chair; but we have neither the space nor the learning to do it as it should be done. Yet no one who has studied with tolerable care the learned Gentilism of the third, fourth, and fifth centuries of our era, and is passably well acquainted with the modern Rationalism of France and Germany, and the movements of the various heretical sects in our day can doubt that our own nineteenth century is distinguished for its return to Gentilism, and has nearly reproduced it under its most perfect form. These various forms of heathenism had become effete; no one of them any longer satisfied the minds or the hearts of its adherents. An age of skepticism and indifference had intervened, attended by a licentiousness of manners and public and private corruption which threatened the universal dissolution of society. Individuals rose who saw it, and felt the necessity of a general reform, and that a general reform was impossible without religion. But they would not, on the one hand, accept the Church, and could not, on the other, hope anything from any of the old forms of heathenism. The world must have a religion, and could not get on without it. But how get a religion, when all religions were discarded, when all forms of religion were treated with general neglect or contempt?

The Reformers saw that they must have a religion, and, since, none existed which was satisfactory, none which was powerful enough to meet the exigency of the times, they must make one for themselves;—that is, form one to their purpose out of the old particular religions no longer needed. Alexandria was their proper workshop, for there were collected or lying about in glorious confusion all the necessary materials. They began with the assumption, that all religions are at a bottom equally true, and that the error of each is in its exclusiveness, in its claim to be the whole of religion, and the only true religion. Take, then, the elements of each, mould them together into a complete and harmonious whole, and you will have the true religion, a religion which will meet the wants of all minds and hearts, rally the human race around it, and be "The Church of the Future." Hence arose the Alexandrian Syncretism, combining in one systematic whole, as far as reason could combine them, all the known religions of the world, which, under the name of philosophy, but which became a veritable superstition, disputed the empire of the world with Christianity for full three hundred years.

What is the movement of our day, but an attempt of the same sort? By the beginning of the eighteenth century, the various forms of heresy, in which the Protestant spirit had developed itself, and which had attempted to reproduce Gentilism without forfeiting their title to Christianity, had exhausted their moral force, and the age began to lapse again into the old license and corruption. Never in its worst days was there grosser immorality and corruption in the Roman Empire than prevailed in England during the earlier half of the last century, under the reigns of George the First and George the Second. Deism was rife in the court, in the schools, in the Church, among the nobility and the people. Germany was hardly better, if so good; and of France under the regency of the profligate Duke of Orleans, or under Louis the Fifteenth with his *parc au cerfs*, we need not speak. Literature was infidel throughout, and atheism became fashionable. To the rabid infidel propagandism, begun by the English deists, and carried on by Voltaire and his associates, under the motto *Écrasez l'infame*, soon succeeded, as of old, profound skepticism and indifference. Neither false religion nor no religion could rouse the mind from the torpidity into which it sank. Exclusive heresy, or, as we may say, sectarianism, born from the Protestant Reformation, though producing its effects far beyond the limits of the so-called Protestant world, had caused all forms of religion, about the beginning of this century, to be treated as equally false and contemptible.

But, once more, individuals started up frightened at the prospect they beheld. They felt and owned the eternal truth, *Man cannot be an atheist*. They saw the necessity of a general reform, and that a general reform could be effected only by religion. But, disdaining the Church as did the old Alexandrians, and seeing clearly that all the particular forms of Protestantism were worn out, they felt that they must have a new religion, and to have it they must either make it for themselves, or reconstruct it out of such materials as the old religions supplied. The principle on which they proceed is precisely the Alexandrian. To them all religious are equally true or equally false,—true as parts of a whole, false when regarded each as a whole in itself. Take, then, the several religions which have been and are, mould them into complete, uniform, and systematic whole, and you will have what the Editor of *The Boston Quarterly Review*, and Chevalier Bunsen after him, call "The Church of the Future," and Dr. Bushnell and his friends call "Comprehensive Christianity,"—what Saint-Simon denominated *Nouveau Christianisme*, and M. Victor Cousin brilliantly advocates under the name of Eclecticism, borrowed avowedly from the Neoplatonists.

In perfect harmony with this, you see everywhere attempts to amalgamate sects, to form the un-Catholic world into one body, with a common creed, a common worship, and a common purpose. While, the philosophers elaborate the bases of the union, statesmen and ministers attempt its practical realization. This is what we see in "Evangelical Alliances" and "World Conventions," in the formation of "The Evangelical Church" in Prussia, and the union of Prussia and England in establishing the bishopric of Jerusalem. The aim is everywhere the same that it was with the Alexandrians, the principles of proceeding are the same, and the result, if obtained, must be similar. The movement of the un-Catholic world now, how much soever it may borrow from Christianity, however near it may approach the Catholic model, can be regarded, by those who understand it, only as a conscious or unconscious effort to reproduce the Gentile Rationalism of the old Alexandrian school.

The identity of the two movements might be established even down to minute details. The most fanciful dreams of our Transcendentalists may be found among the Alexandrians, either with those who disavowed Christianity, or the sects, professing to retain it, allied to them. The very principle of Transcendentalism, namely, an element or activity in the human soul above reason, by which man is placed in immediate communion with the Divine mind, is nothing but the *Ecstasy* or *Trance* of the Neoplatonists, or their *fifth* source of science; and the Alexandrian theurgy and magic are reproduced in your Swedenborgianism and Mesmerism. Moreover, the Protestant Reformation itself not only involved as its legitimate consequence a return to the Alexandrian Rationalism, but was in some measure the effect of such return. To be satisfied of this, we need but study the history of the Revival of Letters and the controversies of the schools in the fifteenth century. We say nothing of the Revival in so far as it was simply a revival of classical antiquity under the relation of art, or beauty of form, under which relation it was not censurable, but relatively, perhaps a progress. Christian piety and learning can coexist with barbarism in taste, and want of elegance and polish in manners, but do not demand them. The Revival, however, was, in fact, something more than this, and something far different from it. Those Greek scholars who escaped from Constantinople when it was taken by the Turks, and who spread themselves over Western Europe, did not bring with them merely the poets, orators, and historians of ancient Greece, nor merely more complete editions of Plato and Aristotle; they brought with them Proclus and Plotinus, and the old Alexandrian Rationalism, with its Oriental comprehensiveness and its Greek subtlety. They made no attacks on the Church,—they professed profound respect for Catholicity, and with Eastern suppleness readily submitted to her authority; but they deposited in the minds and hearts of their disciples the germs of a system the rival of hers, which weakened their attachment to her doctrines, disgusted them with the barbarous Latin and *un-Greek* taste of her Monks, and the rigid, sometimes frigid, Scholasticism of her Doctors. These germs were not slow in developing, and very soon gave us the Neoplatonists in philosophy, and the Humanists in literature, of the fifteenth and sixteenth centuries. The former destroyed the authority of the Schoolmen; the latter, at the head of whom stood Erasmus, the Voltaire of his time, covered the clergy, especially the Monks, with ridicule, and sowed the seeds of practical, as the others had of speculative infidelity. Combined or operating to the same end, they prepared, and, favored by the politics of the period, produced the Protestant Reformation. Not accidentally, then, has Protestantism from its birth manifested a Gentile spirit, misrepresented and ridiculed everything distinctively Christian, or that it is now undeniably developing in pure Alexandrian Syncretism, gathering itself up a grand and well-organized superstition to wage war once more on the old Alexandrian battleground, with the old Alexandrian forces and arms, against the Nazarene, as Julian the Apostate always terms our Lord. Was it by accident that Protestantism, wherever permitted to follow its instincts, began by pulling down, breaking, or defacing the CROSS, the sacred symbol of Christianity?

The identity of the modern movement with that which resulted in Alexandrian Syncretism may be traced also in the pantheistic tendencies of the day. The Alexandrian school rejected none of the popular gods; it placed Apis and Jove, Isis and Hercules, and sometimes even Christ himself, in the same temple; but all under the Shadow of the god Serapis, the symbol of unity, or rather of THE WHOLE, THE ALL, that is, of pure pantheism, in which all pure Rationalism is sure to end. To what does all modern philosophy tend, but to pantheism? Have we not seen Spinoza in our own day rehabilitated, and commented upon as the greatest of modern philosophers? Cousin's Eclecticism is undeniably pantheistic, and less cannot be said of Schellingism or Hegelism. Socialism, now so rife, is simply pantheism adapted to the apprehensions of the vulgar,—refined and voluptuous with the Fourierists and Saint-Simonians, coarse and revolting, with the Chartists and Red Republicans.

But we are pursuing this line of remark beyond our original purpose. We may return to it hereafter. In the meantime we invite those who have the requisite leisure and learning to take up the subject, and consider the relation of all the ancient and modern sects to Gentilism, the persistence of Gentilism in Christian nations down to our own times, in spite of the anathemas of the Church and the unwearied efforts of the Catholic clergy to exterminate it, and its all but avowed revival in our own day under the most comprehensive, scientific, erudite, subtle, and dangerous form it has ever assumed. In doing this, great attention should be paid to chronology; for *the* Gentilism with which it is the fashion among Protestants and unbelievers to compare Christianity, and from which it is pretended the Church has largely borrowed, will be found to have been formed two centuries and a half after the birth of our Lord. That stupendous fabric, that systematic organization of Gentilism, which we find in the time of Julian the Apostate, and which fell with him, was not the model copied by the Church, but was itself modeled after the Christian hierarchy, and it is heathenism that has *Christianized*, not the Church that has *heathenized*. The Platonism of modern times, whether on the Continent or in England, is not the Platonism of Plato, but of the Alexandrians, as everyone knows who has studied Plato himself in his own inimitable Dialogues, not merely in the speculations of Plotinus, or the commentaries of Proclus.

That our author, born and brought up in the Protestant world, and formed by its Gentile spirit and tendencies, should even unconsciously fall into the Alexandrian order of thought, and labor to reconstruct a system intended to rival the Christian, is nothing strange. In doing so, he only yields to the spirit of the age, and follows the lead of those whom the age owns and reverences as its chiefs. That his system is not Christian, although he would have us receive it as Christian, is evident enough from his *dictum* with regard to miracles. "The miracles ascribed to Christ and his Apostles," he says "however conclusive to those who witnessed them, are no evidence to us, until *by other means* we have established the truth of the writings which record them—that is to say, *until we have proved all that we wish to prove*." There is a sophism in this, which, probably, the author does not perceive. If the writings are the only authority for the miracles as historical facts, that we must establish their historical authenticity before the miracles can be evidence to us, we concede; but not their truth, that is, the truth of the mysteries they teach, the material object of faith, therefore the matter we want proved. The miracles are not proofs of the mysteries, but simply motives of credibility. "Rabbi, we know that thou art come a teacher from God; for no man could do these miracles which thou doest, unless God were with him." Ordinary historical testimony, though wholly inadequate to prove the mysteries, is sufficient to prove the miracles as facts, and, when so proved, they are evidence to us in the same manner and in the same degree that they were to those who witnessed them. It does not, therefore, follow that we must prove, without them, all we want proved, before they can be evidence to us.

But this by the way. The author in his *dictum* asserts either that Christianity is not provable at all, or that it is provable without miracles; but no Christian can assert either the one or the other. The former is absurd, if Christianity came from God and is intended for reasonable beings. God, as the author of reason, cannot require us to believe, and we as reasonable beings cannot believe, without reason, or authority sufficient to satisfy reason. The latter cannot be said without reducing Christianity to the mere order of nature; for a supernatural religion is, in the nature of things, provable only by supernaturally accredited witnesses, and witnesses cannot be supernaturally accredited without miracles of some sort. To deny the necessity of miracles as motives of credibility, or to assert the provability of Christianity without them, is to deny the supernatural character of Christianity, and therefore to deny Christianity itself; for Christianity is essentially and distinctively supernatural. Without the miracles, Christianity is provable only as a philosophy, and as a philosophy it must lie wholly within the order of nature; since philosophy, by its very definition, is the science of principles cognizable by the light of natural reason. Rationalism turns for ever within the limits of nature, and, do its best, it can never overleap them. It can never rise to Christianity; all it can do is, by rejecting or explaining away the mysteries, discard all that transcends reason, to bring Christianity down to itself,—a fact we commend to the serious consideration of all who pretend that our religion, even to the loftiest mysteries, is rationally or philosophically demonstrable. The Christianity they can prove as a philosophy is no more the Christianity of the Gospel than the Neoplatonism of Proclus and Plotinus was the Christianity of the Gregories, the Basils, and the Austins.

The author also betrays the unchristian character of his order of thought in his third discourse, entitled *Spiritual Despotism and the Reformation*. He says, indeed, in this part of his work, some very handsome things—in his own estimation—of the Church; but, as he says them from the humanitarian point of view, on the hypothesis that she is a purely human institution, and therefore a gigantic imposition upon mankind, we cannot take them as evidences of his Christian mode of thinking. If the Church is what we hold her to be, these humanitarian compliments and apologies are impertinent; and if what be holds her to be, they betray on his part a very unchristian laxity of moral principle. An infallible Church, the Church of God, needs no apologies; man's Church, or the Synagogue of Satan, deserves none. But, although the author maintains that the Church was very necessary from the fifth to the fifteenth century,—that she preserved our holy religion, and without her Christian faith and piety would have been lost, Christianity would have been unable to fulfill her mission, and the European nations would have remained uncivilized, ignorant, illiterate, ruthless barbarians,—he yet holds that she was a spiritual despotism, and the Protestant Reformation was inevitable and necessary to emancipate the human mind from her thraldom, and to prepare the way for mental and civil freedom.

According to the author, the spiritual despotism of the Church consisted in her claiming and exercising authority over faith and morals,—over the minds, the hearts, and the consciences of the faithful. If we catch his meaning, which does not appear to lie very clear or distinct even in his own mind, the despotism is in the authority itself, not simply in the fact that the Church claims and exercises it. It would be equally despotism, if claimed and exercised by anyone else, because it is intrinsically hostile to the rights of the mind and to the principles of civil liberty. Consequently, he objects not merely to the *claimant*, but to the thing *claimed*, and rejects the authority, let who will claim it, or let it be vested where or in whom it may.

But this is obviously unchristian. If we suppose Christianity at all, we must suppose it as an external revelation from God, a definite and authoritative religion, given by the Supreme Lawgiver to all men as the Supreme Law, binding upon the whole man, against which no one has the right to think, speak, or act, and to which everyone is bound to conform in thought, word, and deed. All this is implied in the very conception of Christianity, and must be admitted, if we admit the Christian religion at all. The authority objected to is, therefore, included in the fundamental conception of the Christian revelation, and consequently we cannot denominate it a spiritual despotism without denominating Christianity itself a spiritual despotism, which, we need not say, would be anything but Christian.

The author's order of thought would carry him even farther. If the authority of the Church is a spiritual despotism for the reason he assigns, the authority of God is also a spiritual despotism. The principle on which he objects to the Church is, that the mind and the state are free, and that any authority over either is unjust. The essence of despotism is not that it is authority, but that it is authority without right, will without reason, power without justice. We cannot suppose the existence of God without supposing the precise authority over the mind and the state objected to. If this authority, claimed and exercised in his name by the Church, is despotism, it must be, their, because he has no right to it; if no right to it, he is not sovereign; if not sovereign, he does not exist. If God does not exist, there is no conscience, no law, no accountability, moral or civil. To this conclusion the author's notions of mental freedom and civil liberty, pushed to their logical consequences, necessarily lead.

Every Christian is obliged to recognize, in the abstract, to say the least, the precise authority claimed and exercised by the Church over faith and morals, over the intellect and the conscience, in spirituals and in temporals; and it is a well-known fact, that all Christian sects, as long as they retain any thing distinctively Christian, do claim, and, as far as able, exercise it, and never practically abandon it, till they lapse into pure Rationalism, from which all that is distinctively Christian disappears. It cannot be otherwise; because Christianity is essentially law, and the Supreme Law, for the reason, the will, the conscience, for individuals and nations, for the subject and for the prince. If our author's order of thought were Christian, he could not object to authority in itself; he would feel himself obliged to assert and vindicate it somewhere for someone; and if he objected to the Church at all, he would do so, not because of the authority, but because it is not rightfully hers, but another's,—which would be a legitimate objection, and conclusive, if sustained, as of course it cannot be, by the facts in the case. His failure to object on this ground is a proof that his thought is not Christian.

The author's notions of authority and liberty are not only unchristian, but exceedingly unphilosophical and confused. He has no just conception of either, and is evidently unable to draw any intelligible distinction between authority and despotism on the one hand, or between liberty and license on the other. He can conceive of authority and liberty only as each is the antagonist or the limitation of the other; he strenuously confesses that he is unable to reconcile them, and presents their reconciliation as a problem that Protestantism has yet to solve. "To adjust the respective limits of these antagonists,—Liberty of thought and Ecclesiastical authority,—and bring about a lasting treaty of peace between them, is the yet unsolved problem of the Reformation. The Reformers attempted to solve it, and strove in vain to confine the torrent they had set in motion, within certain dikes of their own construction. The spring-tide of free inquiry, not yet perhaps at its flood, is sweeping away their barriers, and ages may elapse before it subsides into its proper channel, after cleansing the earth of a thousand follies and abuses." All this proves that his order of thought is unchristian, and that his conceptions of authority and of liberty are not taken from the Gospel. No intelligent Christian, no sound philosopher even, ever conceives of authority and liberty as antagonists, as limiting one the other, or admits that their conciliation is an unsolved problem, or even a problem at all.

The Christian, even the philosopher, derives all from God, and nothing from man, and therefore escapes the difficulty felt by our author and the Reformers. He knows that authority is not authority, if limited, and liberty is not liberty, if bounded. Consequently, he never conceives of the two in the same sphere, but distributes them in separate spheres, where each may be supreme. God is the absolute, underived, and unlimited Sovereign and Proprietor of the universe. Here is the foundation of all authority, and also of all liberty. Before God we have no liberty. We are his, and not our own. We are what he creates us, have only what he gives us, and lie completely at his mercy. We hold all from him, even to the breath in our nostrils, and he has the sovereign right to dispose of us according to his own will and pleasure. In his presence, and in presence of his law, we have duties, but no rights, and our duty and his right is the full, entire, and unconditional submission of ourselves, soul and body, to his will. Here is authority, absolute, full, entire, and unbounded,—as must be all authority, in order to be authority.

In the presence of authority there is no liberty; where, then, is liberty?

It is not before God, but it is between man and man, between man and society, and between society and society. The absolute and plenary sovereignty of God excludes all other sovereignty, and our absolute and unconditional subjection to him excludes all other subjection. Hence no liberty before God, and no subjection before man; and therefore liberty is rightly defined, full and entire freedom from all authority but the authority of God. Here is liberty, liberty in the human sphere, and liberty full and entire, without restraint or limit in the sphere to which it pertains. Man is subjected to God, but to God only. No man, in his own right, has any, the least, authority over man; no body or community of men, as such, has any rightful authority either in spirituals or temporals. All merely human authorities are usurpations, and their acts are without obligation, null and void from the beginning. If the parent, the pastor, the prince has any right to command, it is as the vicar of God, and in that character alone; if I am bound to obey my parents, my pastor, or my prince, it is because my God commands me to obey them, and because in obeying them I am obeying him. Here is the law of liberty, and here, too, is the law of authority. Understand now why religion must found the state, why it is nonsense or blasphemy to talk of an alliance between religion and liberty, a reconciliation between authority and freedom. Both proceed from the same fountain, the absolute, underived, unlimited sovereignty of God, and can be no more opposed one to the other than God can be opposed to himself. Hence, absolute and unconditional subjection to God is absolute and unlimited freedom. Therefore says our Lord, "If the Son makes you free, you shall be free indeed."

The sovereignty of God does not oppose liberty; it founds and guaranties it. Authority is not the antagonist of freedom it is its support, its vindicator. It is not religion, it is not Christianity but infidelity, that places authority and liberty one over against the other, in battle array. It is not God who crushes our liberty, robs us of our rights, and binds heavy burdens upon our shoulders, too grievous to be borne; it is man, who at the same time that he robs us of our rights robs God of his. He who attacks our freedom attacks his sovereignty; he who vindicates his sovereignty, the rights of God, vindicates the rights of man; for all human rights are summed up in the one right to be governed by God and by him alone, in the duty of absolute subjection to him, and absolute freedom from all subjection to any other. Maintain, therefore, the rights of God, the supremacy in all departments of the Divine law, and you need not trouble your beads about the rights of man, freedom of thought or civil liberty; for they are secured with all the guaranty Of the Divine sovereignty. The Divine sovereignty is, therefore, as indispensable to liberty as to authority.

We need not stop to show that the Divine sovereignty is not itself a despotism. The essence of despotism, as we have said, is not that it is authority, but that it is authority without right, will without reason, power without justice, which can never be said of God; for his right to universal dominion is unquestionable, and in him will and reason, power and justice are never disjoined, are identical, are one and the same, and are indistinguishable save in our manner of conceiving them. His sovereignty is rightful, his will is intrinsically, eternally, and immutably just will, his power just power. Absolute subjection to him is absolute subjection to eternal, immutable, and absolute justice. Hence, subjection to him alone is, on the one hand, subjection to absolute justice, and, on the other, freedom to be and to do all that absolute justice permits. Here is just authority as great as can be conceived, and true liberty as large as is possible this side of license; and between the two there is and can be in the nature of things no clashing, no conflict, no antagonism. How mean and shallow is infidel philosophy!

Taking this view along with us, a view which is alike that of Christianity and of sound philosophy, we cannot fail to perceive that the objection urged against the Church is exceedingly ill-chosen. The Church, if what she professes to be,—and we have the right here to reason on the supposition that she is,—represents the Divine sovereignty, and is commissioned by God to teach and to govern in his name. Her authority, then, is his authority, and it is he that teaches and governs in her and through her; so far, then, from being hostile to liberty in one department or another, she must be its support and safeguard in every department. The ground and condition of liberty is the presence of the Divine sovereignty, for in its presence there is no other sovereignty, no other authority, consequently no slavery. The objection, that the Church is a spiritual despotism, is grounded on the supposition that all authority is despotism and all liberty license,—that is, that liberty and authority are antagonist forces,—which would require us to deny both, for neither despotism nor license is defensible. Authority and liberty are only the two phases of one and the same principle; suppose the absence of authority, you suppose the presence of liberty or despotism, which, again, are only the two phases of one and the same thing. To remove license or despotism, you must suppose the presence of legitimate authority. The Church being the representative of the Divine sovereignty on the earth, introduces legitimate authority, and by her presence necessarily displaces both despotism and license, that is, establishes both order and liberty.

The difficulty which Protestants and unbelievers suppose must exist in conforming reason, which is not always obedient to will, to the commands of authority, arises from their overlooking the nature of authority. The authority is not only an order to believe, but it is authority *for* believing. The authority of reason in the natural order is derived from God, not from man; and the obligation to believe the axioms of mathematics or the definitions of geometry arises solely from the fact, that reason, which declares them, does, thus far, speak by Divine authority. If it did not, reason would be no reason for believing or asserting them. The same Divine authority in a higher order, speaking through the Church, cannot be less authoritative, or a less authority for believing what the Church teaches. Hence the command of the Church is at once authority for the will and for the reason, an injunction to believe and a reason for believing. The absolute submission of reason to her commands is not, as some fancy, the abnegation of reason. Reason does not, in submitting, fold her hands, shut her eyes, and take a doze, like a fat alderman after dinner, but keeps wide awake, and exercises her highest powers, her most sacred rights, according to her own nature. What more reasonable reason for believing than the command of God?—since, in the order of truth, his sovereignty is identically his veracity. To suppose a Catholic mind can have any difficulty in bringing reason to assent to the teachings of the Church, believed to be God's Church, is as absurd as to suppose that an American who has never been abroad can have any difficulty in believing that there is such a city as Paris, or that Louis Napoleon Bonaparte has recently been elected President of the French Republic; or as to suppose that the logician finds a difficulty in bringing his reason to assent to the proposition that the same is the same, that the same thing cannot both be and not be at the same time, or that two and two make four.

It is not the Church that establishes spiritual despotism; it is she who saves us from it. Spiritual despotism is that which subjects us, in spiritual matters, to a human authority, whether our own or that of others,—for our own is as human as another's; and the only redemption from it is in having in them a divine authority. Protestants themselves acknowledge this, when they call out for the pure word of God. The Church teaches by Divine authority; in submitting to her, we submit to God, and are freed from all human authority. She teaches infallibly; therefore, in believing what she teaches, we believe the truth, which frees us from falsehood and error, to which all men without an infallible guide are subject, and subjection to which is the elemental principle of all spiritual despotism. Her authority admitted excludes all other authority, and therefore frees us from heresiarchs and sects, the very embodiment of spiritual despotism in its most odious forms. Sectarianism is spiritual despotism itself; and to know how far spiritual despotism and spiritual slavery may go, you have only to study the history of the various sects and false religions which have heretofore existed, which now exist.

In the temporal order, again, the authority claimed and exercised by the Church is nothing but the assertion over the state of the Divine sovereignty, which she represents, or the subjection of the prince to the Law of God, in his character of prince as well as in his character of man. That the prince or civil power is subject to the law of God, no man who admits Christianity, at all dares question; and, if the Church be the Divinely commissioned teacher and guardian of that law, as she certainly is, the same subjection to her must be conceded. But this, instead of being opposed to civil liberty, is its only possible condition. Civil liberty, like all liberty, is in being held to no obedience but obedience to God; and obedience to the state can be compatible with liberty only on the condition that God commands it, or on the condition that he governs in the state, which he does not and cannot do, unless the state holds from his law and is subject to it. To deny, then, the supremacy of the Church in temporals is only to release, the temporal order from its selection to the Divine sovereignty, which, so far as regards the state, is to deny its authority, or its right to govern, and, so far as regards the subject, is to assert pure, unmitigated civil despotism. All authority divested of the Divine sanction is despotic, because it is authority without right, will unregulated by reason, power disjoined from justice. Withdraw the supremacy of the Church from the temporal order, and you deprive the state of that sanction, by asserting that it does not hold from God and is not amenable to his law; you give the state simply a human basis, and have in it only a human authority, which has no right to govern, which I am not bound to obey, and which it is intolerable tyranny to compel me to obey. "Let every soul," says the blessed Apostle Paul, the Doctor of the Gentiles, "be subject to the higher powers, for there is no power but from God; and those that are, are ordained of God. Therefore he that resisteth power resisteth the ordinance of God. . . . Wherefore be subject of necessity, not only for wrath, but for conscience' sake." (Rom. xiii, 1–5.) Here the obligation of obedience is grounded on the fact that the civil power is the ordinance of God, that is, as we say, holds from God. But, obviously, this, while it subjects the subject to the state, equally subjects the state to the Divine sovereignty. Take away the subjection of the state to God, and you take away the reason of the subjection of the subject to the state; and we need not tell you that to subject us to an authority which we are not bound to obey is tyranny. See, then, what you get by denying the supremacy of the Church in temporals!

The Church and the state, as administrations, are distinct bodies; but they are not, as some modern politicians would persuade us, two coordinate and mutually independent authorities. The state holds under the law of nature, and has authority only within the limits of that law. As long as it confines itself within that law, and faithfully executes its provisions, it acts freely, without ecclesiastical restraint or interference. But the Church holds from God under the supernatural or revealed law, which includes, as integral in itself, the law of nature, and is therefore the teacher and guardian of the natural as well is of the revealed law. She is, under God, the supreme judge of both laws, which for her are but one law; and hence she takes cognizance, in her tribunals, of the breaches of the natural law as well as of the revealed, and has the right to take cognizance of its breaches by nations as well as of its breaches by individuals, by the prince as well as by the subject, for it is the supreme law for both. The state is, therefore, only an inferior court, bound to receive the law from the supreme court, and liable to have its decisions reversed on appeal.

This must be asserted, if we assert the supremacy of the Christian law, and hold the Church to be its teacher and judge; for no man will deny that Christianity includes the natural as well as the supernatural law. Who, with any just conceptions, or any conceptions at all, of the Christian religion, will pretend that one can fulfil the Christian law and yet violate the natural law?—that one is a good Christian, if he keeps the precepts of the Church, though he break every precept of the Decalogue? —or that Christianity remits the catechumen to the state to learn the law of nature, or what we term natural morality? Grace presupposes nature. The supernatural ordinances of God's law presupposes the natural, and the Church, which is the teacher and guardian of faith and morals, can no more be so without plenary authority with regard to the latter than the former. Who, again, dares pretend that the moral law is not as obligatory on emperors, kings, princes, commonwealths, "upon private individuals?—upon politicians, as upon priests or simple believers? Unless, then, you exempt the state from ill obligation even to the law of nature, you must make it amenable to the moral law as expounded by the Church, divinely commissioned to teach and declare it.

Deny this, and assert the independence of the political order, and declare the state in its own right, without accountability to the Christian law, of which it is not the teacher or guardian, supreme in temporals, and you gain, instead of civil liberty, simply, in principle at least, civil despotism. If you deny that the Church is the teacher and guardian of the law of God, you must either claim the authority you deny her for the state, or you must deny it altogether. If you claim it for the state, you, on your own principles, make the state a spiritual despotism, and on ours also; for the state obviously has not received that authority, is incompetent in spirituals, is no teacher of morals, or director of consciences. If you deny it altogether, you make the state independent of the moral order, independent of the Divine sovereignty, the only real sovereignty, and establish pure, unmitigated civil despotism.

There is no escaping this conclusion; and hence we see the folly and madness of those who assert in the name of liberty the independence of the political order, and exclaim, in a tone of mock heroism, "Neither priest nor bishop shall interfere with my political opinions as long as I am able to resist him!" Bravo! my young Liberal; but did you know what you are doing you would see that you are laying the foundation, not of liberty, but of despotism. Hence, too, we see that our author must be mistaken, when he asserts that the Protestant Reformation, in its essential principle, was "a revolt of free spirits against profligate despotism." It was no such thing. Its objections to the Church, reduced to their substance, were simple, the Church is a spiritual despotism because she claims supremacy over reason, conscience, and the state; and it objected to her, not because it was she who claimed that supremacy, but because it rejected the supremacy itself, let it be claimed by whom it might. This our author himself concedes, contends, and proves. Its argument was, the Church of God cannot claim supremacy over reason, conscience, and the state. But the Church does claim this supremacy, therefore she cannot be the Church of God. The principle of the argument is, that God could not delegate the authority to any Church. But if he could not, it must have been because he himself did not possess it. Therefore the essential principle of the Reformation, in the last analysis, was the denial, on the one hand, of the sovereignty of God over reason, conscience, and the state, and, on the other, the assertion of the absolute independence of man, and of the temporal order, which is either pure license or pure despotism, according to the light in which you choose to consider it. The real character of the Reformation was the substitution of human sovereignty for the Divine; and hence, in its developments, wherever it is free to follow its own law, we see it result either in pure humanism or pure pantheism, as it does or does not combine with religious sentiment. And either is the denial of both authority and liberty; for all authority is in the Divine sovereignty, and all liberty in being bound to it alone, that is, in freedom from all human government resting merely on a human basis, whether ourselves, the one, the few, or the many, as everyone would see, if it were understood that authority over myself, emanating from myself, is as human, and therefore as illegitimate, as much of the essence of despotism, as authority over me emanating from other men. Is it not said in all languages that a man may be the slave of himself, of his own passions, his own ignorance, or his own prejudices? Under Protestantism we may have civil and spiritual despotism, or civil and spiritual license, the only two things that man can found, without a Divine commission and subjection to the Divine law; but authority and liberty are possible and can be practically secured only under the divine order represented by the Church, or an institution precisely similar to what she professes to be, the Divinely commissioned teacher and guardian of both the natural and the revealed law.

That this conclusion will be acceptable to our politicians, young or old, we are not quite so simple as to suppose; but we are not aware that it is necessary to consult their pleasure. They have in these, as they had in other times, the physical power to do with us as seems to them good. They can decry us, they can pull out our tongue, cut off our right hand, and at need burn our body, or cast it to the wild beasts; but this will not alter the nature of things, make wrong right, or right wrong. Civil and spiritual despotism is not the less despotism because practiced by them, and in the name of humanity and the people. We desire to have all due respect for them; but we must confess that we have not yet seen their title-deeds, the papers which prove them to have a chartered right from Almighty God to be the sole governors of mankind. We have no authority for pronouncing them infallible or impeccable; we have seen no reason for supposing their ascendancy, freed from the restraints of the Divine law, is either honorable to God or serviceable to man; we have not found them always exempt from the common infirmities of our nature; and we think we have seen, at least heard of, politicians who were ambitious, selfish, intriguing, greedy of power, place, emolument even. In a word, we have no reason to believe that they monopolize all the wisdom, the virtue, the generosity and disinterestedness of the community, or that they never need looking after, and therefore never need a power above them, under the immediate and supernatural protection of Almighty God, to look after them, and to compel them to keep within their own province, to respect religion, and to retain from inflicting irreparable injuries upon society. Even should they, then, clamor against us, or do worse, it would not greatly move us, and would tend to confirm us in the truth of our doctrine, rather than lead us to distrust its soundness or necessity.

We need hardly say that we advocate no amalgamation of the civil and ecclesiastical administrations. They are in their nature, as we have said, distinct, and the supremacy of the Church which we assert is by no means the supremacy of the clergy as politicians. We have no more respect for clergymen turned politicians than we have for any other class of politicians of equal worth, perhaps not quite so much; for we cannot forget that they, in becoming politicians, descend from their sacerdotal rank, as a judge does in descending from the bench to play the part of an advocate. We have bad political priests ever since there was a Christian state, and many of them have made sad work of both politics and religion. We have nothing to say of them, but that they were politicians, and their censurable acts were performed in their character of politicians, not in their character of priests. The principle we assert does not exact that the Church should turn politician, and thus from the Church become the state, or that the clergy should turn politicians; it exacts that both she and they should not. The clergy as politicians fall into the category of all politicians, and their supremacy as politicians would still be the supremacy of the state, not of the Church. The state is supreme, if politicians as such be supreme, let them be selected from what class of the community they may. The principle exacts, indeed, the supremacy of the clergy, but solely as the Church, in their sacerdotal and pastoral character as teachers, guardians, and judges of the law of God, natural and revealed, supreme for individuals and nations, for prince and subject, king and commonwealth, noble and plebeian, and poor, great and small, wise and simple; not as politicians, in which character they have and can have no preeminence over politicians selected from the laity, and must stand on the same level with them. We do not advocate—far from it—the notion that the Church must administer the civil government; what we advocate is her supremacy as the teacher and guardian of the law of God,—as the supreme court, which must be recognized and submitted to as such by the state, and whose decisions cannot be disregarded, whose prerogatives cannot be abridged or usurped by any power on earth, without rebellion against the Divine majesty, and robbing man of his rights. As Christians, we must insist on this supremacy; as Catholics, it is not only our duty, but our glorious privilege, to assert it, and to understand and practice our religion as God himself, through his own chosen organ, promulgates and expounds it.

We know how hateful this doctrine is to politicians, to the world, and to the devil, who seek always to find a rival in the state to the kingdom of God. We know that the representatives of the state in nearly all ages of Christendom, and in nearly all nations, have resisted it, and been encouraged, sustained, in their resistance, by ambitious priests and courtly prelates. We know that it is now resisted by every civil government on earth, that the kings of the earth stand up, the princes conspire together, the nations rage, and the people imagine vain things, against the Lord and against his Christ, saying, Let us break their bonds asunder, let us cast away their yoke from us; but we cannot help that. We know the truth, and dare assert it; we know the rights of God, and dare not betray them. We cannot be false, because others are,—shrink from proclaiming the supremacy of the moral order, because now more than ever it is necessary to proclaim it. We do not understand the heroism that goes always with the popular party, or the loyalty that deserts to the enemy the moment that his forces appear to be the most numerous. We know the moral order is supreme, and shall we fear to say it, lest sinners tremble, the wicked gnash their teeth, and the multitude threaten? We know our Church is God's Church; that she is the judge of God's law, and has the right to denounce, as from the judgment-seat of the Almighty, whoever violates it, and to place king or peasant under her anathema, if he refuses to obey it. She has the right, the divine right, to denounce moral wrong, spiritual wrong, political wrong, tyranny and oppression, wheresoever or by whomsoever they are practiced, and to vindicate the rights of God, and, in so doing, the rights of man, let who will dare threaten or invade them. We are subject to God, but to him only; and are we afraid to assert the fact? Are we not free before all men?

The Church is the Divinely appointed guardian of truth, virtue, liberty, because she is the representative of the Divine sovereignty on earth. Kings and potentates, commonwealths and mobs, may rise up, as they have often risen up, against her; politicians may murmur or denounce, the timid may quake, the fainthearted may fail, the cowardly shrink away, and the disloyal join her persecutors; but that can neither justify them, nor unmake her rights, nor depose her from her sovereignty under God,—make it not true that she represents the moral order, and that the moral order is supreme. That supremacy is a fact in God's universe, an eternal and primal truth, and let no man dare deny it, who would not be branded on his forehead traitor to God, and therefore to man; and let him who fears to assert it in the hour of thickest danger be branded poltroon. It is the glory of the Church that she has always asserted it. She asserted it in that noble answer of her inspired Apostles to the magistrates, "We must obey God rather than men;" she asserted it in her glorious army of martyrs, who chose rather to die at the stake, in the amphitheatre, under the most cruel and lingering tortures, than to offer incense to Jupiter or to the statue of Caesar; she asserted it by the mouth of holy Ambrose, Archbishop of Milan, when he forbade the emperor Theodosius the Great to enter the Church till he had done public penance for his tyrannical treatment of his subjects, and drove him from the sanctuary, and bade him take his place with the laity, where he belonged; she asserted it in the person of her sovereign Pontiff, St. Gregory the Seventh, when he made the tyrant and brutal Henry the Fourth of Germany wait for three days shivering with cold and hunger at his door, before he would grant him absolution, and when he finally smote him with the sword of Peter and Paul for his violation of his oaths, his wars against religion, and his oppression of his subjects; and she asserted it, again, in the person of her glorious Pontiff, Gregory the Sixteenth, who, standing with one foot in the grave, confronted the tyrant of the North, and made the Autocrat of all the Russias tremble and weep as a child. Never for one moment has she ceased to assert it in face of crowned and uncrowned beads: Jew, Pagan, Arian, Barbarian, Saracen, Protestant, Infidel, Monarchist, Aristocrat, Democrat; and gloriously is she asserting it now in her noble confessor, the Bishop of Lausanne and Geneva, and in her exiled Pontiff, Pius the Ninth.

You talk of religious liberty. Know you what the word means? Know ye that religious liberty is all and entire in the supremacy of the moral order? The Church is a spiritual despotism, is she? Bold blasphemer, miserable apologist for tyrants and tyranny, go trace her track through eighteen hundred years, and behold it marked with the blood of her free and noble-hearted children, whom God loves and honors, shed in defence of religious liberty. From the first moment of her existence has she fought, ay, fought as no other power can fight, for liberty of religion. Every land has been reddened with the blood and whitened with the bones of her martyrs, in that sacred cause; and now, rash upstart, you dare in the face of day proclaim her the friend of despotism! Alas! my brother, may God forgive you, for you know not what you do.

But we have said enough to show the unchristian as well as the unphilosophical character of our author's thought, which we are willing to believe he does not fully comprehend, and from the logical consequences of which, were he to see them, we are anxious to believe he is prepared to recoil with horror. His thought is unphilosophical, because it conceives authority and liberty as antagonists; it is unchristian, because it reduces Christianity to mere Rationalism, and revives Alexandrian Gentilism; because it denies the Divine sovereignty, and the supremacy in all things of the spiritual or moral order; because it denies moral accountability, and involves unmitigated despotism or unbounded license as the inevitable doom of the human race. As a philosopher, we hold his work in contempt; as an historian, we deny its authenticity; as a Christian, we abhor it; as a friend of liberty, civil and religious, we denounce its principles, as fit only for despots or libertines.

There are matters of detail in the work to which we seriously object, but, as we have shown the unsoundness of the book in its principles, it is not worthwhile to waste time or argument in exposing them. The author has expanded no inconsiderable thought and labor in constructing his work, but, like all the works which rank under the head of *philosophy of history*, it is shallow, vague, confused, worthless. The writers of philosophy of history may have great natural talents, they may have varied and extensive learning, but they start wrong, they attempt what is impossible, and never go to the bottom of things or rise to their first principles. They never reach the ultimate; they never attain to science; and only amuse or bewilder us with vague generalities, crude speculations, or unmeaning verbiage. There is an order of thought of which they have no conception, infinitely more profound than theirs, which, when once attained to, makes all their views appear heterogeneous, confused, weak, and childish.

We have no disposition to treat our young Kentuckian rudely, or to discourage him by an unkind reception. We know him only through his book. His book is bad, but we every day receive works which are far worse. We do not believe that he means to be a Pagan; we do not believe that he even means to be a Rationalist; we are sure that he does not mean to deny the moral order; and this is much for him personally, but it is nothing for his book. In judging the man, we look to his intention; in judging, the author, we look only to the principles he inculcates. If these are unsound or dangerous, we have no mercy for the author, though we may abound in charity for the man. Mr. Nourse does not understand his own principles; he has not seen them in all their relations, and does not suspect their logical consequences. He has undertaken, without other guide than a few books which, themselves unsafe guides, he has read, but not digested, to do after the study of a few months, what no mortal man could accomplish with all the libraries in the world, were he to live longer than the world has stood. How could he expect to succeed? We hold him accountable for his rashness in undertaking such a task, not for having failed in its accomplishment.

TWELVE

The Works of Daniel Webster

This is a much more complete edition of Mr. Webster's works than has heretofore appeared, but it does not embrace the entire series of his writings. "Such a series," the editor tells us," would have required a larger number of volumes than was deemed advisable with reference to the general circulation of the work. A few juvenile performances have accordingly been omitted, as not of sufficient importance or maturity to be included in the collection. Of the earlier speeches in Congress, some were either not reported at all, or in a manner too imperfect to be preserved without doing injustice to the author. No attempt has been made to collect from the contemporaneous newspapers or Congressional registers the short conversational speeches and remarks made by Mr. Webster, as by other prominent members of Congress, in the progress of debate, and sometimes exercising greater influence on the result than the set speeches. Of the addresses to public meetings it has been found impossible to embrace more than a selection, without swelling the work to an unreasonable size. It is believed, however, that the contents of these volumes furnish a fair specimen of Mr. Webster's opinions and sentiments on all the subjects treated, and of his manner of discussing them. The responsibility of deciding what should be omitted and what included has been left by Mr. Webster to the friends having the

"Boston: Little and Brown. 1851. 6 vols. 8vo." From *Brownson's Quarterly Review,* New Series, 6 (July 1952): 341–82.

charge of the publication, and his own opinion on details of this kind has rarely been taken. The volumes before us should, therefore, be entitled *A Selection from the Works of Daniel Webster*; although it is but simple justice to the editor to say, that the selection has been made with taste and judgment, and we are aware of no omission that any of Mr. Webster's friends will seriously regret, unless it be some of his earlier speeches in Congress, especially the speech on the Conscription Bill. The speeches, addresses, law arguments, and diplomatic and state papers, on which his fame must rest, and which exhibit his character as a scholar, orator, lawyer, statesman, and diplomatist, are all included.

The editor, himself one of our most distinguished scholars and an eminent publicist, has preceded the collection by an admirable Biographical Memoir of the author, written with great judgment and delicacy. It is no easy task to write the life of an eminent man while he is still living, and yet the editor has done it in a manner to satisfy the partialities of friendship, without offending the modesty of the illustrious subject or the fidelity of history. The tone of the Memoir is of course laudatory, but it is subdued, and probably says no more in praise than posterity will ratify. Some few shades may be necessary to render the portrait a perfect likeness, but the judgments passed upon the talents, opinions, and services of the author are, in general, solid and just, such as time will confirm, not reverse.

Mr. Webster is of Scottish extraction, and was born in Salisbury, New Hampshire, January 18th, 1782. He pursued his preparatory studies at Phillips Academy, Exeter, and graduated, August, 1801, at Dartmouth College, in his native State. He immediately entered the office of Mr. Thompson, the next-door neighbor of his father, as a student of law, and subsequently studied awhile in the office of the Hon. Christopher Gore in this city. He was admitted to the practice of the law for the Court of Common Pleas of the County of Suffolk, Boston, in 1805, and as an attorney and counsellor of the Superior Court of New Hampshire in 1807, when he removed to Portsmouth, where he appears to have been immediately and eminently successful in his profession. In 1812 he was elected a member of Congress, and again in 1815. In 1816 he removed from Portsmouth to Boston, which has continued to be his home ever since, although, when not called away by his official duties, he for a few years past has usually resided on his farm in Marshfield, in the Old Colony. In 1820 he was chosen a member of the Convention called to revise the Constitution of this Commonwealth, and in the autumn of 1822 was elected a member of the Eighteenth Congress, from Boston. Since then, with scarcely an interval, he has been connected with the general government, as Representative, Senator, or Secretary of State, and has, during the whole period of nearly forty years, been identified with the public history of his country, and exerted a large share of influence on our public policy.

It is not our purpose, in the few remarks we propose to offer on the occasion of a new edition of Mr. Webster's works, to speak at much length of his character as a lawyer or as a statesman. As a statesman, we have often spoken of him, and perhaps enough has been said. He has proved himself one of the very few American statesmen who are able to compare favorably with the higher class of European statesmen, and his views are such as may be honestly commended, with very slight exceptions, for their patriotism, comprehensiveness, and practical wisdom. It is rare that we should now, whatever may have been the case formerly, dissent from his domestic policy; but his foreign policy, although more in accordance with the general sentiment of the great body of his countrymen than the one we should approve, appears to us, in some respects, narrow and illiberal, wrong in principle and dangerous in tendency. In his judgment of the Continental monarchical states he is still a disciple of the eighteenth century, a believer, substantially, in the *contrât social*, and what is called a Liberal. He is not, intentionally, a Jacobin, or a Red Republican, and would, most likely, had he been old enough at the time, have sided with Burke in his denunciation of the old French Revolution; but he would, nevertheless, have denounced it in its excesses, rather than in its principle. He and the Jacobin have the same point of departure, and differ only in this,—that the Jacobin will carry out the principle common to them both logically to its last consequence, while Mr. Webster, restrained by his good sense and practical wisdom, shrinks from going so far, and attempts to stop short of the proper logical extreme, apparently not perceiving that a principle that will not bear being pushed to its last logical conclusion is false, and ought not to be admitted at all.

Mr. Webster is, perhaps, not vehemently opposed to what may be called a parliamentary or representative monarchy,—we say not, as he would, *constitutional* monarchy, for every monarchy that governs by laws is a constitutional, even a limited monarchy;—but he evidently understands by a constitutional monarchy a representative or parliamentary monarchy, and recognizes the strict legality of no monarchical government unless it is, to use the expression of Lafayette, a monarchy surrounded by republican institutions, or a monarchy compelled to govern in conjunction with a parliament, in one or both of its branches chosen by popular suffrage. No government that does not recognize in some form the democratic element, or rather the sovereignty of the people, in the Jacobinical sense, is, in his view, a strictly legal or legitimate government. Hence, without sympathizing with the socialistic tendencies of the age in their developments, and without wishing in the least to weaken the foundations of law and of order, he is the determined enemy of all the monarchical governments of Europe which are not based on popular sovereignty, and do not rule by means of parliaments or representative assemblies; and he holds it the duty of our government to exert all the influence it can on and through public opinion in encouragement and aid of the party, in all monarchical countries, exerting themselves to revolutionize them, and establish popular institutions in their place.

Mr. Webster evidently adopts the Canning policy, adopted and pursued with such disastrous success during the last twenty years by Mr. Canning's pupil, Lord Palmerston, late Foreign Secretary of the British government,— the policy of intervention, if not by armed force, at least by diplomacy and public opinion, by exertions to create and foster a public opinion everywhere hostile to strictly monarchical governments, and by encouraging the subjects of such governments to make illegal efforts to subvert them. Mr. Canning and Lord Palmerston adopted and pursued this policy for the sake of introducing into every European Continental state the parliamentary system of Great Britain; Mr. Webster, perhaps, would have little choice whether that system or our own were introduced, but one or the other he insists upon, as we may collect from his speech in Congress on the affairs of Greece in 1823, and his remarkable letter to Chevalier Hülsemann, in December, 1850, in defence of General Taylor's administration for sending Mr. Dudley Mann to treat, if he had a chance, with the rebellious Hungarians, then in arms against their sovereign. We need not say that we regard this policy as, repugnant to the laws of nations, and as founded upon a false theory of the origin and principles of government. The sovereignty of the people, in the Jacobinical sense, is not a truth, and can be consistently asserted by no man who does not deny the existence of God. Its assertion is the assertion of atheism in politics, and hence every system of policy which presupposes it must be condemned by everyone who believes in God and understands himself.

When Mr. Webster speaks as a lawyer, according to the principles and maxims of the Common Law, what he says is remarkable for its good sense, its profound truth, and its practical wisdom; for then he speaks in accordance with the teachings of our holy religion, which forms the basis of that law; but when he leaves that and undertakes to discuss questions which lie further back, he is the disciple of Hampden, Sydney, Locke, and Rousseau, and proceeds from principles which he did not learn from the law, and which are utterly repugnant to it. This is not a peculiarity of Mr. Webster; it was equally the case with the elder Adams, and, indeed, with the whole of the old Federal party; and it was this that prostrated them, notwithstanding their personal respectability and practical wisdom, before their less scrupulous, but more logical and self-consistent rivals, headed by Thomas Jefferson. They were *via media* men, adopting two contradictory sets of principles, and laboring to reconcile them by stopping half way with each; while their rivals had but one set of principles, which they were prepared to follow whithersoever they should lead. Hence Federalism, inferior in a logical, but far superior in a practical point of view, or in practical wisdom and common sense, was obliged to succumb to virtual Jacobinism, greatly to the permanent injury, perhaps to the ultimate ruin, of the country,—certainly much to the regret of every intelligent and true-hearted American.

We own that we admire the English constitution as it originally existed, but we do not admire it in its present state. In the original constitution of England the democratic element in the modern sense, or rather the Jacobinical element, had no place, and the sovereign people were simply the King and Parliament. The excellence of the system consisted in its being a government of estates. The House of Commons did not represent the people of England, but the Commons Estate, with a negative on each of the other estates. The positive power was in the crown, which had the initiative of all measures, and the power of the Lords and Commons was, properly, only a negative power, or the veto which each could place on those measures of the positive power,—the Lords by refusing to advise them or to assent to them, and the Commons by refusing to vote the supplies. Thus the unity and efficiency of the government were preserved, while ample security against its power to oppress either the nobility or the commonalty was provided. But Parliament has now virtually usurped the positive power of government, and indeed formally; for, if we mistake not, the initiative of measures is no longer the exclusive prerogative of the crown, and since the Reform Bill of 1832, the House of Commons has very nearly become a representative assembly in the democratic sense,—representing not simply an estate, but the people of England. It may not do this perfectly as yet, but the clamor and agitation for reform will be continued till it does, and then, when the House of Commons represents, not the Commons Estate; but the English people, the king and peers will be found to be mere excrescences on the body politic; they will then be lopped off, and Great Britain will become a pure democracy, and thence a pure anarchy. The tendency to a pure democracy is now fearfully strong, and a democratic revolution in that country is not an improbable, perhaps not a distant event. Mr. Canning's policy, so steadily pursued by Lord Palmerston, of encouraging democratic revolutions abroad, has reacted and is reacting with terrible force upon England herself, and can hardly fail to produce there the evils it has produced in such abundance on the Continent, especially in the Spanish and Italian peninsulas.

We sympathize fully with Mr. Webster in his love of liberty, and perhaps we should be found, in case of trial, a more unflinching enemy than he of despotism of every kind; but we think he falls into the common mistake of identifying liberty with popular institutions. It is a narrow and unstatesmanlike view to suppose that liberty is possible only where the people are represented in parliament, or have a positive power in enacting the laws under which they are to live. Liberty, we grant, is not possible under a despotism, that is, a government of mere will; but it is possible under any and every government that is a government of laws, where the sovereign governs only by a fixed code, or in accordance with laws previously enacted and promulgated, as is the case with every Christian or nominally Christian government in Europe, even with that of Russia. Laws prejudicial to individual liberty may, no doubt, be enacted and promulgated by governments constituted like the Prussian, the Russian, or the Austrian, and so they may be under governments constituted like the English, or even our own, as we may see in the Ecclesiastical Titles Bill enacted by the British Parliament, and in the " Maine Liquor Law," recently enacted by several of the States of the Union, and among the rest by the free and liberty-loving Massachusetts; for you shall in vain search the archives of the most despotic states of Europe to find enactments more repugnant, at least in principle, to the liberty of the subject, or more really arbitrary in their nature. Parliamentary governments with a king, as, in Great Britain, or without a king, as with us, are a clumsy and a very expensive sort of government, and it is perhaps chiefly prejudice on our part that makes us regard them as necessarily superior, in themselves considered, to all other governments. Whether the state of our country and the habits of our people, which unquestionably demand such government and render every other unwise and impracticable for us, be a real advantage, or in fact only a disadvantage, is a question on which something may be said on both sides. Perhaps the fact that none but a republican government, resting for its basis on universal suffrage, is practicable or to be thought of for our country, is not, after all, any conclusive proof in itself that we are so much in advance of other nations as we commonly suppose. We are not certain that France, if she were prepared for a republic like ours, as she evidently is not, could be said to be farther advanced in civilization than she now is, or than she was under Louis the Fourteenth or Louis the Ninth. A nation's rank in the scale of civilization is determined, not by the mere form of its government, but by the wisdom and justice of its laws, and the alacrity and fidelity with which they are obeyed. In encouraging the subjects of the European Continental states to rebel against their sovereigns, for the purpose of introducing parliamentary or representative governments, whether in the English or American form, it is far from being certain that we are encouraging them to effect a change for the better. God, in his providence, gives to each people the political constitution that is best adapted to its character and wants, and experience as well as philosophy makes it pretty certain that every fundamental change in that constitution invariably becomes a prolific source of evil. Mr. Webster's policy, that our government should take its stand on the side of modern Liberalism, and exert itself officially to create, throughout the world, and in monarchical states, a public opinion hostile to monarchy, and through that public opinion to cherish movements for popular institutions, is not, in our judgment, a policy likely to serve either the cause of good government or that of true liberty.

Mr. Webster is a lawyer, and we are surprised that he should attribute the freedom and prosperity of our citizens to our political institutions, instead of attributing them, as should be done, to the Common Law, or the system of jurisprudence brought here by our fathers, and inherited from the England that was before the Reformation. It is the Common Law, with the independent judiciary under it, which Mr. Webster has on more occasions than one so nobly and so powerfully defended, that constitutes the real ground and support of our liberties. Take away the Common Law, either by substituting a written code for it, or by suffering its principles to be tampered with by the legislatures of the several States, as has been done in those that have adopted the Maine Liquor Law, for instance, and destroy the independence of the judiciary by rendering the judges elective for a brief term of office, and reeligible, and you will soon find that your political forms are impotent to preserve the freedom and prosperity of the citizen. Yet an independent judiciary is discovered to be antidemocratic, and the tendency is now everywhere to sweep it away; public opinion is setting in with a strong tide against the Common Law, and it is discovered to be democratic to abolish it, and substitute for it an inflexible written code, with new and inept systems of practice, which, while they increase litigation, render justice generally unattainable, except by mere chance.

But be all this as it may, the policy which Mr. Webster has adopted from Mr. Canning is in our judgment unjust, and repugnant to the laws of nations. It assumes for us a sort of dictatorship, or at least supervisorship, over other nations, wholly incompatible with their dignity and independence. We will not say that the government is not free to express officially its opinion, whatever it may be, on a fact accomplished in a foreign independent nation, but it has no right to express an official opinion for the purpose of bringing about a violent change in its form of government, except in those cases in which, if it deemed it expedient, it would have the right to support its opinion by an armed force, or a declaration of war. A government may express its opinion on a revolution in a foreign state when once really effected, and, unless bound by treaty to do otherwise, may treat the revolutionary government, or government *de facto*, as the legitimate government of the state; but it has no right to express any official opinion for the purpose of effecting, or causing to be effected, a revolution. There is no difference in principle between effecting a revolution by expressly creating a public opinion that brings it about, and effecting it by direct intervention with armed force. The means by which you effect a revolution cannot justify your effecting it, unless you have the sovereign right to effect it; and if you have the sovereign right to effect it, you may effect it by armed force, if you choose. It is an admitted principle in international law, that every independent nation has the right to choose its own form of government, and to determine its own domestic institutions, without the dictation or interference of its neighbors; and also, that nations exist to each other only in their supreme government, or political sovereign. There can be no right, then, on the part of one independent nation, to intervene in any way in the domestic affairs of another, for the purpose of revolutionizing or changing its government. It has no right officially to address the people of a foreign state, or to hold any official communication with them, save through its sovereign, and it gives just cause of complaint whenever it attempts to do so.

This rule is founded in natural justice, and is necessary for the peace and happiness of mankind. It is as much for our interest to observe this rule, as it is for that of any other nation. We cannot assert the right of rebellion, and encourage the subjects of other states to conspire against their sovereign, without weakening the loyalty of our own citizens, and paving the way for a revolution at home, that is, such a revolution as is possible with us. A rebellion against the constituted authorities, except in certain localities and for a brief moment, is not possible in this country, because the power is already in the hands of the people, and the government is subject to their will. A revolution here must necessarily assume the form of removing the restrictions imposed by the law of the land on the exercise of the popular will, or, in other words, of destroying the independence of the judiciary, and abolishing the Common Law. The Common Law, which we have inherited from our English ancestors, is the law of the land, and the law that regulates the relations not only between individual and individual, but to some extent between the citizen and the state. It is our rule of justice, and as no constitution or legislative enactment has, or can have, the force of law, if contrary to justice, it follows that any constitutional provision or legislative enactment repugnant to the principles of the Common Law is *ipso facto* null and void, and may be declared so and set aside by the Common Law courts. This Mr. Webster has himself proved, if we understand him, in a most triumphant manner, in his masterly argument in the Supreme Court of the United States in the Dartmouth College case,—an argument which does him the highest honor, and which ought to be read and meditated at least once a year by every American citizen. The revolution we have to dread is not a revolution avowedly for the purpose of overthrowing the government, or changing its form, but a revolution which abolishes the Common Law, and leaves us no restraints on lawless power, and no standard of justice but the will or caprice of the majority for the time being. This revolution has commenced and is in process amongst us, and every word we utter in encouragement of revolutions abroad becomes a still greater encouragement to this silent, and as yet bloodless, revolution going on here at home. Liberty here no more than anywhere else is possible without the sacredness of law, and that sacredness is struck here whenever we strike it abroad. A false principle, asserted for the accomplishment of a foreign purpose deemed desirable, is sure, sooner or later, to return and effect a domestic purpose not desirable. There is a moral order in the government of the world, and nations no more than individuals can transgress it with impunity, and nations, as individuals, will find that they are generally punished in that wherein they have sinned, or that their sins prove to be their punishment.

We have dwelt the longer on this point, because it is almost the only thing in Mr. Webster's course as a statesman that we find to disapprove. In almost every other respect we can admire and honor his public life. It is the only instance in which we have found his general policy unjust or dangerous in principle, however we might dissent from it in some of its details. It is the only stain we are aware of on his public character. Yet we ought in justice to say, that in this he has but followed the public sentiment of his country, and of a powerful party in Great Britain. We ourselves once applauded him for it, and we still remember the exultation with which we read, in 1823, his speech in Congress on the affairs of Greece. At that time nobody in the country, to our knowledge, questioned the justice of the policy, however some might doubt its expediency. Under Mr. Monroe's administration the whole country seemed carried away with a spirit of propagandism, and, though the wild democracy against which we have such frequent occasion to warn our readers was then far from being fully developed, as it is now, the youth of that day boiled over with a patriotism and a love of liberty, as they understood or misunderstood the terms, of which we can now hardly form a conception. The movement for constitutional, that is representative government, was going on all over Europe, supported by the mighty influence of England, which she had so extended by the wars growing out of the French Revolution. A constitutional government was set up in Naples, and another in Spain; the Spanish American colonies declared themselves independent of the mother country, and introduced the republican form of government; and hope was high that it was all over with monarchy except in the English sense, and that republicanism would make the circuit of the globe. Our government and that of England acknowledged the independence of the Spanish American colonies, and President Monroe declared that this continent was closed to European colonization, and virtually that we assumed the championship throughout the world of every party struggling for representative government against monarchy. The writer of this was young then, and has outgrown the wild enthusiasm with which he was then carried away; Mr. Webster was older, and has remained unchanged. All we can say of him is, that in this respect he has not shown his ordinary superiority over the great body of his countrymen, and has followed instead of leading public opinion.

We need not say that Mr. Webster is a great man, for that everybody concedes or asserts; but his greatness does not lie in the original apprehension or discovery of first principles. He takes his principles as he finds them in the common sense of his age and country, and where that errs he errs. His mind is English, and practical rather than speculative. His reading has been principally in the ancient Roman and the modern English classics, while his chief study has been history and the Common Law, with the ordinary writers on government. His views have, perhaps, been formed more by the principles of the Common Law than by any other study, and hence are in general sound, and remarkable for their practical wisdom. But in a large class of questions, not immediately solved by these principles, he has taken the principles ordinarily adopted by the old English Republicans, and the modern English Whigs; and consequently, along with the principles that are excellent, true for all times and countries, he has another class of principles, borrowed from modern innovators, which are invariably unsound, and such as he himself would be as ready to condemn as we are, if he were to subject them to the independent action of his own powerful mind, in the light of those principles along with which he has received them, and which he so firmly holds and so frequently appeals to. The modern English mind, therefore modern English literature, is compounded of the traditional wisdom inherited by Englishmen from their ancestors, and of the innovations of modern reformers. The two elements exist side by side, but they will not coalesce. Consequently, the Englishman lacks unity of moral and intellectual life. When he speaks according to the traditional wisdom of his country, no man speaks with more truth, justice, or practical wisdom; when he leaves this traditional wisdom,—the good sense of his countrymen, for which no people are more remarkable,—and speaks according to the principles of modern innovators, he becomes false, impracticable, and absurd. It is somewhat the same with Mr. Webster. Ordinarily he speaks from the wisdom of our ancestors, for ordinarily the topics he treats are such as lie within the range of that portion of tradition which has been generally retained by Englishmen and Americans; but now and then he neglects it, and takes his principles from the modern innovators, or, what is the same thing, from ancient gentilism, and thus falls into the errors so rife and so dangerous in our times,—errors which in principle warrant the most extravagant conclusions of the Jacobin or the Red Republican. And yet, unless he had a sure means of ascertaining tradition in its purity and integrity, as he has, to some extent, in the case of the Common Law, we see not well how he could do otherwise.

Of Mr. Webster's rank as a lawyer, compared with the more eminent members of the legal profession in Great Britain and the United States, we have no occasion to speak, and, not being a lawyer by profession, we shall not attempt to speak. He is generally considered as having long stood at the head of the legal profession in his own country. But of his professional labors devoted to what is termed Constitutional Law, or the application of the Common Law to the constitutionality of legislative enactments, we must say a word or two. This department of law had, when he entered upon his professional career, been but imperfectly cultivated. "It fell to his lot," says his accomplished biographer, "to perform a prominent part in unfolding a most important class of constitutional doctrines, which, either because occasion had not drawn them forth, or the jurists of a former period had failed to deduce and apply them, had not yet grown into a system. It was reserved for Mr. Webster to distinguish himself before most, if not all, of his contemporaries, in this branch of his profession."

The first occasion on which Mr. Webster laid down what he took to be the principle of the Common Law, as applicable to the constitutionality of legislative enactments, was in the celebrated case of Dartmouth College, already referred to. "In the months of June and December, 1816, the legislature of New Hampshire passed acts altering the charter of Dartmouth College (of which the name was changed to Dartmouth University), enlarging the number of the trustees, and generally reorganizing the corporation. These acts, although passed without the consent and against the protest of the trustees of the College, went into operation. The newly created body took possession of the corporate property, and assumed the administration of the institution. The old board were all named as members of the new corporation, but declined acting as such, and brought an action against the treasurer of the new board for the books of record, the original charter, the common seal, and other corporate property of the College." This action was decided in the Superior Court of New Hampshire in favor of the validity of the State laws, and was carried up by writ of error to the Supreme Court of the United States, where, on the 10th of March, 1818, it came, on for argument before all the judges, who, in the term of the court holden the next February, declared, with only one dissenting voice, the acts of the legislature unconstitutional and invalid, and reversed the opinion of the court below.

The question for the Supreme Court to decide was, no doubt, whether the acts of New Hampshire did or did not contravene the Constitution of the United States; but Mr. Webster, in his argument for the plaintiffs in error, in order to facilitate the decision of that question by determining the real character of those acts, opened up the whole question of Common Law involved, and contended that the acts were invalid because against *common right* and the constitution of New Hampshire. He showed that the College was a private corporation, and that the legislature has no power to divest a private corporation, without its consent, of any of its corporate rights, maintaining that those rights can be taken away only in case of abuse or forfeiture, of which the court, not the legislature, is the judge. The principle on which his argument rests, if we have rightly seized it, is, that all chartered eleemosynary institutions, under which head are included all educational institutions founded and endowed by private liberality, are private corporations; and that all the rights of private corporations, or rather that all private rights, whether of persons or of things, or rights of private individuals, whether personal or corporate, are determined or defined by the Common Law, and are inviolable, so that any legislative enactment which infringes them is for that reason alone unconstitutional and invalid. This is certainly a most important principle, and if sound,—and that it is, it would be temerity on our part to doubt,—it proves that we do really live under a government of laws, and not a government of mere will, and that ours is really a free government, or rather a government that recognizes and guaranties freedom. Deny this principle, maintain that private rights, whether of persons or things, are creatures of the political power, and subject to the will of the legislature, and you convert the government at once into an arbitrary government, a government of mere will, under which there is no real liberty, no solid security, for either person or property; and this just as much where the will that obtains is the will of the majority, as where it is the will of only one man,—just as much where the form of the government is democratic as where it is monarchical.

The real excellence or glory of our institutions, we take it, lies in this principle; not, as is too often assumed, in the form of our political organization. If we have not misapprehended Mr. Webster, the Common Law in its principles, maxims, and definitions is with us both logically and historically anterior to our political constitutions, as well as the legislative bodies instituted under them, and is to be regarded as common right, or, in a word, as law for the convention in framing what we call the Constitution, and for the legislature in its enactments. It is for us really and truly the "higher law," and in the temporal order the most authoritative expression, which we as a people have, of the Divine law, from which all human laws derive their legality. It is the supreme civil law of the land, and although the legislature may undoubtedly modify or abrogate such of its special provisions as are temporary or local in their nature, or depend on time and circumstance for their wisdom and justice, or utility, and therefore such as are not essential to it as a system of law, yet no special enactment, whether by the convention or the ordinary legislature, that is repugnant to any one of its essential principles, is or can be law for an American citizen. All such enactments are unconstitutional, and the courts have the right, and are bound, to set them aside as null. The Common Law is the fundamental constitution of the country, older than the political constitutions, and able to survive them. The political constitutions presuppose it, must conform to it, and be interpreted by it; for what we call our political constitutions are in their essence only a part—the more fundamental part if you will—of our written law, not that which creates and sustains us as a living people. They are the source of our political rights or franchises, but all our other rights, what we call our natural rights, both the rights of persons and the rights of things, are prior to and independent of them, and exist and are determined by the Common Law. They cannot be touched by the political power without usurpation, tyranny, and oppression, from which the Common Law courts, if suffered to remain in their legitimate independence, are competent to relieve us. Thus Mr. Webster contends that the courts of New Hampshire ought of themselves to have declared the law essentially modifying the original charter of Dartmouth College invalid, unconstitutional, as violating common right and the well-settled principles of the Common Law in the case of eleemosynary institutions. It would follow from his doctrine, too, that no State in our Union would have the right to pass a law impairing the obligation of contracts, even if not forbidden to do so by the Constitution of the United States. It is enough that such laws are repugnant to the Common Law. The courts of this State may then, unquestionably, set aside the recent enactment of our legislature in regard to the sale of spirituous liquors, as infringing the rights of property as defined by the Common Law, which is law for the legislature as well as for the courts.

Such we understand to be the principle of law in all the States of the Union in which the Common Law obtains, and it is only in this principle, administered by an independent judiciary, that there is under our system of government, any more than under the most despotic governments of the Old World, any reliable support for the rights of person or property.

Mr. Webster has labored long and earnestly to bring out and establish this doctrine, and the services in this respect which he has rendered the country deserve even a far higher appreciation than they have yet received, and entitle him to the warmest gratitude of his countrymen. Their importance may be judged of by the efforts of all our radicals and experimenters in politics and law to get rid of the Common Law, and to destroy the independence of the judiciary. These men follow their instincts, which are all in favor of anarchy on the one hand, and despotism on the other. And the simple fact that they are hostile to an independent judiciary and to the Common Law proves of itself that these are essential alike to the maintenance of order and of liberty.

The distinguishing excellence of the Common Law system is, that it is *lex non scripta*, unwritten law, that is, a living tradition, in the reason, the conscience, the sentiments, the habits, the manners, and the customs of the people, and therefore in some sense independent of mere political organizations, and capable of surviving even their most violent changes, and of preserving a degree of order and justice among individuals, when the political authority is for the moment suspended or subverted. It is probably owing chiefly to the fact that the Common Law is an unwritten law, a living tradition preserved by the people themselves, and administered by an independent judiciary, that political revolutions in England and in this country preserve a character of sobriety and reserve in comparison with those of the Continent of Europe. The Continental nations have inherited the Civil Law, the old Roman Law, which is a system of written law, and theoretically in the keeping of the prince, beginning and ending with the political sovereign. Under this system of law the sovereign is the fountain of justice, as he must be under every system of mere written law; the people are trained for the sovereign, and have no established law to guide or regulate their conduct where he fails to express in a formal manner his will. The state everywhere takes the initiative, and the people without it are incapable of any orderly or regulated civil activity. Hence, whenever the political power receives a shock, all law is suspended, and the judiciary can perform legitimately none of its functions. Consequently, political revolutions in the Continental nations throw the whole of society into disorder, and subvert all social as well as political relations. The people receiving the law immediately from the sovereign, or written codes promulgated by the sovereign, and not having it in their own life, living in their own traditions, in their own habits, manners, and customs, are without law, and destitute of those habits of thought and action which would restrain them within moderate limits, and consequently are left liable to run into every imaginable excess.

But the Common Law, being an unwritten law, and living in the habits and manners of the people, gives them a sort of self-subsistency independent in a degree of the mere political power, and operates to restrain and regulate their social conduct, even when that power is temporarily overthrown or suspended. As long as the people remain in any sense a living people, the law survives, and survives as law, and preserves among them, in the midst of the most violent political convulsions, the elements of liberty and social order. England has gone through many changes, religious and political, but we have never seen English society wholly dissolved, or the main current of private and domestic life wholly interrupted, or even turned far aside from its ordinary channel. She has survived all her changes, and amid them all she has preserved her private and domestic life, social as distinguished from political order, but slightly impaired. She preserved a certain degree of individual freedom, to some extent the rights of persons and things, even under the Tudors, and something of social order under the Commonwealth, which she has continued to do even under the modern Whig rule and a Reformed Parliament. Much the same may be said of this country during what we call our Revolution. There was a time when our political constitutions were suspended, when the political authority was, as we may say, in abeyance, latent, undeveloped, potential, not actual; yet we did not fall into complete social disorder. Irregularity there certainly was, but the courts and the Common Law remained, and justice still continued to be administered, in the way and in the sense with which our people were familiar, and to which from time immemorial they had been accustomed. In France and other Continental countries, the case has usually been different. The subversion of political power there subverts society itself, save so far as it may be preserved by religious institutions, and the people seem destitute of all recuperative energy, or power in themselves to reestablish order; and if they do it at all, it is either through a military chieftain, or by a restoration. These different results, we think, are owing, not to difference of race or blood, or to different degrees of intelligence or moral virtue, as some in our time pretend, but mainly, if not solely, to the difference there is between a system of written and a system of unwritten law.

The great disadvantage of the European Continental nations is in the fact that they have no Common Law, and no Civil Law but written law. These nations are the heirs of the Roman empire, and their Civil Law is substantially the old Roman Law, and like all law embodied in codes is inflexible, and depends for its operation entirely on the political sovereign, who is supposed to prescribe and to administer it, either in person or by his ministers. It has no power to adapt itself to unforeseen emergencies, and to operate regularly in the midst of disorder. Between the written Civil Law and the unwritten Common Law, or between the Roman and the English systems, there is a fundamental difference. The Roman Law extends only to cases foreseen and provided for, the Common Law to all cases not taken out of its jurisdiction; the former is of gentile origin, simply modified by the Christian Emperors so as not to exclude Christian faith and worship; the latter is of Christian origin, and grew up among the Anglo-Saxons as they were converted from paganism and entered under the guidance of the Church upon the career of Christian civilization. The Common Law starts from the principle that society and the state are for man, and it seeks primarily the protection of private rights, the rights of persons and of things; the Roman Law starts from the heathen principle that man is for society, and society for the state, and it seeks primarily the protection of public rights, or the rights of the prince. The former abhors despotism, the latter abhors anarchy; the one makes the state absolute, supreme, omnipresent, the other presupposes a power above the state, limits the political power of the state, and asserts a law to which the state itself owes obedience, which subsists, and can, when need is, operate without the express sanction of the political sovereign. The Roman Law knows no people but the state, the Common Law recognizes the people, so to speak, as a power distinct from, and capable of surviving, the state. A nation that has been trained under the Common Law system may become an orderly republic; a nation trained under the Roman Law system can never be other than monarchical in effect, whatever it may be in name and pretension, or at farthest a close aristocracy. These are some of the characteristic differences between the two systems, and they sufficiently explain the different results of English or American revolutions from those of Continental Europe.

The essential difference between the two systems does not consist in the mere difference between their respective special provisions, which could easily be made the same in both, but in their general principles, the one as the written law of the prince, and the other as the living traditional law of the people, originating and living in their very life as a people. That the advantages are all on the side of the latter, or the English system, we think must be obvious to every lawyer and every well-informed statesman. It is therefore with pain that we find our politicians ascribing what is excellent in our institutions, what constitutes the chief protection of liberty and order among us, to our mere political organization, and overlooking the merits of the Common Law, the immense superiority of an unwritten over a written law, and seeking to abolish it, and to substitute a written code in its place. The Common Law, as an essentially unwritten law, living in the traditional life of a people, can never be introduced into a nation whose character is already formed. It must be born and grow up with the nation. Consequently, when once eliminated from the life of the people, it can never be replaced. Once gone, it is gone forever. It was born with the birth of England as a Christian nation, and grew up with it as the civil part of its Christian life. It became the public reason, the English common sense, and to it must we attribute the marked superiority of England and her institutions in the Middle Ages, and even in modern times, over the Continent of Europe. Happily England, in casting off, in the sixteenth century, the religion which gave her the Common Law, did not cast off the Common Law itself. She preserved it; slightly marred, no doubt, in its beauty and symmetry, yet she preserved it in its substance; and from her we have inherited it, and it should be our study, as we detest anarchy and love liberty, to transmit it unimpaired, in its purity and integrity, to our latest posterity. A richer legacy, aside from the Christianity which gave it birth, we could not even wish to bequeathe to future generations.

But we had no intention, on setting out, to enlarge as we have on either of the topics we have taken up. It was not our intention to speak of Mr. Webster either as a statesman or as a lawyer, for his merits in both respects have been dwelt upon till the public, perhaps, are growing tired of hearing them extolled, and some may be beginning to feel with the poor Athenian who would ostracize Aristides because tired of hearing him always called the Just. As a statesman we do not think that Mr. Webster has upon the whole been overrated. He was educated in the school of Washington and Adams, the old Federalist school, which, though not without its defects, was the only respectable political school we have ever had in New England. Its error was in copying from the English Whig, instead of the English—we say not the *Irish*—Tory, and acceding to the Jacobinical definition of popular sovereignty. It had too great a sympathy with the urban system of government, or government resting for its main support on the commercial and manufacturing classes, and did not sufficiently recognize the importance of a permanent class of landed proprietors to the stability and permanence of government. But, except in the planting States, its errors were all shared, and in an exaggerated form, by the rival or Democratic school, or if not, were opposed by worse errors, and the worst of all errors,—by that of giving to the government a proletarian basis, whether urban or rustic. In the main Mr. Webster has remained faithful to his school, although he seems, as he has grown older, to have departed from some of its best principles, and approached the party it opposed. He seems latterly to have become almost a democrat. Whether from conviction, or because the country is so hopelessly wedded to democracy, that he considers it the part of wisdom to accept democracy and endeavor to regulate it, we cannot say. However this may be, few who know Mr. Webster will question the elevation or honesty of his views, or suspect him of being capable of adopting any line of policy which he does not believe for the time and under the circumstances wise and just.

No man can question Mr. Webster's attachment to the Union, or his ardent love of country. His patriotic addresses prove this, no less than the general character of the measures to which he has always given his support during his connection with the general government, he is warmly attached to the political institutions of his country,—no man more so,—and this attachment sometimes, perhaps, blinds him to the danger of certain popular tendencies amongst us. In his masterly speech on the basis of representation, in the convention called for amending the constitution of this State in 1820, and in his address at Plymouth, December 22 of the same year, in commemoration of the landing of the Pilgrims and the first settlement of New England, he discusses at great length and with rare sagacity the importance, in a political point of view, of laws regulating the descent and distribution of property, and shows that, with our laws on the subject, monarchy becomes an impossibility. But it does not appear to have occurred to him to ask, if, with such laws,—laws which distribute property in minute parcels, which prevent its accumulation in any considerable masses, and thus render impossible the growth and preservation of families,—even a well-ordered republic can long survive, and if the only government that will ultimately be practicable is not mere military despotism. Family with us is destroyed, and the man who can boast a grandfather may think himself fortunate. Family influence there is none, family ties are broken, and we have only a mighty mass of isolated individuals. It may not be long before nothing but military force under a military chieftain will be able to keep them in order.

But leaving the field of politics, it may not be unpleasant to meet Mr.

Webster in the department of literature. It was mainly of his works in a literary point of view that we intended to speak when we set out, and probably we should have done so, only we have lost, if ever we possessed, the faculty of treating any man's works as mere literary productions. We are forced to admit to ourselves, which by the by we will not do to the public, that we have ourselves very little of what is called literary taste or literary culture. We do not mean to say that we have not read the chief literary works of modern, if not of ancient times; but we cannot understand literature for its own sake, or say much of the form of a literary work without reference to its contents. This is no disqualification for writing essays, but it is, very likely, a serious disqualification for writing literary reviews, that will pass for such with our contemporaries, and hence we seldom have much to say of books, except as to their principles. The principles of literature, or which should govern the literary man in the production of literature, we can understand; we can appreciate the principles of art; we can even admire a work of art, whether a poem, a symphony, a picture, a statue, a temple, or an oration; but we could never describe a work of art, or even our raptures on beholding it. We can enjoy it, take in its full effect, and thank God for the genius and talent that has created it; perhaps we could in a homely way tell what it is in it that we enjoy, and in some instances why we enjoy or ought to enjoy it; but we cannot tell it so as to reproduce in our hearers our own emotions, or rather, so as to make them fancy they feel very much as they would on beholding it, which is, if we understand it, the great aim of the modern critic on art. We have not enough of German subjectivity for that, and we always find it difficult to express what we do not distinctly apprehend as objective, and independent of our own subjective state. We cannot pass off our own emotions for criticism, nor for the object criticized, and consequently are unable to aspire to a rank among our modern approved literary critics.

The form of artistic productions, of course, is not a matter of indifference, but it has little separate value, and is seldom worth dwelling on, except in a school for learners, as detached from the merits of its contents. We like to see a man well dressed, but we cannot value the man for the dress, or the dress without the man. We do not undervalue purely literary taste or culture, but we never esteem works merely for the literary taste and culture they display. As merely literary works, having no end, answering no moral purpose, beyond that of gratifying the literary tastes of the reader, no works are worth the labor of criticism. The orator must always have some end beyond that of producing a beautiful oration, the poet beyond that of producing a poem according to the rules of poetic art, and the logician beyond that of producing an argument, and the first thing in one or another of these to be considered by the critic is the end the author has had in view. We utterly protest against the doctrine that excludes morality from art, or the German doctrine of aesthetics, that art itself is moral, nay, religious, and that the chief merit of the artist is to work instinctively, with no distinct consciousness of the end for which he works, as the bee builds her cell, or the blackbird sings her song. We cannot say with Goethe,—

Ich singe wieder Vogel singt
  in dem Zweigen wohnet,
Das Lied das aus der Kehle springt,
  Ist Lohn der reichlich lohnet.

Art may be used for purposes either good or bad; genius may prostitute itself, and display its charms but to corrupt, as any one may see in reopened Pompeii, or in many a modern gallery,—as any one knows who has read Don Juan and *Childe Harold*, by Byron, or *The Loves of the Angels* and *Lalla Rookh*, by Thomas Moore, to say nothing of works transmitted to us from ancient classic authors. Art, restricted in its application to exterior forms, or to the reproduction of exterior beauty, is indifferent to good or evil, and is as readily employed in the service of the one as of the other. Moreover, nothing is moral, save as it is done for the sake of an end. Morality is predicable not of the procession of existences from God, for in that procession God is the sole actor, and existences are created and simply prepared to be actors; it is predicable alone of the return of existences to God, as their final cause, and even here only of such existences as are endowed with free will, and capable of voluntarily choosing God as their ultimate end. If even these merely act instinctively, without apprehension and choice of the end, that is, without acting for the sake of the end, they are not in such actions moral, and their productions have no moral character. The German doctrine of the essential morality of all art is therefore inadmissible. Art must be for an end, and for a good end, or else it either has no moral character, or is immoral.

Our nature, again, is fallen, and, except so far as restored by grace, is the slave of concupiscence and corrupt propensions. It has been turned away from God as the true Final Cause of all creatures, and instead of instinctively returning to him as the Supreme Good, it instinctively tends from him, towards the creature, and through the creature, which has being only in God, towards death and nullity. Consequently, when man foregoes reason, which demands a final no less than a first cause, and simply follows his instincts or his perverted inclinations, he necessarily produces that which is bad, immoral, corrupt, and corrupting. The song of the blackbird which she sings instinctively is not immoral, nor of an immoral tendency, because it does not spring from a perverted or corrupt instinct. External nature is indeed cursed for our sake, but not in itself, for it has never transgressed the law of its Maker, and the curse is to us, in the use we make of it, and in the power which our sin gives it to afflict us. In itself it has no moral character, for it has no free will, and is subjected to a physical and not a moral law. Its beauty and harmony, the song of birds, the flowers of the fields, the silent groves, the dark forests, the lofty mountains, the majestic rivers, the laughing rills, the broad lakes and vast oceans, may all be to us occasions of virtuous affection or of sinful passion. All depends on ourselves and the use we make of them. To the pure all things are pure, to the corrupt all things are corrupt. The saint finds in all nature incentives to virtuous action, inducements to love and praise the glorious Maker of all; the sinner finds in all nature occasions of evil, or incentives to sin.

The artist, whether orator or poet, painter or sculptor, musician or architect, must have, then, an end in whatever he does beyond the mere doing, and also a good end, an end which lies in the moral order, and is referable to God, the Supreme Good and ultimate End of all things. When we have ascertained the end of a literary production, and ascertained it to be one which a wise and just man can approve, we may proceed to consider the literary taste and beauty with which the author has sought to accomplish it. As detached from its end, the work is no proper subject of criticism. As referred to its end, even its adaptation to that end, its form, its style, its diction, are proper and not unimportant considerations for the critic; for whatever is worth doing at all, is worth doing well. We are not purely intellectual beings, and it is not enough that he who writes for us should have the truth, and be able to state it in a strictly logical form. We have will as well as intellect; we have imagination, affections, passions, and emotions,—a perception of the beautiful as well as of the true and the good,—and we can be pleased as well as instructed, and generally we refuse the instruction if not presented in a form that pleases, or at least in one that does not displease. Now, we are far from considering this form under which we present the true or the good to be a matter of mere indifference. A correct literary taste, a lively sensibility to the fit and the beautiful, the command of an easy and noble style, of appropriate, expressive, and graceful diction, are matters of great importance, and which no man who writes at all is at liberty entirely to neglect. Here we prize literary taste and culture, as highly as anyone can, for here they are not for themselves, but for a legitimate purpose beyond themselves, and are prized as means to an end.

Tried by the standard implied, if not distinctly exhibited, in these remarks, we shall look in vain in the whole range of American secular literature for works that can rival these six volumes before us. In general, the end is just and noble, and, with fewer exceptions than we could reasonably expect, the doctrines set forth are sound and important. No man has written amongst us who has given utterance to sounder maxims on politics and law, and no one has done more to elevate political and legal topics to the dignity of science, to embellish them with the charms of a rich and chaste imagination, and to enrich them with the wealth accumulated from the successful cultivation of the classics of ancient and modern times. The author has received from nature a mind of the highest order, and he has cultivated it with care and success. We see in every page, every sentence, of his writings, vast intellectual power, quick sensibility, deep and tender affection, and a rich and fervid imagination; but we see also the hard student, the traces of long and painful discipline under the tutelage of the most eminent ancient and modern masters. Nature has been bountiful, but art has added its full share, in making the author what he is, and the combination of the two has enabled him to produce works which in their line are certainly unrivalled in this country, and we know not where to look for anything in our language of the kind really superior to them. As an orator Mr. Webster has all the terseness of Demosthenes, the grace and fullness of Cicero, the fire and energy of Chatham, and a dignity and repose peculiarly his own.

In these times a man is to be commended for the faults he avoids, as well as for the positive excellence to which he attains. Mr. Webster is free from the ordinary faults of even the more distinguished of the literary men of his country. American literary taste is in general very low and corrupt. Washington Irving and Hawthorne have good taste, are unaffected, natural, simple, easy, and graceful, but deficient in dignity and strength; they are pleasant authors for the boudoir, or to read while resting one's self on the sofa after dinner. No man who has any self-respect will read either of them in the morning. Prescott is gentlemanly, but monotonous, and occasionally jejune. Bancroft is gorgeous, glowing, but always straining after effect, always on stilts, never at his ease, never natural, never composed, never graceful or dignified. He has intellect, fancy, scholarship, all of a high order, but no taste, no literary good-breeding. He gesticulates furiously, and speaks always from the top of his voice. In general we may say of American literature that it is provincial, and its authors are uncertain of themselves, laboring, but laboring in vain, to catch the tone and manner of a distant metropolis. They have tolerable natural parts, often respectable scholarship, but they lack ease, dignity, repose. They do not speak as masters, but as forward pupils. They take too high a key for their voice, and are obliged in order to get through to sing in falsetto. You are never quite at your ease in listening to them; you are afraid they will break down, and that the lofty flights of oratory they promise you will turn out to be only specimens of the bathos. They fail to give one confidence in their strength, for they are always striving to be strong, and laboring to be intense. From all faults of this kind Mr. Webster is free. He inspires you, whether you are listening to his words as they fall from his lips, or read them as reproduced by the reporter, with full confidence in his ability to get through without any break-down, and he seldom disappoints you. He appears always greater than his subject, always to have the full mastery over it, and never to be mastered or carried away by it. In him you see no labor to be strong or intense, no violent contortions, or unnatural efforts to escape being thought weak, tame, or commonplace. He is always himself, collected, calm, and perfectly at his ease. He is so, not only because he really is a strong man, and has thoroughly mastered his subject, but because he is also a modest man, and is not disturbed by a constant recurrence of his thoughts to himself. He has through his natural modesty, which is one of the most striking traits in his character, and through cultivation, the power of forgetting himself, and of not thinking of the impression he is making on others with regard to himself, and consequently is able to employ the whole force of his intellect, imagination, and learning in stating, illustrating, and embellishing his subject. Being at his ease, having all his powers at his command whenever he rises to speak, and naturally a delicate taste, chastened and refined by the assiduous study of the best models, ancient and modern, he without difficulty avoids the ordinary faults of the orators of his country, and reassures, pleases, instructs, and carries along with him his whole audience.

We know not how Mr. Webster compares as an orator with the great orators of other times or other countries, for mere descriptions of oratory are rarely reliable; but he comes up more nearly to our ideal of the finished orator for the bar, the senate, the popular assembly, or a patriotic celebration, than any other to whom our country has given us an opportunity of listening. His elocution and diction harmonize admirably with his person and voice, and both strike you at once as fitted to each other. His majestic person, his strong, athletic frame, and his deep, rich, sonorous voice, set off with double effect his massive thoughts, his weighty sentences, his chaste, dignified, and harmonious periods. Whatever we may say of the elocution, the rhetoric is always equal to it. Mr. Webster is perhaps the best rhetorician in the country. No man better appreciates the choice of words or the construction and collocation of sentences, so as to seize at once the understanding, soothe the passions, charm the imagination, and captivate the affections. He is always classical. His words are pure English, and the proper words for the occasion, the best in the language; and his sentences are simply constructed, never involved, never violently inverted, but straightforward, honest, sincere, and free from all modern trickery. We know in the language no models better fitted than the orations and speeches in these volumes for the assiduous study of the young literary aspirant who would become a perfect rhetorician, or master a style at once free and natural, instructive and pleasing, pure and correct, graceful and elevated, dignified and noble. Mr. Webster's artistic skill is consummate, and evidently has been acquired only by great labor and pains; but you must study his works long and carefully before you will detect it. Such writing as we have here comes not by nature, and no genius, however great, can match it without years of hard labor in preparatory discipline.

The casual reader may be apt to underrate Mr. Webster's merits as a logician, and we recollect hearing a distinguished Senator, who ought to have known him well, characterize him one day as "a magnificent declaimer, but no reasoner." He is not of a speculative turn of mind, nor does he appear to have devoted much time to the study of the speculative sciences, though he evidently has not wholly neglected them,—and he seldom reasons, as we say, in form; but he gives full evidence, after all, of possessing the logical element in as eminent a degree as he does any other element of the human mind. His style of expression and habits of thought are strictly logical, and his conclusions always follow from his premises. The only thing to be said is, that very often one of his premises is understood and not expressed, and sometimes rests on the prejudice, conviction, or actual common sense of his countrymen, not on a true ontological principle. His defect is not a defect of logic, but a defect of original apprehension, resulting from the neglect to go back from the common sense of his countrymen to first principles. In consequence of this, his conclusions are sometimes unsound, not because they do not follow from his premises expressed or understood, but because one or the other of his premises is unsound. This is more or less necessarily the case with all Englishmen and Americans, who follow what is called common sense; for the common sense of Englishmen and Americans, as we have already remarked, is made up from modern innovations, as well as from the traditions of our ancestors, and is therefore on one side untrue. But where his principles are sound, as in his law arguments, and in the greater part of his speeches in Congress, and in several of his diplomatic letters, his logic is sound and invincible, although it is presented in a popular form, the most suitable for his purpose. Ordinarily he strikes us as comprehensive rather than acute, but he can be as acute, as nice in his analyses and distinctions, as need be, as we may know from his argument to the court and jury in the trial of the Knapps for the murder of Captain White of Salem, which upon the whole is one of the most finished of his performances, as they stand in the volumes before us.

Some readers, again, will regard Mr. Webster as chiefly remarkable for his pure intellectual power; and be disposed to deny him much power of imagination. But this would be in the highest degree unjust. He possesses an uncommonly strong and vivid imagination. Take up any one of his speeches, if but tolerably reported, on any subject, no matter how dry or uninteresting in itself, and you find that he at once informs it with life, elevates it, and invests it with a deep interest. This no man destitute of imagination can ever do. The test of imagination is not a florid style, abounding in tropes and metaphors. Such a style indicates fancy, not imagination, and, in fact, it is the general tendency of our countrymen, nay, of our age, to mistake fancy for imagination. Washington Irving and Hawthorne have imagination, though not of the highest order; Bancroft has fancy, a rich and exuberant fancy, but very little imagination. To test the question whether a man has imagination or not, let him take up a dry and difficult subject, and if he can treat it so that without weariness, and even with interest, you can follow him through his discussion of it, although he uses always the language appropriate to it, and seems to employ only the pure intellect in developing it, you may be sure that he has a strong and fervid imagination, so strong and active as to impart life and motion to whatever he touches. Mr. Webster has an exceedingly rich and active imagination, but he does not suffer it to predominate; he makes it subservient to his reason, and so blends it in with the pure intellect, that you feel its effect without being aware of its presence. No matter how apparently dry and technical the subject he has in hand, the moment he begins to unfold it, and to indicate its connections with other subjects, and through these its high social or moral relations, his hearer's or reader's attention is arrested, fixed, and held till he closes. He no sooner speaks, than the dry bones of his subject assume flesh, move, and stand up, living and breathing, in proper human shape, well formed and duly proportioned, not misshapen monsters, that frighten by their hideous or disgust by their grotesque appearance.

What we most admire in the style of Mr. Webster is its simplicity, strength, and repose. The majority of our writers who study to be simple in their manner are plain, dry, or silly. They are simple in a sense in which simplicity is not a compliment. Those who wish to escape this charge become inflated, bombastic, and unable to say anything in an easy and natural manner. They select high-sounding words, pile up adjective upon adjective, and send their fancy over all nature, and through all its departments, animal, vegetable, and mineral, over all nations, among the English, the French, the Italian, the Dutch, the Russian, the Tartars, the Chinese, the Japanese, the Hindoos, the Egyptians, the Abyssinians, the Negroes, the Malays, the savages of Oceanica and of North and South America, and through all times, from the entrance of Satan into the garden of Eden to seduce our great-grandmother Eve, down to the battle of Buena Vista, in which General Taylor flogged General Santa Ana, or the last Baltimore Convention for nominating a Whig or a Democratic President, to cull flowers and collect images to adorn and illustrate some poor, commonplace thought, or some puny conceit, that might have proved stillborn without in the least affecting the flux and reflux of the ocean tides, interrupting the course of nature, or changing the general current of historical events. Mr. Webster avoids both extremes, and speaks always in accordance with the genius of his native idiom, and in his natural key. Take, for instance, the opening paragraph of his speech on the completion of the Bunker Hill Monument.

> A duty has been performed. A work of gratitude and patriotism is completed. This structure, having its foundations in soil which drank deep of early Revolutionary blood, has at length reached its destined height, and now lifts its summit to the skies.—Vol. I p. 83.

Or this from the same speech:

> The Bunker Hill Monument is finished. Here it stands. Fortunate in the high natural eminence on which it is placed, higher, infinitely higher in its objects and purpose, it rises over the land and over the sea; and, visible, at their homes,

to three hundred thousand of the people of Massachusetts, it stands a memorial of the last, and a monitor to the present and to all succeeding generations. I have spoken of the loftiness of its purpose. If it had been without any other design than the creation of a work of art, the granite of which it is composed would have slept in its native bed. It has a purpose, and that purpose gives it its character. That purpose enrobes it with dignity and moral grandeur. That well-known purpose it is which causes us to look up to it with a feeling of awe. It is itself the orator of this occasion. It is not from my lips, it could not be from any human lips, that that strain of eloquence is this day to flow most competent to move and excite the vast multitudes around me. The powerful speaker stands motionless before us. It is a plain shaft. It hears no inscriptions, fronting to the rising sun, from which the future antiquary shall wipe the dust. Nor does the rising sun cause tones of music to issue from its summit. But at the rising of the sun, and at the setting of the sun; in the blaze of noonday, and beneath the milder effulgence of lunar light; it looks, it speaks, it acts, to the full comprehension of every American mind, and the awakening of glowing enthusiasm in every American heart.—p. 86.

With the exception of the phrase "the milder effulgence of lunar light," which we cannot much admire, this is simply and naturally said, and yet it is in the highest strain of genuine oratory, and we shall not easily forget the emotion with which we heard Mr. Webster, standing in front of the monument, pronounce it, or the deep and prolonged applause it received from the some two hundred thousand of our citizens assembled in honor of the occasion. All true greatness is simple and sedate. It affects no display, for it is satisfied with what it is. It speaks and it is done, commands and it stands fast. Take another passage, of a different description indeed, but illustrating the same simplicity of style and expression. The extract is from the opening of his speech on the trial of the Knapps for the murder of Captain Joseph White of Salem.

I am little accustomed, Gentlemen, to the part which I am now attempting to perform. Hardly more than once or twice has it happened to me to be concerned on the side of the government in any criminal prosecution whatever; and never, until the present occasion, in any case affecting life.

But I very much regret that it should have been thought necessary to suggest to you that I am brought here to "hurry you against the law and beyond the evidence." I hope I have too much regard for justice, and too much respect for my own character, to attempt either; and were I to make such attempt, I am sure that in this court nothing can be carried against the law, and that gentlemen, intelligent and just as you are, are not, by any power, to be hurried beyond the evidence. Though I could well have wished to shun this occasion, I have not felt at liberty to withhold my professional assistance, when it is supposed that I may be in some degree useful in investigating and discovering the truth respecting this most extraordinary murder. It has seemed to be a duty incumbent on me, as on every other citizen, to do my best and my utmost to bring to light the perpetrators of this crime. Against the prisoner at the bar, as an individual, I cannot have the slightest prejudice. I would not do him the smallest injury or injustice. But I do not affect to be indifferent to the discovery and the punishment of this deep guilt. I cheerfully share in the opprobrium, how great soever it may be, which is cast on those who feel and manifest an anxious concern that all who had a part in planning, or a hand in executing, this deed of midnight assassination, may be brought to answer for their enormous crime at the bar of public justice.

Gentlemen, it is a most extraordinary case. In some respects, it has hardly a precedent anywhere; certainly none in our New England history. This bloody drama exhibited no suddenly excited, ungovernable rage. The actors in it were not surprised by any lion-like temptation springing upon their virtue, and overcoming it, before resistance could begin. Nor did they do the deed to glut savage vengeance, or satiate long-settled and deadly hate. It was a cool, calculating, money-making murder. It was all "hire and salary, not revenge." It was the weighing of money against life; the counting out of so many pieces of silver against so many ounces of blood.

An aged man, without an enemy in the world, in his own house, and in his own bed, is made the victim of a butcherly murder, for mere pay. Truly, here is a new lesson for painters and poets. Whoever shall hereafter draw the portrait of murder, if he will show it as it has been exhibited, where such example was last to have been looked for, in the very bosom of our New England society, let him not give it the grim visage of Moloch, the brow knitted by revenge, the face black with settled hate, and the blood-shot eye emitting livid fires of malice. Let him draw, rather, a decorous, smooth-faced, bloodless demon; a picture in repose, rather than in action; not so much an example of human nature in its depravity, and in its paroxysms of crime, as an infernal being, a fiend, in the ordinary display and development of his character.

The deed was executed with a degree of self-possession and steadiness equal to the wickedness with which it was planned. The circumstances now clearly in evidence spread out the whole scene before us. Deep sleep had fallen on the destined victim, and on all beneath his roof. A healthful old man, to whom sleep was sweet, the first sound slumbers of the night held him in their soft but strong embrace. The assassin enters, through the window already prepared, into an unoccupied apartment. With noiseless foot he paces the lonely hall, half lighted by the moon; he winds up the ascent of the stairs, and reaches the door of the chamber. Of this, he moves the lock, by soft and continued pressure, till it turns on its hinges without noise; and he enters, and beholds his victim before him. The room is uncommonly open to the admission of light. The face of the innocent sleeper is turned from the murderer, and the beams of the moon, resting on the gray locks of his aged temple, show him where to strike. The fatal blow is given! And the victim passes, without a struggle or a motion, from the repose of sleep to the repose of death! It is the assassin's purpose to make sure work; and he plies the dagger, though it is obvious that life has been destroyed by the blow of the bludgeon. He even raises the aged arm, that he may not fail in his aim at the heart, and replaces it again over the wounds of the poniard! To finish the picture, he explores the wrist for the pulse! He feels for it, and ascertains that it beats no longer! It is accomplished. The deed is done. He retreats, retraces his steps to the window, passes out through it as he came in, and escapes. He has done the murder. No eye has seen him, no ear has heard him. The secret is his own, and it is safe!

Ah! Gentlemen, that was a dreadful mistake. Such a secret can be safe nowhere. The whole creation of God has neither nook nor corner where the guilty can bestow it, and say it is safe. Not to speak of that eye which pierces through all disguises, and beholds everything as in the splendor of noon, such secrets of guilt are never safe from detection, even by men. True it is, generally speaking, that "murder will out." True it is, that Providence hath so ordained, and doth so govern things, that those who break the great law of Heaven by shedding man's blood seldom succeed in avoiding discovery. Especially, in a case exciting so much attention as this, discovery must come, and will come, sooner or later. A thousand eyes turn at once to explore every man, everything, every circumstance, connected with the time and place; a thousand ears catch every whisper; a thousand excited minds intensely dwell on the scene, shedding all their light, and ready to kindle the slightest circumstance into a blaze of discovery. Meantime the guilty soul cannot keep its own secret. It is false to itself; or rather it feels an irresistible impulse of conscience to be true to itself. It labors under its guilty possession, and knows not what to do with it. The human heart was not made for the residence of such an inhabitant. It finds itself preyed on by a torment, which it dares not acknowledge to God or man. A vulture is devouring it, and it can ask no sympathy or assistance, either from heaven or earth. The secret which the murderer possesses soon comes to possess him; and, like the evil spirits of which we read, it overcomes him, and leads him whithersoever it will. He feels it beating at his heart, rising to his throat, and demanding disclosure. He thinks the whole world sees it in his face, reads it in his eyes, and almost hears its workings in the very silence of his thoughts. It has become his master. It betrays his discretion, it breaks down his courage, it conquers his prudence. When suspicions from without begin to embarrass him, and the net of circumstance to entangle him, the fatal secret struggles with still greater violence to burst forth. It must be confessed, it will be confessed; there is no refuge from confession but suicide, and suicide is confession.—Vol. VI. pp. 51–54.

We continue the extract from this same speech, for the sake, not only of the style, but of the sentiment it expresses with regard to the detection of crime, and the merited rebuke it quietly gives to our romantic philanthropists, whose sympathies are all for the criminal, and who would deem it very low and illiberal to make any account of the sufferings of the innocent which his crimes inevitably occasion. The community in which we live is coming to a strange pass. Crimes are daily and hourly multiplying in our midst, both in frequency and magnitude, and yet the great study is to mitigate punishment, and to convert the criminal into a hero. Virtue goes unhonored, and we are doing our best to have crime go unpunished.

Much has been said, on this occasion, of the excitement which has existed, and still exists, and of the extraordinary measures taken to discover and punish the guilty. No doubt there has been, and is, much excitement, and strange indeed it would be had it been otherwise. Should not all the peaceable and well-disposed naturally feel concerned, and naturally exert themselves to bring to punishment the authors of this secret assassination? Was it a thing to be slept upon or forgotten? Did you, Gentlemen, sleep quite as quietly in your beds after this murder as before? Was it not a case for rewards, for meetings, for committees, for the united efforts of all the good, to find out a band of murderous conspirators, of midnight ruffians, and to bring them to the bar of justice and law? If this be excitement, is it an unnatural or an improper excitement?

It seems to me, Gentlemen, that there are appearances of another feeling, of a very different nature and character; not very extensive, I would hope, but still there is too much evidence of its existence. Such is human nature, that some persons lose their abhorrence of crime in their admiration of its magnificent exhibitions. Ordinary vice is reprobated by them, but extraordinary guilt, exquisite wickedness, the high flights and poetry of crime, seize on the imagination, and lead them to forget the depths of the guilt, in admiration of the excellence of the performance, or the unequalled atrocity of the purpose. There are those in our day who have made great use of this infirmity of our nature, and by means of it done infinite injury to the cause of good morals. They have affected not only the taste, but I fear also the principles, of the young, the heedless, and the imaginative, by the exhibition of interesting and beautiful monsters. They render depravity attractive, sometimes by the polish of its manners, and sometimes by its very extravagance; and study to show off crime under all the advantages of cleverness and dexterity. Gentlemen, this is an extraordinary murder, but it is still a murder. We are not to lose ourselves in wonder at its

> origin, or in gazing on its cool and skillful execution. We are to detect and to punish it; and while we proceed with caution against the prisoner, and are to be sure that we do not visit on his head the offences of others, we are yet to consider that we are dealing with a case of most atrocious crime, which has not the slightest circumstance about it to soften its enormity. It is murder; deliberate, concerted, malicious murder.—pp. 54, 55.

Other extracts in abundance we might make, full of interest in themselves, and illustrating the several features of Mr. Webster's style and manner which we have indicated; but we must refer our readers to their own recollections, or, where these fail, to the volumes themselves. The extracts we have made will serve to illustrate, not only the simplicity of his language, but the strength of his expressions, and the repose of his manner. The quiet majesty of his style in the more felicitous moments of the orator, or when the reporter has been the more competent to his task of reporting his speeches word for word as delivered, has seldom been surpassed, if equaled, by any American, or even English writer. Burke is the English writer with whom we most naturally compare him. As an orator he is far superior to Burke, as a profound and comprehensive thinker, perhaps, he falls below him; as a writer he is as classical in his style, as cultivated, and as refined in his tastes, and simpler and more vigorous in his expression. In many-respects Burke has been his model, and it is not difficult to detect in his pages traces of his intimate communion with the great English, or rather Irish statesman, who, perhaps, taken all in all, is the most eminent among the distinguished statesmen who have written or spoken in our language. We have no thought of placing Mr. Webster above him; but he surpasses him in his oratory, for Burke was an uninteresting speaker, and in the simple majesty and repose of his style and manner. Burke is full, but his fancy is sometimes too exuberant for his imagination, and his periods are too gorgeous and too overloaded. Now and then he all but approaches the inflated, and is simply not bombastic. His work on the French Revolution is a splendid work, a vast treasure-house of historical lore, of sound political doctrines and wise maxims for the statesman, but it frequently lacks simplicity, and is sometimes a little overstrained in its manner. The effort of the author to sustain himself at the height from which he sets out is now and then visible, and his voice, in executing some of the higher notes of his piece, well-nigh breaks into falsetto. His strength, though sufficient to carry him through, is not sufficient to carry him through with ease. Our countryman appears to us to possess naturally a stronger and more vigorous mental constitution, and to carry himself more quietly, and more at his natural ease. The only modern writers, as far as our limited reading extends, who in this respect equal or surpass Mr. Webster, are the great Bossuet and the Gorman Goethe, though we must exclude Goethe's earlier writings from the comparison. The simple natural majesty of Bossuet is perhaps unrivalled in any author, ancient or modern, and in his hands the French language loses its ordinary character, and in dignity, grandeur, and strength becomes able to compete successfully with any of the languages of Modern Europe. Goethe is the only German we have ever read who could write German prose with taste, grace, and elegance, and there is in his writings a quiet strength and a majestic repose which are surpassed only by the very best of Greek or Roman classics. Mr. Webster may not surpass, in the respect named, either of these great writers, but he belongs to their order.

We have dwelt the longer on these features of Mr. Webster's style, because they are precisely those which our authors and orators most lack. The American people have no simplicity, no natural ease, no repose. A pebble is a "rock," a leg or arm is a "limb," breeches or trousers are "unnamables," a petticoat is a "skirt," a shift is a *chemise*, the sun is the "solar orb," the moon the "lunar light." Nothing can be called simply by its proper name in our genuine old Anglo-Saxon tongue. We are always striving to be great, sublime; and simple natural expressions are counted tame, commonplace, or vulgar. We must be inflated, grandiloquent, or eccentric. Even in our business habits, we strive after the strange, the singular, or the wonderful, and are never contented with old fashions, quiet and sure ways of prospering. We must make or lose a fortune at a dash. We have no repose, are always, from the moment we are breeched till wrapped in our grave-clothes, in a state of unnatural excitement, hurrying to and fro, without asking or being able to say why or wherefore. We have no homesteads, no family, no fixtures, no sacred ties which bind us, no hearths or altars around which our affections cling and linger. We are all afloat upon a tumultuous ocean, and seem incapable of enjoying ourselves save amid the wildness and fury of the storm. Our authors and orators, as was to be expected, partake of our national character, and reproduce it in their works. The best thing we can do is to give our days and nights to the study of the volumes before us, which present us admirable models of what we are not, but of what we might and should be.

It is very evident from Mr. Webster's writings that his reading has not been confined to Blackstone and Coke upon Littleton, nor to Harrington,

Sydney, and Locke, that he has made frequent excursions from the line of his professional or official studies among the poets and in the fields of polite literature, and that literary or artistic cultivation has been with him a matter of no inconsiderable moment. He is perfectly familiar with the British classics, whether prose or poetry, and well read, if not in the Greek, at least in the ancient Roman literature. His style is to no inconsiderable extent formed after those very different writers, Cicero and Tacitus; but perhaps it owes still more of its peculiar richness and beauty to his diligent reading,—whether for devotion or literary purposes we know not,—of the English Protestant version of the Holy Scriptures. This version is of no value to the theologian, for it has been made from an impure Hebrew and Greek text, and is full of false and corrupt renderings, but in a literary point of view it has many and rare merits. As an accurate rendering of the sacred text it cannot as a whole compare with our Douay Bible, but its language and style are more truly English, or at least present the English with more idiomatic grace, and greater purity and richness. The Douay Bible borrows terms from the Latin, which, though more precise, are less familiar, and less expressive to the ordinary English reader; at least, so it seems to us, who first studied the Scriptures through the medium of the Protestant version. The English language had reached its fullest and richest development in the sixteenth century, and the men who made the Protestant version of the Scriptures, whatever they were as theologians, were among its most accomplished masters. Hence their version has become the first of English classics, and perhaps we have no work in the language that can be so advantageously studied by the orator or the poet, so far as relates to pure English taste, to the formation of style, and richness, aptness, and beauty of idiomatic expression, though we think there is at present a tendency among some of our Catholic scholars to underrate the literary merits of the Douay Bible, and we find ourselves appreciating them much higher in proportion as we become better acquainted with them.

But we have exhausted our space, and must bring our remarks to a close. We have intended to be fair and just towards Mr. Webster, and our readers will readily perceive that we have written on the principle of saying the best we can, and not the worst, without violating the truth. We have done so, because we have never been one of Mr. Webster's partisans, and have on more occasions than one expressed in strong language our dissent from his particular measures, or the line of policy he has recommended. We have also done so, because Mr. Webster is really a great man, and our country is not so rich in great men as to permit us to overlook or to deal harshly with one so eminent as he unquestionably is. He is one of the few survivors of a generation of distinguished men, who are passing away without leaving any successors. Lowndes, Hayne, Calhoun, are gone, Clay is dying, and may be dead before this sees the light, and of the great men who commenced public life with him, and who might claim to be his peers, Mr. Webster alone survives, and at farthest can survive but a few years longer. We could not well forget his merits, and remember only his faults; in doing so, we should have shown little patriotism and less Christianity. There are so few of our authors, orators, and statesmen that we can honor at all, that we are disposed to honor fully everyone who does not strike us as being wholly unworthy.

Our great men are dying, and who is to take their place? The tendency with us is downward. The generation to which Mr. Webster belonged was inferior to the generation of great men who achieved our independence and founded our national government, and he is perhaps the only man born since the Declaration who could compare favorably with the Washingtons, the Adamses, the Hamiltons, the Madisons, and others of the same class, and in many respects not even he can do it. The generation next in time, and the one to which we ourselves belong, is of a yet lower grade of intellect and still more superficial attainments, and the best thing, perhaps, that can be said in our favor is that some of us feel and lament our inferiority. The generation that follows gives no promise of not falling still lower in the scale. Thus we go on, falling lower and lower in the intellectual and moral order with each new generation, and to what depths we shall ultimately sink, it is impossible to foresee. The democratic order is exceedingly unfavorable to either intellectual or moral greatness. If it has a tendency to bring up a degree or two the very low, which may be questioned, it has a still stronger tendency to bring all down to a low and common level. There is no use in quarrelling with this statement, for it is a fact so plain that even the blind may see it. If, then, a man amongst us rises superior to the unfavorable circumstances created by the political order of his country, and places himself on a level with the great men of other times and other countries, let us cherish him, and yield him ungrudgingly all merited honor.

We have written without any reference to the fact that Mr. Webster is or may be a candidate for the Presidency of the United States. Who will be the candidate of either of the great parties of the country, it is impossible to say at the time we are writing, though the question will be settled before our Review issues from the press. In questions of domestic policy Mr. Webster is anti-sectional and conservative, and is unobjectionable to us and our friends; but his foreign policy has been such as we cannot approve. Ostensibly directed against foreign despotism, it has been really directed against our Church, and the liberty and peace of Continental Europe. The sympathy and support Mr. Kossuth obtained here were obtained on the supposition that he represented the Protestant cause, and that he was in league with Mazzini and others, not only for the overthrow of monarchy, but also of the Catholic Church. Hence it is that our Catholic population have almost to a man refused all sympathy with the eloquent Magyarized Sclave. But Kossuth is Mr. Webster's *protégé*; Mr. Webster liberated him from prison and brought him here, and Mr. Webster is the man who in his behalf has insulted Austria, and compelled her representative to retire from the country. It were suicidal in any Catholic to vote to raise him to the Presidency of the United States. He would in so doing, if left to the choice of a better man in this respect, be false to his religion and to his country.

We love our country and delight to honor her really great men; but our God before our country, and our country before men, however great or distinguished. What we have censured in Mr. Webster he owes to his age and country, what we have commended he owes to himself and the traditional wisdom of our ancestors, and we honor him all the more that he is one of the very few of our countrymen who respect that wisdom, and do not believe that whatever is novel is true, and whatever is a change is an improvement. We have read his writings from time to time and as here collected, we would fain hope not without profit, for which we owe and would willingly pay him a debt of gratitude. If not all that we could wish, they are among the best things which our country has given us. The author has done something, more than any other man in our day, to sustain and enhance the true glory of the American name, and while we live we shall cheerfully honor him, and we shall delight to see him honored by his countrymen. We would willingly see the laurel that binds his brows remain green and fresh, for the honor it bestows is identified with our common country, and is a patrimony to be inherited by our children.

THIRTEEN

Schools of Philosophy

The author of the first named of these works is a French Sulpician of rare merit, formerly Professor of Philosophy at Clermont, now, we believe, at Issy. He is a young man, but he has made good philosophical studies, and is animated by a noble philosophical spirit. His work, which might, perhaps, gain by condensation and vigor of style, is certainly one of great value, and, saving the part which treats of ethics, one of the best manuals of philosophy we are acquainted with. It strikes us as a very great advance, as to its principles, we say not as to the ability of the author, on the *Lugdenensis*, the popular work of Bouvier, the manuals of Liberatore, Dmowski, and even Rothenflue. The author, perhaps, adheres too closely to Malebranche, but he rejects Cartesianism and modern psychologism, and bases his system on sound ontological principles. If we should object at all to his *metaphysics*, it would be to his having failed to adapt his method to his principles. But we are so thankful to find a philosophical work, in these days, generally sound in its fundamental principles, that we can overlook minor faults, and give it a most hearty welcome, although we may not regard it as perfect. The philosophical student will not fail to prize the author's *Prolegomena* very highly, and his refutation of pantheism is decidedly the best we have ever

"*Praelectiones Philosophicae.* Claramon-Ferrandi. 1849. 3 tom. 12 mo. 2. *L'Autocrazia dell'Ente. Comedia in tre Atti.* Roma: La Civiltà Cattolica. Vol. III. 1853." From *Brownson's Quarterly Review,* 3rd Series, 2 (January 1854): 30–60.

seen, and leaves on that head, as far as we can judge, nothing to be desired.

The author, undoubtedly, departs in some respects from the philosophical system of our more generally used manuals, and many will regard him as an innovator; but if he innovates, he innovates antiquity, for the school to which he inclines is older than the school which will oppose him. The ontological school, both among the Gentiles and among Catholics, is older than the psychological or Peripatetic school, as it was formerly called. The latter school hardly makes its appearance in the Catholic world till the Middle Ages, and owes its introduction in a great measure to the influence of the Mahometan schools in the East, on the coast of Africa, and in Spain. If its adherents can produce a catena of great saints and doctors from the twelfth or thirteenth century down to our times, their opponents can produce a catena of no less eminent saints and doctors from the Apostolic age down to our own. If the school which would charge the author with innovating can plead in its favor an Abelard, an Alesius, an Albertus Magnus, a St. Thomas, an Occam, a Suarez, he can plead in his favor a St. Augustine, and nearly all the fathers, St. Anselm, Hugh and Richard of St. Victor, St. Bonaventura, a Duns Scotus, a Gerson, a Ficinus, a Malebranche, a Thomassin, a Vico, a Gerdil, and a Bossuet and a Fénelon, who were Cartesians only in name. If it comes to the authority of great names, our author has nothing to fear; for if the single name of St. Thomas is a host, that of St. Augustine is not inferior to it, nor to any other name in philosophy; besides, it is evident to the student of the works of the Angelic Doctor, that, if he adopted the Peripatetic philosophy, it was not so much because he preferred it as because he found it generally received, and because he would use it against the enemies of religion, who for the most part professed it, and compel it as a slave to serve the cause of revealed truth. Wherever he breaks from the old Stagirite, and philosophizes freely, so to speak, on his own hook, he accepts and defends ontological and realistic principles.

The second work named at the head of this article is from the modern psychological school, and is a very successful attempt to turn the shafts of wit and ridicule against those who have the temerity to defend the principles and method of the ontological school. As a *jeu d'esprit* we can read and enjoy it, but as an argument we cannot respect it so highly as we could wish, for it confounds the bastard ontology of the heterodox with the views of the so-called ontologists among Catholics, and concludes against the truth of the latter from the absurdity of the former. We are sorry to see this mode of warfare adopted by any philosophical school, because it presents a false issue to the public, and is calculated to arouse passions in poor human nature anything but favorable to the cause of truth. We are ourselves as strongly opposed to that bastard ontology as is the writer of *L'Autocrazia dell' Ente*, and it is not pleasant to be held up to the public as embracing it, because we do not happen to embrace the psychological school. There is an ontological school as far removed from the heterodox German ontological school, or the Rosminian *ens ingenere*, as from the school defended by the *Civiltà Cattolica*.

We like earnestness, we like zeal in the defense of what one holds to be truth, but we should not dare to defend even dogmatic truth by unfairness towards its opponents, much less mere philosophical opinions. Two schools of philosophy, it is well known, exist among Catholics, each aspiring to the throne of the philosophical world. These schools, under different forms and different names, have subsisted among us for a long time, and both are tolerated by the Church, which leaves each free to maintain its own opinion in Christian charity, and to dispute that of the other, so long as it does not advance its opinion as Catholic dogma, or maintain anything repugnant to the decisions and definitions of Popes and Councils, and the unanimous teaching of the Fathers. Undoubtedly this does not imply that both schools are equally sound, that their respective opinions are equally probable, and that there is no ground for preferring one to the other; but it does prove that one may belong to either without imperiling the salvation of his soul, and therefore that the differences between the two schools may be discussed without heat or passion on either side. These matters of difference lie in that sphere where the Church wills us to be free, and where, as long as we advance nothing immediately against faith, or that immediately tends to weaken its defenses, she leaves us to follow our own reason and will, as she does in political or domestic economy. We say immediately, because, no doubt, every error even in the natural order has some bearing, more or less remote, on revealed truth, since the revealed order presupposes the natural. But to tolerate no error of reason, however remote from the revealed dogma, would be to deny to man all free intellectual activity, which is contrary to the uniform practice of the Church. Her authority is full and universal as representing the Divine authority on earth, but her uniform practice is to leave men in philosophy, in government, in social and domestic economy, all the freedom compatible with the end for which she has been instituted; for her wish is to rear, not a race of mere slaves, but free and loyal worshippers of God.

The philosophy more generally taught in our schools is what we term the psychological, though of course free from the glaring defects of the psychologism which obtains in the schools of the heterodox. But though permitted to be taught, there is a wide and growing feeling among earnest and devout Catholics, that it does not afford that strong defense to religion and society, and those facilities for the refutation of modern heresies, which we have the right to demand of a philosophy taught to Catholic youth. That we, to some extent, share this feeling, we have no disposition to deny, but we are not very warm on the subject, and we guard against blaming, in any degree, our professors. That philosophy may have, in our opinion, remote bearings injurious to faith; but it is not heretical, and may be held without any impeachment of one's orthodoxy. Moreover, it is not the professor's business to construct a new or revive an obsolete system of philosophy; his business is to teach a system already constructed, and approved by his superiors. The introduction of new, or the revival of old systems, by individual professors, each on his own responsibility, would produce no little confusion in philosophical teaching, and tend to generate that skepticism in the minds of youth which it is so important to guard against. It is always dangerous to disturb the settled order of things, even though that order may not answer to the highest and most perfect ideal. If the hostility of kings and princes to the Pope, and their desire to possess themselves of the goods of the Church, had the principal share in preparing the revolt of the sixteenth century, the quarrels of the Schoolmen, the attempt to dislodge Aristotle and enthrone Plato as the philosopher, had no little to do in detaching the minds of men from the theology of the Church, and preparing the way for the Protestant heresies. When the whole method of public teaching was adjusted to the scholastic philosophy, it was not easy to attack that philosophy without seeming in the minds of many to be attacking the Church, who had permitted her theology to be cast in its mould, and some of whose most revered saints had professed it.

However objectionable many may regard the philosophical system embodied in our more generally used textbooks, it must be conceded that the objections which might be urged against it are to no inconsiderable extent modified and practically obviated by the manner in which it is applied; and even if it were not so, what have we to take its place? Its modern opponents have criticized it, and written able essays on the principles and method of philosophy, but we are not aware that there is any better system of philosophy drawn out in that systematic order and completeness which fit it for the professor's use. Suppose, for a moment, that the ontological principles and methods insisted on by Gioberti are sound, what is the professor to do with them before his class? They are not systematized; there is no philosophy based on them drawn out in all its parts and adjusted to the general system of public teaching. What is the professor to do? Is he to interrupt his lessons till he has constructed all the parts of philosophy in harmony with them,—a work demanding years of patient study and labor, and that high order of metaphysical talent and genius scarcely to be found in one man in a century. Whatever changes may be demanded in the public teaching of philosophy, the time has not yet come for them, as the professor before us, as well as Father Rothenflue, fully proves, for while he adopts in his *Prolegomena* the principles of the ontological or synthetic school, he has not dared to depart from the language and method of the scholastic psychologists.

With these feelings towards the school with which we do not wholly agree, we cannot enlist with much zeal in any controversy against it; or in an animated defense of a rival school; and if we take part now and then in the controversy between them, it is more through our love of fair play than through any strong feeling of the absolute necessity of dispossessing one school and establishing another in its place. On certain questions we undoubtedly sympathize with the so-called Ontologists, but properly speaking, we have for ourselves no philosophical system, belong to no school, and swear by no master, neither by Gioberti nor by Father Curci. We regard, as we often say, philosophy simply as the rational element of supernatural theology, never capable by itself alone of being molded into a complete system even of natural truth, and never worthy of confidence when it aspires to disengage itself from revelation, and to stand alone as a separate and independent science. All we aim at is, to make a right use of reason in discussing those questions pertaining to reason which come in our way when defending Catholic faith and morals. Indeed, logic is the only part of philosophy we set much store by, and if we enter into the discussion of the higher metaphysical problems, it is chiefly for the sake of logic, because we cannot otherwise make sure of a logic which conforms to the real order of things. It is with a view to defend such a logic, not for the sake of one or another school of metaphysics, that we ask our readers to follow us a little into the question in dispute between the two schools respectively represented by the authors of the works we have cited, and perhaps, after all, we shall end by showing them that these two schools can much more easily be made to harmonize with each other than is commonly supposed.

The difference between the ontological and the psychological schools is perpetuated by the very general adoption in our schools of the Aristotelian logic, and what we regard as the errors of the psychological school we think have obtained among Catholics in consequence of that adoption. Aristotle's logic partakes of the general error of his philosophy. We wish to speak with all becoming respect of one whom the great St. Thomas terms the Philosopher; but he was, after all, a Gentile. He went, perhaps, as far as a Gentile could go; but we must remember that all Gentile philosophy was incomplete and fragmentary. The whole Gentile world had lost or corrupted the dogma of creation, and resolved creation into emanation, generation, or formation. They had broken the unity of the primitive language of mankind, had lost the integrity of the primitive tradition, and lacked the light which supernatural theology sheds on the great problems of human science, and hence, whatever their genius, their talent, or their industry, they were utterly unable to construct a complete and self-coherent system of philosophy. Ignorant of the dogma of creation, and holding the doctrine of formation in its place, it was not in Aristotle's power to construct a logic that should correspond to the order of things. He might have a wide and varied knowledge of phenomena, he might have a marvelous sagacity and great subtlety, he might reason powerfully and justly on many aspects of things, but he could never explain the syllogism, or render a just account of reasoning. The fundamental vice of his logic is, that it does not conform to the real order of things, whether taken subjectively or objectively. It does not bring us face to face with reality, although no man ever labored harder to find a logic which would do so; it always interposes a *mundus logicus* between the reason and the real world, and deals with the lifeless forms of abstract thought, instead of the living forms of things. Always is there interposed between the cognitive subject and the intelligible object a world of phantasms and intelligible species, which are neither God nor creature, neither nothing nor yet something, but a *tertium quid*, by means of which in some unintelligible way the cognitive subject comes into relation with the cognizable object. A little meditation on the fact that God has created all things by his own power from nothing, would speedily have made away with these intermeddling phantasms and intelligible species, annihilated this *mundus logicus* unnecessarily interposed between subject and object, by showing that whatever is not *thing* is *nothing*, that whatever thing is not God is creature, and that whatever thing—*entity* in scholastic language—is not creature is God, and that his intelligible light, indistinguishable from him, is the only medium between the cognitive faculty and its object, that can be asserted or conceived.

The old Scholastics, of course, knew and held the dogma of creation, and vindicated it whenever it was an express thesis; but, unhappily, when that dogma was not immediately in question, they adopted without modification the Aristotelian logic, and attempted like him to explain the facts of human cognition and reasoning without its light. Hence their everlasting abstractions, their subtle distinctions of forms of mere thought, not of things, and their unreality, which have so hurt their reputation, and so vitiated no small portion of their philosophical labors. Of course we speak of the Scholastics as philosophers treating freely rational questions, not as theologians treating Catholic dogmas, or even rational questions in their immediate relation to faith. This same Aristotelian logic has served as the model of that still in use, and hence we find in the present scholastic philosophy traces of the original vice. In all that immediately touches dogma, it conforms to the dogma of creation, and is, as we should say, ontological, while in all else it conforms to the Aristotelian notion of formation, and thus is not in harmony with itself.

The psychological school is divided into two principal branches, the Cartesian and the Scholastic. It is possible that the modern Scholastics will object to being termed psychologists, but we see not how they can with propriety. The characteristic of the psychologist is to assert the soul, a contingent existence, as the starting-point of all philosophy, and that the necessary, the absolute, as real and necessary being, is not apprehensible in immediate intuition, and is attained to only by a logical induction from intuition of the contingent, that is, intuition of creatures. The Scholastics of our time, as well as those of mediaeval times, assert this, contend that the contingent only is immediately known, and that God in the natural order is known only logically, as a logical induction, and therefore are really psychologists. We shall so call them, not to offend, but to distinguish them. They differ from the Cartesians as to evidence or the criterion of certainty, and especially as to the methodical doubt, real or feigned, recommended by Descartes. They profess to commence with a certain truth or fact, and to proceed from the known to the unknown, by demonstration, which rests for its certainty on the principle of contradiction; the Cartesians profess to begin by doubting or questioning everything, and they place evidence or certainty in clearness and distinctness of ideas. The Scholastics regard philosophy as *demonstrative*; the Cartesians as *inquisitive*.

The Scholastics have certainly as to method the advantage over their Cartesian brethren. Descartes lays it down that a man should begin by doubting all that he has been taught or hitherto believed, and believe henceforth only what he is able to prove by bringing it to the test of clear and distinct ideas. But this method, which is precisely the Protestant method of examination and private judgment, is obviously inadmissible, for the doubt, if real, is in a Catholic impious and forbidden; if unreal, it is no doubt at all, and amounts to nothing. To begin in a feigned doubt is to begin in a fiction, in falsehood; to begin in a real doubt is to begin in uncertainty, and there is no logical alchemy by which certainty can be extracted from pure uncertainty, or truth from pure falsehood. Descartes himself proves this, for he gets out of the doubt he places as his starting-point only by a shallow sophism, *Cogito, ergo sum*, "I think, therefore I exist,"—which is a sheer begging of the question. We know that, when hard pressed by his opponents, Descartes denied that he intended this as an argument to prove his existence, and maintained that he only gave it as a statement of the fact in which he became conscious of existing. But if so, only so much the worse for him, for it was precisely an argument to prove his existence that he needed. It is true that he might allege that proof in his system consists in clearness and distinctness of ideas; but in the act of thinking he has a clear and distinct idea or conception of his existence, and therefore he really does prove his existence. But that evidence is in clear and distinct ideas he does not anywhere prove, and that always, in thinking, one has a clear and distinct idea of his own existence, is not true, for ordinarily we have only an obscure and indistinct conception of ourselves as existing. Moreover, reasoning is always from premises, and if these be uncertain, so must be the conclusion.

But if the Scholastics are right against the Cartesians in adopting the demonstrative instead of the inquisitive method, they seem to us to fall into a very grave error as to the province of demonstration itself. They assume that demonstration proceeds from the known to the unknown, and enables them to conclude beyond the matter intuitively presented. The whole question between them and us lies precisely in this assumption. They deny all intuition or direct cognition of real and necessary being, and yet they contend that real and necessary being is legitimately concluded from the cognition of contingent existences. They must hold, then, that they can conclude more than they have in their premises, contrary to the well-known rule of logic:—

> Latius hunc quam præmissæ conclusio non vult.

If they contended that the demonstration simply distinguishes real and necessary being from the contingent in the intuition in which it is presented only in an obscure and indistinct manner, their conclusion would not be broader than their premises, and there would be no essential disagreement between them and the Catholic ontological school. But they do not admit this; they deny that we have any direct apprehension of real and necessary being at all, and then either they conclude what is not contained in their premises, and their conclusion is invalid, or the necessary and absolute which they conclude is a mere logical abstraction formed by the mind itself. Their God, then, whom they profess to demonstrate, would be only an abstract God, and they would have no right to laugh at Fichte, who remarked to his class as he concluded one lecture, "In our next lecture, gentlemen, we will make God."

Demonstration is the work of reflection, and reflection is never primary. The Italians happily express it by the word *ripensare*, to re-think, or to think again, and surely the mind must have thought before it can re-think; it must have had the matter of reflection presented before reflecting on it. Reasoning, the syllogism, demonstration, is only the instrument of reflection, whose sole office is to distinguish, clear up, systematize, and verify our immediate intuitions, and though it may and usually does contain less, it can never contain more than the matter presented in our direct cognitions, or by faith, human or divine, in things natural or in things supernatural. As to the reality contained in it, our science begins and ends where begin and end our immediate intuitions or direct cognitions; all beyond is not science, but faith, and can never be legitimately included in our philosophy.

We do not deny that the mediaeval Scholastics—the Peripatetics, we mean—have the air of asserting that the syllogism is an instrument by which we advance from the known to the unknown; but this is to be understood of knowledge under a reflective and scientific form, not as to its matter, and their own expression is from the better to the less known. Reality simply presented or merely apprehended in intuition they do not regard as known, because known only in an obscure and indistinct manner; but they never suppose that in formal science they ever advance beyond the reality thus presented. Their real doctrine is not readily seized, because they do not admit, precisely in our sense, immediate intuition. We know according to them only by means of phantasms and intelligible species; but when we have penetrated to the real fact which they mean to assert, we shall find that the phantasms are simply the means by which we actually cognize sensible or corporeal things, and the intelligible species are the means by which we really apprehend intelligibles or incorporeal things. The sensitive faculty does not, according to St. Thomas, terminate in the phantasms, but by them attains to their objects, and the intellective faculty does not terminate in the intelligible species, but through it attains to the intelligible reality. The phantasms and species present to the intellect their respective objects, and St. Thomas expressly teaches that nothing can be known by us not so presented. But as so presented, the reality is only the *materia informis* of science, and becomes science only as abstracted from the phantasms and species in which it is presented. It is easy to understand, then, why the Angelic Doctor regards the syllogism as the instrument of advancing science; he does so because on his principles it is by it that the intellect impresses on our simple apprehensions the form of science, and it is the form that gives actuality to the matter; but he was too good a logician to hold that the matter concluded can exceed the matter apprehended.

The scholastics followed Aristotle, and held that all cognition begins in sense, *quod principium nostra cognilionis est a sensu*; but we must beware how we suppose that such scholastics as St. Thomas held that only objects of sense are really apprehended in the phantasms or sensible species. They held that the intelligible is really apprehended in the phantasms, but under a sensible form, and is distinctly known only as abstracted or distinguished from them by the reflective intellect; and as nothing is really scientifically known except under an intelligible form, we see again how they could assert that the syllogism, the instrument of reflection, is a means of extending knowledge. But they do not represent it as extending knowledge beyond the matter apprehended, for their meaning is not that the intelligible is obtained from the sensible by a strictly analytic judgment, but that the intelligible is presented in the phantasms, or along with the sensible. That is, in our own language, what is called simple apprehension is simultaneously the apprehension or intuition of the sensible and intelligible as conjoined one with the other.

Under a certain point of view we are disposed on this last point to agree with the Peripatetics in opposition to the Platonists, or at least in opposition to Platonism as represented by Aristotle and understood by St. Thomas after the Neo-Platonists. Aristotle represents Plato as teaching that we have immediate intuition of intelligibles as separate from all apprehension of the sensible. We are far from being satisfied that Plato held this, and certainly, though we have been a somewhat diligent student of his works, we have never found it in them. Plato's problem, as we understand it, was not so much how we know, or by what faculty we are first placed in relation with reality, as what we must know in order to have real science. He placed science in the knowledge of the essences of things, which he called ideas, not in the knowledge of their exterior or sensible forms, which are variable and corruptible. But that these ideas are apprehensible in themselves without apprehension of the sensible to which they are joined, we have not found him teaching. But be this as it may, St. Thomas, after Aristotle, argues, and justly, that the intelligible is to the sensible as the soul is to the body, and that as man is in this present life always soul united to body, he can perform no operations which are not conjointly operations of both. Not being a pure spirit, but spirit united to matter,—not being a pure intelligence, like the angels, but intelligence united to sense,—he can apprehend the intelligible only as united to the sensible, the spiritual only as united in some way to the material. We apprehend the intelligible indeed,—the *idea* in the language of Plato,—but only in conjunction with the sensible, and therefore God never as separate from his works. Thus far we agree with the Peripatetics, and hold that every intuition of the intelligible even includes the sensible.

But we do not accept the doctrine that our cognition begins in sense, or the sensible species. The argument from the union of soul and body admits a double application, and if it proves that we can have no intellections without sensations, it proves equally that we can have no sensations without intellections, no sensible intuition without intelligible intuition. Indeed, it proves more than this. The intellective is to the sensitive, the intelligible is to the sensible, what the soul is to the body. But the soul is *forma corporis*, the form of the body. The intelligible, therefore, is the form of the sensible, intellect the form of sense. The *principium* is in the form, not in the matter, for the matter is potential, simply in *potentia ad formam*, and is made actual by the form. Therefore it is the intellect that gives to sensation its form of cognition, or that renders it actual perception of the objects of sense. Without intelligible intuition, sensation is a mere organic affection, and no actual perception at all. Cognition is the basis of all sensible perception, for whatever the objects or conditions of knowledge, the cognitive faculty is one and the same. We have not, as Aristotle perhaps held, one faculty called sense by which we know particulars, and another called intellect, by which we know universals. We know both corporeals and incorporeals, sensibles and intelligibles, by the intellective faculty, the former through sensible affection, and the latter on the occasion of such affection, or more simply, in conjunction with the former. Properly, then, though both the universal and the particular, the intelligible and the sensible, are presented simultaneously in one and the same intuition, the *principium* of our cognition is in the intellect, not in the senses, for till the intellect is reached there is no commencement of cognition. The Scholastics were misled by Aristotle, who, denying creation and asserting an eternal matter *extra Deum*, in which he placed the possible of determinate things, was obliged to place the *principium* in matter, that is, in the potential, which, since not actual, should be regarded as nothing at all. The Scholastics, knowing perfectly well the dogma of creation, ought not to have fallen into this error, for they were not ignorant that the possibility of things is in the Divine essence, and that the potential in that it is simply potential is a nullity. To say of anything that it is potential, is simply saying that it does not exist, but that God has power, if he chooses, to create it. God is the creator and the creability of all things, is both their formal and their material cause, in so far as material cause they have, and therefore the potential regarded as *extra Deum* is, as we have said, simply nothing. To place the *principium* in the potential is then a simple absurdity, and in the Scholastics wholly uncalled for, an inconsequence. To place the *principium* of cognition in sensation, which is only in *potentia ad cognitionem*, were as absurd as, after having declared the soul *forma corporis*, to pretend that the *principium* of the soul is in the body, or that the soul derives its life and actuality from the body, as pretend our modern materialists, instead of the body being made an actual and living body by the soul, and being, when separate from the soul, not a body, but a carcass.

The Scholastics, having placed the *principium* of our cognition in sense, were obliged to assume intelligibles or universal only as abstracted from the phantasmata or sensible species in which they are originally presented. This abstraction they suppose the intellect is competent to make by its own powers, and does make, as St. Thomas says, *dividendo et componendo*, or by ratiocination. Hence we find them uniformly, after Aristotle, and like all our modern inductionists, reasoning in a vicious circle. They tell us all knowledge begins *a sensu*, and that through the senses we know only particulars, and universals, genera and species, are obtained by reasoning, abstracting them from the particulars. Experience furnishes the particulars, and reason by way of induction obtains from them the universals, which, reapplied to particulars, give *sapientia*, or wisdom, the end of all philosophy. But they also tell us that all reasoning, all demonstration, proceeds from universals to particulars! So they assume universals in order to get particulars, and particulars in order to get universals. They prove their particulars by their universals, and their universals by their particulars. The universals are obtained by reasoning, and yet there is no reasoning without universals. And we are to be held up to ridicule and made the butt of Italian wit, because we cannot accept this as sound logic! Nay, denounced as pantheists, as enemies of religion, and as laboring only to destroy the defences of the Catholic faith! Yet no man who has made himself even superficially acquainted with the Aristotelian logic, can deny that it involves this *vicious* circle.

The mistake of Aristotle was not so much in denying the distinct intuition of universals, as it was in supposing that reflection originally obtains them by abstraction from the sensible species. The intellect does not, and cannot, so obtain them, for the reasons already assigned to prove that we never have intuition of the intelligible without the sensible. Intellect is joined to sense in the reflective order as much as it is in the intuitive, and therefore it cannot in reflection, any more than in direct cognition, apprehend the purely intelligible. As in intuition it is sensibly *presented*, so in reflection it must be sensibly *represented*. Here is a point which, as far as we have seen, neither Aristotle nor even St. Thomas sufficiently elucidates, and in the elucidation of which we must find the method of escaping from the Peripatetic circle. This sensible representation is not furnished by the sensible species or phantasms, for in them the intelligible is presented, not represented,—presented to the intuitive, not represented to the reflective understanding. It is impossible for man himself to furnish the medium of sensible representation, and it cannot be furnished by the objects themselves, for the precise work to be done is to separate the purely intelligible from the sensible species, or the sensible, in the intuition or apprehension of objects themselves. The Creator then must himself furnish it, and he does furnish it in language, which is the sensible sign, symbol, or representation of the intelligible. And hence man cannot reflect, or perform any operation of reasoning, without language, as has been so ably proved by the illustrious De Bonald, although his arguments would have been more conclusive, if he had taken pains to distinguish between reflective and intuitive thought. Intelligibles or universals are intuitively presented, as we say,—presented in the intelligible species, as the Schoolmen say; but they are objects of reflection, of distinct apprehension, or reflex cognition, only as sensibly represented in language. So represented, they are supplied to the mind prior to the intellectual operation of abstracting them from the sensible species or intuitions, and therefore may be legitimately used in reasoning before they are thus obtained. Consequently, by language, which sensibly represents the universals, we can get out of the Peripatetic circle. It is, in fact, by means of the word, of language, that Aristotle himself escapes from that circle; for he very nearly identifies logic with grammar, places the elements of the syllogism in verbal propositions, and makes the explanation of reasoning little else than the explanation of the right use of words. He avails himself of the fact of language, but he does not render a proper account of it, or legitimate the usage he makes of it. His practice was truer than his theory. This fact of the divine origin of language, and its necessity as the sensible representation of the intelligible in the reflective understanding, is one of vast importance, and, if attended to, would save philosophy from that too rationalistic tendency objected by the respectable Bonnetty and others, and teach our scholastic psychologists that to their demonstrative method they must add tradition or history, and prove to the heterodox that true philosophy can be found only where the primitive tradition and the unity and integrity of language have been infallibly preserved, therefore only in the Catholic Society or Church. Outside of that society there is no unity of speech, no integrity of doctrine; the primitive tradition is broken, and there are only fragments, *disjecta membra*, even of truth pertaining to the natural order. Alas! heterodoxy, whether in the natural order or the supernatural, is that wicked Typhon of Egyptian mythology, who seized the good Osiris and hewed him in pieces, and scattered his members far and wide over the land and the sea. So deals it with the fair and lovely form of Truth, and no weeping Isis, however painful her search, can gather them up and mould them anew into a living and reproductive whole!

It is these mistakes into which our Scholastics fall in their laudable efforts to avoid, on the one hand, the pure materialism of old Democritus, and the pure spiritualism or incorporealism of the Platonists on the other, that have induced them to deny all immediate intuition of the intelligible, and to maintain that the necessary is obtained only by induction from the contingent. Correcting these mistakes, dismissing their vexatious phantasms and intelligible species, and understanding that we stand face to face with reality, whether corporeal or incorporeal, spiritual or material, intelligible or sensible, with nothing but the intelligible light of God between as the medium of both intelligible and sensible intuition, they might easily find themselves in accord with the Catholic ontologists, and their philosophy corresponding to the order of things. They might then easily perceive that their principal objections to the ontological method are founded in misapprehension, and that they, though formally denying, do virtually admit all that we ourselves contend for. Their objections to the ontologists are based on the supposition that they assert pure and distinct intuition of God by our natural powers, or clear and distinct intuition of the necessary and intelligible prior to and without the contingent and sensible; but this, though true of the heterodox or bastard ontologists, such as we find among non-Catholics, is by no means the case with all who reject the psychological and assert the ontological method. The alternative presented is not, either that the necessary and intelligible must be concluded, by an analytic judgment, from the intuition of the contingent and sensible, or that the contingent and sensible must be concluded from the necessary and intelligible. These are two extremes alike false and dangerous, the one leading to nihilism through atheism, the other through pantheism. We have already explained that the intelligible is never presented alone, or separate from the sensible, but that both are in this life presented together, in one and the same intuition, and therefore that we have no simple intuitions or apprehensions, but that every apprehension, intuition, or thought is a complex fact, including both the intelligible and the sensible. As the sensible always represents the subject, it follows that there is never intuition of the object without intuition or apprehension of the subject, and none of the subject without the object, and therefore that there can be no intuition of God, real and necessary being, without the apprehension of the soul, contingent and relative being, or existence. Then the *primum philosophicum* can be neither the necessary, the absolute, the *primum ontologicum* alone, as maintain the German ontologists, or rather pantheists, nor the contingent, the relative, the *primum psychologicum*, as maintain the scholastic psychologists, but must be the simultaneous presentation of the two in their real synthesis or union. In this real and necessary being, or God, is really presented in the intuition, not separately, but in relation with the soul, or the contingent, not as clearly and distinctly known, but, as in all direct cognition, as known only in an obscure and indistinct manner.

This view, which we may call the synthetic, is opposed, as our readers cannot fail to perceive, alike to those who make the intuition of real and necessary being their starting-point, and profess to descend, by way of deduction, to contingent existence or to creatures, and to those who profess to start with the soul alone, and to be able from intuition of the contingent to rise by induction to necessary being, that is, to God. When by ontologists are meant the former, we must disclaim the name, for deduction is simple analysis, and attains to no predicates but such as lie already before the mind in the subject, and from the single conception of being can be obtained only being and its attributes. Here is, in our judgment, the principal fault of the work of the excellent Father Rothenflue. Father Rothenflue represents real and necessary being—God—as first in the order of intuition, but he does not take note of the fact that the necessary is never, in this life, presented to us without the contingent; for we never, in this life, see God as he is in himself, and at all only as he is related to us, or in his relation *ad extra*, as the theologians call it, of Creator. We see not, then, how Father Rothenflue's intuition of real and necessary being is to be distinguished, save in degree, from the intuitive vision of the blest; nor do we understand how he contrives to include in his philosophy contingent existences, or, in other words, after having assumed the *primum ontologicum* as his *primum philosophicum*, how he can by any legitimate process escape pantheism. He can relieve himself from this objection only by taking note that along with the necessary, as that on which it depends as its *principium*, is always presented the contingent in the same complex intuition, and therefore that the *primum philosophicum* cannot be being alone, any more than it can be the soul or contingent existence alone.

On the same principle, we object to those who profess to rise from the contingent discursively to the necessary, because, if they have only the *ens contingens*, they can conclude only the contingent and its phenomena. The scholastic psychologists teach that the first object of the intellect is *ens reale et actu*, a real or actual *ens*, but they deny that this is *ens necessarium*, and pretend that it is simply the soul or *ens contingens*. From this *ens contingens* they profess to be able to conclude *ens necessarium*, or God. But this is not possible by deduction, or analytic reasoning, which requires the predicate to be already in the subject, because the *ens necessarium* is not in or a predicate of, *ens contingens*; since if it were the contingent would not be contingent, but necessary,—a manifest contradiction in terms. It is equally impossible by synthetic reasoning, which adds to the subject a predicate not contained in it; for the judgment cannot join to the subject an unknown predicate, or a predicate not intellectually apprehended, as Kant has sufficiently proved in his *Critic der reinen Vernunft*. And here it is denied that the predicate *ens necessarium* is apprehended, since the very object of the process is to find it. In all synthetic or inductive reasoning, the conclusion is invalid if it goes beyond the particulars enumerated or the reality observed, and in the case before us it is contended that the *ens necessarium* which is to be concluded escapes all observation, and is wholly unknown. How, then, is the mind, in its judgment, to add it, bind it, to the subject, *ens contingens*?

The fact is, that our Scholastics do really assume the necessary to be apprehended by the intellect, although they imagine that they do not. They hold that God can be demonstrated by way of induction from contingent existences, and this argument holds a prominent place in their ontology. We do not question, nay, we maintain, the validity of this argument when properly understood. But what is their process? The contingent is known to exist, but, as its very name implies, it does not suffice for itself, has not the reason of its existence in itself, and cannot stand alone, and therefore it is necessary that there be something else on which it depends for its existence, which has caused it to exist, and sustains it. This something, since what is not real cannot act, and since we cannot suppose an infinite series of causes, must be real and necessary being, or the eternal and self-existent God. That is, in the apprehension of *ens contingens* they apprehend or have intuition of the *necessity* of *ens necessarium et reale*. The intuition of this necessity must be conceded, or the argument is good for nothing, and the conclusion cannot be asserted as *necessary*, and, indeed, cannot be asserted at all. Now this *necessity* of real and necessary being which is apprehended in apprehending the contingent, and which is the principle of the conclusion, what is it? The Scholastics, no doubt, regard this necessity as something really distinct from the necessary being itself. Otherwise they could not assert a progress in their argument from the known to the unknown, or deny the immediate intuition of real and necessary being. But is it something distinct? And does not their mistake lie precisely in supposing that it is?

This necessity is either something created or uncreated. It is not something created, for if it were it would be the contingent itself, and a contingent necessity is not admissible. If uncreated, it is either *ens* or *non-ens*. If *non-ens*, a nonentity, it is simply nothing, and can be no medium of concluding the necessary from the contingent. If *ens*, then it is *ens increatum*, and *ens increatum* is God, real and necessary being. Consequently, the distinction contended for, between the apprehension of the necessity of real and necessary being, and the apprehension of real and necessary being itself, does not and cannot in reality exist, and the apprehension of the necessity is *ipso facto* apprehension of real and necessary being, of God himself, although we may not always do, and certainly not always advert to it.

The Scholastics have been misled on this point by their devotion to Aristotle, who was obliged, in his theory, to explain the production of things and human knowledge without the fact of creation. Their error, if they will pardon us the word, lies precisely in supposing a logical necessity distinct from necessary being, and that from the apprehension of the necessity of real and necessary being to the judgment such being is, there is a progress. Hence why we began by insisting so strenuously on the recognition of the fact of the creation of all things from nothing, as essential to the construction of a sound logic, or a logic that conforms to the order of things. It is not till we learn that God has created all things out of nothing, that we are able to say that whatever is not God is creature, and that whatever is not creature is God. God and creature comprise all that is or exists, and what neither is nor exists is simply nothing, and is and can be no object of thought, as both St. Thomas and Aristotle teach. "Ens namque est objectum intellectus primum," says the Angelic Doctor, "cum nihil sciri possit, nisi ipsum quod est ens actu, ut dicitur in 9 Met. Unde nec oppositum ejus intelligere potest intellectus, non ens."[1] Yet Aristotle, who confounds creation with formation, and makes the essences of things consist partly in the form and partly in the matter, imagined a sort of *tertium quid*, neither God nor creature, not precisely something, nor yet absolutely nothing. Corresponding to this *tertium quid*, he imagines a sort of *ens logicum* distinct from *ens physicum*, a sort of middle term between *ens* and *non ens*. Hence a *mundus logicus* distinct from the *mundus physicus*, and a logical necessity distinguishable from physical necessity, or necessary being. Our Scholastics will not say the necessity of necessary being which the mind apprehends is literally nothing, nor yet will they admit it is a real being or entity. They regard it as an *ens logicum*, or as a logical relation between two terms; but relation apart from the related is inconceivable, for it is a sheer nullity. It exists and is apprehensible only in the related. Nothing exists *in abstructo*; all reality is concrete, and it is only in the concrete that things are or can be apprehended.

The Scholastics forget this, and, as they agree that only what is *ens aliquo modo* can be an abject of the intellect, they clothe their abstractions with a sort of entity, and imagine them apprehensible *extra Deum*, and apart from their concretes. It is only by so doing that they can pretend that the necessity they apprehend in apprehending the contingent is distinguishable from real and necessary being. All conceivable necessity is in God, is God, for there can neither be necessity out of being, nor necessity in a non-necessary being. Necessity is in being, not in non-being. The necessity that there should be God is not any other necessity than the necessity of his own being; and the necessity of his being, which we assert when we say he is necessary being, is in him, not out of him, necessitating him to be. It is a necessity in him to be, and to be precisely what he is, and simply implies that his being is itself its sole and sufficient cause or reason of itself. When we say this or that is necessary or unnecessary, we have reference always to his Divine Essence, and the real meaning is, that this or that is or is not necessary in the eternal and immutable nature of God. God is himself, in his own essence, the eternal reason, nature, or fitness of things, of which philosophers speak, that is, in so far as it is necessary, and in his power, in so far as it is contingent. But all this is obscured by the Aristotelian logic, which places the necessary as well as the possible in some sense *extra Deum*. Indeed, an assumption of this sort runs through all Gentile philosophy. Hence the *fatum* of the Stoics, and the Destiny of the Poets, which binds alike gods and men in the invincible chain of an inexorable Necessity. Neither Greek nor Roman philosophy ever succeeds in steering wholly clear of Oriental Dualism. Pythagoras and Plato assert the eternity of matter, and place in it the origin of evil; and Aristotle finds in this same eternal matter a limitation of the power of God. The Scholastics struggle bravely against this Dualism, and to harmonize their Gentile logic with their Catholic theology, but perhaps not always with complete success. They define the possible as that in which there is no repugnance between the subject and predicate, and the impossible as that in which there is such repugnance; but they are not uniformly careful to inform us that the subject is the Divine Essence, and that the possible or impossible is what is or is not repugnant to that, and that both have their reason, not out of God, but in the fullness and perfection of his own being. The same remarks are applicable to the necessary and the unnecessary. Not being ordinarily given as predicates of the Divine Being only, they are not seldom regarded, even by men who pass for philosophers, as predicates, either of no subject, or of an unknown subject, which is neither God nor creation, neither something nor yet nothing.

We do not, say the Scholastics, in apprehending the contingent, apprehend *ens necessarium et reale*, but the necessity there is that there be *ens necessarium et reale*. But can you apprehend the necessity of a thing which you do not apprehend? You apprehend the imperfect, but can you apprehend that it is imperfect, and that it needs something which it has not, if you have not the apprehension of the perfect in which it can find its complement? Not without conceiving the perfect, it is answered, but without apprehending the perfect. Without apprehending or knowing the perfect perfectly, we concede, but without knowing that it is, we deny. We do not pretend that our intuition of real and necessary being gives us a full and comprehensive knowledge of what it is, for our knowledge, at best, whatever its sphere or its object, is extremely imperfect, and hardly deserves the name of knowledge. We do not comprehend real and necessary being, we only apprehend it; and we apprehend it only in its relation to created existences, never in itself. We do not apprehend it at all, say the Scholastics, we apprehend only its necessity. But its necessity is not distinguishable from itself, for necessity can be apprehended only in necessary being, since the abstract apart from the concrete is a mere nullity, and no object of thought. Surely the necessity must be either something or nothing. If nothing, it is nothing, can do nothing, and nothing can be made of it. If something, it is either absolute being, or created existence, for created existence is the only medium between absolute being and nothing. It cannot be created existence, for that would imply a contradiction in terms, and because creation is, on the part of God, a free, not a necessary act. Then it must be absolute being. Then it is God, and then whoever apprehends necessity apprehends God. Then all who accept the argument from the contingent to the necessary, since the reasoning is synthetic, not analytic, do really assume, whether they are aware of it or not, that we have in the apprehension of creature the apprehension of that which is not creature, therefore, of God, the creator. The argument from *entia contingentia* is a good argument, when properly explained, and is objectionable only when presented as an analytic argument, or as a synthesis, which adds to the subject an unknown and unapprehensible predicate.

Every thought, intuitive or reflective, is a judgment, for, as we have seen, we have and can have no apprehension which is not simultaneously apprehension of both subject and object, the mind and that which stands opposed to it and is really distinguishable from it. In every thought, as in every enunciable proposition, there are three terms, subject, predicate, and copula. The subject is *ens necessarium et reale*, real and necessary being; the predicate is *entia contingentia*, or contingent existences. The copula, then, must be the relation of the necessary and contingent. This relation, the nexus that unites subject and predicate, can be nothing else than the creative act of God, which produces the predicate from nothing. We know this is so, from the dogma of creation, and we know furthermore, that *entia contingentia* can exist only inasmuch as they are created, and that the act by which they are created is and must be solely the act of God, for prior to their creation they are nothing, and nothing cannot concur in making itself something. It is of the nature of contingents not to have their cause or the reason of their existence in themselves, and therefore they cannot exist separated or disjoined from the creator. Consequently, the predicate existence can begin or continue to exist only as really joined to the subject, real and necessary being, by the creative act of God. This act must be an *actus perdurans*; for though an existence could be conceived to have been created, it can be conceived as continuing to exist only in its continuing to be created. Suppose the creative act of God to cease, or to be suspended, with regard to any particular existence,—and we may so suppose, because the act is, on the part of God, a free act,—that existence ceases at once, and is literally annihilated. It is only on condition, then, that the creative act is *actus perdurans*, that existences are continued, and what we call conservation is in reality only creation. So that the original and persisting relation between God and the soul, God and existences, is the relation of creator and creature. God, by his creative act, creates existences from nothing, and establishes a relation *ad extra* between them and himself. It is only on condition of the reality of such relation that thought is possible, for it is only by virtue of that relation that we exist at all, or that there is any thinker, except real and necessary being. The relation of creation is then the copula in the real order or in the judgment as the judgment of real and necessary being, and therefore its real apprehension must be the copula of the judgment regarded as ours, or else the order of cognition will not correspond to the order of things. The three terms of the judgment objectively considered are, then, Being, the subject; contingent existences, the predicate; and the creative act of being, the copula. And we may assume as our formula of thought, or *primum philosophicum*, and as the basis of all sound logic, *Ens creat existentias*, or Being creates existences.

This formula has been objected to as pantheistic, as placed first in the order of cognition when it should be last, and as being given as a philosophical when it is a theological truth, known only as supernaturally revealed. It is not easy to understand how it can be pantheistic. The essence of pantheism is in the denial of second causes or the production by the Creator of real effects *ad extra*. The formula, therefore, cannot have a pantheistic sense, unless it denies the predicate existence, or the subject apprehending as existing distinct from God and operating as second cause. This it certainly does not do, for it is given as a formula of thought, and its very purpose is to assert that the mind intuitively apprehends the subject thinking and the object thought as really united by the creative object, and this necessarily asserts the reality of the soul or subject of the intuition distinct from the object God, and its activity as second cause, for without such activity it could not think or be the subject of an intuition. The principle we proceed upon is, that the order of cognition must agree with the order of things, for we hold, with St. Thomas, that the intellect is essentially true, and that truth is in the correspondence of the thought to the thing. We have proved that, in apprehending the object or thing, we invariably and necessarily apprehend ourselves as subject apprehending; that we can never apprehend what is not ourselves without apprehending ourselves, nor ourselves without apprehending what is not ourselves; that is, every thought affirms the subject simultaneously with the object, and the object simultaneously with the subject. The formula then no more denies the subject than the object. It expressly asserts existences distinguished from as well as united to God by his creative act, as really placed *ad extraby* his creative act, which creates them from nothing,—the direct contradiction of pantheism, which denies that any effects are produced *ad extra*, or that there is anything really produced distinguishable *ad extra* from God.

The charge of pantheism, we have been told, is warranted by the fact that the verb in the formula is placed in the present tense. The present tense, it is contended, expresses an action unfinished, whose effect is in the process of completion, but is not yet completed. *Ens creat existentias*, means, God is creating existences, and this means that the existences are only in the process of creation, therefore that they are only incomplete or inchoate existences. Such existences cannot act, and therefore the whole thinking activity asserted is that of God, which, as it denies the proper activity of second causes, is pantheism. But this conclusion, if possible, is not necessary. The verb is placed in the present tense, not to express the act as incomplete in relation to its proper effect, but to express the fact that the act is a present act. The act may be present and yet terminate in its complete effect. The effect is simply the extrinsic terminus of the causative act. Existences cannot be supposed to be once created, and then to be able to subsist of themselves, without the creative energy that produced them. Their conservation is their continuous creation. Being only the extrinsic terminus of the creative act, they are, if separated from it, simply nothing. They are produced and subsist only by virtue of the creative energy of that act, and the cessation of that act would be their annihilation. When I consider myself as having existed, I use the perfect tense, and say, God has created me; but when I wish to consider myself simply as existing, I say, God creates me; for he does literally create me at this very moment, and if his creative act were not a present act to me, and did not this moment create me from nothing, I should not exist, or be an existence at all. The act of creation and conservation is the one creative act, and hence to every actual existence the creative act is necessarily a present act, and can be expressed only in the present tense. The Church indeed, as does Genesis, uses the perfect tense, and says *creavit* instead of *creat*; but because, though she expresses the same fact that the formula does, she does not express it from the same point of view, and it did not enter into her purpose in defining the dogma of creation to assert the identity of creation and conservation; and when it is not necessary to express that identity, the perfect tense must be used.

Our modern Scholastics, who imagine that they detect pantheism in the formula *Ens creat existentias*, have, we must believe, studied it rather for the purpose of finding some error in it, than of ascertaining its real meaning. Their psychological habits and prejudices very naturally dispose them against it, and the fact that they have found some of its most distinguished modern advocates among the worst enemies of the Christian religion and civilization, is not very well fitted to win their respect for it. They seem to have hastily inferred, from the fact that Gioberti—an able but a bad man—used the present tense of the verb, that he meant in his formula to represent Being simply as the immanent cause of existences, in the sense of Spinoza, who opposes *causa immanens* to *causa transiens*. Immanent cause, as thus opposed, means only a cause that operates within its own interior, without placing any real effects *ad extra*. In this sense existences are not an external creation, but effects produced by Being within its own bosom, as modes or modifications of itself, which is pure pantheism. So far as the present tense decides anything, the creative cause asserted in the formula might be understood in this sense, and we suppose our scholastic friends do so understand it. But the character of the cause is determined by the nature, not the tense of the verb. The verb to *create*, according to all Christian usage, means to place real effects *ad extra*, and therefore can no more have the sense of Spinoza in the present than in the perfect tense. The word *existences*, from *ex-stare*, to be from another, by its own force expresses an external effect, distinct, though, like every effect, inseparable, from its cause. Attention to the real sense of the verb to create and of the substantive existences, placed in the plural number expressly to render the idea of plurality distinct, would, we think, have removed all ambiguity occasioned by placing the verb in the present tense, and convinced our scholastic friends that no pantheistic or heterodox sense can fairly be extracted from the formula, regarded as expressing the reality apprehended in the primitive intuition.

The only point on which a reader might doubt Gioberti's orthodoxy is as to the relation of the copula of the judgment, regarded as our judgment, with the real relation of things, or copula of the judgment, regarded as the judgment of God. Thought is composed of three elements, subject, object, and their relation, the soul, God, and the relation between them. Now there can be no doubt that the relation between God and the soul in the real order is the Divine creative act; but if we say that this act is the relation in the order of cognition, we make the judgment God's judgment, not ours, and therefore fall into pantheism. Gioberti, as far as we have examined him, does not seem to us to be very clear on this point, and we are not sure that he does not identify the real relation of the intuitive subject and the intelligible object with the copula of the judgment or the form of the thought. He gives *Ens creat existentias* as his *primum philosophicum*, and calls it a Divine Judgment, and seems to represent the mind as purely passive in regard to it. If so, what is the human judgment, or what is the part of the human intellect in the formation of thought? We have no call to defend Gioberti, and even if he has erred here, it is only an error in his interpretation of the formula, not an error in the formula itself. We have not studied Gioberti's works with any great care, for we felt from the first, long before they were prohibited, that he was a dangerous man, whom it would never do to take as a master, and certainly we cannot bind ourselves to any defence of his philosophy. It seems to us that his explanation of cognition makes intuitive thought an act of God rather than of man, and that he sometimes comes very near identifying the order of cognition with the order of things. Nevertheless, we must remember that he gives *Ens creat existentias* as the ideal formula, which with him means the formula as the intelligible object of the intuition,—not the apprehension, but that which is apprehended; and so taken, it has and can have no pantheistic sense. Whether he sufficiently distinguishes, in the fact of intuition, the intellective action of the subject from the concurrent activity of the intelligible object in the production, not of things, but of intuition, may, perhaps, be a question, and therefore it may be a question whether he has or has not been justly accused of pantheism. But however this may be, it is certain that the formula itself, regarded as the formula of things and the reality asserted in every thought, is in no sense pantheistic.

The objection, that this formula is placed first, at the beginning of the order of cognition, instead of last, or at its conclusion, will vanish the moment we learn to distinguish between direct and reflex intuition. Nobody pretends that, in the historical development of the understanding, we commence with a reflex intuition, or a clear and distinct cognition of this formula, or that the mind is able to say to itself at the first moment of its existence, *Ens creat existentias*. All direct intuition is obscure and indistinct, and although this formula is obscurely and indistinctly apprehended from the first, we are far enough from being aware from the first of the fact. Some men never attain to a reflex intuition of it during their whole lives, and no one ever would or could attain to such intuition of it, if not taught it through the medium of language. It had been lost from the language of the Gentiles, and no Gentile philosopher ever attained to it. All the Gentile schools alike are ignorant of the fact of creation, and even for Pythagoras, Plato, and Aristotle there is no God the creator. Not being able to reflect on the intelligible or idea without the sensible representation of language, the formula, as a *formula of the reflective understanding*, is not attainable till it is represented in language, and a language that has not lost it. But it is represented in language, and children learn it in the Catechism, at a very tender age.

That it is a truth of theology, and known only as supernaturally revealed, we grant; but it does not therefore follow that it is not a truth of the natural order. Superintelligible and supernatural are not by any means the same. There may be truths of philosophy, that is, of the natural order, distinct from the truths of the supernatural order, or the new creation, which we could never by our natural intellect find out, but which when revealed to us we may discover to be evident to natural reason. We do not believe any man could ever have attained to a reflex, that is, a clear and distinct cognition of the formula, without supernatural revelation, and therefore the holy Apostle tells us, "By faith we understand that the world was framed by the word of God." Hence creation is a dogma of faith; but when revealed and represented to us in language, we find it to be really expressed in every one of our direct intuitions, and therefore it is also a truth of philosophy. All the truths of revelation are not also truths of philosophy, but some of them are, for the revelation is not restricted to the Christian mysteries, properly so called. And hence the necessity we before remarked, of adding to the demonstrative method of the Scholastics the traditional or historical method, and the impossibility of constructing a complete science of the natural order without the reflected light of supernatural theology. It is the impossibility of erecting philosophy, in our present state, into a complete and independent science even of natural things, that makes us refuse to embrace any school, or to profess any system of our own. We should as soon think of disengaging our politics or our private and social duties from our theology, as of disengaging our philosophy.

One point more and we have done. We have given as the reality apprehended in every thought, Being creates existences. Here is the basis of all logic. But there are here two errors to be guarded against. The formula as given is the formula of the real order, or the Divine judgment. All the activity it expresses is the Divine activity. It is not the cognition, but that which in cognition is cognized. In other words, it is the formula of the intelligible; but to the intelligible corresponds the intellective, to the order of things the order of cognition. What we have here to guard against, then, is placing, as to the order of cognition, the copula either wholly in the intellective or wholly in the intelligible. The former is the error of the Scholastics, and the latter is the error of the Pantheists. We have found the copula of the Divine judgment; it is the creative act of Being placing existences *ad extra*. The copula of the human judgment is the reverberation of the copula of the Divine judgment, or imitation of it by us as second causes. But what is the nexus or copula which binds the human judgment to the Divine, that is, the intelligible and the intellective? The creative act of Being, says Gioberti, if we understand him; but that makes Being create the intellection, denies our intervention as second causes, and implies pantheism. The intellective, the *intellectus agens* of the Schoolmen? But that is pure Fichteism, and supposes the subject renders actual, that is, creates its object. The solution is in regarding thought as the joint product of both the intelligible and the intellect, and therefore that cognition, formally the act of the mind as second cause, is yet produced only by the active cooperation or concurrence of the intelligible, as is the case with every act of second causes. It is not the *intellectus agens* that renders the intelligible *intelligible in actu*, as the Scholastics teach, but the intelligible is itself by its own light *intelligible in actu*, and it is the concurrence of its intelligibility *in actu* with our own intellective faculty that forms the intuition. As the intelligible concurs only through its creative act, the creative act of God as the objectively concurring force of thought unites our cognition to the Divine judgment, as it does ourselves as existence to the Divine Essence. In this connection of our judgment with Divine judgment lies the explanation of all thought and of all reasoning, as well as the truthfulness of our cognitions.

The explanation of this connection itself, which involves the whole mystery of knowledge and of the whole activity of second causes, we shall not by any means attempt, for if it does not surpass the powers of the human mind, it most assuredly surpasses ours. Its explanation, however, is in the explanation of the Divine cooperation. But the reader will perceive that, in representing the intelligible as *intelligible in actu*, we reject the *intellectus agens* of the Scholastics as a created light, or participated reason, and therefore the intelligible species and phantasms. To intellectual vision as to external, there are necessary the intellect, the object, and the light. As to the purely intelligible, Being, it is intelligible per se, by its own light, and a mediating light distinct from the mind and the object is needed only in apprehending existences, and the light by which we see these is the same Divine light of Being, diffused over them by the Divine creative act. But as we apprehend not the purely intelligible in itself, owing to its excess of light and our weakness, we apprehend God only in the light of his creative act, and therefore only in relation to the things he has made. But as that light proceeds from his essence, and is simply his relation *ad extra* to the things he has made, in apprehending it we do really apprehend him. We apprehend them, not by their phantasms, but by his light, which through the creative act illumines them. And thus, while we maintain that we do really apprehend him, we do not pretend any more than our scholastic friends that we apprehend him separate from the apprehension of his works.

FOURTEEN

Liberalism and Socialism

We have brought these two works together because, though published at distant intervals, and differing almost as widely as it is possible to conceive, they are on the subject treated the two profoundest works to be found in the whole range of modern literature. Both treat the same subject, Donoso Cortés from the point of view of Catholicity, Pierre Leroux from the pantheistic or humanitarian point of view, and each needs to be read and studied by whoever would understand, either in their truth or their falsity, the liberalism and socialism which have made so much noise and stirred up so many commotions throughout the civilized world during the last fifteen or twenty years.

Pierre Leroux has hardly been heard of since 1850. Whether he is still living or not is more than we know; but we remember the time when he was one of the great men of France, and the representative of an important school in philosophy and politics. He belonged originally, we believe, to the Saint-Simonian school or sect, and distinguished himself at a later day as a most bitter enemy of the French eclecticism founded by the eloquent

"1. *Ensayo sobre el Catholicismo, el Liberalism, y el Socialismo, considerados en sus Principios Fundamentales*. Por Don Juan Donoso Cortés, Marqués de Valdegamas. Madrid. 1851. 8vo. pp. 414. 2. *De l'Humanité, de son Principe, et de son Avenir, où se trouve exposée la Vraie Définition de la Religion, et où l'on explique le Sens, la Suite, et l'Enchaînement du Mosaïsme et du Christianisme.* Par Pierre Leroux. Paris: 1840. 2 tomes. 8vo." From *Brownson's Quarterly Review,* 3rd Series, 3 (April 1855): 183–209.

and erudite Cousin. He is decidedly the great man of the modern socialistic school, and the only one with whom we are acquainted who has succeeded in giving it anything like a philosophical basis, he possesses rare philosophical genius, and, though not the soundest, he is the greatest metaphysician that France has produced in modern times, and may as to his genius and erudition take rank with the late Vincenzo Gioberti, who has had no equal since Leibnitz, for we cannot rank very high such men as Fichte, Schelling, and Hegel. Immanuel Kant is the only distinguished German metaphysician in recent times that we should be willing to name, unless one or two Catholics of Germany are to be excepted.

It may be that we attach an undue importance to the writings of Pierre Leroux, because our acquaintance with them marks an epoch in our mental development, and we owe to them more than to those of any other modern writer. They revolutionized our own mind both in regard to philosophy and religion, and by the grace of God became the occasion of our conversion to Catholicity. But we must be permitted to say, that, though his system as a system does not and never did satisfy us, it contains certain great cosmic and metaphysical truths, more distinctly recognized and more clearly and energetically stated than we find even in the ordinary works on theology, and almost wholly wanting in our ordinary systems of philosophy. His grand error is in his having misinterpreted and misapplied the Catholic doctrine of the Incarnation, in confounding the two natures in the one person of our Lord, and in failing to distinguish properly between the natural and the supernatural orders. He starts with the Eutychian heresy, or the confusion of the human and the divine, and really, though perhaps unconsciously, explains the divine by the human, and thus reduces Christianity to pure humanism or naturalism. The Catholic theologian understands at once the reach of this fundamental error, which vitiates and must vitiate the author's whole system. But, after all, there is a human side of truth, for man is made in the image and after the similitude of God. God is, in the language of St. Thomas, *similitudo rerum omnium*, and hence in all nature there is and must be a certain reflection, so to speak, of the Divinity. God is in some sense mirrored by his works. In man and nature we must find, not the elements of Christianity indeed, for they are superhuman and supernatural, but certain analogies or correspondences, which in human language are expressed by the same terms, and through which the Christian mysteries are rendered in a measure intelligible to us. Leroux certainly confounds these analogies or correspondences in the natural and human order with the superhuman and supernatural dogmas of Christianity; but he certainly has studied them profoundly, and tells us, not unmixed with error, some great and important natural truths,—truths recognized and accepted, indeed, by all the great scholastic divines, but which these divines do not set forth in that distinct and prominent light in which we find them in the earlier fathers, or in which it is necessary, perhaps, to set them forth in order to meet the characteristic errors of our age.

The Marquis of Valdegamas has studied the same subject with equal industry, with equal mental strength and acuteness, and with a higher order of genius. He understands it far better, and treats it far more profoundly; for he knows and accepts Catholic theology, which places him in the position to comprehend the natural truth in its true relations with the supernatural, and prevents him from giving a mutilated or distorted view of either. But he writes mainly for the Catholic mind, and is more intent on showing the errors, absurdities, and fatal tendencies of humanitarian or pantheistic socialism to the understanding of the faithful, than he is on distinguishing for the benefit of its adherents the grain of truth in their system, and using it to lead them up to the Catholic doctrine which accepts and completes it. Nothing in the world can be better than his book to guard the faithful against the errors of pantheistic or humanitarian socialism, or to inspire them with a hearty love of Catholic doctrine and morals; but it is not precisely adapted to the wants of the socialists themselves. Ignorant of Catholic faith and theology, they will not always be able to find in his Catholicity the truth they are groping after, and which gives to their speculations a value in their own eyes. We, who happen to know both sides by our own experience, can see that he accepts and vindicates in its true light and place what they really value, and which they erroneously conclude cannot be held in the church, and persuade themselves can be realized without her, and must be, if realized at all.

The noble marquis also takes M. Proudhon as the best representative of Socialism, and confines himself mainly to the refutation of the Proudhonian theory. Here we must be permitted to differ from him. If we would study the Socialistic contradictions and negations, Proudhon is our man; but if we would study Socialism in its affirmations, in what it has that is positive, in its truths, or half-truths, we must, we think, take Leroux. Proudhon is by turns a deist and an atheist, a pantheist and a Manichean, but generally a denier, whose business it is to break with the whole past, to reject all that has hitherto been regarded as sacred, in a word, to destroy all that has been or is. Would we know whither all false theories, religious, political, and social, lead, we must study Proudhon, who under this point of view is the great man of the socialistic and revolutionary world. But Leroux has some religious instincts, is not the veritable Apollyon, and attempts to give the positive and affirmative side of Socialism. If we would know the truth which misleads the Socialists, which they misapprehend and misapply, but which nevertheless is the element which commends to their own judgments and hearts their Socialism, Leroux, not Proudhon, in our judgment, is the great, "the representative man." We say not this to depreciate the work of the lamented Spanish nobleman. We have heretofore expressed our opinion of his remarkable essay, than which, we are assured by those who are more competent than we are to judge, there is nothing more eloquent in the noble Castilian tongue. We are not, we confess, of his political school. We have more confidence in constitutionalism or parliamentary government than he appears to have had. We hold that parliamentary or constitutional government, though by no means perfect, though not all we could wish, and far enough from being all that its partisans pretend, affords the only political guaranty of liberty, civil or religious, which, after so many social changes, and revolutions, is now practicable. Certainly it is to it, not to absolute monarchy, that Catholicity owes the immense progress it has made in Europe during the last fifty years. We have seen nothing in the revolutionary developments during late years to shake our early faith in representative and parliamentary government, and we are satisfied that the Spanish statesman rendered no service to his country by his war against constitutionalism and parliamentary discussion. The great error of the European liberalists is not, in our judgment, so much political as religious. We find no fault with them for seeking what are called checks and balances, or attempting to found government on compromises; for government is a practical affair, and cannot be carried on without an adjustment of opposing interests, which more or less offend theoretic unity. We censure them not for this, but for supposing that these compromises, these balancings of principles and interests, and playing off of one against another, can alone suffice for the maintenance of authority on the one hand and individual freedom on the other. We accept them as far as they go, but we expect no valuable results from them when substituted for religion, or even when intended to operate without it. We do not, therefore, agree with the illustrious author, whose loss the Catholic world justly deplores, in his anti-parliamentary politics and monarchical theory.

But aside from his politics, in which he was more Spanish than American, we have had in modern times no Catholic writer more free and bold in his speculations, more original and brilliant in his genius, more comprehensive in his thought or spirit-stirring in his eloquence, or in general more remarkable for his depth and soundness. He formed himself by the study of the Holy Scriptures and the great fathers, rather than the modern theological compendiums, or the great scholastic doctors; and while for that reason he speculates more freely, and writes with more freshness and vigor, he is less exact in his doctrine and less accurate in his language. There are expressions in his essay, which, if detached from their connection and understood without reference to the obvious intention of the author, are certainly inexact, and perhaps even heretical, as has been shown by the Abbé Gaduel; but if fairly and honestly interpreted by their context and the general scope of the argument, by a liberal-hearted criticism which seeks to unfold the large and comprehensive thoughts of a writer rather than to display its own microscopic accuracy, no very grave objections under the point of view of Catholic doctrine can be sustained against the book. In this essay the author has attempted and executed a work that was much needed in the present time, that of carrying back the faithful to the deepest and most living mysteries of the Catholic faith, and showing the origin and support of human society in God. Starting with the principle already asserted, that God is *similitudo rerum omnium*, or the likeness which all created things copy, and therefore that all things have their ideas or archetypes in his divine essence, he shows that true human society has its origin in the divine society of the ever-adorable Trinity, Father, Son, and Holy Ghost, three persons in one nature or essence. In this divine society, whose characteristic, as he not very accurately expresses it, is unity in diversity and diversity in unity, he finds the original type of all society, and therefore all true human society must reflect this divine society, as all creation reflects the Creator. Here is the fundamental conception, the leading thought, of the Essay on Catholicity, Liberalism, and Socialism. This thought, which is profoundly Catholic, as well as profoundly philosophic, reproduces what is deepest and truest in the Platonic philosophy, although it is perhaps foreign to the Aristotelian. We find it in the Holy Scriptures, we find it in the early fathers, we find it in Catholic theology of all times, but we do not find it always in what passes for philosophy in the schools. The Platonic philosophy is no doubt exposed to dangers from which the Aristotelian is free. It is less rigid in its method; it is more daring in its scope, and opens a wider and richer field to speculation. It gives more play to our emotions, affections, and imagination, and therefore exposes us to greater mental aberrations. It brings into play the mystic elements of our nature, and opens us on that side on which Satan can best approach and seduce us. But there can really be no question that it is far profounder than the Aristotelian philosophy, and penetrates to an order of ideas to which Aristotle was a stranger, and which cannot be brought within the comprehension of a rigid Peripateticism. Peripateticism, considering everything under the form of abstract thought, loses sight of life, of the real living universe, and therefore is unable to detect in the natural order the analogies, resemblances, copies, or reflections, without which the supernatural would be in every sense inapprehensible to our intelligence. Hence it never enables us to connect the intelligible and the superintelligible, and embrace the natural and the supernatural as one harmonious whole, having its unity in the Divine Essence. Donoso Cortés has done a noble service to religion and society by reviving, what was almost lost sight of in popular philosophy, the profound thought of the fathers and the great scholastic doctors, and showing us that even the natural order demands its complement from the supernatural, and that the profoundest mysteries of our faith are the source of all that is true and good, sound and healthy, in our natural life, or, in other words, that the natural has its root in the supernatural, and derives its sap from an order deeper and higher than itself. He thus connects human society with the mystery of the Trinity, which is its norma or type. As all in Catholicity has its origin in the mystery of the Trinity, so all true human society must have its origin and type in Catholicity. This thought reaches far, and must be fully recognized and well understood before we fully comprehend Christian society, and are able to oppose it successfully to the refutation of humanitarian or pantheistic socialism, so rife in our times. Those who seek to do this must study profoundly the essay of Donoso Cortés.

But our purpose at present is not precisely that of the illustrious Spaniard. We have already discussed in our pages the errors and dangerous tendencies of liberalism and socialism; we have pointed out what they have that is opposed to Catholic faith and theology. We wish now to draw attention to what they have that is true. All systems, however erroneous or false, have an element of truth, because the human intellect, being created in the image of the Divine, and made for the apprehension of truth, can never operate with pure falsehood. To rightly comprehend a system is not simply to detect its errors. We understand not even an erroneous system till we understand its truth; and its real refutation lies not so much in detecting and exposing its fallacies, as in detecting, distinguishing, and accepting the truth which it misapprehends, misinterprets, or misapplies. Socialism commends itself to the intellect of its adherents only in the respect that it is true, and to their hearts only in the respect that it is good; for the intellect, St. Thomas teaches, can never be false, nor the will evil. Both falsehood and evil are privative, neither is positive. Error is in the defect of truth, and evil in the defect of good. We must say this or assert falsehood as a real entity and evil as a positive principle, and thus fall into Manicheism. We must beware of the Calvinistic doctrine of total depravity, or total corruption by the fall of human nature. If man cannot embrace pure falsehood nor will what under some aspect is not good, it follows that in every erroneous or mischievous system there is and must be an aspect of truth and goodness, and it is only under this aspect that the system is dear to its adherents. If we wish to produce a favorable effect on them, and to refute their system for their sake, we must begin, not by denouncing their error, but by showing them that we recognize and accept their truth.

Our own views of both liberalism and socialism have so often been expressed in these pages, that none of our readers can suspect us of any undue bias in their favor. We have, as it is well known, no sympathy with them or the movements they have inspired. No one has denounced them in stronger terms, or more strenuously opposed them. But our pages bear ample evidence that we have never denied, or pretended to deny, that each has something true and good in its order. We are not unfrequently accused of being one-sided, narrow-minded, and disposed always to push the principle we may have happened to adopt to extremes. Nothing is more untrue. An opposite charge might with far more propriety be brought against us. In our war against the Red-Republicanism of Europe, we were never known to push our defence of order and authority so far as to express an opinion favorable to absolute monarchy, or to deny the natural equality of all men. We have always made it a point, in combating erroneous or mischievous systems, to recognize the fact that they contain something that we should be sorry to combat, and if we are or have been to a certain extent unpopular with our countrymen, it is precisely because we have never shown ourselves exclusive. But when erroneous systems are in arms or arming themselves against society, we do not think it the proper time to draw attention to their side of truth and goodness, for it is then a more urgent duty to defeat them, and save society from the ruin they threaten, than it is to labor to convert their adherents from their errors. One course is proper when conversion is the end to be sought, another is proper when it is necessary to guard people against falling into error. To have dwelt in 1848 on what there is in liberalism and socialism that may be accepted, would have tended to give the people a false direction. We could not then stop to analyze and distinguish. An imperious duty made it necessary to expose the dangerous errors and tendencies of the revolutionary systems and movements. But in 1855, when the danger comes from the opposite quarter, we are free to labor for the conversion of those whom these false systems have misled, by distinguishing and accepting the truth or half-truth which they misapprehend and misapply. There is a time for all things, and our motto should be, everything in its time.

The liberalists and socialists are not true Christians, but it would be unjust to deny that there are individuals among them who have generous, noble, and even spiritual aspirations, which Christianity teaches us to accept and respect. Much at least of what is most living, least groveling, least servile, most manly, and most elevated, outside of the church, is found today in their ranks. We are never to judge individual members of political and social parties by their mere doctrinal formulas, for men's heads and hearts are often far apart, and sometimes strongly opposed one to the other. Liberalists and socialists are to be judged, under the point of view we wish now to consider them, not solely nor chiefly by their abstract doctrines, but by their sentiments, their cravings, affections, and aspirations. Liberalism and socialism, like all false systems, end at last in pure gentilism, and yet in their modern form they could have originated only in a community which had once been Christian, and which still retained a tradition of the Christian doctrine of love. They originate in philanthropy, the love of mankind, the form, and the only form, which what is purest and best in religion can assume outside of the Christian church.

We condemn as heartily as any man the Liberal and Socialistic revolutions of Europe during the last sixty or seventy years, but we cannot deny that those revolutions have to some extent had a philanthropic origin, and have all been prosecuted with the intention of doing for this world by the state through philanthropy what the church has done or shown she can do through Christian charity. All these movements to popularize government, to mitigate penal codes, to redress political and social grievances, and to elevate the poorer and more numerous classes, although for the most part failing in their object, have originated in benevolent sentiment, though perverted to base, selfish purposes by their chief managers. In their writings at least, in their speculations, the philosophers of the last century overflowed with generous sentiments, and if they attacked old systems, and demanded radical changes in social or religious institutions, in laws, manners, and customs, it was always in the name of virtue, and always for the purpose of realizing, as they pretended, often believed, something better for the nation or the race. No small number of the friends and supporters of the old French revolution were moved by a warm and diffusive benevolence; and we envy not the man who can see nothing not bad in the generous enthusiasm of a very considerable portion of the French people in the early days of that revolution. The state of things which obtained in France prior to the revolution was not so bad as that which the revolution itself introduced, but it was such as no man of a sound mind and an honest heart can approve. The evils may have been exaggerated, but no one can deny that they were great and deplorable. The court and upper classes were corrupt either in their principles or their manners, and the great body of the people were oppressed with burdens too heavy to be borne, and looked upon as born only to minister to the wants and pleasures of the idle and luxurious few. How could men who have the hearts of men be otherwise than indignant, when people were sent to the Bastile for venturing to attack the king's lackey or the king's mistress,—when the king abandoned himself to the most debasing and criminal sensuality, and a painted harlot, a Pompadour or a Dubarry, was virtually the first minister of state, and dispensed the favors or determined the appointments of the crown, while the toiling multitude were overloaded with taxes, reduced to penury, to absolute destitution, and received in answer to their petition for bread "a new gallows forty feet high"? Revolutions are serious things, and no people can be stirred up to make a social revolution against all that they have been accustomed to hold sacred, till they feel the pressure of want, and see gaunt famine staring them in the face. Nations, humanity at large, must bear some traces of that divine similitude which all things more or less faithfully copy, and can no more act without some aspect of truth or shadow of good than individuals; and though it may be generally more in accordance with the fact to say, *Vox populi vox diaboli*, than *Vox populi vox Dei*, yet there is a sense in which it will not do to deny that "the voice of the people is the voice of God." The old French revolution found at least a pretext in the vices of the court, in the corruption of the noblesse, in the dissoluteness of a portion of the clergy, and in the general neglect and distress of the people. And things were not much worse in France than in other European countries at the same time, if indeed they were so bad. It were idle to deny the existence of the evils, or to hold it to have been criminal, or otherwise than praiseworthy, to attempt to redress them. It was a sacred duty, imposed alike by charity and philanthropy, to undertake their removal, though of course not by unlawful means, certainly not by a revolution, which could only make matters worse.

Of course we have no confidence even in philanthropy, when acting alone, to effect anything good, for it seldom fails to make matters worse; but we have very little sympathy with the ordinary shallow and selfish declamation of conservatives against modern revolutionary movements. The only conservatism we can respect is that which frankly acknowledges the wrong, and seeks by proper means to redress it wherever it finds it. It is, after all, less against revolutions that we would direct the virtuous indignation of our conservative friends, now that the reaction has become strong, than against the misgovernment, the tyranny, the vices and the crimes, the heartlessness, the cruelty, the neglect of the poor by those who should love and succor them, or the wrongs inflicted on them, which provoke revolutions, and give Satan an opportunity to possess the multitude, and pervert their purest sentiments and their most generous enthusiasm to evil. Revolution was no fitting remedy for the evils which the system of secular government, attained to its full growth in Louis the Fourteenth, had generated. It was the remedy of madness or wild despair. But the evils had grown beyond all reasonable endurance. They outraged alike natural benevolence and Christian charity. Let not the friends of religion and order have censures only for those who sought madly to remove them by revolutions, and none for those whose vices and crimes caused them, lest they render religion and order odious to all men of human hearts.

Philanthropy is a human sentiment, and by no means Christian charity. We know it perfectly well. But it corresponds to charity as the human corresponds to the divine, copies it as nature copies or imitates God, and we never need persuade ourselves that what is repugnant to it is pleasing to charity. *Gratia supponit naturam*. How often must we repeat, that grace does not supersede nature? St. Ignatius Loyola did not seek to destroy the natural ambition of young Francis Xavier; he accepted it, and sought simply to direct it from earthly to heavenly glory. No wise master of spiritual life ever seeks to root out nature; his aim is always to accept it, and direct it in right paths towards God, the true end of man. Calvin and Jansenius, those subtle enemies of Christ, have done more injury to religion, a thousand times over, than Voltaire and Rousseau, for they placed nature and grace in opposition, and denied nature in order to assert grace. Not enough have been appreciated the services rendered to religion and humanity by the sons of Loyola, in combating as they did, in the seventeenth century and the beginning of the eighteenth, the degrading and demoralizing, though specious, heresy of the Jansenists. Nobly did they defend the freedom, the dignity, and the glorious destiny of human nature. The infamous Maxims of La Rochefoucauld, once so celebrated, were Jansenistic, not Catholic, and were conceived in the spirit of Port Royal, not of the church. They could have been inspired only by a heresy that places grace in opposition to nature, and thinks to exalt the one by degrading and annihilating the other. The Catholic honors nature, and asserts for it a more glorious destiny than do they who madly assert that man in his developments may grow into God. No, we repeat it, God is the similitude of all things, and the human has its type, its exemplar, in the divine. The divine is mirrored, reflected, by the human; grace, therefore, by nature. The natural sentiments of the human heart are below the infused graces of the Christian, but they are not opposed to them. Philanthropy, or the natural benevolence of the human heart, cannot rise to the elevation and power of Christian charity, or aspire to its eternal reward; but charity no more opposes it, and can no more dispense with it, than revelation opposes or can dispense with reason. What is opposed to benevolence is even more opposed to Christian charity. It is a great mistake to suppose that simple human benevolence or philanthropy is sufficient of itself to redress either social or individual grievances; but it is a still greater mistake therefore to condemn it, to neglect it, to make no efforts to redress the grievances, or to deny them to be real grievances, because they can be effectually redressed only by benevolence exalted to Christian charity. Not all the works of infidels are sin. Works of humanity, of genuine human benevolence, which are not always wanting in non-Catholic society, cannot indeed merit eternal life, or even the grace of conversion, for *gratia est omnino gratis*: but they are not sinful; they are good in the natural order, and merit and shall receive in that order their reward. The men of our times, who have lost the sense of Christian charity and seek to substitute philanthropy for it, do yet honor that charity in its pale and evanescent human reflex, and so far have just sentiments, and are unchristian rather than antichristian.

The doctrine of equal rights, so energetically asserted, a few years since, by "the Working-men's party," insisted on under one of its aspects by Abolitionists, and by the democratic party throughout the world, is not all false nor all antichristian, and after all faintly mirrors the Christian doctrine of the unity and solidarity of the race. There is truth in the Jacobinical doctrine of "fraternity," and in Kossuth's doctrine of "the solidarity of peoples." The working-men's party is dead now, and buried in other parties which have absorbed it, but it had a great truth for its basis. It asserted the natural nobility of all men, the nobility of human nature itself, as worthy of our reverence in the humble artisan or laborer as in the titled noble.

> The king can make a belted knight,
> A marquis, duke, and a' that;
> An honest man's aboon his might,
> Guid faith! he maunna fa' that.

There is something that it will not do to sneer at in that free and noble spirit that seeks to break down the artificial barriers which separate man from man and nation from nation, and melt all into one grand brotherhood. If there is any one thing certain, it is that the church has always asserted the unity of the race, and the natural equality of all men. Man equals man the world over, and hence, as Pope St. Gregory the First teaches, man, though he has received the dominion over the lower creation, has not received dominion over man, and princes are required to govern as pastors, not as lords; for since all men are equal by nature, the governed are as men the equals and brothers of the governors.

We are a little surprised to find the historian of the United States, in his earlier volumes, disposed to regard Calvin as in some sense the champion of equal rights, and to give Calvinism credit for the principle of political equality on which our American institutions are based, for his own doctrine is as repugnant to the Calvinistic, as light is to darkness. Calvinism asserts only a negative equality. It reduces all to a common level, we grant, by asserting the total depravity of nature, and therefore the nullity of nature in all men; but this is the equality of death, not of life. All are equal, because all are nothing. But it does not elevate all to a common level by the assertion of a positive equality, an equality founded on what all men are and have by nature. Moreover, Calvinism is unfavorable, nay, decidedly hostile, to that doctrine of equality which Mr. Bancroft so strenuously maintains. By its doctrine of the nullity of nature and particular election and reprobation, whereby only a certain definite number can be elevated by grace, it founds an aristocracy, the aristocracy of the saints, or the elect.

Asserting the moral nullity of nature, it necessarily founds the political order on grace, as it did in Geneva and the early colony of Massachusetts, and excludes from all political rights all whom it does not count among the saints. Maintaining the total depravity of nature, it must deny to nature all rights, and can assert rights only for those who are assumed to be in grace; and hence only the saints have or can have the right to govern,—one of the heresies of Wycliffe, condemned by the Council of Constance. Nature being null, there can be no rights under the law of nature, and if no rights, no possessions. Consequently, they who are counted among the non-elect have nothing which the elect are bound to hold sacred and inviolable. They are at the mercy of the saints, who may at pleasure despoil them of all they call their own, and take possession of their political and civil powers, their houses and lands, their goods and chattels, their wives and children, and even their very persons. Logically and consistently carried out, Calvinism therefore founds, not monarchy indeed, but the aristocracy of the saints, that is, of Calvinists, the most absolute and the most odious aristocracy that it is possible to conceive.

Undoubtedly the regenerate, those who are in grace, alone have rights in regard to eternal salvation, for certainly no man can have a natural right to supernatural beatitude. We are saved not by our natural merits, or merits under the law of nature, but by grace merited for us by Christ our head. The error of the Calvinist does not lie in founding our titles to eternal life on grace and grace alone, but consists in denying the natural law, that man retains all his original rights in the natural order, and that in the natural order all men have equal rights, which even the elect or those elevated by grace must respect as sacred and inviolable. God in promulgating the law of grace does in no respect abrogate the law of nature, nor in the least modify the rights or obligations of men under that law. Hence the Apostle recognizes the legitimacy of the temporal power of his time, and bids the faithful to obey for conscience's sake the Roman emperor, though a pagan, in all things temporal. Hence the Church recognizes and always has recognized the rights of infidel and even heretical princes to the temporal obedience of their subjects, even when those subjects are Catholics, who can be absolved from their allegiance only in case their princes forfeit their rights *by the law* under which they hold. Hence the Church forbids infidels, Jews, or persons who have not come under her spiritual jurisdiction, to be forced to accept the faith. Hence, too, she recognizes the natural rights of life, liberty, and property as fully in infidels and heretics as in the faithful themselves. Here is the grand difference between a positive and a negative natural equality, between the natural equality asserted by Catholicity and that favored by Calvinism. Calvinism asserts the natural equality of all men, by denying alike to all men all natural rights, assuming all rights to have been forfeited by the fall; Catholicity asserts the natural equality of all men, by asserting that all have equal natural rights, and denies that any natural rights were forfeited or lost by the transgression of our first parents. The rights lost by the fall were supernatural, not natural rights,—rights held under the law of grace, not rights held under the law of nature; for it was by grace, not nature, that man was placed prior to the fall on the plane of his supernatural destiny. Hence Catholicity recognizes in nature something sacred and inviolable, which even the church must respect. Hence Catholicity must always respect the natural liberty of man, and can no more tyrannize over the infidel than over the believer,—must, in fact, as to the natural order, place both on the same footing of equality. Calvinism begins by denying all natural rights, nullifying nature, and therefore all natural liberty, and asserts rights for the elect only. Hence it is free from all obligation to the non-elect, that is, to those who are not Calvinists, and is at liberty to play the tyrant over them at pleasure.

This is not mere speculation, or a simple logical conclusion from the Calvinistic premises. It is a conclusion practically drawn by Calvinists themselves, and written out in the blood of non-Calvinists, wherever they have had the power. Never have Calvinists held sacred any liberty except liberty for Calvinists. You may verify the fact by the history of Calvinism in Geneva, by that of the Puritans in England, that of the Covenanters in Scotland, and that of our own Puritan ancestors. Liberty for the elect, but no liberty for the non-elect, is the Calvinistic motto. To the saints belongs the earth. Do you not see this in the Know-Nothing movement against Catholics in our own country? Unbelievers, Unitarians, Universalists, and non-Evangelical sects, may engage in that movement, but its informing and controlling spirit is that of Calvinism, just now galvanized into a sort of spasmodic life. Its very language betrays it. It professes religious liberty, and its very aim is to deny it to Catholics, who in its view, we suppose are reprobates.

We may see here, again, the title of the Jesuits, as true Catholics, to the gratitude of mankind, for the noble energy with which they vindicated the rights and dignity of nature against insidious Jansenism, that improved edition of Calvinism. "Nature," as some one remarks, "is not good for nothing." It is not good for everything, yet it is good for something, and in its place is no more to be denied than grace itself.

That Calvinism has accidentally served the cause of equal rights in this country we are not disposed to deny. It led our Calvinistic ancestors to assert equal rights for the elect, that is, for Calvinists, and to make provisions for protecting them. When Calvinism lost its sway, and had become, as it practically had at the time of the revolution, a dead letter, these provisions were without much difficulty extended so as to apply equally to all citizens, elect or non-elect. But no thanks to Calvinism for that, for they were so extended and made to protect equal rights, not as rights of the elect, but as the rights of man. We think, if Mr. Bancroft had studied more thoroughly the Calvinistic system, he would have seen that, of all conceivable systems, it is the least favorable to that liberty and equality which he so eloquently and so energetically asserts. The equality that results from the equal depravity of nature can never be the basis of the equal rights of all men. To obtain this basis you must assert with the Catholic the inherent freedom, dignity, and nobility of human nature in every man, which requires the assertion of the unity of the race, and the recognition of that great fact, so seldom reflected on, so little understood, and so seldom practically applied, that God made man in his own image and likeness, and therefore man in his very nature must copy, imitate, or mirror his Maker.

The Workingmen were right in asserting the natural equality, or equal natural rights, of all men, and even in asserting the equal natural rights of all men to means and facilities for acquiring; for they did not, as it was alleged, assert the natural right of all men to equal acquisitions. The inequality they complained of was the unequal condition in which men are artificially placed in regard to acquiring, whether it be riches or honors, power or profit. Their error was in seeking to remove this inequality by social or political action. This inequality is, no doubt, in regard to the temporal order, a real grievance; but the difficulty is that it cannot be redressed by society, or if it can, not without striking at the right of property, and thus producing a far greater evil. There are many things very desirable, very proper to be done, which exceed both the ability and the competency of the state to do. The state alone is not competent to all the wants of even natural society. It must protect acquired as well as natural rights, and therefore the right to hold as well as to acquire property; and if it does this, it cannot secure to every man equal means or facilities for acquiring. It is obliged by its very nature to content itself with maintaining the equal right of all to acquire, and to hold what they acquire; when more is needed, we must look to a power of another order,—the moral power. The working-men committed a mistake analogous to that committed by our ultra-temperance people. Intemperance is a sin, a vice, which every man ought to avoid, and temperance is a virtue which every man ought to practice. But the state is competent in the case only to leave full freedom to the virtue, and to punish the intemperance only in so far as it deprives some one of his rights. In that it is a sin or a vice, the state is not competent to deal with it, either by way of prevention or of punishment; it can take cognizance of it only in that it is an injury, or deprives some one of his rights, natural or acquired. The state cannot punish the simple vice of drunkenness; it can punish drunkenness only when it interferes with the rights of others, or disturbs the public peace. Hence the principle of the Maine liquor law is indefensible. A man has a natural right to drink wine, beer, cider, gin, rum, brandy, or whiskey, if he chooses, and can honestly procure it. He has a right to use intoxicating drinks so long as he does not abuse them. That right is and must be sacred and inviolable for the state. The state can have the right to deal only with the abuse. But the Maine liquor law proceeds on the principle that the state has the right to guard against the abuse by prohibiting the use, or by declaring the use itself an abuse. This, as it assumes for the state the right to alter the moral law or to introduce a new principle into morals, cannot be admitted, unless we are prepared to assert civil despotism. The office of the state is not to teach morals, or to interpret the moral law, but to execute it; not to define right, but to protect and vindicate it. To teach morals, to define what is or is not right, is not within the competency of the civil power. That belongs to the spiritual or moral power, distinct from the civil power, and moving in another orbit. The equality, if the working-men had understood it, which they wanted, they would have sought from love, not law, and by means of the church, not the state; for the church alone can introduce equality in the matters of acquired rights, by teaching the doctrine of love, and bringing home to the consciences of rich possessors, that they are stewards, and not absolute proprietors, of their estates, and therefore are to use them for the good of their neighbor, not for their own private good alone, on the principle that each is bound for all and all for each, or that all are members of one body, and members of one another, and that the body cannot suffer without the members, nor a member without the body. It was on this principle that St. Chrysostom told the rich of Constantinople that they were murderers of the poor who died for the want of the means wherewith to live. But it would be perfect madness to attempt to carry out this principle by political organization or legislative action. The right to acquire and to hold property independent of the civil power must be recognized and protected, or the whole community will die of starvation. The evil which the state must tolerate for the sake of the good, the moral power operating on conscience and love must redress.

The doctrine of the solidarity and communion of the race, which Leroux makes the basis of his socialism and the principle of his explanation of Christianity, has something which, perhaps, a Christian may, and even must, accept. If we may be permitted to refer to our personal experience, we must say that it was through that doctrine, as set forth by Leroux in his work on Humanity, that by the grace of God we were led to the Catholic Church; and we may add, that the same was true of several of our friends, one at least of whom is now a most worthy member of the Catholic priesthood, and one of the most indefatigable and successful Catholic missionaries in the country. We thought we saw a great and important truth in the doctrine, but also that, as Leroux laid it down, it was incomplete; and if theoretically and practically completed anywhere, it must be in the Catholic Church. We seized the doctrine with our accustomed ardor, and, developing it in our own way, found ourselves knocking at the door of the church, and demanding entrance. Having been admitted into the church, and commenced the study of Catholic theology in the scholastic authors, in whom we found nothing which seemed to us a recognition of it, we felt that it was our duty to waive its public consideration till we could have time and opportunity of reexamining it in the light of Catholic faith. We saw at once that the doctrine pertained to an order of thought far below Catholic dogma, and that we had erred in supposing it to be the explication and expression of the real sense of the Catholic mysteries; but how far it was or was not in harmony with them, we felt unable to say. It was a problem to be solved, and not by us till we had become somewhat more familiar than we were at the time with Catholic theology. The form under which we had entertained it was, in regard to scholastic theology, a novelty, and therefore to be suspected. It might conceal an error, and even a dangerous error. It was certainly prudent, nay, it was our duty, not to insist on it, and to be content with using the language, arguments, and illustrations which we knew to be safe. Hence the trains of thought with which we made our readers so familiar during our transition state, and which had played so important a part in the process of our conversion, were suddenly interrupted the moment we entered the church and began to write as a Catholic. They who have watched our course, and taken some interest in our progress from a low form of rationalism to Catholicity, were unable to trace in our writings any continuity of thought between what was published the day before we entered the church and what we wrote and published the day after. So abrupt and complete a change seemed to them inexplicable on any rational principles, and was of course ascribed to our fickleness, or to our no longer being suffered to have a mind of our own. People outside of the church lost confidence in us, and if they continued to read us at all, it was mainly to amuse themselves with what they were pleased to look upon as our "feats of intellectual gladiatorship." This of course had its unpleasantness and its inconveniences, but it was not unendurable.

But we may say now, after more than ten years of silent thought and reflection on the subject, that, though not free from trifling errors, and much exaggerated as to their importance in our own mind, the principles which we learned from Leroux and developed and applied in our own way were substantially true, and we can now without lesion to our Catholicity resume the train of thought which appeared to be so abruptly terminated on our entering the Church. The views which we set forth in our Letter to Dr. Channing, in 1842, *on the Mediatorial Life of Christ*, as far as they went, we can accept now, and not without advantage. They were not what we thought them, and did not attain, as we supposed, to Catholic doctrine; yet they embraced elements of natural truth which help us in some respects to understand the Catholic dogma, and which the dogma may accept as charity accepts philanthropy. The basis of the doctrine we set forth in that letter was, that man lives by communion with God, humanity, and nature, and that his life partakes of the qualities of the object with which he communes. Man cannot live by himself alone, and every fact of life is the resultant of two factors, of the concurrent activity of subject and object, and partakes of the character of each. The individual can live and act only by virtue of communion with that which is not himself, and which we call his object, because it is set over against him. This does not mean that he cannot act without some object, or end to which he acts, although that is undoubtedly the case, but without another activity than his own, which meets and concurs with it. The fact of life results from the intershock of the two activities, and is their joint product. The subject is *living* subject, or subject *in actu*, only by virtue of communion with its object. Thus it cannot think without the active presence of the intelligible, or love without the active presence of the amiable, which is really only what St. Thomas teaches when he says the intellect is *in ordinem ad verum*, and the will *in ordinem ad bonum*; that the intellect is never false, and the will can never will only good. Therefore we have frequently brought out the doctrine in order to refute the modern psychologists, and those philosophers who would persuade us that it is not the *mundus physicus*, but an intermediary world, which they call the *mundus logicus*, that the mind in its perceptions immediately apprehends. The mind cannot think without thinking some object, and as to the production of thought, the object must act on or with the subject,—because if purely passive it is as if it were not, for pure passivity is mere potentiality,—the object must be real, being or existence, since what neither is nor exists cannot act or produce any effect. Consequently, either we perceive nothing and perform no act of perception, or the world perceived is the real world itself, not a merely abstract or logical world, or a mere *species* or phantasm.

But thought is an effect, and whoever thinks at all produces or generates something. Every theologian must admit this, or how else can he hold the mystery of the Trinity, and believe in the only begotten Son of God? In God, who is *actus purissimus*, or pure act, as say Aristotle and the schoolmen after him, as he is infinite and contains no passivity, he enters with his whole being into his thought, the word generated is and must be exactly his equal, and identical in nature, consubstantial with himself. But man, not being pure act, nor intelligible in himself, cannot think without another activity that supplies the object necessary to reduce his passivity to act; and as he cannot enter with his whole being into his thought, he cannot, as God, generate the exact image of himself. Nevertheless, in conjunction with the object, since he imitates in his degree the divine intellect, he generates something, and this something we call a fact of life, or life itself considered as the product of living activity. Now, since to production or generation of thought or the fact of life subject and object must concur, it is their joint product, and must participate of the character of each. Here is the basis of what is called the solidarity of the race, under the point of view of intellect.

But man is not pure intellect. He has a heart as well as a head, and can love as well as think. What we have asserted of thought is equally true of love, as we learn from the same adorable mystery of the Trinity. For the Father, the unbegotten, loves the Son, the begotten, and from their mutual love proceeds the third person of the Trinity, the Holy Ghost. Only like can commune with like, and love properly so called can be only of like to like, and therefore under the relation of love man only can be the object of man. By virtue of the unity of the race every human being is the object of every other human being. But by the law of all communion of subject and object, the result generated or proceeding is the joint product of the two factors, and therefore the life of any one man is the joint product of him and every other man; and thus is produced a solidarity of the life of all men, by which it is one and the same life for all and for each, and for each and for all. But as every generation, so to speak, overlaps its successor, and each new generation communes with its predecessor, the solidarity of the race is not only a solidarity of all men in space, but of all men in time, linking together, in one indissoluble life, the first man with the last, and the last man with the first.

Taking this doctrine, but giving a different application from that of Leroux, in order to escape his denial of the personality of God and the personal immortality of the soul, and to be able to assert the Incarnation in the individual man Jesus, instead of the race, we thought we could bridge over the gulf between the Unitarian and the Trinitarian, and accept and explain the Christian church and Christian mysteries. In this respect our letter to Dr. Channing fails. The thought we developed does not rise to the order of Catholic dogma, and at the highest remains in the natural order. Yet the doctrine is substantially true. It is not the supernatural truth of Christianity, but it is in some sense the truth of the natural order which corresponds to it, and by which it is made apprehensible to us. The error of Leroux and ourselves was not in asserting the natural communion and solidarity of the race, but in supposing them to be the real significance of the Christian mysteries, the Incarnation, Holy Communion, the Church, Apostolic Succession, Tradition, etc., or the great truths held by the early Christians, and symbolized by the Catholic dogmas. The error was in assuming that Catholic dogmas symbolize natural truths; it had been more correct to have said the reverse, that the natural truths symbolize the dogmas, or represent them as the human represents the divine. "See that you make all things according to the pattern shown you in the Mount." The earthly symbolizes the heavenly, not the heavenly the earthly. The dogma is not, as Leroux, Cousin, and others have foolishly asserted, the form with which faith, the religious sentiment, or enthusiasm, clothes the natural or philosophic truth. The natural or philosophic truth, on the contrary, is the symbol of which the dogma is the hidden meaning, the divine reality, or the divine likeness which it copies or imitates.

Although the natural communion of the human race does not introduce us to the principle of the Sacraments, as Leroux and we after him supposed, and although the natural solidarity of the race is infinitely below the Christian solidarity effected by the Sacraments, there is no opposition between one and the other. We do not by natural communion receive and incorporate into our life that grace which unites us to God and enables us to live the supernatural life of Christ, and the solidarity resulting from it is infinitely below that of the church, that mystic body of Christ, in which he is as it were continuously incarnated; but it does express the condition of our natural human life, and its assertion, while no disadvantage to the supernatural, is of great advantage to the natural order. It condemns all exclusiveness, whether individual or national, and asserts the necessity to the full development of our natural life of the free and peaceful intercourse of man with man the world over. Man has a threefold nature, and lives by communion with God, man, and nature. He communes with God in religion, with man in society, and with nature in property, and any political or social order that strikes at either of these, or hinders or obstructs this threefold communion, as Leroux well maintains, is alike repugnant to the will of God and the highest interests of humanity; and efforts made to render this communion free and unobstructed, to give freedom in the acquisition and security in the possession of property, to protect the family as the basis of society, and to break down the barriers to social intercourse interposed by prejudices of birth or caste, and to secure freedom of worship or religion, are in principle great and solemn duties, obligatory alike upon all men. Thus far the Liberalists and Socialists can make a valid defence. The end proposed is just and obligatory. The means they adopt of course we do and must condemn. Philanthropy enjoins what they would effect, and Philanthropy here may justify herself by the natural solidarity of the race. Kossuth, when he was here, had much to say of "the solidarity of peoples," from which he concluded the right of the people of every country, irrespective of their government, to run to the assistance of any particular people struggling for its rights. This solidarity of peoples rests on the doctrine of the solidarity of the race. Man lives his social life only by communion with man, and every man thus becomes every man's object, and all are bound together in the unity of one indissoluble life. Man then can never be indifferent to man; never have the right to ask, with Cain, "Am I my brother's keeper?" Your brother is your object, without which you cannot live the life of love. He is your other self, the objective side of your own life. If this may be said of individuals, why not of nations? There is in some sense a solidarity of nations, as well as individuals. The right of the people without the permission of their government to assist a sister people, we cannot absolutely deny. The race is more than the individual, and humanity more than the nation. There is a great and glorious truth in Senator Seward's doctrine of the Higher Law, a truth which every true man will assert, if need be, in exile or the dungeon, on the scaffold or at the stake. I am a man before I am a citizen, and my rights as a man can never be subordinated to my duties as a citizen. Even the Church recognizes and vindicates my rights as a man, and the Church is higher in the order of God's providence than the state, as much so as grace is higher than nature. There are cases in which the state cannot bind the citizen, as the apostles taught us when they refused to obey the magistrates who commanded them to preach no more in the name of Jesus of Nazareth. We are to love our neighbor as ourself; for in one sense our neighbor is ourself, since he is our object, without which we cannot love or live; there are cases when we must rush to his assistance, at least when we *may* rush to his assistance, at the hazard of life. There may then be cases when the solidarity of the race overrides the solidarity of the nation, and permits a people without the national sanction to rush to the assistance of another people struggling against tyranny for its liberty and independence; but not indeed at the call of every discomfited demagogue. The principle we hold to be true, but it can be of only rare application. The struggling people must have a cause manifestly just, and have adopted means manifestly unexceptionable, and the national permission must have been wrongly withheld, before the people of another nation have the right to interfere; and these things must be determined not by private judgment or caprice, but by an authority competent to decide in the case, otherwise an attack may be made against legitimate authority, and a blow be struck at order, which is as sacred as liberty.

We might pursue this subject further, but it is unnecessary at present. We have thus far been intent mainly on pointing out what a Catholic may accept as true and good in modern Liberalism and Socialism. What they want, we mean when sincere, earnest, and disinterested, what they are driving at, under certain aspects, is good, and in its place approved alike by charity and philanthropy. We cannot utterly condemn all we did and said as a Liberalist or as a Socialist, and we find much in Liberalists and Socialists of the present day to approve. When they are not completely beside themselves, we admit that most of the things they call political and social grievances are grievances, and such as ought to be redressed. But with what they contend for that is true and good, they couple great and dangerous errors. They err, above all, as to the means by which they seek to gain their ends. In what they for the most part aim at, we can agree with them. We love liberty as much as they do, we are as indignant at wrong as they are; but we see them trying to effect by the state what can be effected only by the church, and by the natural sentiment of philanthropy what is practicable only by the supernatural virtue of charity.

Every age has its own characteristics, and we must address its dominant sentiment, whether we would serve or disserve it. Our age is philanthropical rather than intellectual. It has lost faith intellectually, but retains a faint echo of it on the side of the affections. It does not think so much as it feels, and it demands the gospel of love with far more earnestness and energy than it does the gospel of truth. Charity had exalted and intensified its affections. Despoiled of charity, it is devoured by its benevolent sentiments. It would do good, it would devote itself to the poor, the enslaved, the neglected, the downtrodden. It would bind up the broken heart, and bring rest to the suffering. These are not bad traits, and we love to dwell on the disinterestedness of the Howards, the Frys, the Nightingales, and the benevolent men and women in our own country who so unreservedly devote themselves to the relief of the afflicted. These prove what the age craves, and what it is looking for. Through its benevolence Satan no doubt often misleads it, but through the same benevolence the missionary of the cross may approach it and lead it up to God.

We have wished, in these times, when the church is assailed so violently by the galvanized Calvinism manifesting itself in Know-Nothing movements, to show, by exhibiting the manner in which she regards those movements which human well-being, that she no more deserves than she fears their violence. What is true and good in the natural order manifested by those outside, though imperfect, she accepts. We have wished, also, in a practical way, to reply to those who are perpetually accusing us of being narrow and exclusive, and a renegade from free principles. What we aimed at before our conversion is still dear to us, and we are still in some sense a man of our age. But having indicated the good side of Liberalism and Socialism, we shall take a future opportunity to show more fully that it is accepted by the church, and is completed only in and through her communion.

FIFTEEN

Civil and Religious Freedom

These admirable Discourses on civil and religious liberty have appeared, we believe, in a separate publication, but we have seen them only in *Le Correspondant*, where they were first published. The *Correspondant*, by the way, published on the 25th of each month, is a periodical that we can conscientiously recommend to the general as well as to the Catholic public. It is able, learned, liberal, spirited, sincere, and earnest. It is the organ of the liberal Catholics of France, the only Catholics in Europe who sympathize with the loyal people of the Union in their war against the slavery Rebellion; and the best account of the struggle in which we are now engaged, that we have seen in any European periodical, has appeared in its pages, written by M. Henri Moreau. Its writers are such men as the Bishop of Orleans, the late Père Lacordaire, Count de Montalembert, Count de Falloux, Auguste Cochin, A. Pontmartin, Henri Moreau, M. de Meaux, Prince de Broglie, and others hardly less eminent, all fervent, orthodox Catholics, devoted heart and soul to civil and religious liberty—men who combine the faith of the martyr ages with the civilization and progressive spirit of the nineteenth century.

These Discourses are able and eloquent, as is every thing from the illustrious author, and exceedingly well timed. They are well matured, well

"*L'Eglise libre dans l' Etat libre. Two Discourses pronounced in the General Assembly of Catholics, held at Mechlin, August 18–22, 1863*. By M. Charles de Montalembert. 'Le Correspondant,' for August and September. Paris: 1863." From *Brownson's Quarterly Review* 1 (July 1864): 258–91.

reasoned, and contain views and advocate a policy which no friend of religion and civilization can prudently disregard. They are grave and earnest, bold and manly, noble and chivalric; and they have been read with surprise by non-Catholics, and with delight by all Catholics who do not happen to have their faces on the backside of their heads. They, however, have not given universal satisfaction, and several journals have entered their protest against them. They have incurred the decided hostility of *La Civiltà Cattolica*, a periodical printed at the Propaganda Press, and published at Rome, under the eye of the General of the Jesuits. They have also incurred the wrath, we are told, of the new *Dublin Review*, said to be the organ of His Eminence Cardinal Wiseman, Archbishop of Westminster. They do not appear, however, to have been opposed by the Catholic organs of the United States, all devoted, as they are, to slavery, and hostile to liberty, whether civil or religious; but this is, probably, owing either to the incapacity of their conductors to understand their hearing, or to the fact that their author is a Frenchman, and a former peer of France. Had he been a plebeian, or had he been born a Yankee, and a Yankee who will not concede that to be a Catholic it is necessary to denationalize himself, and become a foreigner in his native land, they would doubtless have honored him by a more formidable opposition than they have as yet received from any of the Catholic organs of Europe. Becoming a Catholic in this country means becoming an Irishman, or at least a European; and if one becomes a good Irishman, a good European, or a decided anti-American, he is a good Catholic, let him defend what doctrines he may.

That M. de Montalembert's Discourses in favor of civil and religious liberty should incur opposition from *La Civiltà Cattolica* is in the natural course of things. That periodical is the organ of Society which has outlived its day and generation, and which is now not inaptly symbolized by the barren fig-tree of the Gospel. It was a noble and illustrious Society in its origin, and successfully did it labor to check the progress of error, and to place the Church in harmony with the civilization of the age. Its members were men of high character, often of noble birth, with the training and polish of men of the world, the literary tastes and culture of the most accomplished Humanists, the erudition of cloistered monks, the freedom of motion of secular priests, and the ardent charity and burning zeal of apostles. God gave them a great work to do, and they did it, and did it well. They deserved and won the admiration and gratitude of the Catholic world. But the Society being only a human institution, subsidiary to the Church, was not able to adapt itself to the wants of all ages and nations, and the time was sure to come when it would grow old and disappear, like all things human, or remain only to cumber the ground. When it had done the special work assigned it to do, its strength was exhausted, and it became necessarily unable to perform, or even to perceive, the new work demanded by the rapid social changes and new developments of civilization which the movement and progress of events are continually introducing. The world went on, and as it neither would nor could go on with it, the world went on without it, and the once illustrious Society of Jesus stands now calling out for it to stop, for it is going too far, or seizing hold of its skirts and trying with all its might to hold it back.

The Jesuits understood the wants of the age from the middle of the sixteenth century to that of the seventeenth, especially on the Continent, better than any of their contemporaries, and fulfilled with great success that extra-hierarchical mission which, under the new Law, may be termed the mission of genius, and which corresponds in some measure to the mission of the prophets under the old Law. But in their controversy with the Jansenists their glory culminated, and they ceased to lead the civilization of the world. They never understood the eighteenth century; and, holding the chief places of influence, they suffered the world they themselves had educated, to lapse in philosophy into shallow sensism, and in religion into the crudest infidelity. Still less do they understand this nineteenth century. They are out of place in it. They themselves feel it, and, determined to be what they were or not to be at all, they seek to arrest and turn it back to what the world was when they were in their glory. They are good men, learned men, excellent scholars, earnest, devoted, and self-sacrificing priests—none more so in the Church; but they understand not the work of this age. They see not that this age demands men who are to it what St. Ignatius Loyola and his Companions were to theirs—men of large minds and a free spirit, who dare break from routine, to reject the dry technicalities of the schools, to take the world as they find it, to accept the new learning, the new social order, and to Christianize the new civilization by baptizing, not anathematizing it. The Jesuits did their work by harmonizing, not dogma, which is immutable, but theology, the schools, and ecclesiastical administration, with the new developments of civilization in the sixteenth century; but they see not that this is precisely the work now needed in regard to the civilization of the nineteenth century. They wish to retain the world in the mould in which they had cast it. Hence, with all their virtues, with all their private worth, they do little for our age, and still less for our country, with which they have no sympathy. They can no longer restrain or lead the civilized world, and their successes are confined to uncivilized, savage, or barbarous tribes, or to peoples whose civilization is far below the European in the sixteenth century.

But this is not the worst. The Jesuits have formed the Catholic world, at least the ruling portion, in their own image. They have, directly or indirectly, the forming of our Catholic youth, and to a great extent the direction of our consciences: their theology, dogmatic and ascetic, is that generally taught in our ecclesiastical seminaries, and nearly all who pass for earnest, devoted, and devout Catholics are in some sense Jesuits. They have immense influence still in the Church by means of their past, on which they live, if not by their present labors. Catholics who fail to recognize them as virtually the Church, are looked upon by their devouter brethren as wanting, if not in faith, at least in pious fervor and holy obedience. Hence it is that the dominant influence of the Church today is thrown in favor of an order of things that it is impossible to recall, and against a social order that it is usually impossible successfully to resist, even if it were desirable, as it is not, to resist it. There is in the Church a party, and it is at present the dominant party, called in Italy, the *oscurantisti*, who make war *à outrance* on what is called modern civilization. It would be a mistake to suppose that they find their *beau idéal* in the middle ages; they find it rather in the sixteenth and seventeenth centuries, when were consolidated the great centralized monarchies of Europe, and when the ecclesiastical administration was centralized and placed in the Roman bureaucracy. The best, ablest, and most active representatives of this party are unquestionably the Jesuits. It is not strange, then, that the Count de Montalembert finds their organ, opposed to him, just in proportion as he departs from the traditional policy of the *oscurantisti*, and labors to place the Church in harmony with modern civilization. The Jesuits belong to the past; he belongs to the present and the future. If he increases, they must decrease; and if he realizes his idea, they must abandon theirs.

M. de Montalembert loves his Church, is earnestly devoted to his religion, and has from his youth devoted himself, his life, and his fortune, liberally and heartily, to the promotion of Catholic interests. He is, as all the world knows, a man of eminent ability, of brilliant genius, of varied and solid erudition—one of the most accomplished scholars, polished and vigorous writers, and eloquent and graceful orators of France. He is an ardent lover of liberty, a zealous champion of constitutional government, and holds that in the modern world the freedom of the Church can be secured, only in the freedom of the citizen. He defends civil freedom for its own sake, and also as the necessary condition of religious freedom. In the so-called middle ages, churchmen sought the freedom of religion by asserting for the Church the supremacy in temporals as well as in spirituals—in establishing a real *clerocracy*, or government of the world by the clergy. But this, had it succeeded, would have annihilated the state, reduced to naught the lay society, and prevented the development and growth of the people, and the real amelioration of their social condition by their own efforts. Civilization refused to submit to it. The wars between the two orders, which fill the fourteenth and fifteenth centuries, ended finally in its defeat, and, unhappily, in the establishment of the great centralized European monarchies, and the subjection, in turn, of the Church to the temporal order in both Catholic and non-Catholic states. The Church had little more freedom in the Catholic states of Europe, during the sixteenth and seventeenth centuries, than she had in non-Catholic states. She was held by the state in a sort of gilded slavery; she enjoyed large revenues, as does the English Church now, but she dared not oppose the court. In exchange for her freedom, she had the sad consolation of having the state exclude, at least so far as the law went, all heretical or dissentient communions. Externally the Church appeared to be protected by the state, but she was in reality simply enslaved, as in a prior age the clergy had sought to enslave the state. The consequence was that religion everywhere suffered.

M. de Montalembert perfectly well understands that the clerical dream of the middle ages cannot be realized. Men will not and cannot be made to submit to the government of churchmen in temporals. The experiment has been tried and failed. The subjection of the Church to the state, of the spiritual to the temporal, is repugnant to the essential principles of religion, for in principle it is the subjection of God to man. He therefore maintains that the subjection of the state to the clergy, as well as the subjection of the clergy in spirituals to the state, must both be rejected, for both are equally hostile to religion and to civilization. Hence he demands a free Church in a free State, or, as we express it, the freedom of the Church in the freedom of the citizen. That is, the recognition by the Church of the freedom of the state in temporals, or in its own order, and the recognition by the state of the freedom of conscience, and its own incompetence in spirituals. The state does not prescribe or tolerate, it protects the religion of the citizen, not as approving or disapproving it, but as, before it, a natural and inalienable right. As before the state all citizens are equal in their rights, so all religious, not *contra bonos mores*, or incompatible with the public peace, embraced by its citizens, are equal before it, and entitled to equal and full protection. Hence, a free Church in a free State implies the liberty of false religions no less than of the true, the freedom of error no less than the freedom of truth,—the precise order which obtains in the United States.

Now to this order, which is the order of liberty, our *obscurantists* are opposed, because they do not believe in liberty or desire it; because they hold it wrong to guaranty the liberty of error; and because they hold that to do it were to cast reproach on the past conduct of the Church, who, wherever she has been strong enough to have her own way, has approved a contrary policy. The *Civiltà Cattolica* admits that there may be times and countries in which it is wise and even necessary to concede liberty to error, as, for instance, where error is so strong that it cannot be suppressed by civil pains and disabilities, and it is impossible to maintain the unity of faith by the strong hand. It would concede it to France, to Belgium, to Austria, to Great Britain, and to the United States, but as a condescension on the part of the Church, not as a natural right before the state, or as a principle applicable to all times and places. And this seems, in fact, to be all that Montalembert has judged it prudent formally to demand. He asserts his free Church in a free State, not as a universal rule or principle, but as a practical necessity, in our times and in most countries, for the promotion of Catholic interests. He apparently shrinks from its assertion as a natural and indefeasible right. But the concession which the *Civiltà Cattolica* says the Church makes is not all we demand, because in it the Church reserves the right to revoke it when she deems herself strong enough, or judges it for her interest to do so. We venture to assert, as a universal principle, that the State is incompetent in spirituals, and that wherever civilization is sufficiently advanced to admit the organization of the state, or, what is the same thing, the civil organization of lay society, every citizen has the natural right to be protected in the free enjoyment of his religion, or the religion of his free choice.

We except from this rule only tribes or peoples in what may be called their infancy or minority, in which they correspond to the period of childhood in the individual. Here some precautions against error other than instruction may be necessary, and some degree of repression may be resorted to, on the ground that the mind is not yet developed so as to have the right to be remitted to its own judgment, or to be in fact held responsible for its own judgment, either before the human or the divine law with regard to tribes and peoples in this state, which is not that of civilization, we will engage in no dispute. For a certain period I have the authority from God to govern as well as to teach my child, and even to require him to conform to my religion. But that period ends when the child has come to years of discretion, and I can then legitimately use only instruction and moral suasion. So, where a people is or has become civilized, the Church must confine herself to her spiritual authority, and make no resort, directly or indirectly, to force to repress error or to maintain the truth. There is no civilized people on earth to which we would not apply, as an absolute rule, the doctrine asserted simply as a practical doctrine by M. de Montalembert. We accept it not as a concession or as a condescension; we demand it as a right, and we maintain not only that it is impolitic, but that it is wrong, to withhold it. The minority past, the nation, as the individual, is free. "But then you condemn the past and even the present conduct of the Church, which you are well aware that as a good Catholic you cannot do." Be not too fast, my good brother. The Church, we concede, has in all ages and nations been governed by pure and holy motives, and done what her authorities judged to be, under the circumstances, the wisest and best; but we have yet to learn that her authorities are incapable of error in their practical judgments, or that the Church herself is, or claims to be, infallible in anything except dogma. The practice of the Church is not the rule of faith, though it may be cited as throwing light on it. The Church has received the *depositum*, the faith once delivered to the saints, and in the preservation and definition of that, as every Catholic believes, and no one more firmly than we, she is, by the assistance of the indwelling Holy Ghost, infallible. Her dogmatic canons are infallible and irreformable; but we have never heard it pretended that she is infallible in her human legislation, in her administrative canons, or her practical conduct.

The Church, in the sense we now speak of her, means the ecclesiastical authorities, and these have made and continue to make serious blunders, as it would be worse than folly in any one who has studied ecclesiastical history to pretend to deny. A pope has said that England was needlessly lost to the Church by the mismanagement of his predecessor, Clement VII, and we have no doubt that, with a proper degree of prudence, even the East might have been saved, and Protestantism prevented. As to Germany, Scandinavia, and England, there were no dogmatic questions that could not have been adjusted without any serious difficulty. There were bishops in the Council of Trent who differed, before the decisions were arrived at, from the doctrine finally declared by the Council, as widely as did Luther or Calvin. The real source of the defection was in matters of discipline and administration, the former of which was relaxed, and the latter grossly corrupt. There is not much edification in reading the lives of the Popes from Calixtus III to Leo X, inclusive. They live, act, and reign as temporal sovereigns, and apparently think more of strengthening their political influence, and enriching their families, than of feeding the spiritual flock committed to their care.

Nothing is more certain, except in matters of pure doctrine, in what pertains immediately to dogma, than that the Church, that is to say, the authorities of the Church, from the Pope down to the humblest parish priest, are more or less affected by the public opinion of their age or country. The Church has a divine origin, and lives a divine life; but she has also her human element, and lives a human life, often far removed from her divine life. Her divine life is like leaven hidden in three measures of meal, and not all at once, or instantaneously, does it leaven the whole lump. In her human element she is subject to the vicissitudes of time and space, and while she acts upon the world it reacts upon her, and its opinions influence her conduct. She found the doctrine of civil intolerance with the Jews, where it was in place, for the Synagogue was recruited and continued by natural generation, not by the election of grace; she found it also in the Graeco-Roman world, where it survived as a reminiscence of the patriarchal order, and when she became strong enough she adopted it, for it was already in the minds and habits of the great mass of her children. This is a fact which everyone knows, who knows the history of the Church, and in asserting it we assert nothing, even on the supposition that it is an error, that is not consistent with our faith as a Catholic to assert. All forms of government have been developed from the patriarchal; and the doctrine that authority must suppress error, and protect the truth against it, is of patriarchal origin, and grew out of the fact that the patriarch or father of the family was at once priest and king, and never recognized the majority of any member of his family while he lived. The doctrine itself belongs not to dogma, but to civilization, and, so far as regards the Church, comes under the head of discipline, in respect to which no one pretends that the Church is infallible, or that her rules are irreformable.

That the Church has legislative authority, under the divine law, every Catholic maintains; but it is no part of Catholic faith that she is infallible in her legislation or in her disciplinary canons. Nothing forbids us to maintain, if such be our honest conviction, that any human law, borrowed from the Hebrew and Graeco-Roman civilizations, and incorporated into the discipline of the Church, or at least for long ages approved by churchmen and acted on by civil governments, is unnecessary, improper, or prejudicial to the best interests both of religion and of civilization. We find no trace of the doctrine on which the practice is founded among Christian writers, prior to the first Christian Emperor. Many among the greatest doctors and Fathers of the Church have opposed it, and boldly asserted that the only lawful means of maintaining or reestablishing unity of faith are moral, spiritual weapons drawn from the armory of reason and revelation, and addressed to the understanding, the heart, and the conscience. So at one time, at least, held St. Augustine; so held the great St. Dominic, the reputed founder of the Inquisition, who used all his influence to prevent the employment of force against the Albigenses, among whom he was sent to labor as a missionary; so held the illustrious St. Francis de Sales, who, if for a moment he called in the troops of the Duke of Savoy to expel the Calvinistic ministers who gave him so much annoyance, instantly repented of his act, and gave himself no rest till the exiles were recalled and re-established in their homes; and so, it is well known, held the equally illustrious Fénelon, Archbishop of Cambray, who would not undertake the mission for the conversion of the Huguenots, till Louis XIV consented to withdraw his dragoons. We feel, therefore, quite easy as to the past, and have no fear of compromising our orthodoxy by refusing to defend the doctrine, or by openly condemning it, as has been done by the late Archbishop of Baltimore in his learned work on the *Primacy of the Apostolic See*, dedicated to the Supreme Pontiff himself.

That the doctrine we maintain, after M. de Montalembert, concedes the liberty of error, and places it and truth on the footing of equality before the civil authority, we grant, and we would have it so. We do not in this assert the indifference of truth and error, or that a man has the *moral* right to adhere to a false religion. Truth cannot tolerate even so much as the semblance of error, and in the theological order we are as intolerant as any Calvinist in the land, and hold firmly that out of the true Church there is no salvation, any more than there is virtue without obedience to the moral law of God. Nor do we with Milton and Jefferson maintain that "error is harmless where truth is free to combat it." Error makes the circuit of the globe while Truth is pulling on her boots, and no error ever is or ever can be harmless. What we assert is, not what is called theological tolerance, but what is called civil tolerance. Error has no rights, but the man who errs has equal rights with him who errs not. The civil authority is incompetent to discriminate between truth and error, and the Church is a spiritual kingdom without physical force, or the mission to employ it for the one or against the other. The weapons of her warfare are spiritual not carnal; consequently, before the secular or human authority, whether of churchmen or statesmen, truth and error must stand on the same footing, and be equally protected in the equal rights of the citizen. All sects should be equal before the civil law, and each citizen protected in the right to choose and profess his own religion, which we call his conscience, as his natural right, so long as he respects the equal right of others. This is the American order, and we dare maintain that it is the Christian order; for when the Disciples proposed to call down fire from heaven to consume the adversaries of our Lord, he rebuked them, and told them that they "knew not what manner of spirit they were of."

All the doctors of the Church agree that faith is not to be forced, that it must be voluntarily accepted, and that no one can be compelled to receive baptism against his own free will. So much is certain; and hence Charlemagne, who placed before the conquered Saxons the alternative of baptism or perpetual slavery, is never regarded as having conducted himself as a good Christian or as a good Catholic. Yet it is not to be denied that theologians have argued, from the analogy of secular governments, that since by baptism the recipient is born again, and born a subject of Christ's kingdom, he may be compelled by force, when once baptized and become one of the faithful, to keep the unity of the faith, and submit to the authority of the Church, as the natural born subjects of a state may, if rebellious, be reduced to their civil allegiance by the strong hand of power, and, if need be, punished even with death for their treason. But have they not abused this analogy? "My kingdom," says our Lord, "is not of this world,"—is not a secular kingdom, for the government of men in their secular relations, but is a spiritual kingdom, founded to introduce and maintain in human affairs the spiritual or moral law of God. The Church, which is clothed with the authority of this kingdom, or, in a mystical sense, is it, has undoubtedly over her subjects the authority which secular governments have over theirs, only it is an authority of the same kind with her own nature and mission. Since her kingdom is moral and spiritual, she has and can have only moral or spiritual power. She can resort neither directly nor indirectly to physical force, for that would make her a secular kingdom,—a kingdom of this world,—and belie her own spiritual nature.

The mission of the State is one that can be executed by physical force, for its mission is restricted to external acts in the social order. The magistrate bears the sword against evil-doers, and his mission is to watch over the safety of society, and to maintain justice between man and man, or to repress and redress external violence, either against individuals or against society itself. In this, physical force, when needed, may be employed, because there is a congruity between its employment and the end to be obtained. But it is not so with the Church. Her mission being to introduce and maintain the law of God in the interior of man, she affects the exterior only through the interior, that is, the external act only through reason and conscience. This is wherefore she is called a spiritual, not a secular kingdom, or kingdom of this world. She teaches man the truth, tells him what he ought to believe, and what he must be and do in order to render himself acceptable to his Maker, his Redeemer, and his Saviour, or to gain the end for which he has been created. She administers to him the sacraments, through which he receives the new birth, is regenerated, restored, nourished, and strengthened in the life which ends in his supreme beatitude or supernatural union with God. But in all this she can address herself only to his moral or spiritual nature, to his reason or understanding, his free will, his heart, and his conscience. All physical force is here out of place, for physical force can affect only external acts, and all the acts she requires, to be of any value, must be internal, spring from the interior, from real conviction and love, and be the free, voluntary offering of the soul. Faith cannot be forced; she can by exterior force compel no one to receive the sacraments, for though they operate *ex opere operato*, they are inefficacious unless they are received with the proper interior dispositions. "My son, give me thy heart." Obedience in the moral or spiritual order cannot be forced, for it must be voluntary, from the heart; and a forced obedience, or an obedience that springs not from love, and is not yielded by free will, is simply, in her order, no obedience at all. In it the heart is not given. God demands a willing giver, is worshipped with the heart, in spirit and in truth, not with the lips only. External acts, genuflections, prostrations, singing of psalms, and repetitions of the creed, the *Pater-noster*, and the *Ave-Maria*, are of no value if the heart be wanting, if love be absent, and there be not in them acts of free will,—all acts which by their own nature cannot be enforced, or produced by simple external authority or pressure. The Church, then, cannot do her work, cannot produce faith or love, or maintain interior unity, by force, nor could she reduce by force her rebellious subjects to their allegiance and obedience, if she would. The obedience must be voluntary, in the baptized no less than in the unbaptized.

The Church precluded by her own spiritual nature and mission from the employment of force, and the state being incompetent in spirituals, no course is practicable, or even lawful, but that of placing before civil society, before external authority, truth and error on the same footing, and using for the promotion of the former and the correction of the latter moral power alone. Let the state leave the Church free to wield her moral power according to her own divine nature against error, false doctrines, spiritual disobedience, or spiritual defection or rebellion, and it is all that in the Divine Economy is required or admissible. The state can demand only the faithful discharge of one's civil duties, and it can punish only civil offences, and it has no right to make that a civil offence which is not so in its own nature. It has no right or competency to discriminate between the Catholic and the Calvinist, and, if each demeans himself as a good citizen, it is bound to maintain for each the same rights, and to place both, in its own order, on the same footing. The responsibility of the religious error it must remit to the individual conscience, leaving each man to account, in the spiritual order, for himself to God, the only Master of conscience. The spiritual offences being in their very nature such as cannot be redressed by physical force, the Church can use only moral power against them, that is, arguments addressed to reason and conscience. If these fail, she can do no more, and must, as the state, leave those whom she cannot convert to answer to God for themselves. She may, undoubtedly, use moral discipline to correct her delinquent subjects, or to advance them in virtue, and go even so far as to excommunicate those she judges incorrigible, that is, so far as to exclude them from her external communion. She may thus deprive them of many spiritual advantages; but she cannot exclude any from her internal communion unless they first exclude themselves, and she must raise the ban of excommunication from her external communion whenever the excommunicated demand it, and give satisfactory evidence of interior submission. Here her coercive power stops; and even so far her coercive power is moral, not physical, and the moment it becomes physical it is not in her mission. When the priest rides into the mob, and disperses it with the blows of his black-thorn stick or his horsewhip, he may do a very meritorious act, but he does it not in his priestly capacity, but as a peace officer, or as a chieftain of the clan.

The doctrine we contend for, and to which *La Civiltà Cattolica* objects, or which it permits to be held only as a concession or condescension of the Church to the exceptional circumstances of particular localities, has its foundation in the very principle of the Divine Government itself. The Spirit of Christ is the spirit of liberty. God governs the moral world by moral power, never by physical force. He made man free, endows him with reason and free will, that he might have moral worth, be capable of virtue, and merit a reward; and he governs him according to the nature he has given him, as a free agent, and never forces his reason, or does violence to his free will. He governs him as a free man and not as a slave, for he desires his love, and accepts from him only a rational and voluntary service, *obsequium rationabile*, as says St. Paul. The Church, whose mission it is to introduce and maintain the law of God in human affairs and the hearts of men, must imitate the Divine government, and no more than God himself attempt to force reason, or by physical violence constrain free will. She is restricted by the very law of her existence to moral means, and can operate only through reason and conscience. God never suppresses error by the exertion of his omnipotence; he leaves the mind free, and corrects error only by the exhibition of his truth, and wins the heart by displaying his moral beauty. He lets the wheat and the tares grow together in the same field; "maketh his sun to rise on the evil and on the good, and sendeth his rain upon the just and the unjust." This is the law for the Church, and she must bear with error and disobedience as God himself bears with them.

This law, which we call the law of freedom, is universal, and law for both Church and state. The state itself has no right to use force, except to repress or redress external violence, to maintain and vindicate the rights either of individuals or of society against aggressive external acts. Beyond this, all physical force on the part of the state even is unlawful, unauthorized by the law of God, from whom all power is derived. Except in relation to external acts of violence, acts against individual rights, and the rights and peace of society, no government governs legitimately save by the concurrence of the free will of the governed. Hence all despotisms, all arbitrary governments, or governments that do not exist and govern by the free will or free assent of the governed, are repugnant to the law of the Divine government, and therefore are usurpations, without legal authority, and incapable of binding the conscience. Such governments have indeed existed, and been approved and defended even by churchmen, as well as by infidels; but they have done so by misapprehending the principle on which the patriarchal government rested for its justification. The authority of the patriarch is acknowledged as absolute indeed, but it is held to be that of the father over his child, and assumed to be tempered by parental affection and experience. It is wise, just, legitimate, while the governed are infants, incapable of speaking for themselves, but the reverse when the *infans* becomes able to speak, when the child has attained his majority and become a man, Within certain bounds it is just in the government of the family, but never in the government of a state, composed of adults, of members who have arrived at manhood. Here all arbitrary government is unlawful, and only republican government in some form,—elective government, or the government of the people by the people themselves,—is legitimate, or in conformity with the principles of the Divine government. Hence most justly does Count de Montalembert demand a free Church in a *free State*, and maintain that only in a free state is a free Church, or a Church unfettered by the civil authority, practicable, as a free state itself is practicable only with a free Church. There is no freedom for the state under a clerocracy, such as was attempted in the middle ages, and none even for the Church; for spiritual interests are subordinated to secular interests, and the clergy sacrifice or subordinate the spirituals of the Church in order to maintain her temporals, or their own temporal possessions and power, no less than politicians, as the history of what is strangely enough called the "Ages of Faith," but too amply demonstrate. Under Caesarism neither state nor Church is free, for in relation to both Caesar's will or caprice is the law. He can use the law to oppress the Church, and the Church to sustain his oppression of the people. The Church in Russia has no more freedom than have the Russian people, and it had no more freedom in France under Louis XIV or Napoleon I than had the French people themselves. In Great Britain the progress of religious freedom and that of civil freedom have advanced *pari passu*. So is it in Austria; as the Church is emancipated from the shackles imposed by the State under Joseph II the State becomes constitutional; and as the State becomes constitutional and free, the Church becomes free to act as a moral or spiritual power, according to her own constitution. In this country both the Church and the State are free, because here men are governed as freemen, not as slaves, or because here the manhood of the nation is fully recognized.

But the party represented by *La Civiltà Cattolica*, to some extent by the *Dublin Review*, and the first three volumes of our own Review, do not like this, for they, in fact, desire neither a free Church nor a free State. They do not believe in republican government, and they desire a civil government which establishes the Church as the law of the land, and uses its whole force, if needed, to protect her, and to suppress error or dissent. In the United States, they sympathize to a man with the Southern Rebels, not because they love negro slavery, but because they hate the Republic, and wish to see it broken up and its influence destroyed. In France they to a man favored the reestablishment of the Empire on the ruins of the Republic, because they flattered themselves that the new emperor would favor exclusively their church, suppress her enemies, and permit her pastors to bask once more in the sunshine of the Court. In Italy they to a man reject the freedom offered to the Church, because it is offered alike to the sects, and is coupled with constitutional liberty in the state; and if the state has to some extent treated them harshly, it is because they have demanded more than equal rights, and have insisted on special favors to themselves, or on having the government of the country exclusively in their hands. They regret the loss of their former privileges, and believe the Italian world is rushing to the devil because they have been deprived of them, as many people among ourselves fancy that our Constitution will be destroyed, liberty lost, and the country ruined forever and a day after, if negro slavery comes to be abolished. We doubt not the orthodoxy, the honesty, the sincerity, or even the benevolence of these people; but they are like those Jews whom our Lord rebuked for not being able to discern the signs of the times, and who crucified him between two thieves, because he came not precisely in the way they had made up their minds that he was to come, or because he came not in the form, and with the signs, they had expected. They see not that there is more of Christ in what they oppose than there was in what they have lost, and so bitterly regret.

The theory adopted by this party, when reduced to its ultimate principle, is, that even Christian nations are still in the age of barbarism, and that lay society, or the people, are still, and are always to remain, in their infancy, and to be guarded and tended in the nursery. They must be kept in leading-strings, and in no respect be trusted to their own reason and conscience. They are to be treated with all gentleness, with all a father's and all a mother's love; to have plenty of dolls, toys, hobby-horses, wooden swords and wooden guns, miniature drums and flags, plenty of playthings and amusements, pictures, statues, music, processions; but never to be treated as free agents, or to be allowed to speak for themselves. In Church and State they are to be cherished and tenderly cared for, but held to be *infantes*, or mutes, incapable of speech. They cannot think or speak for themselves, and are not to assume the responsibility of their own acts. Supposing the people to be, and always to remain, infants—to have no majority, never to become of age, or to arrive at man's estate—this opposition to civil and religious liberty is reasonable and just. The regimen demanded is the proper regimen for children who have not come to the years of discretion, and perhaps also for savage and barbarous tribes, or nations still in their infancy, not yet brought into the family of civilized nations. We will not say that it was not in some measure proper, even in the barbarous ages which succeeded the overthrow of the Western Roman Empire by the Northern barbarians, and prolonged by new barbarian invasions from the East and the South till the eleventh century, though, perhaps, even in those ages it was at best only partially proper, because, in point of fact, the Graeco-Roman civilization did not wholly perish with the Roman Empire itself, and even the conquering barbarians brought with them many elements of civilization—and of a civilization superior to the Graeco-Roman in its most palmy days. But, be this as it may, nations as well as individuals have a majority; one day they become of age, and are no longer to be treated as minors. They pass from childhood to manhood, and when they have reached their majority, and are men, both Church and state must recognize the fact, acknowledge their freedom, and seek to govern them as men—as free men, not as children or slaves. This doctrine is not new for us, and was amply set forth, though timidly, in our pages for July, 1849.

Modern Christian nations, whether orthodox or heterodox, have unquestionably attained to their majority, and all attempts to remand them to the nursery are only productive of evil. They cannot succeed. Lay society has attained to manhood, and can be governed only under the regimen of liberty, as free rational agents, who can speak, who have the rights of men, which authority must recognize and respect as inviolable. They must be governed through their own reason and conscience. It will not do to treat the nation that breaks away from external unity, and rushes into schism and heresy, as a truant child, to be scourged back, or given up as incorrigible. Force against it is out of the question, except to repress actual violence. Its natural and civil rights remain unaffected, for it derives the former from God through nature, and the latter from God through the people. This we want frankly acknowledged by both ecclesiastics and politicians. So of individuals, whether the majority or minority of the nation, who fall into what the Church condemns as heresy or schism. Natural and civil rights, not being derived from God through the Church, remain the same in both the orthodox and the heterodox, and among these rights is to be reckoned the right of conscience, or right of each one to choose and profess his own religion. All that is to be asked for the Church is, that she be free, by appeals to the reason, intelligence, and conscience of her rebellious subjects, to convert them if she can, and that they be free, in the face of all external authority, to return to her communion if they see proper. This freedom we demand for the Church, not on the ground that she is the Church of God, but on the ground that she is *our* church, *our* religion, *our* conscience, and we are men and citizens, and all men and citizens are equal before the law. This equality of all men and citizens demands equal liberty and protection for the Church and the sects, and for truth and error. The error is always to be deplored, as is every abuse which man makes of his liberty; but its responsibility rests upon the individual, who is accountable for it to no human tribunal, for conscience is accountable to God alone. God gives to every man the means of salvation, and urges him, by all the force of divine wisdom and love, to use them, but leaves him, nevertheless, free to reject them and damn his own soul if he chooses; and what right has Church or state to be more strict than God? And why should either shrink from imitating the example of his government?

The great error of the *oscurantisti* is in persisting in governing men as children. Because the faithful are required to be docile and childlike, they conclude that they are to be retained in perpetual childhood, and never to be allowed the freedom of manhood. Liberty has its inconveniences, we admit, and it requires far less wisdom and virtue to govern men as slaves, than it does to govern them as free men. Men of very small minds, little knowledge, and less virtue, can be despots, and lord it over God's heritage, whether in Church or state; but to govern not as lords, but as pastors, or to govern free men as free men, through their freedom, intelligence, and their moral convictions, requires men of character, of large minds, rare intelligence, rare wisdom, and rarer moral worth,—something divine. Liberty is sure to be abused if recognized, but its abuses never exceed, never equal, the abuses of power. It was not the excesses of liberty, but the excesses of power, that constituted what is called the Reign of Terror in France. Frenchmen were freer under Napoleon than they were under the Convention, or the Committee of Safety. We have ourselves, when shocked or disgusted at the misuse men make of their liberty in our Republican country, allowed ourselves to use expressions in favor of a regimen less free, which we regret, and which must not be taken as our deliberate, settled convictions. If the reader comes across any such expressions in any thing we have written, let him blot them out. They are only the impatient utterances of a transient feeling, of a momentary indignation at the abuses of liberty which we saw daily and hourly before us. Men are permitted to declaim against the abuses of a good thing, without being held to reject the good thing itself. We demand government, and strong government, in both Church and state, but in either a government that recognizes and protects the rights of manhood,—that respects instead of crushing out the natural freedom God gives to every man.

There is no doubt that liberty, in whatever order we assert it, will be abused. Men left to their own reason and conscience, in spite of the teachings and admonitions of the Church, in spite of the Holy Scriptures, in spite of divine revelation and the interior operations of divine grace, in spite of all the moral and spiritual influences that can be brought to bear on them, will abuse it, will fall into pernicious errors, into deadly heresies, and even glory in disobedience. Let no one flatter himself that liberty will never be construed to mean license, or that it will lead to or secure entire unity of doctrine, guard against all dissent, or result in offering to God the pure worship he requires. We know this well. But at all this risk it is better to have liberty than despotism, or else God would not have created man a free moral agent. It is better that men should sometimes err than that they should never think; that they should sometimes act wrong, than that they should never act at all. The great Apostle to the Gentiles tells the faithful to be men: "Be ye no longer children, but be men; howbeit, in innocence be children, but in understanding be men." In the primitive ages there was none of this excessive government and over-direction of the faithful, which render them so weak and timid at the present day. More, far more reliance was then placed on the Christian's own understanding and conscience. He was carefully instructed in his Christian faith and duty, strengthened by the Sacraments, and then left to act as a free, intelligent, conscientious man, who had an interior light that in all ordinary cases could be safely trusted. Hence the faithful, though recruited in great part from the slave population and the humbler classes of society, were men, thinking, reasoning, heroic men, capable of giving a reason for their faith, and, when need was, of dying for it. There was life, moral and intellectual activity of mind, deep energy of soul, which, with God's blessing, converted the world. Heresies and schisms there were, but there were also able and accomplished champions of orthodoxy and unity to meet and vanquish them; and we may say that no heresy or schism has ever been extirpated by the exertion of physical force. Protestantism survives in France, and Catholicity in Ireland. Force may make hypocrites, and, by alienating men from the truth, drive them into infidelity; never can it make sincere and earnest believers. No; mind must be met and conquered by mind, not by brute force.

Even in the middle ages, the modern nursery system hardly obtained. In the bosom of the Church, among the faithful, there was a freedom of thought and action, a reliance on reason and conscience, on self-direction, so to speak, which has been unknown or condemned for the last two hundred years. There was much barbarism, much violence, and there were terrible crimes in those ages, but, as Montalembert has well remarked, in his *Moines d'Occident*, there was more manliness, more strength and elevation of character, than in our times, and if there were great crimes, there were great expiations. There was very little of the weakness, the effeminacy, or the sentimental piety of our days. The party represented by *La Civiltà Cattolica* speak of those ages as "Ages of Faith," as Catholic ages, and regret them. But whatever advantages they had over subsequent ages, they owed them to their greater freedom, to their greater reliance on the individual reason and conscience. The Jesuits had not then invented or perfected that marvelous machinery now in use, which so effectually emasculates the soul, and keeps us at best mere children in the nursery, hardly daring to decide what slip or frock we shall wear for the day, till we have consulted our ghostly father or our spiritual director. We owe our weakness, our lack of self-reliance, of robust faith and manly piety, of strong and elevated character, to our lack of liberty, to our being kept always in leading-strings, and treated as children not to be trusted out of sight of the tutor or governess. What is the consequence? The strong and robust, those who feel themselves men, and have the right to be men, and to think and act as free men even in religion, grow cold in their affections for the religious society, and, confounding faith and piety with the human machinery in vogue for sustaining them, and the Church with a party in the Church that seems to lack all human sympathy and all respect for human rights and human progress, turn away with wrath or disgust, and seek refuge in infidelity or indifference, as men in despair sometimes kill themselves. Under your safeguard system you have no mental activity, or none that has the courage to show itself. Your great men are reduced to silence, or die of broken hearts, and only the voice of mediocrity can be heard. Any other voice is judged unsafe, heretical, revolutionary, or, at best, offensive to pious ears. You see this and deplore it, but, unhappily, labor to remedy it only by new and more vigorous applications of the machinery that has produced it.

Now, both reason and experience prove that we cannot, if we would, keep the nations in perpetual childhood, or remand them to childhood when once they have attained to their majority. We urge, then, the frank abandonment, on the part of the rulers either in Church or state, of the nursery system, and the equally frank adoption of the regimen of liberty. It seems to us worse than idle to resist the spirit of liberty which now moves and agitates nearly all civilized nations—which has created a constitutional Italy and a constitutional Spain; is creating a constitutional Austria, convulsing the Christian populations of Turkey, emancipating the Catholics in Great Britain and Scandinavia, the serfs in Russia, and the slaves in America, and in the name of which the United States have under arms and in the field more than half a million of men. We must accept modern civilization, and, notwithstanding all its infidel and materialistic tendencies, accept it in on faith. After all, if analyzed, this modern civilization will be found to be at bottom, not a revolt against Christianity, nor even against the Church as a spiritual kingdom, as so many worthy people suppose. It is only a revolt against a human authority that seeks to govern men as slaves, not as freemen, and is really more Christian, more catholic than the system it seeks to supplant. It opposes all employment of physical force or secular authority in matters of faith and conscience, and demands for every man the recognition, by all human tribunals, of the liberty that God gives us—a liberty which neither the state, nor the Church in her human legislation, can either grant or alienate,—or, in other words, the full and frank recognition of man's right, before all human authority, to civil and religious freedom. This it demands in all modern nations, Catholic and non-Catholic, for non-Catholic States have been, and still are, even less tolerant than Catholic states. The United States is the only nation in the world, where the majority of the people are non-Catholic, that has not a religion established and supported by the state, or in which all religions are placed on an equal footing before the law. Great Britain tolerates dissent from the national church, but does not recognize the right of dissent; and barbarous laws against recusancy still disgrace her statute-books, though rarely enforced. Civil liberty has made progress in most modern states, but in every country, not excepting our own, it has even yet to struggle to sustain itself. Yet the result is not doubtful, and victory will at last declare itself for the new order of civilization.

The civil and religious liberty, involving the complete separation of Church and state, regarded as governments, which modern civilized society demands, does not, as some suppose, necessarily imply political atheism or a godless state. Religion is by no means, because the state does not establish it, excluded from civil society, and the Church is united with the state through the faith and conscience of the citizen, if the state, as it should be, is republican in its constitution. It would be godless only in case it was an absolute monarchy, in which Caesar can say, *L'état, c'est moi.* But the State being republican, though it professes officially, or enacts no religion, has always in its laws and administration all the religion held and cherished by its citizens. The republican state, or government of the people by the people themselves, must express in its laws and administration, in the long run, the intelligence and will of the people, and, therefore, just so much of religion, of faith and piety, as enter into that intelligence and will; which is all the union of Church and State that is compatible with liberty, or that is really practicable. So far the union is dialectic, living, and indissoluble. But as all citizens are equal, and each has an equal right to assert his own religion, it follows necessarily that the people can bring their religion into the laws and administration only so far as it is common to them all. What each has that is peculiar to himself remains as a part of his individuality, respected by the state, indeed, but incapable of expressing itself in the positive action of civil society. Hence religion only, so far as it is catholic or common to all, can be expressed or recognized in the acts of the government, which is all that is necessary, and to which no one can object. All sects would be free, but the state would be really catholic.

Let no one take any alarm at this. The enemies of religion must understand, that if they require the state to use its power against religion, or to suppress it, they violate the first principle of civil and religious liberty. Religious liberty does not mean the liberty of infidelity to use the state or the civil power to suppress religion. The state, under the control of infidelity, and establishing atheism, is, to say the least, as hostile to religious and civil liberty as the state under the control of the clergy, and establishing the Roman Catholic Church. The French Convention, decreeing that "death is an eternal sleep," violated as flagrantly both civil and religious liberty as does a Catholic State when it deprives Protestants, or a Protestant state when it deprives Catholics, within its dominions, of the free exercise of their faith and worship. The man who denies Christianity has no more right to insist that the state shall give civil effect to his denial, than he who affirms it has that it shall give civil effect to his affirmation—nay, he has altogether less right, because civilized nations are Christian, and nations are really civilized only so far as they are Christian nations. All civilization has its origin and ground in Christian principles or ideas; and the infidel, whatever he may be practically, places himself doctrinally in opposition to civilization itself, and, therefore, to all human development, and individual and social progress. Infidelity is really a return to barbarism, from which Christianity has rescued us. We ask no civil pains and penalties to be enacted against it; but we can consent to none in its favor. Humanity has the right to go on under the law of development, whatever the protests or efforts at resistance of the *oscurantisti*, whether they are churchmen or infidels, and the most thorough-going of all obscurantists are those who reject the Christian religion.

Those of our friends who fear that to accept modern civilization would be to favor schism, heresy, or infidelity, would do well to bear in mind that Christianity, in itself, is one and catholic, and that all Christian nations belong to one and the same family, have the same Christian idea, and are, each in its way, developing and laboring to perfect one and the same order of civilization. The real unity of Christendom, if weakened and obscured, has not been wholly lost. The central life of Christendom, the idea in its purity and integrity, Catholics, of course, hold, is in the Church in communion with the See of Rome, under the pastoral care of the Pope; but they neither hold, nor are bound by the faith to hold, that all life which flows from the central fountain, or which emanates from Christ, who is the Idea of Christendom, is arrested at the external or visible boundaries of the Roman communion, and that there is no Christian life outside of its pale. All civilization is, in some sense, catholic; but all civilization is not confined to so-called Catholic nations. The civilization of Great Britain is, in some important relations, more catholic than that of Austria, Italy, Spain, Portugal, or Spanish and Portuguese America. The Church has lost many nations from her external communion, but the world is more catholic today than it was before the Protestant revolt or even the Greek schism. Neither faith nor charity has failed, or been diminished, and the progress of modern civilization is the real expression of both. No man who understands Christianity can exclude from Christendom the principal Protestant nations, or the nations that adhere, like Russia and modern Greece, to the schismatical Greek communion. We cannot look upon these as heathens, and treat them as aliens from the Christian family. We may often find in these not less catholic truth, save in words, the sense of which is little understood even by Catholics themselves, than we find in many Catholic nations. They are heterodox and externally schismatics, but their civilization and ours is one and the same in principle, and doctrinal and sacramental unity will follow as soon as Catholic nations purge themselves of their sectarianism, understand more fully that Catholicity is catholic, and accept and adhere to the regimen of liberty.

It is necessary to distinguish, in modern civilization, what is central, real, living, from what is merely accidental, temporary, or only simply apparent; and when this is done it will be found that it is essentially Catholic and Christian. Our good souls who are frightened at it, who recoil with horror from it, or anathematize it with so much unction, as does Father Taparelli, Father Curci, or even Father Félix, would do well to study it a little closer, and to ask themselves if they have not failed to give to the Christian dogma its catholic sense and application. They seem to us to seek their Lord among the dead, not the living, and to look for his body in the tomb wherein it was laid by Joseph of Arimathea. They should know that our Lord is risen, and is not to be sought among the tombs. All the words and deeds of our Lord, all the facts of his history, have, aside from their particular sense, a universal sense, applicable alike to all ages and nations. The apparent hostility of modern civilization to Christianity, or its apparent unchristian character, lies in the fact that even churchmen overlook this universal sense and application, and confine themselves too strictly to the particular sense. They accept the Christian dogma, but understand not that every dogma is a catholic or universal principle, and therefore fail to recognize it, when they find it under any other than the particular form in which it is stated in the teaching or definition of the Church. They keep to the letter, forgetting that the letter killeth, and that it is the spirit that quickeneth. The truth is not the sign, but what the sign signifies.

Modern civilization, with all its errors and defects, is, at bottom, the aspiration of the nations to Christ, and is the result of their serious and earnest efforts to realize the Word made flesh, or the Christian Idea, in their social life. No similar civilization is to be found in nations that have received no Christian instruction. The modern demand for liberty is only the assertion of the free will taught by Christian theology applied to our social relations. The demand for the amelioration of the condition of the poor and more numerous classes, or the effort to put the poor in the way of helping themselves, is only a catholic exposition of the precept to give alms; and the movement to place them on a footing of political equality with the rich and prosperous, is only the attempt to fulfill the word of our Lord to the Precursor, "the poor have the Gospel preached unto them." Even democracy, to which the age so strongly tends, is but an earnest effort to realize in society the unity of the race, human brotherhood, and the natural equality of all men, asserted in the Incarnation and Redemption. Your unbeliever, our atheist, whatever his speculative errors, practically follows not seldom the law of Christ, and is a good Christian as a friend, a neighbor, and a citizen. Auguste Comte and his disciples, though they speculatively deny God and vent the grossest sophisms about religion, yet assert the Divine existence under the form of the principles or laws of nature, and hold it man's duty to conform to them, to expiate by his sufferings the faults he commits, and to labor for the development and progress of his race. They reason badly, and have no philosophy, yet they are, intellectually considered, only carried away by a reaction against an exaggerated supernaturalism, and a false theology, which separates God from his works, as a clockmaker is separated from his clock. Unquestionably, in modern civilization there are unchristian and even antichristian tendencies, but these are accidental, and may be separated from it, and would soon disappear were churchmen to accept it, and instead of warring against it, to labor to supply its defects, and restore to it the equilibrium it now lacks. Certainly to do so were the surest and quickest way to put an end to unbelief, and to modern heresies and schisms.

We do not forget here the question of the salvation of the soul, which, after all, is the great thing, since heaven is our end. We hold as firmly as any of our brethren the dogma, *Extra Ecclesiam nulla salus*, but we by no means hold that we are to consign to perdition all who are not visibly in her visible communion. In every age and nation, he that feareth God and worketh righteousness is accepted with him. Not everyone who falls even into dogmatic error is damned. All error is the effect of ignorance, and ignorance, when not culpable in its cause, is excusable. I hope through God's mercy to be saved, but I have not the presumption to pretend that I am free from all error, even in relation to Christian dogma. If all error insures damnation, who can be saved? The greatest and best men that have ever lived have erred, and a man may err without being a heretic. He only is a heretic who rejects the known truth, or voluntarily neglects to use due diligence in seeking for the truth. There are, probably, fewer heretics and schismatics in Christendom than is commonly supposed. The direct labor to convert the individuals we believe in error, or to bring them into our visible communion, is, perhaps, not the best way either to advance orthodoxy or to save the soul. Most of the schisms and heresies, if not all, that the Christian deplores, originate not in pride or obstinacy, in hatred of the truth or impatience of legitimate authority, as is too often pretended, but in the fact that the Church is coupled with an obsolete phase of civilization, and; that in the changes that have taken place, her authorities really do not give to the soul, to the understanding, to the human element its rights. The individual must now, to a great extent, be reached through civilization, and the labors most effective in developing civilization, and making it express the real Christian Idea, will be in the end the most effective in saving the souls of those who are now out of the way. Christ must be formed in society as well as in the individual, and through society the individual must be united with him.

The Christian idea has, hitherto, received from the clergy, whether orthodox or heterodox, a one-sided development. The ascetic and mystic side of Christianity has been insisted upon to the detriment of the social. Heaven and earth, instead of being regarded as parts of one whole, related to each other as medium and end, have been treated as opposites, and what is given to the one has been counted as so much taken from the other. The highest form of Christian life on earth has been assumed to be that which approaches nearest to the life of the saints in glory. Hence the Christian ideal, the ideal of Christian perfection on earth, has been confounded with the monastic life, and, in the monastic life, with the contemplative life. The saint tramples the world beneath his feet, counts this life nothing, suppresses his human instincts and affections, and strives to live, while a mere *viator* or pilgrim, as if he had arrived at home, and become a *comprehensor*—the grand error of both Brahminism and Buddhism. We do not, of course, pretend that this error has ever received the official sanction of the Church, that it has ever been warranted by her authoritative teaching, or that the great masters of spiritual life have failed to warn us against it. The Holy See has never favored it, and has always labored to soften the ascetic rigorism adopted by the founders of religious orders. Yet there has always been a tendency among the devout in this direction; and as nearly all the spiritual reading of the faithful has been for ages furnished by the monastic orders, who were, or profess to be, dead to the world, its virtues and affections, this tendency has been strengthened and become practically predominant in the minds of the faithful. Yet this whole system is one-sided, sophistical, and not seldom mischievous. It mutilates Christianity, and tends to separate in Christ the Divinity from the humanity. This world is not the end for which man was created, but the way to that end lies through it. It does not stand opposed to heaven, but is related to heaven as the means to the end, and the end is attainable only through the means.

This exclusively ascetic view, which has practically prevailed, has led to the neglect of civilization, and to its depreciation in its relation to the salvation of souls, or the elevation of the race to union with God. If I can only save my soul, what need I care for civilization? Men have supposed that nothing should weigh with them but their individual salvation. Yet St. Paul did not so think. He said he could wish himself separated from Christ for his brethren, his kinsmen according to the flesh, showing in the strongest manner possible, that disinterested love which places the good of others above even our own, and which is far removed from that cold-hearted egotism that says, "No matter what becomes of the world, of society, of human life and its affections, if I only save my own soul." The truth is, no man who so feels and so thinks is in the way of saving even his own soul. The commandments, without fulfilling which no man can inherit eternal life, place love to our neighbor on the same level with love to God. Hence the social element, which has love to our neighbor for its basis, and which expresses itself in what we call civilization, is as Christian and lies in as high a plane as the ascetic element. In barbarous ages, or where there is no free State, the development of this social element is, no doubt, obstructed, and hence the reason why such undue prominence has been given to the Ascetic, and why the labors of Churchmen for civilization have been indirect rather than direct, or why they have labored to reach civilization through the individual, rather than the individual through civilization. Hence a reason why we demand a free Church in a *free* State, where both elements may be developed *pari passu*, in dialectic harmony.

Now, if we study modern civilization, that is, the civilization struggling to establish itself, not that which is struggling to hold its old place, we shall find that, at bottom, it is nothing else on the one side than protest against this exclusive asceticism, and, on the other, the assertion of the rights and position of the lay society. It protests against the false mysticism to which exclusive asceticism always gives birth, and asserts that Christian life is a human-divine life, and that man is not pure spirit, or pure spirit inhabiting a body, but the union or complex of soul and body, as implied in the fact that our Lord, in assuming human nature, assumed a human body as well as a human soul, and in the last article but one of the Creed, "I believe in the resurrection of the body,"—*carnis resurrectionem*. No doubt modern civilization, like all reactions, has a tendency to run to the opposite extreme, and, in its turn, to undervalue the ascetic, the mystic, the personal culture hitherto predominant in the Christian world; no doubt it tends to be exclusive, and, therefore, sophistical, but this is a point to be guarded against, for all exclusiveness is opposed to truth, since all truth is catholic. Yet underlying this modern civilization, and pervading it as its informing and moving spirit, is the principle that this world has its place in the Christian order, and civilization its work in the economy of salvation, or that the Word was made flesh and dwelt among us.

Taking what is substantive in each element, and rejecting in each its exclusiveness, or rejecting what is sophistical and accidental in each, and bringing both into dialectic union, we have the truly catholic order, and a really catholic civilization, together with the principle and conditions of the unity and peace of Christendom. We, in this way, secure unity of faith, unity of charity, unity of the sacraments, unity of discipline, unity of communion, without requiring any one to give up anything positive that he really holds and desires to retain, or to accept anything to which he is or ever has been really opposed. There is no compromise of principle or surrender of any positive condition required. All parties are right in what they affirm, and none err except in what they deny. Their affirmations are catholic, for none other are possible; only their denials are exclusive, sectarian, sophistical. The word *catholic* asserts unity as well as universality, for nothing lacking unity can be universal. That which you assert to be universal must be one and the samc, for no addition of one thing to another can ever give you universality, any more than the accumulation of finites can give you infinity. It is not without a profound meaning, therefore, that the true religion, or the Church of Christ, is called *Catholic*. It is so called because it is catholic in itself, in its principles, and because what is not catholic is not true, is not of the Church of God, and can be no art of true religion. What are called false religions, are religions only in so far as they are one and catholic, for there is and can be but one religion. All Christendom repeats daily, "I believe in the Holy Catholic Church—sanctam ecclesiam catholicam," and the word *catholic* is not technical, naming a particular church, sect, or congregation, but an adjective applied to express the quality, nature, and character of the Church herself. Christianity itself is catholic, and hence St. Vincent of Lerins gives us as the criterion or mark of Christian faith, the fact that it has been believed always, everywhere, and by all. Men can all agree only in what is true.

The trouble now is, that the profound significance of the word *catholic* is unheeded,—that the word is taken in a technical sense, and made the rallying-cry of division instead of unity. This is because not all who are called Catholics are really Catholics; for many of them restrict Catholicity to their own external communion, and recognize no Catholic truth outside of it, and consider it their duty to condemn the world outside as all wrong, to convict it of error, instead of recognizing the truth it really has, and seeking to enlighten it and to supply its defects, by presenting it the truth in its unity and integrity, or the truth it has not in dialectic union with the truth it has. These people seem to think, because the Holy Ghost dwells in the Church into which they have been incorporated, that his operations are confined to them. They fail to note that, though the Holy Ghost speaks to men in the Written Word, and in the external authority of the Church, when teaching or defining the faith, he speaks also to them through reason and conscience, common to all men. Peter marveled, no doubt, when he found the Holy Ghost was given to the Gentiles as well as to the Jews; but when he saw his manifest operations, witnessed the effects of his presence, he recognized them for what they really were, and in the joy of his heart exclaimed, "Who can forbid water that these be baptized?" The Holy Ghost is God; God the Consummator; and his presence is therefore universal, as universal as that of God the Creator, or God the Mediator. He is in the new phase assumed by civilization, no less than he was in the old, and, rightly understood, the new developments, which frighten so many of our friends, and make them think the world is about to end, are only a step forward in the great work of consummation. The feebleness of character so marked in our modern conservatives, whether in Church or state, is owing to the fact that they do really, without knowing or intending it, resist the Holy Ghost, and force him to work against them, not with them. The living, beating, aspiring heart of Christendom is not with them, is against them, and on the side of the men who represent the progressive spirit of the age. Only the voice of these, the radicals, as they are called, fetch an echo; and, even when not free from many sad errors, their voices stir the souls of men, and kindle in them noble aspirations, and fire them with heroic daring. Had the President of these United States been one of these men, instead of being a feeble and timid conservative; had he been able to plant himself firmly on the principle of progress, without feeling that he must shuffle backwards and forwards between the party of the past and the party of the future, he would long before this have suppressed the Rebellion, and restored the Republic to unity and peace. It has been a far more difficult task to conquer him than to conquer the Rebels.

We have gone thus at length into this argument, in order to show that neither the friends nor the enemies of religion have anything to fear from adopting the great principle of civil and religious liberty, and asserting a free Church in a free State. We now add, that this regimen of liberty, however it may be resisted and delayed, is inevitable. The struggle may be protracted through long years; there may be still, for more than a generation, a state of war, in which alternate successes and defeats may await each party; but victory is sure at last to crown the party of liberty and progress, for on its side are humanity, and, what is more than humanity, humanity's God. Why, then, war against it? *La Civiltà Cattolica*, which might better be called *La Civiltà Acattolica*, apparently resists, only because it wishes to preserve the old system in Rome and Italy, where the introduction of the new would destroy much old machinery, and break up many old habits. But we are aware of no part of Christendom where the retention of the old régime does so much harm as in Rome and Italy. Leave the old there, and *La Civiltà Cattolica* and its party would permit us the regimen of liberty everywhere else, as a concession to our weakness, our intractableness, or to a local and temporary necessity. But we cannot accept as a concession what we demand as a right. Say what we will, Rome is the centre and capital of Christendom, and while the ecclesiastical authorities there maintain the old order and resist the new, or even refuse indignantly to accept it as a deliverance, it is impossible to give the necessary assurance to the friends of civil and religious liberty elsewhere that the Church is not herself really opposed to them, and that she will not, the moment she feels herself strong enough to do it, revoke her concessions, and insist on the re-establishment of the old system everywhere.

We belong to the Catholic Church; we love her as our mother, and we mean to conduct ourselves towards her as an obedient son. But we distinguish at Rome, as elsewhere, between what is divine and what is human; between what God has established and what men have invented. The Pontificate is divine, and it speaks with divine authority. It, and all that immediately pertains to it, we accept as infallible, to be by us believed, obeyed, loved, and neither judged nor disputed. But the men at Rome are human, and the human at Rome is neither more nor less respectable than at Paris, London, Vienna, or Washington. If we have the right to defend civil and religious liberty, so far as asserted in the Divine Government of men, and as not forbidden by any dogma of faith or law promulgated by Divine authority, at Washington, Baltimore, New York, London, Mechlin, Vienna, the Hague, St. Petersburg, or Paris, we have the right to defend it and insist on it at Rome, providing we do not do it, as we are not at liberty to do it anywhere, in a disorderly manner, or in a turbulent and seditious spirit. As long as Rome repels the regimen the world now demands, it can be looked upon as only provisional and temporary elsewhere. Here we differ from our friends the illustrious Count de Montalembert, and the learned, intrepid, and venerable Bishop of Orleans, who are apparently satisfied with the practical concessions *La Civiltà Cattolica* says may be made. We know no reason why Rome and Italy should be excepted, unless they put in the plea of infancy, the only ground on which the old system, in our judgment, is defensible.

We enter into no discussion of the Pope's temporal sovereignty, the last stronghold of the old system of Prince Bishops; but we must be permitted to say, that it seems strange to us that the wise heads at Rome do not see that the Pope holds that sovereignty only on sufferance, or because at present it does not suit the plans of the Emperor of the French to allow the new Italian kingdom to have Rome for its capital. The Emperor wants an Italy strong enough to be a useful ally, but not strong enough to be a dangerous enemy. So he maintains the Prince-Bishop at Rome and the Austrians in Venice. But the sentiment of the great body of the people of Christendom is against his temporal sovereignty, whatever may be the pastorals of their Bishops, issued in obedience to the mandates of Rome. When Pio Nono a few years since undertook to raise an army, and bid for volunteers from all parts of the Catholic world, to recover his revolted provinces, and to defend his sovereignty against the armed invasion of Sardinia, very few flocked to his standard, and those who did so, did not cover themselves with glory. The Pontiff is strong; the Prince is weak. We are all ready to die for our spiritual Father; but we have not heard of a dozen soldiers who went from the United States to fight for the Prince. The Italian kingdom, *aut fas, aut nefas*, is every day becoming consolidated and stronger, and, as far as men can foresee, if not prevented by France, will before long, in spite of the Tiara and the Quadrilateral, embrace the whole Peninsula, and be in reality, as well as in name, one of the great Powers of the world. If the Roman Sovereign relies on the address of the Bishops assembled at Rome, on the occasion of the canonization of the Japanese martyrs, he will most likely be deceived, for these Bishops have comparatively little power over their flocks save in spirituals, and we are sure that in their address they did not represent the sentiments of the great body of the Catholic people, especially of that people who must do the fighting, if fighting is to be done. Where, then, is he to look for human support? He can look only to diplomacy; only to the embroilment of the European nations in a fierce and general war, from which religion would be sure to lose more than it could possibly gain.

Indeed, it seems to us that Rome feels that her position is insecure. Her whole conduct indicates it. *Non possumus* is the cry of weakness, not of strength. We hear no longer from Rome the voice of Hildebrand, of Innocent III, nor of the stern old Sixtus Quintus. The excommunicatory bulls issued venture to excommunicate no one by name, and, seemingly at least, fall without effect. The scholars and *savans* of Rome explore the catacombs and devote themselves to the study of antiquities, as if they had no promise of the future. If a living man appears he must be silent, or be silenced. No voice of generous inspiration comes to us from the Eternal City; no voice of encouragement to those of us who are toiling day and night, with our heart's richest devotion, to advance the interests of religion and civilization. It is much if we are tolerated,—if we escape an interdict. We have found nothing more disheartening than the Letter of the Holy Father to the Archbishop of Munich, in relation to the Congress last September in Munich of a large number of the most distinguished Catholic scholars and authors of Catholic Germany. It is replete with the spirit of fear, and betrays a total lack of confidence in the human mind. The only determination we discover in it is to persist in the warfare against the irrepressible instincts of civilized humanity. Rome speaks only to repress; she has ceased to speak to encourage. We hear not from her, "Forward!" and we find her landing only those who are foremost in the work of repression. All this indicates that she feels herself insecure, and lives in constant dread of some great and terrible convulsion.

Our readers know that we are no revolutionists in either Church or state; that we respect vested rights, and that we hold that the Pope has as valid a vested right to the sovereignty of the Roman States, as any prince has or can have to the sovereignty of his dominions. We are not aware that his sovereignty has escheated either to his people or to Victor Emmanuel. But vested rights, not being natural rights, are not indefeasible. They may be forfeited, and if not forfeited, they may be alienated or ransomed. The Pope can alienate his authority as Prince by restoring it to the people, or for a just ransom, if he sees proper; and so the *non possumus* is really *non volumus*. The Roman sovereign can do as he pleases; but he knows little of a real movement party who flatters himself that when it finds vested rights in its way, and the owner refusing to put them to ransom, it will not, if strong enough, take them without ransom. The Pope need not then be surprised to find his Italian countrymen, aided by his own subjects, one day taking from him his Roman Principality, without stopping to say, "By your leave." It seems to us, therefore, as there is no reasonable prospect of resisting permanently the movement and retaining the Principality, at least without grave detriment to the highest religious and social interests, it would be wise and prudent for the Holy Father to abandon it for a reasonable ransom and proper guaranties for civil and religious freedom—for a free Church in a free State, as offered by Count Cavour. It is easy to denounce us for saying this. It will not be so easy to prove that what we say is not true, or that it is disloyally said, or with a heart not as devoted to the Church as that of the sovereign of Rome himself.

But we simply add, in conclusion, that we; have in what we have said only defended our own American order of civilization, and the rights conceded and claimed by our own nation, as is in our province, and in our duty as the conductor of a periodical that professes to be National. In the order we have defended, we have the fullest confidence, and we hold it to be not only national, but Catholic, because in accordance with the law of God, or the principles of the Divine Government.

SIXTEEN

Liberalism and Progress

This work, which has not yet found a publisher, and which exists only in the author's autograph, has come honestly into our possession, with permission to make such use of it as we see proper. The author seems to have been only a civilian General, as his name does not appear in the Army Register, and we suspect that he has never served in any army, hardly in a band of filibusters. From his English, and his inability to see anything in our habits or in our civil or military service, to commend, we should judge him some disappointed foreigner, who, at the breaking out of our civil war, had offered his services to the Government and had them refused. He regards himself as qualified for any post from Pathmaster to President, or from Corporal to Commander-in-Chief of the Armies of the United States, which makes against the theory that he is a foreigner, and would indicate that he is a native, and "to the manner born." He finds everything amiss with us, and that things can come right only by his being placed at the head of our civil and military affairs.

The General (?) is very profuse in his military criticisms, and shows a very hostile spirit towards our Military Academy. He blames the Government for intrusting important commands to men who have been educated

"Tendencies of Modern Society, with Remarks on the American People, Government, and Military Administration. By General Croaker. MS." From *Brownson's Quarterly Review*, 1 (October 1864): 450–70.

at West Point, and insists that if it will appoint Americans to the command of its armies, it should appoint civilians, who have not been narrowed, belittled, and cramped by the pedantry of a military education. He prefers instinct to study, and the happy inspirations of ignorance to the calculations of science. He thinks our true course is to invite hither the military adventurers so numerous on the continent of Europe, and who can find, in consequence of their devotion to democracy, no employment at home, and give them the command of our armies. He does not seem to be aware that we have tried his theory pretty thoroughly in both respects, and have found it not to work well. We passed in the beginning over the Army, and made nearly all our high military appointments from civil life. In our first batch of Major-Generals, not one was taken from the Army, and only one was taken who had been educated at West Point. The Government commenced with as great a distrust of West Point and a military education and military experience, and with as great a confidence in the military instincts and inspirations of civilians or political aspirants, as our author himself could desire, and with what wisdom the country knows, to its sorrow. Most of our civilian Generals have proved sad failures; West Point is now at a premium, and would remain so, but for the wretched policy of making most new appointments in the Army from the ranks, thereby spoiling good sergeants and making poor officers. Something besides bravery even is demanded of an officer. Gentlemanly tastes, habits, education, and manners, a knowledge of his profession, and an aptitude to command men, are necessary. Appointments from the ranks, as a reward of extraordinary merit, is well; but they should be sparingly and judiciously made. When we make appointments from the ranks the rule, they cease to be the reward of merit, and degrade the Army and impair its efficiency.

In the beginning of the war, we had almost any number of foreign adventurers in our service, but we have been obliged to get rid of the larger portion of them. Some among the foreign officers who have received commissions from our Government are men of real merit, and have served with intelligence and success; but the majority of them have proved to be men "who left their country for their country's good." No national army can be worth anything that is to any considerable extent officered by foreigners. If the nation cannot from itself officer its own army, it had better not go to war; for it is pretty sure to fail if it does. Then war as made here assumes a peculiar character. Carried on over our vast extent of country, much of it either a wilderness, or sparingly settled, in a manner so different from what the training and experience acquired in European armies and wars fit one for, that foreign officers can be of little use to us. Neither the strategy nor the tactics of a Napoleon would secure success here. The men who enter a foreign service are, besides, rarely the best officers in the army of their native country, and are usually such as their own government does not care to employ. We maintain, too, that though West Point is susceptible of improvement, nowhere are young men better trained for the profession of arms, and it is very little that the men from abroad, who seek commissions in our Army, can teach our West Pointers. The great objection to our army officers at the opening of the war was their lack of experience in commanding, moving, and maneuvering large bodies of men; but the foreigners who seek to enter our armies equally lack that experience. They have had only a Lieutenant's, a Captain's, a Major's, or at most a Colonel's command in their own country, or in the foreign service to which they have been attached. At the opening of the war, there were some who were mad enough to wish the Government to invite Garibaldi to come and take command of our Army; but Garibaldi, however successful he might have been as the tool of Piedmont or Mazzini in stirring up insurrection, and as a partisan commander, had never commanded nor proved himself capable of commanding an army of thirty thousand men. Besides, his proper place in this country would not have been in the Federal Army, but in that of the Rebels. To fight against rebellion and revolution in defence of legal authority and established government would have been a novelty to him, and contrary to his native instincts.

Our author is a decided democrat, in the European sense of the word, and complains that the American people are not truly and thoroughly democratic. He has no sympathy with our people, and thinks them false to their own democratic principles. What brought him here, if a foreigner, and induced him to offer us his valuable services, which appear to have been rejected, was his sympathy with democracy, and hostility to all other actual or possible forms of government. He wanted to sustain democracy here, not for our sake, but as a *point d'appui* for his operations against monarchy and aristocracy in Europe. All this may be very well in him, only he is on the wrong side, as would have been his friend Garibaldi. The struggle in which we are engaged, notwithstanding what some silly journalists write and publish, is not a struggle for the triumph of democracy. So to understand it is to misunderstand it; and we always regret to find friends of the Union urging the war as a war between the Northern democracy and the Southern aristocracy. Such many have tried and are still trying to make it; but such is not its real and legitimate character. On our side it is a war in defence of government, of authority, and the supremacy of law. It is a war in vindication of national integrity, and in defence of American constitutionalism. The very thing our author would have us make the principle and end of the war, is that which the war is waged against. We wish to abolish slavery so far as it can be done without appealing to humanitarian or revolutionary principles: but we have neither the right nor the wish to seek to revolutionize Southern society. Politically, Southern society is no more aristocratic in its constitution than Northern society: if socially it is more so, that is an advantage, not a disadvantage. In the present struggle, Southern society has proved relatively stronger and more energetic than Northern society, because in Southern society the people are marshaled under their natural leaders, under men who are intrinsically superior to the mass, and felt to be so; while in the Northern States they have been marshaled under no leaders or under artificial leaders, not superior, and often inferior, to those they are commissioned to lead. No society that has not a natural aristocracy, if we may borrow a phrase from Thomas Jefferson, has any really cohesive power, or any more strength than a rope of sand.

We have some madmen amongst us who talk of exterminating the Southern leaders, and of New-Englandizing the South. We wish to see the free-labor system substituted for the slave-labor system, but beyond that we have no wish to exchange or modify Southern society, and would rather approach Northern society to it, than it to Northern society. The New Englander has excellent points, but is restless in body and mind, always scheming, always in motion, never satisfied with what he has, and always seeking; to make all the world like himself, or as uneasy as himself. He is smart, seldom great; educated, but seldom learned; active in mind, but rarely a profound thinker; religious, but thoroughly materialistic: his worship is rendered in a temple founded on Mammon, and he expects to be carried to heaven in a softly-cushioned railway car, with his sins carefully checked and deposited in the baggage crate with his other luggage, to be duly delivered when he has reached his destination. He is philanthropic, but makes his philanthropy his excuse for meddling with everybody's business as if it were his own, and under pretense of promoting religion and morality, he wars against every generous and natural instinct, and aggravates the very evils he seeks to cure. He has his use in the community; but a whole nation composed of such as he would be short-lived, and resemble the community of the lost rather than that of the blest. The Puritan is a reformer by nature, but he never understands the true law of progress, and never has the patience to wait till the reform he wishes for can be practically effected. He is too impatient for the end ever to wait the slow operations of the means, and defeats his own purpose by his inconsiderate haste. He needs the slower, the more deliberate, and the more patient and enduring man of the South to serve as his counterpoise.

The South has for its natural leaders, not simply men of property, but men of large landed estates, and who are engaged in agricultural pursuits: the North has for its natural leaders business men and their factors, who may or may not be men of wealth, or who, if rich today, may be poor tomorrow, and who necessarily seek to subordinate everything to business interests. They of course are less fitted, in a country like ours, to lead than the landholders, because agriculture with us is a broader and more permanent interest of the nation than trade or manufactures.

We insist that it were a gross perversion of the war to make it a war against Southern society or the Southern people. The war is just and defensible only when it is conducted as a war of the nation for its own existence and rights against an armed rebellion. In the war the nation seeks to reduce the rebels to their allegiance, not to destroy them, not to exile them, not to deprive them of their property or their franchises; it seeks to make them once more loyal citizens, and an integral portion of the American people, standing on a footing of perfect equality with the rest, not slaves or tributaries. Southern society must be respected, and any attempt to build up a new South out of the few Union men left there, Northern speculators, sharpers, adventurers, and freed negroes, is not only impolitic, but unconstitutional and wrong. Such a South would be a curse to itself and to the whole nation; we want it not. With here and there an individual exception, the real people of the South are united in the Rebellion, and under their natural leaders, and any scheme of settlement that does not contemplate their remaining with their natural leaders, the real, substantial, ruling people of the Southern States, will not only fail, but ought not to be entertained. They must have the control of affairs in their respective States, and represent them in the councils of the nation. The nation cannot afford to lose them; if it could, it need not have gone to war against them. The bringing of the negro element, except in States where it is too feeble to amount to anything, into American political society will never be submitted to by either the North or the South. We must suppress the Rebellion; but with the distinct understanding that the Southern States are to be restored, when they submit, to all the rights of self-government in the Union, and that no attempt in the mean time shall be made to revolutionize their society in favor of Northern or European ideas. If in our haste, our wrath, or our zeal we have said anything that can bear a different sense, it must be retracted.

Friends of constitutional government, and of liberty with law, may justly sympathize with our Government m the present struggle; but not European radicals, democrats, and revolutionists, for the principle of the struggle is as hostile to them as it is to the Southern rebels. In this war the nation is fighting Northern democracy or Jacobinism as much as it is Southern aristocracy, and the evidence of it is in the fact, that the people cease to support willingly the war just in proportion as it assumes a Jacobinical character, and loses its character of a war in defence of government and law. The Administration may not see it; and the philosophers of the *New York Tribune* and *Evening Post*, well convinced as they may be that something is wrong, may deny it, and propose to cure the evil by doubling the dose of radicalism; even the people, while they instinctively feel it, may not be fully aware that it is that which holds them back; but so it is, and nothing for years has given us so much hope for our country as this very fact. It proves that, after all, the popular instincts are right, and that while the people are ready to carry on a war to preserve the Constitution and Government, they are not prepared to carry on a war for revolutionizing either. These foreign radicals and revolutionists who complain of our democracy, that it is not thoroughgoing and consistent, and does not press straight to its end, ought to understand that there is no legitimate sympathy between them and us, and that they cannot fight their battles in ours. We are not fighting their battles, and those of our own countrymen who think we are, begin already to find themselves deserted by the nation. The American people, however ready they have been to sympathize with revolution, and encourage insurrection and rebellion in foreign nations, therein imitating the English Whigs, are yet very far from being revolutionists in the interior of their souls, and for their own country.

Our author, who professes to side with the Federalists, keeps an eye on the revolutionary movements in Europe, and a considerable part of his work is written with the express intention of forwarding them. He rejoices at the spread of democratic ideas in England, in Germany, and in Italy, and he expresses his hope that the democratic party will rise again in France, and hurl the Emperor from his throne. We trust we love liberty and free government as much as does this disappointed foreigner, or American with foreign sympathies and notions: but, in our judgment, what Europe most wants at present is repose in the interior of her several nations, and freedom for their respective governments to devote themselves to the welfare and progress of the people, for which they can do nothing, so long as they have to use all their power and energy to maintain their own existence. Every enlightened well-wisher to European society would rejoice to see the whole race of European revolutionists exterminated, or converted into loyal and peaceful subjects. True liberty was never yet advanced by subverting the established government of a country. Europe has lost far more than it has gained by its century of insurrections, revolutions, and civil wars, and the new *régimes* introduced have left fewer effective guaranties of civil freedom and personal liberty than existed before them. Providence may overrule evil for good, but good is never the natural product of evil.

We know, in censuring the revolutionary spirit of modern society, we are placing ourselves in opposition to the whole so-called Liberal party of the civilized world; but that is not our fault. The Liberal party so called has its good side and its bad side. Some things in it are to be commended, and other things in it, whoever would not stultify himself must condemn. Man is by nature a social being, and cannot live and thrive out of society; society is impracticable without strong and efficient government; and strong and efficient government is impracticable, where the people have no loyal sentiments, and hold themselves free to make war on their government and subvert it whenever they please. Men and governments, no doubt, are selfish, and prone to abuse power when they have it; but no government can stand that rests only on the selfishness of the human heart, or on what in the last century, they called "enlightened self-interest," *intérêt bien entendu*, and not on the sense of duty, strengthened by loyal affection. People must feel not only that it is their interest to sustain government, but that it is their moral and religious duty to sustain it; and when they have no moral sense, no religion, and no loyal affection, they should know that they cannot sustain it, and society must cease to exist. A nation of Atheists were a solecism in history. A few Atheists may, perhaps, live in society, and even serve it for a time, where the mass of the people are believers and worshippers, but an entire nation of real Atheists was never yet found, and never could subsist any longer than it would take it to dissipate the moral wealth acquired while it was as yet a religious nation. It was well said by the Abbe de La Mennais, before his unhappy fall: "Religion is always found by the cradle of nations, philosophy only at their tombs"—meaning, as he did, philosophy in the sense of unbelief and irreligion; not philosophy in the sense of the rational exercise of the faculties of the human mind on divine and human things, aided by the light of revelation. The ancient Lawgivers always sought for their laws not only a moral, but a religious sanction, and where the voice of God does not, in some form, speak to men's consciences, and bid them obey the higher power, government can subsist only as craft or as sheer force, which nobody is bound to respect or obey.

The great misfortune of modern Liberalism is, that it was begotten of impatience and born of a reaction against the tyranny and oppression, the licentiousness and despotism of governments and the governing classes; and it is more disposed to hate than to love, and is abler to destroy than to build up. Wherever you find it, it bears traces of its origin, and confides more in human passion than in Divine Providence. The great majority of its adherents, even if they retain a vague and impotent religious sentiment, and pay some slight outward respect to the religion of their country, yet place the State above the Church, the officers of government above the ministers of religion, and maintain that priests have nothing to do with the affairs of this world. They forget that it is precisely to introduce the elements of truth, justice, right, duty, conscience into the government of individuals and nations in this world, as the means of securing the next, that institutions of religion exist, and priests are consecrated. Politicians may do as they please, so long as they violate no rule of right, no principle of justice, no law of God; but in no world, in no order, in no rank, or condition, have men the right to do wrong. Religion, if anything, is the *lex suprema*, and what it forbids, no man has the right to do. This is a lesson Liberalism has forgotten, or never learned.

In our last review we defended civil and religious freedom, and pointed out to the *oscurantisti* in Church and State, wherein and wherefore they mistake this age, are laboring for an impossibility, and fail to recall men to faith, and to re-establish in its integrity the unity of Christendom; but whoever inferred from what we then said that we have any sympathy with political Atheism, reasoned from premises of his own, not from any we ever laid down or entertained. Almost entire volumes of this Review are filled with refutations, such as they are, of political Atheism, and the defence of the authority of religion for the human conscience in all the affairs of human life. There are elements in modern Liberalism that it will not do to oppose, because, though Liberalism misapplies them, they are borrowed from the Gospel, are taken from Christian civilization, and are, in themselves, true, noble, just, and holy. Not can we recall modern society to that old order of things, that Liberalism began by opposing, even if it were desirable, which it is not. Many things we may seek to save from being overthrown, which, when overthrown, it would be madness to attempt to re-establish. But we have never denied that modern Liberalism has an odor of infidelity and irreligion, and assumes an independence of religion, that is, of conscience, of God, which is alike incompatible with the salvation of souls and the progress of society. Liberals, if they would study the question, would soon find that religion offers no obstacle to anything true and good they wish to effect, and even offers them that very assistance without which they cannot effect or preserve it.

It is the mad attempt to separate the progress of society from religion that has rendered modern Liberalism everywhere destructive, and everywhere a failure. It has sapped the foundation of society, and rendered government, save as a pure despotism, impracticable, by taking from law its sacredness, and authority its inviolability, in the understanding and consciences of men. The world, since the opening of modern history, in the fifteenth century, has displayed great activity, and in all directions; but its progress in the moral and intellectual orders has been in losing rather than in gaining. Its success in getting rid of old ideas, old beliefs, old doctrines, old sentiments, old practices, and in cutting itself loose from all its old moorings, has been marvelous, and well-nigh complete. Taste has, indeed, been refined, and manners, habits, and sentiments have been softened, and become more humane, but we have not learned that they have gained much in purity or morality. There has been a vast development of material resources, great progress in the application of science to the productive arts, and a marvelous augmentation of material goods; but it may well be doubted if there has been any increase even of material happiness. Happiness is not in proportion to what one is able to consume, as our political economists would lead one to suppose, but in proportion of the supply to one's actual wants. We, with our present wants and habits, would be perfectly miserable for a time, if thrown back into the condition of the people of the middle ages; and yet it is probable they were better able to satisfy even such material or animal wants as were developed in them than we are to satisfy those developed in us. Human happiness is not augmented by multiplying human wants, without diminishing the proportion between them, and the means of satisfaction, and that proportion has not been diminished, and cannot be, because such is human nature, that men's wants multiply always in even a greater ratio than the means of meeting them, as affirmed by our political economists, in their maxims of trade and production, that demand creates a supply, and supply creates a demand. Under the purely material relation, as a human animal, there is no doubt that the negro slave, well fed and well clothed, and not unkindly treated, is happier than the free laborer at wages. We suspect that it would be difficult to find in the world's history any age, in which the means of supply were less in proportion to the wants actually developed than in our own. There was more wisdom than our Liberals are disposed to admit in the old maxim: If you would make a man happy, study not to augment his goods, but to diminish his wants. One of the greatest services Christianity has rendered the world has been its consecration of poverty, and its elevation of labor to the dignity of a moral duty. The tendency of modern society is in the opposite direction. England and the United States, the most modern of all modern nations, and the best exponents the world has of the tendencies of modern civilization, treat poverty as a crime, and hold honest labor should be endured by none who can escape it.

There is no question that education has been more generally diffused than it was in the middle ages, but it is doubtful if the number of thinkers has been increased, or real mental culture extended. Education loses in thoroughness and depth what it gains in surface. Modern investigators have explored nature to a greater extent than it appears to have ever been done by the ancients, and accumulated a mass of facts, or materials of science, at which many heads are turned; but little progress has been made in their really scientific classification and explanation. Theories and hypotheses in any number we have, each one of which is held by the simpletons of the age to be a real contribution to science when it is first put forth, but most of them are no better than soap-bubbles, and break and disappear as soon as touched. Christianity has taught the world to place a high estimate on the dignity of human nature, and has developed noble and humane sentiments, but under the progress of modern society in losing it, characters have been enfeebled and debased, and we find no longer the marked individuality, the personal energy, the manliness, the force, the nobility of thought and purpose, and the high sense of honor, so common in the medieval world, and the better periods of antiquity. There is in our characters a littleness, a narrowness, a meanness, coupled with an astuteness and unscrupulousness to be matched only in the later stages of the Bas Empire. In military matters we have introduced changes, but may still study with advantage the Grecian phalanx and the Roman legion. Ulpian and Papinian can still, save in what we have learned from Christianity, teach us law, and we improve modern legislation and jurisprudence only by borrowing from the Civil Law as digested by the lawyers of Justinian, in the *Institutes* and *Novellae*. In political science, properly so called, Aristotle, and any of the great medieval doctors, are still competent to be our masters. He who has read Aristotle's *Politics* has read the history of American democracy, and the unanswerable refutation of all the democratic theories and tendencies of modern Liberals. For the most part we are prone to regard what is new to us as new to the world, and, what is worse, what is new to us as a real scientific acquisition, and a real progress of the race.

We have never read or heard of an age that had so high an opinion of its own acquisitions, that believed so firmly in its own intelligence, and that so little questioned its own immense superiority over all preceding ages, as the eighteenth century. It believed itself enlightened, highly cultivated, profound, philosophic, humane, and yet the doctrines and theories that it placed in vogue, and over which the upper classes grew enthusiastic in their admiration, are so narrow, so shallow, so directly in the face and eyes of common sense, so manifestly false and absurd, that one finds it difficult to believe that anybody out of a madhouse ever entertained them. What think you of a philosopher who defines man—"A digesting tube, open at both ends?" And of another who ascribes all the difference between a man and a horse, for instance, to "the fact that man's fore limbs terminate in hands and flexible fingers, while those of a horse terminate in hoofs?" Yet these philosophers were highly esteemed in their day, and gave a tone to public opinion. We laugh at them as they did, with the disciples of Epicurus, at the superstitions of past ages, the belief in sorcery, magic, necromancy, demons, witches, wizards, magicians, and yet all these things flourished in the eighteenth century, and are believed in this nineteenth century in our own country, in England, France, and Germany, by men of all professions, and in all ranks of society. Wherein, then, consists the progress of our enlightenment?

But "we are more liberal, more tolerant in matters of opinion, and have ceased to persecute men for religious differences," says our author. Hardly; yet if so, it may as well be because we are more indifferent, and less in earnest than our predecessors, believe less in mind, and more in matter. We have read no public document more truly liberal and more tolerant in its spirit and provisions than the Edict of Constantine the Great, giving liberty to Christians, and not taking it from Pagans. Even Julian the Apostate professed as much liberality and tolerance as Voltaire, or Mazzini, and practiced them as well as the Liberals in Europe usually do, when in power. "But the age tends," replies our author, "to democracy, and, therefore, to the amelioration, and the social and political elevation of the people." Fine words; but, in fact, while demagogues spout democracy, and modern literature sneers at law, mocks at loyalty, and preaches insubordination, insurrection, revolution, governments have a fine pretext for tightening their bonds, and rendering their power despotic; nay, in some respects, are compelled to do so, as the only means left of preventing the total dissolution of society and the lapse of the race into complete barbarism. If the system of repression is carried too far, and threatens its own defeat, the exaggerations of Liberalism provoke, and in part justify it, for the Liberalistic tendencies, if unchecked, could lead only to anarchy. Democracy, understood not as a form of government, but as the end government is to seek, to wit, the common good, the advance in civilization of the people, the poorer and more numerous, as well as the richer and less numerous classes, not of a privileged caste or class, is a good thing, and a tendency towards it is really an evidence of social progress. But this is only what the great Doctors of the Church have always taught, when they have defined the end of government to be the good of the community, the public good, or the common good of all,—not the special good of a few, nor yet the greatest good of the greatest number, as taught by that grave and elaborate humbug, Jeremy Bentham, but the common good of all, that good which is common to all the members of the community, whether great or small, rich or poor.

But that democracy as the form of the government is the best practicable means of securing this end, unless restrained by constitutions, the most earnest and enlightened faith, and the most pure and rigid religions discipline, is, to say the least, a perfectly gratuitous assumption. We defend here and everywhere, now and always, the political order established in our own country, and our failure—for failed, substantially, we have—is owing solely to our lack of real Christian faith, of the Christian conscience, and to our revolutionary attempts to interpret that order by the democratic theory. Our political order is republican, not democratic. But, in point of fact, the Liberals have never advocated democracy for the end we have stated, from love of liberty, or for the sake of ameliorating the condition of the people, though they may have so pretended, and at times even so believed, but really as a means of elevating themselves to power. Their democracy is, practically—I am as good as you, and you have no more right than I to be in power or place. We believe in the disinterestedness or the patriotism of no man who can conspire to overthrow the Government of his country, and whenever we hear a man professing great love for the dear people, praising their wisdom and virtue, their intelligence and sagacity, and telling them that they are sovereign, and their will ought to prevail, we always regard him as a self-seeker, and as desirous of using the people simply to elevate himself to be one of their rulers. Democracy elevates to places of honor, profit, and trust, men who could not be so elevated under any other form of government; but that this operates to the advantage of the public we have yet to learn.

What our author praises as the tendency of democracy, is the tendency to reduce all things to a low average, and to substitute popular opinion for truth, justice, reason, as the rule of action, and the criterion even of moral judgment. Democracy, when social as well as political, elevates not the best men to office, but the most available men, usually the most cunning, crafty, or empty-headed demagogues. When, two years ago, the editor of this Review received the nomination in his district for Member of Congress, he was interiorly alarmed, and began a self-examination to ascertain what political folly or iniquity he had committed; and he became reconciled to himself, and his conscience was at ease, only when he found his election defeated by an overwhelming majority. His own defeat consoled him for his nomination, and restored his confidence in his own integrity, loyalty, and patriotism. The men democracy usually elevates are petty attorneys or small lawyers, men of large selfishness and small capacity, and less political knowledge. The Southern States, whose democracy is less socially diffused than that of the Northern States, have always as a rule elevated abler men than has the North, which has given them an ascendency in the Union that has provoked Northern jealousy. They have selected to represent them in Congress, in Diplomacy, in the Cabinet, in the Presidential Chair, their ablest men, while we have selected our feeblest men; or, if abler men, we have, with rare exceptions, "rotated" them from their places before they could acquire experience enough to be useful. Democracy, in the sense we are considering it, has shown what men it selects, when left to itself, in the present Administration, and in the last and present Congresses. Were there no better men in the country? Then is democracy condemned, as tending to degrade intellect and abase character, for greater and better men we certainly had, who were formed while we were yet British Colonies. If there were greater or better men, and democracy passed them over as unavailable, then it is incapable of employing the best talent and the highest character produced by the country in its service, and therefore should also be condemned. President Lincoln we need not speak of; we have elsewhere given his character. But we have not had a single statesman, worthy of the name, in his Cabinet or in Congress since the incoming of the present Administration, and hardly one from the Free States since the Whigs, in 1840, descended into the forum, took the people by the hand, and, led on by the *Boston Atlas* and the *New York Tribune*, undertook to be more democratic than the Democratic party itself, and succeeded in out-Heroding Herod. When they dropped the name *Whig*, and assumed that of *Republican*, which we had recommended in place of *Democratic*, we, in our simplicity, supposed that they really intended to abandon Jacobinism, and to contend for Constitutionalism, else had we never for a moment supported them. But they did, and intended to do nothing of the sort.

There is nothing in the American experiment thus far to justify the Liberals in identifying the progress of liberty and social well-being with the progress of democracy. On this point our author is wholly at fault. Since Mr. Van Buren, more incompetent men in the presidential chair we could not have had, if we had depended on the hereditary principle, than popular election has given us. Prince John would have been better than Harrison or Taylor, and Prince Bob can hardly fall below his father. We want no hereditary Executive, but probably the chances of getting a wise man for President, if the Executive were hereditary, would be greater than they have been under the elective principle, as our elections have been, for a long time, conducted. Seldom has our Senate been equal to the English House of Peers. Democracy opens a door to office to men who, under no other system, would ever attain to office; but their attainment to office is of no conceivable advantage to the public, and very little to themselves. It opens a door to every man's ambition, at least permits every man to indulge ambitious aspirations. When such a man as Abraham Lincoln can become President, who may not hope one day also to be President? It stimulates every one's ambition, every one's hope of office, perhaps of the highest in the gift of the people, but it does not stimulate any one to study or labor to qualify himself for honorably discharging the duties of office. It is rare to find any man who does not think himself qualified for any office to which the people can be induced to elect him. The plurality of votes is a sovereign endorsement of his qualification. The people, in electing me, have judged me qualified, and would you, proud aristocrat, arraign the judgment of the people? Enough said.

The same tendency to democracy, lauded by our author, leads in nearly everything, everyone to struggle to be other than he is, to get what he has not, and to fill another place than the one he is in, and hence produces universal competition, and general uneasiness and discontent in society. No man is contented to live and die in the social position in which he was born, and pride and vanity, not love and humility, become the principle of all individual and social action. I am as good as Abraham Lincoln, and why should he be President and not I? He was a rail-splitter and I am a hod-carrier. Let me throw down the hod, as he did the beetle and wedge, become an Attorney, and I may one day be President as well as he. John Jacob Astor was once a poor German boy, who landed alone and friendless in the streets of New York, and he died worth, some say, twenty-five millions, all made by himself in trade; and why not I do as much, and make as much money as he? So every boy is discontented to remain at home and follow the occupation of his father, that of a mechanic or small farmer, and becomes anxious to get a place in a counting-house, and to engage in trade and speculation. Where all are free to aim to be first, no one is contented to be second, especially to be last. This is the effect of Liberalism, and an effect which our author cites as an evidence of its merit. He dwells on it with enthusiasm, and contrasts the movement, the activity, the aspirations of the common people at present with that of the lower classes under feudalism, and even the monarchical *régime* of the sixteenth and seventeenth centuries.

We, although a true-born Yankee, think very differently. Liberalism, taken in its practical workings in a Society, with weak faith, a movable religion, and no loyalty, tends to develop wants which it is impossible to satisfy, because the wants it develops all demand their satisfaction from the material order. In the moral, intellectual, and spiritual world, the multiplication of wants is in itself not an evil, because the means of satisfaction are liberally supplied, and even the very craving for moral or spiritual good,—what the Gospel calls "a hungering and thirsting after righteousness," is itself a good, and blessed are they who do so, for they shall be filled. But the multiplication of wants which can be satisfied only with material or sensible goods, is not a good, but an evil. Political equality and equality before the law is practicable, but social equality, equality of wealth and social condition, is impracticable, and even undesirable. Only one man, once in four years, out of many millions, can be President of the United States; and if all set their hearts on it, all but the one must be disappointed. The sufferings of disappointed office-seekers more than overbalance the pleasures of office-holders. All can not be rich, for if all were rich, paradoxical as it may sound, all would be poor. Real wealth is not in the magnitude of one's possessions, but in the amount of the labor of others one is able to command; and if all are rich, no one can command any labor of another at all, for there is no one to sell his labor, and the rich man is reduced precisely to the level of the poor man. Though his possessions are counted by millions, he must produce for himself, and actually have only what he can produce with the labor of his own hands. All your schemes of an equal division of property, and for keeping all the members of a community equal in their condition, are fallacious, and, if they could be carried out, would end only in establishing universal poverty, universal ignorance, and universal barbarism. The human race would soon sink everywhere below the condition of our North American savages: and, indeed, Liberalism is practically a tendency to the savage state, as any one may learn even from Jean Jacques Rousseau.

We want no privileged caste or class; we want no political aristocracy, recognized and sustained as such by law. Let all be equal before the law. But we do want a social aristocracy, families elevated by their estates, their public services, their education, culture, manners, tastes, refinement, above the commonalty; and we do not believe a community can long even subsist where such an aristocracy is wanting, to furnish models and leaders for the people. It is the presence of such an aristocracy, that in the present fearful struggle gives to the Southern States their unity and strength. It is the want of such a class, enjoying the confidence and respect of the people in the loyal States, that constitutes our national weakness, as we have elsewhere shown. The people, we have said, and we all know, must have leaders, and leaders must be born, not made. The number in a nation who have the qualities to be leaders, whether in peace or war, are comparatively few. All cannot lead; the mass must follow, and those who are born to follow should be content to follow, and not aspire to lead. If you stir up in them the ambition to lead, make them discontented with their lot, and determined to pass from followers to leaders, you reverse the natural order of things, introduce confusion into society, disorder into all ranks, and do good to nobody. We ourselves, we know it well, were never born to lead, and should only be misplaced, and ruin ourselves and others, were we put in the position of a leader. Our author professes to be a philosopher, and to have mastered what just now is called the science of Sociology,—a barbarous term, which we detest,—and therefore he ought to understand that he is calling things by wrong names; that practically he says, Evil be thou my good! and, if successful, would erect a pandemonium, not a well ordered human society, or a temple of liberty and peace.

Yet our author swims with the current, and is sustained by all the force of what is regarded as the advanced opinion of the age, and for the moment is stronger than we, who are sustained only by certain moral instincts and traditions which are generally unheeded. He has, too, the ear of the public, if not for himself personally, yet for innumerable others who agree with him, and can speak with even far more force and eloquence than he; while we are repudiated by all parties, by all sects, and only a few will listen or heed our voice, harsh and discordant as it is in most ears. We are neither an *Obscurantist* nor a Liberal, but agreeing in some things, and disagreeing in others, with both; precisely the sort of man no party likes, for we can support no party through thick and thin,—a legitimate child of the nineteenth century, yet believing that all wisdom was neither born nor will die with it. We believe there were "brave men before Agamemnon," and that there will be brave men even after we are dead and forgotten. We belong not to the party that would restore the past, but to that which would retain what was true and good, and for all ages, in the past; we are not of those who would destroy the past, and compel the human race to begin *de novo*, but of those, few in number they may be, who see something good even in Liberalism, and would accept it without breaking the chain of tradition, or severing the continuity of the life of the race, separate it from the errors and falsehoods, and bitter and hateful passions with which it is mixed up, and carry it onward. We are too much of the present to please the men of the past, and too much of the past to please the men of the present: so we are not only doomed, Cassandra-like, to utter prophecies which nobody believes, but prophecies which nobody heeds enough either to believe or disbelieve. We know it well, and therefore we said, we were not born to be a leader, although we have been long since spoiled as a follower, like most of our contemporaries. Hence, though we know that we speak the words of truth and soberness, we expect not our words to be heeded. Popular opinion decides us all questions of wisdom and folly, of truth and falsehood, and popular opinion we do not and cannot echo.

Our author is a Liberal, an ultra-democrat, a revolutionist,—has been, and probably still is, a conspirator,—a man who sees no sacredness in law, no inviolability in authority, and no charm in loyalty. His political creed is short, and very precise. It is: "The people are sovereign; the people are divine; the people are infallible and impeccable; I and my fellow-conspirators and revolutionists are the people; and because you Americans will not permit us to assume the direction of your civil and military affairs, you are no true Liberals, no consistent Democrats, and are really hostile to the progressive tendencies of the modern world. This is his creed, and the creed of all such as he, whether at home or abroad. We do not believe his creed, and have no wish to see it prevail. Many Americans profess it: few of them, however, really believe it, or, in fact, much else. They have been in the habit of hearing it, of reading it in newspapers and novels, and listening to it from the lips of impassioned orators on the Fourth of July and in political meetings, and they have repeated it, as a matter of course, without giving it one moment's serious thought; but their instincts are truer than the creed they now and then fancy they believe, and there still linger in their minds faint reminiscences of something better, which was once believed by most men, and approved by Christian faith and conscience.

If the American people could only once understand that the present war is not a war between democracy and aristocracy, but a war in defence of government and law, that is, in defence of authority in principle as well as in practice, against popular license and revolutionism, the war, however it might terminate, would prove the richest boon they have ever as a people received from the hand of Heaven. It would arrest that lawless and revolutionary tendency they have hitherto thoughtlessly followed, which they have fancied it belonged to them to encourage both at home and abroad, and which at times has threatened to make us the pest of the civilized world. We trust it will yet have this effect. We are Radical, if you will, in our determination, at the earliest moment it can be legally done, to get rid of the system of slave-labor, but, thank God, a Radical in nothing else, and sympathize in little else with those who are called Radicals: and, after all, we suspect the mass of the American people agree more nearly with us than with our General Croaker, and that we are a truer exponent of their real interior convictions and social instincts than he, although they will never believe it, because they will never read us; and the journals, if they notice us at all, will only misrepresent and pervert our words. Yet we rely greatly on military discipline and the effects of the war, to bring back the people to sounder political and social views.

PART III | Freedom and Communion

SEVENTEEN

The American Republic

Its Constitution, Tendencies, and Destiny

Preface

In the volume which, with much diffidence, is here offered to the public, I have given, as far as I have considered it worth giving, my whole thought in a connected form on the nature, necessity, extent, authority, origin, ground, and constitution of government, and the unity, nationality, constitution, tendencies, and destiny of the American Republic. Many of the points treated have been from time to time discussed or touched upon, and many of the views have been presented, in my previous writings; but this work is newly and independently written from beginning to end, and is as complete on the topics treated as I have been able to make it.

I have taken nothing bodily from my previous essays, but I have used their thoughts as far as I have judged them sound and they came within the scope of my present work. I have not felt myself bound to adhere to my own past thoughts or expressions any farther than they coincide with my present convictions, and I have written as freely and as independently as if I had never written or published anything before. I have never been the slave of my own past, and truth has always been dearer to me than my own

Originally published by P. O'Shea (New York, 1865). This chapter contains several selections from the original book as noted in the table of contents following the preface.

opinions. This work is not only my latest, but will be my last on politics or government, and must be taken as the authentic, and the only authentic statement of my political views and convictions, and whatever in any of my previous writings conflicts with the principles defended in its pages, must be regarded as retracted, and rejected.

The work now produced is based on scientific principles; but it is an essay rather than a scientific treatise, and even good-natured critics will, no doubt, pronounce it an article or a series of articles designed for a review, rather than a book. It is hard to overcome the habits of a lifetime. I have taken some pains to exchange the reviewer for the author, but am fully conscious that I have not succeeded. My work can lay claim to very little artistic merit. It is full of repetitions; the same thought is frequently recurring,—the result, to some extent, no doubt, of carelessness and the want of artistic skill; but to a greater extent, I fear, of "malice aforethought." In composing my work I have followed, rather than directed, the course of my thought, and, having very little confidence in the memory or industry of readers, I have preferred, when the completeness of the argument required it, to repeat myself to encumbering my pages with perpetual references to what has gone before.

That I attach some value to this work is evident from my consenting to its publication; but how much or how little of it is really mine, I am quite unable to say. I have, from my youth up, been reading, observing, thinking, reflecting, talking, I had almost said writing, at least by fits and starts, on political subjects, especially in their connection with philosophy, theology, history, and social progress, and have assimilated to my own mind what it would assimilate, without keeping any notes of the sources whence the materials assimilated were derived. I have written freely from my own mind as I find it now formed; but how it has been so formed, or whence I have borrowed, my readers know as well as I. All that is valuable in the thoughts set forth, it is safe to assume has been appropriated from others. Where I have been distinctly conscious of borrowing what has not become common property, I have given credit, or, at least, mentioned the author's name, with three important exceptions which I wish to note more formally.

I am principally indebted for the view of the American nationality and the Federal Constitution I present, to hints and suggestions furnished by the remarkable work of John C. Hurd, Esq., on *The Law of Freedom and Bondage in the United States*, a work of rare learning and profound philosophic views. I could not have written my work without the aid derived from its suggestions, any more than I could without Plato, Aristotle, St. Augustine, St. Thomas, Suarez, Pierre Leroux, and the Abbate Gioberti. To these two last-named authors, one a humanitarian sophist, the other a Catholic priest, and certainly one of the profoundest philosophical writers of this century, I am much indebted, though I have followed the political system of neither. I have taken from Leroux the germs of the doctrine I set forth on the solidarity of the race, and from Gioberti the doctrine I defend in relation to the creative act, which is, after all, simply that of the *Credo* and the first verse of *Genesis*.

In treating the several questions which the preparation of this volume has brought up, in their connection, and in the light of first principles, I have changed or modified, on more than one important point, the views I had expressed in my previous writings, especially on the distinction between civilized and barbaric nations, the real basis of civilization itself, and the value to the world of the Graeco-Roman civilization. I have ranked feudalism under the head of barbarism, rejected every species of political aristocracy, and represented the English constitution as essentially antagonistic to the American, not as its type. I have accepted universal suffrage in principle, and defended American democracy, which I define to be territorial democracy, and carefully distinguish from pure individualism on the one hand, and from pure socialism or humanitarianism on the other.

I reject the doctrine of State sovereignty, which I held and defended from 1828 to 1861, but still maintain that the sovereignty of the American Republic vests in the States, though in the States collectively, or united, not severally, and thus escape alike consolidation and disintegration. I find, with Mr. Madison, our most philosophic statesman, the originality of the American system in the division of powers between a General government having sole charge of the foreign and general, and particular or State governments having, within their respective territories, sole charge of the particular relations and interests of the American people; but I do not accept his concession that this division is of conventional origin, and maintain that it enters into the original Providential constitution of the American state, as I have done in my Review for October, 1863, and January and October, 1864.

I maintain, after Mr. Senator Sumner, one of the most philosophic and accomplished living American statesmen, that "State secession is State suicide," but modify the opinion I too hastily expressed that the political death of a State dissolves civil society within its territory and abrogates all rights held under it, and accept the doctrine that the laws in force at the time of secession remain in force till superseded or abrogated by competent authority, and also that, till the State is revived and restored as a State in the Union, the only authority, under the American system, competent to supersede or abrogate them is the United States, not Congress, far less the Executive. The error of the Government is not in recognizing the territorial laws as surviving secession but in counting a State that has seceded as still a State in the Union, with the right to be counted as one of the United States in amending the Constitution. Such State goes *out* of the Union, but comes *under* it.

I have endeavored throughout to refer my particular political views; to their general principles, and to show that the general principles asserted have their origin and ground in the great, universal, and unchanging principles of the universe itself. Hence, I have labored to show the scientific relations of political to theological principles, the real principles of all science, as of all reality. An atheist, I have said, may be a politician; but if there were no God, there could be no politics. This may offend the sciolists of the age, but I must follow science where it leads, and cannot be arrested by those who mistake their darkness for light.

I write throughout as a Christian, because I am a Christian; as a Catholic, because all Christian principles, nay, all real principles are catholic, and there is nothing sectarian either in nature or revelation. I am a Catholic by God's grace and great goodness, and must write as I am. I could not write otherwise if I would, and would not if I could. I have not obtruded my religion, and have referred to it only where my argument demanded it; but I have had neither the weakness nor the bad taste to seek to conceal or disguise it. I could never have written my book without the knowledge I have, as a Catholic, of Catholic theology, and my acquaintance, slight as it is, with the great fathers and doctors of the church, the great masters of all that is solid or permanent in modern thought, either with Catholics or non-Catholics.

Moreover, though I write for all Americans, without distinction of sect or party, I have had more especially in view the people of my own religious communion. It is no discredit to a man in the United States at the present day to be a firm, sincere, and devout Catholic. The old sectarian prejudice may remain with a few, "whose eyes," as Emerson says, "are in their hind-head, not in their fore-head;" but the American people are not at heart sectarian, and the nothingarianism so prevalent among them only marks their state of transition from sectarian opinions to positive Catholic faith. At any rate, it can no longer be denied that Catholics are an integral, living, and growing element in the American population, quite too numerous, too wealthy, and too influential to be ignored. They have played too conspicuous a part in the late troubles of the country, and poured out too freely and too much of their richest and noblest blood in defence of the unity of the nation and the integrity of its domain, for that. Catholics henceforth must be treated as standing, in all respects, on a footing of equality with any other class of American citizens, and their views of political science, or of any other science, be counted of equal importance, and listened to with equal attention.

I have no fears that my book will be neglected because avowedly by a Catholic author, and from a Catholic publishing house. They who are not Catholics will read it, and it will enter into the current of American literature, if it is one they must read in order to be up with the living and growing thought of the age. If it is not a book of that sort, it is not worth reading by any one.

Furthermore, I am ambitious, even in my old age, and I wish to exert an influence on the future of my country, for which I have made, or, rather, my family have made, some sacrifices, and which I tenderly love. Now, I believe that he who can exert the most influence on our Catholic population, especially in giving tone and direction to our Catholic youth, will exert the most influence in forming the character and shaping the future destiny of the American Republic. Ambition and patriotism alike, as well as my own Catholic faith and sympathies, induce me to address myself primarily to Catholics. I quarrel with none of the sects; I honor virtue wherever I see it, and accept truth wherever I find it; but, in my belief, no sect is destined to a long life, or a permanent possession. I engage in no controversy with any one not of my religion, for, if the positive, affirmative truth is brought out and placed in a clear light before the public, whatever is sectarian in any of the sects will disappear as the morning mists before the rising sun.

I expect the most intelligent and satisfactory appreciation of my book from the thinking and educated classes among Catholics; but I speak to my countrymen at large. I could not personally serve my country in the field: my habits as well as my infirmities prevented, to say nothing of my age; but I have endeavored in this humble work to add my contribution, small though it may be, to political science, and to discharge, as far as I am able, my debt of loyalty and patriotism. I would the book were more of a book, more worthy of my countrymen, and a more weighty proof of the love I bear them, and with which I have written it. All I can say is, that it is an honest book, a sincere book, and contains my best thoughts on the subjects treated. If well received, I shall be grateful; if neglected, I shall endeavor to practice resignation, as I have so often done.

O. A. BROWNSON
ELIZABETH, N.J., SEPTEMBER 16, 1865

Contents

Chapter I: Introduction

The ancients summed up the whole of human wisdom in the maxim, Know Thyself, and certainly there is for an individual no more important as there is no more difficult knowledge, than knowledge of himself, whence he comes, whither he goes, what he is, what he is for, what he can do, what he ought to do, and what are his means of doing it.

Nations are only individuals on a larger scale. They have a life, an individuality, a reason, a conscience, and instincts of their own, and have the same general laws of development and growth, and, perhaps, of decay, as the individual man. Equally important, and no less difficult than for the individual, is it for a nation to know itself, understand its own existence, its own powers and faculties, rights and duties, constitution, instincts, tendencies, and destiny. A nation has a spiritual as well as a material, a moral as well as a physical existence, and is subjected to internal as well as external conditions of health and virtue, greatness and grandeur, which it must in some measure understand and observe, or become weak and infirm, stunted in its growth, and end in premature decay and death.

Among nations, no one has more need of full knowledge of itself than the United States, and no one has hitherto had less. It has hardly had a distinct consciousness of its own national existence, and has lived the irreflective life of the child, with no severe trial, till the recent rebellion, to throw it back on itself and compel it to reflect on its own constitution, its own separate existence, individuality, tendencies, and end. The defection of the slaveholding States, and the fearful struggle that has followed for national unity and integrity, have brought it at once to a distinct recognition of itself, and forced it to pass from thoughtless, careless, heedless, reckless adolescence to grave and reflecting manhood. The nation has been suddenly compelled to study itself, and henceforth must act from reflection, understanding, science, statesmanship, not from instinct, impulse, passion, or caprice, knowing well what it does, and wherefore it does it. The change which four years of civil war have wrought in the nation is great, and is sure to give it the seriousness, the gravity, the dignity, the manliness it has heretofore lacked.

Though the nation has been brought to a consciousness of its own existence, it has not, even yet, attained to a full and clear understanding of its own national constitution. Its vision is still obscured by the floating mists of its earlier morning, and its judgment rendered indistinct and indecisive by the wild theories and fancies of its childhood. The national mind has been quickened, the national heart has been opened, the national disposition prepared, but there remains the important work of dissipating the mists that still linger, of brushing away these wild theories and fancies, and of enabling it to form a clear and intelligent judgment of itself, and a true and just appreciation of its own constitution tendencies,—and destiny; or, in other words, of enabling the nation to understand its own idea, and the means of its actualization in space and time.

Every living nation has an idea given it by Providence to realize, and whose realization is its special work, mission, or destiny. Every nation is, in some sense, a chosen people of God. The Jews were the chosen people of God, through whom the primitive traditions were to be preserved in their purity and integrity, and the Messiah was to come. The Greeks were the chosen people of God, for the development and realization of the beautiful or the divine splendor in art, and of the true in science and philosophy; and the Romans, for the development of the state, law, and jurisprudence. The great despotic nations of Asia were never properly nations; or if they were nations with a mission, they proved false to it, and count for nothing in the progressive development of the human race. History has not recorded their mission, and as far as they are known they have contributed only to the abnormal development or corruption of religion and civilization. Despotism is barbaric and abnormal.

The United States, or the American Republic, has a mission, and is chosen of God for the realization of a great idea. It has been chosen not only to continue the work assigned to Greece and Rome, but to accomplish a greater work than was assigned to either. In art, it will prove false to its mission if it do not rival Greece; and in science and philosophy, if it do not surpass it. In the state, in law, in jurisprudence, it must continue and surpass Rome. Its idea is liberty, indeed, but liberty with law, and law with liberty. Yet its mission is not so much the realization of liberty as the realization of the true idea of the state, which secures at once the authority of the public and the freedom of the individual—the sovereignty of the people without social despotism, and individual freedom without anarchy. In other words, its mission is to bring out in its life the dialectic union of authority and liberty, of the natural rights of man and those of society. The Greek and Roman republics asserted the state to the detriment of individual freedom; modern republics either do the same, or assert individual freedom to the detriment of the state. The American republic has been instituted by Providence to realize the freedom of each with advantage to the other.

The real mission of the United States is to introduce and establish a political constitution, which, while it retains all the advantages of the constitutions of states thus far known, is unlike any of them, and secures advantages which none of them did or could possess. The American constitution has no prototype in any prior constitution. The American form of government can be classed throughout with none of the forms of government described by Aristotle, or even by later authorities. Aristotle knew only four forms of government: Monarchy, Aristocracy, Democracy, and Mixed Governments. The American form is none of these, nor any combination of them. It is original, a new contribution to political science, and seeks to attain the end of all wise and just government by means unknown or forbidden to the ancients, and which have been but imperfectly comprehended even by American political writers themselves. The originality of the American constitution has been overlooked by the great majority even of our own statesmen, who seek to explain it by analogies borrowed from the constitutions of other states rather than by a profound study of its own principles. They have taken too low a view of it, and have rarely, if ever, appreciated its distinctive and peculiar merits.

As the United States have vindicated their national unity and integrity, and are preparing to take a new start in history, nothing is more important than that they should take that new start with a clear and definite view of their national constitution, and with a distinct understanding of their political mission in the future of the world. The citizen who can help his countrymen to do this will render them an important service and deserve well of his country, though he may have been unable to serve in her armies and defend her on the battle-field. The work now to be done by American statesmen is even more difficult and more delicate than that which has been accomplished by our brave armies. As yet the people are hardly better prepared for the political work to be done than they were at the outbreak of the civil war for the military work they have so nobly achieved. But, with time, patience, and good-will, the difficulties may be overcome, the errors of the past corrected, and the Government placed on the right track for the future.

It will hardly be questioned that either the constitution of the United States is very defective or it has been very grossly misinterpreted by all parties. If the slave States had not held that the States are severally sovereign, and the Constitution of the United States a simple agreement or compact, they would never have seceded; and if the Free States had not confounded the Union with the General government, and shown a tendency to make it the entire national government, no occasion or pretext for secession would have been given. The great problem of our statesmen has been from the first, How to assert union without consolidation, and State rights without disintegration? Have they, as yet, solved that problem? The war has silenced the State sovereignty doctrine, indeed, but has it done so without lesion to State rights? Has it done it without asserting the General government as the supreme, central, or national government? Has it done it without striking a dangerous blow at the federal element of the constitution? In suppressing by armed force the doctrine that the States are severally sovereign, what barrier is left against consolidation? Has not one danger been removed only to give place to another?

But perhaps the constitution itself, if rightly understood, solves the problem; and perhaps the problem itself is raised precisely through misunderstanding of the constitution. Our statesmen have recognized no constitution of the American people themselves; they have confined their views to the written constitution, as if that constituted the American people a state or nation, instead of being, as it is, only a law ordained by the nation already existing and constituted. Perhaps, if they had recognized and studied the constitution which preceded that drawn up by the Convention of 1787, and which is intrinsic, inherent in the republic itself, they would have seen that it solves the problem, and asserts national unity without consolidation, and the rights of the several States without danger of disintegration. The whole controversy, possibly, has originated in a misunderstanding of the real constitution of the United States, and that misunderstanding itself in the misunderstanding of the origin and constitution of government in general. The constitution, as will appear in the course of this essay is not defective; and all that is necessary to guard against either danger is to discard all our theories of the constitution, and return and adhere to the constitution itself, as it really is and always has been.

There is no doubt that the question of Slavery had much to do with the rebellion, but it was not its sole cause. The real cause must be sought in the program that had been made, especially in the States themselves, in forming and administering their respective governments, as well as the General government, in accordance with political theories borrowed from European speculators on government, the so called Liberals and Revolutionists, which have and can have no legitimate application in the United States. The tendency of American politics, for the last thirty or forty years, has been, within the several States themselves, in the direction of centralized democracy, as if the American people had for their mission only the reproduction of ancient Athens. The American system is not that of any of the simple forms of government, nor any combination of them. The attempt to bring it under any of the simple or mixed forms of government recognized by political writers, is an attempt to clothe the future in the cast-off garments of the past. The American system, wherever practicable, is better than monarchy, better than aristocracy, better than simple democracy, better than any possible combination of these several forms, because it accords more nearly with the principles of things, the real order of the universe.

But American statesmen have studied the constitutions of other states more than that of their own, and have succeeded in obscuring the American system in the minds of the people, and giving them in its place pure and simple democracy, which is its false development or corruption. Under the influence of this false development, the people were fast losing sight of the political truth that, though the people are sovereign, it is the organic, not the inorganic people, the territorial people, not the people as simple population, and were beginning to assert the absolute God-given right of the majority to govern. All the changes made in the bosom of the States themselves have consisted in removing all obstacles to the irresponsible will of the majority, leaving minorities and individuals at their mercy. This tendency to a centralized democracy had more to do with provoking secession and rebellion than the anti-slavery sentiments of the Northern, Central, and Western States.

The failure of secession and the triumph of the National cause, in spite of the short-sightedness and blundering of the Administration, have proved the vitality and strength of the national constitution, and the greatness of the American people. They say nothing for or against the democratic theory of our demagogues, but everything in favor of the American system or constitution of government, which has found a firmer support in American instincts than in American statesmanship. In spite of all that had been done by theorists, radicals, and revolutionists, no-government men, non-resistants, humanitarians, and sickly sentimentalists to corrupt the American people in mind, heart, and body, the native vigor of their national constitution has enabled them to come forth triumphant from the trial. Every American patriot has reason to be proud of his countrymen, and every American lover of freedom to be satisfied with the institutions of his country. But there is danger that the politicians and demagogues will ascribe the merit, not to the real and living national constitution, but to their miserable theories of that constitution, and labor to aggravate the several evils and corrupt tendencies which caused the rebellion it has cost so much to suppress. What is now wanted is, that the people, whose instincts are right, should understand the American constitution as it is, and so understand it as to render it impossible for political theorists, no matter of what school or party, to deceive them again as to its real import, or induce them to depart from it in their political action.

A work written with temper, without passion or sectional prejudice, in a philosophical spirit, explaining to the American people their own national constitution, and the mutual relations of the General government and the State governments, cannot, at this important crisis in our affairs, be inopportune, and, if properly executed, can hardly fail to be of real service. Such a work is now attempted—would it were by another and abler hand—which, imperfect as it is, may at least offer some useful suggestions, give a right direction to political thought, although it should fail to satisfy the mind of the reader.

This much the author may say, in favor of his own work, that it sets forth no theory of government in general, or of the United States in particular. The author is not a monarchist, an aristocrat, a democrat, a feudalist, nor an advocate of what are called mixed governments like the English, at least for his own country; but is simply an American, devoted to the real, living, and energizing constitution of the American republic as it is, not as some may fancy it might be, or are striving to make it. It is, in his judgment, what it ought to be, and he has no other ambition than to present it as it is to the understanding and love of his countrymen.

Perhaps simple artistic unity and propriety would require the author to commence his essay directly with the United States; but while the constitution of the United States is original and peculiar, the government of the United States has necessarily something in common with all legitimate governments, and he has thought it best to precede his discussion of the American republic, its constitution, tendencies, and destiny, by some considerations on government in general. He does this because he believes, whether rightly or not, that while the American people have received from Providence a most truly profound and admirable system of government, they are more or less infected with the false theories of government which have been broached during the last two centuries. In attempting to realize these theories, they have already provoked or rendered practicable a rebellion which has seriously threatened the national existence, and come very near putting an end to the American order of civilization itself. These theories have received already a shock in the minds of all serious and thinking men; but the men who think are in every nation a small minority, and it is necessary to give these theories a public refutation, and bring back those who do not think, as well as those who do, from the world of dreams to the world of reality. It is hoped, therefore, that any apparent want of artistic unity or symmetry in the essay will be pardoned for the sake of the end the author has had in view.

Chapter II: Government

Man is a dependent being, and neither does nor can suffice for himself. He lives not in himself, but lives and moves and has his being in God. He exists, develops, and fulfills his existence only by communion with God, through which he participates of the divine being and life. He communes with God through the divine creative act and the Incarnation of the Word, through his kind, and through the material world. Communion with God through Creation and Incarnation is religion, distinctively taken, which binds man to God as his first cause, and carries him onward to God as his final cause; communion through the material world is expressed by the word property; and communion with God through humanity is society. Religion, society, property, are the three terms that embrace the whole of man's life, and express the essential means and conditions of his existence, his development, and his perfection, or the fulfilment of his existence, the attainment of the end for which he is created.

Though society, or the communion of man with his Maker through his kind, is not all that man needs in order to live, to grow, to actualize the possibilities of his nature, and to attain to his beatitude, since humanity is neither God nor the material universe, it is yet a necessary and essential condition of his life, his progress, and the completion of his existence. He is born and lives in society, and can be born and live nowhere else. It is one of the necessities of his nature. "God saw that it was not good for man to be alone." Hence, wherever man is found he is found in society, living in more or less strict intercourse with his kind.

But society never does and never can exist without government of some sort. As society is a necessity of man's nature, so is government a necessity of society. The simplest form of society is the family—Adam and Eve. But though Adam and Eve are in many respects equal, and have equally important though different parts assigned them, one or the other must be head and governor, or they cannot form the society called family. They would be simply two individuals of different sexes, and the family would fail for the want of unity. Children cannot be reared, trained, or educated without some degree of family government, of some authority to direct, control, restrain, or prescribe. Hence the authority of the husband and father is recognized by the common consent of mankind. Still more apparent is the necessity of government the moment the family develops and grows into the tribe, and the tribe into the nation. Hence no nation exists without government; and we never find a savage tribe, however low or degraded, that does not assert somewhere in the father, in the elders, or in the tribe itself, the rude outlines or the faint reminiscences of some sort of government, with authority to demand obedience and to punish the refractory. Hence, as man is nowhere found out of society, so nowhere is society found without government.

Government is necessary: but let it be remarked by the way, that its necessity does not grow exclusively or chiefly out of the fact that the human race by sin has fallen from its primitive integrity, or original righteousness. The fall asserted by Christian theology, though often misinterpreted, and its effects underrated or exaggerated, is a fact too sadly confirmed by individual experience and universal history; but it is not the cause why government is necessary, though it may be an additional reason for demanding it. Government would have been necessary if man had not sinned, and it is needed for the good as well as for the bad. The law was promulgated in the Garden, while man retained his innocence and remained in the integrity of his nature. It exists in heaven as well as on earth, and in heaven in its perfection. Its office is not purely repressive, to restrain violence, to redress wrongs, and to punish the transgressor. It has something more to do than to restrict our natural liberty, curb our passions, and maintain justice between man and man. Its office is positive as well as negative. It is needed to render effective the solidarity of the individuals of a nation, and to render the nation an organism, not a mere organization—to combine men in one living body, and to strengthen all with the strength of each, and each with the strength of all—to develop, strengthen, and sustain individual liberty, and to utilize and direct it to the promotion of the common weal—to be a social providence, imitating in its order and degree the action of the divine providence itself, and, while it provides for the common good of all, to protect each, the lowest and meanest, with the whole force and majesty of society. It is the minister of wrath to wrong-doers, indeed, but its nature is beneficent, and its action defines and protects the right of property, creates and maintains a medium in which religion can exert her supernatural energy, promotes learning, fosters science and art, advances civilization, and contributes as a powerful means to the fulfilment by man of the Divine purpose in his existence. Next after religion, it is man's greatest good; and even religion without it can do only a small portion of her work. They wrong it who call it a necessary evil; it is a great good, and, instead of being distrusted, hated, or resisted, except in its abuses, it should be loved, respected, obeyed, and if need be, defended at the cost of all earthly goods, and even of life itself.

The nature or essence of government is to govern. A government that does not govern, is simply no government at all. If it has not the ability to govern and governs not, it may be an agency, an instrument in the bands of individuals for advancing their private interests, but it is not government. To be government it must govern both individuals and the community. If it is a mere machine for making prevail the will of one man, of a certain number of men, or even of the community, it may be very effective sometimes for good, sometimes for evil, oftenest for evil, but government in the proper sense of the word it is not. To govern is to direct, control, restrain, as the pilot controls and directs his ship. It necessarily implies two terms, governor and governed, and a real distinction between them. The denial of all real distinction between governor and governed is an error in politics analogous to that in philosophy or theology of denying all real distinction between creator and creature, God and the universe, which all the world knows is either pantheism or pure atheism—the supreme sophism. If we make governor and governed one and the same, we efface both terms; for there is no governor nor governed, if the will that governs is identically the will that is governed. To make the controller and the controlled the same is precisely to deny all control. There must, then, if there is government at all, be a power, force, or will that governs, distinct from that which is governed. In those governments in which it is held that the people govern, the people governing do and must act in a diverse relation from the people governed, or there is no real government.

Government is not only that which governs, but that which has the right or authority to govern. Power without right is not government. Governments have the right to use force at need, but might does not make right, and not every power wielding the physical force of a nation is to be regarded as its rightful government. Whatever resort to physical force it may be obliged to make, either in defence of its authority or of the rights of the nation, the government itself lies in the moral order, and politics is simply a branch of ethics—that branch which treats of the rights and duties of men in their public relations, as distinguished from their rights and duties in their private relations.

Government being not only that which governs, but that which has the right to govern, obedience to it becomes a moral duty, not a mere physical necessity. The right to govern and the duty to obey are correlatives, and the one cannot exist or be conceived without the other. Hence loyalty is not simply an amiable sentiment but a duty, a moral virtue. Treason is not merely a difference in political opinion with the governing authority, but a crime against the sovereign, and a moral wrong, therefore a sin against God, the Founder of the Moral Law. Treason, if committed in other countries, unhappily, has been more frequently termed by our countrymen patriotism and loaded with honor than branded as a crime, the greatest of crimes, as it is, that human governments have authority to punish. The American people have been chary of the word loyalty, perhaps because they regard it as the correlative of royalty; but loyalty is rather the correlative of law, and is, in its essence, love and devotion to the sovereign authority, however constituted or wherever lodged. It is as necessary, as much a duty, as much a virtue in republics as in monarchies; and nobler examples of the most devoted loyalty are not found in the world's history than were exhibited in the ancient Greek and Roman republics, or than have been exhibited by both men and women in the young republic of the United States. Loyalty is the highest, noblest, and most generous of human virtues, and is the human element of that sublime love or charity which the inspired Apostle tells us is the fulfilment of the law. It has in it the principle of devotion, of self-sacrifice, and is, of all human virtues, that which renders man the most Godlike. There is nothing great, generous, good, or heroic of which a truly loyal people are not capable, and nothing mean, base, cruel, brutal, criminal, detestable, not to be expected of a really disloyal people. Such a people no generous sentiment can move, no love can bind. It mocks at duty, scorns virtue, tramples on all rights, and holds no person, no thing, human or divine, sacred or inviolable.

The assertion of government as lying in the moral order, defines civil liberty, and reconciles it with authority. Civil liberty is freedom to do whatever one pleases that authority permits or does not forbid. Freedom to follow in all things one's own will or inclination, without any civil restraint, is license, not liberty. There is no lesion to liberty in repressing license, nor in requiring obedience to the commands of the authority that has the right to command. Tyranny or oppression is not in being subjected to authority, but in being subjected to usurped authority—to a power that has no right to command, or that commands what exceeds its right or its authority. To say that it is contrary to liberty to be forced to forego our own will or inclination in any case whatever, is simply denying the right of all government, and falling into no-governmentism. Liberty is violated only when we are required to forego our own will or inclination by a power that has no right to make the requisition; for we are bound to obedience as far as authority has right to govern, and we can never have the right to disobey a rightful command. The requisition, if made by rightful authority, then, violates no right that we have or can have, and where there is no violation of our rights there is no violation of our liberty. The moral right of authority, which involves the moral duty of obedience, presents, then, the ground on which liberty and authority may meet in peace and operate to the same end.

This has no resemblance to the slavish doctrine of passive obedience, and that the resistance to power can never be lawful. The tyrant may be lawfully resisted, for the tyrant, by force of the word itself, is a usurper, and without authority. Abuses of power may be resisted even by force when they become too great to be endured, when there is no legal or regular way of redressing them, and when there is a reasonable prospect that resistance will prove effectual and substitute something better in their place. But it is never lawful to resist the rightful sovereign, for it can never be right to resist right, and the rightful sovereign in the constitutional exercise of his power can never be said to abuse it. Abuse is the unconstitutional or wrongful exercise of a power rightfully held, and when it is not so exercised there is no abuse or abuses to redress. All turns, then, on the right of power, or its legitimacy. Whence does government derive its right to govern? What is the origin and ground of sovereignty? This question is fundamental and without a true answer to it politics cannot be a science, and there can be no scientific statesmanship. Whence, then, comes the sovereign right to govern?

Chapter III: Origin of Government

Government is both a fact and a right. Its origin as a fact, is simply a question of history; its origin as a right or authority to govern, is a question of ethics. Whether a certain territory and its population are a sovereign state or nation, or not—whether the actual ruler of a country is its rightful ruler, or not—is to be determined by the historical facts in the case; but whence the government derives its right to govern, is a question that can be solved only by philosophy, or, philosophy failing, only by revelation.

Political writers, not carefully distinguishing between the fact and the right, have invented various theories as to the origin of government, among which may be named—

I. Government originates in the right of the father to govern his child.
II. It originates in convention, and is a social compact.
III. It originates in the people, who, collectively taken, are sovereign.
IV. Government springs from the spontaneous development of nature.
V. It derives its right from the immediate and express appointment of God;—

VI. From God through the Pope, or visible head of the spiritual society;—
VII. From God through the people;—
VIII. From God through the natural law.

I. The first theory is sound, if the question is confined to the origin of government as a fact. The patriarchal system is the earliest known system of government, and unmistakable traces of it are found in nearly all known governments—in the *tribes* of Arabia and Northern Africa, the Irish *septs* and the Scottish *clans*, the Tartar *hordes*, the Roman *gentes*, and the Russian and Hindoo *villages*. The right of the father was held to be his right to govern his family or household, which, with his children, included his wife and servants. From the family to the tribe the transition is natural and easy, as also from the tribe to the nation. The father is chief of the family; the chief of the eldest family is chief of the tribe; the chief of the eldest tribe becomes chief of the nation, and, as such, king or monarch. The heads of families collected in a senate form an aristocracy, and the families themselves, represented by their delegates, or publicly assembling for public affairs, constitute a democracy. These three forms, with their several combinations, to wit, monarchy, aristocracy, democracy, and mixed governments, are all the forms known to Aristotle, and have generally been held to be all that are possible.

Historically, all governments have, in some sense, been developed from the patriarchal, as all society has been developed from the family. Even those governments, like the ancient Roman and the modern feudal, which seem to be founded on landed property, may be traced back to a patriarchal origin. The patriarch is sole proprietor, and the possessions of the family are vested in him, and he governs as proprietor as well as father. In the tribe, the chief is the proprietor, and in the nation, the king is the landlord, and holds the domain. Hence, the feudal baron is invested with his fief by the suzerain, holds it from him, and to him it escheats when forfeited or vacant. All the great Asiatic kings of ancient or modern times hold the domain and govern as proprietors; they have the authority of the father and the owner; and their subjects, though theoretically their children, are really their slaves.

In Rome, however, the proprietary right undergoes an important transformation. The father retains all the power of the patriarch within his family, the patrician in his *gens* or house, but, outside of it, is met and controlled by the city or state. The heads of houses are united in the senate, and collectively constitute and govern the state. Yet, not all the heads of houses have seats in the senate, but only the tenants of the sacred territory of the city, which has been surveyed and marked by the god Terminus. Hence the great plebeian houses, often richer and nobler than the patrician, were excluded from all share in the government and the honors of the state, because they were not tenants of any portion of the sacred territory. There is here the introduction of an element which is not patriarchal, and which transforms the patriarch or chief of a tribe into the city or state, and founds the civil order, or what is now called civilization. The city or state takes the place of the private proprietor, and territorial rights take the place of purely personal rights.

In the theory of the Roman law, the land owns the man, not the man the land. When land was transferred to a new tenant, the practice in early times was to bury him in it, in order to indicate that it took possession of him, received, accepted, or adopted him; and it was only such persons as were taken possession of, accepted or adopted by the sacred territory or domain that, though denizens of Rome, were citizens with full political rights. This, in modern language, means that the state is territorial, not personal, and that the citizen appertains to the state, not the state to the citizen. Under the patriarchal, the tribal, and the Asiatic monarchical systems, there is, properly speaking, no state, no citizens, and the organization is economical rather than political. Authority—even the nation itself—is personal, not territorial. The patriarch, the chief of the tribe, or the king, is the only proprietor. Under the Graeco-Roman system all this is transformed. The nation is territorial as well as personal, and the real proprietor is the city or state. Under the Empire, no doubt, what lawyers call the eminent domain was vested in the emperor, but only as the representative and trustee of the city or state.

When or by what combination of events this transformation was effected, history does not inform us. The first-born of Adam, we are told, built a city, and called it after his son Enoch; but there is no evidence that it was constituted a municipality. The earliest traces of the *civil* order proper are found in the Greek and Italian republics, and its fullest and grandest developments are found in Rome, imperial as well as republican. It was no doubt preceded by the patriarchal system, and was historically developed from it, but by way of accretion rather than by simple explication. It has in it an element that, if it exists in the patriarchal constitution, exists there only in a different form, and the transformation marks the passage from the economical order to the political, from the barbaric to the civil constitution of society, or from barbarism to civilization.

The word civilization stands opposed to barbarism, and is derived from *civitas*—city or state. The Greeks and Romans call all tribes and nations in which authority is vested in the chief, as distinguished from the state, barbarians. The origin of the word *barbarian, barbarus,* or βάρβαρος, is unknown, and its primary sense can be only conjectured. Webster regards its primary sense as foreign, wild, fierce; but this could not have been its original sense; for the Greeks and Romans never termed all foreigners barbarians, and they applied the term to nations that had no inconsiderable culture and refinement of manners, and that had made respectable progress in art and sciences—the Indians, Persians, Medians, Chaldeans, and Assyrians. They applied the term evidently in a political, not an ethical or an aesthetical sense, and as it would seem to designate a social order in which the state was not developed, and in which the nation was personal, not territorial, and authority was held as a private right, not as a public trust, or in which the domain vests in the chief or tribe, and not in the state; for they never term any others barbarians.

Republic is opposed not to monarchy, in the modern European sense, but to monarchy in the ancient or absolute sense. Lacedaemon had kings; yet it was no less republican than Athens; and Rome was called and was a republic under the emperors no less than under the consuls. Republic, *respublica,* by the very force of the term, means the public wealth, or, in good English, the commonwealth; that is, government founded not on personal or private wealth, but on the public wealth, public territory, or domain, or a Government that vests authority in the nation, and attaches the nation to a certain definite territory. France, Spain, Italy, Holland, Belgium, Denmark, even Great Britain in substance though not in form, are all, in the strictest sense of the word, republican states; for the king or emperor does not govern in his own private right, but solely as representative of the power and majesty of the state. The distinctive mark of republicanism is the substitution of the state for the personal chief, and public authority for personal or private right. Republicanism is really civilization as opposed to barbarism, and all civility, in the old sense of the word, or *civiltà* in Italian, is republican, and is applied in modern tiles to breeding or refinement of manners, simply because these are characteristics of a republican, or polished [from πολίς, city] people. Every people that has a real civil order, or a fully developed state or polity, is a republican people; and hence the church and her great doctors when they speak of the state as distinguished from the church, call it the *republic,* as may be seen by consulting even a late Encyclical of

Pius IX, which some have interpreted wrongly in an anti-republican sense.

All tribes and nations in which the patriarchal system remains, or is developed without transformation, are barbaric, and really so regarded by all Christendom. In civilized nations the patriarchal authority is transformed into that of the city or state, that is, of the republic; but in all barbarous nations it retains its private and personal character. The nation is only the family or tribe, and is called by the name of its ancestor, founder, or chief, not by a geographical denomination. Race has not been supplanted by country; they are a people, not a state. They are not fixed to the soil, and though we may find in them ardent love of family, the tribe, or the chief, we never find among them that pure love of country or patriotism which so distinguished the Greeks and Romans, and is no less marked among modern Christian nations. They have a family, a race, a chief or king, but no *patria*, or country. The barbarians who overthrew the Roman Empire, whether of the West or the East, were nations, or confederacies of nations, but not states. The nation with them was personal, not territorial. Their country was wherever they fed their flocks and herds, pitched their tents, and encamped for the night. There were Germans, but no German state, and even today the German finds his "father-land" wherever the German speech is spoken. The Polish, Sclavonian, Hungarian, Illyrian, Italian, and other provinces held by German states, in which the German language is not the mother-tongue, are excluded from the Germanic Confederation. The Turks, or Osmanlis, are a race, not a state, and are encamped, not settled, on the site of the Eastern Roman or Greek Empire.

Even when the barbaric nations have ceased to be nomadic, pastoral, or predatory nations, as the ancient Assyrians and Persians or modern Chinese, and have their geographical boundaries, they have still no state, no country. The nation defines the boundaries, not the boundaries the nation. The nation does not belong to the territory, but the territory to the nation or its chief. The Irish and Anglo-Saxons, in former times, held the land in gavelkind, and the territory belonged to the tribe or sept; but if the tribe held it as indivisible, they still held it as private property. The shah of Persia holds the whole Persian territory as private property, and the landholders among his subjects are held to be his tenants. They hold it from him, not from the Persian state. The public domain of the Greek empire is in theory the private domain of the Ottoman emperor or Turkish sultan. There is in barbaric states no republic, no commonwealth; authority is parental, without being tempered by parental affection. The chief is a despot, and rules with the united authority of the father and the harshness of the proprietor. He owns the land and his subjects.

Feudalism, established in Western Europe after the downfall of the Roman Empire, however modified by the Church and by reminiscences of Graeco-Roman civilization retained by the conquered, was a barbaric constitution. The feudal monarch, as far as he governed at all, governed as proprietor or landholder, not as the representative of the commonwealth. Under feudalism there are estates, but no state. The king governs as an estate, the nobles hold their power as an estate, and the commons are represented as an estate. The whole theory of power is, that it is an estate; a private right, not a public trust. It is not without reason, then that the common sense of civilized nations terms the ages when it prevailed in Western Europe barbarous ages.

It may seem a paradox to class democracy with the barbaric constitutions, and yet as it is defended by many stanch democrats, especially European democrats and revolutionists, and by French and Germans settled in our own country, it is essentially barbaric and anti-republican. The characteristic principle of barbarism is, that power is a private or personal right, and when democrats assert that the elective franchise is a natural right of man, or that it is held by virtue of the fact that the elector is a man, they assert the fundamental principle of barbarism and despotism. This says nothing in favor of restricted suffrage, or against what is called universal suffrage. To restrict suffrage to property-holders helps nothing, theoretically or practically. Property has of itself advantages enough, without clothing its holders with exclusive political rights and privileges, and the laboring classes any day are as trustworthy as the business classes. The wise statesman will never restrict suffrage, or exclude the poorer and more numerous classes from all voice in the government of their country. General suffrage is wise, and if Louis Philippe had had the sense to adopt it, and thus rally the whole nation to the support of his government, he would never have had to encounter the revolution of 1848. The barbarism, the despotism, is not in universal suffrage, but in defending the elective franchise as a private or personal right. It is not a private, but a political right, and, like all political rights, a public trust. Extremes meet, and thus it is that men who imagine that they march at the head of the human race and lead the civilization of the age, are really in principle retrograding to the barbarism of the past, or taking their place with nations on whom the light of civilization has never yet dawned. All is not gold that glistens.

The characteristic of barbarism is, that it makes all authority a private or personal right; and the characteristic of civilization is, that it makes it a public trust. Barbarism knows only persons; civilization asserts and maintains the state. With barbarians the authority of the patriarch is developed simply by way of explication; in civilized states it is developed by way of transformation. Keeping in mind this distinction, it may be maintained that all systems of government, as a simple historical fact, have been developed from the patriarchal. The patriarchal has preceded them all, and it is with the patriarchal that the human race has begun its career. The family or household is not a state, a civil polity, but it is a government, and, historically considered, is the initial or inchoate state as well as the initial or inchoate nation. But its simple direct development gives us barbarism, or what is called Oriental despotism, and which nowhere exists, or can exist, in Christendom. It is found only in pagan and Mohammedan nations; Christianity in the secular order is republican, and continues and completes the work of Greece and Rome. It meets with little permanent success in any patriarchal or despotic nation, and must either find or create civilization, which has been developed from the patriarchal system by way of transformation.

But, though the patriarchal system is the earliest form of government, and all governments have been developed or modified from it, the right of government to govern cannot be deduced from the right of the father to govern his children, for the parental right itself is not ultimate or complete. All governments that assume it to be so, and rest on it as the foundation of their authority, are barbaric or despotic, and, therefore, without any legitimate authority. The right to govern rests on ownership or dominion. Where there is no proprietorship, there is no dominion; and where there is no dominion, there is no right to govern. Only he who is sovereign proprietor is sovereign lord.

Property, ownership, dominion rests on creation. The maker has the right to the thing made. He, so far as he is sole creator, is sole proprietor, and may do what he will with it. God is sovereign lord and proprietor of the universe because He is its sole creator. He hath the absolute dominion, because He is absolute maker. He has made it, He owns it; and one may do what he will with his own. His dominion is absolute, because He is absolute creator, and He rightly governs as absolute and universal lord; yet is He no despot, because He exercises only His sovereign right, and His own essential wisdom, goodness, justness, rectitude, and immutability, are the highest of all conceivable guaranties that His exercise of His power will always be right, wise, just, and good. The despot is a man attempting to be God upon earth, and to exercise a usurped power. Despotism is based on the parental right, and the parental right is assumed to be absolute. Hence, your despotic rulers claim to reign, and to be loved and worshipped as gods. Even the Roman emperors, in the fourth and fifth centuries, were addressed as divinities; and Theodosius the Great, a Christian, was addressed as "Your Eternity," *Eternitas vestras*—so far did barbarism encroach on civilization, even under Christian emperors.

The right of the father over his child is an imperfect right, for he is the generator, not the creator of his child. Generation is in the order of second causes, and is simply the development or explication of the race. The early Roman law, founded on the confusion of generation with creation, gave the father absolute authority over the child—the right of life and death, as over his servants or slaves; but this was restricted under the Empire, and in all Christian nations the authority of the father is treated, like all power, as a trust. The child, like the father himself, belongs to the state, and to the state the father is answerable for the use he makes of his authority. The law fixes the age of majority, when the child is completely emancipated; and even during his nonage, takes him from the father and places him under guardians, in case the father is incompetent to fulfill or grossly abuses his trust. This is proper, because society contributes to the life of the child, and has a right as well as an interest in him. Society, again, must suffer if the child is allowed to grow up a worthless vagabond or a criminal; and has a right to intervene, both in behalf of itself and of the child, in case his parents neglect to train him up in the nurture and admonition of the Lord, or are training him up to be a liar, a thief, a drunkard, a murderer, a pest to the community. How, then, base the right of society on the right of the father, since, in point of fact, the right of society is paramount to the right of the parent?

But even waiving this, and granting what is not the fact that the authority of the father is absolute, unlimited, it cannot be the ground of the right of society to govern. Assume the parental right to be perfect and inseparable from the parental relation, it is no right to govern where no such relation exists. Nothing true, real, solid in government can be founded on what Carlyle calls a "sham." The statesman, if worthy of the name, ascertains and conforms to the realities, the verities of things; and all jurisprudence that accepts legal fictions is imperfect, and even censurable. The presumptions or assumptions of law or politics must have a real and solid basis, or they are inadmissible. How, from the right of the father to govern his own child, born from his loins, conclude his right to govern one not his child? Or how, from my right to govern my child, conclude the right of society to found the state, institute government, and exercise political authority over its members?

Chapter IV: Origin of Government (Continued)

II. Rejecting the patriarchal theory as untenable, and shrinking from asserting the divine origin of government, lest they should favor theocracy, and place secular society under the control of the clergy, and thus disfranchise the laity, modern political writers have sought to render government purely human, and maintain that its origin is conventional, and that it is founded in compact or agreement. Their theory originated in the seventeenth century, and was predominant in the last century and the first third of the present. It has been, and perhaps is yet, generally accepted by American politicians and statesmen, at least so far as they ever trouble their heads with the question at all, which it must be confessed is not far.

The moral theologians of the Church have generally spoken of government as a social pact or compact, and explained the reciprocal rights and obligations of subjects and rulers by the general law of contracts; but they have never held that government originates in a voluntary agreement between the people and their rulers, or between the several individuals composing the community. They have never held that government has only a conventional origin or authority. They have simply meant, by the social compact, the mutual relations and reciprocal rights and duties of princes and their subjects, as implied in the very existence and nature of civil society. Where there are rights and duties on each side, they treat the fact, not as an agreement voluntarily entered into, and which creates them, but as a compact which binds alike sovereign and subject; and in determining whether either side has sinned or not, they inquire whether either has broken the terms of the social compact. They were engaged, not with the question whence does government derive its authority, but with its nature, and the reciprocal rights and duties of governors and the governed. The compact itself they held was not voluntarily formed by the people themselves, either individually or collectively, but was imposed by God, either immediately, or mediately, through the law of nature. "Every man," says Cicero, "is born in society, and remains there." They held the same, and maintained that every one born into society contracts by that fact certain obligations to society, and society certain obligations to him; for under the natural law, everyone has certain rights, as life, liberty, and the pursuit of happiness, and owes certain duties to society for the protection and assistance it affords him.

But modern political theorists have abused the phrase borrowed from the theologians, and made it cover a political doctrine which they would have been the last to accept. These theorists or political speculators have imagined a state of nature antecedently to civil society, in which men lived without government, law, or manners, out of which they finally came by entering into a voluntary agreement with some one of their number to be king and to govern them, or with one another to submit to the rule of the majority. Hobbes, the English materialist, is among the earliest and most distinguished of the advocates of this theory. He held that men lived, prior to the creation of civil society, in a state of nature, in which all were equal, and every one had an equal right to everything, and to take anything on which he could lay his hands and was strong enough to hold. There was no law but the will of the strongest. Hence, the state of nature was a state of continual war. At length, wearied and disgusted, men sighed for peace, and, with one accord, said to the tallest, bravest, or ablest among them: Come, be our king, our master, our sovereign lord, and govern us; we surrender our natural rights and our natural independence to you, with no other reserve or condition than that you maintain peace among us, keep us from robbing and plundering one another or cutting each other's throats.

Locke followed Hobbes, and asserted virtually the same theory, but asserted it in the interests of liberty, as Hobbes had asserted it in the interests of power. Rousseau, a citizen of Geneva, followed in the next century with his *Contrat Social*, the text-book of the French revolutionists—almost their Bible—and put the finishing stroke to the theory. Hitherto the compact or agreement had been assumed to be between the governor and the governed; Rousseau supposes it to be between the people themselves, or a compact to which the people are the only parties. He adopts the theory of a state of nature in which men lived, antecedently to their forming themselves into civil society, without government or law. All men in that state were equal, and each was independent and sovereign proprietor of himself. These equal, independent, sovereign individuals met, or are held to have met, in convention, and entered into a compact with themselves, each with all, and all with each, that they would constitute government, and would each submit to the determination and authority of the whole, practically of the fluctuating and irresponsible majority. Civil society, the state, the government, originates in this compact, and the government, as Mr. Jefferson asserts in the Declaration of American Independence, "derives its just powers from the consent of the governed."

This theory, as so set forth, or as modified by asserting that the individual delegates instead of surrendering his rights to civil society, was generally adopted by the American people in the last century, and is still the more prevalent theory with those among them who happen to have any theory or opinion on the subject. It is the political tradition of the country. The state, as defined by the elder Adams, is held to be a voluntary association of individuals. Individuals create civil society, and may uncreate it whenever they judge it advisable. Prior to the Southern Rebellion, nearly every American asserted with Lafayette, "the sacred right of insurrection" or revolution, and sympathized with insurrectionists, rebels, and revolutionists, wherever they made their appearance. Loyalty was held to be the correlative of royalty, treason was regarded as a virtue, and traitors were honored, feasted, and eulogized as patriots, ardent lovers of liberty, and champions of the people. The fearful struggle of the nation against a rebellion which threatened its very existence may have changed this.

That there is, or ever was, a state of nature such as the theory assumes, may be questioned. Certainly nothing proves that it is, or ever was, a real state. That there is a law of nature is undeniable. All authorities in philosophy, morals, politics, and jurisprudence assert it; the state assumes it as its own immediate basis, and the codes of all nations are founded on it; universal jurisprudence, the *jus gentium* of the Romans, embodies it, and the courts recognize and administer it. It is the reason and conscience of civil society, and every state acknowledges its authority. But the law of nature is as much in force in civil society as out of it. Civil law does not abrogate or supersede natural law, but presupposes it, and supports itself on it as its own ground and reason. As the natural law, which is only natural justice and equity dictated by the reason common to all men, persists in the civil law, municipal or international, as its informing soul, so does the state of nature persist in the civil state, natural society in civil society, which simply develops, applies, and protects it. Man in civil society is not out of nature, but is in it—is in his most natural state; for society is natural to him, and government is natural to society, and in some form inseparable from it. The state of nature under the natural law is not, as a separate state, an actual state, and never was; but an abstraction, in which is considered, apart from the concrete existence called society, what is derived immediately from the natural law. But as abstractions have no existence, out of the mind that forms them, the state of nature has no actual existence in the world of reality as a separate state.

But suppose with the theory the state of nature to have been a real and separate state, in which men at first lived, there is great difficulty in understanding how they ever got out of it. Can a man divest himself of his nature, or lift himself above it? Man is in his nature, and inseparable from it. If his primitive state was his natural state, and if the political state is supernatural, preternatural, or subnatural, how passed he alone, by his own unaided powers, from the former to the latter? The ancients, who had lost the primitive tradition of creation, asserted, indeed, the primitive man as springing from the earth, and leading a mere animal life, living in eaves or hollow trees, and feeding on roots and nuts, without speech, without science, art, law, or sense of right and wrong; but prior to the prevalence of the Epicurean philosophy, they never pretended, that man could come out of that state alone by his own unaided efforts. They ascribed the invention of language, art, and science, the institution of civil society, government, and laws, to the intervention of the gods. It remained for the Epicureans—who, though unable, like their modern successors, the Positivists or Developmentists, to believe in a first cause, believed in effects without causes, or that things make or take care of themselves—to assert that men could, by their own unassisted efforts, or by the simple exercise of reason, come out of the primitive state, and institute what in modern times is called *civiltà*, civility, or civilization.

The partisans of this theory of the state of nature from which men have emerged by the voluntary and deliberate formation of civil society, forget that if government is not the sole condition, it is one of the essential conditions of progress. The only progressive nations are civilized or republican nations. Savage and barbarous tribes are unprogressive. Ages on ages roll over them without changing anything in their state; and Niebuhr has well remarked with others, that history records no instance of a savage tribe or people having become civilized by its own spontaneous or indigenous efforts. If savage tribes have ever become civilized, it has been by influences from abroad, by the aid of men already civilized, through conquest, colonies, or missionaries; never by their own indigenous efforts, nor even by commerce, as is so confidently asserted in this mercantile age. Nothing in all history indicates the ability of a savage people to pass of itself from the savage state to the civilized. But the primitive man, as described by Horace in his *Satires*, and asserted by Hobbes, Locke, Rousseau, and others, is far below the savage. The lowest, most degraded, and most debased savage tribe that has yet been discovered has at least some rude outlines or feeble reminiscences of a social state, of government, morals, law, and religion, for even in superstition the most gross there is a reminiscence of true religion; but the people in the alleged state of nature have none.

The advocates of the theory deceive themselves by transporting into their imaginary state of nature the views, habits, and capacities of the civilized man. It is, perhaps, not difficult for men who have been civilized, who have the intelligence, the arts, the affections, and the habits of civilization, if deprived by some great social convulsion of society, and thrown back on the so-called state of nature, or cast away on some uninhabited island in the ocean, and cut off from all intercourse with the rest of mankind, to reconstruct civil society, and re-establish and maintain civil government. They are civilized men, and bear civil society in their own life. But these are no representatives of the primitive man in the alleged state of nature. These primitive men have no experience, no knowledge, no conception even of civilized life, or of any state superior to that in which they have thus far lived. How then can they, since, on the theory, civil society has no root in nature, but is a purely artificial creation, even conceive of civilization, much less realize it?

These theorists, as theorists always do, fail to make a complete abstraction of the civilized state, and conclude from what they feel they could do in case civil society were broken up, what men may do and have done in a state of nature. Men cannot divest themselves of themselves, and, whatever their efforts to do it, they think, reason, and act as they are. Every writer, whatever else he writes, writes himself. The advocates of the theory, to have made their abstraction complete, should have presented their primitive man as below the lowest known savage, unprogressive, and in himself incapable of developing any progressive energy. Unprogressive, and, without foreign assistance, incapable of progress, how is it possible for your primitive man to pass, by his own unassisted efforts, from the alleged state of nature to that of civilization, of which he has no conception, and towards which no innate desire, no instinct, no divine inspiration pushes him?

But even if, by some happy inspiration, hardly supposable without supernatural intervention repudiated by the theory—if by some happy inspiration, a rare individual should so far rise above the state of nature as to conceive of civil society and of civil government, how could he carry his conception into execution? Conception is always easier than its realization, and between the design and its execution there is always a weary distance. The poetry of all nations is a wail over unrealized ideals. It is little that even the wisest and most potent statesman can realize of what he conceives to be necessary for the state: political, legislative or judicial reforms, even when loudly demanded, and favored by authority, are hard to be effected, and not seldom generations come and go without effecting them. The republics of Plato, Sir Thomas More, Campanella, Harrington, as the communities of Robert Owen and M. Cabet, remain Utopias, not solely because intrinsically absurd, though so in fact, but chiefly because they are innovations, have no support in experience, and require for their realization the modes of thought, habits, manners, character, life, which only their introduction and realization can supply. So to be able to execute the design of passing from the supposed state of nature to civilization, the reformer would need the intelligence, the habits, and characters in the public which are not possible without civilization itself. Some philosophers suppose men have invented language, forgetting that it requires language to give the ability to invent language.

Men are little moved by mere reasoning, however clear and convincing it may be. They are moved by their affections, passions, instincts, and habits. Routine is more powerful with them than logic. A few are greedy of novelties, and are always for trying experiments; but the great body of the people of all nations have an invincible repugnance to abandon what they know for what they know not. They are, to a great extent, the slaves of their own *vis inertiae*, and will not make the necessary exertion to change their existing mode of life, even for a better. Interest itself is powerless before their indolence, prejudice, habits, and usages. Never were philosophers more ignorant of human nature than they, so numerous in the last century, who imagined that men can be always moved by a sense of interest, and that enlightened self-interest, *L'intérêt bien entendu*, suffices to found and sustain the state. No reform, no change in the constitution of government or of society, whatever the advantages it may promise, can be successful, if introduced, unless it has its root or germ in the past. Man is never a creator; he can only develop and continue, because he is himself a creature, and only a second cause. The children of Israel, when they encountered the privations of the wilderness that lay between them and the promised land flowing with milk and honey, fainted in spirit, and begged Moses to lead them back to Egypt, and permit them to return to slavery.

In the alleged state of nature, as the philosophers describe it, there is no germ of civilization, and the transition to civil society would not be a development, but a complete rupture with the past, and an entire new creation. When it is with the greatest difficulty that necessary reforms are introduced in old and highly civilized nations and when it can seldom be done at all without terrible political and social convulsions, how can we suppose men without society, and knowing nothing of it, can deliberately, and, as it were, with "malice aforethought," found society? Without government, and destitute alike of habits of obedience and habits of command, how can they initiate, establish, and sustain government? To suppose it, would be to suppose that men in a state of nature, without culture, without science, without any of the arts, even the most simple and necessary, are infinitely superior to the men formed under the most advanced civilization. Was Rousseau right in asserting civilization as a fall, as a deterioration of the race?

But suppose the state of nature, even suppose that men, by some miracle or other, can get out of it and found civil society, the origin of government as authority in compact is not yet established. According to the theory, the rights of civil society are derived from the rights of the individuals who form or enter into the compact. But individuals cannot give what they have not, and no individual has in himself the right to govern another. By the law of nature all men have equal rights, are equals, and equals have no authority one over another. Nor has an individual the sovereign right even to himself, or the right to dispose of himself as he pleases. Man is not God, independent, self-existing and self-sufficing. He is dependent, and dependent not only on his Maker, but on his fellow-men, on society, and even on nature, or the material world. That on which he depends in the measure in which be depends on it, contributes to his existence, to his life, and to his well-being, and has, by virtue of its contribution, a right in him and to him; and hence it is that nothing is more painful to the proud spirit than to receive a favor that lays him under an obligation to another. The right of that on which man depends, and by communion with which he lives, limits his own right over himself.

Man does not depend exclusively on society, for it is not his only medium of communion with God, and therefore its right to him is neither absolute nor unlimited; but still he depends on it, lives in it, and cannot live without it. It has, then, certain rights over him, and he cannot enter into any compact, league, or alliance that society does not authorize, or at least permit. These rights of society override his rights to himself, and he can neither surrender them nor delegate them. Other rights, as the rights of religion and property, which are held directly from God and nature, and which are independent of society, are included in what are called the natural rights of man; and these rights cannot be surrendered in forming civil society, for they are rights of man only before civil society, and therefore not his to cede, and because they are precisely the rights that government is bound to respect and protect. The compact, then, cannot be formed as pretended, for the only rights individuals could delegate or surrender to society to constitute the sum of the rights of government are hers already, and those which are not hers are those which cannot be delegated or surrendered, and in the free and full enjoyment of which, it is the duty, the chief end of government to protect each and every individual.

The convention not only is not a fact, but individuals have no authority without society, to meet in convention, and enter into the alleged compact, because they are not independent, sovereign individuals. But pass over this: suppose the convention, suppose the compact, it must still be conceded that it binds and can bind only those who voluntarily and deliberately enter into it. This is conceded by Mr. Jefferson and the American Congress of 1776, in the assertion that government derives its "just powers from the consent of the governed." This consent, as the matter is one of life and death, must be free, deliberate, formal, explicit, not simply an assumed, implied, or constructive consent. It must be given personally, and not by one for another without his express authority.

It is usual to infer the consent or the acceptance of the terms of the compact from the silence of the individual, and also from his continued residence in the country and submission to its government. But residence is no evidence of consent, because it may be a matter of necessity. The individual may be unable to emigrate, if he would; and by what right can individuals form an agreement to which I must consent or else migrate to some strange land? Can my consent, under such circumstances, even if given, be anything but a forced consent, a consent given under duress, and therefore invalid? Nothing can be inferred from one's silence, for he may have many reasons for being silent besides approval of the government. He may be silent because speech would avail nothing; because to protest might be dangerous—cost him his liberty, if not his life; because he sees and knows nothing better, and is ignorant that he has any choice in the case; or because, as very likely is the fact with the majority, he has never for moment thought of the matter, or ever had his attention called to it, and has no mind on the subject.

But however this may be, there certainly must be excluded from the compact or obligation to obey the government created by it all the women of a nation, all the children too young to be capable of giving their consent, and all who are too ignorant, too weak of mind to be able to understand the terms of the contract. These several classes cannot be less than three-fourths of the population of any country. What is to be done with them? Leave them without government? Extend the power of the government over them? By what right? Government derives its just powers from the consent of the governed, and that consent they have not given. Whence does one-fourth of the population get its right to govern the other three-fourths?

But what is to be done with the rights of minorities? Is the rule of unanimity to be insisted on in the convention and in the government, when it goes into operation? Unanimity is impracticable, for where there are many men there will be differences of opinion. The rule of unanimity gives to each individual a veto on the whole proceeding, which was the grand defect of the Polish constitution. Each member of the Polish Diet, which included the whole body of the nobility, had an absolute veto, and could, alone, arrest the whole action of the government. Will you substitute the rule of the majority, and say the majority must govern? By what right? It is agreed to in the convention. Unanimously, or only by a majority? The right of the majority to have their will is, on the social compact theory, a conventional right, and therefore cannot come into play before the convention is completed, or the social compact is framed and accepted. How, in settling the terms of the compact, will you proceed? By majorities? But suppose a minority objects, and demands two-thirds, three-fourths, or four-fifths, and votes against the majority rule, which is carried only by a simple plurality of votes, will the proceedings of the convention bind the dissenting minority? What gives to the majority the right to govern the minority who dissent from its action?

On the supposition that society has rights not derived from individuals, and which are entrusted to the government, there is a good reason why the majority should prevail within the legitimate sphere of government, because the majority is the best representative practicable of society itself; and if the constitution secures to minorities and dissenting individuals their natural rights and their equal rights as citizens, they have no just cause of complaint, for the majority in such case has no power to tyrannize over them or to oppress them. But the theory under examination denies that society has any rights except such as it derives from individuals who all have equal rights. According to it, society is itself conventional, and created by free, independent, equal, sovereign individuals. Society is a congress of sovereigns, in which no one has authority over another, and no one can be rightfully forced to submit to any decree against his will. In such a congress the rule of the majority is manifestly improper, illegitimate, and invalid, unless adopted by unanimous consent.

But this is not all. The individual is always the equal of himself, and if the government derives its powers from the consent of the governed, he governs in the government, and parts with none of his original sovereignty. The government is not his master, but his agent, as the principal only delegates, not surrenders, his rights and powers to the agent. He is free at any time he pleases to recall the powers he has delegated, to give new instructions, or to dismiss him. The sovereignty of the individual survives the compact, and persists through all the acts of his agent, the government. He must, then, be free to withdraw from the compact whenever he judges it advisable. Secession is perfectly legitimate if government is simply a contract between equals. The disaffected, the criminal, the thief the government would send to prison, or the murderer it would hang, would be very likely to revoke his consent, and to secede from the state. Any number of individuals large enough to count a majority among themselves, indisposed to pay the government taxes, or to perform the military service exacted, might hold a convention, adopt a secession ordinance, and declare themselves a free, independent, sovereign state, and bid defiance to the tax-collector and the provost-marshall, and that, too, without forfeiting their estates or changing their domicile. Would the government employ military force to coerce them back to their allegiance? By what right? Government is their agent, their creature, and no man owes allegiance to his own agent, or creature.

The compact could bind only temporarily, and could at any moment be dissolved. Mr. Jefferson saw this, and very consistently maintained that one generation has no power to bind another; and, as if this was not enough, he asserted the right of revolution, and gave it as his opinion that in every nation a revolution once in every generation is desirable, that is, according to his reckoning, once every nineteen years. The doctrine that one generation has no power to bind its successor is not only a logical conclusion from the theory that governments derive their just powers from the consent of the governed, since a generation cannot give its consent before it is born, but is very convenient for a nation that has contracted a large national debt; yet, perhaps, not so convenient to the public creditor, since the new generation may take it into its head not to assume or discharge the obligations of its predecessor, but to repudiate them. No man, certainly, can contract for anyone but himself; and how then can the son be bound, without his own personal or individual consent, freely given, by the obligations entered into by his father?

The social compact is necessarily limited to the individuals who form it, and as necessarily, unless renewed, expires with them. It thus creates no state, no political corporation, which survives in all its rights and powers, though individuals die. The state is on this theory a voluntary association, and in principle, except that it is not a secret society, in no respect differs from the Carbonari, or the Knights of the Golden Circle. When Orsini attempted to execute the sentence of death on the Emperor of the French, in obedience to the order of the Carbonari, of which the Emperor was a member, he was, if the theory of the origin of government in compact be true, no more an assassin than was the officer who executed on the gallows the rebel spies and incendiaries Beal and Kennedy.

Certain it is that the alleged social compact has in it no social or civil element. It does not and cannot create society. It can give only an aggregation of individuals, and society is not an aggregation nor even an organization of individuals. It is an organism, and individuals live in its life as well as it in theirs. There is a real living solidarity, which makes individuals members of the social body, and members one of another. There is no society without individuals, and there are no individuals without society; but in society there is that which is not individual, and is more than all individuals. The social compact is an attempt to substitute for this real living solidarity, which gives to society at once unity of life and diversity of members, an artificial solidarity, a fictitious unity for a real unity, and membership by contract for real living membership, a cork leg for that which nature herself gives. Real government has its ground in this real living solidarity, and represents the social element, which is not individual, but above all individuals, as man is above men. But the theory substitutes a simple agency for government, and makes each individual its principal. It is an abuse of language to call this agency a government. It has no one feature or element of government. It has only an artificial unity, based on diversity; its authority is only personal, individual, and in no sense a public authority, representing a public will, a public right, or a public interest. In no country could government be adopted and sustained if men were left to the wisdom or justness of their theories, or in the general affairs of life, acted on them. Society, and government as representing society, has a real existence, life, faculties, and organs of its own, not derived or derivable from individuals. As well might it be maintained that the human body consists in and derives all its life from the particles of matter it assimilates from its food, and which are constantly escaping as to maintain that society derives its life, or government its powers, from individuals. No mechanical aggregation of brute matter can make a living body, if there is no living and assimilating principle within; and no aggregation of individuals, however closely bound together by pacts or oaths, can make society where there is no informing social principle that aggregates and assimilates them to a living body, or produce that mystic existence called a state or commonwealth.

The origin of government in the *Contrat Social* supposes the nation to be a purely personal affair. It gives the government no territorial status, and clothes it with no territorial rights or jurisdiction. The government that could so originate would be, if anything, a barbaric, not a republican government. It has only the rights conferred on it, surrendered or delegated to it by individuals, and therefore, at best, only individual rights. Individuals can confer only such rights as they have in the supposed state of nature. In that state there is neither private nor public domain. The earth in that state is not property, and is open to the first occupant, and the occupant can lay no claim to any more than he actually occupies. Whence, then, does government derive its territorial jurisdiction, and its right of eminent domain claimed by all national governments? Whence its title to vacant or unoccupied lands? How does any particular government fix its territorial boundaries, and obtain the right to prescribe who may occupy, and on what conditions the vacant lands within those boundaries? Whence does it get its jurisdiction of navigable rivers, lakes, bays, and the seaboard within its territorial limits, as appertaining to its domain? Here are rights that it could not have derived from individuals, for individuals never possessed them in the so-called state of nature. The concocters of the theory evidently overlooked these rights, or considered them of no importance. They seem never to have contemplated the existence of territorial states, or the division of mankind into nations fixed to the soil. They seem not to have supposed the earth could be appropriated; and, indeed, many of their followers pretend that it cannot be, and that the public lands of a nation are open lands, and who so chooses may occupy them, without leave asked of the national authority or granted. The American people retain more than one reminiscence of the nomadic and predatory habits of their Teutonic or Scythian ancestors before they settled on the banks of the Don or the Danube, on the Northern Ocean, in Scania, or came in contact with the Graeco-Roman civilization.

Yet mankind are divided into nations, and all civilized nations are fixed to the soil. The territory is defined, and is the domain of the state, from which all private proprietors hold their title-deeds. Individual proprietors hold under the state, and often hold more, than they occupy; but it retains in all private estates the eminent domain, and prohibits the alienation of land to one who is not a citizen. It defends its domain, its public unoccupied lauds, and the lands owned by private individuals, against all foreign powers. Now whence, if government has only the rights ceded it by individuals, does it get this domain, and hold the right to treat settlers on even its unoccupied lands as trespassers? In the state of nature the territorial rights of individuals, if any they have, are restricted to the portion of land they occupy with their rude culture, and with their flocks and herds, and in civilized nations to what they hold from the state, and, therefore, the right as held and defended by all nations, and without which the nation has no status, no fixed dwelling, and is and can be no state, could never have been derived from individuals. The earliest notices of Rome show the city in possession of the sacred territory, to which the state and all political power are attached. Whence did Rome become a landholder, and the governing people a territorial people? Whence does any nation become a territorial nation and lord of the domain? Certainly never by the cession of individuals, and hence no civilized government ever did or could originate in the so-called social compact.

Chapter V: Origin of Government (Continued)

III. The tendency of the last century was to individualism; that of the present is to socialism. The theory of Hobbes, Locke, Rousseau, and Jefferson, though not formally abandoned, and still held by many, has latterly been much modified, if not wholly transformed. Sovereignty, it is now maintained, is inherent in the people; not individually, indeed, but collectively, or the people as society. The constitution is held not to be simply a compact or agreement entered into by the people as individuals creating civil society and government, but a law ordained by the sovereign people, prescribing the constitution of the state and defining its rights and powers.

This transformation, which is rather going on than completed, is, under one aspect at least, a progress, or rather a return to the sounder principles of antiquity. Under it government ceases to be a mere agency, which must obtain the assassin's consent to be hung before it can rightfully hang him, and becomes authority, which is one and imperative. The people taken collectively are society, and society is a living organism, not a mere aggregation of individuals. It does not, of course, exist without individuals, but it is something more than individuals, and has rights not derived from them, and which are paramount to theirs. There is more truth, and truth of a higher order, in this than in the theory of the social compact. Individuals, to a certain extent, derive their life from God through society, and so far they depend on her, and they are hers; she owns them, and has the right to do as she will with them. On this theory the state emanates from society, and is supreme. It coincides with the ancient Greek and Roman theory, as expressed by Cicero, already cited. Man is born in society and remains there, and it may be regarded as the source of ancient Greek and Roman patriotism, which still commands the admiration of the civilized world. The state with Greece and Rome was a living reality, and loyalty a religion. The Romans held Rome to be a divinity, gave her statues and altars, and offered her divine worship. This was superstition, no doubt, but it had in it an element of truth. To every true philosopher there is something divine in the state, and truth in all theories. Society stands nearer to God, and participates more immediately of the Divine essence, and the state is a more lively image of God than the individual. It was man, the generic and reproductive man, not the isolated individual, that was created in the image and likeness of his Maker. "And God created man in his own image; in the image of God created he him; male and female created he them."

This theory is usually called the democratic theory, and it enlists in its support the instincts, the intelligence, the living forces, and active tendencies of the age. Kings, kaisers, and hierarchies are powerless before it, and war against it in vain. The most they can do is to restrain its excesses, or to guard against its abuses. Its advocates, in returning to it, sometimes revive in its name the old pagan superstition. Not a few of the European democrats recognize in the earth, in heaven, or in hell, no power superior to the people, and say not only people-king but people-God. They say absolutely, without any qualification, the voice of the people is the voice of God, and make their will the supreme law, not only in politics, but in religion, philosophy, morals, science, and the arts. The people not only found the state, but also the church. They inspire or reveal the truth, ordain or prohibit worships, judge of doctrines, and decide cases of conscience. Mazzini said, when at the bead of the Roman Republic in 1848, the question of religion must be remitted to the judgment of the people. Yet this theory is the dominant theory of the age, and is in all civilized nations advancing with apparently irresistible force.

But this theory has its difficulties. Who are the collective people that have the rights of society, or, who are the sovereign people? The word *people* is vague, and in itself determines nothing. It may include a larger or a smaller number; it may mean the political people, or it may mean simply population; it may mean peasants, artisans, shopkeepers, traders, merchants, as distinguished from the nobility; hired laborers or workmen as distinguished from their employer, or slaves as distinguished from their master or owner. In which of these senses is the word to be taken when it is said, "The people are sovereign?" The people are the population or inhabitants of one and the same country. That is something. But who or what determines the country? Is the country the whole territory of the globe? That will not be said, especially since the dispersion of mankind and their division into separate nations. Is the territory indefinite or undefined? Then indefinite or undefined are its inhabitants, or the peoplc invested with the rights of society. Is it defined and its boundaries fixed? Who has done it? The people. But who are the people? We are as wise as we were at starting. The logicians say that the definition of *idem* per *idem*, or the same by the same, is simply no definition at all.

The people are the nation, undoubtedly, if you mean by the people the sovereign people. But who are the people constituting the nation? The sovereign people? This is only to revolve in a vicious circle. The nation is the tribe or the people living under the same regimen, and born of the same ancestor, or sprung from the same ancestor or progenitor. But where find a nation in this the primitive sense of the word? Migration, conquest, and intermarriage, have so broken up and intermingled the primitive races, that it is more than doubtful if a single nation, tribe, or family of unmixed blood now exists on the face of the earth. A Frenchman, Italian, Spaniard, German, or Englishman, may have the blood of a hundred different races coursing in his veins. The nation is the people inhabiting the same country, and united under one and the same government, it is further answered. The nation, then, is not purely personal, but also territorial. Then, again, the question comes up, who or what determines the territory? The government? But not before it is constituted, and it cannot be constituted till its territorial limits are determined. The tribe doubtless occupies territory, but is not fixed to it, and derives no jurisdiction from it, and therefore is not territorial. But a nation, in the modern or civilized sense, is fixed to the territory, and derives from it its jurisdiction, or sovereignty; and, therefore, till the territory is determined, the nation is not and cannot be determined.

The question is not an idle question. It is one of great practical importance; for, till it is settled, we can neither determine who are the sovereign people, nor who are united under one and the same government. Laws have no extra-territorial force, and the officer who should attempt to enforce the national laws beyond the national territory would be a trespasser. If the limits are undetermined, the government is not territorial, and can claim as within its jurisdiction only those who choose to acknowledge its authority. The importance of the question has been recently brought home to the American people by the secession of eleven or more States from the Union. Were these States a part of the American nation, or were they not? Was the war which followed secession, and which cost so many lives and so much treasure, a civil war or a foreign war? Were the secessionists traitors and rebels to their sovereign, or were they patriots fighting for the liberty and independence of their country and the right of self-government? All on both sides agreed that the nation is sovereign; the dispute was as to the existence of the nation itself, and the extent of its jurisdiction. Doubtless, when a nation has a generally recognized existence as an historical fact, most of the difficulties in determining who are the sovereign people can be got over; but the question here concerns the institution of government, and determining who constitute society and have the right to meet in person, or by their delegates in convention, to institute it. This question, so important, and at times so difficult, the theory of the origin of government in the people collectively, or the nation, does not solve, or furnish any means of solving.

But suppose this difficulty surmounted, there is still another, and a very grave one, to over-come. The theory assumes that the people collectively, "in their own native right and might," are sovereign. According to it the people are ultimate, and free to do whatever they please. This sacrifices individual freedom. The origin of government in a compact entered into by individuals, each with all and all with each, sacrificed the rights of society, and assumed each individual to be in himself an independent sovereignty.

If logically carried out, there could be no such crime as treason, there could be no state, and no public authority. This new theory transfers to society the sovereignty which that asserted for the individual, and asserts social despotism, or the absolutism of the state. It asserts with sufficient energy public authority, or the right of the people to govern; but it leaves no space for individual rights, which society must recognize, respect, and protect. This was the grand defect of the ancient Graeco-Roman civilization. The historian explores in vain the records of the old Greek and Roman republics for any recognition of the rights of individuals not held as privileges or concessions from the state. Society recognized no limit to her authority, and the state claimed over individuals all the authority of the patriarch over his household, the chief over his tribe, or the absolute monarch over his subjects. The direct and indirect influence of the body of freemen admitted to a voice in public affairs, in determining the resolutions and action of the state, no doubt tempered in practice to some extent the authority of the state, and prevented acts of gross oppression; but in theory the state was absolute, and the people individually were placed at the mercy of the people collectively, or, rather, the majority of the collective people.

Under ancient republicanism, there were rights of the state and rights of the citizen, but no rights of man, held independently of society, and not derived from God through the state. The recognition of these rights by modern society is due to Christianity: some say to the barbarians, who overthrew the Roman empire; but this last opinion is not well founded. The barbarian chiefs and nobles had no doubt a lively sense of personal freedom and independence, but for themselves only. They had no conception of personal freedom as a general or universal right, and men never obtain universal principles by generalizing particulars. They may give a general truth a particular application, but not a particular truth—understood to be a particular truth—a general or universal application. They are too good logicians for that. The barbarian individual freedom and personal independence was never generalized into the doctrine of the rights of man, any more than the freedom of the master has been generalized into the right of his slaves to be free. The doctrine of individual freedom before the state is due to the Christian religion, which asserts the dignity and worth of every human soul, the accountability to God of each man for himself, and lays it down as law for every one that God is to be obeyed rather than men. The church practically denied the absolutism of the state, and asserted for every man rights not held from the state, in converting the empire to Christianity, in defiance of the state authority, and the imperial edicts punishing with death the profession of the Christian faith. In this she practically, as well as theoretically, overthrew state absolutism, and infused into modern society the doctrine that every individual, even the lowest and meanest, has rights which the state neither confers nor can abrogate; and it will only be by extinguishing in modern society the Christian faith, and obliterating all traces of Christian civilization, that state absolutism can be revived with more than a partial and temporary success.

The doctrine of individual liberty may be abused, and so explained as to deny the rights of society, and to become pure individualism; but no political system that runs to the opposite extreme, and absorbs the individual in the state, stands the least chance of any general or permanent success till Christianity is extinguished. Yet the assertion of principles which logically imply state absolutism is not entirely harmless, even in Christian countries. Error is never harmless, and only truth can give a solid foundation on which to build. Individualism and socialism are each opposed to the other, and each has only a partial truth. The state founded on either cannot stand, and society will only alternate between the two extremes. Today it is torn by a revolution in favor of socialism; tomorrow it will be torn by another in favor of individualism, and without effecting any real progress by either revolution. Real progress can be secured only by recognizing and building on the truth, not as it exists in our opinions or in our theories, but as it exists in the world of reality, and independent of our opinions.

Now, social despotism or state absolutism is not based on truth or reality. Society has certain rights over individuals, for she is a medium of their communion with God, or through which they derive life from God, the primal source of all life; but she is not the only medium of man's life. Man, as was said in the beginning, lives by communion with God, and he communes with God in the creative act and the Incarnation, through his kind, and, through nature. This threefold communion gives rise to three institutions—religion or the church, society or the state, and property. The life that man derives from God through religion and property, is not derived from him through society, and consequently so much of his life be holds independently of society; and this constitutes his rights as a man as distinguished from his rights as a citizen. In relation to society, as not held from God through her, these are termed his natural rights, which, she must hold inviolable, and government protect for everyone, whatever his complexion or his social position. These rights—the rights of conscience and the rights of property, with all their necessary implications—are limitations of the rights of society, and the individual has the right to plead them against the state. Society does not confer them, and it cannot take them away, for they are at least as sacred and as fundamental as her own.

But even this limitation of popular sovereignty is not all. The people can be sovereign only in the sense in which they exist and act. The people are not God, whatever some theorists may pretend—are not independent, self-existent, and self-sufficing. They are as dependent collectively as individually, and therefore can exist and act only as second cause, never as first cause. They can, then, even in the limited sphere of their sovereignty, be sovereign only in a secondary sense, never absolute sovereign in their own independent right. They are sovereign only to the extent to which they impart life to the individual members of society, and only in the sense in which she imparts it, or is its cause. She is not its first cause or creator, and is the medial cause or medium through which they derive it from God, not its efficient cause or primary source. Society derives her own life from God, and exists and acts only as dependent on him. Then she is sovereign over individuals only as dependent on God. Her dominion is then not original and absolute, but secondary and derivative.

This third theory does not err in assuming that the people collectively are more than the people individually, or in denying society to be a mere aggregation of individuals with no life, and no rights but what it derives from them; nor even in asserting that the people in the sense of society are sovereign, but in asserting that they are sovereign in their own native or underived right and might. Society has not in herself the absolute right to govern, because she has not the absolute dominion either of herself or her members. God gave to man dominion over the irrational creation, for he made irrational creatures for man; but he never gave him either individually or collectively the dominion over the rational creation. The theory that the people are absolutely sovereign in their own independent right and might, as some zealous democrats explain it, asserts the fundamental principle of despotism, and all despotism is false, for it identifies the creature with the Creator. No creature is creator, or has the rights of creator, and consequently no one in his own right is or can be sovereign. This third theory, therefore, is untenable.

IV. A still more recent class of philosophers, if philosophers they may be called, reject the origin of government in the people individually or collectively. Satisfied that it has never been instituted by a voluntary and deliberate act of the people, and confounding government as a fact with government as authority, maintain that government is a spontaneous development of nature. Nature develops it as the liver secretes bile, as the bee constructs her cell, or the beaver builds his dam. Nature, working by her own laws and inherent energy, develops society, and society develops government. That is all the secret. Questions as to the origin of government or its rights, beyond the simple positive fact, belong to the theological or metaphysical stage of the development of nature, but are left behind when the race has passed beyond that stage, and has reached the epoch of positive science, in which all, except the positive fact, is held to be unreal and non-existent. Government, like everything else in the universe, is simply a positive development of nature. Science explains the laws and conditions of the development, but disdains to ask for its origin or ground in any order that transcends the changes of the world of space and time.

These philosophers profess to eschew all theory, and yet they only oppose theory to theory. The assertion that reality for the human mind is restricted to the positive facts of the sensible order, is purely theoretic, and is anything but a positive fact. Principles are as really objects of science as facts, and it is only in the light of principles that facts themselves are intelligible. If the human mind had no science of reality that transcends the sensible order, or the positive fact, it could have no science at all. As things exist only in their principles or causes, so can they be known only in their principles and causes; for things can be known only as they are, or as they really exist. The science that pretends to deduce principles from particular facts, or to rise from the fact by way of reasoning to an order that transcends facts, and in which facts have their origin, is undoubtedly chimerical, and as against that the positivists are unquestionably right. But to maintain that man has no intelligence of anything beyond the fact, no intuition or intellectual apprehension of its principle or cause, is equally chimerical. The human mind cannot have all science, but it has real science as far as it goes, and real science is the knowledge of things as they are, not as they are not. Sensible facts are not intelligible by themselves, because they do not exist by themselves; and if the human mind could not penetrate beyond the individual fact, beyond the mimetic to the methexic, or transcendental principle, copied or imitated by the individual fact, it could never know the fact itself. The error of modern philosophers, or philosopherlings, is in supposing the principle is deduced or inferred from the fact, and in denying that the human mind has direct and immediate intuition of it.

Something that transcends the sensible order there must be, or there could be no development; and if we had no science of it, we could never assert that development is development, or scientifically explain the laws and conditions of development. Development is explication, and supposes a germ which precedes it, and is not itself a development; and development, however far it may be carried, can never do more than realize the possibilities of the germ. Development is not creation, and cannot supply its own germ. That at least must be given by the Creator, for from nothing can be developed. If authority has not its germ in nature, it cannot be developed from nature spontaneously or otherwise. All government has a governing will; and without a will that commands, there is no government; and nature has in her spontaneous developments no will, for she has no personality. Reason itself, as distinguished from will, only presents the end and the means, but does not govern; it prescribes a rule, but cannot ordain a law. An imperative will, the will of a superior who has the right to command what reason dictates or approves, is essential to government; and that will is not developed from nature, because it has no germ in nature. So something above and beyond nature must be asserted, or government itself cannot be asserted, even as a development. Nature is no more self-sufficing than are the people, or than is the individual man.

No doubt there is a natural law, which is law in the proper sense of the word law; but this is a positive law under which nature is placed by a sovereign above herself, and is never to be confounded with those laws of nature so-called, according to which she is productive as second cause, or produces her effects, which are not properly laws at all. Fire burns, water flows, rain falls, birds fly, fishes swim, food nourishes, poisons kill, one substance has a chemical affinity for another, the needle points to the pole, by a natural law, it is said; that is, the effects are produced by an inherent and uniform natural force. Laws in this sense are simply physical forces, and are nature herself. The natural law, in an ethical sense, is not a physical law, is not a natural force, but a law imposed by the Creator on all moral creatures, that is, all creatures endowed with reason and free-will, and is called *natural* because promulgated in natural reason, or the reason common and essential to all moral creatures. This is the moral law. It is what the French call *le droit naturel*, natural right, and, as the theologians teach us, is the transcript of the eternal law, the eternal will or reason of God. It is the foundation of all law, and all acts of a state that contravene it are, as St. Augustine maintains, violences rather than laws. The moral law is no development of nature, for it is above nature, and is imposed on nature. The only development there is about it is in our understanding of it.

There is, of course, development in nature, for nature considered as creation has been created in germ, and is completed only in successive developments. Hence the origin of space and time. There would have been no space if there had been no external creation, and no time if the creation had been completed externally at once, as it was in relation to the Creator. Ideal space is simply the ability of God to externalize his creative act, and actual space is the relation of coexistence in the things created; ideal time is the ability of God to create existences with the capacity of being completed by successive developments, and actual time is the relation of these in the order of succession, and when the existence is completed or consummated development ceases, and time is no more. In relation to himself the Creator's works are complete from the first, and hence with him there is no time, for there is no succession. But in relation to itself creation is incomplete, and there is room for development, which may be continued till the whole possibility of creation is actualized. Here is the foundation of what is true in the modern doctrine of progress. Man is progressive, because the possibilities of his nature are successively unfolded and actualized.

Development is a fact, and its laws and conditions may be scientifically ascertained and defined. All generation is development, as is all growth, physical, moral, or intellectual. But everything is developed in its own order, and after its kind. The Darwinian theory of the development of species is not sustained by science. The development starts from the germ, and in the germ is given the law or principle of the development. From the acorn is developed the oak, never the pine or the linden. Every kind generates its kind, never another. But no development is, strictly speaking, spontaneous, or the result alone of the inherent energy or force of the germ developed. There is not only a solidarity of race, but in some sense of all races, or species; all created things are bound to their Creator, and to one another. One and the same law or principle of life pervades all creation, binding the universe together in a unity that copies or imitates the unity of the Creator. No creature is isolated from the rest, or absolutely independent of others. All are parts of one stupendous whole, and each depends on the whole, and the whole on each, and each on each. All creatures are members of one body, and members one of another. The germ of the oak is in the acorn, but the acorn left to itself alone can never grow into the oak, any more than a body at rest can place itself in motion. Lay the acorn away in your closet, where it is absolutely deprived of air, heat, and moisture, and in vain will you watch for its germination. Germinate it cannot without some external influence, or communion, so to speak, with the elements from which it derives its sustenance and support.

There can be no absolutely spontaneous development. All things are doubtless active, for nothing exists except in so far as it is an active force of some sort; but only God himself alone suffices for his own activity. All created things are dependent, have not their being in themselves, and are real only as they participate, through the creative act, of the Divine being. The germ can no more be developed than it could exist without God, and no more develop itself than it could create itself. What is called the law of development is in the germ; but that law or force can operate only in conjunction with another force or other forces. All development, as all growth, is by accretion or assimilation. The assimilating force is, if you will, in the germ, but the matter assimilated comes and must come from abroad. Every herdsman knows it, and knows that to rear his stock he must supply them with appropriate food; every husbandman knows it, and knows that to raise a crop of corn, be must plant the seed in a soil duly prepared, and which will supply the gases needed for its germination, growth, flowering, boiling, and ripening. In all created things, in all things not complete in themselves, in all save God, in whom there is no development possible, for He is, as say the schoolmen, most pure act, in whom there is no unactualized possibility, the same law holds good. Development is always the resultant of two factors, the one the thing itself, the other some external force co-operating with it, exciting it, and aiding it to act. Hence the *praemotio physica* of the Thomists, and the *praevenient* and *adjuvant* grace of the theologians, without which no one can begin the Christian life, and which must needs be supernatural when the end is supernatural. The principle of life in all orders is the same, and human activity no more suffices for itself in one order than in another.

Here is the reason why the savage tribe never rises to a civilized state without communion in some form with a people already civilized, and why there is no moral or intellectual development and progress without education and instruction, consequently without instructors and educators. Hence the value of tradition; and hence, as the first man could not instruct himself, Christian theologians, with a deeper philosophy than is dreamed of by the sciolists of the age, maintain that God himself was man's first teacher, or that he created Adam a full-grown man, with all his faculties developed, complete, and in full activity. Hence, too, the heathen mythologies, which always contain some elements of truth, however they may distort, mutilate, or travesty them, make the gods the first teachers of the human race, and ascribe to their instruction even the most simple and ordinary arts of everyday life. The gods teach men to plough, to plant, to reap, to work in iron, to erect a shelter from the storm, and to build a fire to warm them and to cook their food. The common sense, as well as the common traditions of mankind, refuses to accept the doctrine that men are developed without foreign aid, or progressive without divine assistance. Nature of herself can no more develop government than it can language. There can be no language without society, and no society without language. There can be no government without society, and no society without government of some sort.

But even if nature could spontaneously develop herself, she could never develop an institution that has the right to govern, for she has not herself that right. Nature is not God, has not created us, therefore has not the right of property in us. She is not and cannot be our sovereign. We belong not to her, nor does she belong to herself, for she is herself creature, and belongs to her Creator. Not being in herself sovereign, she cannot develop the right to govern, nor can she develop government as a fact, to say nothing of its right, for government, whether we speak of it as fact or as authority, is distinct from that which is governed; but natural developments are nature, and indistinguishable from her. The governor and the governed, the restrainer and the restrained, can never as such be identical. Self-government, taken strictly, is a contradiction in terms. When an individual is said to govern himself, he is never understood to govern himself in the sense in which he is governed. He by his reason and will governs or restrains his appetites and passions. It is man as spirit governing man as flesh, the spiritual mind governing the carnal mind.

Natural developments cannot in all cases be even allowed to take their own course without injury to nature herself. “Follow nature” is an unsafe maxim, if it means, leave nature to develop herself as she will, and follow thy natural inclinations. Nature is good, but inclinations are frequently bad. All our appetites and passions are given us for good, for a purpose useful and necessary to individual and social life, but they become morbid and injurious if indulged without restraint. Each has its special object, and naturally seeks it exclusively, and thus generates discord and war in the individual, which immediately find expression in society, and also in the state, if the state be a simple natural development. The Christian maxim, Deny thyself, is far better than the Epicurean maxim, Enjoy thyself, for there is no real enjoyment without self-denial. There is deep philosophy in Christian asceticism, as the Positivists themselves are aware, and even insist. But Christian asceticism aims not to destroy nature, as voluptuaries pretend, but to regulate, direct, and restrain its abnormal developments for its own good. It forces nature in her developments to submit to a law which is not in her, but above her. The Positivists pretend that this asceticism is itself a natural development, but that cannot be a natural development which directs, controls, and restrains natural development.

The Positivists confound nature at one time with the law of nature, and at another the law of nature with nature herself, and take what is called the natural law to be a natural development. Here is their mistake, as it is the mistake of all who accept naturalistic theories. Society, no doubt, is authorized by the law of nature to institute and maintain government. But the law of nature is not a natural development, nor is it in nature, or any part of nature. It is not a natural force which operates in nature, and which is the developing principle of nature. Do they say reason is natural, and the law of nature is only reason? This is not precisely the fact. The natural law is law proper, and is reason only in the sense that reason includes both intellect and will, and nobody can pretend that nature in her spontaneous developments acts from intelligence and volition. Reason, as the faculty of knowing, is subjective and natural; but in the sense in which it is coincident with the natural law, it is neither subjective nor natural, but objective and divine, and is God affirming himself and promulgating his law to his creature, man. It is, at least, an immediate participation of the divine by which He reveals himself and His will to the human understanding, and is not natural, but supernatural, in the sense that God himself is supernatural. This is wherefore reason is law, and every man is bound to submit or conform to reason.

That legitimate governments are instituted under the natural law is frankly conceded, but this is by no means the concession of government as a natural development. The reason and will of which the natural law is the expression are the reason and will of God. The natural law is the divine law as much as the revealed law itself, and equally obligatory. It is not a natural force developing itself in nature, like the law of generation, for instance, and therefore proceeding from God as first cause, but it proceeds from God as final cause, and is, therefore, theological, and strictly a moral law, founding moral rights and duties. Of course, all morality and all legitimate government rest on this law, or, if you will, originate in it. But not therefore in nature, but in the Author of nature. The authority is not the authority of nature, but of Him who holds nature in the hollow of His hand.

V. In the seventeenth century a class of political writers who very well understood that no creature, no man, no number of men, not even, nature herself, can be inherently sovereign, defended the opinion that governments are founded, constituted, and clothed with their authority by the direct and express appointment of God himself. They denied that rulers hold their power from the nation; that, however oppressive may be their rule, that they are justiciable by any human tribunal, or that power, except by the direct judgment of God, is amissible. Their doctrine is known in history as the doctrine of "the divine right of kings, and passive obedience." All power, says St. Paul, is from God, and the powers that be are ordained of God, and to resist them is to resist the ordination of God. They must be obeyed for conscience' sake.

It would, perhaps, be rash to say that this doctrine had never been broached before the seventeenth century, but it received in that century, and chiefly in England, its fullest and most systematic developments. It was patronized by the Anglican divines, asserted by James I of England, and lost the Stuarts the crown of three kingdoms. It crossed the Channel, into France, where it found a few hesitating and stammering defenders among Catholics, under Louis XIV, but it has never been very generally held, though it has had able and zealous supporters. In England it was opposed by all the Presbyterians, Puritans, Independents, and Republicans, and was forgotten or abandoned by the Anglican divines themselves in the Revolution of 1688, that expelled James II and crowned William and Mary. It was ably refuted by the Jesuit Suarez in his reply to a *Remonstrance for the Divine Right of Kings* by the James I; and a Spanish monk who had asserted it in Madrid, under Philip II, was compelled by the Inquisition to retract it publicly in the place where he had asserted it. All republicans reject it, and the Church has never sanctioned it. The Sovereign Pontiffs have claimed and exercised the right to deprive princes of their principality, and to absolve their subjects from the oath of fidelity. Whether the Popes rightly claimed and exercised that power is not now the question; but their having claimed and exercised it proves that the Church does not admit the inamissibility of power and passive obedience; for the action of the Pope was judicial, not legislative. The Pope has never claimed the right to depose a prince till by his own act he has, under the moral law or the constitution of his state, forfeited his power, nor to absolve subjects from their allegiance till their oath, according to its true intent and meaning, has ceased to bind. If the Church has always asserted with the Apostle there is no power but from God—*non est potestas nisi a Deo*—she has always through her doctors maintained that it is a trust to be exercised for the public good, and is forfeited when persistently exercised in a contrary sense. St. Augustine, St. Thomas, and Suarez all maintain that unjust laws are violences rather than laws, and do not oblige, except in charity or prudence, and that the republic may change its magistrates, and even its constitution, if it sees proper to do so.

That God, as universal Creator, is Sovereign Lord and proprietor of all created things or existences, visible or invisible, is certain; for the maker has the absolute right to the thing made; it is his, and he may do with it as he will. As he is sole creator, he alone hath dominion; and as he is absolute creator, he has absolute dominion over all the things which he has made. The guaranty against oppression is his own essential nature, is in the plenitude of his own being, which is the plenitude of wisdom and goodness. He cannot contradict himself, be other than he is, or act otherwise than according to his own essential nature. As he is, in his own eternal and immutable essence, supreme reason and supreme good, his dominion must always in its exercise be supremely good and supremely reasonable, therefore supremely just and equitable. From him certainly is all power; he is unquestionably King of kings, and Lord of lords. By him kings reign and magistrates decree just things. He may, at his will, set up or pull down kings, rear or overwhelm empires, foster the infant colony, and make desolate the populous city. All this is unquestionably true, and a simple dictate of reason common to all men. But in what sense is it true? Is it true in a supernatural sense? Or is it true only in the sense that it is true that by him we breathe, perform any or all of our natural functions, and in him live, and move, and have our being?

Viewed in their first cause, all things are the immediate creation of God, and are supernatural, and from the point of view of the first cause the Scriptures usually speak, for the great purpose and paramount object of the sacred writers, as of religion itself, is to make prominent the fact that God is universal creator, and supreme governor, and therefore the first and final cause of all things. But God creates second causes, or substantial existences, capable themselves of acting and producing effects in a secondary sense, and hence he is said to be *causa causarum*, cause of causes. What is done by these second causes or creatures is done eminently by him, for they exist only by his creative act, and produce only by virtue of his active presence, or effective concurrence. What he does through them or through their agency is done by him, not immediately, but mediately, and is said to be done naturally, as what he does immediately is said to be done supernaturally. Natural is what God does through second causes, which he creates; supernatural is that which he does by himself alone, without their intervention or agency. Sovereignty, or the right to govern, is in him, and he may at his will delegate it to men either mediately or immediately, by a direct and express appointment, or mediately through nature. In the absence of all facts proving its delegation direct and express, it must be assumed to be mediate, through second causes. The natural is always to be presumed, and the supernatural is to be admitted only on conclusive proof.

The people of Israel had a supernatural vocation, and they received their law, embracing their religious and civil constitution and their ritual directly from God at the hand of Moses, and various individuals from time to time appear to have been specially called to be their judges, rulers, or kings. Saul was so called, and so was David. David and his line appear, also, to have been called not only to supplant Saul and his line, but to have been supernaturally invested with the kingdom forever; but it does not appear that the royal power with which David and his line were invested was inamissible. They lost it in the Babylonish captivity, and never afterwards recovered it. The Asmonean princes were of another line, and when our Lord came the sceptre was in the hands of Herod, an Idumean or Edomite. The promise made, to David and his house is generally held by Christian commentators to have received its fulfilment in the everlasting spiritual royalty of the Messiah, sprung through Mary from David's line.

The Christian Church is supernaturally constituted and supernaturally governed, but the persons selected to exercise powers supernaturally defined, from the Sovereign Pontiff down to the humblest parish priest are selected and inducted into office through human agency. The Gentiles very generally claimed to have received their laws from the gods, but it does not appear, save in exceptional cases, that they claimed that their princes were designated and held their powers by the direct and express appointment of the god. Save in the case of the Jews, and that of the Church, there is no evidence that any particular government exists or ever has existed by direct or express appointment, or otherwise than by the action of the Creator through second causes, or what is called his ordinary providence. Except David and his line, there is no evidence of the express grant by the Divine

Sovereign to any individual or family, class or caste of the government of any nation or country. Even those Christian princes who professed to reign "by the grace of God," never claimed that they received their principalities from God otherwise than through his ordinary providence, and meant by it little more than an acknowledgment of their dependence on him, their obligation to use their power according to his law and their accountability to him for the use they make of it.

The doctrine is not favorable to human liberty, for it recognizes no rights of man in face of civil society. It consecrates tyranny, and makes God the accomplice of the tyrant, if we suppose all governments have actually existed by his express appointment. It puts the king in the place of God, and requires us to worship in him the immediate representative of the Divine Being. Power is irresponsible and inamissible, and however it may be abused, or however corrupt and oppressive may be its exercise, there is no human redress. Resistance to power is resistance to God. There is nothing for the people but passive obedience and unreserved submission. The doctrine, in fact, denies all *human* government, and allows the people no voice in the management of their own affairs, and gives no place for human activity. It stands opposed to all republicanism, and makes power an hereditary and indefeasible right, not a trust which he who holds it may forfeit, and of which he may be deprived if he abuses it.

Chapter VII: Constitution of Government

The Constitution is twofold: the constitution of the state or nation, and the constitution of the government. The constitution of the government is, or is held to be, the work of the nation itself; the constitution of the state, or the people of the state, is, in its origin at least, providential, given by God himself, operating through historical events or natural causes. The one originates in law, the other in historical fact. The nation must exist, and exist as a political community, before it can give itself a constitution; and no state, any more than an individual, can exist without a constitution of some sort.

The distinction between the providential constitution of the people and the constitution of the government, is not always made. The illustrious Count de Maistre, one of the ablest political philosophers who wrote in the last century, or the first quarter of the present, in his work on the *Generative Principle of Political Constitutions*, maintains that constitutions are generated, not made, and excludes all human agency from their formation and growth. Disgusted with French Jacobinism, from which he and his kin and country had suffered so much, and deeply wedded to monarchy in both church and state, he had the temerity to maintain that God creates expressly royal families for the government of nations, and that it is idle for a nation to expect a good government without a king who has descended from one of those divinely created royal families. It was with some such thought, most likely, that a French journalist, writing home from the United States, congratulated the American people on having a Bonaparte in their army, so that when their democracy failed, as in a few years it was sure to do, they would have a descendant of a royal house to be their king or emperor. Alas! the Bonaparte has left us, and besides, he was not the descendant of a royal house, and was, like the present Emperor of the French, a decided *parvenu*. Still, the Emperor of the French, if only a *parvenu*, bears himself right imperially among sovereigns, and has no peer among any of the descendants of the old royal families of Europe.

There is a truth, however, in De Maistre's doctrine that constitutions are generated, or developed, not created *de novo*, or made all at once. But nothing is more true than that a nation can alter its constitution by its own deliberate and voluntary action, and many nations have done so, and sometimes for the better, as well as for the worse. If the constitution once given is fixed and unalterable, it must be wholly divine, and contain no human element, and the people have and can have no hand in their own government—the fundamental objection to the theocratic constitution of society. To assume it is to transfer to civil society, founded by the ordinary providence of God, the constitution of the church, founded by his gracious or supernatural providence, and to maintain that the divine sovereignty governs in civil society immediately and supernaturally, as in the spiritual society. But such is not the fact. God governs the nation by the nation itself, through its own reason and free-will. De Maistre is right only as to the constitution the nation starts with, and as to the control which that constitution necessarily exerts over the constitutional changes the nation can successfully introduce.

The disciples of Jean-Jacques Rousseau recognize no providential constitution, and call the written instrument drawn up by a convention of sovereign individuals the constitution, and the only constitution, both of the people and the government. Prior to its adoption there is no government, no state, no political community or authority. Antecedently to it the people are an inorganic mass, simply individuals, without any political or national solidarity. These individuals, they suppose, come together in their own native right and might, organize themselves into a political community, give themselves a constitution, and draw up and vote rules for their government, as a number of individuals might meet in a public hall and resolve themselves into a temperance society or a debating club. This might do very well if the state were, like the temperance society or debating club, a simple voluntary association, which men are free to join or not as they please, and which they are bound to obey no farther and no longer than suits their convenience. But the state is a power, a sovereignty; speaks to all within its jurisdiction with an imperative voice; commands, and may use physical force to compel obedience, when not voluntarily yielded. Men are born its subjects, and no one can withdraw from it without its express or tacit permission, unless for causes that would justify resistance to its authority. The right of subjects to denationalize or expatriate themselves, except to escape a tyranny or an oppression which would forfeit the rights of power and warrant forcible resistance to it, does not exist, any more than the right of foreigners to become citizens, unless by the consent and authorization of the sovereign; for the citizen or subject belongs to the state, and is bound to it.

The solidarity of the individuals composing the population of a territory or country under one political head is a truth; but "the solidarity of peoples," irrespective of the government or political authority of their respective countries, so eloquently preached a few years since by the Hungarian Kossuth, is not only a falsehood, but a falsehood destructive of all government and of all political organization. Kossuth's doctrine supposes the people, or the populations of all countries, are, irrespective of their governments, bound together *in solido*, each for all and all for each, and therefore not only free, but bound, wherever they find a population struggling nominally for liberty against its government, to rush with arms in their hands to its assistance—a doctrine clearly incompatible with any recognition of political authority or territorial rights. Peoples or nations commune with each other only through the national authorities, and when the state proclaims neutrality or non-intervention, all its subjects are bound to be neutral, and to abstain from all intervention on either side. There may be, and indeed there is, a solidarity, more or less distinctly recognized, of Christian nations, but of the populations with and through their governments, not without them. Still more strict is the solidarity of all the individuals of one and the same nation. These are all bound together, all for each and each for all. The individual is born into society and under the government, and without the authority of the government, which represents all and each, he cannot release himself from his obligations. The state is then by no means a voluntary association. Every one born or adopted into it is bound to it, and cannot without its permission withdraw from it, unless, as just said, it is manifest that he can have under it no protection for his natural rights as a man, more especially for his rights of conscience. This is Vattel's doctrine, and the dictate of common sense.

The constitution drawn up, ordained, and established by a nation for itself is a law—the organic or fundamental law, if you will, but a law, and is and must be the act of the sovereign power. That sovereign power must exist before it can act, and it cannot exist, if vested in the people or nation, without a constitution, or without some sort of political organization of the people or nation. There must, then, be for every state or nation a constitution anterior to the constitution which the nation gives itself, and from which the one it gives itself derives all its vitality and legal force.

Logic and historical facts are here, as elsewhere, coincident, for creation and providence are simply the expression of the Supreme Logic, the Logos, by whom all things are made. Nations have originated in various ways, but history records no instance of a nation existing as an inorganic mass organizing itself into a political community. Every nation, at its first appearance above the horizon, is found to have an organization of some sort. This is evident from the only ways in which history shows us nations originating. These ways are: 1. The union of families in the tribe. 2. The union of tribes in the nation. 3. The migration of families, tribes, or nations in search of new settlements. 4. Colonization, military, agricultural, commercial, industrial, religious, or penal. 5. War and conquest. 6. The revolt, separation, and independence of provinces. 7. The intermingling of the conquerors and conquered, and by amalgamation forming a new people. These are all the ways known to history, and in none of these ways does a people, absolutely destitute of all organization, constitute itself a state, and institute and carry on civil government.

The family, the tribe, the colony are, if incomplete, yet incipient states, or inchoate nations, with an organization, individuality, and a center of social life of their own. The families and tribes that migrate in search of new settlements carry with them their family and tribal organizations, and retain it for a long time. The Celtic tribes retained it in Gaul till broken up by the Roman conquest, under Caesar Augustus; in Ireland, till the middle of the seventeenth century; and in Scotland, till the middle of the eighteenth.

It subsists still in the *hordes* of Tartary, the Arabs of the Desert, and the Berbers or Kabyles of Africa.

Colonies, of whatever description, have been founded, if not by, at least under, the authority of the mother country, whose political constitution, laws, manners, and customs they carry with them. They receive from the parent state a political organization, which, though subordinate, yet constitutes them embryonic states, with a unity, individuality, and center of public life in themselves, and which, when they are detached and recognized as independent, render them complete states. War and conquest effect great national changes, but do not, strictly speaking, create new states. They simply extend and consolidate the power of the conquering state.

Provinces revolt and become independent states or nations, but only when they have previously existed as such, and have retained the tradition of their old constitution and independence; or when the administration has erected them into real though dependent political communities. A portion of the people of a state not so erected or organized, that has in no sense had a distinct political existence of its own, has never separated from the national body and formed a new and independent nation. It cannot revolt; it may rise up against the government, and either revolutionize and take possession of the state, or be put down by the government as an insurrection. The amalgamation of the conquering and the conquered forms a new people, and modifies the institutions of both, but does not necessarily form a new nation or political community. The English of today are very different from both the Normans and the Saxons, or Dano-Saxons, of the time of Richard Coeur de Lion, but they constitute the same state or political community. England is still England.

The Roman empire, conquered by the Northern barbarians, has been cut up into several separate and independent nations, but because its several provinces had, prior to their conquest by the Roman arms, been independent nations or tribes, and more especially because the conquerors themselves were divided into several distinct nations or confederacies. If the barbarians had been united in a single nation or state, the Roman empire most likely would have changed masters, indeed, but have retained its unity and its constitution, for the Germanic nations that finally seated themselves on its ruins had no wish to destroy its name or nationality, for they were themselves more than half Romanized before conquering Rome. But the new nations into which the empire has been divided have never been, at any moment, without political or governmental organization, continued from the constitution of the conquering tribe or nation, modified more or less by what was retained from the empire.

It is not pretended that the constitutions of states cannot be altered, or that every people starts with a constitution fully developed, as would seem to be the doctrine of De Maistre. The constitution of the family is rather economical than political, and the tribe is far from being a fully developed state. Strictly speaking, the state, the modern equivalent for the city of the Greeks and Romans, was not fully formed till men began to build and live in cities, and became fixed to a national territory. But in the first place, the eldest born of the human race, we are told, built a city, and even in cities we find traces of the family and tribal organization long after their municipal existence—in Athens down to the Macedonian conquest, and in Rome down to the establishment of the Empire; and, in the second place, the pastoral nations, though they have not precisely the city or state organization, yet have a national organization, and obey a national authority. Strictly speaking, no pastoral nation has a civil or political constitution, but they have what in our modern tongues can be expressed by no other term. The feudal *régime*, which was in full vigor even in Europe from the tenth to the close of the fourteenth century, had nothing to do with cities, and really recognized no state proper; yet who hesitates to speak of it as a civil or political system, though a very imperfect one?

The civil order, as it now exists, was not fully developed in the early ages. For a long time the national organizations bore unmistakable traces of having been developed from the patriarchal, and modeled from the family or tribe, as they do still in all the non-Christian world. Religion itself, before the Incarnation, bore traces of the same organization. Even with the Jews, religion was transmitted and diffused, not as under Christianity by conversion, but by natural generation or family adoption. With all the Gentile tribes or nations, it was the same. At first the father was both priest and king, and when the two offices were separated, the priests formed a distinct and hereditary class or caste, rejected by Christianity, which, as we have seen, admits priests only after the order of Melchisedech. The Jews had the synagogue, and preserved the primitive revelation in its purity and integrity; but the Greeks and Romans, more fully than any other ancient nations, preserved or developed the political order that best conforms to the Christian religion; and Christianity, it is worthy of remark, followed in the track of the Roman armies, and it gains a permanent establishment only where was planted, or where it is able to plant, the Graeco-Roman civilization. The

Graeco-Roman republics were hardly less a schoolmaster to bring the world to Christ in the civil order, than the Jewish nation was to bring it to Him in the spiritual order, or in faith and worship. In the Christian order nothing is by hereditary descent, but everything is by election of grace. The Christian dispensation is teleological, palingenesiac, and the whole order, prior to the Incarnation, was initial, genesiac, and continued by natural generation, as it is still in all nations and tribes outside of Christendom. No non-Christian people is a civilized people, and, indeed, the human race seems not anywhere, prior to the Incarnation, to have attained to its majority: and it is, perhaps, because the race were not prepared for it, that the Word was not sooner incarnated. He came only in the fullness of time, when the world was ready to receive him.

The providential constitution is, in fact, that with which the nation is born, and is, as long as the nation exists, the real living and efficient constitution of the state. It is the source of the vitality of the state, that which controls or governs its action, and determines its destiny. The constitution which a nation is said to give itself, is never the constitution of the state, but is the law ordained by the state for the government instituted under it. Thomas Paine would admit nothing to be the constitution but a written document which he could fold up and put in his pocket, or file away in a pigeon-hole. The Abbé Sieyès pronounced politics a science which he had finished, and he was ready to turn you out constitutions to order, with no other defect than that they had, as Carlyle wittily says, no feet, and could not go. Many in the last century, and some, perhaps, in the present, for folly as well as wisdom has her heirs, confounded the written instrument with the constitution itself. No constitution can be written on paper or engrossed on parchment. What the convention may agree upon, draw up, and the people ratify by their votes, is no constitution, for it is extrinsic to the nation, not inherent and living in it—is, at best, legislative instead of constitutive. The famous Magna Charta drawn up by Cardinal Langton, and wrung from John Lackland by the English barons at Runnymede, was no constitution of England till long after the date of its concession, and even then was no constitution of the state, but a set of restrictions on power. The constitution is the intrinsic or inherent and actual constitution of the people or political community itself; that which makes the nation what it is, and distinguishes it from every other nation, and varies as nations themselves vary from one another.

The constitution of the state is not a theory, nor is it drawn up and established in accordance with any preconceived theory. What is theoretic in a constitution is unreal. The constitutions conceived by philosophers in their closets are constitutions only of Utopia or Dreamland. This world is not governed by abstractions, for abstractions are nullities. Only the concrete is real, and only the real or actual has vitality or force. The French people adopted constitution after constitution of the most approved pattern, and amid bonfires, beating of drums, sound of trumpets, roar of musketry, and thunder of artillery, swore, no doubt, sincerely as well as enthusiastically, to observe them, but all to no effect; for they had no authority for the nation, no hold on its affections, and formed no element of its life. The English are great constitution-mongers—for other nations. They fancy that a constitution fashioned after their own will fit any nation that can be persuaded, wheedled, or bullied into trying it on; but, unhappily, all that have tried it on have found it only an embarrassment or encumbrance. The doctor might as well attempt to give an individual a new constitution, or the constitution of another man, as the statesman to give a nation any other constitution than that which it has, and with which it is born.

The whole history of Europe, since the fall of the Roman empire, proves this thesis. The barbarian conquest of Rome introduced into the nations founded on the site of the empire, a double constitution—the barbaric and the civil—the Germanic and the Roman in the West, and the Tartaric or Turkish and the Graeco-Roman in the East. The key to all modern history is in the mutual struggles of these two constitutions and the interests respectively associated with them, which created two societies on the same territory, and, for the most part, under the same national denomination. The barbaric was the constitution of the conquerors; they had the power, the government, rank, wealth, and fashion, were reinforced down to the tenth century by fresh hordes of barbarians, and had even brought the external ecclesiastical society to a very great extent into harmony with itself. The Pope became a feudal sovereign, and the bishops and mitred abbots feudal princes and barons. Yet, after eight hundred years of fierce struggle, the Roman constitution got the upper hand, and the barbaric constitution, as far as it could not be assimilated to the Roman, was eliminated. The original Empire of the West is now as thoroughly Roman in its constitution, its laws, and its civilization, as it ever was under any of its Christian emperors before the barbarian conquest.

The same process is going on in the East, though it has not advanced so far, having begun there several centuries later, and the Graeco-Roman constitution was far feebler there than in the West at the epoch of the conquest. The Germanic tribes that conquered the West had long had close relations with the empire, had served as its allies, and even in its armies, and were partially Romanized. Most of their chiefs had received a Roman culture; and their early conversion to the Christian faith facilitated the revival and permanence of the old Roman constitution. In the East it was different. The conquerors had no touch of Roman civilization, and, followers of the Prophet, they were animated with an intense hatred, which, after the conquest, was changed into a superb contempt, of Christians and Romans. They had their civil constitution in the Koran; and the Koran, in its principles, doctrines, and spirit, is exclusive and profoundly intolerant. The Graeco-Roman constitution was always much weaker in the East, and had far greater obstacles to overcome there than in the West; yet it has survived the shock of the conquest. Throughout the limits of the ancient Empire of the East, the barbaric constitution has received and is daily receiving rude blows, and, but as reenforced by barbarians lying outside of the boundaries of that empire, would be no longer able to sustain itself. The Greek or Christian populations of the empire are no longer in danger of being exterminated or absorbed by the Mohammedan state or population. They are the only living and progressive people of the Ottoman Empire, and their complete success in absorbing or expelling the Turk is only a question of time. They will, in all present probability, reestablish a Christian and Roman East in much less time from the fall of Constantinople in 1453, than it took the West from the fall of Rome in 476 to put an end to the feudal or barbaric constitution founded by its Germanic invaders.

Indeed, the Roman constitution, laws, and civilization not only gain the mastery in the nations seated within the limits of the old Roman Empire, but extend their power throughout the whole civilized world. The Graeco-Roman civilization is, in fact, the only civilization now recognized, and nations are accounted civilized only in proportion as they are Romanized and Christianized. The Roman law, as found in the Institutes, Pandects, and Novellae of Justinian, or the *Corpus Legis Civilis*, is the basis of the law and jurisprudence of all Christendom. The Graeco-Roman civilization, called not improperly Christian civilization, is the only progressive civilization. The old feudal system remains in England little more than an empty name. The king is only the first magistrate of the kingdom, and the House of Lords is only an hereditary senate. Austria is hard at work in the Roman direction, and finds her chief obstacle to success in Hungary, with the Magyars whose feudalism retains almost the full vigor of the Middle Ages. Russia is moving in the same direction; and Prussia and the smaller Germanic states obey the same impulse. Indeed, Rome has survived the conquest—has conquered her conquerors, and now invades every region from which they came. The Roman Empire may be said to be acknowledged and obeyed in lands lying far beyond the farthest limits reached by the Roman eagles, and to be more truly the mistress of the world than under Augustus, Trajan, or the Antonines. Nothing can stand before the Christian and Romanized nations, and all pagandom and Mohammedom combined are too weak to resist their onward march.

All modern European revolutions result only in reviving the Roman Empire, whatever the motives, interests, passions, or theories that initiate them. The French Revolution of the last century and that of the present prove it. France, let people say what they will, stands at the head of the European civilized world, and displays *en grand* all its good and all its bad tendencies. When she moves, Europe moves; when she has a vertigo, all European nations are dizzy; when she recovers her health, her equilibrium, and good sense, others become sedate, steady, and reasonable. She is the head, nay, rather, the heart of Christendom—the head is at Rome—through which circulates the pure and impure blood of the nations. It is in vain Great Britain, Germany, or Russia disputes with her the hegemony of European civilization. They are forced to yield to her at last, to be content to revolve around her as the center of the political system that masters them. The reason is, France is more completely and sincerely Roman than any other nation. The revolutions that have shaken the world have resulted in eliminating the barbaric elements she had retained, and clearing away all obstacles to the complete triumph of Imperial Rome. Napoleon III is for France what Augustus was for Rome. The revolutions in Spain and Italy have only swept away the relics of the barbaric constitution, and aided the revival of Roman imperialism. In no country do the revolutionists succeed in establishing their own theories; Caesar remains master of the field. Even in the United States, a revolution undertaken in favor of the barbaric system has resulted in the destruction of what remained of that system—in sweeping away the last relics of disintegrating feudalism, and in the complete establishment of the Graeco-Roman system, with important improvements, in the New World.

The Roman system is republican, in the broad sense of the term, because under it power is never an estate, never the private for the public good. As it existed under the Caesars, and is revived in modern times, whether under the imperial or the democratic form, it, no doubt, tends to centralism, to the concentration of all the powers and forces of the state in one central government, from which all local authorities and institutions emanate. Wise men oppose it as affording no guaranties to individual liberty against the abuses of power. This it may not do, but the remedy is not in feudalism. The feudal lord holds his authority as an estate, and has over the people under him all the power of Caesar and all the rights of the proprietor. He, indeed, has a guaranty against his liege-lord, sometimes a more effective guaranty than his liege-lord has against him; but against his centralized power his vassals and serfs have only the guaranty that a slave has against his owner.

Feudalism is alike hostile to the freedom of public authority and of the people. It is essentially a disintegrating element in the nation. It breaks the unity and individuality of the state, embarrasses the sovereign, and guards against the abuse of public authority by overpowering and suppressing it. Every feudal lord is a more thorough despot in his own domain than Caesar ever was or could be in the empire; and the monarch, even if strong enough, is yet not competent to intervene between him and his people, any more than the General government in the United States was to intervene between the negro slave and his master. The great vassals of the crown singly, or, if not singly, in combination—and they could always combine in the interest of their order—were too strong for the king, or to be brought under any public authority, and could issue from their fortified castles and rob and plunder to their hearts' content, with none to call them to an account. Under the most thoroughly centralized government there is far more liberty for the people, and a far greater security for person and property, except in the case of the feudal nobles themselves, than was even dreamed of while the feudal *régime* was in full vigor. Nobles were themselves free, it is conceded, but not the people. The king was too weak, too restricted in his action by the feudal constitution to reach them, and the higher clergy were *ex officio* sovereigns, princes, barons, or feudal lords, and were led by their private interests to act with the feudal nobility, save when that nobility threatened the temporalities of the church. The only reliance, under God, left in feudal times to the poor people was in the lower ranks of the clergy, especially of the regular clergy. All the great German emperors in the twelfth and thirteenth centuries, who saw the evils of feudalism, and attempted to break it up and revive imperial Rome, became involved in quarrels with the chiefs of the religious society, and failed, because the interest of the Popes, as feudal sovereigns and Italian princes, and the interests of the dignified clergy, were for the time bound up with the feudal society, though their Roman culture and civilization made them at heart hostile to it. The student of history, however strong his filial affection towards the visible head of the church, cannot help admiring the grandeur of the political views of Frederic the Second, the greatest and last of the Hohenstaufen, or refrain from dropping a tear over his sad failure. He had great faults as a man, but he had rare genius as a statesman; and it is some consolation to know that he died a Christian death, in charity with all men, after having received the last sacraments of his religion.

The Popes, under the circumstances, were no doubt justified in the policy they pursued, for the Swabian emperors failed to respect the acknowledged rights of the church, and to remember their own incompetency in spirituals; but evidently their political views and aims were liberal, far-reaching, and worthy of admiration. Their success, if it could have been effected without lesion to the church, would have set Europe forward some two or three hundred years, and probably saved it from the schisms of the fourteenth and sixteenth centuries. But it is easy to be wise after the event. The fact is, that during the period when feudalism was in full vigor, the king was merely a shadow; the people found their only consolation in religion, and their chief protectors in the monks, who mingled with them, saw their sufferings, and sympathized with them, consoled them, carried their cause to the castle before the feudal lord and lady, and did, thank God, do something to keep alive religious sentiments and convictions in the bosom of the feudal society itself. Whatever opinions may be formed of the monastic orders in relation to the present, this much is certain, that they were the chief civilizers of Europe, and the chief agents in delivering European society from feudal barbarism.

The aristocracy have been claimed as the natural allies of the throne, but history proves them to be its natural enemies, whenever it cannot be used in their service, and kings do not consent to be their ministers and to do their bidding. A political aristocracy has at heart only the interests of its order, and pursues no line of policy but the extension or preservation of its privileges. Having little to gain and much to lose, it opposes every political change that would either strengthen the crown or elevate the people. The nobility in the French Revolution were the first to desert both the king and the kingdom, and kings have always found their readiest and firmest allies in the people. The people in Europe have no such bitter feelings towards royalty as they have towards the feudal nobility—for kings have never so grievously oppressed them. In Rome the patrician order opposed alike the emperor and the people, except when they, as chivalric nobles sometimes will do, turned courtiers or demagogues. They were the people of Rome and the provinces that sustained the emperors, and they were the emperors who sustained the people, and gave to the provincials the privileges of Roman citizens.

Guaranties against excessive centralism are certainly needed, but the statesman will not seek them in the feudal organization of society—in a political aristocracy, whether founded on birth or private wealth, nor in a privileged class of any sort. Better trust Caesar than Brutus, or even Cato. Nor will he seek them in the antagonism of interests intended to neutralize or balance each other, as in the English constitution. This was the great error of Mr. Calhoun. No man saw more clearly than Mr. Calhoun the utter worthlessness of simple paper constitutions, on which Mr. Jefferson placed such implicit reliance, or that the real constitution is in the state itself, in the manner in which the people themselves are organized; but his reliance was in constituting, as powers in the state, the several popular interests that exist, and pitting them against each other—the famous system of checks and balances of English states men. He was led to this, because be distrusted power, and was more intention guarding against its abuses than on providing for its free, vigorous, and healthy action, going on the principle that "that is the best government which governs least." But, if the opposing interests could be made to balance one another perfectly, the result would be an equilibrium, in which power would be brought to a stand-still; and if not, the stronger would succeed and swallow up all the rest. The theory of checks and balances is admirable if the object be to trammel power, and to have as little power in the government as possible; but it is a theory which is born from passions engendered by the struggle against despotism or arbitrary power, not from a calm and philosophical appreciation of government itself. The English have not succeeded in establishing their theory, for, after all, their constitution does not work so well as they pretend. The landed interest controls at one time, and the mercantile and manufacturing interest at another. They do not perfectly balance one another, and it is not difficult to see that the mercantile and manufacturing interest, combined with the moneyed interest, is henceforth to predominate. The aim of the real statesman is to organize all the interests and forces of the state dialectically, so that they shall unite to add to its strength, and work together harmoniously for the common good.

Chapter IX: The United States

Sovereignty, under God, inheres in the organic people, or the people as the republic; and every organic people fixed to the soil, and politically independent of every other people, is a sovereign people, and, in the modern sense, an independent sovereign nation.

Sovereign states may unite in an alliance, league, or confederation, and mutually agree to exercise their sovereign powers or a portion of them in common, through a common organ or agency; but in this agreement they part with none of their sovereignty, and each remains a sovereign state or nation as before. The common organ or agency created by the convention is no state, is no nation, has no inherent sovereignty, and derives all its vitality and force from the persisting sovereignty of the states severally that have united in creating it. The agreement no more affects the sovereignty of the several states entering into it, than does the appointment of an agent affect the rights and powers of the principal. The creature takes nothing from the Creator, exhausts not, lessens not his creative energy, and it is only by his retaining and continuously exerting his creative power that the creature continues to exist.

An independent state or nation may, with or without its consent, lose its sovereignty, but only by being merged in or subjected to another. Independent sovereign states cannot by convention, or mutual agreement, form themselves into a single sovereign state, or nation. The compact, or agreement, is made by sovereign states, and binds by virtue of the sovereign power of each of the contracting parties. To destroy that sovereign power would be to annul the compact, and render void the agreement. The agreement can be valid and binding only on condition that each of the contracting parties retains the sovereignty that rendered it competent to enter into the compact, and states that retain severally their sovereignty do not form a single sovereign state or nation. The states in convention cannot become a new and single sovereign state, unless they lose their several sovereignty, and merge it in the new sovereignty; but this they cannot do by agreement, because the moment the parties to the agreement cease to be sovereign, the agreement, on which alone depends the new sovereign state, is vacated, in like manner as a contract is vacated by the death of the contracting parties.

That a nation may voluntarily cede its sovereignty is frankly admitted, but it can cede it only to something or somebody actually existing, for to cede to nothing and not to cede is one and the same thing. They can part with their own sovereignty by merging themselves in another national existence, but not by merging themselves in nothing; and, till they have parted with their own sovereignty, the new sovereign state does not exist. A prince can abdicate his power, because by abdicating he simply gives back to the people the trust he had received from them; but a nation cannot, save by merging itself in another. An independent state not merged in another, or that is not subject to another, cannot cease to be a sovereign nation, even if it would.

That no sovereign state can be formed by agreement or compact has already been shown in the refutation of the theory of the origin of government in convention, or the so-called social compact. Sovereign states are as unable to form themselves into a single sovereign state by mutual compact as are the sovereign individuals imagined by Rousseau. The convention, either of sovereign states or of sovereign individuals, with the best will in the world, can form only a compact or agreement between sovereigns, and an agreement or compact, whatever its terms or conditions, is only an alliance, a league, or a confederation, which no one can pretend is a sovereign state, nation, or republic.

The question, then, whether the United States are a single sovereign state or nation, or a confederacy of independent sovereign states depends on the question whether the American people originally existed as one people or as several independent states. Mr. Jefferson maintains that before the convention of 1787 they existed as several independent sovereign states, but that since that convention, or the ratification of the constitution it proposed, they exist as one political people in regard to foreign nations, and several sovereign states in regard to their internal and domestic relations. Mr. Webster concedes that originally the States existed as severally sovereign states, but contends that by ratifying the constitution they have been made one sovereign political people, state, or nation, and that the General government is a supreme national government, though with a reservation in favor of State rights. But both are wrong. If the several States of the Union were severally sovereign states when they met in the convention, they are so now; and the constitution is only an agreement or compact between sovereigns, and the United States are, as Mr. Calhoun maintained, only a confederation of sovereign states, and not a single state or one political community.

But if the sovereignty persists in the States severally, any State, saving its faith, may whenever it chooses to do so, withdraw from the Union, absolve its subjects from all obligation to the Federal authorities, and make it treason in them to adhere to the Federal government. Secession is, then, an incontestable right; not a right held under the constitution or derived from the convention but a right held prior to it, independently of it, inherent in the State sovereignty, and inseparable from it. The State is bound by the constitution of the Union only while she is in it, and is one of the States united. In ratifying the constitution she did not part with her sovereignty, or with any portion of it, any more than France has parted with her sovereignty, and ceased to be an independent sovereign nation, by vesting the imperial power in Napoleon III. and his legitimate heirs male. The principal parts not with his power to his agent, for the agent is an agent only by virtue of the continued power of the principal. Napoleon is emperor by the will of the French people, and governs only by the authority of the French nation, which is as competent to revoke the powers it has conferred on him, when it judges proper, as it was to confer them. The Union exists and governs, if the States are sovereign, only by the will of the State, and she is as competent to revoke the powers she has delegated as she was to delegate them. The, Union, as far as she is concerned, is her creation, and what she is competent to make she is competent to unmake.

In seceding or withdrawing from the Union a State may act very unwisely, very much against her own interests and the interests of the other members of the confederacy; but, if sovereign, she in doing so only exercises her unquestionable right. The other members may regret her action, both for her sake and their own, but they cannot accuse her or her citizens of disloyalty in seceding, nor of rebellion, if in obedience to her authority they defend their independence by force of arms against the Union. Neither she nor they, on the supposition, ever owed allegiance to the Union. Allegiance is due from the citizen to the sovereign state, but never from a sovereign state or from its citizens to any other sovereign state. While the State is in the Union the citizen owes obedience to the United States, but only because his State has, in ratifying the Federal constitution, enacted that it and all laws and treaties made under it shall be law within her territory. The repeal by the State of the act of ratification releases the citizen from the obligation even of obedience, and renders it criminal for him to yield it without her permission.

It avails nothing, on the hypothesis of the sovereignty of the States as distinguished from that of the United States, to appeal to the language or provisions of the Federal constitution. That constitutes the government, not the state or the sovereign. It is ordained by the sovereign, and if the States were severally independent and sovereign states, that sovereign is the States severally, not the States united. The constitution is law for the citizens of a State only so long as the State remains one of the United States. No matter, then, how clear and express the language, or stringent the provisions of the constitution, they bind only the citizens of the States that enact the constitution. The written constitution is simply a compact, and obliges only while the compact is continued by the States, each for itself. The sovereignty of the United States as a single or political people must be established before anything in the constitution can be adduced as denying the right of secession.

That this doctrine would deprive the General government of all right to enforce the laws of the Union on a State that secedes, or the citizens thereof, is no doubt true; that it would weaken the central power and make the Union a simple voluntary association of states, no better than a rope of sand, is no less true; but what then? It is simply saying that a confederation is inferior to a nation, and that a federal government lacks many of the advantages of a national government. Confederacies are always weak in the center, always lack unity, and are liable to be dissolved by the influence of local passions, prejudices, and interests. But if the United States are a confederation of states or nations, not a single nation or sovereign state, then there is no remedy.

If the Anglo-American colonies, when their independence of Great Britain was achieved and acknowledged, were severally sovereign states, it has never since been in their power to unite and form a single sovereign state, or to form themselves into one indivisible sovereign nation. They could unite only by mutual agreement, which gives only a confederation, in which each retains its own sovereignty, as two individuals, however closely united, retain each his own individuality. No sovereignty is of conventional origin, and none can emerge from the convention that did not enter it. Either the states are one sovereign people or they are not. If they are not, it is undoubtedly a great disadvantage; but a disadvantage that must be accepted, and submitted to without a murmur.

Whether the United States are one sovereign people or only a confederation is a question of very grave importance. If they are only a confederation of states—and if they ever were severally sovereign states, only a confederation they certainly are—state secession is an inalienable right, and the government has had no right to make war on the secessionists as rebels, or to treat them, when their military power is broken, as traitors, or disloyal persons. The honor of the government, and of the people who have sustained it, is then deeply compromised.

What then is the fact? Are the United States politically one people, nation, state, or republic, or are they simply independent sovereign states united in close and intimate alliance, league, or federation, by a mutual pact or agreement? Were the people of the United States who ordained and established the written constitution one people, or were they not? If they were not before ordaining and establishing the government, they are not now; for the adoption of the constitution did not and could not make them one. Whether they are one or many is then simply a question of fact, to be decided by the facts in the case, not by the theories of American statesmen, the opinion of jurists, or even by constitutional law itself. The old Articles of Confederation and the later Constitution can serve here only as historical documents. Constitutions and laws presuppose the existence of a national sovereign from which they emanate, and that ordains them, for they are the formal expression of a sovereign will. The nation must exist as an historical fact, prior to the possession or exercise of sovereign power, prior to the existence of written Constitutions and laws of any kind, and its existence must be established before they can be recognized as having any legal force or vitality.

The existence of any nation, as an independent sovereign nation, is a purely historical fact, for its right to exist as such is in the simple fact that it does so exist. A nation *de facto* is a nation *de jure*, and when we have ascertained the fact, we have ascertained the right. There is no right in the case separate from the fact—only the fact must be really a fact. A people hitherto a part of another people, or subject to another sovereign, is not in fact a nation, because they have declared themselves independent, and have organized a government, and are engaged in what promises to be a successful struggle for independence. The struggle must be practically over; the former sovereign must have practically abandoned the effort to reduce them to submission, or to bring them back under his authority, and if he continues it, does it as a matter of mere form; the postulant must have proved his ability to maintain civil government, and to fulfill within and without the obligations which attach to every civilized nation, before it can be recognized as an independent sovereign nation; because before it is not a fact that it is a sovereign nation. The prior sovereign, when no longer willing or able to vindicate his right, has lost it, and no one is any longer bound to respect it, for humanity demands not martyrs to lost causes.

This doctrine may seem harsh, and untenable even, to those sickly philanthropists who are always weeping over extinct or oppressed nationalities; but nationality in modern civilization is a fact, not a right antecedent to the fact. The repugnance felt to this assertion arises chiefly from using the word *nation* sometimes in a strictly political sense, and sometimes in its original sense of tribe, and understanding by it not simply the body politic, but a certain relation of origin, family, kindred, blood, or race. But God has made of one blood, or race, all the nations of men; and, besides, no political rights are founded by the law of nature on relations of blood, kindred, or family. Under the patriarchal or tribal system, and, to some extent, under feudalism, these relations form the basis of government, but they are economical relations rather than civil or political, and, under Christian and modern civilization, are restricted to the household, are domestic relations, and enter not the state or body politic, except by way of reminiscence or abuse. They are protected by the state, but do not found or constitute it. The vicissitudes of time, the revolutions of states and empires, migration, conquest, and intermixture of families and races, have rendered it impracticable, even if it were desirable, to distribute people into nations according to their relations of blood or descent.

There is no civilized nation now existing that has been developed from a common ancestor this side of Adam, and the most mixed are the most civilized. The nearer a nation approaches to a primitive people of pure unmixed blood, the farther removed it is from civilization. All civilized nations are political nations, and are founded in the fact, not on rights antecedent to the fact. A hundred or more lost nationalities went to form the Roman empire, and who can tell us how many layers of crushed nationalities, superposed one upon another, serve for the foundation of the present French, English, Russian, Austrian, or Spanish nationalities? What other title to independence and sovereignty, than the fact, can you plead in behalf of any European nation? Everyone has absorbed and extinguished—no one can say how many—nationalities, that once had as good a right to be as it has, or can have. Whether those nationalities have been justly extinguished or not, is no question for the statesman; it is the secret of Providence. Failure in this world is not always a proof of wrong; nor success, of right. The good is sometimes overborne, and the bad sometimes triumphs; but it is consoling, and even just, to believe that the good oftener triumphs than the bad.

In the political order, the fact, under God, precedes the law. The nation holds not from the law, but the law holds from the nation. Doubtless the courts of every civilized nation recognize and apply both the law of nature and the law of nations, but only on the ground that they are included, or are presumed to be included, in the national law, or jurisprudence. Doubtless, too, the nation holds from God, under the law of nature, but only by virtue of the fact that it is a nation; and when it is a nation dependent on no other, it holds from God all the rights and powers of any independent sovereign nation. There is no right behind the fact needed to legalize the fact, or to put the nation that is in fact a nation in possession of full national rights. In the case of a new nation, or people, lately an integral part of another people, or subject to another people the right of the prior sovereign must be extinguished indeed, but the extinction of that right is necessary to complete the fact, which otherwise would be only an initial, inchoate fact, not a *fait accompli*. But that right ceases when its claimant, willingly or unwillingly, formally or virtually, abandons it; and he does so when he practically abandons the struggle, and shows no ability or intention of soon renewing it with any reasonable prospect of success.

The notion of right, independent of the fact as applied to sovereignty, is founded in error. Empty titles to states and kingdoms are of no validity. The sovereignty is, under God, in the nation and the title and the possession are inseparable. The title of the Palaeologi to the Roman Empire of the East, of the king of Sicily, the king of Sardinia, or the king of Spain—for they are all claimants—to the kingdom of Jerusalem founded by Godfrey and his crusaders, of the Stuarts to the thrones of England, Ireland, and Scotland, or of the Bourbons to the throne of France, are vacated and not worth the parchment on which they are engrossed. The contrary opinion, so generally entertained, belongs to barbarism, not to civilization. It is in modern society a relic of feudalism, which places the state in the government, and makes the government a private estate—a private, and not a public right—a right to govern the public, not a right to govern held from or by the public.

The proprietor may be dispossessed in fact of his estate by violence, by illegal or unjust means, without losing his right, and another may usurp it, occupy it, and possess it in fact without acquiring any right or legal title to it. The man who holds the legal title has the right to oust him and re-enter upon his estate whenever able to do so. Here, in the economical order, the fact and the right are distinguishable, and the actual occupant may be required to show his title-deeds. Holding sovereignty to be a private estate, the feudal lawyers very properly distinguish between governments *de facto* and governments *de jure*, and argue very logically that violent dispossession of a prince does not invalidate his title. But sovereignty, it has been shown, is not in the government, but in the state, and the state is inseparable from the public domain. The people organized and held by the domain or national territory, are under God the sovereign nation, and remain so as long as the nation subsists without subjection to another. The government, as distinguished from the state or nation, has only a delegated authority, governs only by a commission from the nation. The revocation of the commission vacates its title and extinguishes its rights. The nation is always sovereign, and every organic people fixed to the soil, and actually independent of every other, is a nation. There can then be no independent nation *de facto* that is not an independent nation *de jure*, nor *de jure* that is not *de facto*. The moment a people cease to be an independent nation in fact, they cease to be sovereign, and the moment they become in fact an independent nation, they are so of right. Hence in the political order the fact and the right are born and expire together; and when it is proved that a people, are in fact an independent nation, there is no question to be asked as to their right to be such nation.

In the case of the United States there is only the question of fact. If they are in fact one people they are so in right, whatever the opinions and theories of statesmen, or even the decisions of courts; for the courts hold from the national authority, and the theories and opinions of statesmen may be erroneous. Certain it is that the States in the American Union have never existed and acted as severally sovereign states. Prior to independence, they were colonies under the sovereignty of Great Britain, and since independence they have existed and acted only as states united. The colonists, before separation and independence, were British subjects, and whatever rights the colonies had they held by charter or concession from the British crown. The colonists never pretended to be other than British subjects, and the alleged ground of their complaint against the mother country was not that she had violated their natural rights as men, but their rights as British subjects—rights, as contended by the colonists, secured by the English constitution to all Englishmen or British subjects. The denial to them of these common rights of Englishmen they called tyranny, and they defended themselves in throwing off their allegiance to George III, on the ground that he had, in their regard, become a tyrant, and the tyranny of the prince absolves the subject from his allegiance.

In the Declaration of Independence they declared themselves independent states indeed, but not severally independent. The declaration was not made by the states severally, but by the states jointly, as the United States. They unitedly declared their independence; they carried on the war for independence, won it, and were acknowledged by foreign powers and by the mother country as the *United* States, not as severally independent sovereign states. Severally they have never exercised the full powers of sovereign states; they have had no flag—symbol of sovereignty—recognized by foreign powers, have made no foreign treaties, held no foreign relations, had no commerce foreign or interstate, coined no money, entered into no alliances or confederacies with foreign states or with one another, and in several respects have been more restricted in their powers in the Union than they were as British colonies.

Colonies are initial or inchoate states, and become complete states by declaring and winning their independence; and if the English colonies, now the United States, had separately declared and won their independence, they would unquestionably have become separately independent states, each invested by the law of nature with all the rights and powers of a sovereign nation. But they did not do this. They declared and won their independence jointly, and have since existed and exercised sovereignty only as states united, or the United States, that is, states sovereign in their union, but not in their separation. This is of itself decisive of the whole question.

But the colonists have not only never exercised the full powers of sovereignty save as citizens of states united, therefore as one people, but they were, so far as a people at all, one people even before independence. The colonies were all erected and endowed with their rights and powers by one and the same national authority, and the colonists were subjects of one and the same national sovereign. Mr. Quincy Adams, who almost alone among our prominent statesmen maintains the unity of the colonial people, adds indeed to their subjection to the same sovereign authority, community of origin, of language, manners, customs, and law. All these, except the last, or common law, may exist without national unity in the modern political sense of the term nation. The English common law was recognized by the colonial courts, and in force in all the colonies, not by virtue of colonial legislation, but by virtue of English authority, as expressed in English jurisprudence. The colonists were under the Common Law, because they were Englishmen, and subjects of the English sovereign. This proves that they were really one people with the English people, though existing in a state of colonial dependence, and not a separate people having nothing politically in common with them but in the accident of having the same royal person for their king. The union with the mother country was national, not personal, as was the union existing between England and Hanover, or that still existing between the empire of Austria, formerly Germany, and the kingdom of Hungary; and hence the British parliament claimed, and not illegally, the right to tax the colonies for the support of the empire, and to bind them in all cases whatsoever—a claim the colonies themselves admitted in principle by recognizing and observing the British navigation laws. The people of the several colonies being really one people before independence, in the sovereignty of the mother country, must be so still, unless they have since, by some valid act, divided themselves or been divided into separate and independent states.

The king, say the jurists, never dies, and the heralds cry, "The king is dead! Live the king!" Sovereignty never lapses, is never in abeyance, and the moment it ceases in one people it is renewed in another. The British sovereignty ceased in the colonies with independence, and the American took its place. Did the sovereignty, which before independence was in Great Britain, pass from Great Britain to the States severally, or to the States united? It might have passed to them severally, but did it? There is no question of law or antecedent right in the case, but a simple question of fact, and the fact is determined by determining who it was that assumed it, exercised it, and has continued to exercise it. As to this there is no doubt. The sovereignty as a fact has been assumed and exercised by the United States, the States united, and never by the States separately or severally. Then as a fact the sovereignty that before independence was in Great Britain, passed, on independence to the States united, and reappears in all its vigor in the United States, the only successor to Great Britain known to or recognized by the civilized world.

As the colonial people were, though distributed in distinct colonies, still one people, the people of the United States, though distributed into distinct and mutually independent States, are yet one sovereign people, therefore a sovereign state or nation, and not a simple league or confederacy of nations.

There is no doubt that all the powers exercised by the General Government, though embracing all foreign relations and all general interests and relations of all the States, might have been exercised by it under the authority of a mutual compact of the several States, and practically the difference between the compact theory and the national view would be very little, unless in cases like that of secession. On the supposition that the American people are one political people, the government would have the right to treat secession, in the sense in which the seceders understand it, as rebellion, and to suppress it by employing all the physical force at its command; but on the compact theory it would have no such right. But the question now under discussion turns simply on what has been and is the historical fact. Before the States could enter into the compact and delegate sovereign powers to the Union, they must have severally possessed them. It is historically certain that they did not possess them before independence; they did not obtain them by independence, for they did not severally succeed to the British sovereignty, to which they succeeded only as States united. When, then, and by what means did they or could they become severally sovereign States? The United States having succeeded to the British sovereignty in the Anglo-American colonies, they came into possession of full national sovereignty, and have alone held and exercised it ever since independence became a fact. The States severally succeeding only to the colonies, never held, and have never been competent to delegate sovereign powers.

The old Articles of Confederation, it is conceded, were framed on the assumption that the States are severally sovereign; but the several States, at the same time, were regarded as forming one nation, and, though divided into separate States, the people were regarded as one people. The Legislature of New York, as early as 1782, calls for an essential change In the Articles of Confederation, as proved to be inadequate to secure the peace, security, and prosperity of "the nation." All the proceedings that preceded and led to the call of the convention of 1781 were based on the assumption that the people of the United States were one people. The States were called *united*, not confederated States, even in the very Articles of Confederation themselves, and officially the United States were called "the Union." That the united colonies by independence became united States, and formed really one and only one people, was in the thought, the belief, the instinct of the great mass of the people. They acted as they existed through State as they had previously acted through colonial organization, for in throwing off the British authority there was no other organization through which they could act. The States, or people of the States, severally sent their delegates to the Congress of the United States, and these delegates adopted the rule of voting in Congress by States, a rule that might be revived without detriment to national unity. Nothing was more natural, then, than that Congress, composed of delegates elected or appointed by States, should draw up articles of confederation rather than articles of union, in order, if for no other reason, to conciliate the smaller States, and to prevent their jealousy of the larger States such as Virginia, Massachusetts, and Pennsylvania.

Moreover, the Articles of Confederation were drawn up and adopted during the transition from colonial dependence to national independence. Independence was declared in 1776, but it was not a fact till 1782, when the preliminary treaty acknowledging it was signed at Paris. Till then the United States were not an independent nation; they were only a people struggling to become an independent nation. Prior to that preliminary treaty, neither the Union nor the States severally were sovereign. The articles were agreed on in Congress in 1777, but they were not ratified by all the States till May, 1781, and in 1782 the movement was commenced in the Legislature of New York for their amendment. Till the organization under the constitution ordained by the people of the United States in 1787, and which went into operation in 1789, the United States had in reality only a provisional government, and it was not till then that the national government was definitively organized, and the line of demarcation between the General Government and the particular State governments was fixed.

The Confederation was an acknowledged failure, and was rejected by the American people, precisely because it was not in harmony with the unwritten or Providential constitution of the nation; and it was not in harmony with that constitution precisely because it recognized the States as severally sovereign, and substituted confederation for union. The failure of confederation and the success of union are ample proofs of the unity of the American nation. The instinct of unity rejected State sovereignty in 1787 as it did in 1861. The first and the last attempt to establish State sovereignty have failed, and the failure vindicates the fact that the sovereignty is in the States united, not in the States severally.

EIGHTEEN

The Democratic Principle

During our late civil war it was almost proverbial to call our government the best government under heaven; and whoever in the loyal states expressed an opinion to the contrary ran some risk of being sent to Fort Lafayette, Fort Warren, or to some other Federal place of imprisonment. I defended the government during those fearful times, and stood by it when many a stout heart failed, because it was the government of *my* country, and I owed it the allegiance due from the citizen; but never since the "Hard-Cider" campaign have I believed it practically "the best government under heaven," or superior to almost any other civilized government. "Tippecanoe and Tyler too" upset my democracy, by showing how easily the people can be humbugged and carried away by a song. Till then I had believed in democracy, though I believed in little else.

My friend, the Hon. George Bancroft, defined democracy, in a lecture which I published in my *Boston Quarterly Review,* to be "Eternal justice ruling through the people": I defined it in a series of Resolutions adopted by a democratic state convention, to be the "Supremacy of man over his accidents"—meaning thereby that democracy regards the man as more than his possessions, social position, or anything separable from his manhood—and got most unmercifully ridiculed for it; but the ridicule did not move me,

"Democracy Favors Inequality, and Is a Heavy Burden to the People." From *Brownson's Quarterly Review,* Last Series, 1 (April 1873): 235–59.

and I held fast to the doctrine, that the will of the people is the most direct and authentic expression of the divine will that can be had or desired. The people held with us then, in some respects, the place the church now holds with us. We labored under the comfortable illusion that, in order to secure wise and just government, all we had to do was to remove all restrictions on the free and full expression of the popular will, and to leave the people free to follow in all things their own divine instincts. The defects of bad legislation to which I could not shut my eyes, I attributed not to democracy, but to the fact that the democratic principle was obstructed, and the will of the people could not have its free and full expression. There were still many restraints on their will, retained from old monarchical and aristocratic institutions; such as an independent judiciary, and the English Common Law with its subtleties and technicalities. These should all be swept away, and the unrestrained will of the people be supreme, and make itself felt alike in the administration of justice, and the election of representatives in the legislature and in all the offices of the government, state or national. To secure the rule of justice and the recognition of the man over his accidents, everything should be swept away that imposed the least check on the direct and immediate action of the popular will. People, though adopting the democratic principle, told me I went too far, but I knew I was logical; and I have never in my life been able to persuade myself that a principle, really sound and true, will not bear pushing to its last logical consequences. If the democratic principle will not bear being so pushed, it is simply a proof that it is untrue, and cannot be safely adopted. This was my reasoning then, and is my reasoning now. The country, public opinion, gave me the principle, furnished me the democratic premises, and I took it for granted that the principle was sound and the premises indisputable, as do the majority of my countrymen.

The "Hard-Cider" campaign of 1840 came. In it I took an active part on the democratic side, in behalf of Martin Van Buren, the last first-class man that sat, or probably that ever will sit, in the presidential chair of the United States; and my party was, as all the world knows, woefully defeated. It was the first presidential campaign in which I had ever taken an active part, and almost my first experience in practical politics. It was enough. What I saw served to dispel my democratic illusions, to break the idol I had worshipped, and shook to its foundation my belief in the divinity of the people, or in their will as the expression of eternal justice. I saw that they could be easily duped, easily made victims of the designing, and carried away by an irresistible passion in the wrong as easily as in the right. I was forced by the shock my convictions received, to review first my logic, and then to examine the premises which I had taken on trust from my democratic countrymen, which I had not hitherto thought of questioning. I found them untenable and absurd. I ceased henceforth to believe in democracy, but I did not cease to be a loyal citizen, nor did I deem it necessary to abandon the Democratic party so called, which, after all, was less unsound, less radical, and more conservative than the Whig party, which had carried the elections; but I labored day and night with voice and pen, in the *Boston Quarterly Review* and in the *Democratic Review,* to make it still more conservative, and to convince its leaders that the people as the state need governing no less than the people as individuals. So I labored till my happy conversion to the church, when, having no associations with the Catholic population of the country, except our common Catholic faith, I ceased to have any political influence; and if I resume the discussion of political topics, it is solely with the hope of being of some service to my ingenuous, pure-minded, and educated young Catholic friends, destined to exert a powerful influence for good or for evil on the political future of the republic.

The great democratic principle was asserted by the Congress of 1776, in the declaration that "Governments derive their just powers from the assent of the governed." They thus declared that governments originate in convention, and that law derives its force as law from the will of those it is to bind. This asserts the purely human origin of government, and rejects all law enjoined by any authority above the people. It denies the right or authority of any government to command, for no such right or authority can be created by any convention or agreement; it denies, also, all law that restrains the will of the governed. That the law binds only by virtue of the assent of those on whom it is to operate, Gallicans asserted in principle, in asserting that papal constitutions do not bind the conscience unless assented to, at least tacitly, by the church. This principle, which reverses all one's natural ideas of government and law, the recent Council of the Vatican has condemned, when applied in the spiritual or ecclesiastical order; and we see no reason why a Catholic should not condemn it, when applied in the political and civil order. No government that has real authority to govern, can originate in convention alone; for the convention itself needs to be authorized by a law or an authority superior to itself, since St. Paul teaches, *Non est potestas nisi a Deo*. Where there is no law of nations, which the nation itself is bound to obey, there may be national force, but no national right or authority to govern. Laws that emanate from the people, or that are binding only by virtue of the assent of the governed, or that emanate from any human source alone, have none of the essential characteristics of law, for they bind no conscience, and restrain, except by force, no will.

We do not allege that human governments have no legislative authority or power to enact laws and bind the conscience; but that authority, that power is not derived from a human source, and is held only from the divine law under which they are constituted. Governments that have only a conventional origin, and only such powers as are held from the assent of the governed, have no such authority, no such power. The grand objection to democracy, then, is, that it rejects the law of nations, the *jus gentium*, denies the rule of eternal and immutable right, and resolves eternal justice into more conventionalism, and, if a government at all, it is simply a government of force, under which, as we have seen in the foregoing article, might makes right. I am not arguing against a republic, or a government largely popular in its constitution and administration, such as ours was intended to be; but against the democratic principle, that founds government in convention, and derives its powers from the consent of the governed, or which applies to the civil order the Gallican principle, condemned by the Council of the Vatican, when applied in the spiritual or ecclesiastical order. It makes the people who are to be governed superior to the government, and leaves their will supreme, subject to no authority, bound by no law. It is, therefore, simply the principle of political atheism. So far as the national authority is concerned, the principle is not confined to a popularly constituted government, but is accepted and acted on by most modern governments, especially by the Sardinian, the Prussian, the Russian, and we fear also the Austrian, in none of which is the law of nations, binding the conscience of the nation itself, recognized.

The American constitution is not founded on political atheism, but recognizes, as we showed in our article last January on *The Papacy and the Republic*, the rights of man, and, therefore, the rights of God. There remain as yet among us some traces of the law of nations, as asserted by Lord Arundel of Wardour in his work on *Tradition*, reviewed in the preceding article, in distinction from the international law of the Benthamites and diplomates, which consists solely in conventional pacts and precedents, without any recognition of the rule of right, or of eternal and immutable justice. Something of Christian tradition lives among us and is kept alive by the common law and the judicial department of the government, though, latterly, too often overruled by the legislative department which is continually encroaching on the province of the judiciary, as we see in much recent Congressional legislation. What we complain of is the tendency of American public opinion, formed and directed to a great extent by popular journalism, to apply the naked, unmitigated democratic principle to the interpretation of the Constitution and what we call our American institutions; though what is really meant by this phrase which is in every one's mouth, it would be hard to say. Public opinion with us asserts and applies the democratic principle, which, as we have seen, liberates the people as the state from all government, and their will from all restraint; and leaves them perfectly untrammelled, free to do whatever they have the physical force to do. Their might founds and measures their right.

Is it not so? If not, why are the public so sensitive to the assertion of any authority above the people, or of a law which does not emanate from the people, and which they are bound in conscience, collectively as well as individually, to obey? Why does our American public opinion applaud Prince von Bismarck and Victor Emmanuel for their efforts to subject all authorities or powers in the nation to the national will? The principle is the same whatever the form of government. In our country our Protestant fellow-citizens, being the majority, take great credit to themselves for "tolerating," as Dr. Bellows puts it, the Catholic faith and worship. Why, if not because they hold themselves free to prohibit them, if they should choose? Are they not, in fact, using the power numbers give them, to invade the Catholic conscience and deprive Catholics of their equal rights as parents and citizens, by compelling them to pay for the support of schools to which they are forbidden by conscience to send their children? Evidently they recognize no law of right or justice to which their will is subject, and which we may plead as our protection. The plea of justice in regard to public measures is rarely heard. Utility or expediency, not right or justice, is the standard adopted in politics, as external decorum or propriety is the rule in ethics. Even the late William H. Seward, when he appealed from the Constitution of the United States, which as senator he had sworn to observe, to the "higher law," only appealed from one human law to another, or from the particular to the general; for he appealed only to general humanity, whose rights he never dreamed of identifying with the rights of God. If the abolition party he represented appealed to the law of God as the law of nations, it was to that law without any court or tribunal to declare and apply it, and as interpreted and applied by the party itself. The abolitionist, with all his fine talk, fierce declamation in favor of a law above the state, would have recoiled from the assertion of a divinely instituted court or tribunal to interpret it and give it practical efficacy in the government of men and nations. He asserted it, but only on the condition that he should be free to interpret and apply it for himself; and hence his individualism nullified the law, and his humanitarianism was resolved, sometimes even avowedly, into no-governmentism.

I repeat, I am not warring against the political constitution of my country, nor am I seeking in any respect to change it; for I am no revolutionist, no monarchist, no aristocrat. It is the spirit and opinions of the American people, or of the majority of them, that I want changed, and so changed as to interpret the constitution of American political society by the principles of law and justice, not by the democratic principle, which asserts the sovereignty of the arbitrary will of the people, or, practically, the unrestricted rule of the majority for the time: which is tyranny, and repugnant to the very essence of liberty, which is will ruled by right, or power controlled by justice.

The philosophers and statesmen of the last century supposed that the evil could be prevented, and the necessary restraints on the popular will or ruling majority could be imposed, by means of written constitutions, which, in the words of the Thetford stay-maker, author of the *Age of Reason*, could be "folded up and filed away in a pigeon hole." They supposed the people emancipated from superstition, as they called religion, and from priests and priestcraft, and left to the promptings of their simple nature, would always be guided by reason, and therefore needed only to be governed in their action by a wise and just written constitution. They held the people could be safely entrusted with the guardianship of the constitution, which was very much like locking up a man in prison, and giving him the key. But experience has proved that written constitutions, unless they are written in the sentiments, convictions, consciences, manners, customs, habits, and organization of the people, are no better than so much waste paper, and can no more restrain them than the green withes with which the Philistines bound his limbs, could restrain the mighty Samson.

John C. Calhoun, the most sagacious and accomplished statesman our republic has ever produced, and who appreciated the tyranny of majorities better than any other man amongst us, placed no confidence in written constitutions; but he hoped to restrain the popular will by dividing and organizing the people according to their different sectional pursuits and interests, or by organizing a system of "concurrent majorities." This would be, no doubt, an advance on simply written constitutions; but it is only in communities where the pursuits and interests of different sections of the population are very distinct, that it is practicable, or could be efficacious. Since the abolition of slavery, the population, pursuits, and interests of the whole country are too homogeneous to allow the organization he demanded, or to admit the system of concurrent majorities. If introduced, it would be rendered ineffective by the great homogeneous interests and pursuits of the majority of the population, which would overpower and trample on all minorities opposed to them.

We hold that whatever constitutional or organic provisions may be adopted, the stronger interest of a country, in the absence of all recognition of the law of nations, limiting and defining the rights and powers of the nation, will govern the country, whether the interest and pursuits of the numerical majority or not; or at least dictate the policy of its government. For a time, the Southern States could protect their interests, and, to some extent, shape the policy of the government, because they represented the strongest of any one interest of the country, the interest of capital invested in labor; but when short crops and wars in Europe had created a demand for our breadstuff's and provisions, the products of the non-slave-holding states, and the produce of the California mines had strengthened the commercial and manufacturing interests, which already controlled the free states, and enabled the representatives of these interests to meet their foreign exchanges,—they were stronger than any interests the South could oppose to them. The South had then no alternative, but either to submit to be controlled by them, as the people of the non-slave-holding states were, or to secede from the Union, and endeavor to establish an independent republic for themselves. The struggle was a struggle of interests. The abolition fanatics were only the fly on the wheel, and the question they raised amounted to nothing in itself, and was of importance only as it was seized upon as a pretext, and had only this significance, that the business interests of the North could subject the interests of the South to their control only by destroying the southern capital invested in labor. Mr. Calhoun's policy, if carried out, might have staved off the crisis for a few years, but could not have prevented it or its final results.

I have said, in the absence of the law of nations, which, it cannot be too often repeated, is law for the nation as well for the individual, therefore law emanating from an authority above the nation, above and over the people. The attempt of modern statesmen, Mr. Calhoun among the rest, to constitute the state without any power or authority above the people, so that by its own spontaneous working it should maintain order with liberty, and liberty with order, and promote the highest utility and the greatest happiness of the nation, is a vain attempt. The thing is impossible. No simply human wisdom, no adjustment of positive and negative forces, no organization of interests, or system of checks and balances, will do it. The English in their Constitution have carried to perfection their system of checks and balances, or of the organization of separate interests, classes, or estates, each with a negative on the others; yet, in spite of the national boasts, it works with difficulty, and one of the separately organized estates is swallowing up the others. It, in its present form, is hardly a century and a half old, and it undergoes a greater or less change every few years. The prosperity of England under it is commercial and industrial, and is due less to it, than to the fact that she has invented the art of converting debt into capital; and by means of the revolutions, and the wars growing out of them, of the continental states, she has contrived to bring the nations of the Old World and the New into debt to her, and to compel them to pour their surplus earnings into her lap. The nations live and labor to enrich her; and yet her overgrown wealth consists chiefly in paper evidences of credit, and might vanish in a day. Then her wealth is unequally distributed: a few are very rich in paper values, but in no country on earth is there greater poverty or more squalid wretchedness. Then we must take into the account her government of Ireland and India, worse than any of the proconsular governments of ancient Rome. She, also, owes more to her mines of tin, lead, iron, and coal, soon to be exhausted, than to the excellence of her political constitution, or the wisdom of her statesmen.

I cannot conceive a more profoundly philosophic, or more admirably devised constitution, than that of our own government, as I have endeavored truthfully to present it in my *American Republic*, published by O'Shea in this city, in the autumn of 1865. Yet, for the lack of the moral element in the American people, for the lack of a recognition of the law of nations emanating from an authority above the people, and binding the conscience of the nation, it is practically disregarded, and its wisest and most vital provisions are treated by the ruling people as *non avenues*. The people have forgotten its providential origin, treat it as their own creature, as a thing they have made, and may alter or unmake at their pleasure. It is not a law enjoined on them, and has no hold on their conscience. They give it a purely democratic interpretation. Men talk of loyalty, but men cannot be loyal to what is below them and dependent on their breath; and, therefore, they violate it without compunction, as often as prompted to so do by their interests or their passions. Nothing was more striking during the late civil war than the very general absence of loyalty or feeling of duty, on the part of the adherents of the Union, to support the government because it was the legal government of the country, and every citizen owed it the sacrifice of his life, if needed. The administration never dared confide in the loyalty of the Federal people. The appeals made were to interest, to the democracy of the North against the aristocracy of the South; to anti-slavery fanaticism, or to the value and utility of the Union, rarely to the obligation in conscience to support the legitimate or legal authority; prominent civilians were bribed by high military commissions; others, by advantageous contracts for themselves or their friends for supplies to the army; and the rank and file, by large bounties and high wages. There were exceptions, but such was the rule.

"I will have a draft," said the Secretary of War, Mr. Stanton, to me one day in his office: "I will have a draft, if I get but one man by it, for I wish to assert the majesty of this government, its right to command the support of citizens in the ranks of the army, or elsewhere, in its hour of need. This reliance on large bounties and high wages, that is running up an enormous bill of expenses which the people must ultimately pay, is derogatory to the majesty of the government, obscures and weakens its authority, and appeals only to the lowest and most sordid motives of the human heart."—Well, the draft was ordered, and, as we all know, proved a failure. The government, indeed, asserted its majesty, but the people did not recognize it; they effectively resisted it, or came to a compromise. How could they see a majesty in a government they themselves had made and could unmake? The universal conviction of the conventional origin of the government despoiled it of its majesty. It had no majesty, no authority, but what it held from the people, and could command no obedience but such as they chose to give it. If it went farther, it was by force, not by right: and fully did the administration feel it.

The conventional origin of the constitution excludes its moral or divine right, and therefore denies all obligations in conscience of the people, either collectively or individually, to obey it. It has nothing in it that one is morally bound to treat as sacred and inviolable. Its violation is no moral offence, for it is the violation of no moral law, of no eternal and immutable right. Nothing hinders the people, when they find the Constitution in the way of some favorite project on which they are bent, from trampling it under their feet, and passing on as if it never had any existence. The Constitution, to be respected, must be clothed with a moral authority, an authority for conscience, which it cannot be, if of conventional origin; and the government constituted has no just powers not derived from the assent of the governed.

This is wherefore no constitutional contrivances or combinations, however artistic or skilful, can be successful that have no support in the divine order. The government which has no authority for conscience, and none that holds not from God, and under his law, has or can have no authority for conscience, having no moral support, is impotent to govern, except by sheer force, as we have already shown over and over again. Now, as modern statesmen exclude the moral order, and make no account of the divine element in society, and rely on the human element alone, they are unable to clothe power with right, or to give it any stability. The revolutionary spirit is everywhere at work, and is kept down and a semblance of order maintained in Europe only by five millions of armed soldiers. In our own country, we owe such order as we have, first, to the fact that the government acts less as a government, than as the factor or agent of the controlling, that is, the business interests of the country; and second, to the fact that the American people are not yet completely democratized, but retain, in spite of their theory of the conventional origin of power, no little of their traditionary respect for authority, and their obligation in conscience to obey the law. Yet, under the influence of their democratic training, they are fast losing what they have thus far retained from an epoch prior to the rejection of divine order by statesmen and the constitution of states.

Democracy which asserts the conventional origin of government, and thus excludes the divine order from the state, necessarily denies with Jeremy Bentham all rule of right, eternal and immutable, and can at best assert only the rule of utility, or, as commonly expressed, "the greatest happiness of the greatest number;" though Benthan himself changed in his later days the formula, and, for the greatest happiness of the greatest number, substituted as his political, juridical, and ethical formula, simply "the greatest happiness." This is the only formula of the sort that the purely democratic principle can adopt or accept. Democrats tell us this end is to be gained by getting rid of the burden of kings and aristocrats, and introducing not only equality before the law, but equality of rights and privileges, and carrying out the great principle, "All men are created equal." Equality of privileges is an absurdity, and there can be no rights where there is no right. But pass over this. "Democracy asserts and maintains equality!" Yes, *asserts* it, we grant, but it tends to promote the contrary. It operates practically, almost exclusively, in favor of those who command and employ capital or credit in business, and against the poorer and more numerous classes.

The political equality, expressed by universal suffrage and eligibility, is of no practical value; for, however elections may go, or whoever may be elected, the legislation will invariably follow the stronger interest, therefore the business interests of the country: it may be now the commercial interests, now the industrial or manufacturing interests, or, in fine, the railroad, and other business corporation interests. There is no help for it in universal suffrage. By excluding the moral element and founding the state on utility, democracy tends to materialize the mind, and to create a passion for sensible goods, or material wealth and well-being. Take any ten thousand electors at random, and ask them what they want of government, and the honest answer will be: "Such legislative action as will facilitate the acquisition of wealth." Suppose such action taken—and most of our legislation is of that sort—how many of the ten thousand are in a position to profit by it? perhaps, ten; perhaps, not more than one. Democracy excludes aristocracy in the European sense, an aristocracy founded on large landed estates, noble birth, education, and manners; and substitutes and substitutes for it an aristocracy founded on business capacity and capital or credit, a thousand times worse and more offensive, because more exacting, more insolent and haughty, always afraid of compromising its dignity by mingling with the poor or unfashionable, feeling that it is a sort of usurper, without any hereditary or legitimate claims to respect,—an aristocracy of *rôturiers*, the most contemptible as well as, socially and politically, the most galling of all possible aristocracies. We do not object to a man, or refuse to honor him, because he has risen from a gutter; but we do refuse to honor a man who was born in a gutter and has remained there, but claims respect simply because he has succeeded in gathering a mass of gold around him.[1]

Democracy, following the lead of the business classes, builds up, and with us has covered the land over with huge business and moneyed corporations, which the government itself cannot control. We complain of the great feudal barons, that they were often more powerful than their suzerain; but our railroad "kings" can match the most powerful vassals, either of the king of France, or of the king of England, in feudal times. Louis XI was not weaker against Charles the Bold, than is Congress against the Pennsylvania Central Railroad and its connections, or the Union Pacific, built at the expense of the government itself. The great feudal lords had souls, railroad corporations have none. Congress cannot resume specie payments, for the National-Bank interest opposes it; and so our commercial interests must bear the loss of a depreciated currency, and the laboring classes must continue to pay the higher prices for the necessaries of life it creates. In a word, the business classes, according to the old whig party, the "Urban Party" of the time of Swift and Addison, or of Queen Anne's reign, have permanent possession of the government, and use it to further their own interests, which is a damage; for this country is fitted to be, and really is, a great agricultural country.

In the *Review* for January, I showed the disastrous influence which the equality, asserted by democracy, and supposed to be favored by universal suffrage and eligibility, has on the laboring classes. It is to the honor of the church that she has always had a special regard and tenderness for the poor; and it is no less to her honor that she has never attempted to remove poverty. She always relieves distress when able, and solaces suffering whatever its cause; but she honors the poor, and treats poverty as a blessing, not as a misfortune. In her view, the poor are really the more favored class, and she never attempts, and has never enjoined it upon her children to attempt, to place them, as to the goods of this world, on an equality with the rich. She holds the thing neither practicable nor desirable. Democracy regards the poor as unfortunate, and undertakes to remove poverty by opening to them all the avenues of wealth, and to elevate them by establishing their political and civil equality; and thus leads them, as we see in the recently enfranchised negroes, to aspire to social equality. This causes them to be discontented with their lot, and makes them feel their poverty a real misery. It greatly enhances the expenses of their living. As a rule, men live for their families, especially for their wives and daughters, whom they would see live as well, be as well educated, and as well dressed as the wives and daughters of the better-to-do, whom democracy teaches them to regard as equals. The evil this causes is immeasurable. It induces not a few to live beyond their means, or to make a show of wealth which they have not; it creates a universal struggle to escape poverty, and to acquire riches as the means of equality and respectability. The passion for wealth, so strong in most Americans, and which is called by foreigners "the worship of the almighty dollar," is at bottom only the desire to escape poverty and the disgrace attached to it by democracy. Political economists regard this struggle with favor, for it stimulates production and increases the wealth of the nation, which would be true enough, if consumption did not fully keep pace with production; though, if true, we could hardly see, in the increased wealth of the nation, a compensation for the private and domestic misery it causes, and the untold amount of crime of which it is the chief instigator. We regard it as an unmixed evil which could and would be avoided, if poverty were honored, and the honest and virtuous poor were respected according to their real worth, as they are by the church, and were in all old Catholic countries till the modern democratic spirit invaded them: "A contented mind is a continual feast," says the proverb.

Democracy, by its delusive universal suffrage and eligibility, stimulates a universal passion, as we have seen, for social equality, which can be gratified only by the possession of wealth or material goods; for democracy, excluding the moral order, can content no one with moral equality. "I am as good as you, and why should you be rich and I poor? Why should you live in a palace, and I in a mud hovel? Why should you ride in your coach and live in luxury, while I must trudge on foot, be thinly clad, and live on the coarsest and most meagre fare, which I can procure only with difficulty, sometimes not at all."—Just consider that there are in this city of New York, at least, forty thousand children, orphans or worse than orphans, absolutely homeless, who live by begging and thieving, and lodge on doorsteps, under the wharves, and in miserable dens; initiated, almost as soon as able to speak, into every vice and crime that finds opportunity or shelter in a great city: contrast these with the children brought up in elegant and luxurious homes, bearing in mind that democracy asserts equality, and say, if there is any thing singular in the logic that concludes communism from democratic premises, or if a Wendell Phillips is not a true and consistent democrat in defending the Paris Commune and the Internationale? Or if, when you denounce either as infamous, you do not forget your democracy, and borrow from an order of ideas that, though approved by Christian tradition, democracy excludes, or at least makes no account of?

But communism, which demands equality in material goods, is not only an impossibility, but an absurdity. Equality of wealth is equivalent to equality of poverty. Wealth consists in its power to purchase labor, and no matter how great it is, it can purchase no labor, if there is none in the market; and, if all were equally rich, there would be none in the market, for no one would sell his labor to another. Then each man would be reduced to what he can produce with his own hands, wealth would lose all the advantages it has where there are rich and poor, and society would lapse after a generation or two into the lowest barbarism. Communism, if it could be carried out, would not, then, as the communists dream, secure to all the advantages of wealth, but would result in the reduction of all to the most abject poverty,—the very thing which they are ready to commit any crime or sacrilege in order to escape. All projects of reform of any sort, undertaken without divine authority and guidance, inevitably defeat themselves, and aggravate the evils they would redress.

Reject the communistic conclusion. The Democratic Equality asserted, then, can be, practically, only free competition, making all equally free to compete for wealth, and the good things of this world, and leaving each free to possess what he acquires. This is the interpretation democracy receives with us. But in this competition there is only a delusive equality. In it the honest man stands no chance with the dishonest. The baker who feels bound to furnish thirty-two ounces in his two-pound loaf, cannot compete with him who has no scruple in charging the full price of a two-pound loaf for eighteen ounces. So throughout the whole business world. It would be undemocratic for the law to interfere to protect those who are unable, no matter from what cause, to protect themselves. The law must leave all things of the sort to free competition, and to regulate themselves. We thus, under our democratic system, pay a premium for dishonesty, cheatery, and knavery, and then are astonished at the daily increase of fraud and crime in the business world. We tempt men to get rich—honestly if they may, but at any rate to get rich—by the contempt in which we hold poverty, and the honor which we pay to wealth, as I have already intimated. Universal suffrage and eligibility can at best secure only this so-called free competition, and enact laws favorable to the acquisition of wealth. But men's natural capacities are unequal; and these laws, which on their face seem perfectly fair and equal, create monopolies which enrich a few individuals at the expense of the many. There is far less equality, as well as less honesty and integrity, in American society, than there was fifty or sixty years ago. The honor paid to wealth, or what is called success in the world, is greater; people are less contented with moderate means, a moderate style of living, as well as with moderate gains, and have a much greater horror of honest labor. I remember when it was, in the country at least, regarded as an act of prudence for a young couple with little or nothing but health, industrious habits, and a willingness to earn their living by hard work, to marry and set up housekeeping for themselves. Now, except to a very limited extent, it would be regarded as the greatest imprudence. No little of that remarkable purity and morality for which the Catholic peasantry of Ireland are noted the world over, is due to early marriages, which the habits of the people encourage. Yet English and American economists denounce them, and represent them as due to the craft of the clergy who encourage them for the sake of the wedding-fee, and of the baptismal fees most likely in due time to follow. The purity and morality of our New-England people—I speak of them, for I was brought up among them—have diminished in very nearly the same ratio in which early marriages have been discontinued as imprudent, except with the very rich. The class of small farmers who cultivated their own farms, and by their labor, economy, and frugality obtained a comfortable living, and were able to establish one son in business, and to educate another to be a lawyer, a doctor, or a minister, to provide moderate portions for the daughters, and to leave the homestead to the eldest son,—has disappeared; and they have been obliged to emigrate, to exile themselves from their early homes and all the endearing associations of childhood and youth, though they go not beyond the limits of their own country. I myself am even more an exile in my present residence, than my Irish or German neighbor; for he has near him those whom he was brought up with, knew him in his youth, while I have not one,—not one with whom I can talk over old times, or who knew me before I had reached middle age: and my case has in it nothing peculiar. But the fact, that no small portion of the American people have been separated from the old homestead and scattered among strangers, has a fatal influence in checking the development of their finer qualities, and in throwing them for relief upon the coarser passions and grosser pleasures of sense.

There is less equality than there was in my boyhood, and the extremes are greater. The rich are richer, and the poor are poorer. The rich are also more extravagant and more fond of displaying their wealth, for, to the great majority of them, wealth is a novelty. Shoddy and petroleum, as well as successful speculation, have made millionaires and thrice millionaires of men of low and vulgar minds, destitute of social refinement and gentle breeding, whose wives and daughters know no way of commanding consideration or of attracting admiration, but by their furs and diamonds and their extravagant expenditures. The effect of this on the community at large, in producing a competition in extravagance, and enhancing the average expense and difficulty of living, is not easily estimated. There is no country in the world where the general extravagance is so great as in our own, or where the cost of living is greater for all classes. Some provision is made for paupers as for prisoners and criminals, but there is a larger class who are too honest to steal, too proud to beg, and too high-spirited to allow themselves to be sent to the almshouse; mostly women, many of them widows with one, two, or more small children, whose sufferings from want of sufficient food, decent clothing, and comfortable shelter, are not to be told. I attribute the sufferings of these to the delusive doctrine of equality, and the worship of wealth which democracy encourages, and the disgrace it attaches to poverty, and to humble labor for a living; for otherwise most of them could find relief and ample provision for their wants in domestic service. A really hereditary aristocracy produces no such evil, for between them and such aristocracy there is no competition. It is the burgher aristocracy and burgher wealth that treat poverty as a crime or a nuisance, and make our women and girls of American parentage shrink from domestic service as hardly less disgraceful than a life of shame.

The corruption generated by the struggle for wealth which democracy stimulates, is not confined to private and domestic life. It pervades public life. Señor Calderon de la Barca, the Spanish minister for several years to our government at Washington, told me in April, 1852, that when he was first sent by his government to ours at Washington, in 1822, he was charmed with every thing he saw or heard. "The government struck me," he said, "as strictly honest, and your statesmen as remarkable for their public spirit, integrity, and incorruptibility. I was subsequently sent to Mexico; and when, recalled from that mission, I was offered my choice between Rome and Washington, such was my high opinion of the American republic, and the honesty and integrity of its government, that I chose Washington in preference to Rome, though the latter was more generally coveted. I have been here now for several years a close observer, and I have seen every thing change under my eyes. All my admiration for the republic and for republican government has vanished. I cannot conceive a government more corrupt than this government of yours. I see men come here worth only their salary as members of Congress, and in two or four years return home worth from a hundred thousand to two hundred thousand dollars."—This was said in 1852, when corruption was very little in comparison with what it has become. In 1822, the great body of the people were far from being democratized, and no party in the country bore or would consent to bear the democratic name. There was no democratic party in the country known as such, till after the inauguration of General Jackson as president, March 4, 1829; and none became predominantly democratic, till the success of the democratic whigs in 1840, who far outdid the Jackson-Van Buren party in their democracy. The late Horace Greeley always called that party the "sham democracy," and treated at first the whig party, and, after 1856, the republican party, as the genuine Simon-Pure democracy. He was right in one sense; for the whig-republican party was always farther gone in democracy, that is, in asserting the supremacy of the popular will and the exclusion of the moral order from politics, than was the party that bore the democratic name.

Up to the election of General Jackson, the American people, if adopting the democratic theory, were not governed by it; they still were influenced by ante-revolutionary traditions, recognized the moral order, the rule of right to which the people as the state as well as individuals were bound to conform; and I believed then and believe now that no purer government, indeed, no better government, existed under heaven. But since then the democratic principle has passed from theory into the practical life of the people, and become the ruling principle of their political judgments and conduct, at least, to an alarming extent. The result we saw during the war, and still more plainly see in the corruption developed by the recent very imperfect investigations in Congress. We were told the main facts with regard to the Credit Mobilier over two years ago; and the real facts are far more damaging than any that appear from the investigation in Congress. But this, though perhaps on a larger scale, is yet in reality no grosser than the corruption that has for years obtained in Congress, the state legislature, the municipal governments, and the elections all over the country. It is in vain to look to legislation for a remedy. The laws are good enough as they are, and stringent enough; but laws are impotent where the people have become venal, and are easily evaded or openly violated with impunity, when they are not consecrated and rendered inviolable by the national conscience: and it is of the essence of democracy to dispense with conscience, and to attempt to maintain wise and beneficent government, without drawing on the moral order, by considerations of public and private utility alone.

The actual burden imposed by our democratic administrations, whether called democratic or republican, and including both the general government and the several state governments due to the democratic principle itself, cannot be even approximately ascertained. The extravagance of the American people, and the expensiveness of their style of living in proportion to their means, we attribute to democracy, which measures a man's respectability by his wealth, and his wealth by his expenditures; for the American people are naturally both frugal and economical. The American people are directly and indirectly more heavily taxed by government, counting the General government and the State and municipal governments, than any other people known. The population of the United States, and that of France before her late dismemberment, are about equal; and yet the taxes imposed by our government are more than double the taxes imposed by the French government; and if we have to provide for the expenses of a disastrous civil war, France has to provide for the expenses and losses of an equally disastrous foreign war, carried on in her own territory. The cost of living in this country should be much less than in any European country, owing to the average mildness of our climate, the extent, fertility, and cheapness of land, and the variety of its productions; and yet the cost of living with us, I am told, is greater even than in England, the dearest country in Europe, and which is obliged to import annually from a hundred million to a hundred and fifty million dollars' worth of breadstuffs and provisions to feed her population. We attribute this to democracy, as we do the dearness of living in England; for England is almost as democratic as the United States. The election of a president once every four years costs, besides the derangement of business, the American people more than the Civil List of Great Britain costs the British people. The Aristocracy is hardly a check on the Commons; and as not engaged in business, and living on its own revenues derived principally from land and mines, hardly affects the course of the business operations of the nation, or the general cost and style of living. In Italy and Germany the democratic principle, combined with the monarchical form, prevails; and in both taxation is rapidly approaching the British and the American standard, notwithstanding the confiscation of the goods of the church by the former, and the heavy French indemnity to the latter.

But we have singularly failed to make ourselves understood, if the reader infers that we are defending monarchy or aristocracy, or that we have had any other purpose in our remarks than to show that the assertion of the people as the source of all legitimate authority, and that governments derive all their just powers from the assent of the governed, which makes all authority, all law of purely human origin, excludes the divine order which alone has authority for conscience, divorces politics from ethics, substitutes utility for right, and makes it the measure of justice, fails of the end of all just government, the promotion of the public good, and is either no government at all, but a mere agency of the controlling private interests of the people, or a government of mere force. This with me is no new doctrine: I defended it in the *Democratic Review* thirty years ago, while I was yet a Protestant, and it has been steadily maintained in this *Review* from its first number in January, 1844. To assert and defend it, was a main purpose for which I originally commenced it.

Now, it is easy to see that what we object to is not popular government, but the doctrine that the people as the state or nation are the origin and source of all authority and all law, that they are absolutely supreme, and bound by no law or authority that does not emanate from themselves. We call this the democratic principle; but as the people are here taken in the sense of state or nation, it may be applied equally to any political order which asserts the national will as supreme, and free from all authority or law which does not emanate from the nation itself. The principle is applied in Russia, where the czar, as representing the nation, claims absolute autocratic power; it is applied in Germany in a more absolute sense than in the United States, and is the principle on which Prince von Bismarck suppresses the Jesuits and kindred religious orders, and expels them from the empire, and on which he persecutes the church, denies her independence, and demands the enactment of statutes that subject her to the imperial will, that is, the national authority. It is the principle on which the London *Times* asserted the other day that no Catholic can be a loyal Englishman, and on which the sectarian press of this country maintain that we cannot be Catholics and loyal American citizens. It is the principle which inspires and underlies the whole revolutionary party in Europe. It is the liberty of the people, not from aristocracies, kings, kaisers, or arbitrary power, but from all authority or law, that does not emanate from the people, or from the nation, and therefore from a purely human source, that the party is struggling for. That is, the revolutionary party, the democratic party of Europe, are struggling to eliminate from modern society the *jus gentium* of Roman jurisprudence under the protection of religion, or what Lord Arundel of Wardour, as we have seen in the foregoing article, calls the "law of nations," that is, a law emanating from God himself, and founding and binding the national conscience; and, in this struggle, the mass of the American people sympathize with them, and loudly applaud them.

This is what our age calls liberty, what it means by liberty of conscience, that is, getting rid of all laws that bind the national conscience, and thus severing politics from the moral order, and subjecting the moral order itself to the secular authority, however constituted. The moral order, that is, justice, eternal and immutable right, or the law of nations, is by the divine will and appointment, according to Christian tradition, placed in charge of the pope, or the Vicar of Christ on earth. To effect this object and emancipate politics from the law of nations, or the people, the state, or the nation, from the law of eternal and immutable right, that is, the law of God, it is necessary to get rid of the papacy, and to effect the utter destruction of the Catholic Church, its divinely appointed defender; and we see that the democratic, the liberal party, are willing to sustain so unmitigated a despot as the chancellor of the new German empire, if he will only join them in their war against the papacy, and aid them in their efforts to effect the complete destruction of the church. It is to conciliate and gain the support of this liberal party that the several governments of Europe, even of Catholic nations, have abandoned the papacy, even when they have not, like Germany, Italy, and Spain, turned against the pope. No head could wear a crown, no government could stand a day, at least, according to all human calculations, were it to take up the defence of the papacy, or adhere to it, as did the Frank Emperor Charlemagne.

We have called the attention of our readers to the principle that, as we have said, inspires and underlies this so-called liberal party, because it is precisely the principle that in our country is called the democratic principle. As thousands, perhaps, hundreds of thousands of Catholics in the Old World, have been led to adopt and defend this principle, without understanding its real character; so some Catholics in our own country, fired by political ambition, and engrossed in political affairs, may have also been led to adopt it in equal ignorance of its real anticatholic character, supposing they might adopt it and act on it, without injury to .the church, or detriment to their Catholic faith and influence. We do not write with any expectation of undeceiving these, if any such there are. If they read us at all, they will not understand us, and will feel towards us only anger or contempt. But there is a large class of Catholic young men, graduates from our colleges, whose minds are fresh and malleable, whose hearts are open and ingenuous, who love truth and justice, and who take a deep interest in the future of their country. We write for them, to warn them against the dangers which threaten us, and against which there were none to warn us when we were young like them.

There is also even a larger number of Catholic young women annually coming forth from our conventual schools and academies, with fresh hearts, and cultivated minds, and noble aspirations, who are no less interested in the welfare of the country, and no less capable of exerting an influence on its destiny. They have no more sympathy than we have, with so-called "strong-minded women," who give from the rostrum or platform public lectures on politics or ethics; but we have much mistaken the training they have received from the good Sisters who have educated them, if they have not, along with the accomplishments that fit them to grace the drawing-room, received that high mental culture which prepares them to be wives and mothers of men; or, if such should be their vocation, to be accomplished and efficient teachers in their turn. Men are but half men, unless inspired and sustained in whatever is good and noble by woman's sympathy and co-operation. We want no *bas bleus*, no female pedants, nor male pedants either, as to that matter; but we do want cultivated, intelligent women, women who not only love their country, but understand its interests and see its dangers, and can, in their proper sphere, exert a domestic and social influence to elevate society and protect it from the principles and corruption which lead to barbarism. This is no time and no country in which to waste one's life in frivolities or on trifles: *Ernst ist das Leben*. And seriously should those of either sex whom the world has not yet corrupted, soured, or discouraged, take it, and labor to perform its high and solemn duties.

What we want, what the church wants, what the country wants, is a high-toned Catholic public opinion, independent of the public opinion of the country at large, and in strict accordance with Catholic tradition and Catholic inspirations, so strong, so decided, that every Catholic shall feel it, and yield intelligently and lovingly to its sway. It is to you, my dear Catholic young men and Catholic young women, with warm hearts, and cultivated minds, and noble aims, that I appeal to form and sustain such a true Catholic public opinion. You, with the blessing of God and directed by your venerable pastors, can do it. It is already forming, and you can complete it. Every good deed done, every pure thought breathed, every true word spoken, shall quicken some intelligence, touch some heart, inspire some noble soul. Nothing true or good is ever lost, no brilliant example ever shines in vain. It will kindle some fire, illumine some darkness, and gladden some eyes. Be active, be true, be heroic, and you will be successful beyond what you can hope.

NOTES

Introduction: Orestes Brownson's American Search for the Truth

1. H. F. Brownson, ed., *Orestes A. Brownson's Middle Life* (Detroit, Mich.: H. F. Brownson, 1899).

2. Arthur M. Schlesinger Jr., *A Life in the Twentieth Century* (New York: Houghton Mifflin, 2000), 177.

3. Russell Kirk, introduction to *Selected Essays of Orestes Brownson* (Chicago: Henry Regnery Company, 1955): 1.

4. Brownson battled throughout his life for the principles he thought were worth defending. Among his opponents at different points were leaders of the Universalist Church upon his departure, the transcendentalists, various American Catholic bishops, most notably Archbishop of New York John Hughes, Ralph Waldo Emerson, John Henry Newman, the Know-Nothing Party, and others. For historical accounts of these disputes see Thomas R. Ryan, *Orestes A. Brownson: A Definitive Biography* (Huntington, Ind.: Our Sunday Visitor, 1976): 42–46, 143–50, 532–38, 367–80, 474–86 (hereinafter cited as *OAB Biography*).

5. Peter Augustine Lawler, introduction to the ISI Edition of Orestes A. Brownson, *The American Republic: Its Constitution, Tendencies and Destiny*, Vol. I, *Orestes A. Brownson: Works in Political Philosophy*, ed. Gregory S. Butler (Wilmington, Del.: ISI Books, 2003): xx–xxi (hereafter cited as *AR*).

6. "The Mediatorial Life of Jesus," in *The Works of Orestes A. Brownson*, Vol. 4, ed. by Henry Brownson (Detroit, Mich.: 1882–1887), 140–72 (hereafter cited as *Works*). Other work evidencing Brownson's belief in the catholicity of truth include "Schools of Philosophy," in *Works*, 1:276–305; "Rationalism and Traditionalism," in *Works*, 1:490–520; "An Old Quarrel," in *Works*, 2:284–305; "An Essay in Refutation of Atheism," in *Works*, 2: 380–406; "Nature and Grace," in *Works*, 4:350–74; "Science and the Sciences," in *Works*, 9:254–68; and "Liberalism and Progress," in *Works*, 20:342–60.

7. Brownson, "Schools of Philosophy," 302–3.

8. Pope Benedict XVI, "Deus Caritas Est," No. 9, quoting from Aristotle's *Metaphysics*, 7:7. Peter Lawler alerted me to this comparison in his collection of essays titled *Modern and American Dignity* (Wilmington, Del.: ISI Books, 2010). Lawler argued in the chapter "American Nominalism" that "Aristotle attempted to grasp God as the object of every human desire

or love. He understood God only as the object of love, as a wholly self-sufficient or unerotic or unmovable being, not as a person at all. Aristotle's God is certainly not a 'relational' God, one who cares or even knows about the existence of particular human beings. According to Aristotle, our pursuit of divine knowledge, or what God knows, becomes progressively more impersonal" (142).

9. *OAB Biography*, 18–19.

10. Ibid.

11. *The Convert* (one of Brownson's autobiographies) incorporated in *Works*, 5:11–19. *The Convert*, published in 1857, is Brownson's autobiographical account of his conversion to Catholicism. His first semidisguised autobiography was titled *Charles Elwood, or the Infidel Converted*, published in 1840. This recollection sets forth Brownson's conversion from skepticism to belief.

12. "Kant's Critique of Pure Reason I–III," in *Works*, 1:130–213; "Essays on the Reformation, I and III," in *Works*, 8:519–21, 523, 576, and 579; and "Newman's Development of Doctrine," "Newman's Theory of Christian Doctrine," "The Dublin Review on Developments," "The Dublin Review and Ourselves," and "Doctrinal Developments," in *Works*, 14:1–140. Brownson's strong criticism of Newman's theory was partially rethought later in his life. He stated, "We have long suspected that we did him an injustice, though we have not changed our own views of the soundness of the theology we opposed to him, or thought we were opposing to him. The fact is, his book was profounder that we supposed and was designed to solve theological difficulties which we had not then encountered in our own intellectual life and experience." "Explanations to Catholics," in *Works*, 20:361–80, 372.

13. Brownson's understanding of federalism is greatly apparent in his essays on slavery and its expansion into the federal territories as well as in his essays evaluating the abolitionist movement. Brownson's thoughts on the related subjects of slavery, the Constitution and federalism, and the abolitionist movement unfold in a series of essays beginning with the 1838 essay "Slavery–Abolitionism," in which he noted that the Declaration of Independence had for once and all settled the issue of the wrongness of slavery in America but that the constitutional principle of federalism made resolving the issue of slavery difficult. Slavery, Brownson rightly argued, was not guaranteed by the Constitution but was given legal establishment by state law, not federal law. The Constitution merely recognized its existence. As such, the attempt by the abolitionists to abolish slavery at the federal level recognized the triumph of majority will against the principle of the freedom of communities to order their domestic affairs, that is, slavery. If the abolitionists were to be triumphant, then the deconstruction of the republic would be at hand with the resolution of differences proceeding on pure democratic procedures and not the republican constitution and its federalism that acknowledged differences among the states on the slavery question. For this reason, Brownson found the abolitionist movement opposed to the Constitution. As a result, he generally opposed their efforts. Similarly, when the south's stranglehold on the federal government became apparent in the 1850s with the Kansas–Nebraska Act, the Dred Scott opinion's removal of territorial prohibitions on slavery, and the recognition of Kansas's fraudulent Lecompton Constitution by the Buchanan administration, Brownson argued that the south was using federal power to centralize its beliefs and practices regarding slavery. Brownson believed that slavery in the federal territories was constitutionally illegitimate. Slavery, he emphasized, could only be established by state law. Consequently, the territories, nursed under the protection of federal law, even as federal law recognized the provincial territorial authorities, could not legally affirm slavery within their borders.

Despite his earlier reluctance on constitutional grounds to support federal action to emancipate slaves, Brownson ultimately sided with Abraham Lincoln and the Republican Party in the election of 1860, perceiving that the south was the dominant threat to the continued existence to the Union. In a series of essays during the war, Brownson ultimately favored immediate emancipation of the slaves and personally urged Lincoln to use this device as a war measure. However, he also insisted that the war was about the Union and the Constitution, not liberating slaves or achieving equality. See the following essays for Brownson's views on the slavery issue: "Slavery–Abolitionism," *Boston Quarterly Review* 1 (April 1838): 238–60; "Letter to William Lloyd Garrison," *The Liberator* 8 (May 11, 1838): 73; and "The Higher Law," The Fugitive Slave Law," "Sumner on Fugitive Slaves," "Slavery and the Incoming Administration," "The Slavery Question Once More," "Politics at Home," "The Great Rebellion," "Slavery and the War," "Archbishop Hughes on Slavery," "The Struggle of the Nation for Life," "State Rebellion, State Suicide," "Emancipation and Colonization," "What the Rebellion Teaches," "Confiscation and Emancipation," and "Slavery and the Church," in *Works*, 17:1–352.

14. "The Works of Daniel Webster," in *Works*, 19:343–81. *AR*, 136–37.

15. "The Works of Daniel Webster," 348–54.

16. "Church and Monarchy," in *Works*, 8:107–26, 117.

17. R. A. Herrera, prologue to *Orestes Brownson: Sign of Contradiction* (Wilmington, Del.: ISI Books, 1999), xv.

18. Gregory S. Butler, *In Search of the American Spirit: The Political Thought of Orestes Brownson* (Carbondale: Southern Illinois University Press, 1992): 18–19. In volume 5 of *Works*, Brownson recorded that his commitment to Universalism in 1824 commenced his intellectual life (19).

19. *OAB Biography*, 63. Ryan quoted from Brownson that he saw Christ as "the model man, who sought, by teaching the truth under a religious envelope, and practicing the purist morality, to meliorate the earthly condition of mankind" (63).

20. Patrick W. Carey, ed., introduction to *The Early Works of Orestes A. Brownson: The Early Years, 1826–29*, ed., Patrick W. Carey (Milwaukee, Wisc.: Marquette University Press, 2000), 24–25. Also evidencing Brownson's belief in religion as a deeper motivating source for social reform are the essays "Priest and Infidel" and "Calvinism and Infidelity" appearing, respectively, in *Philanthropist* 2 (May 29, 1832): 209–21, 221–22.

21. H. F. Brownson, *Orestes A. Brownson's Middle Life*, 116–17.

22. Patrick W. Carey, ed., introduction to *The Early Works of Orestes A. Brownson: The Free Thought and Unitarian Years, 1830–35* (Milwaukee, Wisc.: Marquette University Press, 2000), 7–10. Channing's sermon argued that there is divinity within humanity that is a source of human perfectibility. Brownson is greatly affected by Channing's work and aimed his pastorate from this point to the moral and social uplift of the poor.

23. Benjamin Constant's *Religion, Considered in its Origin, its Forms, and its Developments* had an effect on Brownson's thinking similar in part to Channing's. Brownson stated, "Never shall we forget the joy with which my heart bounded, when we fancied that Benjamin Constant had proved that religion has a firm and solid foundation in a law of nature, universal, personal, and indestructible as that nature itself—not indeed because it saved us from the necessity of believing the Bible or submitting to an external authoritative revelation, but because for the moment it seemed to restore us to communion with the religious world." "The Eclipse of Faith," in *Works*, 7:289.

24. Orestes A. Brownson, "Memoir of Saint-Simon," *Unitarian* 1 (June 1834): 279–89, 285.

25. Ibid., 286. "New Christianity is given to the world! Moses promised to mankind

universal brotherhood; Jesus Christ prepared it; Saint-Simon realizes it. The church really universal is about to be born. The reign of Caesar ends; a pacific takes the place of military society; and the universal church governs the temporal as well as the spiritual, in the outer as well as in the inner court. Science is holy, industry is holy, for they seem to improve the condition of the poorest classes and to bring them near to God." Id.

26. Henry F. Brownson, *Orestes A. Brownson's Early Life, 1803–1844* (Detroit, Mich.: H. F. Brownson, 1898), 138–39. Estimates were that Boston had a population of twenty to thirty thousand who were no longer attending church services.

27. "Reform and Conservatism," in *Works*, 4:80–82.

28. Orestes A. Brownson, "A Discourse on the Wants of the Times, Delivered in Lyceum Hall, Hanover Street, Boston, Sunday, May 29, 1836" (Boston, 1836).

29. Orestes A. Brownson, *New Views of Christianity, Society and the Church* (Boston: James Munroe and Company, 1836).

30. *OAB Biography*, 116.

31. Brownson, *New Views*, 18–32, 56–57.

32. Ibid., 68.

33. *OAB Biography*, 107. Quoting Brownson from *The Convert*, "[t]he book is remarkable for its protest against Protestantism, and its laughable blunders as to the doctrines and tendencies of the Catholic Church, to which I was by no means hostile, but of which I was profoundly ignorant" (84–85).

34. Brownson, *New Views*, 87.

35. Ibid.

36. Ibid., 107.

37. Perry Miller, *The Transcendentalists* (Cambridge, Mass.: Harvard University Press, 1950), 114–15.

38. Butler, *In Search of the American Spirit*, 18. I also note a more sobering essay by Brownson, actuated by his sense of evil, but also presciently analyzing the spectacle of a public execution in upstate New York. The crowd, Brownson said, that gathered to watch the execution was in the thousands. Many were drunk and given to various forms of public disorder, the event being a form of entertainment that impoverished the community morally, Brownson judged. "An Address ... on the Day of [Guy C. Clark's] Execution," *Philanthropist* 2 (February 14, 1832): 127.

39. Orestes A. Brownson, "The Essayist," *The Gospel Advocate and Impartial Investigator* (July 19, 1828): 230–31.

40. Orestes A. Brownson, "An Essay on the Progress of Truth," *The Gospel Advocate and Impartial Investigator* 5–6 (November 17, 1827): 362.

41. Ibid.

42. Orestes A. Brownson, "An Address, Delivered at Dedham, on the Fifty-Eighth Anniversary of American Independence, July 4, 1834," (Dedham, Mass.: H. Hamm, 1834).

43. Ibid.

44. Ibid. Brownson's essay "Observations and Hints on Education" sets forth a vision of education as liberation from conventional belief and social practice so that the student would break with "servile dependence on the thoughts of others, the reverence for the past, the acquiescence in authority." *Boston Quarterly Review* 3 (January 1840): 137–66.

45. Orestes A. Brownson, "Democracy and Reform," *Boston Quarterly Review* 2 (October 1839): 506.

46. Brownson, *New Views*, 49.

47. Orestes A. Brownson, "The Laboring Classes," *Boston Quarterly Review* V (July 1840): 358–95, 373.

48. On this point, Arthur Schlesinger Jr. called the essay an anticipation of Karl Marx's diagnosis of the modern economic problem, written nearly a decade in advance of Marx's *Communist Manifesto*: "The analysis that Orestes Brownson arrived at is perhaps disconcerting to a generation which believes that Marx invented the Marxian theory of history. In 1838, a decade before *The Communist Manifesto*, Brownson interpreted history in the terms of the inescapable conflict between those who profited by the existing order and those on whom its burden chiefly fell." Arthur Schlesinger, Jr., "An American Marxist before Marx," *Sewanee Review* 48 (July–September 1939): 319.

49. Brownson, "The Laboring Classes," 375.

50. Ibid., 378–79.

51. Ibid., 394.

52. Ibid., 395.

53. "Democracy," in *Works*, 15:1–34, 4.

54. Ibid., 9.

55. Herrera, "The Saturnalia of Faith," in *Orestes Brownson*, chapter 3, contains a concrete description of Brownson's involvement in transcendentalism and his relationships with Thoreau, Emerson, and other members.

56. Patrick W. Carey, *Orestes A. Brownson: American Religious Weathervane* (Grand Rapids, Mich.: Eerdmans Publishing, 2004), 55–96. This book provides an excellent description of Brownson's complicated relationship with the transcendentalist movement, its central philosophical and religious aims, and Brownson's later critique of the movement.

57. *AR*, xiv.

58. "Transcendentalism, or the Latest Form of Infidelity," in *Works*, 6:42.

59. Orestes A. Brownson, "Mr. Emerson's Address," *Brownson's Quarterly Review* (October 1838): 501, 504–10.

60. Sidney E. Ahlstron, *A Religious History of the American People* (New Haven, Conn.: Yale University Press, 1972), 603.

61. In 1842 Brownson rejected much of the learning he received from Cousin's eclectic school of thought. Subjectivism, the prison that Kant's idealism created, Brownson held, had not been surmounted by Cousin. This had been the chief merit of Cousin's spontaneous reason and primitive revelation, but the person could never get to the external world without the self, rendering his knowledge of it unsure.

62. *The Convert*, 130–31.

63. *OAB Biography*, 254–55.

64. "The Mediatorial Life of Jesus," in *Works*, 4:140–72, 149.

65. Ralph Hancock, "Brownson's Political Providence, with Some Preliminary Comparisons with Tocqueville's Providential Statesmanship," *Perspectives on Political Science* 37, no. 1 (2008): 17–22, 18.

66. "Rights and Duties," in *Works*, 14:290–317, 303–307, 315.

67. Lawler, introduction to the ISI Edition of *AR*, xxv.

68. *AR*, 76.

69. Orestes A. Brownson, *Essays and Reviews Chiefly on Theology, Politics, and Socialism* (New York: D. and J Sadlier and Co., 1852): 368–85.

70. "Socialism and the Church," in *Works*, 10:79–110; "Channing on Social Reform I," in *Works*, 10:136–68; and "Channing on Social Reform II," in *Works*, 10:169–206.

71. "Socialism and the Church," 92.

72. "Liberalism and Socialism," in *Works*, 10:526–50.

73. Lawler, introduction to the ISI Edition of *AR*, lxv–lxvii; "The Church and the Republic," in *Works*, 7:1–33, 9–15; and "The Temporal Power of the Pope," in *Works*, 9:137–64, 157–59.

74. "Civil and Religious Freedom," in *Works*, 20:308–41. Other essays evidencing Brownson's support for religious freedom include the following: "Temporal and Spiritual," "The Spiritual Not For the Temporal," "The Spiritual Order Supreme," "Temporal Power of the Popes," and "Mission of America," in *Works*, 1–94, 114–36, 551–84; and "The Church and the Republic," "The Day Star of Freedom," "The Church and Modern Civilization," "Rights of the Temporal," and "Separation of Church and State" in *Works*, 7:1–32, 103–35, 406–38.

75. "The Day Star of Freedom," in *Works*, 9:103–16.

76. "The Church and the Republic," 1–32, 23.

77. Ibid., 23.

78. *AR*, 32–35.

79. Ibid., 33–34.

80. Ibid., 33.

81. Russell Hittinger, *The First Grace: Rediscovering the Natural Law in a Post-Christian World* (Wilmington, Del.: ISI Press, 2003), 13. Hittinger also points us to Thomas Hobbes's rendering of man in *De Homine*: "Politics and ethics can be demonstrated a priori; because we ourselves make the principles—that is, the causes of justice (namely, laws and covenants)—whereby it is known what justice and equity, and their opposites injustice and inequity, are" (X.5).

82. Ibid., 14.

83. *AR*, 32–35.

84. Ibid., 36–37.

85. Ibid., 11–14.

86. Ibid., cix–cx.

87. Ibid., cxii–cxiii.

88. Ibid., 11.

89. Ibid., 12.

90. Ibid., 13. It has something more to do than restrict our natural liberty, curb our passions, and maintain justice between man and man. Its office is positive as well as negative. It is needed to render effective the solidarity of the individuals of a nation, and to render the nation an organism, not a mere organization—to combine men in one living body, and to strengthen all with the strength of each, and each with the strength of all—to develop, strengthen, and sustain individual liberty, and to utilize and direct it to the promotion of the common weal—to be a social providence, imitating in its order and degree the action of the divine providence itself, and, while it provides for the common good of all, to protect each, the lowest and meanest, with the whole force and majesty of society. Id.

91. Ibid., 3.

92. Ibid., 4.

93. Ibid., 21.

94. Ibid., 221.

95. Ibid., 189.

96. Ibid., 257.

97. Ibid., 225.

98. Ibid., 234.

99. Ibid., 246.

100. "The Democratic Principle," "Constitutional Guaranties," and "The Executive Power," in *Works*, 18:223–80.

101. "The Political State of the Country," in *Works* 18:520–34, 523, and 530.

102. "The Woman Question I and II," in *Works*, 18:381–417.

Chapter 1: An Essay on the Progress of Truth

1. When I attribute the doctrine of election and reprobation to John Calvin I would not be understood as asserting that the sentiment originated with him, for I believe it was held by Luther in a light not less abhorrent; but as we know the sentiment now only as a part of the antiquated system of the Genevan Reformer it may receive his name.

Chapter 5: New Views of Christianity, Society, and the Church

1. I use these terms, Spiritualism and Materialism, to designate two social, rather than two philosophical systems. They designate two orders, which, from time out of mind, have been called *spiritual* and *temporal* or carnal, *holy* and *profane*, *heavenly* and *worldly*, etc.

2. Benjamin Constant.

3. See my Article on Cousin's Philosophy in the *Christian Examiner*, for September, 1836. Also, Cousin's Philosophical Works everywhere, especially the V. and VI. Lectures of his "Cours," in 1828, and the Preface to the 2d Edition of his *Fragmens philosophiques*.

Chapter 7: The Laboring Classes

1. I am aware that I broach in this place a delicate subject, though I by no means advance a novel doctrine. In justice to those friends with whom I am in the habit of thinking and acting on most subjects, as well as to the political party with which I am publicly connected, I feel bound to say, that my doctrine, on the hereditary descent of property, is put forth by myself alone, and on my own responsibility. There is to my knowledge, none of my friends who entertain the doctrine, and who would not, had I consulted them, have labored to convince me of its unsoundness. Whatever then may be the measure of condemnation the community in its wisdom may judge it proper to mete out for its promulgation, that condemnation should fall on my head alone. I hold not myself responsible for others' opinions, and I wish not others to be held responsible for mine.

I cannot be supposed to be ignorant of the startling nature of the proposition I have made, nor can I, if I regard myself of the least note in the commonwealth, expect to be able to put forth such propositions, and go scathless. Because I advance singular doctrines, it is not necessary to suppose that I am ignorant of public opinion, or that I need to be informed as to the manner in which my doctrines are likely to be received. I have made the proposition, which I have, deliberately, with what I regard a tolerably clear view of its essential bearings, and after having meditated it, and been satisfied of its soundness, for many years. I make it then with my eyes open, if the reader please, "with malice prepense." I am then entitled to no favor, and I ask as I expect none. But I am not quite so unfortunate as to be wholly without friends in this world. There are those to whom I am linked by the closest ties of affection, and whose approbation and encouragement, I have ever found an ample reward for all the labors I could perform. Their reputations are dear to me. For their sake I add this note, that they may not be in the least censured for the fact, that one whom they have honored with their friendship, and in a journal which, in its general character, they have not hesitated to commend, has seen proper to put forth a doctrine, which, to say the least, for long years to come must be condemned almost unanimously.

Chapter 18: The Democratic Principle

1. There is no mistake in saying that the mass of the electoral people demand of government such legislation in relation to business interests, as will facilitate the acquisition of wealth; nor in saying that all legislation of the sort does and must, as far as it has any effect, favor inequality, and enrich the few at the expense of the many. If all could avail themselves equally of such legislation, nobody would or could derive any advantage from it, and it would facilitate the acquisition of wealth for no one. Where there has been bad legislation, legislation creating monopolies, or conferring special business privileges on individuals, or a particular class or corporation, the repeal by the government of such legislation, may have, to a

certain extent, the effect demanded, by removing restrictions. But no other legislation, save such as secures the citizen an open field for exertion, and the full possession of the fruits of his honest industry for facilitating acquisition of wealth, is possible except by facilitating the transference of the earnings of the many to the pockets of the few. Such is the effect of all laws designed to facilitate the operations of the business classes, and to promote business interests. Whether this is a good or an evil, certainly the inevitable tendency of universal suffrage and eligibility is to inequality, not to equality, as is pretended.

Seeking the Truth: An Orestes Brownson Anthology was designed in Garamond and composed by Kachergis Book Design of Pittsboro, North Carolina. It was printed on 60-pound Natural Recycled and bound by McNaughton and Gunn of Saline, Michigan.